Glenn's Flat Rate Manual

AMERICAN CARS 1966-1975

Clarence W. Coles and Harold T. Glenn

Henry Regnery Company • Chicago

Library of Congress Cataloging in Publication Data

Glenn, Harold T.
  Glenn's Flat rate manual

  1. Automobiles — Maintenance and repair — Rates.
I. Coles, Clarence W., joint author.   II. Title.
III. Title: Flat rate manual.
TL152.G552   338.4′3629′28722   75-11748
ISBN 0-8092-8193-7

Copyright © 1975 by Harold T. Glenn

All rights reserved. This volume
may not be reproduced in whole or
in part in any form without
written permission from the publisher.

Printed in the United States of America
Library of Congress Catalog Card Number 75-11748
International Standard Book Number 0-8092-8193-7

Books by HAROLD T. GLENN

Youth at the Wheel
Safe Living
Automechanics
Glenn's Auto Troubleshooting Guide
Exploring Power Mechanics
Automobile Engine Rebuilding and Maintenance
Automobile Power Accessories
Glenn's Auto Repair Manual
Automotive Smog Control Manual
Glenn's Emission-Control Systems
Glenn's Tune-Up and Repair Manual for American and Imported Car Emission-Control Systems
Glenn's Foreign Car Repair Manual
Glenn's Triumph Repair and Tune-Up Guide
Glenn's Alfa Romeo Repair and Tune-Up Guide
Glenn's Austin, Austin-Healey Repair and Tune-Up Guide
Glenn's Sunbeam-Hillman Repair and Tune-Up Guide
Glenn's MG, Morris and Magnette Repair and Tune-Up Guide
Glenn's Volkswagen Repair and Tune-Up Guide
Glenn's Volkswagen Repair and Tune-Up Guide (Spanish Edition)
Glenn's Mercedes-Benz Repair and Tune-Up Guide
Glenn's Foreign Carburetors and Electrical Systems Guide
Glenn's Renault Repair and Tune-Up Guide
Glenn's Jaguar Repair and Tune-Up Guide
Glenn's Volvo Repair and Tune-Up Guide
Glenn's Peugeot Repair and Tune-Up Guide
Glenn's Fiat Repair and Tune-Up Guide
Glenn's Toyota Tune-Up and Repair Guide
Glenn's Mazda Tune-Up and Repair Guide
Glenn's Chrysler Outboard Motor Repair and Tune-Up Guide for 1 & 2 Cylinder Engines
Glenn's Chrysler Outboard Motor Repair and Tune-Up Guide for 3 & 4 Cylinder Engines
Glenn's Evinrude Outboard Motor Repair and Tune-Up Guide for 1 & 2 Cylinder Engines
Glenn's Evinrude Outboard Motor Repair and Tune-Up Guide for 3 & 4 Cylinder Engines
Glenn's Johnson Outboard Motor Repair and Tune-Up Guide for 1 & 2 Cylinder Engines
Glenn's Johnson Outboard Motor Repair and Tune-Up Guide for 3 & 4 Cylinder Engines
Glenn's McCulloch Outboard Motor Repair and Tune-Up Guide
Glenn's Mercury Outboard Motor Repair and Tune-Up Guide
Glenn's Sears Outboard Motor Repair and Tune-Up Guide
Honda One-Cylinder Repair and Tune-Up Guide
Glenn's Honda Two-Cylinder Repair and Tune-Up Guide
Suzuki One-Cylinder Tune-Up and Repair Guide
Yamaha Enduro Tune-Up and Repair Guide
Triumph Two-Cylinder Motorcycle Tune-Up and Repair Guide
Glenn's Chevrolet Tune-Up and Repair Guide
Glenn's Chevrolet Camaro Tune-Up and Repair Guide
Glenn's Chevrolet Vega Tune-Up and Repair Guide
Glenn's Ford/Lincoln/Mercury Tune-Up and Repair Guide
Glenn's Chrysler/Plymouth/Dodge Tune-Up and Repair Guide
Glenn's Pontiac Tune-Up and Repair Guide
Glenn's Pontiac Firebird Tune-Up and Repair Guide
Glenn's Oldsmobile Tune-Up and Repair Guide
Glenn's Buick Tune-Up and Repair Guide
Glenn's Basic Repair Guide
Glenn's OMC Inboard/Outboard Repair and Tune-Up Guide
Glenn's Pinto Tune-Up and Repair Guide
Glenn's Mustang II Tune-Up and Repair Guide
Glenn's Opel Tune-Up and Repair Guide
Glenn's Datsun Tune-Up and Repair Guide
Glenn's Mercury Bobcat Tune-Up and Repair Guide
Glenn's Capri and Capri II Tune-Up and Repair Guide
Glenn's Flat Rate Manual
Glenn's Complete Bicycle Manual

acknowledgment

The authors wish to express their appreciation to the scores of IGO members (too numerous to acknowledge individually) throughout Southern California who assisted in proving the realistic times given in the schedules by performing the work under actual garage conditions. We also wish to thank them for their many helpful suggestions, constructive criticism, and constant encouragement toward the completion of this work. Without their cooperation, this book would not have been possible.

Clarence W. Coles
Harold T. Glenn

foreword

This is a comprehensive, easty-to-understand American car flat rate manual designed for the independent garage owner, service station operator, or shop foreman who must estimate repair costs intelligently and accurately if he expects to realize a profit for his labor.

The labor schedules in this manual are shop-tested, rather than conventional factory flat rate times, which are developed by using highly-trained mechanics working on new cars under favorable conditions. Manufacturer's factory times are so low that few mechanics can match them because of rusted parts, broken bolts, and layers of oil and grime found on older cars.

With today's exacting laws, it is essential that accurate estimates be given before work is started, and this is where GLENN'S FLAT RATE MANUAL gives the garage owner the chance to realize a fair profit, which is necessary to stay in business.

The time schedules in GLENN'S FLAT RATE MANUAL are presented in a highly efficient manner. In this manual, each table is preceded by a consise statement of the specific tasks that have been timed. This extremely valuable feature for saving estimator time is worth much more than the price of the book, each time it is used.

GLENN'S FLAT RATE MANUAL tells the estimator exactly what work is scheduled with a realistic time addition for vehicles or engines having special time-consuming equipment. These additions are arranged in tabular form so that it is not necessary to use an adding machine to figure the times required to do a complete job.

The schedules in this manual contain (on the same page) related job time schedules, closely allied to the main job. This format eliminates time lost looking back-and-forth through other sections as is the case with all other manuals. Main headings lead the estimator directly to the job title needed, and the allied jobs are added to the schedule in such a way that no ambiguity exists.

Part cost estimates assist the mechanic to determine, within a workable range, how much to price replacement items. With today's inflationary trends, it is impossible to give precise figures, but the range given in this manual permits intelligent interpretations. Because parts are being constantly improved and older ones superseded, requiring part-number revisions and price changes, no attempt has been made to include individual part numbers. Such numbers would be obsolete when the manual was printed and ridiculous a few years later.

contents

AMERICAN MOTORS

SERVICE STATION MAINTENANCE

- General Lubrication 1
- Battery 1
- Cooling System 1
- Ignition System 1
- Fuel System 2
- Driveshaft 2
- Hydraulic Brake System 2
- Parking Brakes 2
- Suspension System 2
- Front End & Steering System 2
- Charging System 2
- Cranking System 3
- Lighting System 3
- Minor Tune-up 3
- Major Tune-up 3

INDEPENDENT GARAGE SCHEDULES

- **Minor Tune-up** 3
- **Major Tune-up** 4
- **Emission Control Systems**
  - Exhaust-Gas Recirculation (EGR) 4
  - Smog Station Certification 5
  - Complete Test or Service 6
  - Heated-Air System 6
  - Evaporative Emission Control System 7
  - Air-Guard (AIR) 7
  - Transmission Controlled Spark (TCS) 8
  - Positive Crankcase Ventilation (PCV) 8
- **Engine Service**
  - Ignition System 8
  - Cranking System 9
  - Charging System 10
  - Fuel System 10
  - Short Block, Replace 11
  - Engine Overhaul, Out-of-Car 12
  - Engine Overhaul, In-Car 12
  - Timing Chain Mechanism 13
  - Oil Pump 14
  - Bearings, Main or Rod 14
  - Valve Mechanism 15
  - Cylinder Head or Gasket 15
  - Exhaust System 16
  - Cooling System 16
- **Clutch & Standard Transmission**
  - Clutch Mechanism 17
  - Shift Linkage 18
  - Standard Transmission, Overhaul 19
- **Automatic Transmission**
  - Major Service 19
  - Shift and Linkage Controls 20
  - Performance Check 20
- **Driveshaft & Rear Axle**
  - Driveshaft 21
  - Rear Axle 21
  - Rear Suspension 22
- **Steering & Front End**
  - Steering Linkage 22
  - Standard Steering Gear 23
  - Power Steering Unit 23
  - Front End 24
- **Brake System**
  - Brakes, Service 25
  - Hydraulic Brake System 25
  - Parking Brakes 26
- **Air Conditioning System**
  - Major Service 26
  - Spring Tune-up 27
  - Blower Motor or Controls 27
- **Heating System**
  - Test & Service 27
- **Lighting System**
  - Adjust & Service 28

BUICK

SERVICE STATION MAINTENANCE

- General Lubrication 29
- Battery 29
- Cooling System 29
- Ignition System 29
- Fuel System 30
- Driveshaft 30
- Hydraulic Brake System 30
- Parking Brakes 30

Suspension System 30	Automatic Transmission
Front End & Steering System 30	Shift & Linkage Controls 47
Charging System 31	Performance Check 47
Cranking System 31	Major Service 48
Lighting System 31	**Driveshaft & Rear Axle**
Minor Tune-up 31	Driveshaft 49
Major Tune-up 31	Rear Axle 49
	Rear Suspension 50

INDEPENDENT GARAGE SCHEDULES

Minor Tune-up 32
Major Tune-up 32
Emission Control Systems

Steering & Front End
  Front End 50
  Steering Linkage 51
  Standard Steering Gear 51
  Power Steering Unit 52

Brake System
  Hydraulic Brake System 53
  Power Brake Unit 53
  Service Brakes 54
  Parking Brakes 54

INDEPENDENT GARAGE SCHEDULES

Minor Tune-up 32
Major Tune-up 32
Emission Control Systems
  Smog Station Certification 33
  Complete Test or Service 34
  Positive Crankcase Ventilation (PCV) 34
  Exhaust-Gas Recirculation (EGR) 35
  Transmission Controlled Spark (TCS) 35
  Air Injection Reactor (AIR) 35
  Heated-Air System 36
  Evaporative Emission Control System 36

Engine Service
  Ignition Service 37
  Cranking System 37
  Charging System 38
  Fuel System 38
  Engine Overhaul, In-Car 39
  Short Block, Replace 40
  Engine Overhaul, Out-of-Car 41
  Timing Chain Mechanism 41
  Oil Pump 42
  Bearings, Main or Rod 42
  Cylinder Head or Gasket 43
  Valve Mechanism 44
  Exhaust System 44
  Cooling System 45

Clutch & Standard Transmission
  Clutch Mechanism 46
  Shift Linkage 46
  Transmission Overhaul 47

Lighting System
  Adjust & Service 55

Heating System
  Test & Service 55

Air Conditioning System
  Spring Tune-up 56
  Blower Motor or Controls 56
  Major Service 57

CADILLAC

SERVICE STATION MAINTENANCE

General Lubrication & Systems Check 58
Battery 58
Cooling System 58
Ignition System 58
Fuel System 58
Driveshaft 58
Hydraulic Brake System 59
Parking Brakes 59
Suspension System 59
Front End & Steering System 59
Charging System 59
Cranking System 59
Lighting System 60
Minor Tune-up 60
Major Tune-up 60

INDEPENDENT GARAGE SCHEDULES

Minor Tune-up 60
Major Tune-up 61
Emission Control Systems
  Complete Test or Service 61
  Smog Station Certification 62
  Positive Crankcase Ventilation (PCV) 62
  Evaporative Emission Control System 63
  Transmission or Speed Controlled Spark (TCS/SCS) 63
  Exhaust-Gas Recirculation (EGR) 64
  Air Injection Reactor (AIR) 64
  Heated-Air System 64
Engine Service
  Ignition System 65
  Charging System 65
  Cranking System 66
  Engine Overhaul In-Car 66
  Engine Overhaul Out-of-Car 67
  Short Block, Replace 67
  Fuel System 68
  Timing Chain Mechanism 68
  Valve Mechanism 69
  Cylinder Head or Gasket 69
  Oil Pump 69
  Bearings, Main or Rod 70
  Cooling System 70
  Exhaust System 71
Automatic Transmission
  Performance Check 72
  Shift & Linkage Controls 72
  Major Service 73
Driveshaft, Rear Axle/Final Drive
  Driveshaft 73
  Rear Axle/Final Drive 74
  Rear Suspension 75
Front End Steering
  Front End 75
  Power Steering Unit 77
  Steering Linkage 78
Brake System
  Brakes 78
  Hydraulic Brake System 79
  Power Brake Unit 79
  Parking Brakes 80

Lighting System
  Adjust & Service 80
Heating System
  Test & Service 80
Air Conditioning System
  Spring Tune-up 81
  Major Service 81
  Blower Motor or Controls 82

CHEVROLET-CORVETTE

SERVICE STATION MAINTENANCE

General Lubrication 83
Battery 83
Cooling System 83
Ignition System 83
Fuel System 84
Driveshaft 84
Hydraulic Brake System 84
Parking Brakes 84
Suspension System 85
Front End & Steering System 85
Charging System 85
Cranking System 86
Lighting System 86
Minor Tune-up 86
Major Tune-up 86

INDEPENDENT GARAGE SCHEDULES

Minor Tune-up 87
Major Tune-up 87
Emission Control Systems
  Smog Station Certification 88
  Complete Test or Service 89
  Heated-Air System 90
  Evaporative System 91
  Positive Crankcase Ventilation 91
  Exhaust-Gas Recirculation (EGR) 91
  Transmission Controlled Spark 92
  Air Injection Reactor 92
Engine Service
  Ignition System 93
  Cranking System 94
  Charging System 94
  Fuel System 95

Engine Overhaul In-Car	96
Engine Overhaul Out-of-Car	97
Timing Chain Mechanism	98
Oil Pump	99
Bearings, Main or Rod	100
Cylinder Head or Gasket	101
Valve Mechanism	102
Exhaust System	102
Cooling System	103

Clutch & Standard Transmission

Shift Linkage	104
Clutch Mechanism	105
Standard Transmission, Overhaul	105

Automatic Transmission

Shift & Linkage Controls	106
Performance Check	106
Major Service	107

Driveshaft & Rear Axle

Driveshaft	107
Rear Axle	108
Rear Suspension	109

Steering & Front End

Standard Steering Gear	109
Front End	110
Power Steering Unit	111
Steering Linkage	112

Brake System

Hydraulic Brake System, Overhaul	112
Brakes, Service	113
Power Brake Unit	113
Parking Brakes	114

Lighting System

Adjust & Service	114

Heating System

Test & Service	115

Air Conditioning System

Spring Tune-up	116
Major Service	116
Blower Motor or Controls	117

CHRYSLER-PLYMOUTH-DODGE

SERVICE STATION MAINTENANCE

General Lubrication	118
Battery	118
Cooling System	118
Hydraulic Brake System	118
Parking Brakes	118
Suspension System	119
Front End & Steering System	119
Ignition System	119
Minor Tune-up	119
Major Tune-up	119
Fuel System	120
Driveshaft	120
Charging System	120
Cranking System	120
Lighting System	120

INDEPENDENT GARAGE SCHEDULES

Minor Tune-up	121
Major Tune-up	121

Emission Control Systems

Smog Station Certification	122
Complete Test or Service	123
Positive Crankcase Ventilation	124
NOx Control System	124
Air Injection System	125
Evaporative System	125
Heated-Air System	126
Exhaust-Gas Recirculation (EGR)	126
Orfice Spark Advance Control (OSAC)	126

Engine Service

Fuel System	127
Ignition System	128
Charging System	128
Cranking System	129
Engine Overhaul In-Car	129
Engine Overhaul Our-of-Car	130
Short Block, Replace	131
Timing Chain Mechanism	132
Oil Pump	132
Bearings, Main or Rods	133
Cylinder Head or Gasket	133
Valve Mechanism	134
Cooling System	135
Exhaust System	136

Clutch & Standard Transmission

Clutch Mechanism	136
Shift Linkage	137

Standard Transmission, Overhaul 137
Automatic Transmission
   Shift & Linkage Controls 138
   Performance Check 138
   Major Service 139
Driveshaft & Rear Axle
   Driveshaft 140
   Rear Axle 140
   Rear Suspension 141
Steering & Front End
   Standard Steering Gear 141
   Steering Linkage 141
   Front End 142
   Power Steering Unit 143
Brake System
   Power Brake Unit 143
   Brakes, Service 144
   Hydraulic Brake System 145
Lighting System
   Adjust & Service 145
Heating System
   Test & Service 146
Air Conditioning
   Spring Tune-up 146
   Major Service 147
   Blower Motor or Controls 147

FORD-LINCOLN-MERCURY

SERVICE STATION MAINTENANCE

   General Lubrication 148
   Battery 148
   Cooling System 148
   Ignition System 149
   Minor Tune-up 149
   Major Tune-up 149
   Fuel System 150
   Driveshaft 150
   Hydraulic Brake System 150
   Parking Brakes 150
   Suspension System 150
   Front End & Steering System 150
   Charging System 151
   Cranking System 151
   Lighting System 151

INDEPENDENT GARAGE SCHEDULES

Minor Tune-up 152
Major Tune-up 152
Emission Control Systems
   Smog Station Certification 153
   Complete Test or Service 154
   Positive Crankcase Ventilation (PCV) 155
   Transmission Regulated Spark (TRS) 155
   Electronic Spark Control (ESC) 155
   Heated-Air System 156
   Evaporative Control System 156
   Exhaust-Gas Recirculation (EGR) 156
   Spark Delay System (SDS) 157
   Thermactor (AIR) 157
Engine Service
   Cranking System 157
   Charging System 158
   Ignition System 159
   Fuel System 160
   Engine Overhaul, In-Car 161
   Engine Overhaul, Out-of-Car 162
   Short Block, Replace 163
   Cylinder Head or Gasket 163
   Valve Mechanism 164
   Oil Pump 165
   Timing Chain Mechanism 166
   Bearings, Main or Rod 167
   Cooling System 168
   Exhaust System 169
Clutch & Standard Transmission
   Shift Linkage 170
   Clutch Mechanism 170
   Standard Transmission, Overhaul 171
Automatic Transmission
   Performance Check 171
   Shift and Linkage Controls 172
   Major Service 172
Driveshaft & Rear Axle
   Driveshaft 173
   Rear Axle 173
   Rear Suspension 174
Steering & Front End
   Standard Steering Gear 174
   Power Steering Unit 175
   Front End 176
   Steering Linkage 177

Brake System
- Brakes, Service 177
- Hydraulic Brake System 178
- Parking Brakes 178
- Brake Booster or Skid Control 179

Lighting System
- Adjust & Service 179

Heating System
- Test & Service 180

Air Conditioning System
- Spring Tune-up 181
- Major Service 181
- Blower Motor or Controls 182

OLDSMOBILE

SERVICE STATION MAINTENANCE

- General Lubrication 183
- Battery 183
- Cooling System 183
- Ignition System 183
- Minor Tune-up 184
- Major Tune-up 184
- Fuel System 184
- Driveshaft 184
- Hydraulic Brake System 184
- Parking Brakes 184
- Suspension System 184
- Front End & Steering System 185
- Charging System 185
- Cranking System 185
- Lighting System 185

INDEPENDENT GARAGE SCHEDULES

Minor Tune-up 186
Major Tune-up 186

Emission Control Systems
- Smog Station Certification 187
- Complete Test or Service 188
- Air Injection Reactor (AIR) 189
- Transmission Controlled Spark (TCS) 189
- Positive Crankcase Ventilation (PCV) 190
- Evaporative Emission Control System 190
- Exhaust-Gas Recirculation (EGR) 190
- Heated-Air System 191

Engine Service
- Ignition System 191
- Cranking System 192
- Charging System 192
- Fuel System 193
- Engine Overhaul, In-Car 193
- Engine Overhaul, Out-of-Car 194
- Short Block, Replace 195
- Timing Chain Mechanism 196
- Oil Pump 196
- Bearings, Main or Rod 197
- Valve Mechanism 198
- Cylinder Head or Gasket 198
- Exhaust System 199
- Cooling System 200

Clutch & Standard Transmission
- Clutch Mechanism 200
- Shift Linkage 201
- Standard Transmission, Overhaul 201

Automatic Transmission
- Major Service 202
- Performance Check 203
- Shift & Linkage Controls 203

Driveshaft & Rear Axle
- Rear Axle/Final Drive 204
- Driveshaft 205
- Rear Suspension 205

Steering & Front End
- Steering Linkage 205
- Standard Steering Gear 206
- Power Steering Unit 206
- Front End 207

Brake System
- Hydraulic Brake System 209
- Parking Brakes 209
- Brakes, Service 210
- Power Brake Unit 210

Lighting System
- Adjust & Service 211

Heating System
- Test & Service 211

Air Conditioning System
- Spring Tune-up 212
- Major Service 212
- Blower Motor or Controls 213

PONTIAC

SERVICE STATION MAINTENANCE

- General Lubrication 215
- Battery 215
- Cooling System 215
- Ignition System 215
- Minor Tune-up 216
- Major Tune-up 216
- Fuel System 216
- Driveshaft 216
- Hydraulic Brake System 216
- Parking Brakes 216
- Suspension System 217
- Front End & Steering System 217
- Charging System 217
- Cranking System 217
- Lighting System 217

INDEPENDENT GARAGE SCHEDULES

- **Minor Tune-up** 218
- **Major Tune-up** 218
- **Emission Control Systems**
  - Complete Test or Service 219
  - Smog Station Certification 220
  - Positive Crankcase Ventilation (PCV) 221
  - Evaporative Emission Control System . 221
  - Heated-Air System 221
  - Air Injection Reactor (AIR) 222
  - Transmission Controlled Spark (TCS) 222
  - Exhaust-Gas Recirculation (EGR) 223
- **Engine Service**
  - Ignition System 223
  - Cranking System 224
  - Charging System 224
  - Fuel System 225
  - Engine Overhaul, In-Car 226
  - Engine Overhaul, Out-of-Car 227
  - Short Block, Replace 228
  - Timing Chain Mechanism 228
  - Oil Pump 229
  - Bearings, Main or Rod 230
  - Valve Mechanism 230
  - Cylinder Head or Gasket 231
  - Cooling System 232
  - Exhaust System 233
- **Clutch & Standard Transmission**
  - Shift Linkage 233
  - Clutch Mechanism 234
  - Standard Transmission, Overhaul 234
- **Automatic Transmission**
  - Major Service 235
  - Performance Check 236
  - Shift & Linkage Controls 236
- **Driveshaft & Rear Axle**
  - Driveshaft 237
  - Rear Axle 237
  - Rear Suspension 237
- **Steering & Front End**
  - Front End 238
  - Steering Linkage 239
  - Standard Steering Gear 239
  - Power Steering Unit 239
- **Brake System**
  - Parking Brakes 240
  - Brakes, Service 241
  - Power Brake Unit 241
  - Hydraulic Brake System 242
- **Lighting System**
  - Adjust & Service 242
- **Heating System**
  - Test & Service 243
- **Air Conditioning System**
  - Spring Tune-up 244
  - Major Service 244
  - Blower Motor or Controls 245

AMERICAN MOTORS 1

SERVICE STATION MAINTENANCE

Includes:
   Basic Job: Lubricate chassis, drain oil, change filters, repack front wheel bearings, repack U-joints, and lubricate front end. Check fluid levels of battery, radiator, air conditioner, brake master cylinder, power steering reservoir, transmission, and differential. Check condition of hoses and drive belts. Lubricate miscellaneous moving parts and joints, hinges, etc.
   Related Jobs: Service individual system or components. See detailed description of work included for each job in separate major section.
   Additions to Basic or Related Jobs: Allowances for special equipment installed.

MODEL	1966	1967	1968	1969	1970	1971	1972	1973	1974	1975
Basic Job:										
General lubrication & systems check,										
6-cylinder	1.0	1.0	1.0	1.0	1.0	1.0	1.0	1.0	1.0	1.0
V-8 engine	1.3	1.3	1.3	1.3	1.3	1.3	1.3	1.3	1.3	1.3
With air conditioning, **ADD:**	.3	.3	.3	.3	.3	.3	.3	.3	.3	.3
With air-Guard, **ADD:**	.2	.2	.2	.2	.2	.2	.2	.2	.2	.2
With disc brakes, **ADD:**	.9	.9	.9	.9	.9	.9	.9	.9	.9	.9
Related Jobs:										
Service Battery										
Clean, test, & fill	.3	.3	.3	.3	.3	.3	.3	.3	.3	.3
Clean terminals	.2	.2	.2	.2	.2	.2	.2	.2	.2	.2
Replace ground cable	.2	.2	.2	.2	.2	.2	.2	.2	.2	.2
Replace starter cable	.3	.3	.3	.3	.3	.3	.3	.3	.3	.3
Replace battery	.4	.4	.4	.4	.4	.4	.4	.4	.4	.4
Service Cooling System										
Back-flush, fill & pressure-test cap & sys.	.6	.6	.6	.6	.6	.6	.6	.6	.6	.6
Replace upper hose	.4	.4	.4	.4	.4	.4	.4	.4	.4	.4
Replace lower hose	.5	.5	.5	.5	.5	.5	.5	.5	.5	.5
With air conditioning, **ADD:**	.2	.2	.2	.2	.2	.2	.2	.2	.2	.2
Replace thermostat, includes test,										
6-cylinder	.5	.5	.5	.5	.5	.5	.5	.5	.5	.5
V-8 engine	.7	.7	.7	.7	.7	.7	.7	.7	.7	.7
With air conditioning, **ADD:**	.2	.2	.2	.2	.2	.2	.2	.2	.2	.2
Replace water pump drive belt & adjust	.4	.4	.4	.4	.4	.4	.4	.4	.4	.4
With air cond., Air-Guard, or P.S., **ADD:**	.2	.2	.2	.2	.2	.2	.2	.2	.2	.2
Replace water pump, incl. check system,										
6-cylinder	1.0	1.0	1.0	1.0	1.0	1.0	1.0	1.0	1.0	1.0
With air conditioning, **ADD:**	.1	.1	.1	.1	.1	.1	.1	.1	.1	.1
V-8 engine	1.5	1.5	1.5	1.5	1.5	1.5	1.5	1.5	1.5	1.5
With air conditioning, **ADD:**	.3	.3	.3	.3	.3	.3	.6	.6	.6	.6
With power steering, all models, **ADD:**	.2	.2	.2	.2	.2	.2	.2	.2	.2	.2
With Air-Guard, all models, **ADD:**	.2	.2	.2	.2	.2	.2	.2	.2	.2	.2
Service Ignition System										
Adjust & install new spark plugs,										
6-cylinder	.6	.6	.6	.6	.6	.6	.6	.6	.6	.6
V-8 engine	.8	.8	.8	.8	.8	.8	.8	.8	.8	.8
With air conditioning, **ADD:**	.3	.3	.3	.3	.3	.3	.3	.3	.3	.3
With Air-Guard, **ADD:**	.3	.3	.3	.3	.3	.3	.3	.3	.3	.3
Replace points & condenser & adjust ignition timing	.7	.7	.7	.7	.7	.7	.7	.7	.7	—
Replace distributor cap, **ADD:**	.4	.4	.4	.4	.4	.4	.4	.4	.4	.4
Adjust reluctor air gap and adj. ign. timing	—	—	—	—	—	—	—	—	—	.3
Replace spark plug wires,										
6-cylinder	.5	.5	.6	.6	.8	.8	.6	.6	.6	.6
V-8 engine	.7	.7	.8	.8	.8	.8	.8	.8	.8	.8
With air conditioning, **ADD:**	.3	.3	.3	.3	.3	.3	.3	.3	.3	.3
Replace ignition coil	.5	.5	.5	.5	.5	.5	.5	.5	.5	.5

(THIS SCHEDULE CONTINUED ON NEXT PAGE.)

2 AMERICAN MOTORS

SERVICE STATION MAINTENANCE Continued

MODEL	1966	1967	1968	1969	1970	1971	1972	1973	1974	1975
Service Fuel System										
Complete carburetor adjustments,										
Single barrel	.4	.4	.4	.4	.4	.4	.4	.4	.4	.4
Two-barrel	.6	.6	.6	.6	.6	.6	.6	.6	.6	.6
Four-barrel	.7	.7	.7	.7	.7	.7	.7	.7	.7	.7
Replace fuel filter	.3	.3	.3	.3	.3	.3	.3	.3	.3	.3
Test & replace fuel pump,										
6-cylinder	.9	.9	.9	.9	.9	.9	.9	.9	.9	.9
V-8 engine	1.1	1.1	1.1	1.1	1.1	1.1	1.1	1.1	1.1	1.1
With air conditioning, **ADD:**	.2	.2	.2	.2	.2	.2	.2	.2	.2	.2
With power steering, **ADD:**	.1	.1	.1	.1	.1	.1	.1	.1	.1	.1
With Air-Guard, **ADD:**	.1	.1	.1	.1	.1	.1	.1	.1	.1	.1
Replace flexible fuel line	.3	.3	.3	.3	.3	.3	.3	.3	.3	.3
Service Driveshaft										
R&R driveshaft & overhaul both U-joints and adjust pinion nose angle.										
Ambassador	2.1	2.1	2.1	2.1	2.2	2.2	2.2	2.2	2.2	
All others	1.6	1.6	1.6	1.6	1.6	1.6	1.6	1.6	1.6	1.6
Service Hydraulic Brake System										
Adjust drum brakes	.5	.5	.5	.5	.5	.5	.5	.5	.5	.5
Replace drum brake shoes	3.5	3.5	3.5	3.5	3.5	3.5	3.5	3.5	3.5	3.5
Replace disc brake pads	.6	.6	.6	.6	.6	.6	.6	.6	.6	.6
Bleed hydraulic system	.6	.6	.6	.6	.6	.6	.6	.6	.6	.6
O/h 4 wheel cylinders, incl. hone & bleed	1.6	2.3	2.3	2.3	2.3	2.4	2.4	2.4	2.4	2.4
O/h calipers, incl. turn rotors	3.5	3.5	3.5	2.9	2.9	2.9	2.9	2.9	2.9	2.9
O/h master cylinder, incl. bleed sys.	1.5	1.5	1.5	1.5	1.5	1.8	1.8	1.8	1.8	1.8
Service Parking Brakes										
Adjust parking brakes	.4	.4	.4	.4	.4	.4	.4	.4	.4	.4
Replace forward cable	1.0	1.0	1.0	1.0	1.0	1.0	1.0	1.1	1.1	1.1
Replace rear cable, one side	.8	.8	.8	.8	.8	.8	.8	.8	.8	.8
Service Suspension System										
Replace front shock absorber, both sides	.9	.9	.9	.9	.9	.9	.9	.9	.9	.9
Replace rear shock absorber, both sides	.9	.9	.9	.9	.8	.8	.8	.8	.8	.8
Replace shackle and bushings; eye bolt and bushings	.7	.7	.7	.7	.7	.7	.7	.7	.7	.7
Replace rear leaf spring & shim to align pinion angle	1.7	1.7	1.7	1.7	1.7	1.7	1.7	1.7	1.7	1.7
Service Front End & Steering System										
Adjust toe-in only	.6	.6	.6	.6	.6	.6	.6	.6	.6	.6
Replace tie-rods or tie-rod ends, (4)	1.6	1.6	1.5	1.5	1.5	1.5	1.5	1.5	1.5	1.5
Repl. Pitman arm, incl. adj. toe-in	.8	.8	.8	.8	.8	.8	.8	.8	.8	.8
Repl. steering idler arm or bushing, including adjust toe-in	.8	.8	.8	.8	.8	.8	.8	.8	.8	.8
Repl. pwr. steer. pump drive belt & adj.	.3	.3	.3	.3	.3	.3	.3	.3	.3	.3
With air conditioning, **ADD:**	.2	.2	.2	.2	.2	.2	.2	.2	.2	.2
Check & replenish reservoir fluid	.2	.2	.2	.2	.2	.2	.2	.2	.2	.2
Repl. press. hose, incl. adj. dr. belt	.5	.5	.6	.6	.6	.6	.6	.6	.6	.6
Repl. return hose, incl. adj. dr. belt	.4	.4	.4	.4	.4	.4	.4	.4	.4	.4
Balance four wheels on car	2.0	2.0	2.0	2.0	2.0	2.0	2.0	2.0	2.0	2.0
Service Charging System										
Test system and adjust regulator	.6	.6	.6	.6	.6	.6	.6	.6	.6	.6
R&R alternator incl. pulley	.6	.6	.6	.6	.7	.7	.7	.7	.7	.7
With air conditioning, **ADD:**	.1	.1	.1	.1	.1	.1	.1	.1	.1	.1
With Air-Guard, **ADD:**	.2	.2	.2	.2	.2	.2	.2	.2	.2	.2
Overhaul alternator after removal	2.3	2.3	1.5	1.5	1.5	1.5	1.5	1.5	1.5	1.5
Replace regulator	.3	.3	.3	.3	.4	.4	.4	.4	.4	.4

(THIS SCHEDULE CONTINUED ON NEXT PAGE.)

AMERICAN MOTORS 3

SERVICE STATION MAINTENANCE Continued

MODEL	1966	1967	1968	1969	1970	1971	1972	1973	1974	1975
Service Cranking System										
R&R starter,										
6-cylinder	.7	.7	.7	.7	.7	.8	.8	.8	.8	.8
V-8 engine	.8	.8	.8	.8	.9	.9	1.0	1.0	1.0	1.0
Overhaul starter after removal	1.7	1.7	1.7	1.7	1.7	1.7	1.7	1.7	1.7	1.7
Replace starter battery cable	.3	.3	.3	.3	.3	.3	.3	.3	.3	.3
Replace starter solenoid switch	.2	.2	.2	.2	.2	.2	.2	.2	.2	.2
Service Lighting System										
Adjust two headlights	.4	.4	.4	.4	.4	.4	.4	.4	.4	.4
Adjust four headlights	.6	.6	.6	.6	.6	.6	.6	.6	.6	.6
Replace sealed beam unit, ea.	.3	.3	.3	.3	.3	.3	.3	.3	.3	.3
Replace foot dimmer switch	.3	.3	.3	.3	.3	.3	.3	.3	.3	.3
Replace signal/hazard flasher	.3	.3	.3	.3	.3	.3	.3	.3	.3	.3
Replace signal/hazard switch,										
With standard column	.8	.8	.8	.8	.8	.8	.8	.8	.8	.8
With tilt wheel	1.0	1.0	1.0	1.0	1.0	1.0	1.0	1.0	1.0	1.0
Perform Minor Tune-up										
6-cylinder	2.2	2.2	2.2	2.2	2.4	2.4	2.5	2.5	2.5	2.5
V-8 engine	2.7	2.7	2.7	2.7	2.9	2.9	3.0	3.0	3.0	3.0

Note: See minor tune-up section for work included and additions.

Perform Major Tune-up										
6-cylinder	5.8	5.8	5.8	5.8	6.1	6.1	6.1	6.3	6.3	6.5
V-8 engine	6.3	6.3	6.3	6.5	6.5	6.5	6.5	6.8	6.8	7.0

Note: See major tune-up section for work included and additions.

TUNE-UP, MINOR

Includes:

Basic Job: Perform the following work.

1. Service air cleaner element.
2. Replace PCV valve.
3. Replace crankcase ventilation filter in air cleaner.
4. Clean battery terminals.
5. Check condition and tension of all drive belts.
6. Check all hoses and hose connections.
7. Check operation of heated-air system (air cleaner), manifold heat valve, and automatic choke. Service where necessary.
8. Replace fuel filter.
9. Perform compression test.
10. Replace spark plugs.
11. Replace ignition points and condenser.
12. Adjust dwell or sensor air gap and ignition timing.
13. Adjust carburetor idle mixture and speed.
14. Make necessary ignition-and carburetor adjustments to obtain satisfactory scope or HC/CO exhaust system analyzer readings.

Additions to Basic Job: Allowances for special equipment and carburetor.

MODEL	1966	1967	1968	1969	1970	1971	1972	1973	1974	1975
Basic Job:										
Perform minor tune-up,										
6-cylinder	2.2	2.2	2.2	2.2	2.4	2.4	2.5	2.5	2.5	2.5
V-8 engine	2.7	2.7	2.7	2.7	2.9	2.9	3.0	3.0	3.0	3.0
V-8 small block with 4-bbl. carb., **ADD:**	.2	.2	.2	.2	.2	.2	.2	.2	.2	.2
With Air-Guard, **ADD:**	.3	.3	.3	.3	.3	.3	.3	.3	.3	.3
With air conditioning, **ADD:**	.6	.6	.6	.6	.6	.6	.6	.6	.6	.6

Approximate parts cost:

Spark plugs, each	$1.50	Air cleaner element	$5.50
Points & condenser	5.00	Fuel filter	3.50
PCV valve	3.00		

4 AMERICAN MOTORS

TUNE-UP, MAJOR

Includes:
    Basic Job: Perform the following work.
        1. Service air cleaner element.
        2. Replace crankcase ventilation filter in air cleaner.
        3. Replace PCV valve.
        4. Check drive belts and adjust for proper tension.
        5. Check all hoses and hose connections.
        6. Clean battery terminals.
        7. Check operation of manifold heat valve and automatic choke. Service where necessary.
        8. Check operation of heated-air system.
        9. Check exhaust and evaporative emission control systems for proper operation.
        10. Replace fuel filter.
        11. Perform compression check.
        12. Replace spark plugs.
        13. Replace ignition points and condenser.
        14. Adjust dwell or sensor air gap and ignition timing.
        15. Check distributor cap and rotor.
        16. Tighten cylinder head bolts.
        17. Adjust valve lash (where applicable).
        18. Overhaul carburetor.
        19. Adjust carburetor idle mixture and speed.
        20. Make necessary ignition and carburetor adjustments to obtain satisfactory scope or HC/CO exhaust system analyzer readings.
    Additions to Basic Job: Allowances for special equipment and carburetor.

MODEL	1966	1967	1968	1969	1970	1971	1972	1973	1974	1975
Basic Job:										
Perform major tune-up.										
6-cylinder	5.8	5.8	5.8	5.8	6.1	6.1	6.1	6.3	6.3	6.5
V-8 engine	6.3	6.3	6.3	6.5	6.5	6.5	6.5	6.8	6.8	7.0
Additions to Basic Job:										
Replace hydraulic valve lifter, one, ea.	2.0	2.0	2.0	2.0	2.0	2.0	2.0	2.0	2.0	2.0
V-8 small block with 4-bbl. carb., **ADD:**	1.0	1.0	1.0	1.0	1.0	1.0	1.0	1.0	1.0	1.0
With Air-Guard, **ADD:**	.3	.3	.3	.3	.3	.3	.3	.3	.3	.3
With air conditioning, **ADD:**	.6	.6	.6	.6	.6	.6	.6	.6	.6	.6

Approximate parts cost:

Spark plugs, each	$1.50	Fuel filter	$3.50
Points & condenser	5.00	Carburetor repair kit	6.00-15.00
PCV valve	3.00	Carburetor gasket kit	2.50
Air cleaner element	5.50	Hydraulic valve lifter, each	4.00

EXHAUST-GAS RECIRCULATION (EGR), TEST AND SERVICE

Includes:
    Basic Job: Test EGR valve, control system, and engine idling condition.
    Additions to Basic Job: Service or replace defective parts. Test & repair EGR thermostatic control system.

MODEL	1966	1967	1968	1969	1970	1971	1972	1973	1974	1975
Basic Job:										
Test EGR system, all models	—	—	—	—	—	—	—	.4	.4	.4

(THIS SCHEDULE CONTINUED ON NEXT PAGE.)

AMERICAN MOTORS 5

EXHAUST-GAS RECIRCULATION (EGR) TEST AND SERVICE Continued

MODEL	1966	1967	1968	1969	1970	1971	1972	1973	1974	1975
Additions to Basic Job:										
Service EGR valve, **ADD:**	—	—	—	—	—	—	.7	.7	.7	.7
Replace EGR valve, **ADD:**	—	—	—	—	—	—	.4	.4	.4	.4
Test & service thermo. control sys., **ADD:**	—	—	—	—	—	—	.6	.6	.6	.6

Approximate parts cost:
EGR valve $10.00

EMISSION CONTROL SYSTEMS, TESTS FOR SMOG STATION CERTIFICATION

Includes:
Basic Job: Test crankcase, exhaust and evaporative emission control systems. Check heated-air system. Check HC/CO level with exhaust analyzer. Sign certification certificate. (No adjustments or repairs included in basic job.)
Related Jobs: Service any defective emission control system. Perform minor or major tune-up as required.
Additions to Related Jobs: Service or replace defective part(s) in the system and allowances for special equipment and carburetor.

MODEL	1966	1967	1968	1969	1970	1971	1972	1973	1974	1975
Basic Job:										
Test all systems & sign certificate										
Ambassador	.8	.8	.8	.8	.8	.8	.8	.8	.8	
All others	1.0	1.0	1.0	1.0	1.0	1.0	1.0	1.0	1.0	1.0
Related Jobs:										
Service crankcase emission control sys.	.3	.3	.3	.3	.3	.3	.3	.3	.3	.3
Service evaporative emission contr. sys.	—	—	—	—	.4	.4	.4	.4	.4	.4
Exhaust emission control systems,										
Service heated-air system	.3	.3	.3	.3	.3	.3	.3	.3	.3	.3
Service TCS system	—	—	—	—	—	.5	.5	.5	.5	.5
Service EGR system	—	—	—	—	—	—	.4	.4	.4	.4
Service Air-Guard (AIR) system	.5	.5	.5	.5	.5	—	.5	.5	.5	.5
Replace catalytic converter	—	—	—	—	—	—	—	—	—	1.8

Note: See separate section for replacement of components in each system.

	1966	1967	1968	1969	1970	1971	1972	1973	1974	1975
Perform minor tune-up,										
6-cylinder	2.2	2.2	2.2	2.2	2.4	2.4	2.5	2.5	2.5	2.5
V-8 engine	2.7	2.7	2.7	2.7	2.9	2.9	3.0	3.0	3.0	3.0
Perform major tune-up,										
6-cylinder	5.8	5.8	5.8	5.8	6.1	6.1	6.1	6.3	6.3	6.5
V-8 engine	6.3	6.3	6.3	6.5	6.5	6.5	6.5	6.8	6.8	7.0
Additions to Related Jobs:										
Major Tune-up										
V-8 small block with 4-bbl. carb., **ADD:**	1.0	1.0	1.0	1.0	1.0	1.0	1.1	1.1	1.1	1.1
Minor Tune-up										
V-8 small block with 4-bbl. carb., **ADD:**	.2	.2	.2	.2	.2	.2	.2	.2	.2	.2
With Air-Guard, **ADD:**	.3	.3	.3	.3	.3	.3	.3	.3	.3	.3
With air conditioning, **ADD:**	.6	.6	.6	.6	.6	.6	.6	.6	.6	.6

Approximate parts cost:
Catalytic converter $175.00
See major or minor tune-up section for cost of tune-up parts.

6 AMERICAN MOTORS

EMISSION CONTROL SYSTEMS, COMPLETE TEST OR SERVICE

Includes:
Basic Job: Make all necessary tests and repairs. Sign certification certificate.
1. Replace PCV valve, check all vacuum passageways and hoses.
2. Replace crankcase ventilation filter in air cleaner.
3. Test evaporative emission system gas tank filler cap and vent lines, and hoses for leakage.
4. Replace evaporation system charcoal canister filter.
5. Clean EGR valve and test the control system.
6. Check TCS system.
7. Check Spark-Control System (SCS).
8. Check operation of manifold heat control valve and automatic choke. Free up where necessary.
9. Check and adjust tension of drive belts.
10. Check operation of heated air system.
11. Check AIR pump air flow.
12. Check routing and condition of hoses.
13. Check operation of diverter or bypass valve.
14. Inspect air manifold and hoses.
15. Replace catalytic converter, if necessary.
16. Measure exhaust HC/CO levels with analyzer to determine if an engine tune-up is required.

Related Jobs: Minor or major tune-up as required.

MODEL	1966	1967	1968	1969	1970	1971	1972	1973	1974	1975
Basic Job:										
Perform emission control sys. tune-up,										
6-cylinder	2.8	2.8	2.8	2.8	3.3	3.3	3.3	3.3	3.3	3.5
V-8 engine	3.3	3.3	3.3	3.3	3.8	3.8	3.8	3.8	3.8	4.0
With Air-Guard, **ADD:**	.5	.5	.5	.5	.5	.5	.5	.5	.5	.5
Related Jobs:										
Perform minor tune-up,										
6-cylinder	2.2	2.2	2.2	2.2	2.4	2.4	2.5	2.5	2.5	2.5
V-8 engine	2.7	2.7	2.7	2.7	2.9	2.9	3.0	3.0	3.0	3.0
Perform major tune-up,										
6-cylinder	5.8	5.8	5.8	5.8	6.1	6.1	6.1	6.3	6.3	6.5
V-8 engine	6.3	6.3	6.3	6.5	6.5	6.5	6.5	6.8	6.8	7.0
Additions to Related Jobs:										
V-8 small block with 4-bbl. carb., **ADD:**	1.0	1.0	1.0	1.0	1.0	1.0	1.0	1.0	1.0	1.0
With air conditioning, **ADD:**	.6	.6	.6	.6	.6	.6	.6	.6	.6	.6

Approximate parts cost:
PCV valve	$3.00
Hose, per ft.	.75
Canister filter	1.00
Purge control valve	4.00
Drive belt	$ 3.00
Catalytic converter	175.00
Diverter valve	12.00
Air-Guard (AIR) pump	75.00

See major or minor tune-up section for cost of tune-up parts.

HEATED-AIR SYSTEM, TEST AND SERVICE

Includes:
Basic Job: Check cold/heated-air door, temperature sensor, and vacuum motor.
Additions to Basic Job: Replace defective parts.

MODEL	1966	1967	1968	1969	1970	1971	1972	1973	1974	1975
Basic Job:										
Test heated-air system	—	—	—	.3	.3	.3	.3	.3	.3	.3

(THIS SCHEDULE CONTINUED ON NEXT PAGE.)

AMERICAN MOTORS

HEATED-AIR SYSTEM, TEST AND SERVICE Continued

MODEL	1966	1967	1968	1969	1970	1971	1972	1973	1974	1975
Additions to Basic Job:										
Replace temperature sensor, **ADD**:	—	—	—	.5	.5	.5	.5	.5	.5	.5
Replace vacuum motor, **ADD**:	—	—	—	.4	.4	.4	.4	.4	.4	.4

Approximate parts cost:
Vacuum motor assembly ....$5.00   Temperature sensor $4.50

EVAPORATIVE EMISSION CONTROL SYSTEM, TEST AND SERVICE

Includes:
Basic Job: Test gas tank filler cap, vent lines, and hoses.
Additions to Basic Job: Replace defective parts.

MODEL	1966	1967	1968	1969	1970	1971	1972	1973	1974	1975
Basic Job:										
Test evap. emission control system	—	—	—	—	.4	.4	.4	.4	.4	.4
Additions to Basic Job:										
Replace purge control valve, **ADD**:	—	—	—	—	—	—	.5	—	—	—
Replace fuel vapor canister filter, **ADD**:	—	—	—	—	.3	.3	.3	.3	.3	.3
Replace fuel vapor canister, **ADD**:	—	—	—	—	.5	.5	.5	.5	.5	.5
Replace hose, each, **ADD**:	—	—	—	—	.2	.2	.2	.2	.2	.2

Approximate parts cost:
Purge control valve ....$4.00   Hose, per ft. ....$ .75
Fuel vapor canister filter ....1.00   Fuel vapor canister 25.00

AIR-GUARD (AIR) SYSTEM, TEST AND SERVICE

Includes:
Basic Job: Test air pump flow, check routing and condition of hoses, determine operation of diverter valve, verify check valve operation, inspect air manifold and hoses. Check and adjust drive belt tension.
Additions to Basic Job: Replace defective part. Replace drive belt includes adjust tension. Replacement of hose(s) includes soapy water test.

MODEL	1966	1967	1968	1969	1970	1971	1972	1973	1974	1975
Basic Job:										
Test AIR system, all models	.5	.5	.5	.5	.5	.5	.5	.5	.5	.5
Additions to Basic Job:										
Replace and adjust drive belt, **ADD**:	.5	.5	.5	.5	.5	.5	.5	.5	.5	.5
Replace AIR pump,										
Ambassador, **ADD**:	.8	.8	.8	.8	.8	.8	.8	.8	.8	—
All others, **ADD**:	.6	.6	.6	.6	.6	.6	.6	.6	.6	.6
Replace diverter valve, **ADD**:	.4	.4	.4	.4	.4	.4	.4	.4	.4	.4
Replace hose, incl. soapy wtr. test,										
Ambassador, **ADD**:	.5	.5	.5	.5	.5	.5	.5	.5	.5	—
All others, **ADD**:	.4	.4	.4	.4	.4	.4	.4	.4	.4	.4

Approximate parts cost:
Drive belt ....$ 3.00   Diverter valve $12.00-25.00
Air-Guard (AIR) pump ....60.00   Hose, per ft. 75

8 AMERICAN MOTORS

TRANSMISSION CONTROLLED SPARK (TCS) SYSTEM, TEST AND SERVICE

Includes:
Basic Job: Check engine speed in gear using tachometer and timing light, test TRS solenoid and transmission switch.
Additions to Basic Job: Replace defective parts.

MODEL	1966	1967	1968	1969	1970	1971	1972	1973	1974	1975
Basic Job:										
Test TCS system, all models	—	—	—	—	—	.5	.5	.5	.5	.5
Additions to Basic Job:										
Replace TCS solenoid vacuum valve, **ADD:**	—	—	—	—	—	1.1	1.1	1.1	1.1	1.1
Replace TCS trans. speed sensor,										
Manual transmission, **ADD:**	—	—	—	—	—	.8	.8	.8	.8	.8
Automatic transmission, **ADD:**	—	—	—	—	—	1.1	1.1	1.1	1.1	1.1
Replace TCS temp. override switch, **ADD:**	—	—	—	—	—	1.1	1.1	1.1	1.1	1.1
Replace idle stop solenoid, **ADD:**	—	—	—	—	—	.7	.7	.7	.7	.7

Approximate parts cost:
Solenoid vacuum valve .... $12.00 TCS temperature override switch .... $ 6.00
Transmission speed sensor .... 6.00 Idle stop solenoid 11.00

POSITIVE CRANKCASE VENTILATION (PCV) SYSTEM, TEST AND SERVICE

Includes:
Basic Job: Test PCV valve, check all vacuum passageways, and inspect hoses. Clean or replace air filter.
Additions to Basic Job: Replace defective parts. (Do not attempt to clean PCV valve; replace if valve is not free.)

MODEL	1966	1967	1968	1969	1970	1971	1972	1973	1974	1975
Basic Job:										
Test PCV system, all models	.3	.3	.3	.3	.3	.3	.3	.3	.3	.3
Additions to Basic Job:										
Replace PCV valve, **ADD:**	.3	.3	.3	.3	.3	.3	.3	.3	.3	.3
Replace all hoses, **ADD:**	.6	.6	.6	.6	.6	.6	.6	.6	.6	.6

Approximate parts cost:
PCV valve .... $3.00 Hose, per ft. .... $ .75

IGNITION SYSTEM, SERVICE

Includes:
Basic Jobs: 1. Adjust and install new spark plugs.
             2. Replace points and condenser, adjust dwell and ignition timing.
             3. R&R distributor, overhaul and test centrifugal and vacuum advances, set dwell or adjust sensor air gap and ignition timing.
Related Jobs: Replace additional defective part(s) as required.
Additions: Allowances for special equipment installed or replacement of associated defective part(s).

MODEL	1966	1967	1968	1969	1970	1971	1972	1973	1974	1975
Basic Job #1										
Adjust & install new spark plugs,										
6-cylinder	.6	.6	.6	.6	.6	.6	.6	.6	.6	.6
V-8 engine	.8	.8	.8	.8	.8	.8	.8	.8	.8	.8
With air conditioning, **ADD:**	.3	.3	.3	.3	.3	.3	.3	.3	.3	.3
With Air-Guard, **ADD:**	.3	.3	.3	.3	.3	.3	.3	.3	.3	.3

(THIS SCHEDULE CONTINUED ON NEXT PAGE.)

AMERICAN MOTORS

IGNITION SYSTEM, SERVICE Continued

MODEL	1966	1967	1968	1969	1970	1971	1972	1973	1974	1975
Basic Job #2										
Replace points and condenser & adjust	.7	.7	.7	.7	.7	.7	.7	.7	.7	—
Replace distributor cap, **ADD:**	.4	.4	.4	.4	.4	.4	.4	.4	.4	.4
Basic Job #3										
R&R and overhaul distributor & adjust,										
6-cylinder	1.9	1.9	1.9	1.9	1.9	1.9	1.9	1.9	1.9	1.4
V-8 engine	2.3	2.3	2.3	2.3	2.3	2.3	2.3	2.3	2.3	1.8
Replace vacuum advance unit, **ADD:**	.2	.2	.2	.2	.2	.2	.2	.2	.2	.2
Related Jobs:										
Replace ignition coil	.5	.5	.5	.5	.5	.5	.5	.5	.5	.5
Replace spark plug wires,										
6-cylinder	.5	.5	.6	.6	.8	.8	.6	.6	.6	.6
V-8 engine	.7	.7	.8	.8	.8	.8	.8	.8	.8	.8
With air conditioning, **ADD:**	.3	.3	.3	.3	.3	.3	.3	.3	.3	.3
Replace ignition switch,										
With standard column	.6	.6	.6	.6	1.1	1.1	1.1	1.1	1.1	1.1
With tilt or telescopic column	.8	.8	.8	.8	.8	.8	.8	.8	.8	.8

Approximate parts cost:

Spark plugs, each	$ 1.50
Point set	4.00
Condenser	1.50
Distributor cap	4.50
Distributor parts	10.00
Vacuum control unit	$10.00
Ignition coil	12.50
Spark plug wires, 6-cylinder	8.00
V-8 engine	12.00-27.00
Ignition switch	9.00

CRANKING SYSTEM, TEST AND SERVICE

Includes:
Basic Jobs: Test battery and cranking system. Clean battery cable terminals.
Related Jobs: Replace defective part including test when necessary.

MODEL	1966	1967	1968	1969	1970	1971	1972	1973	1974	1975
Basic Job:										
Test cranking system	.5	.5	.5	.5	.5	.5	.5	.5	.5	.5
Related Jobs:										
R&R starter,										
6-cylinder	.7	.7	.7	.7	.7	.8	.8	.8	.8	.8
V-8 engine	.8	.8	.8	.8	.9	.9	1.0	1.0	1.0	1.0
Overhaul starter after removal	1.7	1.7	1.7	1.7	1.7	1.7	1.7	1.7	1.7	1.7
Replace starter-battery cable	.3	.3	.3	.3	.3	.3	.3	.3	.3	.3
Replace starter solenoid switch	.2	.2	.2	.2	.2	.2	.2	.2	.2	.2
Repl. starter/neutral switch & adjust,										
With column shift	.4	.4	.4	.4	.4	.4	.4	.4	.4	.4
With floor shift	.7	.7	.7	.7	.7	.7	.7	.7	.7	.7

Approximate parts cost:

Starter, new	$70.00
Starter, rebuilt	30.00
Starter-battery cable	2.00-6.00
Starter solenoid switch	$17.00
Starter neutral switch	7.00

10 AMERICAN MOTORS

CHARGING SYSTEM, TEST AND SERVICE

Includes:
Basic Job: Test battery voltage and gravity, clean battery cable terminals, test alternator output, test and adjust regulator.
Related Jobs: Replace or overhaul defective component.

MODEL	1966	1967	1968	1969	1970	1971	1972	1973	1974	1975
Basic Job:										
Test system and adjust regulator	.6	.6	.6	.6	.6	.6	.6	.6	.6	.6
Related Jobs:										
R&R alternator incl. pulley	.6	.6	.6	.6	.7	.7	.7	.7	.7	.7
With air conditioning, **ADD:**	.1	.1	.1	.1	.1	.1	.1	.1	.1	.1
With AIR, **ADD:**	.2	.2	.2	.2	.2	.2	.2	.2	.2	.2
Overhaul alternator after removal	1.5	1.5	1.5	1.5	1.5	1.5	1.5	1.5	1.5	1.5
Replace regulator	.3	.3	.3	.3	.4	.4	.4	.4	.4	.4

Approximate parts cost:
Alternator, new .... $75.00-95.00 Regulator $18.00
Alternator, rebuilt 35.00

FUEL SYSTEM, ADJUST AND SERVICE

Includes:
Basic Job: Adjust idle speed, fast-idle speed and idle mixture for performance and to obtain satisfactory exhaust system analyzer readings.
Related Jobs: R&R carburetor, overhaul carburetor R&R associated fuel components.

MODEL	1966	1967	1968	1969	1970	1971	1972	1973	1974	1975
Basic Job:										
Complete carburetor adjustments,										
Single barrel	.4	.4	.4	.4	.4	.4	.4	.4	.4	.4
Two-barrel	.6	.6	.6	.6	.6	.6	.6	.6	.6	.6
Four-barrel	.7	.7	.7	.7	.7	.7	.7	.7	.7	.7
Related Jobs:										
Replace carb. incl. compl. adjustments,										
Single or 2-barrel	.6	.6	.5	.5	.7	.7	.7	.7	.7	.7
Four-barrel	1.0	1.0	1.0	1.0	1.0	1.0	1.0	1.0	1.0	1.0
O/H carb., incl. R&R and compl. adjust.,										
Singel or two-barrel	2.6	2.6	2.6	2.5	2.7	2.2	2.4	2.4	2.4	2.4
Four-barrel	4.0	4.0	4.0	4.0	3.2	3.2	3.2	3.2	3.4	3.4
Test & replace fuel pump,										
6-cylinder	.9	.9	.9	.9	.9	.9	.9	.9	.9	.9
V-8 engine	1.1	1.1	1.1	1.1	1.1	1.1	1.1	1.1	1.1	1.1
With air conditioning, **ADD:**	.2	.2	.2	.2	.2	.2	.2	.2	.2	.2
With pwr. steer., **ADD:**	.1	.1	.1	.1	.1	.1	.1	.1	.1	.1
With Air-Guard, **ADD:**	.1	.1	.1	.1	.1	.1	.1	.1	.1	.1
Replace fuel filter	.3	.3	.3	.3	.3	.3	.3	.3	.3	.3
Replace fuel tank sending unit	.8	.8	.8	.8	.8	.8	.8	.8	.8	.8
Replace fuel gauge, instrument panel,										
Javelin, AMX	1.5	1.5	1.5	1.5	1.5	1.1	1.1	1.1	1.1	1.1
All others	1.0	1.0	1.0	1.0	1.0	1.0	1.0	1.0	1.0	1.0
Replace fuel tank	.9	.9	.9	.9	1.1	1.1	1.1	1.1	1.1	1.1
Clean fuel tank, **ADD:**	.6	.6	.6	.6	.6	.6	.6	.6	.6	.6
Replace flexible fuel line	.3	.3	.3	.3	.3	.3	.3	.3	.3	.3

(THIS SCHEDULE CONTINUED ON NEXT PAGE.)

AMERICAN MOTORS 11

FUEL SYSTEM, ADJUST AND SERVICE Continued

MODEL	1966	1967	1968	1969	1970	1971	1972	1973	1974	1975
Related Jobs: Continued										
Replace intake manifold gasket, includes adjust carburetor & ignition timing,										
6-cylinder	1.5	1.5	1.5	1.5	1.5	1.5	1.5	1.5	1.5	1.5
V-8 engine	2.0	2.0	2.0	2.0	2.0	2.0	2.0	2.0	2.0	2.0
With Air-Guard, **ADD**:	.2	.2	.2	.2	.2	.2	.2	.2	.2	.2
With air conditioning, **ADD**:	.3	.3	.3	.3	.3	.3	.3	.3	.3	.3
V-8 small block with 4-bbl. carb., **ADD**:	.2	.2	.2	.2	.2	.2	.2	.2	.2	.2

Approximate parts cost:
Carburetor repair kit	$6.00-15.00
Carburetor, new, single bbl.	40.00
Two bbl.	40.00
Four bbl.	80.00
Carburetor, rebuilt, single bbl.	15.00
Two bbl.	22.00
Four bbl.	40.00
Fuel pump	$15.00-25.00
Fuel tank sending unit	10.00
Fuel gauge, dashboard	7.00-15.00
Fuel tank	50.00-65.00
Gasket, manifold	4.00
Air cleaner element	4.00

SHORT BLOCK, REPLACE

Includes:
Basic Job: R&R engine, clean and reface valves, scrape carbon, grind valve seats, replace valve seals, overhaul rocker arm mechanism, transfer all parts, and perform major tune-up.

Additions to Basic Job: Associated work that is required during basic job and allowances for special equipment and/or carburetor.

MODEL	1966	1967	1968	1969	1970	1971	1972	1973	1974	1975
Basic Job:										
Replace short block										
6-cylinder	14.8	14.8	14.8	14.8	15.1	15.1	15.1	15.3	15.3	15.5
V-8 engine	19.6	19.6	18.5	18.7	18.7	18.7	18.7	19.0	19.2	19.4
Additions to Basic Job:										
Ream valve guides oversize, **ADD**:										
6-cylinder	.7	.7	.7	.7	.7	.7	.7	.7	.7	.7
V-8 engine	.9	.9	.9	.9	.9	.9	.9	.9	.9	.9
Replace rocker arm stud, each, **ADD**:										
All models	.3	.3	.3	.3	.3	.3	.3	.3	.3	.3
With air cond., incl. chg. sys., **ADD**:	1.5	1.5	1.5	1.5	1.5	1.5	1.5	1.5	1.5	1.5
Replace all engine mounts, **ADD**:	.6	.6	.6	.6	.6	.6	.6	.6	.6	.6
Replace worn clutch parts, **ADD**:	.5	.5	.5	.5	.5	.5	.5	.5	.5	.5
With Air-Guard, **ADD**:	.7	.7	.7	.7	.7	.7	.7	.7	.7	.7
V-8 small block with 4-bbl. carb., **ADD**:	.2	.2	.2	.2	.2	.2	.2	.2	.2	.2

Approximate parts cost:
Major tune-up parts	$35.00
Complete gasket set, 6-cyl.	26.00
V-8	30.00
Short block: Call supplier for price.	
Engine mounts, each	6.00
Oil and air filters	$9.00
Pressure plate	$30.00-60.00
Clutch disc	21.00-40.00
Thrust bearing	5.00-15.00
Carburetor repair kit	6.00-15.00

12 AMERICAN MOTORS

ENGINE OVERHAUL, OUT-OF-CAR

Includes:
Basic Job: R&R engine, remove ring ridge, rebore or hone cylinder walls, regrind crankshaft and camshaft, replace camshaft bushings and line ream, replace timing chain and gears and oil seal, install main bearing inserts and seals, install piston pins, align connecting rods, install new piston rings and rod bearings, overhaul oil pump, clean carbon, grind valves, overhaul rocker arm mechanism, and perform major tune-up.

Additions to Basic Job: Associated work that is required during basic job and allowances for special equipment installed.

MODEL	1966	1967	1968	1969	1970	1971	1972	1973	1974	1975
Basic Job:										
Overhaul engine,										
6-cylinder	34.5	34.5	34.5	34.5	34.8	34.8	34.8	35.0	35.3	35.5
V-8 engine	42.4	42.4	40.7	40.9	41.7	41.7	41.1	41.7	41.7	42.1
Additions to Basic Job:										
Regroove top piston ring groove,										
6-cylinder, **ADD:**	1.8	1.8	1.8	1.8	1.8	1.8	1.8	1.8	1.8	1.8
V-8 engine, **ADD:**	2.4	2.4	2.4	2.4	2.4	2.4	2.4	2.4	2.4	2.4
Replace rocker arm stud, each, **ADD:**	.3	.3	.3	.3	.3	.3	.3	.3	.3	.3
Ream valve guides oversize,										
6-cylinder, **ADD:**	.7	.7	.7	.7	.7	.7	.7	.7	.7	.7
V-8 engine, **ADD:**	.9	.9	.9	.9	.9	.9	.9	.9	.9	.9
Replace all engine mounts, **ADD:**	.6	.6	.6	.6	.6	.6	.6	.6	.6	.6
Replace worn clutch parts, **ADD:**	.5	.5	.5	.5	.5	.5	.5	.5	.5	.5
With Air-Guard, **ADD:**	.7	.7	.7	.7	.7	.7	.7	.7	.7	.7
With air conditioning, incl. rechg. sys., **ADD:**	1.8	1.8	1.8	1.8	1.8	1.8	1.8	1.8	1.8	1.8
V-8 small block with 4-bbl. carb., **ADD:**	.2	.2	.2	.2	.2	.2	.2	.2	.2	.2

Approximate parts cost:

Complete gasket set, 6-cylinder	$26.00	Engine mounts, 6-cylinder	$ 6.00
V-8 engine	30.00	V-8 engine	7.50
Piston ring set, 6-cylinder	36.00	Pressure plate	30.00-60.00
V-8 engine	50.00	Clutch disc	21.00-40.00
Connecting rod bearing set, 6-cylinder	18.00	Thrust bearing	5.00-15.00
V-8 engine	32.00	Major tune-up parts	35.00
Main bearing oil seals	5.00	Carburetor repair kit	6.00-15.00
Main bearing insert set, 6-cylinder	15.00	Piston assy., std., ea.	12.00-22.00
V-8 engine	27.00		

ENGINE OVERHAUL, IN-CAR

Includes:
Basic Job: Remove ring ridge, deglaze cylinders walls, fit piston pins, align connecting rods, install new piston rings and rod bearings, install new main bearing inserts and oil seals, overhaul oil pump, clean carbon, grind valves, and perform major tune-up.

Additions to Basic Job: Associated work that is required during basic job and allowances for special equipment installed.

MODEL	1966	1967	1968	1969	1970	1971	1972	1973	1974	1975
Basic Job:										
Overhaul engine										
6-cylinder	21.5	21.5	21.5	21.5	21.8	21.8	21.0	21.2	21.2	21.4
V-8 engine	26.4	26.4	26.4	26.6	26.6	26.6	26.3	26.5	26.5	26.9

(THIS SCHEDULE CONTINUED ON NEXT PAGE.)

AMERICAN MOTORS 13

ENGINE OVERHAUL, IN-CAR Continued

MODEL	1966	1967	1968	1969	1970	1971	1972	1973	1974	1975
Additions to Basic Job:										
Rebore cylinders,										
6-cylinder, **ADD:**	4.0	4.0	4.0	4.0	4.0	4.0	4.0	4.0	4.0	4.0
V-8 engine, **ADD:**	5.0	5.0	5.0	5.0	5.0	5.0	5.0	5.0	5.0	5.0
Expand pistons,										
6-cylinder, **ADD:**	1.8	1.8	1.8	1.8	1.8	1.8	1.8	1.8	1.8	1.8
V-8 engine, **ADD:**	2.4	2.4	2.4	2.4	2.4	2.4	2.4	2.4	2.4	2.4
Regroove top piston ring groove,										
6-cylinder, **ADD:**	1.8	1.8	1.8	1.8	1.8	1.8	1.8	1.8	1.8	1.8
V-8 engine, **ADD:**	2.4	2.4	2.4	2.4	2.4	2.4	2.4	2.4	2.4	2.4
Replace hydraulic valve lifters, **ADD:**	1.0	1.0	1.0	1.0	1.0	1.0	1.0	1.0	1.0	1.0
Replace rocker arm stud, each, **ADD:**	.3	.3	.3	.3	.3	.3	.3	.3	.3	.3
Overhaul rocker arm mechanism,										
6-cylinder, **ADD:**	1.0	1.0	1.0	1.0	1.0	1.0	1.0	1.0	1.0	1.0
V-8 engine, **ADD:**	1.9	1.9	1.9	1.9	1.9	1.9	1.9	1.9	1.9	1.9
Ream valve guides oversize,										
6-cylinder, **ADD:**	.7	.7	.7	.7	.7	.7	.7	.7	.7	.7
V-8 engine, **ADD:**	.9	.9	.9	.9	.9	.9	.9	.9	.9	.9
With Air-Guard, **ADD:**	.7	.7	.7	.7	.7	.7	.7	.7	.7	.7
V-8 small block with 4-bbl. carb., **ADD:**	.2	.2	.2	.2	.2	.2	.2	.2	.2	.2
With air conditioning, **ADD:**	.6	.6	.6	.6	.6	.6	.6	.6	.6	.6

Approximate parts cost:

Hydraulic valve lifters, each	$ 4.00
Valve spring, each	2.00
Major tune-up parts	35.00
Piston pin, std., ea.	1.75
Piston assy., std., ea.	12.00-22.00
Connecting rod brg. insert, ea.	2.50-4.00
Complete gasket set, 6-cyl.	$26.00
V-8 engine	30.00
Piston ring set, 6-cylinder	36.00
V-8 engine	53.00
Carburetor repair kit	6.00-15.00

TIMING CHAIN MECHANISM, SERVICE

Includes:
   Basic Job: Replace timing cover oil seal and timing chain. Perform minor tune-up.
   Additions to Basic Job: Replace camshaft timing sprocket or crankshaft timing sprocket.

MODEL	1966	1967	1968	1969	1970	1971	1972	1973	1974	1975
Basic Job:										
Replace timing cover oil seal & chain; perform minor tune-up,										
6-cylinder	4.2	4.2	4.2	4.2	4.4	4.4	4.4	4.2	4.2	4.2
V-8 engine	3.6	3.6	3.6	3.6	3.8	3.8	4.1	4.1	4.1	4.1
Additions to Basic Job:										
Replace camshaft sprocket, **ADD:**	.2	.2	.2	.2	.2	.2	.2	.2	.2	.2
Replace crankshaft sprocket, **ADD:**	.2	.2	.2	.2	.2	.2	.2	.2	.2	.2
With air conditioning, **ADD:**	.5	.5	.5	.5	.5	.5	.5	.5	.5	.5

Approximate parts cost:

Timing cover gasket	$ 1.00
Timing cover oil seal	2.00
Timing chain	11.00
Camshaft sprocket	$ 8.00
Crankshaft sprocket	6.00
Minor tune-up parts	25.00

14 AMERICAN MOTORS

OIL PUMP, SERVICE

Includes:
  Basic Job: R&R oil pan, service oil pump and replace oil filter element.
  Additions to Basic Job: Allowances for associated work that is required during basic job.

MODEL	1966	1967	1968	1969	1970	1971	1972	1973	1974	1975
Basic Job:										
R&R oil pan, serv. pump & repl. filter element										
6-cylinder	2.8	2.8	2.8	2.4	2.4	2.4	2.4	2.4	2.4	2.4
V-8 engine	2.0	2.0	2.0	2.0	2.2	2.2	2.2	2.2	2.2	2.2
Additions to Basic Job:										
Overhaul oil pump, **ADD:**	.5	.5	.5	.5	.5	.5	.5	.5	.5	.5
Replace rear main bearing insert and seals,										
6-cylinder, **ADD:**	.3	.3	.3	.3	.3	.3	.3	.3	.3	.3
V-8 engine, **ADD:**	.4	.4	.4	.4	.4	.4	.4	.4	.4	.4
Replace other main brg. inserts, ea. pair, **ADD:**	.6	.6	.6	.6	.6	.6	.6	.6	.6	.6

Approximate parts cost:
Oil pan gasket	$ 4.00	Oil filter element	$4.50
Oil pan	25.00	Oil pump shaft and rotor kit	8.00
Oil pump assembly, new	30.00		

BEARINGS, MAIN AND/OR RODS, REPLACE

Includes:
  Basic Job: R&R oil pan, measure connecting rod bearing oil clearance with Plastigage, install new connecting rod bearing inserts, and oil filter element.
  Additions to Basic Job: Measure main bearing oil clearance with Plastigage, replace all main bearing inserts and lower rear main bearing oil seals, repair or replace oil pump.

MODEL	1966	1967	1968	1969	1970	1971[1]	1972	1973	1974	1975
Basic Job:										
R&R pan, measure, clearance install inserts & oil filter,										
6-cylinder	4.8	4.8	4.8	4.8	5.2	5.2	5.2	5.2	4.3	4.3
V-8 engine	6.6	6.6	6.6	6.6	5.9	6.1	6.1	6.1	5.0	5.0
Additions to Basic Job:										
Use Plastigage — all main brgs.,										
6-cylinder, **ADD:**	.4	.4	.4	.4	.4	.4	.4	.4	.4	.4
V-8 engine, **ADD:**	.5	.5	.5	.5	.5	.5	.5	.5	.5	.5
Repl. main inserts & rear oil seals,										
6-cylinder, **ADD:**	1.2	1.2	1.2	1.2	1.2	1.2	1.2	1.2	1.2	1.2
V-8 engine, **ADD:**	2.0	2.0	2.0	2.0	2.0	2.0	2.0	2.0	2.0	2.0
R&R oil pump,										
6-cylinder, **ADD:**	.5	.5	.5	.5	.5	.5	.5	.5	.5	.5
V-8 engine, **ADD:**	.3	.3	.3	.3	1.0	1.0	.4	.4	.6	.6
Overhaul oil pump, **ADD:**	.8	.8	.8	.8	.8	.8	.8	.8	.8	.8

Approximate parts cost:
Oil pan gasket	$ 4.00	Rear main brg. oil seal, set	$3.00
Rod bearing inserts, set, each	4.00	Oil filter element	4.50
Main bearing inserts, set, each	4.00-7.00	Oil pump shaft & rotor kit	8.00
Oil pump	30.00		

AMERICAN MOTORS

VALVE MECHANISM, SERVICE

Includes:
  Adjustment and Tune-up: Adjust valve lash and perform minor tune-up.
  Basic Job: Clean and reface valves, scrape carbon, grind valve seats, replace valve seals, adjust valves, and perform major tune-up.
  Additions to Basic Job: Associated work required during basic job and allowances for special equipment and carburetor.

MODEL	1966	1967	1968	1969	1970	1971	1972	1973	1974	1975
Adjustment & tune-up,										
6-cylinder	2.8	2.8	2.8	2.8	3.0	3.0	3.1	3.1	3.1	3.1
Basic Job:										
Service valve mechanism,										
6-cylinder	10.4	10.4	10.4	10.8	10.8	11.1	11.1	10.9	10.9	11.1
V-8 engine	16.9	15.1	14.1	14.3	14.3	14.7	14.7	15.0	14.2	14.4
Additions to Basic Job:										
Ream valve guides oversize,										
6-cylinder, **ADD:**	.7	.7	.7	.7	.7	.7	.7	.7	.7	.7
V-8 engine, **ADD:**	.9	.9	.9	.9	.9	.9	.9	.9	.9	.9
Replace rocker arm stud, ea., **ADD:**	.3	.3	.3	.3	.3	.3	.3	.3	.3	.3
Overhaul rocker arm mechanism,										
6-cylinder, **ADD:**	1.0	1.0	1.0	1.0	1.0	1.0	1.0	1.0	1.0	1.0
V-8 engine, **ADD:**	1.9	1.9	1.9	1.9	1.9	1.9	1.9	1.9	1.9	1.9
Replace hydraulic valve lifters, **ADD:**	1.0	1.0	1.0	1.0	1.0	1.0	1.0	1.0	1.0	1.0
V-8 small block with 4-bbl. carb., **ADD:**	.2	.2	.2	.2	.2	.2	.2	.2	.2	.2
With Air-Guard, **ADD:**	.3	.3	.3	.3	.3	.3	.3	.3	.3	.3
With air conditioning, **ADD:**	.6	.6	.6	.6	.6	.6	.6	.6	.6	.6

Approximate parts cost:
Major tune-up parts $35.00
Valve grind gasket set, 6-cylinder 9.00
  V-8 engine 18.00
Hydraulic valve lifters, each $4.00
Valve spring, each 2.00

CYLINDER HEAD AND/OR GASKET, REPLACE

Includes:
  Basic Jobs: 1. R&R intake manifold and cylinder head to install new gasket. Clean head and block surfaces, scrape carbon, recondition valves, and perform minor tune-up.
  2. Install new cylinder head, including recondition valves and perform minor tune-up.
  Additions to Basic Jobs: Allowances for special equipment and/or carburetor.

MODEL	1966	1967	1968	1969	1970	1971	1972	1973	1974	1975
Basic Job #1										
Replace head gasket, incl. minor tune-up,										
6-cylinder	4.2	4.6	4.6	4.6	4.8	4.8	4.8	4.8	4.8	4.8
V-8 engine, one side	6.2	6.2	5.7	5.7	5.9	5.9	6.0	6.0	6.0	6.0
V-8 engine, both sides	7.8	7.8	7.3	7.3	7.5	7.5	7.5	7.5	7.5	7.5
Basic Job #2										
Install new cyl. head, incl. minor tune-up,										
6-cylinder	6.9	7.3	7.3	7.3	7.3	7.5	7.5	7.5	7.5	7.5
V-8 engine, ea. head	8.6	8.6	8.1	8.1	8.1	8.1	8.4	8.4	8.4	8.4

(THIS SCHEDULE CONTINUED ON NEXT PAGE.)

16 AMERICAN MOTORS

CYLINDER HEAD AND/OR GASKET, REPLACE Continued

MODEL	1966	1967	1968	1969	1970	1971	1972	1973	1974	1975
Additions to Basic Jobs:										
V-8 small block with 4-bbl. carb., **ADD:**	.2	.2	.2	.2	.2	.2	.2	.2	.2	.2
With Air-Guard, **ADD:**	.3	.3	.3	.3	.3	.3	.3	.3	.3	.3
With air conditioning, **ADD:**	.6	.6	.6	.6	.6	.6	.6	.6	.6	.6

Approximate parts cost:

Head gasket, each .... $ 4.00	Valve grind gasket set, 6-cylinder .... $ 9.00
Cylinder head, each 90.00	V-8 engine 18.00-30.00
Minor tune-up parts 25.00	

EXHAUST SYSTEM, TEST AND SERVICE

Includes:
  Basic Job: Test exhaust system for leaks and/or exhaust odors. Use HC/CO exhaust analyzer to trace carbon monoxide leaks.
  Related Jobs: Replace defective parts. Each job includes basic job tests and install new hangers as required.

MODEL	1966	1967	1968	1969	1970	1971	1972	1973	1974	1975
Basic Job:										
Complete test of exhaust system	.4	.4	.4	.4	.4	.4	.4	.4	.4	.4
Related Jobs:										
Replace muffler,										
Single or dual, one	1.0	1.0	1.0	1.0	1.0	1.0	1.0	1.0	1.0	1.0
Dual, both	1.4	1.4	1.4	1.4	1.4	1.4	1.4	1.4	1.4	1.4
Replace tail pipe,										
Single or dual, one	1.1	1.1	1.1	1.1	1.1	1.1	1.1	1.1	1.1	1.1
Dual, both	1.4	1.4	1.4	1.4	1.4	1.4	1.4	1.4	1.4	1.4
Replace exhaust pipe flange gasket, each	.5	.5	.5	.5	.5	.5	.5	.5	.5	.5
Free-up or o/h heat control valve,										
6-cylinder	1.5	1.5	1.5	1.5	1.5	1.5	1.5	1.5	1.5	1.5
V-8 engine	1.8	1.8	1.8	1.8	1.8	1.8	1.8	1.8	1.8	1.8
Replace exhaust pipe,										
6-cylinder	1.3	1.3	1.3	1.3	1.3	1.3	1.3	1.3	1.3	1.3
V-8 engine, single exhaust	1.4	1.4	1.4	1.4	1.4	1.4	1.4	1.4	1.4	1.4
V-8 engine, dual exhaust, one pipe	1.2	1.2	1.2	1.2	1.2	1.2	1.2	1.2	1.2	1.2
V-8 engine, dual exhaust, both pipes	2.0	2.0	2.0	2.0	2.0	2.0	2.0	2.0	2.0	2.0

Approximate parts cost:

Muffler $25.00	Heat control valve $12.00
Exhaust pipe 15.00	

COOLING SYSTEM, TEST AND SERVICE

Includes:
  Basic Job: Drain and back-flush system, check for leaks and tighten all hose connections, pressure-test radiator cap and system.
  Related Jobs: Replace defective parts. Work performed independently of basic job.
  Additions to Related Jobs: Allowances for special equipment installed.

MODEL	1966	1967	1968	1969	1970	1971	1972	1973	1974	1975
Basic Job:										
Drain, flush, fill, & press.-test sys.	.9	.9	.9	.9	.9	.9	.9	.9	.9	.9

(THIS SCHEDULE CONTINUED ON NEXT PAGE.)

AMERICAN MOTORS

COOLING SYSTEM, TEST AND SERVICE Continued

MODEL	1966	1967	1968	1969	1970	1971	1972	1973	1974	1975
Related Jobs:										
Replace upper hose	.4	.4	.4	.4	.4	.4	.4	.4	.4	.4
Replace lower hose	.5	.5	.5	.5	.5	.5	.5	.5	.5	.5
With air conditioning, **ADD:**	.2	.2	.2	.2	.2	.2	.2	.2	.2	.2
Replace thermostat, includes, test,										
6-cylinder	.5	.5	.5	.5	.5	.5	.5	.5	.5	.5
V-8 engine	.7	.7	.7	.7	.7	.7	.7	.7	.7	.7
With air conditioning, **ADD:**	.2	.2	.2	.2	.2	.2	.2	.2	.2	.2
Replace water pump drive belt & adjust	.4	.4	.4	.4	.4	.4	.4	.4	.4	.4
With air cond., Air-Guard, or P.S., **ADD:**	.2	.2	.2	.2	.2	.2	.2	.2	.2	.2
Replace water pump, incl. check sys.,										
6-cylinder	1.0	1.0	1.0	1.0	1.0	1.0	1.0	1.0	1.0	1.0
With air conditioning, **ADD:**	.1	.1	.1	.1	.1	.1	.1	.1	.1	.1
V-8 engine	1.5	1.5	1.5	1.5	1.5	1.5	1.5	1.5	1.5	1.5
With air conditioning, **ADD:**	.3	.3	.3	.3	.3	.3	.6	.6	.6	.6
With power steering, all models, **ADD:**	.2	.2	.2	.2	.2	.2	.2	.2	.2	.2
With Air-Guard, all models, **ADD:**	.2	.2	.2	.2	.2	.2	.2	.2	.2	.2
Replace radiator,										
6-cylinder	.6	.6	.6	.6	.6	.6	.6	.6	.6	.6
V-8 engine	.9	.9	.9	.9	.9	.9	.9	.9	.9	.9
With air conditioning, **ADD:**	.2	.2	.2	.2	.2	.2	.2	.2	.2	.2
With automatic transmission, **ADD:**	.1	.1	.1	.1	.1	.1	.1	.1	.1	.1
Replace water temp. sending unit, engine	.5	.5	.5	.5	.5	.5	.5	.5	.5	.5
Replace water temp. gauge, dash,										
Javelin, AMX	.8	.8	.9	.9	.9	1.2	1.2	1.2	1.2	1.2
All others	.9	.9	.9	.9	.9	.9	.9	.9	.9	.9
Replace water jacket expansion plug,										
6-cylinder										
Front	1.4	1.4	1.4	1.4	1.4	1.4	.9	.9	.9	.9
Side ctr., incl. R&R manifold	1.5	1.5	1.5	1.5	1.5	1.5	1.8	1.8	1.8	1.8
Rear	1.6	1.6	1.6	1.6	1.6	1.6	2.2	2.2	2.2	2.2
With Air-Guard, **ADD:**	.2	.2	.2	.2	.2	.2	.2	.2	.2	.2
With air conditioning, **ADD:**	.3	.3	.3	.3	.3	.3	.3	.3	.3	.3
V-8 engine										
Front or center	1.2	1.2	1.2	1.2	1.2	1.2	1.3	1.3	1.3	1.3
Left rear	.8	.8	.8	.8	.8	.8	.9	.9	.9	.9
Right rear, incl. R&R starter	1.0	1.0	1.0	1.0	1.0	1.0	1.0	1.0	1.0	1.0

Approximate parts cost:

Radiator, new	$100.00
Upper or lower hose, ea.	5.00
Thermostat	4.00
Water pump	25.00
Drive belt, ea.	$4.00
Temperature sending unit	4.00
Temperature gauge, dash	3.00-14.00
Expansion plug, ea.	1.50

CLUTCH MECHANISM, SERVICE

Includes:
Adjust: Adjust clutch pedal play.
Basic Job: Replace thrust bearing, pressure plate and disc. Adjust clutch pedal play.
Additions to Basic Job: Associated work that is required during basic job.

MODEL	1966	1967	1968	1969	1970	1971	1972	1973	1974	1975
Adjust:										
Clutch pedal play	.3	.3	.3	.3	.3	.3	.3	.3	.3	.3

(THIS SCHEDULE CONTINUED ON NEXT PAGE.)

18 AMERICAN MOTORS

CLUTCH MECHANISM, SERVICE Continued

MODEL	1966	1967	1968	1969	1970	1971	1972	1973	1974	1975
Basic Job:										
Repl. thrust brg., press. plate & disc.,										
3-speed transmission	2.1	2.1	2.1	2.1	2.1	2.1	2.2	2.2	2.2	2.2
4-speed transmission	2.6	2.6	2.6	2.6	3.0	3.0	3.0	2.8	2.8	2.8
Transmission with overdrive	2.8	2.8	2.8	2.8	—	—	—	—	—	—
Additions to Basic Job:										
Remove, reface, and instl. flywheel, **ADD**:	1.8	1.8	1.8	1.8	1.8	1.8	1.8	1.8	1.8	1.8
Replace flywheel ring gear, **ADD**:	1.0	1.0	1.0	1.0	1.0	1.0	1.0	1.0	1.0	1.0
Resurface clutch pressure plate, **ADD**:	.8	.8	.8	.8	.8	.8	.8	.8	.8	.8
Replace clutch pilot bearing, **ADD**:	.2	.2	.2	.2	.2	.2	.2	.2	.2	.2
With self adjusting clutch, **ADD**:	.3	.3	.3	.3	.3	.3	.3	.3	.3	.3

Approximate parts cost:

Pressure plate	$30.00-60.00	Pilot bearing	$ 2.00
Clutch disc	30.00-55.00	Flywheel w/ring gear	40.00-70.00
Thrust bearing	5.00-17.00	Throw-out bearing	8.00-15.00
Throwout bearing	8.00-15.00		

SHIFT LINKAGE, SERVICE

Includes:
Adjust: Adjust shift linkage.
Basic Job: Replace one control rod and/or grommet and adjust linkage. Replace overdrive parts.
Additions to Basic Job: Associated work that is required during basic job.

MODEL	1966	1967	1968	1969	1970	1971	1972	1973	1974	1975
Adjust Shift Linkage:										
3-speed transmission	.5	.5	.5	.5	.5	.5	.5	.5	.5	.5
4-speed transmission	.6	.6	.6	.6	.6	.6	.6	.6	.6	.6
Transmission with overdrive	.6	.6	.6	.6	—	—	—	—	—	—
Basic Job:										
Repl. one rod and/or grommet & adjust,										
3-speed transmission	.8	.8	.8	.8	.8	.8	.8	.8	.8	.8
4-speed transmission	.9	.9	.9	.9	.9	.9	.9	.9	.9	.9
Transmission with overdrive	1.0	1.0	1.0	1.0	—	—	—	—	—	—
Replace overdrive solenoid	.5	.5	.5	.5	—	—	—	—	—	—
Replace overdrive relay	.4	.4	.4	.4	—	—	—	—	—	—
Replace overdrive kickdown switch	.4	.4	.4	.4	—	—	—	—	—	—
Replace overdrive governor	.5	.5	.5	.5	—	—	—	—	—	—
Additions to Basic Job:										
Replace additional rod, **ADD**:	.3	.3	.3	.3	.3	.3	.3	.3	.3	.3
Repl. shift lever oil seals, both, **ADD**:	.5	.5	.5	.5	.5	.5	.5	.5	.5	.5

Approximate parts cost:

Shift rod, each	$ 2.00	Shift lever oil seals	$ 1.50
Rear oil seal	2.50	Kickdown switch	5.00
Overdrive solenoid	30.00	Overdrive relay	21.00
Overdrive governor	25.00		

AMERICAN MOTORS

STANDARD TRANSMISSION, OVERHAUL

Includes:
  Basic Job: R&R transmission, disassemble, replace worn parts, and adjust linkage.
  Additions to Basic Job: Associated work that is required during basic job.

MODEL	1966	1967	1968	1969	1970	1971	1972	1973	1974	1975
Basic Job:										
R&R, overhaul, and adjust linkage,										
3-speed transmission	5.4	5.4	5.4	5.4	5.4	5.4	5.4	5.4	5.4	5.4
4-speed transmission	6.9	6.9	6.9	6.9	6.9	6.9	6.9	6.9	6.9	6.9
Transmission with overdrive	7.9	7.9	7.9	7.9	—	—	—	—	—	—
Additions to Basic Job:										
Recondition transmission cover,										
3-speed trans., **ADD:**	.3	.3	.3	.3	.3	.3	.3	.3	.3	.3
4-speed trans., **ADD:**	.4	.4	.4	.4	.4	.4	.4	.4	.4	.4
Resurface clutch pressure plate, **ADD:**	.8	.8	.8	.8	.8	.8	.8	.8	.8	.8
R&R and resurface flywheel, **ADD:**	1.8	1.8	1.8	1.8	1.8	1.8	1.8	1.8	1.8	1.8
Replace flywheel ring gear, **ADD:**	1.0	1.0	1.0	1.0	1.0	1.0	1.0	1.0	1.0	1.0
Replace clutch pilot bearing, **ADD:**	.2	.2	.2	.2	.2	.2	.2	.2	.2	.2
Repl. crankshaft trans. drive pinion bushing, **ADD:**	.7	.7	.7	.7	.7	.7	.7	.7	.7	.7

Approximate parts cost:
Phone supplier for price quote on transmission parts required.
Speedometer gear $10.00
Gasket and seals 8.00
Clutch pressure plate 30.00-60.00
Crankshaft trans. drive pinion bushing $1.50
Clutch pilot bearing 2.00
Throw-out bearing 8.00-15.00

AUTOMATIC TRANSMISSION, MAJOR SERVICE

Includes:
  Basic Jobs:
    1. **Overhaul transmission.** R&R transmission. Disassemble, clean, inspect and replace all worn parts as needed. Replace all oil seals. Adjust throttle and shift linkage as required. Flush converter and cooler lines. Perform pressure-checks of main line, throttle, and accumulator. Road test.
    2. **Replace torque converter.** R&R transmission. Flush oil cooler and lines. Replace transmission oil and oil filter. Perform pressure checks of main line, throttle, and accumulator. Adjust throttle and shift linkage as required. Road test.
    3. **Reseal transmission.** R&R transmission. Replace all seals and gaskets. Replace transmission oil and oil filter. Check oil cooler for leaks. Perform pressure checks of main line, throttle, and accumulator. Adjust throttle and shift linkage as required. Road test.
  Additions to Basic Jobs: Associated work that is performed while the transmission is out during one of basic jobs.

MODEL	1966	1967	1968	1969	1970	1971	1972	1973	1974	1975
Basic Job #1										
Overhaul transmission,										
Flash-O-Matic	9.2	9.2	9.2	9.2	9.2	9.2	—	—	—	—
Shift Command	10.0	10.0	10.0	10.0	10.0	10.0	—	—	—	—
Torque Command	—	—	—	—	—	—	11.9	11.9	11.9	11.9
Basic Job #2										
Replace torque converter. Flush and clean lines,										
Flash-O-Matic	5.1	5.1	5.1	5.1	5.1	5.1	—	—	—	—
Shift Command	5.7	5.7	5.7	5.7	5.7	5.7	—	—	—	—
Torque Command	—	—	—	—	—	—	5.2	5.2	5.2	5.2

(THIS SCHEDULE CONTINUED ON NEXT PAGE.)

20 AMERICAN MOTORS

AUTOMATIC TRANSMISSION, MAJOR SERVICE Continued

MODEL	1966	1967	1968	1969	1970	1971	1972	1973	1974	1975
Basic Job #3										
Reseal transmission,										
Flash-O-Matic	6.8	6.8	6.8	6.8	6.8	6.8	—	—	—	—
Shift Command	7.6	7.6	7.6	7.6	7.6	7.6	—	—	—	—
Torque Command	—	—	—	—	—	—	9.5	9.5	9.5	9.5
Additions to Basic Jobs:										
Replace oil cooler pipes, both, **ADD:**	.9	.9	.9	.9	.9	.9	.9	.9	.9	.9
Replace oil filler pipe and/or seal, **ADD:**	.5	.5	.5	.5	.5	.5	.5	.5	.5	.5
Replace torque converter ring gear, **ADD:**	.5	.5	.5	.5	.5	.5	.5	.5	.5	.5

Approximate parts cost:
Transmission seal and gasket kit ... $20.00	Oil filler pipe ... $3.00
Oil cooler pipe, each ... 9.00	Oil filler pipe seal ... .25
Torque converter assembly ... 200.00	Oil pan ... 5.00
Torque converter ring gear ... 8.00	Oil pan gasket ... 1.00
Transmission fluid, per qt. ... 1.20	Governor kit ... 16.00

AUTOMATIC TRANSMISSION, SHIFT AND LINKAGE CONTROLS, REPLACE AND ADJUST

Includes:
Replace defective part and make necessary adjustment(s).

MODEL	1966	1967	1968	1969	1970	1971	1972	1973	1974	1975
Repl. control rob, carb. or trans. & adjust	.9	.9	.9	.9	.9	.9	.9	.9	.9	.9
Replace each additional rod, **ADD:**	.4	.4	.4	.4	.4	.4	.4	.4	.4	.4
Repl. carb./throttle link, **ADD:**	.3	.3	.3	.3	.3	.3	.3	.3	.3	.3
Repl. throttle control cable, **ADD:**	.5	.5	.5	.5	.5	.5	.5	.5	.5	.5
Repl. front contr. rod, column shift, **ADD:**	.3	.3	.3	.3	.3	.3	.3	.3	.3	.3
Repl. rear contr. rod or swivel, **ADD:**	.4	.4	.4	.4	.4	.4	.4	.4	.4	.4
Repl. contr. torque shaft or bushings, **ADD:**	.6	.6	.6	.6	.6	.6	.6	.6	.6	.6
Repl. shift contr. key lock assy.	.7	.7	.7	.7	.7	.7	.7	.7	.7	.7
Replace neutral safety switch	.5	.5	.5	.5	.5	.5	.5	.5	.5	.5
Repl. and adjust floor shift contr. assy.	.8	.8	.8	.8	.8	.8	.8	.8	.8	.8

Approximate parts cost:
Linkage rod, ea. ... $1.50	Neutral safety switch ... $5.00
Control cable ... 8.00	Floor shift contr. assy. ... 40.00

AUTOMATIC TRANSMISSION, PERFORMANCE CHECK

Includes:
Basic Job: Conduct transmission performance check. Clean transmission case and operate unit to check case, oil cooler and oil cooler lines for external leaks. Remove oil pan, clean pan, screen or filter. Torque valve body mounting bolts. Adjust kickdown and reverse bands. Adjust throttle and shift linkage. Perform pressure checks of main line, throttle, and accumulator. Road test.
Related Jobs: Work which does not include R&R transmission and may be done as separate job.

MODEL	1966	1967	1968	1969	1970	1971	1972	1973	1974	1975
Basic Job:										
Complete trans. performance check	2.1	2.1	2.1	2.1	2.1	2.1	2.1	2.1	2.1	2.1

(THIS SCHEDULE CONTINUED ON NEXT PAGE.)

AMERICAN MOTORS

AUTOMATIC TRANSMISSION, PERFORMANCE CHECK Continued

MODEL	1966	1967	1968	1969	1970	1971	1972	1973	1974	1975
Related Jobs:										
Drain & fill trans., clean filter	.8	.8	.8	.8	.8	.8	.8	.8	.8	.8
Check for oil leaks	.7	.7	.7	.7	.7	.7	.7	.7	.7	.7
Repl. oil pan gasket, incl. clean filter	.9	.9	.9	.9	.9	.9	.9	.9	.9	.9
Repl. rear oil seal & O-ring	1.0	1.0	.7	.5	.5	.5	.5	.5	.5	.5
Repl. neutral safety switch	.5	.5	.5	.5	.5	.5	.5	.5	.5	.5
R&R and overhaul governor, press. & road tests,										
Flash-O-Matic	2.3	2.3	2.3	2.3	2.3	2.3	—	—	—	—
Shift Command	2.5	2.5	2.5	2.5	2.5	2.5	—	—	—	—
Torque Command	—	—	—	—	—	—	2.7	2.7	2.7	2.7
R&R and o/h control valve assy. and test	2.9	2.9	2.9	2.9	2.9	2.9	2.9	2.9	2.9	2.9
Adjust throttle and shift linkage	1.0	1.0	1.0	1.0	1.0	1.0	1.0	1.0	1.0	1.0
Adjust low and reverse band or kickdown band	1.0	1.0	1.0	1.0	1.0	1.0	1.0	1.0	1.0	1.0

Approximate parts cost:
Transmission fluid, per qt. $1.20	Neutral safety switch $5.00-12.00
Oil pan gasket 1.00	Governor body repair kit 16.00
Rear oil seal 4.50	Valve body assy., new 80.00

DRIVESHAFT, SERVICE

Includes:
   Basic Job: R&R driveshaft and overhaul or replace front and rear U-joints, adjust pinion nose angle.

MODEL	1966	1967	1968	1969	1970	1971	1972	1973	1974	1975
Basic Job:										
R&R driveshaft & overhaul both U-joints, and adjust pinion nose angle.										
Ambassador	2.1	2.1	2.1	2.1	2.2	2.2	2.2	2.2	2.2	2.2
All others	1.6	1.6	1.6	1.6	1.6	1.6	1.6	1.6	1.6	1.6
Replace axle drive pinion oil seal, **ADD:**	.5	.5	.5	.5	.5	.5	.5	.5	.5	.5

Approximate parts cost:
Universal joint kit $12.00	Pinion shaft oil seal $3.50

REAR AXLE, SERVICE

Includes:
   Basic Jobs: 1. R&R driveshaft, R&R axle shafts, overhaul differential assembly, and check and adjust pinion nose angle.
               2. R&R driveshaft and replace pinion bearing oil seal.
   Related Jobs: Associated work that is performed independently of basic jobs.

MODEL	1966	1967	1968	1969	1970	1971	1972	1973	1974	1975
Basic Job #1										
Overhaul differential assembly										
Standard	5.8	5.8	5.8	5.8	5.8	5.8	5.8	5.8	5.8	5.8
Locking differential	5.5	5.5	5.5	5.5	5.5	5.5	5.5	5.5	5.5	5.5
With Twin Grip, **ADD:**	.5	.5	.5	.5	.5	.5	.5	.5	.5	.5
Basic Job #2										
Repl. drive pinion bearing oil seal	1.0	1.0	1.0	1.0	1.0	1.0	1.0	1.0	1.0	1.0

(THIS SCHEDULE CONTINUED ON NEXT PAGE.)

22 AMERICAN MOTORS

REAR AXLE, SERVICE Continued

MODEL	1966	1967	1968	1969	1970	1971	1972	1973	1974	1975
Related Jobs:										
R&R axle shaft (one side), and/or bearing and seals and adjust end-play	1.5	1.5	1.5	1.5	1.5	1.5	1.5	1.5	1.5	1.5
Repl. axle shaft wheel mounting stud	.8	.8	.8	.8	.8	.8	.8	.8	.8	.8

Approximate parts cost:

Axle shaft & bearing assy.	$40.00	Cover gasket	$ 1.00
Axle shaft oil seal	2.00	Ring & pinion gear set	80.00
Pinion shaft oil seal	3.50	Pinion gear kit	9.00
Side gear kit	18.00	Wheel bearing oil seal	3.00
Universal joint flange assembly	12.00	Rear wheel bearing	16.00

REAR SUSPENSION, SERVICE

Includes:
Service for the rear suspension system is listed as individual jobs. Add times if more than one job is performed.

MODEL	1966	1967	1968	1969	1970	1971	1972	1973	1974	1975
Repl. rear spring & shim to align pinion angle	1.7	1.7	1.7	1.7	1.7	1.7	1.7	1.7	1.7	1.7
Replace rear coil spring	.8	.8	.8	.8	.8	.8	.8	.8	.8	.8
Replace shackle and bushings; eye bolt & bushings	.7	.7	.7	.7	.7	.7	.7	.7	.7	.7
Replace control arm including pinion angle adjustment,										
Upper arm, one	1.5	1.5	1.5	1.5	1.5	1.5	1.1	1.1	1.1	1.1
Lower arm, one	1.1	1.1	1.1	1.1	1.1	1.1	1.1	1.1	1.1	1.1
Replace shock absorber, both sides	.9	.9	.9	.9	.8	.8	.8	.8	.8	.8
Replace torque link, incl. adjust	—	—	.8	.8	.8	.8	.6	—	—	—

Approximate parts cost:

Rear leaf spring	$40.00	Shackle bushing package	$1.00
Torque link, kit	33.00	Control arm, upper	6.00
Shackle package	7.50	Control arm, lower	8.00
Coil spring, ea.	18.00		

STEERING LINKAGE, SERVICE AND ADJUST

Includes:
Basic Job: Adjust toe-in.
Related Jobs: Replace defective parts and adjust toe-in.

MODEL	1966	1967	1968	1969	1970	1971	1972	1973	1974	1975
Basic Job:										
Adjust toe-in	.4	.4	.4	.4	.4	.4	.4	.4	.4	.4
Related Jobs:										
Replace tie-rods or tie-rod ends, (4)	1.6	1.6	1.5	1.5	1.5	1.5	1.5	1.5	1.5	1.5
Repl. Pitman arm, includes adjust toe-in	.8	.8	.8	.8	.8	.8	.8	.8	.8	.8
Repl. steering idler arm or bushing, including adjust toe-in	1.4	1.4	1.4	1.4	1.4	1.4	1.4	1.4	1.4	1.4

Approximate parts cost:

Tie-rod end pkg.	$ 7.00	Idler arm, kit	$9.00-20.00
Pitman arm	14.00	Tie rod	9.00

AMERICAN MOTORS

STANDARD STEERING GEAR, ADJUST AND SERVICE

Includes:
Basic Job: Adjust steering gear end play, worm and sector mesh; adjust wheel bearings and toe-in.
Related Job: Replace steering gear assembly.
Addition to Related Job: Overhaul steering gear.

MODEL	1966	1967	1968	1969	1970	1971	1972	1973	1974	1975
Basic Job:										
Complete gear, wheel brgs. & toe-in adj.	1.4	1.4	1.4	1.4	1.4	1.4	1.4	1.4	1.4	1.4
Related Job:										
Repl. steering gear assembly	2.4	2.6	2.6	2.6	2.4	2.4	2.4	2.4	2.0	2.0
Overhaul steering gear, **ADD:**	1.2	1.2	1.2	1.2	1.2	1.2	1.2	1.2	.9	.9

Approximate parts cost:
Tube & worm assembly .... $25.00-45.00 Oil seal $1.50
Housing & bushing assembly 40.00

POWER STEERING UNIT, TEST AND SERVICE

Includes:
Basic Job: Adjust drive belt tension; hook-up gauges to check pressure on left and right turns. Adjust steering gear box over-center torque and control valve to balance left and right steering effort.
Additions to Basic Job: Service power steering unit.
Related Jobs: R&R power steering unit, pump, or other associated parts.
Additions to Related Jobs: Overhaul steering unit or pump including replacement of all seals and worn parts.

MODEL	1966	1967	1968	1969	1970	1971	1972	1973	1974	1975
Basic Job:										
Compl. test and adj. pwr. steer. unit	1.0	1.0	1.0	1.0	1.0	1.0	1.0	1.0	1.0	1.0
Additions to Basic Job:										
Repl. pwr. steer. pump drive belt, **ADD:**	.3	.3	.3	.3	.3	.3	.3	.3	.3	.3
With air conditioning, **ADD:**	.2	.2	.2	.2	.2	.2	.2	.2	.2	.2
Check & replenish reservoir fluid, **ADD:**	.2	.2	.2	.2	.2	.2	.2	.2	.2	.2
Related Jobs:										
Repl. press. hose, incl. adjust dr. belt	.5	.5	.6	.6	.6	.6	.6	.6	.6	.6
Repl. return hose, incl. adjust dr. belt	.4	.4	.4	.4	.4	.4	.4	.4	.4	.4
Repl. pump reservoir or O-ring seals	1.0	1.3	1.0	1.0	1.0	1.0	1.0	1.0	1.0	1.0
Repl. pump, includes pressure-test original pump and transfer pulley	1.6	1.6	1.6	1.6	1.6	1.6	1.8	1.8	1.8	1.8
With air conditioning, **ADD:**	.2	.2	.2	.2	.2	.2	.2	.2	.2	.2
With Air-Guard, **ADD:**	.2	.2	.2	.2	.2	.2	.2	.2	.2	.2
Repl. pwr. steering unit, includes test original unit and complete adjustment	2.0	2.0	2.0	2.0	2.0	2.0	2.0	2.0	2.0	2.0
Additions to Related Jobs:										
Overhaul pwr. steering unit, **ADD:**	2.2	2.2	2.2	2.4	2.4	2.4	2.4	2.4	2.4	2.4
Overhaul pump, incl. new kit & seals, **ADD:**	.6	.6	.6	.6	.6	.6	.6	.6	.6	.6

Approximate parts cost:
Drive belt .... $ 4.00 Pump assembly $65.00-95.00
Pressure hose .... 12.00 Shaft seal kit 5.00
Return hose .... 4.00 Valve seal kit 5.00
Pwr. steering gear valve assy. .... 55.00 O-ring kit 6.00
Adjuster assy. .... 20.00 Seal & ring kit 19.00

24 AMERICAN MOTORS

FRONT END, TEST, SERVICE, AND ADJUST

Includes:
  Basic Jobs: Check caster, camber, steering axis inclination, turning radius, toe-in, adjust car height, pack and adjust front wheel bearings, replace seals.
  Related Jobs: Perform individual adjustments. Replace or overhaul defective components and make necessary adjustments.

MODEL	1966	1967	1968	1969	1970	1971	1972	1973	1974	1975
Basic Jobs:										
Complete test and adjustments,										
With drum brakes	2.5	2.5	2.5	2.5	2.5	2.5	2.5	2.5	2.5	2.5
With disc brakes	3.0	3.0	3.0	3.0	3.0	3.0	3.0	3.0	3.0	3.0
Related Jobs:										
Adjust toe-in only	.6	.6	.6	.6	.6	.6	.6	.6	.6	.6
Repack wheel brgs. only, incl. new seals,										
Drum brakes, both sides	.9	.9	.9	.9	.9	.9	.9	.9	.9	.9
Disc brakes, both sides	1.5	1.5	1.5	1.2	1.9	1.9	1.9	1.5	1.5	1.5
Replace wheel brgs. only, each side,										
Drum brakes, inner or outer brg.	.5	.5	.5	.5	.5	.5	.5	.5	.5	.5
Disc brakes, inner or outer brg.	.8	.8	.8	.7	1.1	1.1	1.1	.9	.9	.9
Balance all four wheels	2.0	2.0	2.0	2.0	2.0	2.0	2.0	2.0	2.0	2.0
Overhaul front suspension, incl. disassemble, replace nec. parts, lube., & complete adjust.,										
With drum brakes	7.9	7.9	7.9	7.9	7.9	7.9	7.9	7.9	7.9	7.9
With disc brakes	8.8	8.8	8.8	8.8	8.8	8.8	8.8	8.8	8.8	8.8
Replace coil spring, one side, incl. complete front end adjustments,										
Ambassador	2.8	2.8	2.8	2.8	2.8	2.8	2.8	2.8	2.8	
All others	2.6	2.6	2.6	2.6	2.6	2.6	2.6	2.6	2.6	2.6
Replace upper ball joints, both sides, incl. complete front end adjustments	3.7	3.7	3.7	3.7	3.7	3.7	3.7	3.7	3.7	3.7
Replace steering knuckle, one side, incl. complete front end adjustment,										
With drum brakes	2.9	2.9	2.9	2.9	2.9	2.9	2.9	2.9	2.9	2.9
With disc brakes	3.2	3.2	3.2	3.2	3.2	3.2	3.2	3.2	3.2	3.2
Replace shock absorber, both sides	.9	.9	.9	.9	.9	.9	.9	.9	.9	.9
Repl. lwr. control arm struts or bushing,										
With drum brakes	1.2	1.2	1.2	1.2	1.4	1.4	1.4	1.4	1.4	1.4
With disc brakes	1.6	1.6	1.6	1.6	1.8	1.8	1.8	1.8	1.8	1.8
Replace control arm rubber bumper, one	.8	.8	.8	.8	.4	.4	.4	.4	.4	.4
Repl. stabilizer bar and bushings	.7	.7	.7	.7	.7	.7	.7	.7	.7	.7

Approximate parts cost:

Front wheel brg., outer	$ 2.00
Wheel bearing inner	3.00
Wheel bearing, package	4.50
Seals	1.50
Stabilizer bar & bushing	25.00
Coil spring, ea.	20.00
Steering knuckle	$50.00
Rubber bumper, each	1.50
Shock absorber, each	13.00
Control arm strut	10.00
Ball joint	13.00

AMERICAN MOTORS

BRAKES, SERVICE

Includes:
Basic Job: Install new linings or pads, turn brake drums or rotors, lubricate and adjust front wheel bearings, replace rear oil seals, bleed hydraulic system, and adjust brakes.
Additions to Basic Job: Overhaul four wheel cylinders, overhaul or replace front calipers, overhaul master cylinder.
Related Jobs: Performed at time other than during basic job. Overhaul or replace front calipers, overhaul master cylinder.

MODEL	1966	1967	1968	1969	1970	1971	1972	1973	1974	1975
Basic Job:										
Complete job incl. turn drums or rotors,										
Drum (4), all models	6.4	6.4	6.4	6.4	6.6	6.6	6.6	6.1	6.1	6.0
Disc front, drum rear, all models	7.3	7.3	7.3	7.3	7.3	7.3	6.7	6.7	6.7	6.7
Additions to Basic Job:										
Overhaul 4 wheel cyl. hone, **ADD:**	1.6	2.3	2.3	2.3	2.3	2.4	2.4	2.4	2.4	2.4
Overhaul front calipers (both), **ADD:**	3.5	3.5	3.5	2.9	2.9	2.9	2.9	2.9	2.9	2.9
Replace front calipers (both), **ADD:**	.4	.4	.4	.4	.4	.4	.4	.4	.4	.4
Overhaul master cylinder, **ADD:**	.8	.8	.8	.8	.8	.8	.8	.8	.8	.8
Related Jobs: (Not during basic job)										
Bleed hyd. system, 4 wheels	.6	.6	.6	.6	.6	.6	.6	.6	.6	.6
Adjust drum brakes, 4 wheels	.5	.5	.5	.5	.5	.5	.5	.5	.5	.5
Replace disc brake pads, fr. wheels	1.6	1.6	1.6	1.6	1.6	1.6	1.0	1.0	1.0	1.0
O/h fr. calipers, incl. turn rotors	5.3	5.3	5.3	5.3	4.6	4.6	4.6	4.6	4.6	4.6
Rpl. fr. caliper, incl. turn rotor, ea.	2.4	2.4	2.4	2.4	2.4	2.4	2.4	2.4	2.4	2.4
Overhaul master cylinder	1.2	1.2	1.2	1.2	1.2	1.2	1.2	1.2	1.2	1.2

Approximate parts cost:
Master cylinder repair kit $16.00	Wheel cylinder repair kit, ea. . . . . . $ 2.00
Wheel cyl. seal, boot & bushing pkg. 6.00	Caliper brake housing 50.00
Disc brake pads, one wheel, set of 2 . . . . 24.00	Oil seal, ea. 2.00
Brake shoes & lining sets, front or rear 25.00	

HYDRAULIC BRAKE SYSTEM, OVERHAUL

Includes:
Basic Job: Overhaul or replace master cylinder, all wheel cylinders including hone if necessary, overhaul calipers, replace rear wheel oil seals, bleed hydraulic system, and adjust brakes.
Related Jobs: Work performed at time other than during basic job. Front wheel work includes pack & adjust wheel bearings. Rear wheel work includes R&R rear oil seals.

MODEL	1966	1967	1968	1969	1970	1971	1972	1973	1974	1975
Basic Job:										
Compl. job, incl. mstr. & wh. cylinders,										
Drum brakes, all models	4.7	4.7	4.7	4.7	4.7	4.7	4.7	4.6	4.6	4.6
Disc front, drum rear, all models	3.9	3.9	3.9	3.9	3.9	3.9	3.9	3.9	3.9	3.9
Related Jobs: (Not during basic job)										
Bleed hyd. system, 4 wheels	.6	.6	.6	.6	.6	.6	.6	.6	.6	.6
Overhaul master cylinder, incl. hone,										
Drum brakes	1.4	1.4	1.2	1.2	1.2	1.2	1.2	1.2	1.2	1.2
Disc brakes	1.6	1.6	1.2	1.2	1.2	1.2	1.2	1.2	1.2	1.2
Replace master cylinder	1.2	1.2	1.2	1.0	1.0	1.0	1.0	1.0	1.1	1.1
O/h wheel cylinders, drum brakes (4)	4.4	4.4	4.4	4.4	4.4	4.4	4.1	4.1	4.1	4.1
O/h fr. calipers, incl. turn rotors	4.0	4.0	4.0	4.0	4.0	4.0	4.0	4.0	4.0	4.0
With power brakes, **ADD:**	.2	.2	.2	.2	.2	.2	.2	.2	.2	.2
R&R and overhaul pwr. brake unit	1.8	1.8	1.8	1.8	1.8	1.8	1.8	1.8	1.8	1.8
Replace vacuum check valve	.4	.4	.4	.4	.4	.4	.4	.4	.4	.4

(THIS SCHEDULE CONTINUED ON NEXT PAGE.)

AMERICAN MOTORS

HYDRAULIC BRAKE SYSTEM, OVERHAUL Continued

MODEL	1966	1967	1968	1969	1970	1971	1972	1973	1974	1975

Approximate parts cost:

Master cylinder repair kit	$16.00	Master cylinder	$35.00
Wheel cylinder repair kit, ea.	2.00	Power brake vacuum check valve	5.00
Wheel cyl. seal, boot & bushing pkg.	6.00	Power brake assembly repair kit	21.00

PARKING BRAKES, SERVICE AND ADJUST

Includes:
   Basic Jobs: Replace defective cable or brake shoes and adjust parking brakes.

MODEL	1966	1967	1968	1969	1970	1971	1972	1973	1974	1975
Basic Job:										
Adjust parking brakes	.4	.4	.4	.4	.4	.4	.4	.4	.4	.4
Replace forward cable	1.0	1.0	1.0	1.0	1.0	1.0	1.0	1.1	1.1	1.1
Replace rear cable, one side	.8	.8	.8	.8	.8	.8	.8	.8	.8	.8
Replace rear cables, both sides	1.4	1.4	1.4	1.4	1.4	1.4	1.4	1.4	1.4	1.4

Approximate parts cost:

Front cable	$9.00-15.00	Rear cable, each	6.00-10.00

AIR CONDITIONING SYSTEM, MAJOR SERVICE

Includes:
   Basic Job: Drain system in order to replace defective component, evacuate, dehydrate, and recharge system, pressure-test, and leak-check. Clean condenser fins, adjust drive belt tension, tighten compressor, condenser, and evaporator mounts, and conduct performance test.
   Additions to Basic Job: Replace or overhaul compressor. Replace other defective parts.

MODEL	1966	1967	1968	1969	1970	1971	1972	1973	1974	1975
Basic Job:										
Drain, evacuate, dehydrate, charge & test	3.0	3.0	3.0	3.0	3.0	3.0	3.0	3.0	3.0	3.0
Additions to Basic Job:										
Replace compressor, ADD:	1.2	1.2	1.2	1.2	1.2	1.2	1.2	1.2	1.2	1.2
Overhaul compressor, incl. R&R, ADD:	2.9	2.9	2.9	2.9	2.9	2.9	2.9	2.9	2.9	2.9
Replace compressor oil pump seal, ADD:	.9	.9	.9	.9	.9	.9	.9	.9	.9	.9
Replace suction throttling valve, ADD:	.6	.6	.6	.6	.6	.6	.6	.6	.6	.6
Replace condenser, ADD:	1.3	1.3	1.3	1.3	1.3	1.3	1.3	1.3	1.3	1.3
Replace evaporator core, ADD:	1.6	1.6	1.6	1.6	1.6	1.6	1.6	1.6	1.6	1.6
Replace sight-glass, ADD:	1.4	1.4	1.4	1.4	1.4	1.4	.9	.9	.9	.9
Replace dehydrator-receiver tank, ADD:	1.0	1.0	1.0	.8	.8	.8	.8	.8	.8	.8
Replace expansion valve, ADD:	1.1	1.1	1.1	.8	.8	.8	.8	.8	.8	.8
Replace one hose, ADD:	.4	.4	.4	.4	.4	.4	.4	.4	.4	.4

Approximate parts cost:

Compressor	$ 90.00	Suction throttling valve	$40.00
Compressor repair kit	15.00	Expansion valve	35.00
Compressor seal kit	7.00	Hose, per ft.	2.75
Condenser	120.00	Freon, per 14 oz. can	2.50
Evaporator core	100.00	Anti-freeze, per gal.	9.50

(THIS SCHEDULE CONTINUED ON NEXT PAGE.)

AMERICAN MOTORS 27

AIR CONDITIONING SYSTEM, SPRING TUNE-UP

Includes:
  Basic Job: Clean condenser fins; adjust drive belt tension; test anti-freeze; tighten compressor condenser, and evaporator mounts. Pressure-test and leak-check system. Check system for performance.
  Additions to Basic Job: Replace defective parts not involving evacuate and charge system.

MODEL	1966	1967	1968	1969	1970	1971	1972	1973	1974	1975
Basic Job:										
Perform complete spring tune-up	2.0	2.0	2.0	2.0	2.0	2.0	2.0	2.0	2.0	2.0
Additions to Basic Job:										
Replace compressor belt & adjust, **ADD:**	.5	.5	.5	.5	.5	.5	.5	.5	.5	.5
Repl. compr. clutch pulley & bearing, **ADD:**	.8	.8	.8	.8	.8	.8	1.0	1.0	1.0	1.2
Replace compr. clutch, **ADD:**	.8	.8	.8	.8	.8	.8	.8	.8	.8	.8

Approximate parts cost:
Compressor drive belt .... $ 3.00   Compressor clutch $50.00
Compressor pulley & bearing .... 40.00   Anti-freeze, per gal. 9.50
Freon, per 14 oz. can 2.50

AIR CONDITIONING SYSTEM BLOWER MOTOR OR CONTROLS, SERVICE

Includes:
  Basic Job: Performance-test system to determine defective part, R&R component, and test system following installation.

MODEL	1966	1967	1968	1969	1970	1971	1972	1973	1974	1975
Basic Jobs:										
R&R blower mtr., test sys. after install.	1.6	1.6	1.6	1.6	1.6	1.6	1.6	1.6	1.4	1.4
R&R blower mtr. switch., test system	1.8	1.8	1.8	1.8	1.8	1.8	1.8	1.8	1.8	1.8
R&R compr. clutch switch, test system	1.4	1.4	1.4	1.4	1.4	1.4	1.3	1.3	1.3	1.3
R&R evap. thermostatic sw., test system,										
Javelin	1.6	1.6	1.6	1.6	1.6	1.6	1.6	1.6	1.6	1.6
All others	.9	.9	.9	.9	.9	.9	1.1	1.1	1.1	1.1
Weather Eye controls, replace	.5	.5	.5	.7	.7	.7	.7	.7	.7	.7

Approximate parts cost:
Blower motor .... $27.00   Compressor clutch switch $10.00
Blower motor switch .... 4.50   Evaporator thermostatic switch 25.00

HEATING SYSTEM, TEST AND SERVICE

Includes:
  Basic Job: Drain, back-flush, and fill radiator, check radiator and heater hoses and connections, pressure-test radiator cap and system.
  Related Jobs: Replace defective parts. Work performed individually and independently of basic job.

MODEL	1966	1967	1968	1969	1970	1971	1972	1973	1974	1975
Basic Job:										
Drain, flush, fill, check, & press-test	.9	.9	.9	.9	.9	.9	.9	.9	.9	.9
Related Jobs:										
Replace heater hose, one, inlet or outlet	.5	.5	.5	.5	.5	.5	.5	.5	.5	.5
Replace ea. additional hose, **ADD:**	.2	.2	.2	.2	.2	.2	.2	.2	.2	.2

(THIS SCHEDULE CONTINUED ON NEXT PAGE.)

AMERICAN MOTORS

HEATING SYSTEM, TEST AND SERVICE Continued

MODEL	1966	1967	1968	1969	1970	1971	1972	1973	1974	1975
R&R heater core with air conditioning,										
Includes partial charge system	2.5	2.5	2.5	2.5	2.5	2.5	2.9	2.9	2.9	2.9
Boil-out and repair core, **ADD:**	1.2	1.2	1.2	1.2	1.2	1.2	1.2	1.2	1.2	1.2
Replace heater core without air cond.	1.2	1.2	1.2	1.2	1.2	1.2	1.6	1.6	1.6	1.6
Boil-out and repair core, **ADD:**	1.2	1.2	1.2	1.2	1.2	1.2	1.2	1.2	1.2	1.2
Replace heater blower motor, test system	1.4	1.4	1.4	1.4	1.4	1.4	1.4	1.4	1.4	1.4
Replace heater switch	.7	.7	.7	.7	.7	.7	.7	.7	.7	.7

Approximate parts cost:
- Heater hose, per ft. .... $ .75
- Heater switch 4.50
- Heater core $35.00
- Blower motor 27.00

LIGHTING SYSTEM, ADJUST AND SERVICE

Includes:
Basic Jobs: 1. Adjust headlights to inspection requirements.
2. Replace defective parts in rear lighting system.
Additions to Basic Job: Replace associated parts affecting headlight adjustment.
Related Jobs: Replace associated parts not affecting headlight adjustment.

MODEL	1966	1967	1968	1969	1970	1971	1972	1973	1974	1975
Basic Job #1										
Adjust two lights	.4	.4	.4	.4	.4	.4	.4	.4	.4	.4
Adjust four lights	.6	.6	.6	.6	.6	.6	.6	.6	.6	.6
Basic Job #2										
Replace stoplight switch	.4	.4	.4	.4	.4	.4	.4	.4	.4	.4
Replace back-up light switch	.4	.4	.4	.4	.4	.4	.4	.4	.4	.4
Additions to Basic Job:										
Replace sealed beam unit, each, **ADD:**	.3	.3	.3	.3	.3	.3	.3	.3	.3	.3
Related Jobs:										
Replace headlamp switch,										
AMX, Gremlin	.6	.6	.6	.6	.6	.8	.8	.8	.8	.8
All others	.7	.7	.7	.7	.7	.8	.8	.8	.8	.8
Replace foot dimmer switch	.3	.3	.3	.3	.3	.3	.3	.3	.3	.3
Replace signal/hazard flasher	.3	.3	.3	.3	.3	.3	.3	.3	.3	.3
Replace signal/hazard switch,										
With standard column	.8	.8	.8	.8	.8	.8	.8	.8	.8	.8
With tilt wheel	1.0	1.0	1.0	1.0	1.0	1.0	1.0	1.0	1.0	1.0

Approximate parts cost:
- Sealed beam unit $4.00
- Signal/hazard flasher 2.00
- Signal/hazard switch 4.00
- Headlamp switch $8.00
- Back-up light switch 7.00

BUICK 29

SERVICE STATION MAINTENANCE

Includes:

Basic Job: Lubricate chassis, drain oil, change filters, repack front wheel bearings, repack U-joints, and lubricate front end. Check fluid levels of battery, radiator, air conditioner, brake master cylinder, power steering reservoir, transmission, and differential. Check condition of hoses and drive belts. Lubricate miscellaneous moving parts, latches, hinges, etc.

Related Jobs: Service individual systems or components. See detailed description of work included for each job in separate major section.

Additions to Basic or Related Jobs: Allowances for special equipment installed.

MODEL	1966	1967	1968	1969	1970	1971	1972	1973	1974	1975
Basic Job:										
General lubrication & system check,										
L-6 engine	—	—	1.0	1.0	1.0	1.0	—	—	1.0	1.0
V-6 engine	1.2	1.2	—	—	—	—	—	—	—	1.3
V-8 engine	1.4	1.4	1.4	1.4	1.4	1.4	1.4	1.4	1.5	1.5
With air conditioning, **ADD:**	.3	.3	.3	.3	.3	.3	.3	.3	.3	.3
With AIR pump, **ADD:**	.2	.2	.2	.2	.2	.2	.2	.2	.2	.2
With disc brakes, **ADD:**	—	.9	.9	.9	.9	.9	.9	.9	.9	.9
Related Jobs:										
Service Battery										
Clean, test, & fill	.3	.3	.3	.3	.3	.3	.3	.3	.3	.3
Replace ground cable	.2	.2	.2	.2	.2	.2	.2	.2	.2	.2
Replace starter cable	.3	.3	.3	.3	.3	.3	.3	.3	.3	.3
Replace battery	.4	.4	.4	.4	.4	.4	.4	.4	.4	.4
Service Cooling System										
Back-flush, fill, & press. test system	.9	.9	.9	.9	.9	.9	.9	.9	.9	.9
Replace upper hose	.4	.4	.4	.4	.4	.4	.4	.4	.4	.4
Replace lower hose	.5	.5	.5	.5	.5	.5	.5	.5	.5	.5
Replace both hoses	.7	.7	.7	.7	.7	.7	.7	.7	.7	.7
Replace thermostat & press-test system,										
L-6 engine	—	—	.5	.5	.5	.5	—	—	.5	.5
V-6 or V-8 engine	.7	.7	.7	.7	.7	.7	.7	.7	.7	.7
Replace water pump drive belt & adjust	.4	.4	.4	.4	.4	.4	.4	.4	.4	.4
With air conditioning, **ADD:**	.1	.1	.1	.1	.1	.1	.1	.1	.1	.1
Replace water pump,										
L-6 engine	—	—	1.0	1.0	1.0	1.0	—	—	1.0	1.0
With air conditioning, **ADD:**	—	—	.1	.1	.1	.1	—	—	.1	.1
V-6 or V-8 engine	1.5	1.5	1.5	1.5	1.5	1.5	1.5	1.5	1.5	1.5
With air conditioning, **ADD:**	.3	.3	.3	.3	.3	.3	.3	.3	.3	.3
With power steering, **ADD:**	.2	.2	.2	.2	.2	.2	.2	.2	.2	.2
With AIR, **ADD:**	.2	.2	.2	.2	.2	.2	.2	.2	.2	.2
Service Ignition System										
Adjust & install spark plugs										
L-6 or V-6 engine	.6	.6	.6	.6	.6	.6	—	—	.6	.6
V-8 engine	.8	.8	.8	.8	.8	.8	.8	.8	.8	.8
With air conditioning, **ADD:**	.3	.3	.3	.3	.3	.3	.3	.3	.3	.3
With AIR, **ADD:**	.3	.3	.3	.3	.3	.3	.3	.3	.3	.3
Replace points & condenser & adjust										
L-6 or V-6 engine	.5	.5	.5	.5	.5	.5	—	—	.5	—
V-8 engine	.7	.7	.7	.7	.7	.7	.7	.7	.7	—
Replace distributor cap,										
L-6 or V-6 engine, **ADD:**	.3	.3	.3	.3	.3	.3	—	—	.3	.4
V-8 engine, **ADD:**	.4	.4	.4	.4	.4	.4	.4	.4	.4	.5
Check reluctor air gap, and adjust ignition timing	—	—	—	—	—	—	—	—	—	.4

30 BUICK
SERVICE STATION MAINTENANCE Continued

MODEL	1966	1967	1968	1969	1970	1971	1972	1973	1974	1975
Replace spark plug wires,										
L-6 engine	—	—	.5	.5	.5	.5	—	—	.5	.5
V-6 engine	.6	.6	—	—	—	—	—	—	—	.6
V-8 engine	.8	.8	.8	.8	.8	.8	.8	.8	.8	.8
Replace ignition coil	.4	.4	.4	.4	.4	.4	.4	.4	.4	.4
Service Fuel System										
Adjust idle speed and mixture,										
Single barrel	.4	.4	.4	.4	.4	.4	.4	.4	.4	.4
Two and four-barrel	.6	.6	.6	.6	.6	.6	.6	.6	.6	.6
Replace fuel filter	.3	.3	.3	.3	.3	.3	.3	.3	.3	.3
Test & replace fuel pump,										
L-6 engine	—	—	.5	.5	.5	.5	—	—	.5	.5
V-6 or V-8 engine	.7	.7	.7	.7	.7	.7	.8	.8	.8	.8
Replace flexible fuel line	.3	.3	.3	.3	.3	.3	.3	.3	.3	.3
Service Driveshaft										
R&R driveshaft & overhaul U-joints. Measure and adjust U-joint & driveshaft angles.										
Cross & roller joints	1.5	1.5	1.5	1.5	1.5	1.5	1.5	1.5	1.5	1.5
Constant velocity joint	1.8	1.8	1.8	1.8	1.8	1.6	1.6	1.6	1.6	1.6
Service Hydraulic Brake System										
Adjust drum brakes	.5	.5	.5	.5	.5	.5	.5	.5	.5	.5
Replace drum brake shoes, 4 wheels	3.5	3.5	3.5	3.5	3.5	3.5	3.5	3.5	3.5	3.5
Bleed hydraulic system, 4 wheels	.6	.6	.6	.6	.6	.6	.6	.6	.6	.6
Replace front disc brake pads	—	1.5	1.5	1.5	1.5	1.5	1.0	1.0	1.0	1.0
Overhaul master cylinder	1.3	1.3	1.5	1.5	1.5	1.5	1.8	1.8	1.8	1.8
O/H wheel cylinders, drum brakes (4)	4.1	4.1	4.1	4.1	4.1	4.1	4.2	4.2	4.2	4.2
O/H fr. calipers incl. turn rotors	—	4.6	4.6	4.0	4.0	4.0	4.0	4.0	4.0	4.0
Service Parking Brakes										
Replace forward cable,										
Apollo	—	—	—	—	—	—	—	.5	.5	.5
All others	.9	.9	.9	.9	.9	.9	.9	.9	.9	.9
Replace rear cable, one side,										
Apollo	—	—	—	—	—	—	—	1.0	1.0	1.0
All others	.9	.9	.9	.9	.9	.9	.9	.9	.9	.9
Service Suspension System										
Replace front shock absorber, both sides	.9	.9	.9	.9	.9	.9	.9	.9	.9	.9
Replace rear shock absorber, both sides	.8	.8	.8	.8	.8	.8	.8	.8	.8	.8
Replace rear spring shackle and bushings; eye bolt and bushings	.7	.7	.7	.7	.7	.7	.7	.7	.7	.7
Replace rear leaf spring & shim to align pinion angle,										
Station wagon	1.5	1.5	1.5	1.5	1.5	1.5	1.5	1.5	1.5	1.5
Apollo	—	—	—	—	—	—	—	1.7	1.7	1.7
Service Front End & Steering System										
Adjust toe-in only	.4	.4	.4	.4	.4	.4	.4	.4	.4	.4
Replace tie-rods or tie-rod ends, (4)	1.4	1.4	1.4	1.4	1.4	1.4	1.4	1.4	1.4	1.4
Repl. Pitman arm, incl. adjust toe-in	.8	.8	.8	.8	.8	.8	.8	.8	.8	.8
Repl. steering idler arm or bushing, including adjust toe-in	.7	.7	.7	.7	.7	.7	.7	.7	.7	.7
Repl. pwr. steering pump drive belt	.3	.3	.3	.3	.3	.3	.3	.3	.3	.3
With air conditioning, **ADD:**	.2	.2	.2	.2	.2	.2	.2	.2	.2	.2

(THIS SCHEDULE CONTINUED ON NEXT PAGE.)

BUICK 31

SERVICE STATION MAINTENANCE Continued

MODEL	1966	1967	1968	1969	1970	1971	1972	1973	1974	1975
Check & replenish reservoir fluid	.2	.2	.2	.2	.2	.2	.2	.2	.2	.2
Replace pressure hoses, either set, includes adjust drive belt,										
L-6 engine	.3	.3	.3	.3	.3	.3	.3	.3	.3	.3
V-6 or V-8 engine	.6	.6	.6	.6	.6	.6	.6	.6	.6	.6
With air conditioning, **ADD:**	.1	.1	.1	.1	.1	.1	.1	.1	.1	.1
Balance four wheels on car,										
With drum brakes	1.2	1.2	1.2	1.2	1.2	1.2	1.2	1.2	1.2	1.2
With drum/disc brakes	—	1.5	1.5	1.5	1.5	1.5	1.5	1.5	1.5	1.5
Rotate five wheels	.6	.6	.6	.6	.6	.6	.6	.6	.6	.6
Service Charging System										
Test system and/or adjust regulator	.6	.6	.6	.6	.6	.6	.6	.6	.6	.6
R&R alternator including pulley	.6	.6	.6	.6	.7	.7	.7	.7	.7	.7
With air conditioning, **ADD:**	.1	.1	.1	.1	.1	.1	.1	.1	.1	.1
With AIR, **ADD:**	.2	.2	.2	.2	.2	.2	.2	.2	.2	.2
Overhaul alternator after removal	2.3	2.3	1.5	1.5	1.5	1.5	1.5	1.5	1.5	1.5
Replace regulator	.3	.3	.3	.3	.4	.4	.4	.3	.3	.3
Service Cranking System										
R&R starter,										
L-6 engine	—	—	.7	.7	.7	.8	—	—	.8	.8
V-6 engine	1.8	1.8	—	—	—	—	—	—	—	1.3
V-8 engine	.9	.9	.9	.9	.9	.9	1.1	1.1	1.1	1.1
Overhaul starter after removal	1.7	1.7	1.7	1.7	1.7	1.7	1.7	1.7	1.7	1.7
Replace starter-battery cable	.3	.3	.3	.3	.3	.3	.3	.3	.3	.3
Replace starter solenoid, incl. test sys.,										
L-6 engine	—	—	1.7	1.7	1.7	1.7	—	—	1.7	1.7
V-6 engine	2.7	2.6	—	—	—	—	—	—	—	1.8
V-8 engine	1.9	1.9	1.9	1.9	2.4	2.4	2.3	2.0	2.0	2.0
Service Lighting System										
Adjust two headlights	.4	.4	.4	.4	.4	.4	.4	.4	.4	.4
Adjust four headlights	.6	.6	.6	.6	.6	.6	.6	.6	.6	.6
Replace sealed beam unit, ea.	.3	.3	.3	.3	.3	.3	.3	.3	.3	.3
Replace foot dimmer switch	.3	.3	.3	.3	.3	.3	.3	.3	.3	.3
Replace signal/hazard flasher	.2	.2	.2	.2	.2	.2	.2	.2	.2	.2
Replace turn signal/hazard switch,										
With standard column	1.2	1.2	1.2	1.0	1.0	1.0	1.0	1.0	1.0	1.0
With tilt or telescopic column	1.5	1.5	1.5	1.3	1.3	1.3	1.3	1.3	1.3	1.3
Replace back-up light switch	.4	.4	.4	.4	.4	.4	.4	.4	.4	.4
Replace stoplight switch	.3	.3	.3	.3	.3	.3	.3	.3	.3	.3
Perform Minor Tune-up										
L-6 engine	—	—	1.8	1.8	1.8	2.0	—	—	2.3	2.3
V-6 engine	2.2	2.2	—	—	—	—	—	—	—	2.7
V-8 engine	2.7	2.7	2.7	2.7	2.7	2.7	2.5	2.5	2.8	3.0
Note: See minor tune-up section for work included and additions.										
Perform Major Tune-up										
L-6 engine	—	—	5.3	5.6	5.6	5.6	—	—	5.8	6.0
V-6 engine	5.8	5.8	—	—	—	—	—	—	—	6.7
V-8 engine	6.6	6.6	6.6	6.8	6.8	6.8	6.8	7.0	7.0	7.3
Note: See major tune-up section for work included and additions.										

32 BUICK

TUNE-UP, MAJOR Continued

MODEL	1966	1967	1968	1969	1970	1971	1972	1973	1974	1975

Includes:

Basic Job: Perform the following work:
1. Service air cleaner element.
2. Replace PCV valve.
3. Replace crankcase ventilation filter in air cleaner.
4. Clean battery terminals.
5. Check condition and tension of all drive belts.
6. Check all hoses and hose connections.
7. Check operation of heated-air system (air cleaner), manifold heat valve, and automatic choke. Service where necessary.
8. Replace fuel filter.
9. Perform compression test.
10. Replace spark plugs.
11. Replace ignition points and condenser.
12. Check dwell or reluctor air gap and adjust ignition timing.
13. Adjust carburetor idle mixture and speed.
14. Make necessary ignition and carburetor adjustments to obtain satisfactory exhaust system analyzer readings.

Additions to Basic Job: Allowances for special equipment.

MODEL	1966	1967	1968	1969	1970	1971	1972	1973	1974	1975
Basic Job: Perform minor tune-up,										
L-6 engine	—	—	1.8	1.8	1.8	2.0	—	—	2.3	2.3
V-6 engine	2.2	2.2	—	—	—	—	—	—	—	2.7
V-8 engine	2.7	2.7	2.7	2.7	2.7	2.7	2.5	2.5	2.8	3.0
Additions to Basic Job:										
With AIR pump, **ADD**:	.3	.3	.3	.3	.3	.3	.3	.3	.3	.3
With air conditioning, **ADD**:	.6	.6	.6	.6	.6	.6	.6	.6	.6	.6

Approximate parts cost:

Spark plugs, each	$1.50	Air cleaner element	$5.50
Points & condenser	5.00	Fuel filter	3.50
PCV valve	3.00		

TUNE-UP, MAJOR

Includes:

Basic Job: Perform the following work.
1. Service air cleaner element.
2. Replace crankcase ventilation filter in air cleaner.
3. Replace PCV valve.
4. Check drive belts and adjust for proper tension.
5. Check all hoses and hose connections.
6. Clean battery terminals.
7. Check operation of manifold heat valve and automatic choke. Service where necessary.
8. Check operation of heated-air system.
9. Check exhaust and evaporative emission control systems for proper operation:
10. Replace fuel filter.
11. Perform compression check.
12. Replace spark plugs.
13. Replace ignition points and condenser.
14. Check dwell or reluctor air gap and adjust ignition timing.
15. Check distributor cap and rotor.
16. Tighten cylinder head bolts.
17. Adjust valve lash (where applicable).
18. Overhaul carburetor.
19. Adjust carburetor idle mixture and speed.
20. Make necessary ignition and carburetor adjustments to obtain satisfactory exhaust system analyzer readings.

Additions to Basic Job: Allowances for special equipment.

MODEL	1966	1967	1968	1969	1970	1971	1972	1973	1974	1975
Basic Job: Perform major tune-up.										
L-6 engine	—	—	5.3	5.6	5.6	5.6	—	—	5.8	6.0
V-6 engine	5.8	5.8	—	—	—	—	—	—	—	6.7
V-8 engine	6.6	6.6	6.6	6.8	6.8	6.8	6.8	7.0	7.0	7.3

(THIS SCHEDULE CONTINUED ON NEXT PAGE.)

BUICK 33

TUNE-UP, MAJOR Continued

MODEL	1966	1967	1968	1969	1970	1971	1972	1973	1974	1975
Additions to Basic Job:										
With AIR pump, ADD:	.7	.7	.7	.7	.7	.7	.7	.7	.7	.7
Replace hydraulic valve lifter, one, ADD:	2.0	2.0	2.0	2.0	2.0	2.0	2.0	2.0	2.0	2.0
With air conditioning, ADD:	.6	.6	.6	.6	.6	.6	.6	.6	.6	.6

Approximate parts cost:

Spark plugs, each	$1.50
Points & condenser	5.00
PCV valve	3.00
Air cleaner element	5.50
Fuel filter	$3.50
Carburetor repair kit	10.00-20.00
Ignition coil	14.00
HEI coil	25.00

EMISSION CONTROL SYSTEMS, TESTS FOR SMOG STATION CERTIFICATION

Includes:

Basic Job: Test crankcase, exhaust, and evaporative emission control systems. Check heated-air system. Check HC/CO level with exhaust analyzer. Sign certification certificate. (No adjustments or repairs included in basic job.)

Related Jobs: Service any defective emission control system. Perform minor or major tune-up as required.

Additions to Related Jobs: Service or replace defective part(s) in the system. Allowances for special equipment installed.

MODEL	1966	1967	1968	1969	1970	1971	1972	1973	1974	1975
Basic Job:										
Test all systems & sign certificate,										
L-6 engine	—	—	.5	.5	.5	.8	—	—	.9	.9
V-6 engine	.7	.7	—	—	—	—	—	—	—	1.0
V-8 engine	1.0	1.0	1.0	1.0	1.0	1.0	1.3	1.3	1.3	1.3
Related Jobs:										
Service crankcase emission control system	.3	.3	.3	.3	.3	.3	.3	.3	.3	.3
Service evaporative emission control system	—	—	—	—	.4	.4	.4	.4	.4	.4
Exhaust emission control systems,										
Service heated-air system	—	—	—	.3	.3	.3	.3	.3	.3	.3
Service transmission controlled spark (TCS)	—	—	—	—	.5	.5	.5	.5	.5	.5
Service EGR system	—	—	—	—	—	—	.4	.4	.4	.4
Service air inj. (AIR) system	.5	.5	.5	.5	.5	.5	.5	.5	.5	.5
Replace catalytic converter pellets	—	—	—	—	—	—	—	—	—	1.0
Note: See separate section for replacement of components in each system.										
Perform minor tune-up,										
L-6 engine	—	—	1.8	1.8	1.8	2.0	—	—	2.3	2.3
V-6 engine	2.2	2.2	—	—	—	—	—	—	—	2.7
V-8 engine	2.7	2.7	2.7	2.7	2.7	2.7	2.5	2.5	2.8	3.0
Perform major tune-up,										
L-6 engine	—	—	5.3	5.6	5.6	5.6	—	—	5.8	6.0
V-6 engine	5.8	5.8	—	—	—	—	—	—	—	6.7
V-8 engine	6.6	6.6	6.6	6.8	6.8	6.8	6.8	7.0	7.0	7.3
Additions to Related Jobs:										
With AIR pump, ADD:	.3	.3	.3	.3	.3	.3	.3	.3	.3	.3
With air conditioning, ADD:	.6	.6	.6	.6	.6	.6	.6	.6	.6	.6

Approximate parts cost:

Catalytic converter pellets .... $70.00   See minor or major tune-up section for cost of tune-up parts.

34 BUICK

EMISSION CONTROL SYSTEMS, COMPLETE TEST OR SERVICE

Includes:

Basic Job: Make all necessary tests and repairs. Sign certification certificate.
1. Replace PCV valve, check all vacuum passageways and hoses.
2. Replace crankcase ventilation filter in air cleaner.
3. Test purge-control valve, gas tank filler cap and vent lines, and hoses for leakage.
4. Replace evaporation canister filter.
5. Clean EGR valve and test the control system.
6. Check transmission control spark (TCS) system.
7. Check operation of manifold heat valve and automatic choke. Free-up where necessary.
8. Check and adjust tension of drive belts.
9. Check operation of heated-air system.
10. Check AIR air pump flow.
11. Check routing and condition of hoses.
12. Check operation of diverter or bypass valve.
13. Check AIR manifold and hoses.
14. Replace catalytic converter or pellets, if necessary.
15. Determine if engine tune-up is required.

Related Jobs: Minor or major tune-up as required.

MODEL	1966	1967	1968	1969	1970	1971	1972	1973	1974	1975
Basic Job:										
Perform emission control sys. tune-up,										
L-6 engine	—	—	2.8	2.8	2.8	3.3	—	—	3.5	3.5
V-6 engine	3.0	3.0	—	—	—	—	—	—	—	3.8
V-8 engine	3.3	3.3	3.3	3.3	3.8	3.8	3.8	3.8	3.8	4.0
Additions to Basic Job:										
With AIR, **ADD:**	.5	.5	.5	.5	.5	.5	.5	.5	.5	.5
Related Jobs:										
Perform minor tune-up,										
L-6 engine	—	—	1.8	1.8	1.8	2.0	—	—	2.3	2.3
V-6 engine	2.2	2.2	—	—	—	—	—	—	—	2.7
V-8 engine	2.7	2.7	2.7	2.7	2.7	2.7	2.5	2.5	2.8	3.0
Perform major tune-up,										
L-6 engine	—	—	5.3	5.6	5.6	5.6	—	—	5.8	6.0
V-6 engine	5.8	5.8	—	—	—	—	—	—	—	6.7
V-8 engine	6.6	6.6	6.6	6.8	6.8	6.8	6.8	7.0	7.0	7.3
Additions to Related Jobs:										
With AIR pump, **ADD:**	.3	.3	.3	.3	.3	.3	.3	.3	.3	.3
With air conditioning, **ADD:**	.6	.6	.6	.6	.6	.6	.6	.6	.6	.6

Approximate parts cost:

Catalytic converter pellets	$70.00	Drive belt	$ 3.00
PCV valve	3.00	Diverter valve	12.00
Hose, per ft.	0.75	Air pump	50.00
Canister filter	1.00	Catalytic converter	175.00
Purge control valve	4.00	See minor or major tune-up section for cost of tune-up parts.	

POSITIVE CRANKCASE VENTILATION (PCV) SYSTEM, TEST AND SERVICE

Includes:

Basic Job: Test PCV valve, check all vacuum passageways, and inspect hoses. Clean or replace air filter.
Additions to Basic Job: Replace defective parts. (Do not attempt to clean PCV valve, replace if valve is not free.)

MODEL	1966	1967	1968	1969	1970	1971	1972	1973	1974	1975
Basic Job:										
Test PCV system, all models	.3	.3	.3	.3	.3	.3	.3	.3	.3	.3
Additions to Basic Job:										
Replace PCV valve, **ADD:**	.3	.3	.3	.3	.3	.3	.3	.3	.3	.3
Replace all hoses, **ADD:**	.6	.6	.6	.6	.6	.6	.6	.6	.6	.6

Approximate parts cost:

PCV valve	$3.00	Hose, per ft.	$0.75

BUICK 35

EXHAUST-GAS RECIRCULATION (EGR), TEST AND SERVICE

Includes:
Basic Job: Test EGR valve, control system, and engine idling condition.
Additions to Basic Job: Replace defective parts. Test & repair thermostatic control system.

MODEL	1966	1967	1968	1969	1970	1971	1972	1973	1974	1975
Basic Job:										
Test EGR system, all models	—	—	—	—	—	—	.4	.4	.4	.4
Additions to Basic Job:										
Service EGR valve, **ADD:**	—	—	—	—	—	—	.7	.7	.7	.7
Replace EGR valve, **ADD:**	—	—	—	—	—	—	.4	.4	.4	.4
Test & repair thermo. control sys., **ADD:**	—	—	—	—	—	—	.6	.6	.6	.6

Approximate parts cost:
EGR valve .... $10.00   Thermal vacuum switch $12.00

TRANSMISSION CONTROLLED SPARK (TCS) SYSTEM, TEST AND SERVICE

Includes:
Basic Job: Check engine speed in gear using tachometer and timing light, test TCS solenoid or CEC valve, and transmission switch.
Additions to Basic Job: Replace defective parts.

MODEL	1966	1967	1968	1969	1970	1971	1972	1973	1974	1975
Basic Job:										
Test TCS system, all models	—	—	—	—	.6	.5	.5	.5	.5	.5
Additions to Basic Job:										
Replace TCS or CEC solenoid, **ADD:**	—	—	—	—	.3	.3	.3	.3	.3	.3
Adjust CEC valve, **ADD:**	—	—	—	—	—	—	—	—	.2	.2
Replace TCS switch,										
With standard transmission, **ADD:**	—	—	—	—	.4	.4	.4	.4	.4	.4
With THM 400 transmission, **ADD:**	—	—	—	—	.8	.8	.8	.8	.8	.8
All other automatic transmissions, **ADD:**	—	—	—	—	.5	.5	.5	.5	.5	.5
Replace TCS relay, **ADD:**	—	—	—	—	.2	.2	.2	.2	.2	.2
Replace thermostatic vacuum switch or TCS temperature switch, **ADD:**	—	—	—	—	.3	.3	.3	.3	.3	.3
Replace idle stop solenoid, **ADD:**	—	—	—	—	.3	.3	.3	.3	.3	.3

Approximate parts cost:
TCS switch ....$5.00   TCS solenoid $11.50
Thermostatic vacuum switch .... 6.50   Idle stop solenoid 11.00
TCS relay .... 2.50   CEC solenoid 12.00

AIR INJECTION REACTOR (AIR) SYSTEM, TEST AND SERVICE

Includes:
Basic Job: Test AIR air pump flow, check routing and condition of hoses, determine operation of diverter valve, verify check valve operation, inspect air manifold and hoses. Check and adjust drive belt tension.
Additions to Basic Job: Replace defective parts. Replace drive belt, includes adjust tension. Replacement of hose(s), includes soapy water test.

MODEL	1966	1967	1968	1969	1970	1971	1972	1973	1974	1975
Basic Job:										
Test AIR system, all models	.5	.5	.5	.5	.5	.5	.5	.5	.5	.5

36 BUICK

AIR INJECTION REACTOR SYSTEM Continued

MODEL	1966	1967	1968	1969	1970	1971	1972	1973	1974	1975
Additions to Basic Job:										
Replace and adjust drive belt,										
L-6 engine, **ADD**:	—	—	.4	.4	.4	.4	—	—	.4	.4
V-6 or V-8 engine, **ADD**:	.5	.5	.5	.5	.5	.5	.5	.5	.5	.5
Replace AIR pump,										
L-6 engine, **ADD**:	—	—	.5	.5	.5	.5	—	—	.5	.5
V-6 or V-8 engine, **ADD**:	.7	.7	.7	.7	.7	.7	.7	.7	.7	.7
Replace diverter valve, all models, **ADD**:	.4	.4	.4	.4	.4	.4	.4	.4	.4	.4
Replace check valve assembly, **ADD**:	.3	.3	.3	.3	.3	.3	.3	.3	.3	.3
Repl. hose, incl. soapy water test, **ADD**:	.4	.4	.4	.4	.4	.4	.4	.4	.4	.4

Approximate parts cost:

Drive belt	$3.00	Diverter valve	$12.00
Air pump	50.00	Hose, per ft.	0.75
Check valve	7.00		

HEATED-AIR SYSTEM, TEST AND SERVICE

Includes:
  Basic Job: Check cold/heated-air door, temperature sensor, and vacuum motor.
  Additions to Basic Job: Replace defective parts.

MODEL	1966	1967	1968	1969	1970	1971	1972	1973	1974	1975
Basic Job:										
Test heated-air system	—	—	—	.3	.3	.3	.3	.3	.3	.3
Additions to Basic Job:										
Replace vacuum motor, **ADD**:	—	—	—	.4	.4	.4	.4	.4	.4	.4
Replace temperature sensor, **ADD**:	—	—	—	.5	.5	.5	.5	.5	.5	.5

Approximate parts cost:

Vacuum motor assembly	$5.00	Temperature sensor	$4.50

EVAPORATIVE EMISSION CONTROL SYSTEM, TEST AND SERVICE

Includes:
  Basic Job: Test purge control valve, gas tank filler cap, vent lines, and hoses.
  Additions to Basic Job: Replace defective parts.

MODEL	1966	1967	1968	1969	1970	1971	1972	1973	1974	1975
Basic Job:										
Test evap. emission control system	—	—	—	—	.4	.4	.4	.4	.4	.4
Additions to Basic Job:										
Replace purge control valve, **ADD**:	—	—	—	—	—	—	.5	—	—	—
Replace charcoal canister filter, **ADD**:	—	—	—	—	.3	.3	.3	.3	.3	.3
Replace charcoal canister, **ADD**:	—	—	—	—	.5	.5	.5	.5	.5	.5
Replace hose, each, **ADD**:	—	—	—	—	.2	.2	.2	.2	.2	.2

Approximate parts cost:

Purge control valve	$4.00	Hose, per ft.	$0.75
Canister filter	1.50	Charcoal canister	32.00

BUICK 37

IGNITION SYSTEM, SERVICE

Includes:
Basic Jobs: 1. Adjust and install new spark plugs.
2. Replace points and condenser, adjust dwell and ignition timing.
3. R&R distributor, overhaul and test centrifugal and vacuum advances, set dwell or check reluctor air gap and ignition timing.
Related Jobs: Replace additional defective part(s) as required.
Additions: Allowances for special equipment installed or replacement of associated defective part(s).

MODEL	1966	1967	1968	1969	1970	1971	1972	1973	1974	1975
Basic Job #1										
Adjust & install new spark plugs,										
L-6 or V-6 engine	.6	.6	.6	.6	.6	.6	—	—	.6	.6
V-8 engine	.8	.8	.8	.8	.8	.8	.8	.8	.8	.8
With air conditioning, **ADD:**	.3	.3	.3	.3	.3	.3	.3	.3	.3	.3
With AIR, **ADD:**	.3	.3	.3	.3	.3	.3	.3	.3	.3	.3
Basic Job #2										
Replace points and condenser and adjust ignition timing,										
L-6 or V-6 engine	.5	.5	.5	.5	.5	.5	—	—	.5	—
V-8 engine	.7	.7	.7	.7	.7	.7	.7	.7	.7	—
Replace distributor cap,										
L-6 or V-6 engine, **ADD:**	.3	.3	.3	.3	.3	.3	—	—	.3	.4
V-8 engine, **ADD:**	.4	.4	.4	.4	.4	.4	.4	.4	.4	.5
Check reluctor air gap and adjust ignition timing	—	—	—	—	—	—	—	—	—	.4
Basic Job #3										
R&R and overhaul distributor and adjust ignition timing,										
All models	1.4	1.4	1.4	1.4	1.4	1.4	1.4	1.4	1.4	.8
Replace vacuum advance unit, **ADD:**	.2	.2	.2	.2	.2	.2	.2	.2	.2	.2
Related Jobs:										
Replace ignition coil	.4	.4	.4	.4	.4	.4	.4	.4	.4	.4
Replace spark plug wires,										
L-6 engine	—	—	.5	.5	.5	.5	—	—	.5	.5
V-6 engine	.6	.6	—	—	—	—	—	—	—	.6
V-8 engine	.8	.8	.8	.8	.8	.8	.8	.8	.8	.8
With air conditioning, **ADD:**	.3	.3	.3	.3	.3	.3	.3	.3	.3	.3
Replace ignition switch, all models	.6	.6	.6	.6	.6	.6	.6	.6	.6	.6
Replace ign. sw. lock cyl. or buzzer sw.	.4	.4	.4	.4	.4	.7	.7	.7	.7	.7

Approximate parts cost:

Spark plugs, each	$ 1.50
Point set	3.00
Condenser	1.50
Distributor cap	4.50
Distributor parts	10.00
Ignition switch	7.00
H.E.I. ignition coil	25.00
Vacuum control unit	$ 4.00
Ignition coil	12.50
Spark plug wires, L-6 engine	7.00
V-6 engine	10.00
V-8 engine	10.00-17.00
Ignition buzzer switch	2.50

CRANKING SYSTEM, TEST AND SERVICE

Includes:
Basic Job: Test battery and cranking system. Clean battery cable terminals.
Related Jobs: Replace defective part, including test when necessary.

MODEL	1966	1967	1968	1969	1970	1971	1972	1973	1974	1975
Basic Job:										
Test cranking system	.5	.5	.5	.5	.5	.5	.5	.5	.5	.5

38 BUICK

CRANKING SYSTEM, TEST AND SERVICE Continued

MODEL	1966	1967	1968	1969	1970	1971	1972	1973	1974	1975
Related Jobs:										
R&R starter,										
L-6 engine	—	—	.7	.7	.7	.8	—	—	.8	.8
V-6 engine	1.8	1.8	—	—	—	—	—	—	—	1.3
V-8 engine	.9	.9	.9	.9	.9	.9	1.1	1.1	1.1	1.1
Overhaul starter after removal	1.7	1.7	1.7	1.7	1.7	1.7	1.7	1.7	1.7	1.7
Replace starter-battery cable	.3	.3	.3	.3	.3	.3	.3	.3	.3	.3
Repl. starter solenoid, incl. sys. test,										
L-6 engine	—	—	1.7	1.7	1.7	1.7	—	—	1.7	1.7
V-6 engine	2.7	2.6	—	—	—	—	—	—	—	1.8
V-8 engine	1.9	1.9	1.9	1.9	2.4	2.4	2.3	2.0	2.0	2.0
Repl. starter/neutral switch & adjust,										
With column shift	.4	.4	.4	.4	.4	.4	.4	.4	.4	.4
With floor shift	.6	.6	.6	.6	.6	.6	.6	.6	.6	.6

Approximate parts cost:
Starter, new $80.00
Starter, rebuilt w/o solenoid 30.00
Starter-battery cable 4.50-8.50
Solenoid switch $14.00
Starter/neutral switch 4.00

CHARGING SYSTEM, TEST AND SERVICE

Includes:
Basic Job: Test battery voltage and gravity, clean battery cable terminals, test alternator output, test and/or adjust regulator.
Related Jobs: Replace or overhaul defective component.

MODEL	1966	1967	1968	1969	1970	1971	1972	1973	1974	1975
Basic Job:										
Test system and/or adjust regulator	.6	.6	.6	.6	.6	.6	.6	.6	.6	.6
Related Jobs:										
R&R alternator, incl. pulley	.6	.6	.6	.6	.7	.7	.7	.7	.7	.7
With air conditioning, **ADD:**	.1	.1	.1	.1	.1	.1	.1	.1	.1	.1
With AIR, **ADD:**	.2	.2	.2	.2	.2	.2	.2	.2	.2	.2
Overhaul alternator after removal	2.3	2.3	1.5	1.5	1.5	1.5	1.5	1.5	1.5	1.5
Replace regulator	.3	.3	.3	.3	.4	—	—	—	—	—

Approximate parts cost:
Alternator, new $90.00
Alternator, rebuilt 35.00
Regulator $20.00-40.00

FUEL SYSTEM, ADJUST AND SERVICE

Includes:
Basic Job: Adjust idle mixture and speed for performance and to obtain satisfactory exhaust system analyzer readings.
Related Jobs: R&R carburetor, overhaul carburetor, R&R associated fuel system components.

MODEL	1966	1967	1968	1969	1970	1971	1972	1973	1974	1975
Basic Job:										
Complete carburetor adjustments,										
Single or two-barrel	.4	.4	.4	.4	.4	.4	.4	.4	.4	.4
Four-barrel	.5	.5	.5	.5	.5	.5	.5	.5	.5	.5

(THIS SCHEDULE CONTINUED ON NEXT PAGE.)

BUICK 39

FUEL SYSTEM, ADJUST AND SERVICE Continued

MODEL	1966	1967	1968	1969	1970	1971	1972	1973	1974	1975
Related Jobs:										
Replace carb. incl. compl. adjustments,										
Single or 2-barrel	.6	.6	.5	.5	.7	.7	.7	.7	.7	.7
Four-barrel	1.0	1.0	1.0	1.0	1.0	1.0	1.0	1.0	1.0	1.0
O/H carb., incl. R&R and compl. adjust.,										
Single or two-barrel	2.6	2.6	2.6	2.5	2.7	2.2	2.4	2.4	2.4	2.4
Four-barrel	4.0	4.0	4.0	4.0	3.2	3.2	3.2	3.2	3.4	3.4
Test & replace fuel pump,										
L-6 engine	—	—	.5	.5	.5	.5	—	—	.5	.5
V-6, V-8 engine	.7	.7	.7	.7	.7	.7	.8	.8	.8	.8
Replace fuel filter	.3	.3	.3	.3	.3	.3	.3	.3	.3	.3
Replace fuel tank sending unit,										
Station Wagon	1.0	1.0	1.0	1.0	1.0	1.0	1.0	1.0	1.0	1.0
All others	.9	.8	.8	.8	.8	.8	.8	.8	.8	.8
Replace dashboard fuel gauge,										
LeSabre, Centurion, Electra, Riviera	1.1	1.1	*2.0	*2.0	*2.0	.4	.4	.4	.4	.4
*Includes disconnect and connect instrument cluster.										
All others	.4	.4	.4	.4	.4	.4	.4	.4	.4	.4
With air conditioning, **ADD:**	.1	.1	.1	.1	.1	.1	.1	.1	.1	.1
Replace fuel tank,										
Station Wagon	1.2	1.2	1.2	1.2	1.2	1.3	1.3	1.3	1.3	1.3
All others	.9	.9	.9	.9	.9	.9	.9	.9	.9	.9
Clean fuel tank, **ADD:**	.3	.3	.3	.3	.3	.3	.3	.3	.3	.3
Replace flexible fuel line	.3	.3	.3	.3	.3	.3	.3	.3	.3	.3

Approximate parts cost:

Carburetor repair kit, ea.	$10.00-20.00
Carburetor, new, ea., single bbl.	40.00
Two bbl.	75.00
Four bbl.	100.00
Flexible fuel line, per ft.	0.50
Fuel tank	50.00-65.00
Carburetor, rebuilt, single bbl.	$15.00
Two bbl.	22.00
Four bbl.	40.00
Fuel pump	15.00
Fuel tank sending unit	13.00-24.00
Fuel gauge, dash	9.00-14.00

ENGINE OVERHAUL, IN-CAR

Includes:

Basic Job: Remove ring ridge, deglaze cylinder walls, fit piston pins, align connecting rods, install new piston rings and rod bearings, install new main bearing inserts and oil seals, overhaul oil pump, clean carbon, grind valves, and perform major tune-up.

Additions to Basic Job: Associated work that is required during basic job and allowances for special equipment.

MODEL	1966	1867	1968	1969	1970	1971	1972	1973	1974	1975
Basic Job:										
Overhaul engine,										
L-6 engine	—	—	22.0	22.0	22.0	22.0	—	—	22.5	22.5
V-6 engine	24.5	24.5	—	—	—	—	—	—	—	25.0
V-8 engine	29.0	29.0	29.0	29.4	29.4	29.4	29.0	29.0	29.0	29.5
Additions to Basic Job:										
Rebore cylinders,										
6-cylinder, **ADD:**	4.0	4.0	4.0	4.0	4.0	4.0	—	—	4.0	4.0
V-8 engine, **ADD:**	5.0	5.0	5.0	5.0	5.0	5.0	5.0	5.0	5.0	5.0
Expand pistons,										
6-cylinder, **ADD:**	1.8	1.8	1.8	1.8	1.8	1.8	—	—	1.8	1.8
V-8 engine, **ADD:**	2.4	2.4	2.4	2.4	2.4	2.4	2.4	2.4	2.4	2.4

(THIS SCHEDULE CONTINUED ON NEXT PAGE.)

40 BUICK

ENGINE OVERHAUL, IN-CAR Continued

MODEL	1966	1967	1968	1969	1970	1971	1972	1973	1974	1975
Regroove top piston ring groove,										
6-cylinder, **ADD**:	1.8	1.8	1.8	1.8	1.8	1.8	—	—	1.8	1.8
V-8 engine, **ADD**:	2.4	2.4	2.4	2.4	2.4	2.4	2.4	2.4	2.4	2.4
Replace hydraulic valve lifters, **ADD**:	1.0	1.0	1.0	1.0	1.0	1.0	1.0	1.0	1.0	1.0
Overhaul rocker arm mechanism,										
V-6 engine, **ADD**:	1.5	1.5	—	—	—	—	—	—	—	1.5
V-8 engine, **ADD**:	1.9	1.9	1.9	1.9	1.9	1.9	1.9	1.9	1.9	1.9
Ream valve guides oversize,										
6-cylinder, **ADD**:	.7	.7	.7	.7	.7	.7	—	—	.7	.7
V-8 engine, **ADD**:	.9	.9	.9	.9	.9	.9	.9	.9	.9	.9
With AIR pump, **ADD**:	.7	.7	.7	.7	.7	.7	.7	.7	.7	.7
With air conditioning, **ADD**:	.7	.7	.7	.7	.7	.7	.7	.7	.7	.7

Approximate parts cost:

Hydraulic valve lifters, ea.	$ 4.00
Major tune-up parts	22.00-35.00
Carburetor repair kit	10.00-20.00
Rod bearing inserts, 6-cylinder engine	24.00
V-8 engine	32.00
Rear main brg. oil seal set	3.00
Complete gasket set, L-6 engine	26.00
V-6 engine	28.00
V-8 engine	30.00
Main bearing inserts, L-6 engine	$ 35.00
V-6 engine	20.00
V-8 engine	25.00
Piston rings, complete set, 6-cylinder	27.00
V-8 engine	36.00
Piston pins, 6-cylinder	10.50
V-8 engine	14.00
Piston assemblies, set, 6-cylinder	108.00
V-8, set	144.00

SHORT BLOCK, REPLACE

Includes:

  Basic Job: R&R engine, clean and reface valves, scrape carbon, grind valve seats, replace valve seals, overhaul rocker arm mechanism, transfer all parts, and perform major tune-up.

  Additions to Basic Job: Associated work that is required during basic job and allowances for special equipment installed.

MODEL	1966	1967	1968	1969	1970	1971	1972	1973	1974	1975
Basic Job:										
Replace short block,										
L-6 engine	—	—	15.5	15.5	14.7	14.7	—	—	15.0	15.5
V-6 engine	17.6	17.6	—	—	—	—	—	—	—	17.2
V-8 engine	20.5	20.5	20.5	20.0	20.0	20.0	20.0	20.2	20.2	20.4
Additions to Basic Job:										
Ream valve guides oversize,										
6-cylinder, **ADD**:	.7	.7	.7	.7	.7	.7	—	—	.7	.7
V-8 engine, **ADD**:	.9	.9	.9	.9	.9	.9	.9	.9	.9	.9
Service/replace hyd. valve lifters, **ADD**:	2.0	2.0	2.0	2.0	2.0	2.0	2.0	2.0	2.0	2.0
Replace all engine mounts, **ADD**:	.6	.6	.6	.6	.6	.6	.6	.6	.6	.6
Replace worn clutch parts, **ADD**:	.5	.5	.5	.5	.5	.5	.5	.5	.5	.5
With AIR pump, **ADD**:	.7	.7	.7	.7	.7	.7	.7	.7	.7	.7
With air conditioning, incl. chg. sys., **ADD**:	1.8	1.8	1.8	1.8	1.8	1.8	1.8	1.8	1.8	1.8

Approximate parts cost:

Complete gasket set, L-6 engine	$26.00
V-6 engine	28.00
V-8 engine	30.00
Engine mounts	7.00
Short block: Call supplier for price quote.	
Oil and air filters	$ 9.00
Pressure plate	30.00-60.00
Clutch disc	21.00-40.00
Thrust bearing	5.00-15.00
Carburetor repair kit	10.00-20.00

BUICK 41

ENGINE OVERHAUL, OUT-OF-CAR

Includes:
Basic Job: R&R engine, remove ring ridge, rebore or hone cylinder walls, regrind crankshaft and camshaft, replace camshaft bushings and line ream, replace timing chain and/or gears and oil seal, install main bearing inserts and seals, install piston pins, align connecting rods, install new piston rings and rod bearings, overhaul oil pump, clean carbon, grind valves, overhaul rocker arm mechanism, and perform major tune-up.

Additions to Basic Job: Associated work that is required during basic job and allowances for special equipment installed.

MODEL	1966	1967	1968	1969	1970	1971	1972	1973	1974	1975
Basic Job:										
Overhaul engine,										
L-6 engine	—	—	34.5	34.5	34.5	34.5	—	—	35.2	35.4
V-6 engine	38.4	38.4	—	—	—	—	—	—	—	39.0
V-8 engine	42.5	42.5	42.5	42.5	42.5	42.0	42.0	42.5	42.5	42.5
Additions to Basic Job:										
Regroove top piston ring grooves,										
6-cylinder, **ADD:**	1.8	1.8	1.8	1.8	1.8	1.8	1.8	1.8	1.8	1.8
V-8 engine, **ADD:**	2.4	2.4	2.4	2.4	2.4	2.4	2.4	2.4	2.4	2.4
Ream valve guides oversize,										
6-cylinder, **ADD:**	.7	.7	.7	.7	.7	.7	—	—	.7	.7
V-8 engine, **ADD:**	.9	.9	.9	.9	.9	.9	.9	.9	.9	.9
Replace all engine mounts, **ADD:**	.6	.6	.6	.6	.6	.6	.6	.6	.6	.6
Replace worn clutch parts, **ADD:**	.5	.5	.5	.5	.5	.5	.5	.5	.5	.5
With AIR pump, **ADD:**	.7	.7	.7	.7	.7	.7	.7	.7	.7	.7
With air conditioning, incl. chg. sys., **ADD:**	1.8	1.8	1.8	1.8	1.8	1.8	1.8	1.8	1.8	1.8

Approximate parts cost:

Complete gasket set, L-6 engine	$26.00	Main bearing inserts, L-6 engine	$ 35.00
V-6 engine	28.00	V-6 engine	20.00
V-8 engine	30.00	V-8 engine	25.00
Hydraulic valve lifters, ea.	4.00	Piston rings, complete set, 6-cylinder	27.00
Major tune-up parts	22.00-35.00	V-8 engine	36.00
Carburetor repair kit	10.00-20.00	Piston pins, standard 6-cylinder	10.50
Rod bearing inserts, 6-cylinder engine	24.00	V-8 engine	14.00
V-8 engine	32.00	Piston assemblies, 6-cylinder, set	108.00
Rear main bearing oil seal set	3.00	V-8, set	144.00
Engine mounts	7.00	Clutch disc	21.00-48.00
Pressure plate	30.00-60.00	Clutch release bearing	12.00
Flywheel pilot bushing or bearing	1.50		

TIMING CHAIN MECHANISM, SERVICE

Includes:
Basic Job: Replace timing cover oil seal and timing chain. Perform minor tune-up.
Additions to Basic Job: Replace camshaft timing sprocket or crankshaft timing sprocket.

MODEL	1966	1967	1968	1969	1970	1971	1972	1973	1974	1975
Basic Job:										
Replace timing cover oil seal & chain and perform minor tune-up,										
L-6 engine	—	—	*7.3	*7.3	*7.3	5.0	—	—	5.3	5.3
V-6 engine	4.4	4.4	—	—	—	—	—	—	—	5.1
V-8 engine	4.8	4.8	4.8	4.8	4.5	4.5	4.3	4.4	4.8	5.0

*Includes R&R engine, 1968 all models, and 1969 & 70 with manual transmission.

42 BUICK

TIMING CHAIN MECHANISM, SERVICE Continued

MODEL	1966	1967	1968	1969	1970	1971	1972	1973	1974	1975
Additions to Basic Job:										
Replace camshaft sprocket, **ADD**:	.2	.2	.2	.2	.2	.2	.2	.2	.2	.2
Replace crankshaft sprocket, **ADD**:	.2	.2	.2	.2	.2	.2	.2	.2	.2	.2
With air conditioning, **ADD**:	.5	.5	.5	.5	.5	.5	.5	.5	.5	.5
With AIR, **ADD**:	.2	.2	.2	.2	.2	.2	.2	.2	.2	.2
With power steering, **ADD**:	.3	.3	.3	.3	.3	.3	.3	.3	.3	.3

Approximate parts cost:
Timing cover gasket	$1.00	Camshaft sprocket	$6.00-12.00
Timing cover oil seal	2.00	Crankshaft sprocket	4.50
Timing chain	9.00	Minor tune-up parts	25.00-30.00

OIL PUMP SERVICE

Includes:
Basic Job: R&R oil pan, service oil pump, and replace oil filter element.

MODEL	1966	1967	1968	1969	1970	1971	1972	1973	1974	1975
Basic Job:										
R&R oil pan, service oil pump, and replace oil filter element.										
L-6 engine	—	—	4.5	4.5	2.0	2.0	—	—	1.8	1.8
V-6 engine	1.1	1.1	—	—	—	—	—	—	—	.8
V-8 engine	.8	.8	.8	.8	.8	.8	.8	.8	.8	.8
Additions to Basic Job:										
Overhaul oil pump, **ADD**:	.8	.8	.8	.8	.8	.8	.8	.8	.8	.8
Replace rear main bearing insert & seals,										
L-6 engine, **ADD**:	—	—	.3	.3	.3	.3	—	—	.3	.3
V-6 engine, **ADD**:	.4	.4	—	—	—	—	—	—	—	.4
V-8 engine, **ADD**:	.3	.3	.3	.3	.3	.3	.3	.3	.3	.3
Replace other main brg. inserts, ea., **ADD**:	.6	.6	.6	.6	.6	.6	.6	.6	.6	.6

Approximate parts cost:
Oil pan	$24.00	Oil pump	$18.00
Oil pan gasket	4.00	Oil pump screen	2.50
Oil pump shaft & rotor kit	8.00	Oil filter element	5.00

BEARINGS, MAIN AND/OR RODS, REPLACE

Includes:
Basic Job: R&R oil pan, measure connecting rod bearing oil clearance with Plastigage, install new connecting rod bearing inserts, service oil pump, and install new oil filter.

Additions to Basic Job: Measure main bearing oil clearance with Pastigage, replace all main bearing inserts and rear main bearing oil seals, repair or replace oil pump.

MODEL	1966	1967	1968	1969	1970	1971	1972	1973	1974	1975
Basic Job:										
R&R pan, measure, install inserts & filter,										
L-6 engine	—	—	6.0	6.0	3.5	3.5	—	—	4.0	4.0
V-6 engine	3.6	3.6	—	—	—	—	—	—	—	3.6
V-8 engine	3.9	3.9	3.9	3.9	3.9	3.9	3.9	3.9	4.0	4.0

(THIS SCHEDULE CONTINUED ON NEXT PAGE.)

BUICK 43

BEARINGS, MAIN AND/OR RODS, REPLACE Continued

MODEL Additions to Basic Job:	1966	1967	1968	1969	1970	1971	1972	1973	1974	1975
Use Plastigage — all main brgs,										
L-6 engine, **ADD**:	—	—	.7	.7	.7	.7	—	—	.7	.7
V-6 engine, **ADD**:	.4	.4	—	—	—	—	—	—	—	.4
V-8 engine, **ADD**:	.5	.5	.5	.5	.5	.5	.5	.5	.5	.5
Replace main inserts & rear oil seals,										
L-6 engine, **ADD**:	—	—	3.5	3.5	3.5	3.5	—	—	3.5	3.5
V-6 engine, **ADD**:	2.0	2.0	—	—	—	—	—	—	—	2.0
V-8 engine, **ADD**:	2.5	2.5	2.5	2.5	2.5	2.5	2.5	2.5	2.5	2.5
Overhaul oil pump, **ADD**:	.8	.8	.8	.8	.8	.8	.8	.8	.8	.8

Approximate parts cost:
Oil pan gasket .... $ 4.00	Main bearing inserts, L-6 engine $35.00
Rod bearing inserts, 6-cylinder engine 24.00	V-6 engine 20.00
V-8 engine 32.00	V-8 engine 25.00
Rear main brg. oil seal set 3.00	Oil filter element 5.00
Oil pump shaft & rotor kit 8.00	

CYLINDER HEAD AND/OR GASKET, REPLACE

Includes:
Basic Jobs: 1. R&R intake manifold and cylinder head to install new gasket. Clean head and block surfaces and perform minor tune-up.
                2. Install new cylinder head, including recondition valves and perform minor tune-up.
Additions to Basic Job: Allowances for special equipment.

MODEL	1966	1967	1968	1969	1970	1971	1972	1973	1974	1975
Basic Job #1										
Replace head gasket, including minor tune-up,										
L-6 engine	—	—	4.6	4.6	4.6	4.8	—	—	4.7	4.7
V-6 engine, left side	4.3	4.3	—	—	—	—	—	—	—	5.0
V-6 engine, right side	4.6	4.6	—	—	—	—	—	—	—	5.3
V-6 engine, both sides	5.8	5.8	—	—	—	—	—	—	—	6.5
V-8 engine, one side	5.4	5.4	5.4	5.4	5.4	5.4	5.2	5.2	5.5	5.7
V-8 engine, both sides	6.7	6.7	6.7	6.7	6.7	6.7	6.7	6.7	7.0	7.4
Basic Job #2										
Install new head, including minor tune-up,										
L-6 engine	—	—	5.6	5.6	5.6	5.8	—	—	6.0	6.0
V-6 engine, left side	5.1	5.1	—	—	—	—	—	—	—	5.8
V-6 engine, right side	5.4	5.4	—	—	—	—	—	—	—	6.1
V-6 engine, both sides	7.4	7.4	—	—	—	—	—	—	—	7.8
V-8 engine, one side	6.4	6.4	6.4	6.4	6.4	6.4	6.2	6.2	6.5	6.7
V-8 engine, both sides	8.7	8.7	8.7	8.7	8.7	8.7	8.5	8.5	8.8	9.0
Additions to Basic Jobs:										
With power steering, left side, **ADD**:	.3	.3	.3	.3	.3	.3	.3	.3	.3	.3
With air conditioning, **ADD**:	.4	.4	.4	.4	.4	.4	.4	.4	.4	.4
With AIR pump, **ADD**:	.3	.3	.3	.3	.3	.3	.3	.3	.3	.3

Approximate parts cost:
Head gasket, ea. .... $ 4.00	Valve grind gasket set, L-6 engine .... $ 9.00
Cylinder head, ea. 90.00	V-6 or V-8 engine 20.00
Minor tune-up parts 22.00-30.00	

44 BUICK

VALVE MECHANISM, SERVICE

Includes:
  Adjustment and Tune-up: Adjust valve lash and perform minor tune-up.
  Basic Job: Clean and reface valves, scrape carbon, grind valve seats, replace valve seals, adjust valves, and perform major tune-up.
  Additions to Basic Job: Associated work required during basic job and allowances for special equipment installed.

MODEL	1966	1967	1968	1969	1970	1971	1972	1973	1974	1975
Adjustment & tune-up,										
L-6 engine	—	—	2.8	2.8	3.0	3.0	—	—	3.0	3.0
Basic Job:										
Service valve mechanism,										
L-6 engine	—	—	10.4	10.8	10.8	11.1	—	—	10.9	11.1
V-6 engine	16.9	15.1	—	—	—	—	—	—	—	14.4
V-8 engine	14.4	15.6	15.6	15.8	15.8	16.0	16.0	15.3	15.3	15.5
Additions to Basic Job:										
Ream valve guides oversize,										
L-6 or V-6 engine, **ADD:**	.7	.7	.7	.7	.7	.7	—	—	.7	.7
V-8 engine, **ADD:**	.9	.9	.9	.9	.9	.9	.9	.9	.9	.9
Replace rocker arm stud, ea., **ADD:**	.3	.3	.3	.3	.3	.3	.3	.3	.3	.3
Overhaul rocker arm mechanism,										
V-6 or V-8 engine, **ADD:**	1.9	1.9	1.9	1.9	1.9	1.9	1.9	1.9	1.9	1.9
Replace hydraulic valve lifters, **ADD:**	1.0	1.0	1.0	1.0	1.0	1.0	1.0	1.0	1.0	1.0
With air conditioning, **ADD:**	.6	.6	.6	.6	.6	.6	.6	.6	.6	.6
With AIR pump, **ADD:**	.7	.7	.7	.7	.7	.7	.7	.7	.7	.7

Approximate parts cost:
Major tune-up parts ... $35.00
Valve grind gasket set, L-6 engine ... 9.00
  V-6 or V-8 engine ... 20.00
Hydraulic valve lifters, each ... $4.00
Valve spring, each ... 2.00

EXHAUST SYSTEM, TEST AND SERVICE

Includes:
  Basic Job: Test exhaust system for leaks and/or exhaust odors. Use HC/CO exhaust analyzer to trace carbon monoxide leaks.
  Related Jobs: Replace defective parts. Each job includes basic job tests and installation of new hangers as required.

MODEL	1966	1967	1968	1969	1970	1971	1972	1973	1974	1975
Basic Job:										
Complete test of exhaust system	.4	.4	.4	.4	.4	.4	.4	.4	.4	.4
Related Jobs:										
Replace muffler,										
Front, single or dual, one	1.3	1.3	1.3	1.3	1.3	1.3	1.3	1.3	1.3	1.3
Rear, single or dual, one	1.2	1.2	1.2	1.2	1.2	1.2	1.2	1.2	1.2	1.2
One side, single or dual, one	1.8	1.8	1.8	1.8	1.8	1.8	1.8	1.8	1.8	1.8
One each side, dual, two	1.9	1.9	1.9	1.9	1.9	1.9	1.9	1.9	1.9	1.9
Replace tail pipe,										
Single or dual, one	1.1	1.1	1.1	1.1	1.1	1.1	1.1	1.1	1.1	1.1
Dual, two	1.4	1.4	1.4	1.4	1.4	1.4	1.4	1.4	1.4	1.4
Replace exhaust pipe flange gasket, ea.	1.0	1.0	1.0	1.0	1.0	1.0	1.0	1.0	1.0	1.0
Replace exhaust manifold gasket,										
L-6 engine	—	—	1.4	1.4	1.4	1.4	—	—	1.6	1.6
Free-up or O/H heat-control valve,										
Single exhaust	—	—	1.2	1.2	1.2	1.2	—	—	1.2	1.2
Dual exhaust	.7	.7	.7	.7	.7	.7	.7	.7	.7	.7

(THIS SCHEDULE CONTINUED ON NEXT PAGE.)

BUICK 45

EXHAUST SYSTEM, TEST AND SERVICE Continued

MODEL	1966	1967	1968	1969	1970	1971	1972	1973	1974	1975
Replace exhaust pipe,										
Single exhaust, front, L-6 engine	—	—	1.2	1.2	1.2	1.2	—	—	1.2	1.2
Single exhaust, front, V-6 or V-8	1.4	1.4	1.4	1.4	1.4	1.4	1.4	1.4	1.4	1.4
Dual exhaust, front	1.0	1.0	1.0	1.0	1.0	1.0	1.0	1.0	1.0	1.0
Center, includes muffler	.9	.9	.9	.9	.9	.9	.9	.9	.9	.9
Rear, each side	.8	.8	.8	.8	.8	.8	.8	.8	.8	.8
Replace catalytic converter, ea.	—	—	—	—	—	—	—	—	—	1.0
Replace catalytic converter catalyst	—	—	—	—	—	—	—	—	—	1.5
Replace bottom cover, ADD:	—	—	—	—	—	—	—	—	—	.5

Approximate parts cost:

Catalytic converter	$175.00	Catalytic converter pellets	$70.00
Muffler	28.00	Exhaust pipe, each	15.00
Tail pipe, each	12.00	Exhaust manifold gasket	3.00

COOLING SYSTEM, TEST AND SERVICE

Includes:
  Basic Job: Drain and back-flush system, check for leaks and tighten all hose connections, pressure-test radiator cap and system.
  Related Jobs: Replace defective part. Work performed independently of basic job.
  Additions to Related Jobs: Allowances for special equipment installed.

MODEL	1966	1967	1968	1969	1970	1971	1972	1973	1974	1975
Basic Job:										
Drain, flush, fill, and press.-test system	.9	.9	.9	.9	.9	.9	.9	.9	.9	.9
Related Jobs:										
Replace upper hose	.4	.4	.4	.4	.4	.4	.4	.4	.4	.4
Replace lower hose	.5	.5	.5	.5	.5	.5	.5	.5	.5	.5
Replace both hoses	.7	.7	.7	.7	.7	.7	.7	.7	.7	.7
Replace thermostat & press.-test system,										
L-6 engine	—	—	.5	.5	.5	.5	—	—	.5	.5
V-6 or V-8 engine	.7	.7	.7	.7	.7	.7	.7	.7	.7	.7
Replace water pump drive belt & adjust	.4	.4	.4	.4	.4	.4	.4	.4	.4	.4
With air conditioning, ADD:	.1	.1	.1	.1	.1	.1	.1	.1	.1	.1
Replace water pump,										
L-6 engine	—	—	1.0	1.0	1.0	1.0	—	—	1.0	1.0
With air conditioning, ADD:	—	—	.1	.1	.1	.1	—	—	.1	.1
V-6 or V-8 engine	1.5	1.5	1.5	1.5	1.5	1.5	1.5	1.5	1.5	1.5
With air conditioning, ADD:	.3	.3	.3	.3	.3	.3	.3	.3	.3	.3
With power steering, ADD:	.2	.2	.2	.2	.2	.2	.2	.2	.2	.2
With AIR, ADD:	.2	.2	.2	.2	.2	.2	.2	.2	.2	.2
Replace radiator, incl. press.-test system,										
L-6 engine	.7	.7	.7	.7	.7	.7	.7	.7	.7	.7
V-6 or V-8 engine	1.0	1.0	1.0	1.0	1.0	1.0	1.0	1.0	1.0	1.0
With automatic transmission, ADD:	.2	.2	.2	.2	.2	.2	.2	.2	.2	.2
Replace water temp. gauge, engine	.5	.5	.5	.5	.5	.5	.5	.5	.5	.5
With air conditioning, ADD:	.1	.1	.1	.1	.1	.1	.1	.1	.1	.1
Replace water temp. gauge, dash,										
Riviera	1.5	1.5	1.5	1.5	1.5	1.1	1.1	.5	.5	.5
LeSabre, Centurion, Electra,	—	—	—	—	—	1.1	1.1	.5	.5	.5
All others	—	—	—	—	—	.5	.5	.5	.5	.5
Replace water jacket expansion plug	.5	.5	.5	.5	.5	.5	.5	.5	.5	.5
Add time req'd to gain access to plug.										

46 BUICK

COOLING SYSTEM, TEST AND SERVICE Continued

MODEL	1966	1967	1968	1969	1970	1971	1972	1973	1974	1975

Approximate parts cost:

Radiator, new $125.00-175.00	Drive belt, ea. 3.00
Upper or lower hose, ea. 5.00	Temperature gauge, engine 4.00
Thermostat 4.00	Temperature gauge, dash 9.50
Water pump 35.00	Expansion plug, ea. 1.50

CLUTCH MECHANISM, SERVICE

Includes:
Adjustment: Adjust clutch pedal play.
Basic Job: Replace thrust bearing, pressure plate, and disc. Adjust clutch pedal play.
Additions to Basic Job: Associated work that is required during basic job.

MODEL	1966	1967	1968	1969	1970	1971	1972	1973	1974	1975
Adjustment:										
Adjust clutch pedal play	.3	.3	.3	.3	.3	.3	.3	.3	.3	.3
Basic Job:										
Repl. thrust bearing, pressure plate & disc,										
3-speed transmission	2.1	2.1	2.1	2.1	2.1	2.1	2.2	2.2	2.2	2.2
4-speed transmission	2.6	2.6	2.6	2.6	3.0	3.0	3.0	2.8	2.8	2.8
Additions to Basic Job:										
Remove, reface, and instl. flywheel, **ADD:**	1.8	1.8	1.8	1.8	1.8	1.8	1.8	1.8	1.8	1.8
Replace flywheel ring gear, **ADD:**	1.0	1.0	1.0	1.0	1.0	1.0	1.0	1.0	1.0	1.0
Resurface clutch pressure plate, **ADD:**	.8	.8	.8	.8	.8	.8	.8	.8	.8	.8
Replace clutch pilot bearing, **ADD:**	.2	.2	.2	.2	.2	.2	.2	.2	.2	.2

Approximate parts cost:

Pressure plate $25.00-60.00	Pilot bearing .... $ 1.00
Clutch disc 20.00-35.00	Flywheel w/ring gear 36.00-56.00
Thrust bearing 5.00-17.00	

SHIFT LINKAGE, SERVICE

Includes:
Adjust: Adjust manual transmission shift linkage.
Basic Job: Replace one control rod and/or grommet and adjust linkage.
Additions to Basic Job: Associated work that is required during basic job.

MODEL	1966	1967	1968	1969	1970	1971	1972	1973	1974	1975
Adjust shift linkage:										
3-speed transmission	.5	.5	.5	.5	.5	.5	.5	.5	.5	.5
4-speed transmission	.6	.6	.6	.6	.6	.6	.6	.6	.6	.6
Basic Job:										
Repl. one rod and/or grommet & adjust.										
3-speed transmission	.8	.8	.8	.8	.8	.8	.8	.8	.8	.8
4-speed transmission	.9	.9	.9	.9	.9	.9	.9	.9	.9	.9
Additions to Basic Job:										
Replace additional rod, **ADD:**	.3	.3	.3	.3	.3	.3	.3	.3	.3	.3
Repl. shift lever oil seals, both, **ADD:**	.5	.5	.5	.5	.5	.5	.5	.5	.5	.5

Approximate parts cost:

Shift rod, each $2.50	Shift lever oil seals $1.50
Rear oil seal 2.50	

BUICK 47

STANDARD TRANSMISSION, OVERHAUL

Includes:
Basic Job: R&R transmission, disassemble, replace worn parts, and adjust linkage.
Additions to Basic Job: Associated work that is required during basic job.

MODEL	1966	1967	1968	1969	1970	1971	1972	1973	1974	1975
Basic Job:										
R&R, overhaul transmission, and adjust linkage,										
3-speed transmission	5.4	5.4	5.4	5.4	5.4	5.4	5.4	5.4	5.4	5.4
4-speed transmission	6.9	6.9	6.9	6.9	6.9	6.9	6.9	6.9	6.9	6.9
Additions to Basic Job:										
Recondition transmission cover,										
3-speed trans., **ADD:**	.3	.3	.3	.3	.3	.3	.3	.3	.3	.3
4-speed trans., **ADD:**	.4	.4	.4	.4	.4	.4	.4	.4	.4	.4
Resurface clutch pressure plate, **ADD:**	.8	.8	.8	.8	.8	.8	.8	.8	.8	.8
R&R and resurface flywheel, **ADD:**	1.8	1.8	1.8	1.8	1.8	1.8	1.8	1.8	1.8	1.8
Replace flywheel ring gear, **ADD:**	1.0	1.0	1.0	1.0	1.0	1.0	1.0	1.0	1.0	1.0
Replace flywheel pilot bushing or bearing, **ADD:**	.2	.2	.2	.2	.2	.2	.2	.2	.2	.2
Replace clutch release or throwout bearing, **ADD:**	.7	.7	.7	.7	.7	.7	.7	.7	.7	.7

Approximate parts cost:
Speedometer gear .... $ 2.00
Gasket set 8.00
Clutch pressure plate 30.00-60.00
Clutch pilot bearing .... $ 1.00
Flywheel pilot bushing or bearing 1.50
Clutch release bearing 12.00
Phone supplier for price quote on additional transmission parts required.

AUTOMATIC TRANSMISSION, SHIFT AND LINKAGE CONTROLS, REPLACE AND ADJUST

Includes:
Replace defective part and make necessary adjustments.

MODEL	1966	1967	1968	1969	1970	1971	1972	1973	1974	1975
Replace control rod, carb. or trans. & adj:	.9	.9	.9	.9	.9	.9	.9	.9	.9	.9
Replace each additional rod, **ADD:**	.4	.4	.4	.4	.4	.4	.4	.4	.4	.4
Replace carb./throttle link, **ADD:**	.3	.3	.3	.3	.3	.3	.3	.3	.3	.3
Replace throttle control cable, **ADD:**	.5	.5	.5	.5	.5	.5	.5	.5	.5	.5
Replace front contr. rod, column shift, **ADD:**	.3	.3	.3	.3	.3	.3	.3	.3	.3	.3
Replace rear contr. rod or swivel, **ADD:**	.4	.4	.4	.4	.4	.4	.4	.4	.4	.4
Replace control torque shaft or bushings, **ADD:**	.6	.6	.6	.6	.6	.6	.6	.6	.6	.6
Repl. shift control key lock assy.	.7	.7	.7	.7	.7	.7	.7	.7	.7	.7
Repl. vac. modulator hose & adj. linkage	.6	.6	.6	.6	.6	.6	.6	.6	.6	.6
Repl. and adjust floor shift control assy.	.8	.8	.8	.8	.8	.8	.8	.8	.8	.8
With console equipped, **ADD:**	.5	.5	.5	.5	.5	.5	.5	.5	.5	.5

Approximate parts cost:
Linkage rod, ea. $1.50
Control cable 8.00
Modulator hose, per ft. .... $ 0.25
Floor shift control assy. 40.00

AUTOMATIC TRANSMISSION, PERFORMANCE CHECK

Includes:
Basic Job: Conduct transmission performance check. Clean transmission case and operate unit to check case, oil cooler, and oil cooler lines for external leaks. Remove oil pan, clean pan, screen, or filter. Torque valve body mounting bolts. Adjust band/s where applicable. Adjust throttle and shift linkage. Perform pressure checks of main line, throttle, and accumulator. Road test.
Related Jobs: Work which does not include R&R transmission and may be done as separate job.

48 BUICK

AUTOMATIC TRANSMISSION, PERFORMANCE CHECK Continued

MODEL	1966	1967	1968	1969	1970	1971	1972	1973	1974	1975
Basic Job:										
Complete trans. performance check	2.1	2.1	2.1	2.1	2.1	2.1	2.1	2.1	2.1	2.1
Related Jobs:										
Drain & fill trans., clean filter	.8	.8	.8	.8	.8	.8	.8	.8	.8	.8
Check for oil leaks	.7	.7	.7	.7	.7	.7	.7	.7	.7	.7
Repl. oil pan gasket, incl. clean filter	.9	.9	.9	.9	.9	.9	.9	.9	.9	.9
Repl. rear oil seal & O-ring	1.0	1.0	.7	.5	.5	.5	.5	.5	.5	.5
Repl. neutral safety switch	.5	.5	.5	.5	.5	.5	.5	.5	.5	.5
Overhaul governor, includes complete trans. performance check,										
250/ST300/350 THM	3.1	3.1	3.1	3.1	3.1	3.1	3.1	3.1	2.9	2.9
375/400 THM	2.9	2.9	2.9	2.9	2.9	2.9	2.9	2.9	2.8	2.8
Overhaul valve body assembly	2.0	2.0	2.0	2.0	2.0	2.0	2.0	2.0	2.0	2.0
Adjust throttle and shift linkage	1.0	1.0	1.0	1.0	1.0	1.0	1.0	1.0	1.0	1.0
Adjust band/s where applicable	1.3	1.3	1.3	1.3	1.3	1.3	1.3	1.3	1.3	1.3

Approximate parts cost:

Transmission fluid, per qt.	$1.20
Oil pan gasket	1.00
Rear oil seal	4.50
Neutral safety switch	$ 3.50
Governor body repair kit	18.00
Valve body assy., new	80.00

AUTOMATIC TRANSMISSION, MAJOR SERVICE

Includes:

Basic Jobs:
1. **Overhaul transmission.** Disassemble, clean, inspect and replace all worn parts as needed. Replace all oil seals. Adjust throttle and shift linkage as required. Flush converter and cooler lines. Perform pressure checks of main line, throttle, and accumulator. Road test.
2. **Replace torque converter.** R&R transmission. Flush oil cooler and lines. Replace transmission oil and oil filter. Perform pressure checks of main line, throttle, and accumulator. Adjust throttle and shift linkage as required.
3. **Reseal transmission.** R&R transmission. Replace all seals and gaskets. Replace transmission oil and oil filter. Check oil cooler for leaks. Perform pressure checks of main line, throttle, and accumulator. Adjust throttle and shift linkage as required. Road test.

Additions to Basic Jobs: Associated work that is performed while the transmission is out during one of basic jobs.

MODEL	1966	1967	1968	1969	1970	1971	1972	1973	1974	1975
Basic Job #1										
Overhaul transmission,										
250/ST300/350 THM	8.0	8.0	8.0	8.0	8.0	8.0	8.0	8.7	8.7	8.7
375/400 THM	7.2	7.2	7.2	7.2	7.2	7.2	7.2	7.9	8.6	8.6
Basic Job #2										
Replace torque converter,										
250/ST300/350 THM	4.8	4.8	4.8	4.8	4.8	4.8	4.8	4.8	4.6	4.6
375/400 THM	4.4	4.4	4.4	4.4	4.4	4.4	4.4	4.6	4.6	4.6
Replace oil pump front seal, **ADD:**	.2	.2	.2	.2	.2	.2	.2	.2	.2	.2
Basic Job #3										
Reseal transmission,										
250/ST300/350 THM	6.3	6.3	6.3	6.3	6.3	6.3	6.3	6.8	6.8	6.8
375/400 THM	5.8	5.8	5.8	5.8	5.8	5.8	5.8	6.3	6.3	6.3
Additions to Basic Jobs:										
Replace oil cooler pipes, both, **ADD:**	.9	.9	.9	.9	.9	.9	.9	.9	.9	.9
Replace oil filler pipe and/or seal, **ADD:**	.5	.5	.5	.5	.5	.5	.5	.5	.5	.5
Replace torque converter ring gear, **ADD:**	.5	.5	.5	.5	.5	.5	.5	.5	.5	.5

(THIS SCHEDULE CONTINUED ON NEXT PAGE.)

BUICK 49

AUTOMATIC TRANSMISSION, MAJOR SERVICE Continued

Approximate parts cost:
Transmission seal and gasket kit	$20.00	Oil filler pipe	$ 4.00
Transmission partial overhaul kit	56.00	Oil filler pipe seal	0.25
Oil cooler pipe, each	9.00	Oil pan	8.00
Torque converter	75.00	Oil pan gasket	1.00
Torque converter ring gear	8.00	Governor kit	19.00

DRIVESHAFT, SERVICE

Includes:
Basic Job: R&R driveshaft and overhaul or replace front and rear U-joints. Measure and adjust U-joint and driveshaft angles. Balance driveshaft.

MODEL	1966	1967	1968	1969	1970	1971	1972	1973	1974	1975
Basic Job:										
R&R driveshaft & overhaul both U-joints,										
Cross & roller joints	1.5	1.5	1.5	1.5	1.5	1.5	1.5	1.5	1.5	1.5
Constant velocity joint	1.8	1.8	1.8	1.8	1.8	1.6	1.6	1.6	1.6	1.6
R&R driveshaft with joints	1.1	1.1	1.1	1.1	1.1	1.1	1.1	1.1	1.1	1.1

Approximate parts cost:
U-joint package, cross & roller	$11.00	Driveshaft with joints	$120.00
Constant velocity joint	60.00	Constant velocity joint kit	12.00

REAR AXLE, SERVICE

Includes:
Basic Jobs: 1. R&R driveshaft, R&R axle shafts, overhaul differential assembly, check and adjust pinion nose angle. Measure and adjust U-joint and driveshaft angles. Balance driveshaft.
             2. R&R driveshaft and replace pinion bearing oil seal. Check pinion bearing preload. Measure and adjust driveshaft angles. Balance driveshaft.

Related Jobs: R&R axle shaft (one side) and/or bearing and seals. Replace axle shaft wheel mounting stud.

MODEL	1966	1967	1968	1969	1970	1971	1972	1973	1974	1975
Basic Job #1										
Overhaul differential assembly,										
Removable-type	5.5	5.5	5.5	5.5	5.5	5.5	5.5	5.5	5.5	5.5
Integral-type	5.0	5.0	5.0	5.0	5.0	5.0	5.0	5.0	5.0	5.0
With Positive Traction, **ADD:**	.6	.6	.6	.6	.6	.6	.6	.6	.6	.6
Basic Job #2										
Replace drive pinion bearing oil seal	1.2	1.2	1.2	1.7	1.7	1.7	1.7	1.7	1.7	1.7
Related Jobs:										
R&R axle shaft (one side), and/or bearing and seals	1.3	1.3	1.3	1.3	1.3	1.3	1.3	1.3	1.3	1.3
Replace axle shaft wheel mounting stud	.8	.8	.8	.8	.8	.8	.8	.8	.8	.8

Approximate parts cost:
Axle shaft	$45.00	Pinion bearing oil seal	$ 3.00
Inner or outer seal	2.00	Cover gasket	1.00
Positive Traction repair kit	25.00	Ring & pinion gear set	100.00-120.00

50 BUICK

REAR SUSPENSION, SERVICE

Includes:
Service for the rear suspension system listed as individual jobs. Add times if more than one job is performed.

MODEL	1966	1967	1968	1969	1970	1971	1972	1973	1974	1975
Replace rear leaf spring & shim to align pinion angle,										
Station Wagon	1.5	1.5	1.5	1.5	1.5	1.5	1.5	1.5	1.5	1.5
Apollo	—	—	—	—	—	—	—	1.7	1.7	1.7
Replace rear coil spring	.8	.8	.8	.8	.8	.8	.8	.8	.8	.8
Replace control arm, incl. pinion angle adjustment,										
Upper arm, one	1.1	1.1	1.1	1.1	1.1	1.1	1.1	1.1	1.1	1.1
Lower arm, one	1.5	1.5	1.5	1.5	1.5	1.5	1.1	1.1	1.1	1.1
Replace shackle and bushings; eye bolt & bushings	.7	.7	.7	.7	.7	.7	.7	.7	.7	.7
Replace shock absorber, both sides	.8	.8	.8	.8	.8	.8	.8	.8	.8	.8
Replace tie rod & stabilizer shaft (one)	.9	.9	.9	.9	.9	.9	.9	.9	.9	.9
Service Automatic Level Control										
Replace compressor assembly	.4	.4	.4	.4	.4	.4	.4	.4	.4	.4
Overhaul compressor assembly, **ADD:**	.7	.7	.7	.7	.7	.7	.7	.7	.7	.7
Replace level control regulator	.3	.3	.3	.3	.3	.3	.3	.3	.3	.3
Replace level & height control valve	.4	.4	.4	.4	.4	.4	.4	.4	.4	.4

Approximate parts cost:

Shock absorber	$14.00
Coil spring	40.00
Leaf spring	65.00
Tie rod & stabilizer shaft	23.00
Auto. level control compressor assy.	70.00
Shackle package	$4.00-7.00
Shackle bushing package	1.00
Auto. level control regulator	24.00
Level & height control valve	68.00

FRONT END, TEST, SERVICE, AND ADJUST

Includes:
Basic Job: Check and adjust car height, caster, camber, steering axis inclination, turning radius, toe-in, pack and adjust front wheel bearings, replace seals.
Related Jobs: Perform individual adjustments. Replace or overhaul defective components and make necessary adjustments.

MODEL	1966	1967	1968	1969	1970	1971	1972	1973	1974	1975
Basic Job:										
Complete test and adjustments,										
With drum brakes	2.5	2.5	2.5	2.5	2.5	2.5	2.5	2.5	2.5	2.5
With disc brakes	—	3.0	3.0	3.0	3.0	3.0	3.0	3.0	3.0	3.0
Related Jobs:										
Adjust toe-in only	.4	.4	.4	.4	.4	.4	.4	.4	.4	.4
Repack wheel brgs. only, incl. new seals,										
Drum brakes, both sides	.9	.9	.9	.9	.9	.9	.9	.9	.9	.9
Disc brakes, both sides	—	1.3	1.3	1.3	1.3	1.3	1.3	1.3	1.3	1.3
Replace wheel brgs. only each side,										
Drum brakes, inner or outer brg.	.5	.5	.5	.5	.5	.5	.5	.5	.5	.5
Disc brakes, inner or outer brg.	—	.8	.8	.8	.8	.9	.9	.9	.9	.9
Balance four wheels on car	1.5	1.5	1.5	1.5	1.5	1.5	1.5	1.5	1.5	1.5
Overhaul front suspension, incl. disassemble, replace nec. parts, lube., & complete front end adjustments,										
With drum brakes	7.9	7.9	7.9	7.9	7.9	7.9	7.9	7.9	7.9	7.9
With disc brakes, Electra, Riviera	—	8.8	8.8	8.8	8.8	8.8	8.8	8.8	8.8	8.8
With disc brakes, all others	—	8.5	8.5	8.5	8.5	8.5	8.5	8.5	8.5	8.5

(THIS SCHEDULE CONTINUED ON NEXT PAGE.)

BUICK 51

FRONT END, TEST, SERVICE, AND ADJUST Continued

MODEL	1966	1967	1968	1969	1970	1971	1972	1973	1974	1975
Replace coil spring, one side, incl. complete front end adjustments,										
With drum brakes	3.9	3.9	3.9	3.9	3.9	3.6	3.6	3.6	3.6	3.6
With disc brakes	—	4.4	4.4	4.4	4.4	4.1	4.1	4.1	4.1	4.1
Replace upper and lower ball joints, both sides, incl. complete front end adjustment,										
With drum brakes	3.9	3.9	3.9	3.9	3.9	3.9	3.7	3.7	3.7	3.7
With disc brakes	—	4.4	4.4	4.4	4.4	4.4	4.2	4.2	4.2	4.2
Replace steering knuckle, one side, incl. complete front end adjustment,										
With drum brakes	3.1	3.1	3.1	3.1	3.1	3.1	3.1	3.1	3.1	3.1
With disc brakes	—	3.6	3.6	3.6	3.6	3.6	3.6	3.6	3.6	3.6
Replace shock absorber, both sides	.9	.9	.9	.9	.9	.9	.9	.9	.9	.9
Repl. control arm rubber bumpers, ea. side	.3	.3	.3	.3	.3	.3	.3	.3	.3	.3
Replace strut rod or bushings, ea. side	.4	.4	.4	.4	.4	.4	.4	.4	.4	.4
Replace stabilizer shaft & bushings	1.1	1.1	1.1	1.1	1.1	1.1	1.1	1.1	1.1	1.1
Replace both stabilizer links or grommets	.7	.7	.7	.7	.7	.7	.7	.7	.7	.7

Approximate parts cost:
Coil spring, ea.	$16.00	Control arm rubber bumpers, ea.	$ 1.50
Upper ball joint	12.00	Strut rod & bushing	6.00
Lower ball joint	14.00	Stabilizer shaft & bushings	15.00
Steering knuckle	40.00	Stabilizer links or grommets	2.00
Shock absorber, ea.	15.00	Wheel bearing seals	2.00
Wheel bearing, outer	5.00	Wheel bearing, inner	6.00

STEERING LINKAGE, SERVICE AND ADJUST

Includes:
Basic Job: Adjust toe-in.
Related Jobs: Replace defective parts and adjust toe-in.

MODEL	1966	1967	1968	1969	1970	1971	1972	1973	1974	1975
Basic Job:										
Adjust toe-in	.4	.4	.4	.4	.4	.4	.4	.4	.4	.4
Related Jobs:										
Replace tie-rods or tie-rod ends, (4)	1.4	1.4	1.4	1.4	1.4	1.4	1.4	1.4	1.4	1.4
Repl. Pitman arm, includes adjust toe-in	.8	.8	.8	.8	.8	.8	.8	.8	.8	.8
Repl. steering idler arm or bushing	.7	.7	.7	.7	.7	.7	.7	.7	.7	.7

Approximate parts cost:
Tie-rod end pkg.	$10.00-15.00	Idler arm	$17.00
Pitman arm	15.00	Tie rod	15.00

STANDARD STEERING GEAR, ADJUST AND SERVICE

Includes:
Basic Job: Adjust steering gear, worm and sector mesh, adjust wheel bearings and toe-in.
Related Job: R&R steering gear assembly and complete adjustments.
Additions to Related Job: Overhaul steering gear.

MODEL	1966	1967	1968	1969	1970	1971	1972	1973	1974	1975
Basic Job:										
Complete steering gear, wheel bearings, & toe-in adjustments,										
With drum brakes	1.4	1.4	1.4	1.4	1.4	1.4	1.4	1.4	1.4	1.4
With disc brakes	—	1.8	1.8	1.8	1.8	1.8	1.8	1.8	1.8	1.8

52 BUICK

STANDARD STEERING GEAR, ADJUST AND SERVICE Continued

MODEL	1966	1967	1968	1969	1970	1971	1972	1973	1974	1975
Related Job:										
R&R steering gear assembly & complete adjustments	1.9	1.9	1.9	1.9	1.9	1.9	1.9	1.9	1.9	1.9
Additions to Related Job:										
Overhaul steering gear assembly, **ADD:**	1.0	1.0	1.0	1.0	1.0	1.0	1.0	1.0	1.0	1.0

Approximate parts cost:
Pitman shaft bushing ....$2.00 Worm thrust bearing $1.00
Pitman shaft seal ....1.50 Shaft dust seal 1.00

POWER STEERING UNIT, TEST AND SERVICE

Includes:
Basic Job: Adjust drive belt tension; hook up gauges to check pressure on left and right turns. Adjust steering gear box overcenter torque and control valve to balance left and right steering effort.
Additions to Basic Job: Service power steering unit.
Related Jobs: R&R power steering unit, pump, or other associated parts.
Additions to Related Jobs: Overhaul steering unit or pump, including replacement of all seals and worn parts.

MODEL	1966	1967	1968	1969	1970	1971	1972	1973	1974	1975
Basic Job:										
Complete test and adjustment of power steering unit	1.0	1.0	1.0	1.0	1.0	1.0	1.0	1.0	1.0	1.0
Additions to basic Job:										
Replace power steering pump drive belt, **ADD:**	.3	.3	.3	.3	.3	.3	.3	.3	.3	.3
With air conditioning, **ADD:**	.2	.2	.2	.2	.2	.2	.2	.2	.2	.2
Check & replenish reservoir fluid, **ADD:**	.2	.2	.2	.2	.2	.2	.2	.2	.2	.2
Related Jobs:										
Replace pressure hoses, either set, includes adjust drive belt,										
L-6 engine	—	—	.3	.3	.3	.3	—	—	.3	.3
V-6 or V-8 engine	.6	.6	.6	.6	.6	.6	.6	.6	.6	.6
With air conditioning, **ADD:**	.1	.1	.1	.1	.1	.1	.1	.1	.1	.1
Replace pump reservoir or O-ring seals,										
L-6 engine	—	—	1.0	1.0	1.0	1.0	—	—	1.1	1.1
V-6 engine	1.4	1.4	—	—	—	—	—	—	—	1.5
V-8 engine	1.1	1.1	1.1	1.1	1.1	1.1	1.2	1.2	1.2	1.2
With air conditioning, **ADD:**	.1	.1	.1	.1	.1	.1	.1	.1	.2	.2
Replace pump, includes pressure-test original pump and transfer pulley,										
L-6 engine	—	—	.7	.7	.7	.7	—	—	.7	.7
V-6 engine	1.1	1.1	—	—	—	—	—	—	—	1.1
V-8 engine	.8	.8	.8	.8	.8	.8	.8	.8	.8	.8
With air conditioning, **ADD:**	.1	.1	.1	.1	.1	.1	.1	.1	.2	.2
Replace control valve, includes adjust	1.1	1.1	1.1	1.1	1.1	1.1	1.1	1.1	1.1	1.1
Overhaul control valve, **ADD:**	.6	.6	.6	.6	.6	.6	.6	.6	.6	.6
R&R power steering unit, includes test original unit and complete adjustment,										
L-6 engine	—	—	1.9	1.9	1.9	1.9	—	—	1.9	1.9
V-6 engine	2.6	2.6	—	—	—	—	—	—	—	2.6
V-8 engine	2.3	2.3	2.3	2.3	2.3	2.3	2.3	2.3	2.3	2.3
Additions to Related Jobs:										
Overhaul power steering unit, **ADD:**	2.2	2.2	2.2	2.2	2.4	2.4	2.4	2.4	3.0	3.0
O/H pump, incl. new kit & seals, **ADD:**	.8	.8	.8	.8	.8	.8	.8	.6	.6	.6

(THIS SCHEDULE CONTINUED ON NEXT PAGE.)

BUICK 53

POWER STEERING UNIT, TEST AND SERVICE Continued

Approximate parts cost:

Drive belt .... $ 4.00	Power cylinder $33.00
Pressure hose 12.00	Power steering gear & seal kit 18.00
Return hose 4.00	Hydraulic pump 50.00
Control valve 8.00	Hydraulic reservoir 24.00
Control valve seal kit 2.00	Hydraulic pump seals 4.00
Power steering unit, valve assembly 85.00	Hydraulic pump repair kit 14.00

HYDRAULIC BRAKE SYSTEM, OVERHAUL

Includes:

Basic Job: Overhaul including hone or replace master cylinder, all wheel cylinders or calipers; bleed hydraulic system; and adjust brakes.
Related Jobs: Performed at time other than during basic job. Overhaul or replace master cylinder only; overhaul wheel cylinders or calipers.
Addition to Related Jobs: Allowance for power brakes.

MODEL	1966	1967	1968	1969	1970	1971	1972	1973	1974	1975
Basic Job:										
Complete job, including master & wheel cylinders,										
Drum brakes	4.7	4.7	4.7	4.7	4.7	4.7	4.7	4.6	4.6	4.6
Disc front, drum rear	—	4.5	4.5	3.9	3.9	3.9	3.9	3.9	3.9	3.9
Related Jobs: (Not during basic job)										
Overhaul master cylinder, including hone,										
Drum or disc brakes	1.3	1.3	1.5	1.5	1.5	1.5	1.8	1.8	1.8	1.8
Replace master cylinder	.5	.5	.8	.8	.8	.8	1.1	1.1	1.1	1.1
O/H wheel cylinders, drum brakes (4)	4.1	4.1	4.1	4.1	4.1	4.1	4.2	4.2	4.2	4.2
O/H front calipers, incl. turn rotors	—	4.0	4.0	4.0	4.0	4.0	4.0	4.0	4.0	4.0
Bleed hydraulic system, 4 wheels	.6	.6	.6	.6	.6	.6	.6	.6	.6	.6
Replace combination valve, includes bleed system	—	—	—	—	—	.6	.6	.6	.6	.6
Addition to Related Jobs:										
With power brakes, **ADD:**	.2	.2	.2	.2	.2	.2	.2	.2	.2	.2

Approximate parts cost:

Master cylinder repair kit $18.00	Master cylinder $27.00-40.00
Wheel cylinder repair kit, ea. 2.00	Wheel cylinder seal, boot & bushing pkg. 6.00
Caliper repair kit 4.00	Combination valve 26.00

POWER BRAKE UNIT, SERVICE

Includes:

Basic Job: R&R with new unit, test, and adjust brakes.
Additions to Basic Job: Replace vacuum hose or vacuum check valve. Allowance for air conditioning.

MODEL	1966	1967	1968	1969	1970	1971	1972	1973	1974	1975
Basic Job:										
R&R power unit, test, & adj. brakes	1.6	1.6	1.6	1.6	1.5	1.5	1.5	1.5	1.5	1.5
Additions to Basic Job:										
With air conditioning, **ADD:**	.3	.3	.3	.3	.3	.3	.3	.3	.3	.3
Install new hose, **ADD:**	.2	.2	.2	.2	.2	.2	.2	.2	.2	.2
Install new vacuum check valve, **ADD:**	.2	.2	.2	.2	.2	.2	.2	.2	.2	.2

Approximate parts cost:

Power brake unit $50.00-70.00	Vacuum check valve $1.75
Vacuum hose, per ft. 0.90	

54 BUICK

BRAKES, SERVICE

Includes:
  Basic Job: Install new linings or pads, turn brake drums or rotors, lubricate and adjust front wheel bearings, replace rear oil seals, bleed hydraulic system, and adjust brakes.
  Additions to Basic Job: Overhaul four wheel cylinders, overhaul or replace front calipers.
  Related Jobs: Performed at time other than during basic job.

MODEL	1966	1967	1968	1969	1970	1971	1972	1973	1974	1975
Basic Job:										
Complete job incl. turn drums or rotors,										
Drum (4), all models	6.5	6.5	6.5	6.5	6.5	6.5	6.5	6.5	6.5	6.5
Disc front, drum rear, all models	—	6.9	6.9	6.9	6.9	6.9	6.9	6.9	6.9	6.9
Additions to Basic Job:										
O/H 4 wheel cylinders, incl. hone, **ADD:**	2.3	2.3	2.3	2.3	2.3	2.4	2.4	2.4	2.4	2.4
Overhaul front calipers (both), **ADD:**	—	3.5	3.5	2.9	2.9	2.9	2.9	2.9	2.9	2.9
Replace front calipers (both), **ADD:**	—	.4	.4	.4	.4	.4	.4	.4	.4	.4
Overhaul master cylinder, **ADD:**	.8	.8	.8	.8	.8	.8	.8	.8	.8	.8
Related Jobs: (Not during basic job)										
Bleed hydraulic system, 4 wheels	.6	.6	.6	.6	.6	.6	.6	.6	.6	.6
Adjust drum brakes, 4 wheels	.5	.5	.5	.5	.5	.5	.5	.5	.5	.5
Replace disc brake pads, front wheels	—	1.5	1.5	1.5	1.5	1.5	1.0	1.0	1.0	1.0
Replace drum brake shoes, 4 wheels	3.5	3.5	3.5	3.5	3.5	3.5	3.5	3.5	3.5	3.5
O/H front calipers, incl. turn rotors	—	4.6	4.6	4.0	4.0	4.0	4.0	4.0	4.0	4.0
Repl. fr. caliper, incl. turn rotor, ea.	—	3.0	3.0	2.4	2.4	2.4	2.4	2.4	2.4	2.4
Overhaul master cylinder	1.3	1.3	1.5	1.5	1.5	1.5	1.8	1.8	1.8	1.8

Approximate parts cost:

Wheel cylinder seal, boot & bushing pkg.	$ 6.00	Wheel cylinder repair kit, ea.	$ 2.00
Brake shoes and lining sets, front or rear	25.00	Caliper brake housing	50.00
Disc brake pads, set of 2	24.00	Oil seal, ea.	2.00
Master cylinder repair kit	18.00		

PARKING BRAKES, SERVICE AND ADJUST

Includes:
  Basic Jobs: Replace defective cable and adjust parking brakes.

MODEL	1966	1967	1968	1969	1970	1971	1972	1973	1974	1975
Basic Jobs:										
Adjust parking brakes,										
Skyhawk	—	—	—	—	—	—	—	—	—	.6
All others	.4	.4	.4	.4	.4	.4	.4	.4	.4	.4
Replace forward cable,										
Apollo	—	—	—	—	—	—	—	.5	.5	.5
All others	.9	.9	.9	.9	.9	.9	.9	.9	.9	.9
Replace rear cable, one side,										
Apollo	—	—	—	—	—	—	—	1.0	1.0	1.0
All others	.9	.9	.9	.9	.9	.9	.9	.9	.9	.9
Replace rear cable both sides,										
Apollo	—	—	—	—	—	—	—	1.5	1.5	1.5
All others	1.5	1.5	1.5	1.5	1.5	1.7	1.7	1.7	1.7	1.7
Replace center cable	.8	.8	.8	.8	.8	.5	.5	.5	.5	.5

Approximate parts cost:

Front cable	$5.00	Rear cable	8.00
Center cable	3.50		

BUICK 55

LIGHTING SYSTEM, ADJUST AND SERVICE

Includes:
Basic Job: 1. Adjust headlights to inspection requirements.
2. Replace defective parts in rear lighting system.
Additions to Basic Job: Replace associated parts affecting headlight adjustment.
Related Jobs: Replace associated parts not affecting headlight adjustment.

MODEL	1966	1967	1968	1969	1970	1971	1972	1973	1974	1975
Basic Job #1										
Adjust two lights	.4	.4	.4	.4	.4	.4	.4	.4	.4	.4
Adjust four lights	.6	.6	.6	.6	.6	.6	.6	.6	.6	.6
Basic Job #2										
Replace stoplight switch	.3	.3	.3	.3	.3	.3	.3	.3	.3	.3
Replace back-up light switch	.4	.4	.4	.4	.4	.4	.4	.4	.4	.4
Additions to Basic Job:										
Replace sealed beam unit, ea., **ADD:**	.3	.3	.3	.3	.3	.3	.3	.3	.3	.3
Related Jobs:										
Replace headlamp door electric motor	.7	.7	—	—	—	—	—	—	—	—
Replace headlamp door vacuum motor	—	—	.8	.8	—	—	—	—	—	—
Replace headlamp switch,										
Riviera	.8	.8	1.2	1.2	1.2	.5	.5	.5	.5	.5
Apollo, Skyhawk	—	—	—	—	—	—	—	.8	.8	.9
All others	.5	.5	.5	.5	.5	.5	.5	.5	.5	.5
With air conditioning, **ADD:**	.1	.1	.1	.1	.1	.1	.1	.1	.2	.2
Replace foot dimmer switch	.3	.3	.3	.3	.3	.3	.3	.3	.3	.3
Replace signal/hazard flasher	.2	.2	.2	.2	.2	.2	.2	.2	.2	.2
Replace signal/hazard switch,										
With standard column	1.2	1.2	1.2	1.0	1.0	1.0	1.0	1.0	1.0	1.0
With tilt or telescopic column	1.5	1.5	1.5	1.3	1.3	1.3	1.3	1.3	1.3	1.3

Approximate parts cost:

Sealed beam unit	$ 4.00	Headlamp vacuum actuator	$20.00
Signal/hazard flasher	2.00	Headlamp switch	7.00
Signal/hazard switch	15.00	Back-up light switch, col. shift	4.50
Electric motor	75.00	Floor shift, 1966-1968 w/s.t.	14.00

HEATING SYSTEM, TEST AND SERVICE

Includes:
Basic Job: Drain back-flush, and fill radiator, check radiator and heater hoses and connections, pressure-test radiator cap and system.
Related Jobs: Replace defective parts. Work performed individually and independently of basic job.

MODEL	1966	1967	1968	1969	1970	1971	1972	1973	1974	1975
Basic Job:										
Drain, flush, fill, check, & pressure-test	.9	.9	.9	.9	.9	.9	.9	.9	.9	.9
Related Jobs:										
Replace heater hose, one, inlet or outlet	.5	.5	.5	.5	.5	.5	.5	.5	.5	.5
Replace ea. additional hose, **ADD:**	.2	.2	.2	.2	.2	.2	.2	.2	.2	.2
With air conditioning, **ADD:**	.3	.3	.3	.3	.3	.3	.3	.3	.3	.3
Replace blower motor and/or impeller										
LeSabre, Centurion, Electra, Skylark	*2.2	*2.2	*1.4	*1.4	*1.4	1.0	.6	.6	.6	.6
Riviera	.9	.9	*2.0	*2.0	*2.0	1.0	1.0	1.0	1.0	1.0
Apollo	—	—	—	—	—	—	—	1.2	1.2	1.2
All others	*2.0	*1.8	*1.8	*1.8	*1.8	1.0	.5	.5	.5	.5

*Includes loosening front fender.

56 BUICK

LIGHTING SYSTEM, ADJUST AND SERVICE Continued

MODEL	1966	1967	1968	1969	1970	1971	1972	1973	1974	1975
Replace heater core without air conditioning,										
Riviera	1.4	1.4	2.9	2.9	2.9	2.1	2.1	2.1	2.1	2.1
Apollo	—	—	—	—	—	—	—	1.6	1.6	1.6
All others	1.7	1.7	2.1	2.1	2.1	2.1	2.1	2.1	2.1	2.1
Replace heater core with air conditioning										
Riviera	1.2	1.2	1.2	1.2	1.2	1.9	1.9	1.9	1.9	1.9
Apollo	—	—	—	—	—	—	—	3.2	3.2	3.2
All others	3.0	3.0	4.2	4.2	4.2	4.2	4.2	1.9	1.9	1.9
With automatic climate control, **ADD:**	.5	.5	.5	.5	.5	.5	.5	.5	.5	.5
Replace blower motor switch,										
Riviera	.5	.5	1.5	1.5	1.5	.8	.8	.8	.8	.8
All others	.8	.8	.8	.5	.5	.8	.8	.8	.8	.8

Approximate parts cost:
Heater hose, per ft. .... $ 0.75	Heater core $43.00
Blower motor 32.00	Blower motor switch 9.00

AIR CONDITIONING SYSTEM, SPRING TUNE-UP

Includes:
Basic Job: Clean condenser fins; adjust drive belt tension; test anti-freeze; tighten compressor, condenser, and evaporator mounts. Pressure-test and leak-check system. Check system for performance.
Additions to Basic Job: Replace defective parts.

MODEL	1966	1967	1968	1969	1970	1971	1972	1973	1974	1975
Basic Job:										
Perform complete spring tune-up	2.0	2.0	2.0	2.0	2.0	2.0	2.0	2.0	2.0	2.0
Additions to Basic Job:										
Replace compressor belt & adjust, **ADD:**	.4	.4	.4	.4	.4	.4	.4	.4	.4	.4
Repl. compr. clutch pulley w/hub assy., **ADD:**	.5	.5	.5	.5	.5	.5	.5	.5	.5	.5
Repl. compr. clutch coil, **ADD:**	.8	.8	.8	.8	.8	.8	.8	.8	.8	.8
Repl. compr. clutch bearing, **ADD:**	.8	.8	.8	.8	.8	.8	.8	.8	.8	.8

Approximate parts cost:
Compressor drive belt .... $ 3.00	Compressor clutch coil $28.00
Compressor clutch pulley w/hub 75.00	Compressor clutch bearing 23.00
Freon, per 14 oz. can 2.50	Anti-freeze, per gal. 9.50

AIR CONDITIONING SYSTEM BLOWER MOTOR OR CONTROLS, SERVICE

Includes:
Basic Jobs: Conduct performance test of system to determine defective part; R&R component; clean condenser fins; adjust drive belt tension; tighten all mounts; and test system.

MODEL	1966	1967	1968	1969	1970	1971	1972	1973	1974	1975
Basic Jobs:										
R&R blower motor, test sys. after install.,										
LeSabre, Centurion, Electra, Skylark	*2.2	*2.2	*1.4	*1.4	*1.4	1.0	.6	.6	.6	.6
Riviera	.9	.9	*2.0	*2.0	*2.0	1.0	1.0	1.0	1.0	1.0
Apollo	—	—	—	—	—	—	—	1.2	1.2	1.2
All others	*2.0	*1.8	*1.8	*1.8	*1.8	1.0	.5	.5	.5	.5
*Includes loosening front fender.										
R&R blower motor switch, test system	1.8	1.8	1.8	1.8	1.8	1.8	1.8	1.8	1.8	1.8

(THIS SCHEDULE CONTINUED ON NEXT PAGE.)

BUICK 57

AIR CONDITIONING SYSTEM BLOWER MOTOR OR CONTROLS, SERVICE Continued

MODEL	1966	1967	1968	1969	1970	1971	1972	1973	1974	1975
R&R compressor clutch switch, test system,										
Riviera	1.1	1.1	2.2	1.1	1.1	—	—	—	—	—
All others	1.4	1.4	1.4	1.4	1.4	—	—	—	—	—
R&R evaporator thermostatic switch	1.1	1.1	1.1	1.1	1.1	1.1	1.1	1.1	1.1	1.1
R&R control assembly, test system	1.6	1.6	1.6	1.6	1.6	1.6	1.6	1.6	1.6	1.6
Replace control cable, temperature door	.7	.7	.7	.7	.7	.7	1.0	1.0	1.0	1.0
Replace programmer, including test system	—	—	—	—	—	1.0	1.0	1.0	1.0	1.0

Approximate parts cost:

Blower motor	$23.00	Control cable, per ft.	$ 0.80
Blower motor switch	3.00	Control cable fittings, ea.	0.75
Evaporator thermostatic switch	4.00	Control assembly	24.00
Compressor clutch switch	2.50	Programmer	75.00

AIR CONDITIONING SYSTEM, MAJOR SERVICE

Includes:

Basic Job: Drain system in order to replace defective component; evacuate, dehydrate, and recharge system; pressure-test and leak-check; clean condenser fins; adjust drive belt tension; tighten compressor, condenser, and evaporator mounts; and conduct performance test.

Additions to Basic Job: Replace or overhaul compressor. Replace other defective parts.

MODEL	1966	1967	1968	1969	1970	1971	1972	1973	1974	1975
Basic Job:										
Drain, evacuate, dehydrate, charge & test	3.0	3.0	3.0	3.0	3.0	3.0	3.0	3.0	3.0	3.0
Additions to Basic Job:										
Replace compressor, ADD:	1.2	1.2	1.2	1.2	1.2	1.2	1.2	1.2	1.2	1.2
Overhaul compressor, incl. R&R, ADD:	2.9	2.9	2.9	2.9	2.9	2.9	2.9	2.9	2.9	2.9
Replace relief valve, ADD:	1.5	1.5	1.5	1.5	.8	.8	.8	.8	.8	.8
Repl. compr. front head or reed valve, ADD:	1.4	1.4	1.4	1.4	1.4	1.4	.5	.5	.5	.5
Repl. compr. rear hd. or reed valve, ADD:	1.1	1.1	1.1	1.1	1.1	1.1	.6	.6	.6	.6
Replace suction throttling valve, ADD:	.6	.6	.6	.6	.6	.6	.6	.6	.6	.6
Replace condenser, ADD:	1.3	1.3	1.3	1.3	1.3	1.3	1.3	1.3	1.3	1.3
Replace evaporator core,										
Riviera, ADD:	1.1	1.1	1.1	1.1	1.1	1.1	.8	.8	.8	.8
Skylark and Station Wagons, ADD:	1.8	1.8	1.8	1.8	1.8	1.8	1.3	1.3	1.3	1.3
All others, ADD:	1.0	1.0	1.0	1.0	1.0	1.0	1.0	1.0	1.0	1.0
With AIR, ADD:	.2	.2	.2	.2	.2	.2	.2	.2	.2	.2
Replace sight glass, ADD:	1.4	1.4	1.4	1.4	1.4	1.4	.9	.9	.9	.9
Replace dehydrator-receiver tank, ADD:	1.0	1.0	1.0	.8	.8	.8	.5	.5	.5	.5
Replace expansion valve, ADD:	1.5	1.5	1.5	.8	.8	.8	.8	.8	.8	.8
Replace POA valve, ADD:	.7	.7	.7	.7	.7	.7	.5	.5	.5	.5
Replace compressor shaft seal, ADD:	1.4	1.4	1.4	1.4	1.4	1.4	.9	.9	.9	.9
Replace valves-in-receiver (VIR) assy., ADD:	—	—	—	—	—	—	—	.5	.5	.5
O/H VIR assy. incl. repl. nec. parts, ADD:	—	—	—	—	—	—	—	1.0	1.0	1.0
Replace one hose, ADD:	.4	.4	.4	.4	.4	.4	.4	.4	.4	.4

Approximate parts cost:

Compressor	$150.00	Expansion valve	$36.00
Compressor front head & valve assy.	20.00	Pressure-operated absolute (POA) valve	30.00
Compressor rear head & valve assy.	65.00	Hose, per ft.	2.75
Compressor pressure relief valve	7.00	Hose fitting, ea.	1.00
Condenser	125.00	Freon, per 14 oz. can	2.50
Evaporator core assy.	90.00-160.00	Anti-freeze, per gal.	9.50
Compressor shaft seal assy.	8.00		

58 CADILLAC

SERVICE STATION MAINTENANCE

Includes:

Basic Job: Lubricate chassis, drain oil, change filters, repack front wheel bearings, repack U-joints, and lubricate front end. Check fluid levels of battery, radiator, air conditioner, brake master cylinder, power steering reservoir, transmission, and differential. Check condition of hoses and drive belts. Lubricate miscellaneous moving parts, latches, hinges, etc.

Related Jobs: Service individual systems or components. See detailed description of work included for each job in separate major section.

Additions to Basic or Related Jobs: Allowances for special equipment installed.

MODEL	1966	1967	1968	1969	1970	1971	1972	1973	1974	1975
Basic Job:										
General lubrication & system check	1.5	1.5	1.5	1.5	1.5	1.5	1.5	1.5	1.7	1.7
With air conditioning, **ADD:**	.3	.3	.3	.3	.3	.3	.3	.3	.3	.3
With AIR pump, **ADD:**	.2	.2	.2	.2	.2	.2	.2	.2	.2	.2
Related Jobs:										
Service Battery										
Clean, test & fill	.3	.3	.3	.3	.3	.3	.3	.3	.3	.3
Replace ground cable	.2	.2	.2	.2	.2	.2	.2	.2	.2	.2
Replace starter cable	.3	.3	.3	.3	.3	.3	.3	.3	.3	.3
Replace battery	.4	.4	.4	.4	.4	.4	.4	.4	.4	.4
Service Cooling System										
Back-flush, fill, & pressure-test system	.9	.9	.9	.9	.9	.9	.9	.9	.9	.9
Replace upper hose	.3	.3	.3	.3	.3	.3	.3	.3	.3	.3
Replace lower hose	.4	.4	.4	.4	.4	.4	.4	.4	.4	.4
Replace both hoses	.5	.5	.5	.5	.5	.5	.5	.5	.5	.5
Replace thermostat & pressure-test system	.7	.7	.7	.7	.7	.7	.7	.7	.7	.7
With air conditioning, **ADD:**	.2	.2	.2	.2	.2	.2	.2	.2	.2	.2
Replace water pump drive belt & adjust	.4	.4	.4	.4	.4	.4	.4	.4	.4	.4
With air conditioning, **ADD:**	.1	.1	.1	.1	.1	.1	.1	.1	.1	.1
Replace water pump	2.5	2.5	2.5	2.0	2.0	2.0	2.0	2.0	1.5	1.5
Overhaul pump after removal, **ADD:**	.3	.3	.3	.3	.3	.3	.3	.3	.3	.3
With air conditioning, **ADD:**	.3	.3	.3	.3	.3	.3	.3	.3	.3	.3
With AIR pump, **ADD:**	.2	.2	.2	.2	.2	.2	.2	.2	.2	.2
Service Ignition System										
Adjust & install spark plugs	.8	.8	.8	.8	.8	.8	.8	.8	.8	.8
With air conditioning, **ADD:**	.3	.3	.3	.3	.3	.3	.3	.3	.3	.3
With AIR, **ADD:**	.3	.3	.3	.3	.3	.3	.3	.3	.3	.3
Replace points and condenser and adjust ignition timing	.7	.7	.7	.7	.7	.7	.7	.7	.7	—
Replace distributor cap	.4	.4	.4	.4	.4	.4	.4	.4	.3	.3
Check reluctor air gap & adjust ignition timing	—	—	—	—	—	—	—	—	—	.4
Replace spark plug wires	.8	.8	.8	.8	.8	.8	.8	.8	.8	.8
With air conditioning, **ADD:**	.3	.3	.3	.3	.3	.3	.3	.3	.3	.3
Replace ignition coil	.4	.4	.4	.4	.4	.4	.4	.4	.4	.4
Service Fuel System										
Adjust carburetor idle mixture & speed	.7	.7	.7	.7	.7	.7	.7	.7	.7	.7
Replace fuel filter	.3	.3	.3	.3	.3	.3	.3	.3	.3	.3
Test and replace fuel pump	.9	.9	.9	.9	.9	.9	1.0	1.0	1.0	1.0
Replace flexible fuel line	.3	.3	.3	.3	.3	.3	.3	.3	.3	.3
Service Driveshaft										
R&R driveshaft & O/H or replace U-joints. Measure and adjust U-joint and driveshaft angles. Balance driveshaft,										
Constant velocity joints (2)	1.8	1.8	1.8	1.8	1.8	1.8	1.8	1.8	1.8	1.8
Constant velocity joints (3)	2.2	2.2	2.2	2.2	2.2	2.2	2.2	2.2	2.2	2.2

(THIS SCHEDULE CONTINUED ON NEXT PAGE.)

CADILLAC 59

SERVICE STATION MAINTENANCE Continued

MODEL	1966	1967	1968	1969	1970	1971	1972	1973	1974	1975
Service Hydraulic Brake System										
Adjust drum brakes, 4 wheels	.5	.5	—	—	—	—	—	—	—	—
Adjust drum brakes, 2 wheels	.3	.3	.3	.3	.3	.3	.3	.3	.3	.3
Replace drum brake shoes, 4 wheels	3.5	3.5	—	—	—	—	—	—	—	—
Replace drum brake shoes, rear wheels	1.6	1.6	1.6	1.6	1.6	1.6	1.6	1.6	1.6	1.6
Bleed hydraulic system, 4 wheels	.6	.6	.6	.6	.6	.6	.6	.6	.6	.6
Replace front disc brake pads, both sides	—	—	1.5	1.5	1.5	1.5	1.0	1.0	1.0	1.0
Overhaul master cylinder	1.3	1.3	1.5	1.5	1.5	1.5	1.8	1.8	1.8	1.8
O/H front calipers, incl. turn rotors,										
Eldorado	—	—	5.1	4.5	4.5	4.5	4.5	4.5	4.5	4.5
All others	—	—	4.6	4.0	4.0	4.0	4.0	4.0	4.0	4.0
R&R skid control modulator	—	—	—	—	—	.7	.7	.7	.7	.7
Service Parking Brakes										
Adjust parking brakes	.4	.4	.4	.4	.4	.4	.4	.4	.4	.4
Replace forward cable	.5	.5	.5	.5	.5	.5	.5	.5	.5	.5
Replace rear cable, one side	.4	.4	.4	.4	.4	.4	.4	.4	.4	.4
Replace rear cable, both sides	.6	.6	.6	.6	.6	.6	.6	.6	.6	.6
Replace center cable	.5	.5	.5	.5	.5	.5	.5	.5	.5	.5
Service Suspension System										
Replace front shock absorber, both sides	.9	.9	.9	.9	.9	.9	.9	.9	.9	.9
Replace rear shock absorber, both sides	.8	.8	.8	.8	.8	.8	.8	.8	.8	.8
With automatic level control, **ADD:**	.2	.2	.2	.2	.2	.2	.2	.2	.2	.2
Replace rear spring shackle & bushings; eye bolt and bushings, Commercial chassis only	.7	.7	.7	.7	.7	.7	.7	.7	.7	.7
Replace rear leaf spring & shim to align pinion angle, Commercial chassis	1.6	1.6	1.6	1.6	1.8	1.8	1.8	1.7	1.7	1.7
Replace rear coil spring, both	2.5	2.5	2.5	2.5	2.5	2.5	2.5	2.5	2.5	2.5
Service Front End & Steering System										
Adjust toe-in only	.4	.4	.4	.4	.4	.4	.4	.4	.4	.4
Replace steering idler arm or bushing	.7	.7	.7	.7	.7	.5	.5	.5	.5	.5
Replace tie-rods or tie-rod ends, (4)	1.4	1.4	1.4	1.4	1.4	1.6	1.6	1.6	1.6	1.6
Replace steering pump drive belt	.3	.3	.3	.3	.3	.3	.3	.3	.3	.3
With air conditioning, **ADD:**	.2	.2	.2	.2	.2	.2	.2	.2	.2	.2
Check & replenish reservoir fluid	.2	.2	.2	.2	.2	.2	.2	.2	.2	.2
Replace pressure hose, incl. adjust drive belt	.6	.6	.6	.6	.6	.6	.6	.6	.6	.6
Replace return hose incl. adjust drive belt	.4	.4	.4	.4	.4	.4	.4	.4	.4	.4
With air conditioning, **ADD:**	.1	.1	.1	.1	.1	.1	.1	.1	.1	.1
Balance four wheels on car,										
With drum brakes	1.2	1.2	1.2	—	—	—	—	—	—	—
With disc brakes	—	—	1.5	1.5	1.5	1.5	1.5	1.5	1.5	1.5
Rotate five wheels	.6	.6	.6	.6	.6	.6	.6	.6	.6	.6
Service Charging System										
Test system and/or adjust regulator	.6	.6	.6	.6	.6	.4	.4	.4	.4	.4
R&R alternator including pulley	.6	.6	.6	.6	.6	.6	.6	.6	.6	.6
With air conditioning, **ADD:**	.1	.1	.1	.1	.1	.1	.1	.1	.1	.1
With AIR, **ADD:**	.2	.2	.2	.2	.2	.2	.2	.2	.2	.2
Overhaul alternator after removal	2.3	2.3	1.5	1.5	1.5	1.5	1.5	1.5	1.5	1.5
Replace regulator	.5	.5	.5	.5	.5	—	—	—	—	—
Service Cranking System										
Test battery & cranking system	.5	.5	.5	.5	.5	.5	.5	.5	.5	.5
R&R starter	1.0	1.0	1.0	1.0	1.0	1.0	1.1	1.1	1.1	1.1
Overhaul starter after removal	1.7	1.7	1.7	1.7	1.7	1.7	1.7	1.7	1.7	1.7
Replace starter-battery cable	.3	.3	.3	.3	.3	.3	.3	.3	.3	.3
Repl. starter solenoid, incl. R&R starter	1.9	1.9	1.9	1.9	1.9	1.9	2.3	2.3	2.0	2.0

60 CADILLAC

SERVICE STATION MAINTENANCE Continued

MODEL	1966	1967	1968	1969	1970	1971	1972	1973	1974	1975
Service Lighting System										
Adjust two headlights	.4	.4	.4	.4	.4	.4	.4	.4	.4	.4
Adjust four headlights	.6	.6	.6	.6	.6	.6	.6	.6	.6	.6
Replace sealed beam unit, ea.	.3	.3	.3	.3	.3	.3	.3	.3	.3	.3
Replace foot dimmer switch	.3	.3	.3	.3	.3	.3	.3	.3	.3	.3
Replace signal/hazard flasher	.2	.2	.2	.2	.2	.2	.2	.2	.2	.2
Replace back-up light switch	.4	.4	.4	.4	.4	.4	.4	.4	.4	.4
Replace stoplight switch	.3	.3	.3	.3	.3	.3	.3	.3	.3	.3
Perform Minor Tune-up	2.5	2.5	2.5	2.5	2.7	2.7	2.9	2.9	3.0	3.0
With AIR, **ADD**:	.3	.3	.3	.3	.3	.3	.3	.3	.3	.3
With air conditioning, **ADD**:	.6	.6	.6	.6	.6	.6	.6	.6	.6	.6

Note: See minor tune-up section for work included and additions.

Perform Major Tune-up	6.6	6.6	6.6	6.6	6.8	6.8	7.0	7.0	7.3	7.3
With AIR, **ADD**:	.7	.7	.7	.7	.7	.7	.7	.7	.7	.7
With air conditioning, **ADD**:	.6	.6	.6	.6	.6	.6	.6	.6	.6	.6

Note: See major tune-up section for work included and additions.

TUNE-UP, MINOR

Includes:

Basic Job: Perform the following work:
1. Service air cleaner element.
2. Replace PCV valve.
3. Replace crankcase ventilation filter in air cleaner.
4. Clean battery terminals.
5. Check condition and tension of all drive belts.
6. Check all hoses and hose connections.
7. Check operation of heated air system (air cleaner), manifold heat valve, or EFE system (since 1975), and automatic choke. Service where necessary.
8. Replace fuel filter.
9. Perform compression test.
10. Replace spark plugs.
11. Replace ignition points and condenser.
12. Check dwell or reluctor air gap and adjust ignition timing.
13. Adjust carburetor idle mixture and speed.
14. Make necessary ignition and carburetor adjustments to obtain satisfactory exhaust system analyzer readings.

Additions to Basic Job: Allowances for special equipment and carburetor combinations.

MODEL	1966	1967	1968	1969	1970	1971	1972	1973	1974	1975
Basic Job:										
Perform minor tune-up	2.5	2.5	2.5	2.5	2.7	2.7	2.9	2.9	3.0	3.0
Additions to Basic Job:										
With AIR pump, **ADD**:	.3	.3	.3	.3	.3	.3	.3	.3	.3	.3
With air conditioning, **ADD**:	.6	.6	.6	.6	.6	.6	.6	.6	.6	.6

Approximate parts cost:

Spark plugs, each	$1.50	Fuel filter	$3.50
Points & condenser	5.00	Early Fuel Evaporation (EFE) valve	5.00
PCV valve	3.00	EFE valve vacuum motor	6.00
Air cleaner element	5.50		

CADILLAC 61

TUNE-UP, MAJOR

Includes:

Basic Job: Perform the following work:
1. Service air cleaner element.
2. Replace crankcase ventilation filter in air cleaner.
3. Replace PCV valve.
4. Check drive belts and adjust for proper tension.
5. Check all hoses and hose connections.
6. Clean battery terminals.
7. Check operation of manifold heat valve or EFE system (since 1975), and automatic choke. Service where necessary.
8. Check operation of heated-air system.
9. Check exhaust and evaporative emission control systems.
10. Replace fuel filter.
11. Perform compression check.
12. Replace spark plugs.
13. Replace ignition points and condenser.
14. Check dwell or reluctor air gap and adjust ignition timing.
15. Check distributor cap and rotor.
16. Tighten cylinder head bolts.
17. Adjust valve lash (where applicable).
18. Overhaul carburetor(s).
19. Adjust carburetor(s) idle mixture and speed.
20. Make necessary ignition and carburetor adjustments to obtain satisfactory exhaust system analyzer readings.

Additions to Basic Job: Allowances for special equipment installed.

MODEL	1966	1967	1968	1969	1970	1971	1972	1973	1974	1975
Basic Job:										
Perform major tune-up	6.6	6.6	6.6	6.6	6.8	6.8	7.0	7.0	7.3	7.3
Additions to Basic Job:										
With AIR pump, ADD:	.7	.7	.7	.7	.7	.7	.7	.7	.7	.7
With air conditioning, ADD:	.6	.6	.6	.6	.6	.6	.6	.6	.6	.6
Replace hydraulic valve lifter, one, ADD:	2.0	2.0	2.0	2.0	2.0	2.0	2.0	2.0	2.0	2.0

Approximate parts cost:

Spark plugs, each $1.50	Fuel filter $3.50
Points & condenser 5.00	Carburetor repair kit, ea. 18.00
PCV valve 3.00	Early Fuel Evaporation (EFE) valve 5.00
Air cleaner element 5.50	EFE valve vacuum motor 6.00

EMISSION CONTROL SYSTEMS, COMPLETE TEST OR SERVICE

Includes:

Basic Job: Make all necessary tests and repairs. Sign certification certificate.
1. Replace PCV valve, check all vacuum passageways and hoses.
2. Replace crankcase ventilation filter in air cleaner.
3. Test purge-control valve, gas tank filler cap and vent lines, and hoses for leakage.
4. Replace evaporation canister filter.
5. Clean EGR valve and test the control system.
6. Check speed control spark (SCS) system.
7. Check operation of manifold heat valve or EFE system (since 1975), and automatic choke. Free-up where necessary.
8. Check and adjust tension of drive belts.
9. Check operation of heated-air system.
10. Check AIR air pump flow.
11. Check routing and condition of hoses.
12. Check operation of diverter or bypass valve.
13. Check AIR manifold and hoses.
14. Replace catalytic converter or pellets, if necessary.
15. Determine if engine tune-up is required.

Related Jobs: Perform minor or major tune-up as required.

MODEL	1966	1967	1968	1969	1970	1971	1972	1973	1974	1975
Basic Job:										
Perform emission control system tune-up	3.3	3.3	3.3	3.3	3.8	3.8	4.2	4.2	4.3	4.3
Additions to Basic Job:										
With AIR, ADD:	.5	.5	.5	.5	.5	.5	.5	.5	.5	.5

62 CADILLAC

EMISSION CONTROL SYSTEMS, COMPLETE TEST OR SERVICE Continued

MODEL	1966	1967	1968	1969	1970	1971	1972	1973	1974	1975
Related Jobs:										
Perform minor tune-up, **ADD**:	2.5	2.5	2.5	2.5	2.7	2.7	2.9	2.9	3.0	3.0
With air conditioning, **ADD**:	.6	.6	.6	.6	.6	.6	.6	.6	.6	.6
Perform major tune-up, **ADD**:	6.6	6.6	6.6	6.6	6.8	6.8	7.0	7.0	7.3	7.3
With air conditioning, **ADD**:	.6	.6	.6	.6	.6	.6	.6	.6	.6	.6

Approximate parts cost:

Catalytic converter pellets $70.00	Drive belt $3.00
PCV valve 3.00	Diverter valve 12.00
Hose, per ft. 0.75	Air pump 50.00
Cannister filter 1.00	Catalytic converter 175.00
Purge control valve 4.00	See minor or major tune-up section for cost of tune-up parts.

EMISSION CONTROL SYSTEMS, TESTS FOR SMOG STATION CERTIFICATION

Includes:

Basic Job: Test crankcase, exhaust and evaporative emission control systems. Check heated-air system. Check HC/CO level with exhaust analyzer. Sign certification certificate. (No adjustments or repairs included in basic job.)

Related Jobs: Service any defective emission control system. Perform minor or major tune-up as required.

MODEL	1966	1967	1968	1969	1970	1971	1972	1973	1974	1975
Basic Job:										
Test all systems & sign certificate	1.0	1.0	1.0	1.0	1.2	1.2	1.4	1.4	1.5	1.5
Related Jobs:										
Service crankcase emission control system	.3	.3	.3	.3	.3	.3	.3	.3	.3	.3
Service evaporative emission control system	—	—	—	—	.4	.4	.4	.4	.4	.4
Exhaust emission control systems,										
Service heated-air system.	.3	.3	.3	.3	.3	.3	.3	.3	.3	.3
Service speed controlled spark (SCS)	—	—	—	—	.5	.5	.5	—	—	—
Service EGR system.	—	—	—	—	—	—	.4	.4	.4	.4
Service air injection (AIR) system	.5	.5	.5	.5	.5	.5	.5	.5	.5	.5
Replace catalytic converter pellets	—	—	—	—	—	—	—	—	—	1.0
Note: See separate section for replacement of components in each system.										
Perform minor tune-up	2.5	2.5	2.5	2.5	2.7	2.7	2.9	2.9	3.0	3.0
With air conditioning, **ADD**:	.6	.6	.6	.6	.6	.6	.6	.6	.6	.6
Perform major tune-up	6.6	6.6	6.6	6.6	6.8	6.8	7.0	7.0	7.3	7.3
With air conditioning, **ADD**:	.6	.6	.6	.6	.6	.6	.6	.6	.6	.6

Approximate parts cost:

Catalytic converter pellets $70.00
See minor or major tune-up section for cost of tune-up parts.

POSITIVE CRANKCASE VENTILATION (PCV) SYSTEM, TEST AND SERVICE

Includes:

Basic Job: Test PCV valve, check all vacuum passageways, and inspect hoses. Clean or replace air filter.

Additions to Basic Job: Replace defective parts. (Do not attempt to clean PCV valve, replace if valve is not free.)

MODEL	1966	1967	1968	1969	1970	1971	1972	1973	1974	1975
Basic Job:										
Test PCV system, all models	.3	.3	.3	.3	.3	.3	.3	.3	.3	.3

(THIS SCHEDULE CONTINUED ON NEXT PAGE.)

CADILLAC 63

POSITIVE CRANKCASE VENTILATION (PCV) SYSTEM, TEST AND SERVICE Continued

MODEL	1966	1967	1968	1969	1970	1971	1972	1973	1974	1975
Additions to Basic Job:										
Replace PCV valve, **ADD:**	.3	.3	.3	.3	.3	.3	.3	.3	.3	.3
Replace all hoses, **ADD:**	.6	.6	.6	.6	.6	.6	.6	.6	.6	.6

Approximate parts cost:
PCV valve ....$3.00   Hose, per ft. $0.75

EVAPORATIVE EMISSION CONTROL SYSTEM, TEST AND SERVICE

Includes:
  Basic Job: Test purge control valve, gas tank filler cap, vent lines, and hoses.
  Additions to Basic Job: Replace defective part.

MODEL	1966	1967	1968	1969	1970	1971	1972	1973	1974	1975
Basic Job:										
Test evap. emission control system	—	—	—	—	.4	.4	.4	.4	.4	.4
Additions to Basic Job:										
Replace purge control valve, **ADD:**	—	—	—	—	—	—	.5	—	—	—
Replace charcoal canister filter, **ADD:**	—	—	—	—	.3	.3	.3	.3	.3	.3
Replace charcoal canister, **ADD:**	—	—	—	—	.5	.5	.5	.5	.5	.5
Replace hose, each, **ADD:**	—	—	—	—	.2	.2	.2	.2	.2	.2

Approximate parts cost:
Purge control valve ....$4.00   Charcoal canister $32.00
Canister filter ....1.50   Hose, per ft. 0.75

TRANSMISSION OR SPEED CONTROLLED SPARK (TCS/SCS) SYSTEM, TEST AND SERVICE

Includes:
  Basic Job: Check engine speed in gear using tachometer and timing ight, test TCS solenoid, and transmission switch.
  Additions to Basic Job: Replace defective parts.

MODEL	1966	1967	1968	1969	1970	1971	1972	1973	1974	1975
Basic Job:										
Test TCS or SCS system	—	—	—	—	.6	.5	.5	—	—	—
Additions to Basic Job:										
Replace TCS or SCS solenoid, **ADD:**	—	—	—	—	.3	.3	.3	—	—	—
Replace TCS or SCS switch,										
Eldorado, **ADD:**	—	—	—	—	.8	.8	.8	—	—	—
All others, **ADD:**	—	—	—	—	.5	.5	.5	—	—	—
Replace TCS or SCS relay, **ADD:**	—	—	—	—	.2	.2	.2	—	—	—
Replace thermostatic vacuum switch or										
TCS/SCS temperature switch, **ADD:**	—	—	—	—	.3	.3	.3	—	—	—
Replace idle stop solenoid, **ADD:**	—	—	—	—	.3	.3	.3	—	—	—

Approximate parts cost:
TCS switch ....$5.00   TCS solenoid $11.50
Thermostatic vacuum switch ....6.50   Idle stop solenoid 11.00
TCS relay 2.50

64 CADILLAC

EXHAUST-GAS RECIRCULATION (EGR) SYSTEM, TEST AND SERVICE

Includes:
Basic Job: Test EGR valve, control system, and engine idling condition.
Additions to Basic Job: Replace defective parts. Test & repair thermostatic control system.

MODEL	1966	1967	1968	1969	1970	1971	1972	1973	1974	1975
Basic Job:										
Test EGR system, all models	—	—	—	—	—	—	—	.4	.4	.4
Additions to Basic Job:										
Service EGR valve, **ADD:**	—	—	—	—	—	—	—	.7	.7	.7
Replace EGR valve, **ADD:**	—	—	—	—	—	—	—	.4	.4	.4
Test & repair thermo. control system, **ADD:**	—	—	—	—	—	—	—	.6	.6	.6

Approximate parts cost:
EGR valve .... $10.00   Thermal vacuum switch 12.00

AIR INJECTION REACTOR (AIR) SYSTEM, TEST AND SERVICE

Includes:
Basic Job: Test air pump flow, check routing and condition of hoses, determine operation of diverter valve, verify check valve operation, inspect air manifold and hoses. Check and adjust drive belt tension.
Additions to Basic Job: Replace defective part. Replace drive belt, includes adjust tension. Replacement of hose(s), includes soapy water test.

MODEL	1966	1967	1968	1969	1970	1971	1972	1973	1974	1975
Basic Job:										
Test AIR system	.5	.5	.5	.5	.5	.5	.5	.5	.5	.5
Additions to Basic Job:										
Replace and adjust drive belt, **ADD:**	.5	.5	.5	.5	.5	.5	.5	.5	.5	.5
Replace AIR pump, **ADD:**	1.0	1.0	1.0	1.0	1.0	1.1	1.1	1.1	1.1	1.1
Replace diverter valve, **ADD:**	.7	.7	.7	.7	.7	.7	.7	.7	.7	.7
Replace check valve assembly, **ADD:**	1.2	1.2	1.2	1.2	1.2	1.2	1.2	1.2	1.2	1.2
Replace hose, includes soapy water test, **ADD:**	.4	.4	.4	.4	.4	.4	.4	.4	.4	.4

Approximate parts cost:
Drive belt .... $3.00   Diverter valve $12.00
Air pump .... 50.00   Hose, per ft .... .75
Check valve 7.00

HEATED-AIR SYSTEM, TEST AND SERVICE

Includes:
Basic Job: Check heated-air door, temperature sensor, and vacuum motor operation.
Additions to Basic Job: Replace defective parts.

MODEL	1966	1967	1968	1969	1970	1971	1972	1973	1974	1975
Basic Job:										
Test heated-air system	—	—	—	.3	.3	.3	.3	.3	.3	.3
Additions to Basic Job:										
Replace vacuum motor, **ADD:**	—	—	—	.4	.4	.4	.4	.4	.4	.4
Replace temperature sensor, **ADD:**	—	—	—	.5	.5	.5	.5	.5	.5	.5

Approximate parts cost:
Vacuum motor assembly .... $5.00   Temperature sensor $4.50

CADILLAC 65

IGNITION SYSTEM, SERVICE

Includes:

Basic Jobs: 1. Adjust and install new spark plugs.
2. Replace points and condenser, adjust dwell and ignition timing.
3. R&R distributor, overhaul and test centrifugal and vacuum advances, set dwell or check reluctor air gap and ignition timing.

Related Jobs: Replace additional defective part(s) as required.

Additions: Allowances for special equipment installed or replacement of associated defective part(s).

MODEL	1966	1967	1968	1969	1970	1971	1972	1973	1974	1975
Basic Job #1										
Adjust & install new spark plugs	.8	.8	.8	.8	.8	.8	.8	.8	.8	.8
With air conditioning, **ADD:**	.3	.3	.3	.3	.3	.3	.3	.3	.3	.3
With AIR, **ADD:**	.3	.3	.3	.3	.3	.3	.3	.3	.3	.3
Basic Job #2										
Replace points and condenser and adjust ignition timing	.7	.7	.7	.7	.7	.7	.7	.7	.7	—
Replace distributor cap	.4	.4	.4	.4	.4	.4	.4	.4	.3	.3
Check reluctor air gap & adjust ignition timing	—	—	—	—	—	—	—	—	—	.4
Basic Job #3										
R&R and overhaul distributor & adjust ignition timing	1.4	1.4	1.4	1.4	1.4	1.4	1.4	1.4	1.4	.8
Replace vacuum advance unit, **ADD:**	.2	.2	.2	.2	.2	.2	.2	.2	.2	.2
Related Jobs:										
Replace ignition coil	.4	.4	.4	.4	.4	.4	.4	.4	.4	.4
Replace spark plug wires	.8	.8	.8	.8	.8	.8	.8	.8	.8	.8
With air conditioning, **ADD:**	.3	.3	.3	.3	.3	.3	.3	.3	.3	.3
Replace ignition switch	.6	.6	.6	.6	.6	.6	.6	.6	.6	.6
Replace ignition key buzzer switch	.8	.8	.8	.8	.8	.8	.8	.8	.8	.8

Approximate parts cost:

Spark plugs, each ... $ 1.50	Vacuum control unit ... $ 4.00
Point set ... 3.00	Ignition coil ... 14.00
Condenser ... 1.50	Spark plug wires ... 15.00
Distributor cap ... 4.50	H.E.I. distributor cap ... 10.00
Distributor parts, kit ... 10.00	HEI coil ... 25.00
Ignition switch ... 8.00	

CHARGING SYSTEM, TEST AND SERVICE

Includes:

Basic Job: Test battery voltage and gravity, clean battery cable terminals, test alternator output, test and/or adjust regulator.

Related Jobs: Replace or overhaul defective component.

MODEL	1966	1967	1968	1969	1970	1971	1972	1973	1974	1975
Basic Job:										
Test system and/or adjust regulator	.6	.6	.6	.6	.6	.4	.4	.4	.4	.4
Related Jobs:										
R&R alternator incl. pulley	.6	.6	.6	.6	.7	.7	.7	.7	.7	.7
With air conditioning, **ADD:**	.1	.1	.1	.1	.1	.1	.1	.1	.1	.1
With AIR, **ADD:**	.2	.2	.2	.2	.2	.2	.2	.2	.2	.2
Overhaul alternator after removal	2.3	2.3	1.5	1.5	1.5	1.5	1.5	1.5	1.5	1.5
Replace regulator	.5	.5	.5	.5	.5	—	—	—	—	—

Approximate parts cost:

Alternator, new ... $80.00-160.00	Regulator ... $13.00-27.00
Alternator, rebuilt ... 35.00-70.00	

66 CADILLAC

CRANKING SYSTEM, TEST AND SERVICE

Includes:
  Basic Job: Test battery and cranking system. Clean battery cable terminals.
  Related Jobs: Replace defective parts, including test when necessary.

MODEL	1966	1967	1968	1969	1970	1971	1972	1973	1974	1975
Basic Job:										
Test cranking system	.5	.5	.5	.5	.5	.5	.5	.5	.5	.5
Related Jobs:										
R&R starter	1.0	1.0	1.0	1.0	1.0	1.0	1.1	1.1	1.1	1.1
Overhaul starter after removal	1.7	1.7	1.7	1.7	1.7	1.7	1.7	1.7	1.7	1.7
Replace starter-battery cable	.3	.3	.3	.3	.3	.3	.3	.3	.3	.3
Repl. starter/neutral switch & adjust	.4	.4	.4	.4	.4	.4	.4	.4	.4	.4
Repl. starter solenoid, incl. R&R starter	1.9	1.9	1.9	1.9	1.9	1.9	2.3	2.3	2.0	2.0

Approximate parts cost:
Starter, new	$95.00	Solenoid, service kit	$15.00
Starter, rebuilt w/o solenoid	40.00	Solenoid switch	14.00
Starter-battery cable	15.00	Starter/neutral switch	12.00

ENGINE OVERHAUL, IN-CAR

Includes:
  Basic Job: Remove ring ridge, deglaze cylinder walls, fit piston pins, align connecting rods, install new piston rings and rod bearings, install new main bearing inserts and oil seals, overhaul oil pump, clean carbon, grind valves, and perform major tune-up.
  Additions to Basic Job: Associated work that is required during basic job and allowances for special equipment.

MODEL	1966	1967	1968	1969	1970	1971	1972	1973	1974	1975
Basic Job:										
Overhaul engine, Eldorado, not performed in car. All others	30.2	30.2	30.2	30.6	30.6	30.6	30.6	30.8	30.8	30.8
Additions to Basic Job:										
Rebore cylinders, **ADD:**	5.0	5.0	5.0	5.0	5.0	5.0	5.0	5.0	5.0	5.0
Expand pistons, **ADD:**	2.4	2.4	2.4	2.4	2.4	2.4	2.4	2.4	2.4	2.4
Regroove top piston ring grooves, **ADD:**	2.4	2.4	2.4	2.4	2.4	2.4	2.4	2.4	2.4	2.4
Replace hydraulic valve lifters, **ADD:**	1.0	1.0	1.0	1.0	1.0	1.0	1.0	1.0	1.0	1.0
Overhaul rocker arm mechanism, **ADD:**	1.9	1.9	1.9	1.9	1.9	1.9	1.9	1.9	1.9	1.9
Ream valve guides oversize, **ADD:**	.9	.9	.9	.9	.9	.9	.9	.9	.9	.9
Overhaul oil pump, **ADD:**	.8	.8	.8	.8	.8	.8	.8	.8	.8	.8
With AIR pump, **ADD:**	.7	.7	.7	.7	.7	.7	.7	.7	.7	.7
With air conditioning, **ADD:**	.7	.7	.7	.7	.7	.7	.7	.7	.7	.7

Approximate parts cost:
Hydraulic valve lifters, ea.	$ 4.00	Main bearing inserts (5)	$37.00
Major tune-up parts	40.00	Piston rings, complete set	52.00
Carburetor repair kit	20.00	Piston pins, set	14.00
Rod bearing inserts	36.00	Piston assemblies, set	240.00
Rear main oil seal, set	3.00	Complete gasket set	30.00

CADILLAC 67

ENGINE OVERHAUL, OUT-OF-CAR

Includes:

Basic Job: R&R engine, remove ring ridge, rebore or hone cylinder walls, regrind crankshaft and camshaft, replace camshaft bushings and line ream, replace timing chain and gears and oil seal, install main bearing inserts and seals, install piston pins, align connecting rods, install new piston rings and rod bearings, overhaul oil pump, clean carbon, grind valves, overhaul rocker arm mechanism, and perform major tune-up.

Additions to Basic Job: Associated work that is required during basic job and allowances for special equipment installed.

MODEL	1966	1967	1968	1969	1970	1971	1972	1973	1974	1975
Basic Job:										
Overhaul engine,										
Eldorado	—	42.7	42.7	42.7	42.7	41.0	41.0	41.2	41.2	41.5
All others	42.7	42.7	42.7	42.7	42.7	42.7	42.7	42.9	42.9	43.2
Additions to Basic Job:										
With AIR pump, **ADD:**	.7	.7	.7	.7	.7	.7	.7	.7	.7	.7
With air conditioning, incl. chg. sys., **ADD:**	1.8	1.8	1.8	1.8	1.8	1.8	1.8	1.8	1.8	1.8
With Cruise Control, **ADD:**	.2	.2	.2	.2	.2	.2	.2	.2	.2	.2
Regroove top piston ring grooves, **ADD:**	1.8	1.8	1.8	1.8	1.8	1.8	1.8	1.8	1.8	1.8
Ream valve guides oversize, **ADD:**	.9	.9	.9	.9	.9	.9	.9	.9	.9	.9
Replace all engine mounts, **ADD:**	.6	.6	.6	.6	.6	.6	.6	.6	.6	.6

Approximate parts cost:

Major tune-up parts $40.00	Main bearing inserts (5) $37.00
Complete gasket set 30.00	Piston rings, complete, set 52.00
Carburetor repair kit 20.00	Piston pins, set 14.00
Rod bearing inserts 36.00	Piston assemblies, set 240.00
Rear main oil seal 3.00	

SHORT BLOCK, REPLACE

Includes:

Basic Job: R&R engine, clean and reface valves, scrape carbon, grind valve seats, replace valve seals, overhaul rocker arm mechanism, transfer all parts, and perform major tune-up.

Additions to Basic Job: Associated work that is required during basic job and allowances for special equipment installed.

MODEL	1966	1967	1968	1969	1970	1971	1972	1973	1974	1975
Basic Job:										
Replace short block,										
Eldorado	—	25.1	25.1	25.1	25.3	22.2	22.4	22.4	22.7	22.5
All others	22.6	22.6	22.6	22.6	22.8	22.8	23.0	23.0	23.3	23.1
Additions to Basic Job:										
With AIR pump, **ADD:**	.7	.7	.7	.7	.7	.7	.7	.7	.7	.7
With air conditioning, incl. chg. sys., **ADD:**	1.8	1.8	1.8	1.8	1.8	1.8	1.8	1.8	1.8	1.8
Ream valve guides oversize, **ADD:**	.9	.9	.9	.9	.9	.9	.9	.9	.9	.9
Replace all engine mounts, **ADD:**	.6	.6	.6	.6	.6	.6	.6	.6	.6	.6

Approximate parts cost:

Complete gasket set $30.00	Engine mounts, front or rear $10.00
Major tune-up parts 40.00	Hydraulic valve lifters, ea. 4.00
Carburetor repair kit 20.00	Short block 500.00
Oil & air filters 9.00	

68 CADILLAC

FUEL SYSTEM, ADJUST AND SERVICE

Includes:
Basic Job: Adjust idle mixture and speed for performance and to obtain satisfactory exhaust system analyzer readings.
Related Jobs: R&R carburetor, overhaul carburetor, R&R associated fuel components.

MODEL	1966	1967	1968	1969	1970	1971	1972	1973	1974	1975
Basic Job:										
Complete carburetor adjustments	.7	.7	.7	.7	.7	.7	.7	.7	.7	.7
Related Jobs:										
Replace carb., incl. complete adjustments	1.0	1.0	1.0	1.0	1.0	1.0	1.0	1.0	1.0	1.0
Overhaul carburetor, includes R&R and make idle mixture and speed adjustment	4.0	4.0	4.0	4.0	3.2	3.2	3.2	3.2	3.4	3.4
Test and replace fuel pump	.9	.9	.9	.9	.9	.9	1.0	1.0	1.0	1.0
Replace fuel filter	.3	.3	.3	.3	.3	.3	.3	.3	.3	.3
Replace fuel tank sending unit	1.5	1.5	1.5	1.5	1.5	1.5	1.5	1.5	1.5	1.5
Replace dashboard fuel gauge	2.5	2.5	2.5	1.0	1.0	1.0	1.0	1.0	1.0	1.0
Repl. fuel tank, incl. transfer float unit	1.5	1.5	1.5	1.5	1.5	1.5	1.5	1.5	1.5	1.5
Replace flexible fuel line	.3	.3	.3	.3	.3	.3	.3	.3	.3	.3
Test & repl. Early Fuel Evaporation (EFE) valve	—	—	—	—	—	—	—	—	—	.4

Approximate parts cost:
Carburetor, new	$100.00	Fuel pump	$20.00
Carburetor, rebuilt	45.00	Fuel tank sending unit	20.00
Carburetor, repair kit	20.00	Fuel gauge, dash	14.00
Flexible fuel line, per ft.	0.50	Fuel tank	73.00
In-line fuel filter	4.00	Early Fuel Evaporation (EFE) valve	5.00

TIMING CHAIN MECHANISM, SERVICE

Includes:
Basic Job: Replace timing cover oil seal and timing chain. Perform minor tune-up.
Additions to Basic Job: Replace camshaft timing sprocket or crankshaft timing sprocket.

MODEL	1966	1967	1968	1969	1970	1971	1972	1973	1974	1975
Basic Job:										
Replace timing cover oil seal & chain and perform minor tune-up,										
Eldorado, includes R&R engine	—	11.5	11.5	11.5	11.7	8.2	8.4	8.4	8.5	6.2
With Cruise Control, ADD:	—	.2	.2	.2	.2	.2	.2	.2	.2	.2
With air conditioning, incl. chg. sys. ADD:	—	1.8	1.8	1.8	1.8	1.8	1.8	1.8	1.8	1.8
With AIR, ADD:	—	.2	.2	.2	.2	.2	.2	.2	.2	.2
All other models	6.6	6.6	6.6	6.6	6.8	6.8	7.0	7.0	5.7	6.2
With air conditioning, ADD:	.5	.5	.5	.5	.5	.5	.5	.5	.5	.5
With AIR, ADD:	.2	.2	.2	.2	.2	.2	.2	.2	.2	.2
All models with power steering, ADD:	.3	.3	.3	.3	.3	.3	.3	.3	.3	.3
Additions to Basic Job:										
Replace camshaft sprocket, ADD:	.2	.2	.2	.2	.2	.2	.2	.2	.2	.2
Replace crankshaft sprocket, ADD:	.2	.2	.2	.2	.2	.2	.2	.2	.2	.2
Replace engine mounts, Eldorado, ADD:	.6	.6	.6	.6	.6	.6	.6	.6	.6	.6

Approximate parts cost:
Timing cover gasket	$ 1.00	Camshaft sprocket	$10.00
Timing cover oil seal	2.00	Crankshaft sprocket	8.00
Timing chain	11.00	Minor tune-up parts	30.00
Engine mounts, front or rear	10.00		

CADILLAC 69

VALVE MECHANISM, SERVICE

Includes:
   Basic Job: Clean and reface valves, scrape carbon, grind valve seats, replace valve seals, and perform major tune-up.
   Additions to Basic Job: Associated work required during basic job and allowances for special equipment installed.

MODEL	1966	1967	1968	1969	1970	1971	1972	1973	1974	1975
Basic Job:										
Service valve mechanism	14.1	14.1	14.1	14.1	14.3	14.3	14.5	14.5	14.8	14.8
Additions to Basic Job:										
Ream valve guides oversize, **ADD:**	.9	.9	.9	.9	.9	.9	.9	.9	.9	.9
Replace hydraulic valve lifters, **ADD:**	1.0	1.0	1.0	1.0	1.0	1.0	1.0	1.0	1.0	1.0
With air conditioning, **ADD:**	.6	.6	.6	.6	.6	.6	.6	.6	.6	.6
With Cruise Control, **ADD:**	.2	.2	.2	.2	.2	.2	.2	.2	.2	.2
With AIR, pump, **ADD:**	.7	.7	.7	.7	.7	.7	.7	.7	.7	.7

Approximate parts cost:
Major tune-up parts $40.00	Hydraulic valve lifters, each $4.00
Valve grind gasket set 23.00	Valve spring, each 2.00

CYLINDER HEAD AND/OR GASKET, REPLACE

Includes:
   Basic Jobs: **1.** R&R intake manifold and cylinder head to install new gasket. Clean head and block surfaces and perform minor tune-up.
   2. Install new cylinder head, including recondition valves and perform minor tune-up.
   Additions to Basic Job: Allowances for special equipment installed.

MODEL	1966	1967	1968	1969	1970	1971	1972	1973	1974	1975
Basic Job #1										
Repl. head gasket,										
One side	4.9	4.9	4.9	4.9	5.1	5.1	5.3	5.3	5.4	5.4
Both sides	6.2	6.2	6.2	6.2	6.4	6.4	6.6	6.6	6.7	7.0
Basic Job #2										
Install new head,										
One side	7.0	7.0	7.0	7.0	7.2	7.2	7.4	7.4	7.5	7.8
Both sides	10.4	10.4	10.4	10.4	10.6	10.6	10.8	10.8	10.9	11.2
Additions to Basic Jobs:										
With Cruise Control, **ADD:**	.2	.2	.2	.2	.2	.2	.2	.2	.2	.2
With air conditioning, **ADD:**	.6	.6	.6	.6	.6	.6	.6	.6	.6	.6
With AIR pump, **ADD:**	.3	.3	.3	.3	.3	.3	.3	.3	.3	.3

Approximate parts cost:
Head gasket, ea. . . . . $ 4.00	Valve grind gasket set $23.00
Cylinder head, ea. 110.00	Rocker arm cover gasket, ea. 3.00
Minor tune-up parts 30.00	

OIL PUMP SERVICE

Includes:
   Basic Job: R&R oil filter and pump.
   Additions to Basic Job: Associated work required during basic job.

MODEL	1966	1967	1968	1969	1970	1971	1972	1973	1974	1975
Basic Job:										
R&R oil filter and pump	.5	.5	.5	.5	.5	.5	.5	.5	.5	.5

CADILLAC

OIL PUMP SERVICE Continued

MODEL	1966	1967	1968	1969	1970	1971	1972	1973	1974	1975
Additions to Basic Job:										
Overhaul pump after removal, **ADD:**	.5	.5	.5	.5	.5	.5	.5	.5	.5	.5
Replace oil pressure sending unit, **ADD:**	.2	.2	.2	.2	.2	.2	.2	.2	.2	.2

Approximate parts cost:
- Oil pump gasket $0.60
- Oil pump overhaul kit 7.50
- Oil pressure sending unit $3.00
- Oil filter element 5.00

BEARING, MAIN AND/OR RODS, REPLACE

Includes:
Basic Job: R&R oil pan (includes R&R engine, Eldorado) measure connecting rod bearing oil clearance with Plastigage, install new connecting rod bearing inserts, and oil filter element.

Additions to Basic Job: Measure main bearing oil clearance with Plastigage, replace all main bearing inserts and rear main bearing oil seals, repair or replace oil pump.

MODEL	1966	1967	1968	1969	1970	1971	1972	1973	1974	1975
Basic Job:										
R&R pan, measure, install inserts & filter,										
Eldorado (includes R&R engine)	—	9.7	9.7	9.7	9.7	6.6	6.6	6.6	6.6	6.6
All others	4.4	4.4	4.4	4.4	4.4	4.4	4.4	4.4	4.4	4.4
Additions to Basic Job:										
Use Plastigage — all main brgs., **ADD:**	.5	.5	.5	.5	.5	.5	.5	.5	.5	.5
Replace main inserts & rear oil seals,										
Eldorado, **ADD:**	—	1.0	1.0	1.0	1.0	1.0	1.0	1.0	1.0	1.0
All others, **ADD:**	2.5	2.5	2.5	2.5	2.5	2.5	2.5	2.5	2.5	2.5
Overhaul oil pump, **ADD:**	.5	.5	.5	.5	.5	.5	.5	.5	.5	.5

Approximate parts cost:
- Rod bearing inserts $36.00
- Rear main bearing oil seal set 3.00
- Main bearing inserts (5) 37.00
- Oil pan gasket $4.00
- Oil filter element 5.00
- Oil pump overhaul kit 7.50

COOLING SYSTEM, TEST AND SERVICE

Includes:
Basic Job: Drain and back-flush system, check for leaks and tighten all hose connections, pressure-test radiator cap and system.
Related Jobs: Replace defective part. Work performed independently of basic job.
Additions to Related Jobs: Allowances for special equipment installed.

MODEL	1966	1967	1968	1969	1970	1971	1972	1973	1974	1975
Basic Job:										
Drain, flush, fill, and pressure-test system.	.9	.9	.9	.9	.9	.9	.9	.9	.9	.9
Related Jobs:										
Replace upper hose	.3	.3	.3	.3	.3	.3	.3	.3	.3	.3
Replace lower hose	.4	.4	.4	.4	.4	.4	.4	.4	.4	.4
Replace both hoses	.5	.5	.5	.5	.5	.5	.5	.5	.5	.5
Replace thermostat & pressure-test system	.7	.7	.7	.7	.7	.7	.7	.7	.7	.7
With air conditioning, **ADD:**	.2	.2	.2	.2	.2	.2	.2	.2	.2	.2
Replace water pump drive belt & adjust	.4	.4	.4	.4	.4	.4	.4	.4	.4	.4
With air conditioning, **ADD:**	.1	.1	.1	.1	.1	.1	.1	.1	.1	.1

(THIS SCHEDULE CONTINUED ON NEXT PAGE.)

CADILLAC 71

COOLING SYSTEM, TEST AND SERVICE Continued

MODEL	1966	1967	1968	1969	1970	1971	1972	1973	1974	1975
Related Jobs Continued										
Replace water pump	2.5	2.5	2.5	2.0	2.0	2.0	2.0	2.0	1.5	1.5
Overhaul pump after removal, **ADD:**	.3	.3	.3	.3	.3	.3	.3	.3	.3	.3
With air conditioning, **ADD:**	.3	.3	.3	.3	.3	.3	.3	.3	.3	.3
With AIR, **ADD:**	.2	.2	.2	.2	.2	.2	.2	.2	.2	.2
Repl. radiator, incl. pressure-test system	1.3	1.3	1.3	1.3	1.3	1.3	1.3	1.3	1.3	1.3
Replace water temp. gauge, engine	.5	.5	.5	.5	.5	.5	.5	.5	.5	.5
With air conditioning, **ADD:**	.1	.1	.1	.1	.1	.1	.1	.1	.1	.1
Replace water temp. gauge, dash,										
Eldorado	—	2.5	2.5	2.5	2.5	2.5	2.5	2.5	2.5	2.5
All others	2.0	2.0	2.0	2.0	2.0	2.0	2.0	2.0	2.0	2.0
Replace water jacket expansion plug	.5	.5	.5	.5	.5	.5	.5	.5	.5	.5

Add time required to gain access to plug.

Approximate parts cost:
Radiator, new	$150.00	Water pump	$45.00
Upper or lower hose	5.00	Drive belt, ea.	3.00
Thermostat	4.00	Temperature gauge, engine	5.00
Expansion plug, ea.	1.50	Temperature gauge, dash	12.00

EXHAUST SYSTEM TEST AND SERVICE

Includes:
Basic Job: Test exhaust system for leaks and/or exhaust odors. Use HC/CO exhaust analyzer to trace carbon monoxide leaks.
Related Jobs: Replace defective part(s). Each job includes basic job tests and installation of new hangers as required.

MODEL	1966	1967	1968	1969	1970	1971	1972	1973	1974	1975
Basic Job:										
Complete test of exhaust system	.4	.4	.4	.4	.4	.4	.4	.4	.4	.4
Related Jobs:										
Replace muffler	1.4	1.4	1.4	1.4	1.4	1.4	.9	.9	.9	.9
Replace resonator assembly	.9	.9	.9	.9	.9	.9	.9	.9	.9	.9
Replace intermediate pipe	.9	.9	.9	.9	.9	.9	.9	.9	.9	.9
Replace exhaust pipe, one side	.8	.8	.8	.8	.8	.8	.8	.8	.8	.8
Replace exhaust pipe, both sides	1.1	1.1	1.1	1.1	1.1	1.1	1.1	1.1	1.1	1.1
Replace exhaust Y-pipe, Eldorado	—	—	—	—	—	.8	.8	.8	.8	.8
Replace exhaust pipe flange gasket, one	.9	.9	.9	.9	.9	.9	.9	.9	.9	.9
Free-up or O/H heat control valve	.7	.7	.7	.7	.7	.7	.7	.7	.7	—
Test & repl. Early Fuel Evaporation (EFE) valve	—	—	—	—	—	—	—	—	—	.4
Replace catalytic converter	—	—	—	—	—	—	—	—	—	1.0
Replace catalytic converter catalyst	—	—	—	—	—	—	—	—	—	1.5
Replace bottom cover, **ADD:**	—	—	—	—	—	—	—	—	—	.5

Approximate parts cost:
Muffler	$50.00	Intermediate pipe	$15.00
Resonator assembly	40.00	Exhaust pipe, right or left	12.00
Exhaust manifold gasket, each	3.00	Y-pipe	30.00
Catalytic converter pellets & bottom cover kit	70.00	Catalytic converter	175.00

72 CADILLAC

AUTOMATIC TRANSMISSION, PERFORMANCE CHECK

Includes:
Basic Job: Conduct transmission performance check. Clean transmission case and operate unit to check case, oil cooler and oil cooler lines for external leaks. Remove oil pan, clean pan, screen or filter. Torque valve body mounting bolts. Adjust shift linkage. Perform pressure checks of mainline, throttle, and accumulator. Road test.
Related Jobs: Work which does not include R&R transmission and may be done as separate job.

MODEL	1966	1967	1968	1969	1970	1971	1972	1973	1974	1975
Basic Job:										
Complete trans. performance check	2.1	2.1	2.1	2.1	2.1	2.1	2.1	2.1	2.1	2.1
Related Jobs:										
Drain & fill trans., clean filter	.8	.8	.8	.8	.8	.8	.8	.8	.8	.8
Check for oil leaks	.7	.7	.7	.7	.7	.7	.7	.7	.7	.7
Repl. oil pan gasket, incl. clean filter	.9	.9	.9	.9	.9	.9	.9	.9	.9	.9
Replace parking linkage & detent assy., **ADD:**	.6	.6	.6	.6	.6	.6	.6	.6	.6	.6
Repl. rear oil seal & O-ring	1.0	1.0	.7	.5	.5	.5	.5	.5	.5	.5
Repl. neutral safety switch	.5	.5	.5	.5	.5	.5	.5	.5	.5	.5
Overhaul governor, incl. complete trans. performance check, 375/400/425 THM	3.1	3.1	3.1	3.1	3.1	3.1	3.1	3.1	3.0	3.0
Overhaul valve body assembly	2.0	2.0	2.0	2.0	2.0	2.0	2.0	2.0	2.0	2.0
Remove, test, and replace vacuum modulator	.5	.5	.5	.5	.5	.5	.5	.5	.5	.5

Approximate parts cost:
Transmission fluid, per qt.	$1.20
Oil pan gasket	1.00
Rear oil seal	4.50
Parking linkage & detent assembly	8.50
Neutral safety switch	$ 3.50
Governor body repair kit	18.00
Valve body assy., new	80.00
Vacuum modulator	18.00

AUTOMATIC TRANSMISSION, SHIFT AND LINKAGE CONTROLS, REPLACE AND ADJUST

Includes:
Replace defective part and make necessary adjustment(s).

MODEL	1966	1967	1968	1969	1970	1971	1972	1973	1974	1975
Adjust manual linkage	.4	.4	.4	.4	.4	.4	.4	.4	.4	.4
Replace lower shifter lever	.4	.4	.4	.4	.4	.4	.4	.4	.4	.4
Replace shift rod rubber bushings	.6	.6	.6	.6	.6	.6	.6	.6	.6	.6
Replace shift control key lock assembly	.7	.7	.7	.7	.7	.7	.7	.7	.7	.7
Remove, test, and replace vacuum modulator	.6	.6	.6	.6	.6	.6	.6	.6	.6	.6
Replace neutral safety switch	.5	.5	.5	.5	.5	.5	.5	.5	.5	.5
Replace kickdown switch	.3	.3	.3	.3	.3	.3	.3	.3	.3	.3

Approximate parts cost:
Lower shifter lever	$5.00
Shift rod bushings, pkg.	1.00
Shift control key lock assembly	7.50
Kickdown switch	5.00
Vacuum modulator hose, per ft.	$ 0.25
Vacuum modulator	18.00
Neutral safety switch	12.00

CADILLAC 73

AUTOMATIC TRANSMISSION, MAJOR SERVICE

Includes:

Basic Jobs:
1. Overhaul transmission. Disassemble, clean, inspect and replace all worn parts as needed. Replace all oil seals. Adjust shift linkage as required. Flush converter and cooler lines. Perform pressure checks of mainline, throttle, and accumulator. Road test.
2. Replace torque converter. R&R transmission. Flush oil cooler and lines. Replace transmission oil and oil filter. Perform pressure checks of mainline, throttle, and accumulator. Adjust shift linkage as required.
3. Reseal transmission. R&R transmission. Replace all seals and gaskets. Replace transmission oil and oil filter. Check oil cooler for leaks. Perform pressure checks of mainline, throttle, and accumulator. Adjust shift linkage as required. Road test.

Additions to Basic Jobs: Associated work that is performed while the transmission is out during one of basic jobs.

MODEL	1966	1967	1968	1969	1970	1971	1972	1973	1974	1975
Basic Job #1										
Overhaul transmission,										
Eldorado	—	12.3	12.3	12.3	12.3	12.3	12.3	12.5	12.5	12.5
All others	10.5	10.5	10.5	10.5	10.5	10.5	10.5	9.4	9.4	9.4
Basic Job #2										
Replace torque converter,										
Eldorado	—	6.1	6.1	6.1	6.1	6.3	6.3	6.3	6.3	6.3
All others	5.1	5.1	5.1	5.1	5.1	5.1	5.1	4.0	4.0	4.0
Basic Job #3										
Reseal transmission,										
Eldorado	—	7.7	7.7	7.7	7.7	7.9	7.9	9.5	9.5	9.5
All others	7.0	7.0	7.0	7.0	7.0	7.0	7.0	7.5	7.5	7.5
Additions to Basic Jobs:										
Replace oil cooler pipes, both, **ADD:**	.9	.9	.9	.9	.9	.9	.9	.9	.9	.9
Replace oil filler pipe and/or seal, **ADD:**	.5	.5	.5	.5	.5	.5	.5	.5	.5	.5
Replace torque converter ring gear, **ADD:**	.5	.5	.5	.5	.5	.5	.5	.5	.5	.5

Approximate parts cost:

Transmission seal and gasket kit	$20.00	Oil filler pipe	$ 4.00
Transmission partial overhaul kit	56.00	Oil filler pipe seal	0.25
Oil cooler pipe, each	9.00	Oil pan	8.00
Torque converter assembly	200.00	Oil pan gasket	1.00
Torque converter ring gear	8.00	Governor kit	19.00

DRIVESHAFT, SERVICE

Includes:

Basic Job: R&R driveshaft and overhaul or replace front and rear U-joints. Measure and adjust U-joint and driveshaft angles. Balance driveshaft.

MODEL	1966	1967	1968	1969	1970	1971	1972	1973	1974	1975
Basic Job:										
R&R driveshaft & overhaul both U-joints,										
Constant velocity joints (2)	1.8	1.8	1.8	1.8	1.8	1.8	1.8	1.8	1.8	1.8
Constant velocity joints (3)	2.2	2.2	2.2	2.2	2.2	2.2	2.2	2.2	2.2	2.2
R&R driveshaft with joints	1.1	1.1	1.1	1.1	1.1	1.1	1.1	1.1	1.1	1.1

Approximate parts cost:

Constant velocity joint	$60.00	Driveshaft with joints (2)	$140.00
Constant velocity joint kit	12.00		

74 CADILLAC

REAR AXLE/FINAL DRIVE, SERVICE

Includes:
Basic Jobs: 1. (Except Eldorado) R&R driveshaft, R&R axle shafts, overhaul differential assembly. Measure and adjust U-joint and driveshaft angles. Balance driveshaft.
2. (Except Eldorado) R&R driveshaft and replace pinion bearing oil seal. Check pinion bearing preload. Measure and adjust driveshaft angles. Balance driveshaft.
Related Jobs: R&R axle shaft (one side) and/or bearing and seals. Replace axle shaft wheel mounting stud.
Basic Job: 3. (Eldorado) Replace final drive unit and related parts **Note:** Final drive unit cannot be serviced but must be replaced as an assembly, with the exception of external seals. Jobs listed below in the schedule can be individually performed as indicated.
Related Work to Basic Job 3 (El Dorado): Service axle shafts, constant-velocity joints, and output shaft.

MODEL	1966	1967	1968	1969	1970	1971	1972	1973	1974	1975
Basic Job #1										
Overhaul differential assembly	5.5	5.5	5.5	5.5	5.5	5.5	5.5	5.5	5.5	5.5
With Posi-traction, **ADD:**	.6	.6	.6	.6	.6	.6	.6	.6	.6	.6
Basic Job #2										
Replace drive pinion bearing oil seal	1.2	1.2	1.2	1.7	1.7	1.7	1.7	1.7	1.7	1.7
Related Jobs:										
R&R axle shaft (one side), and/or bearing & seals	1.3	1.3	1.3	1.3	1.3	1.3	1.3	1.3	1.3	1.3
Replace axle shaft wheel mounting stud	.8	.8	.8	.8	.8	.8	.8	.8	.8	.8
Basic Job #3										
R&R final drive unit	—	3.0	3.0	3.0	3.0	3.0	3.0	3.0	3.0	3.0
Repl. pinion brg. cover and/or O-ring seal, **ADD:**	—	.3	.3	.3	.3	.3	.3	.3	.3	.3
Replace pinion bearing seal and/or vent pin seal, **ADD:**	—	.4	.4	.4	.4	.4	.4	.4	.4	.4
Replace output shaft seal, **ADD:**	—	.2	.2	.2	.2	.2	.2	.2	.2	.2
Replace final drive cover gasket, **ADD:**	—	.4	.4	.4	.4	.4	.4	.4	.4	.4
Replace final drive link belt, **ADD:**	—	.6	.6	.6	.6	.6	.6	.6	.6	.6
Related Work to Basic Job #3										
Replace axle shaft assemblies,										
Right axle	—	.7	.7	.7	.7	.7	.7	.7	.7	.7
Left axle	—	1.1	1.1	1.1	1.1	1.1	1.1	1.1	1.1	1.1
Both axles	—	1.7	1.7	1.7	1.7	1.7	1.7	1.7	1.7	1.7
Repack or replace right or left outer C.V. joint, **ADD:**	—	.5	.5	.5	.5	.5	.5	.5	.5	.5
Repack or replace right or left inner C.V. joint, **ADD:**	—	.8	.8	.8	.8	.8	.8	.8	.8	.8
Repack/repl. both right or both left C.V. joints, **ADD:**	—	1.2	1.2	1.2	1.2	1.2	1.2	1.2	1.2	1.2
Replace output shaft,										
Right side	—	.5	.5	.5	.5	.5	.5	.5	.5	.5
Left side	—	1.1	1.1	1.1	1.1	1.1	1.1	1.1	1.1	1.1
Both sides	—	1.5	1.5	1.5	1.5	1.5	1.5	1.5	1.5	1.5
Replace bearing or retainer on right shaft, **ADD:**	—	.3	.3	.3	.3	.3	.3	.3	.3	.3
Replace output shaft seal,										
Right side	—	.6	.6	.6	.6	.6	.6	.6	.6	.6
Left side	—	1.2	1.2	1.2	1.2	1.2	1.2	1.2	1.2	1.2

Approximate parts cost (Except Eldorado)

Axle shaft	$45.00
Inner or outer seal	2.00
Posi-traction repair kit	25.00
Pinion bearing oil seal	$ 3.00
Cover gasket	1.00
Ring & pinion gear set	100.00-125.00

Approximate parts cost (Eldorado)

Final drive housing	$130.00
Axle assy., w/shaft & joints	300.00
Pinion bearing O-ring	1.50
Output shaft seal	3.50
Output shaft bearing	17.00
Link belt & gear pkg.	220.00
Final drive cover gasket	$ 1.00
Right or left outer C.V. joint	160.00
Right or left inner C.V. joint	70.00
Right output shaft	74.00
Left output shaft	32.00

CADILLAC 75

REAR SUSPENSION, SERVICE

Includes:
Service for the rear suspension system listed as individual jobs. Add times if more than one job is performed.

MODEL	1966	1967	1968	1969	1970	1971	1972	1973	1974	1975
Repl. rear leaf spring & shim to align pinion angle, commercial chassis	1.6	1.6	1.6	1.6	1.8	1.8	1.8	1.7	1.7	1.7
Repl. shackle and bushings; eye bolt & bushings	.7	.7	.7	.7	.7	.7	.7	.7	.7	.7
Replace rear coil spring, both	2.5	2.5	2.5	2.5	2.5	2.5	2.5	2.5	2.5	2.5
Replace control arm,										
Upper arm, one	1.1	1.1	1.1	1.1	1.1	1.1	1.1	1.1	1.1	1.1
Lower arm, one	1.5	1.5	1.5	1.5	1.5	1.5	1.1	1.1	1.1	1.1
Replace shock absorber, both sides	.8	.8	.8	.8	.8	.8	.8	.8	.8	.8
With automatic level control, **ADD:**	.2	.2	.2	.2	.2	.2	.2	.2	.2	.2
Replace tie rod & stabilizer shaft (one)	.9	.9	.9	.9	.9	.9	.9	.9	.9	.9
Service Automatic Level Control										
Replace compressor assembly	.4	.4	.4	.4	.4	.4	.4	.4	.4	.4
Overhaul compressor assembly, **ADD:**	.7	.7	.7	.7	.7	.7	.7	.7	.7	.7
Replace level control regulator	.3	.3	.3	.3	.3	.3	.3	.3	.3	.3
Replace level & height control valve	.4	.4	.4	.4	.4	.4	.4	.4	.4	.4

Approximate parts cost:

Shock absorber	$14.00	Shackle package	$ 7.00
Rear leaf spring	72.00	Shackle bushing package	1.00
Rear coil spring	27.00	Auto. level control regulator	24.00
Tie rod & stabilizer shaft	23.00	Level & height control valve	68.00
Auto level control compressor assy.	70.00		

FRONT END, TEST, SERVICE, AND ADJUST

Includes:
  Basic Job: All models; Check and adjust car height, caster, camber, steering axis inclination, turning radius, toe-in, pack and adjust front wheel bearings, replace seals.
  Related Jobs: 1. (Except Eldorado) Perform individual adjustments. Replace or overhaul defective components and make necessary adjustments.
                       2. (Eldorado) Perform individual adjustments. Replace or overhaul defective components and make necessary adjustments.

MODEL	1966	1967	1968	1969	1970	1971	1972	1973	1974	1975
Basic Job:										
Complete front end test and adjustment,										
Eldorado	—	3.0	3.0	3.0	3.0	3.0	3.0	3.0	3.0	3.0
All others	2.7	2.7	2.7	2.7	2.7	2.7	2.7	2.7	2.7	2.7
Related Jobs: #1 (Except Eldorado)										
Adjust toe-in only	.4	.4	.4	.4	.4	.4	.4	.4	.4	.4
Repack wheel bearings only, incl. new seals	1.3	1.3	1.3	1.3	1.3	1.3	1.3	1.3	1.3	1.3
Replace wheel bearings only, each side	.8	.8	.8	.8	.8	.9	.9	.9	.9	.9
Balance four wheels on car,										
With drum brakes	1.2	1.2	1.2	—	—	—	—	—	—	—
With disc brakes	—	—	1.5	1.5	1.5	1.5	1.5	1.5	1.5	1.5
Overhaul front suspension, incl. disassemble, replace necessary parts, lube., & complete front end adjustment	7.9	7.9	7.9	7.9	7.9	7.9	7.9	7.9	7.9	7.9
Repl. coil spring, one side, incl. complete front end adjustment	4.4	4.4	4.4	4.4	4.4	4.1	4.1	4.1	4.1	4.1
Replace lower spherical joint, one side, includes R&R lower control arm and complete front end adjustment	4.6	4.6	4.6	4.6	4.6	4.6	4.6	4.6	4.6	4.6

76 CADILLAC

FRONT END, TEST, SERVICE, AND ADJUST Continued

MODEL	1966	1967	1968	1969	1970	1971	1972	1973	1974	1975
Related Jobs: #1 (Except Eldorado) Continued										
Replace upper spherical joint, one side, (replaced as an assembly with upper control arm), includes complete front end adjustment	5.5	5.5	5.5	5.5	5.5	5.5	5.5	5.5	5.5	5.5
Repl. steering knuckle, one side, incl. complete front end adjustment	3.6	3.6	3.6	3.6	3.6	3.6	3.6	3.6	3.6	3.6
Replace shock absorber, both sides	.9	.9	.9	.9	.9	.9	.9	.9	.9	.9
Repl. control arm rubber bumpers, ea. side	.3	.3	.3	.3	.3	.3	.3	.3	.3	.3
Replace tie strut, one side, incl. disconnect and connect stabilizer link	.6	.6	.6	.6	.6	.6	.6	.6	.6	.6
Replace stabilizer bar and bushings	1.1	1.1	1.1	1.1	1.1	1.1	1.1	1.1	1.1	1.1
Replace both stabilizer links or grommets	.7	.7	.7	.7	.7	.7	.7	.7	.7	.7
Related Jobs #2 (Eldorado)										
Adjust toe-in only	—	.4	.4	.4	.4	.4	.4	.4	.4	.4
Adjust torsion bar (car height)	—	.3	.3	.3	.3	.3	.3	.3	.3	.3
Balance four wheels on car	—	1.2	1.5	1.5	1.5	1.5	1.5	1.5	1.5	1.5
Overhaul front suspension, incl. disassemble, replace necessary parts, lube., & complete front end adjustment	—	10.8	10.8	10.8	10.8	10.8	10.8	10.8	10.8	10.8
Repl. torsion bar, one side, incl. compl. front end adjust.	—	3.3	3.3	3.3	3.3	3.3	3.3	2.8	2.8	2.8
Replace steering knuckle inner seal, one side, incl. complete front end adjustment	—	4.8	4.8	4.8	4.8		4.7	4.7	4.7	4.7
Replace hub, bearings, cups & seals, **ADD:**	—	.7	.7	.7	.7	.7	.7	.7	.7	.7
Replace axle shaft assemblies,										
Right axle	—	.7	.7	.7	.7	.7	.7	.7	.7	.7
Left axle	—	1.1	1.1	1.1	1.1	1.1	1.1	1.1	1.1	1.1
Both axles	—	1.7	1.7	1.7	1.7	1.7	1.7	1.7	1.7	1.7
Repack or replace right or left outer C.V. joint, **ADD:**	—	.5	.5	.5	.5	.5	.5	.5	.5	.5
Repack or replace right or left inner C.V. joint, **ADD:**	—	.8	.8	.8	.8	.8	.8	.8	.8	.8
Repack/replace both right or both left C.V. joints, **ADD:**	—	1.2	1.2	1.2	1.2	1.2	1.2	1.2	1.2	1.2
Replace output shaft,										
Right side	—	.5	.5	.5	.5	.5	.5	.5	.5	.5
Left side	—	1.1	1.1	1.1	1.1	1.1	1.1	1.1	1.1	1.1
Both sides	—	1.5	1.5	1.5	1.5	1.5	1.5	1.5	1.5	1.5
Replace bearing or retainer on right shaft, **ADD:**	—	.3	.3	.3	.3	.3	.3	.3	.3	.3
Replace output shaft seal,										
Right side	—	.6	.6	.6	.6	.6	.6	.6	.6	.6
Left side	—	1.2	1.2	1.2	1.2	1.2	1.2	1.2	1.2	1.2
Replace lower spherical joint, one side, includes R&R lower control arm and complete front end adjustment	—	5.2	5.2	5.2	5.2	5.2	5.2	5.2	5.2	5.2
Replace upper spherical joint, one side, (replaced as an assy. with upper control arm), incl. compl. front end adjust.	—	6.8	6.8	6.8	6.8	6.8	6.1	6.1	6.1	6.1
Replace stabilizer bar & bushings	—	1.1	1.1	1.1	1.1	1.1	1.1	1.1	1.1	1.1
Replace both stabilizer links or grommets	—	.7	.7	.7	.7	.7	.7	.7	.7	.7
Replace tie strut, one side, incl. disconnect and connect stabilizer link	—	.6	.6	.6	.6	.6	.6	.6	.6	.6
Replace shock absorber, both sides	—	.9	.9	.9	.9	.9	.9	.9	.9	.9

Approximate parts cost: (Except Eldorado)

Coil spring, ea.	$25.00
Lower spherical joint kit	16.00
Upper spherical joint and control arm assembly	35.00
Steering knuckle	50.00
Shock absorber, ea.	15.00
Wheel bearing seals	2.00
Stabilizer link kit, ea.	$ 2.50
Stabilizer bar and bushings	17.00
Tie strut	15.00
Wheel bearing, outer	5.00
Wheel bearing, inner	6.00

(THIS SCHEDULE CONTINUED ON NEXT PAGE.)

CADILLAC 77

FRONT END, TEST, SERVICE AND ADJUST Continued

Approximate parts cost: (Eldorado)

Torsion bar, ea.	$30.00
Lower spherical joint kit	16.00
Upper spherical joint and control arm assembly	35.00
Steering knuckle	50.00
Shock absorber, ea.	15.00
Tie strut	15.00
Stabilizer link kit, ea.	2.50
Right or left outer C.V. joint	$160.00
Right or left inner C.V. joint	70.00
Output shaft bearing	17.00
Right output shaft	74.00
Left output shaft	32.00
Output shaft seal	3.50
Stabilizer bar and bushing	17.00

POWER STEERING UNIT, TEST AND SERVICE

Includes:

Basic Job: Adjust drive belt tension; hook-up gauges to check pressure on left and right turns. Adjust steering gear box over-center torque and control valve to balance left and right steering effort.
Additions to Basic Job: Service power steering unit.
Related Jobs: R&R power steering unit, pump, or other associated parts.
Additions to Related Jobs: Overhaul steering unit or pump including replacement of all seals and worn parts.

MODEL	1966	1967	1968	1969	1970	1971	1972	1973	1974	1975
Basic Job:										
Complete test and adjustment of power steering unit	1.0	1.0	1.0	1.0	1.0	1.0	1.0	1.0	1.0	1.0
Additions to basic job:										
Replace power steering pump drive belt, **ADD:**	.3	.3	.3	.3	.3	.3	.3	.3	.3	.3
With air conditioning, **ADD:**	.2	.2	.2	.2	.2	.2	.2	.2	.2	.2
Check & replenish reservoir fluid, **ADD:**	.2	.2	.2	.2	.2	.2	.2	.2	.2	.2
Related Jobs:										
Replace pressure hoses, either set, includes adjust drive belt	.6	.6	.6	.6	.6	.6	.6	.6	.6	.6
With air conditioning, **ADD:**	.1	.1	.1	.1	.1	.1	.1	.1	.1	.1
Replace pump reservoir or O-ring seals	1.1	1.1	1.1	1.1	1.1	1.1	1.2	1.2	1.2	1.2
With air conditioning, **ADD:**	.1	.1	.1	.1	.1	.1	.1	.1	.2	.2
Replace pump, includes pressure-test original pump and transfer pulley, fill and bleed system	.8	.8	.8	.8	.8	.8	.8	.8	.8	.8
With air conditioning, **ADD:**	.1	.1	.1	.1	.1	.1	.1	.1	.1	.1
R&R power steering unit, includes test original unit and complete adjustment,										
Eldorado	2.5	2.5	2.5	2.5	2.5	2.5	2.5	2.5	2.5	2.5
All others	2.3	2.3	2.3	2.3	2.3	2.3	2.3	2.3	2.3	2.3
Additions to Related Jobs:										
Overhaul power steering unit, **ADD:**	2.2	2.2	2.2	2.2	2.4	2.4	2.4	2.4	3.0	3.0
O/H pump, incl. new kit & seals, **ADD:**	.8	.8	.8	.8	.8	.8	.8	.6	.6	.6

Approximate parts cost:

Drive belt	$ 4.00
Pressure hose	16.00
Return hose	4.00
Control valve	8.00
Control valve seal kit	2.00
Power steering unit, valve assembly	85.00
Power cylinder	$33.00
Power cylinder piston rod seal kit	2.50
Hydraulic pump	90.00
Hydraulic reservoir	15.00
Hydraulic pump seal kit	4.00
Hydraulic pump repair kit	32.00

78 CADILLAC

STEERING LINKAGE, SERVICE AND ADJUST

Includes:
  Basic Job: Adjust toe-in.
  Related Jobs: Replace defective parts and adjust toe-in.

MODEL	1966	1967	1968	1969	1970	1971	1972	1973	1974	1975
Basic Job:										
Adjust toe-in	.4	.4	.4	.4	.4	.4	.4	.4	.4	.4
Related Jobs:										
Replace tie-rods or tie-rod ends, (4),	1.4	1.4	1.4	1.4	1.4	1.6	1.6	1.6	1.6	1.6
Replace Pitman arm, includes adjust toe-in,										
Eldorado	—	*1.5	*1.5	*1.5	*1.5	.5	.5	.5	*1.2	*1.2
All others	*1.5	*1.5	*1.5	*1.5	*1.5	.5	.5	.5	.5	.5
*Includes R & R steering gear.										
Repl. steering idler arm or bushing	.7	.7	.7	.7	.7	.5	.5	.5	.5	.5

Approximate parts cost:
Tie-rod end pkg. .... $15.00   Idler arm & bracket $18.00
Pitman arm .... 10.00   Tie rod 12.00

BRAKES, SERVICE

Includes:
  Basic Job: Install new linings or pads, turn brake drums or rotors, lubricate and adjust front wheel bearings, replace rear oil seals, bleed hydraulic system, and adjust brakes.
  Additions to Basic Job: Overhaul wheel cylinders, overhaul or replace front calipers.
  Related Jobs: Performed at time other than during basic job. Overhaul or replace front calipers.

MODEL	1966	1967	1968	1969	1970	1971	1972	1973	1974	1975
Basic Job:										
Complete job incl. turn drums or rotors,										
Drum (4) Eldorado	—	6.8	—	—	—	—	—	—	—	—
Drum (4) All others	6.3	6.3	—	—	—	—	—	—	—	—
Disc front, drum rear, Eldorado	—	—	7.4	7.4	7.4	7.4	7.4	7.4	7.4	7.4
Disc front, drum rear, All others	—	—	6.9	6.9	6.9	6.9	6.9	6.9	6.9	6.9
Additions to Basic Job:										
O/H 4 wheel cylinders, incl. hone, **ADD:**	2.0	2.0	—	—	—	—	—	—	—	—
O/H front calipers (both), **ADD:**	—	—	.5	.5	.5	.5	.5	.5	.5	.5
O/H master cylinder, **ADD:**	.8	.8	.8	.8	.8	.8	.8	.8	.8	.8
Related Jobs: (Not during basic job)										
Bleed hydraulic system, 4 wheels	.6	.6	.6	.6	.6	.6	.6	.6	.6	.6
Adjust drum brakes, 4 wheels	5.	.5	—	—	—	—	—	—	—	—
Adjust parking brake cables	.3	.3	.3	.3	.3	.3	.3	.3	.3	.3
Replace disc brake pads, front wheels	—	—	1.5	1.5	1.5	1.5	1.0	1.0	1.0	1.0
Replace drum brake shoes, 4 wheels	3.5	3.5	—	—	—	—	—	—	—	—
Replace drum brake shoes, rear wheels	1.6	1.6	1.6	1.6	1.6	1.6	1.6	1.6	1.6	1.6
O/H front calipers, incl. turn rotors,										
Eldorado	—	—	5.1	4.5	4.5	4.5	4.5	4.5	4.5	4.5
All others	—	—	4.6	4.0	4.0	4.0	4.0	4.0	4.0	4.0
Replace front caliper, incl. turn rotor, ea.,										
Eldorado	—	—	3.5	2.9	2.9	2.9	2.9	2.9	2.9	2.9
All others	—	—	3.0	2.4	2.4	2.4	2.4	2.4	2.4	2.4
Overhaul master cylinder	1.3	1.3	1.5	1.5	1.5	1.5	1.8	1.8	1.8	1.8
R&R skid control modulator	—	—	—	—	—	.7	.7	.7	.7	.7
R&R wire harness, modulator to controller	—	—	—	—	—	.6	.6	.6	.6	.6

(THIS SCHEDULE CONTINUED ON NEXT PAGE.)

CADILLAC

BRAKES, SERVICE Continued

Approximate parts cost:
Wheel cylinder seal, boot & bushing pkg.	$ 6.00	Wheel cylinder repair kit, ea.	$ 3.50
Brake shoes and lining sets, front or rear	25.00	Caliper brake housing	50.00
Disc brake pads, set of 2	24.00	Oil seal, ea.	2.00
Master cylinder repair kit	18.00	Skid control modulator	150.00
Skid control wire harness, modulator	28.00		

HYDRAULIC BRAKE SYSTEM, OVERHAUL

Includes:
Basic Job: Overhaul, including hone or replace master cylinder, all wheel cylinders or calipers; bleed hydraulic system; and adjust brakes.
Related Jobs: Work performed at time other than during basic job. Overhaul or replace master cylinder only; overhaul wheel cylinders or calipers.

MODEL	1966	1967	1968	1969	1970	1971	1972	1973	1974	1975
Basic Job:										
Complete job, including master & wheel cylinders,										
Drum (4) Eldorado	—	5.2	—	—	—	—	—	—	—	—
Drum (4) All others	4.7	4.7	—	—	—	—	—	—	—	—
Disc front, drum rear, Eldorado	—	—	5.0	4.4	4.4	4.4	4.4	4.4	4.4	4.4
Disc front, drum rear, All others	—	—	4.5	3.9	3.9	3.9	3.9	3.9	3.9	3.9
Related Jobs: (Not during basic job)										
Overhaul master cylinder, including hone	1.3	1.3	1.5	1.5	1.5	1.5	1.8	1.8	1.8	1.8
Replace master cylinder	.5	.5	.8	.8	.8	.8	1.1	1.1	1.1	1.1
Overhaul 4 wheel cylinders, incl. hone	4.1	4.1	—	—	—	—	—	—	—	—
O/H 2 rear wheel cylinders, incl. hone	2.1	2.1	2.1	2.1	2.1	2.1	2.1	2.1	2.1	2.1
O/H front calipers, incl. turn rotors,										
Eldorado	—	—	5.1	4.5	4.5	4.5	4.5	4.5	4.5	4.5
All others	—	—	4.6	4.0	4.0	4.0	4.0	4.0	4.0	4.0

Approximate parts cost:
Master cylinder repair kit	$18.00	Master cylinder	$30.00-55.00
Wheel cylinder repair kit, ea.	3.50	Wheel cylinder seal, boot & bushing pkg.	6.00
Caliper repair kit	4.00		

POWER BRAKE UNIT, SERVICE

Includes:
Basic Job: R&R with new unit, test, and adjust brakes.
Additions to Basic Job: Replace vacuum hose or vacuum check valve. Allowance for air conditioning.

MODEL	1966	1967	1968	1969	1970	1971	1972	1973	1974	1975
Basic Job:										
R&R power unit, test, & adj. brakes	1.6	1.6	1.6	1.6	1.6	1.6	1.6	1.6	1.6	1.6
Additions to Basic Job:										
Install new hose, **ADD:**	.2	.2	.2	.2	.2	.2	.2	.2	.2	.2
Install new vacuum check valve, **ADD:**	.2	.2	.2	.2	.2	.2	.2	.2	.2	.2
With air conditioning, **ADD:**	.3	.3	.3	.3	.3	.3	.3	.3	.3	.3

Approximate parts cost:
Power brake unit	$50.00-70.00	Vacuum check valve	$1.75
Brake booster repair kit	16.00	Vacuum hose, per ft	0.90

80 CADILLAC

PARKING BRAKES, SERVICE AND ADJUST

Includes:
    Basic Jobs: Replace defective cable and adjust parking brakes.

MODEL	1966	1967	1968	1969	1970	1971	1972	1973	1974	1975
Basic Jobs:										
Adjust parking brakes	.4	.4	.4	.4	.4	.4	.4	.4	.4	.4
Replace forward cable	.5	.5	.5	.5	.5	.5	.5	.5	.5	.5
Replace rear cable, one side	.4	.4	.4	.4	.4	.4	.4	.4	.4	.4
Replace rear cable, both sides	.6	.6	.6	.6	.6	.6	.6	.6	.6	.6
Replace center cable	.5	.5	.5	.5	.5	.5	.5	.5	.5	.5

Approximate parts cost:
Front cable ....$5.00   Rear cable 8.00
Center cable 3.50

LIGHTING SYSTEM, ADJUST AND SERVICE

Includes:
    Basic Job: 1. Adjust headlights to inspection requirements.
                      2. Replace defective parts in rear lighting system.
    Additions to Basic Job: Replace associated parts affecting headlight adjustment.
    Related Jobs: Replace associated parts not affecting headlight adjustment.

MODEL	1966	1967	1968	1969	1970	1971	1972	1973	1974	1975
Basic Job #1										
Adjust two headlights	.4	.4	.4	.4	.4	.4	.4	.4	.4	.4
Adjust four headlights	.6	.6	.6	.6	.6	.6	.6	.6	.6	.6
Basic Job #2										
Replace stoplight switch	.3	.3	.3	.3	.3	.3	.3	.3	.3	.3
Replace back-up light switch	.4	.4	.4	.4	.4	.4	.4	.4	.4	.4
Additions to Basic Job:										
Replace sealed beam unit, ea., ADD:	.3	.3	.3	.3	.3	.3	.3	.3	.3	.3
Related Jobs:										
Replace headlamp door vacuum actuator	.8	.8	—	—	—	—	—	—	—	—
Replace headlamp switch	1.2	1.2	1.2	1.2	.4	.4	.4	.4	.4	.4
Replace foot dimmer switch	.3	.3	.3	.3	.3	.3	.3	.3	.3	.3
Replace signal/hazard flasher	.2	.2	.2	.2	.2	.2	.2	.2	.2	.2
Replace signal/hazard switch,										
With standard column	1.2	1.2	1.2	1.2	1.2	1.2	1.2	1.2	1.2	1.2
With tilt column	1.5	1.5	1.5	1.5	1.5	1.5	1.5	1.5	1.5	1.5

Approximate parts cost:
Sealed beam unit ....$ 4.00   Vacuum actuator $20.00
Signal/hazard flasher ....2.00   Headlamp switch 9.00
Signal/hazard switch ....18.00   Back-up light switch 13.00

HEATING SYSTEM, TEST AND SERVICE

Includes:
    Basic Job: Drain, back-flush, and fill radiator; check radiator and heater hoses and connections; pressure-test radiator cap and system.
    Related Jobs: Replace defective parts. Work performed individually and independently of basic job.

MODEL	1966	1967	1968	1969	1970	1971	1972	1973	1974	1975
Basic Job:										
Drain, flush, fill, check & pressure-test	.9	.9	.9	.9	.9	.9	.9	.9	.9	.9

(THIS SCHEDULE CONTINUED ON NEXT PAGE.)

CADILLAC 81

HEATING SYSTEM, TEST AND SERVICE Continued

MODEL	1966	1967	1968	1969	1970	1971	1972	1973	1974	1975
Related Jobs:										
Replace heater hose, one, inlet or outlet	.5	.5	.5	.5	.5	.5	.5	.5	.5	.5
Replace ea. additional hose, **ADD:**	.2	.2	.2	.2	.2	.2	.2	.2	.2	.2
With air conditioning, **ADD:**	.3	.3	.3	.3	.3	.3	.3	.3	.3	.3
Replace blower motor and/or impeller	.4	.4	.4	.4	.4	.4	.4	.4	.4	.4
Lubricate bearings, **ADD:**	.3	.3	.3	.3	.3	.3	.3	.3	.3	.3
Replace blower fan, **ADD:**	.2	.2	.2	.2	.2	.2	.2	.2	.2	.2
Replace heater core,										
Eldorado	—	1.7	1.7	1.7	1.7	1.5	1.5	1.5	1.5	1.5
All others	1.4	1.4	1.4	1.4	1.4	1.4	1.4	1.4	1.4	1.4
With air conditioning, **ADD:**	.2	.2	.2	1.3	1.3	.6	.6	.6	.6	.6
Replace heater switch	1.0	1.0	1.0	1.0	1.0	.5	.5	.5	.5	.5
Replace water control valve	.5	.5	.5	.5	.5	.5	.5	.5	.5	.5

Approximate parts cost:

Heater hose, per ft .... $ 0.75	Heater core 43.00
Blower motor 20.00-50.00	Heater control 5.00
Heater control valve 5.00	

AIR CONDITIONING SYSTEM, MAJOR SERVICE

Includes:
    Basic Job: Drain system in order to replace defective component; evacuate, dehydrate, and recharge system; pressure-test and leak-check; clean condenser fins; adjust drive belt tension; tighten compressor, condenser, and evaporator mounts; and performance test.
    Additions to Basic Job: Replace or overhaul compressor. Replace other defective parts.

MODEL	1966	1967	1968	1969	1970	1971	1972	1973	1974	1975
Basic Job:										
Drain, evacuate, dehydrate, charge & test.	3.0	3.0	3.0	3.0	3.0	3.0	3.0	3.0	3.0	3.0

AIR CONDITIONING SYSTEM, SPRING TUNE-UP

Includes:
    Basic Job: Clean condenser fins; adjust drive belt tension; test anti-freeze; tighten compressor, condenser, and evaporator mounts; pressure-test and leak-check system; check system for performance.
    Additions to Basic Job: Replace defective parts.

MODEL	1966	1967	1968	1969	1970	1971	1972	1973	1974	1975
Basic Job:										
Perform complete spring tune-up	2.0	2.0	2.0	2.0	2.0	2.0	2.0	2.0	2.0	2.0
Additions to Basic Job:										
Replace compressor belt & adjust, **ADD:**	.4	.4	.4	.4	.4	.4	.4	.4	.4	.4
Repl. compr. clutch pulley w/hub assy., **ADD:**	.5	.5	.5	.5	.5	.5	.5	.5	.5	.5
Repl. compr. clutch coil, **ADD:**	.8	.8	.8	.8	.8	.8	.8	.8	.8	.8
Repl. compr. clutch bearing, **ADD:**	.8	.8	.8	.8	.8	.8	.8	.8	.8	.8

Approximate parts cost:

Compressor drive belt .... $ 3.00	Compressor clutch coil $28.00
Compressor clutch pulley w/hub 75.00	Compressor clutch bearing 23.00
Freon, per 14 oz. can 2.50	Anti-freeze, per gal. 9.50

(THIS SCHEDULE CONTINUED ON NEXT PAGE.)

82 CADILLAC

AIR CONDITIONING SYSTEM, MAJOR SERVICE Continued

MODEL	1966	1967	1968	1969	1970	1971	1972	1973	1974	1975
Additions to Basic Job:										
Replace compressor, **ADD**:	1.2	1.2	1.2	1.2	1.2	1.2	1.2	1.2	1.2	1.2
Overhaul compressor, incl. R&R, **ADD**:	2.9	2.9	2.9	2.9	2.9	2.9	2.9	2.9	.29	2.9
Replace relief valve, **ADD**:	1.5	1.5	1.5	1.5	.8	.8	.8	.8	.8	.8
Repl. compr. front head or reed valve, **ADD**:	1.4	1.4	1.4	1.4	1.4	1.4	.5	.5	.5	.5
Repl. compr. rear head or reed valve, **ADD**:	1.1	1.1	1.1	1.1	1.1	1.1	.6	.6	.6	.6
Replace suction throttling valve, **ADD**:	.6	.6	.6	.6	.6	.6	.6	.6	.6	.6
Replace condenser, **ADD**:	1.3	1.3	1.3	1.3	1.3	1.3	1.3	1.3	1.3	1.3
Replace evaporator core,										
Eldorado, **ADD**:	—	1.8	1.8	1.8	1.8	1.8	1.6	1.6	1.6	1.6
All others, **ADD**:	1.6	1.6	1.6	3.0	3.0	1.6	1.6	1.6	1.6	1.6
With AIR, **ADD**:	.2	.2	.2	.2	.2	.2	.2	.2	.2	.2
Replace sight-glass, **ADD**:	1.4	1.4	1.4	1.4	1.4	1.4	.9	.9	.9	.9
Replace dehydrator-receiver tank, **ADD**:	.5	.5	.5	.5	.5	.5	.5	.5	.5	.5
Replace expansion valve, **ADD**:	1.5	1.5	1.5	1.5	1.5	.8	.8	.8	.8	.8
Replace POA valve, **ADD**:	.7	.7	.7	.7	.7	.5	.5	.5	.5	.5
Replace compressor shaft seal, **ADD**:	1.4	1.4	1.4	1.4	1.4	.9	.9	.9	.9	.9
Replace valves-in-receiver (VIR) assy. **ADD**:	—	—	—	—	—	—	—	.6	.6	.6
O/H VIR assy. incl. repl. nec. parts, **ADD**:	—	—	—	—	—	—	—	1.0	1.0	1.0
Replace one hose, **ADD**:	.4	.4	.4	.4	.4	.4	.4	.4	.4	.4

Approximate parts cost:

Compressor	$ 85.00	Expansion valve	$36.00
Compressor front head & valve assy.	20.00	Pressure-operated absolute (POA) valve	30.00
Compressor rear head & valve assy.	65.00	Hose, per ft.	2.75
Compressor pressure relief valve	7.00	Hose fitting, ea.	1.00
Condenser	75.00-125.00	Freon, per 14 oz. can	2.50
Evaporator core assy	90.00-160.00	Anti-freeze, per gal.	9.50
Compressor shaft seal assy	8.00		

AIR CONDITIONING SYSTEM BLOWER MOTOR OR CONTROLS, SERVICE

Includes:

Basic Jobs: Conduct performance test of system to determine defective part; R&R component; clean condenser fins; adjust drive belt tension; tighten all mounts; and test system.

MODEL	1966	1967	1968	1969	1970	1971	1972	1973	1974	1975
Basic Jobs:										
R&R blower motor	1.5	1.5	1.5	1.5	1.5	1.5	1.5	1.5	1.5	1.5
Lubricate bearings, **ADD**:	.3	.3	.3	.3	.3	.3	.3	.3	.3	.3
Replace blower fan, **ADD**:	.2	.2	.2	.2	.2	.2	.2	.2	.2	.2
R&R blower motor switch	2.1	2.1	2.1	2.1	2.1	1.6	1.6	1.6	1.6	1.6
R&R compressor clutch switch	1.1	1.1	1.1	1.1	1.1	—	—	—	—	—
R&R evaporator thermostatic switch	1.1	1.1	1.1	1.1	1.1	1.1	1.1	1.1	1.1	1.1
R&R control assembly										
Replace control cable, temperature door	.7	.7	.7	.7	.7	1.0	1.0	1.0	1.0	1.0
Replace programmer	—	—	—	—	—	1.0	1.0	1.0	1.0	1.0

Approximate parts cost:

Blower motor	$23.00	Control cable, per ft	$ 0.80
Blower motor switch	3.00	Control cable fittings, ea.	0.75
Evaporator thermostatic switch	4.00	Control assembly	24.00
Compressor clutch switch	2.50	Programmer	75.00

CHEVROLET/CORVETTE 83

SERVICE STATION MAINTENANCE

Includes:
Basic Job: Lubricate chassis, drain oil, change filters, repack front wheel bearings, repack U-joints, and lubricate front end. Check fluid levels of battery, radiator, air conditioner, brake master cylinder, power steering reservoir, transmission, and differential. Check condition of hoses and drive belts. Lubricate miscellaneous moving parts, latches, hinges, etc.
Related Jobs: Service individual systems or components. See detailed description of work included for each job in separate major section.
Additions to Basic or Related Jobs: Allowances for special equipment installed.

MODEL	1966	1967	1968	1969	1970	1971	1972	1973	1974	1975
Basic Job:										
General lubrication & system check,										
4-cylinder	1.2	1.2	1.2	1.2	1.2	1.2	1.2	1.2	1.2	1.3
L-6 engine	1.0	1.0	1.0	1.0	1.0	1.0	1.0	1.0	1.1	1.1
V-8, small block (265-400 CID)	1.2	1.2	1.2	1.2	1.2	1.2	1.2	1.2	1.2	1.2
V-8, Mark IV (396-454 CID except 400)	1.4	1.4	1.4	1.4	1.4	1.4	1.4	1.4	1.4	1.4
With air conditioning, **ADD:**	.3	.3	.3	.3	.3	.3	.3	.3	.3	.3
With AIR pump, **ADD:**	.2	.2	.2	.2	.2	.2	.2	.2	.2	.2
With disc brakes, **ADD:**	—	.9	.9	.9	.9	.9	.9	.9	.9	.9
Related Jobs:										
Service Battery										
Clean, test, & fill	.3	.3	.3	.3	.3	.3	.3	.3	.3	.3
Replace ground cable	.2	.2	.2	.2	.2	.2	.2	.2	.2	.2
Replace starter cable	.3	.3	.3	.3	.3	.3	.3	.3	.3	.3
Replace battery	.4	.4	.4	.4	.4	.4	.4	.4	.4	.4
Service Cooling System										
Back-flush, fill, & pressure-test system	.9	.9	.9	.9	.9	.9	.9	.9	.9	.9
Replace upper hose	.4	.4	.4	.4	.4	.4	.4	.4	.4	.4
Replace lower hose	.5	.5	.5	.5	.5	.5	.5	.5	.5	.5
Replace both hoses	.7	.7	.7	.7	.7	.7	.7	.7	.7	.7
Replace thermostat & pressure-test system	.6	.6	.6	.6	.6	.6	.6	.6	.6	.6
Replace water pump drive belt & adjust tension,										
OHC engines	—	—	—	—	—	1.0	1.0	1.0	1.0	1.0
All others	.3	.3	.3	.3	.3	.3	.3	.4	.4	.4
Replace water pump, pressure-test system,										
OHC engines	—	—	—	—	—	1.3	1.3	1.3	1.3	1.3
Corvette	1.4	1.4	1.4	1.4	1.4	1.4	1.4	1.4	1.4	1.4
All others	1.2	1.2	1.2	1.2	1.2	1.2	1.2	1.2	1.2	1.2
With air conditioning, **ADD:**	.2	.2	.2	.2	.2	.2	.2	.2	.2	.2
With power steering, **ADD:**	.2	.2	.2	.2	.2	.2	.2	.2	.2	.2
With AIR pump, **ADD:**	.2	.2	.2	.2	.2	.2	.2	.2	.2	.2
Service Ignition System										
Adjust & install spark plugs,										
4-cylinder	.4	.4	.4	.4	.4	.4	.4	.4	.4	.4
6-cylinder	.6	.6	.6	.6	.6	.6	.6	.6	.6	.6
V-8 engine	.8	.8	.8	.8	.8	.8	.8	.8	.8	.8
Corvette, small block	1.4	1.4	1.4	1.4	1.4	1.4	1.4	1.4	1.4	1.4
Corvette, large block	1.2	1.2	1.2	1.2	1.2	1.2	1.2	1.2	1.2	1.2
With air conditioning, **ADD:**	.3	.3	.3	.3	.3	.3	.3	.3	.3	.3
With AIR, **ADD:**	.3	.3	.3	.3	.3	.3	.3	.3	.3	.3
Note: 1975 Monza 2+2, V-8 engine must be raised to remove #3 spark plug, **ADD:**	—	—	—	—	—	—	—	—	—	1.1
Replace points and condenser and adjust ignition timing,										
4 or 6-cylinder	.5	.5	.5	.5	.5	.5	.5	.5	.5	—
V-8 engine	.7	.7	.7	.7	.7	.7	.7	.7	.7	—

(THIS SCHEDULE CONTINUED ON NEXT PAGE.)

84 CHEVROLET/CORVETTE

SERVICE STATION MAINTENANCE Continued

MODEL	1966	1967	1968	1969	1970	1971	1972	1973	1974	1975
Service Ignition System Continued										
Replace distributor cap,										
4 or 6-cylinder, **ADD:**	.3	.3	.3	.3	.3	.3	.3	.3	.3	.4
V-8, Corvette, **ADD:**	.5	.5	.5	.5	.5	.5	.5	.5	.6	.6
V-8, all others, **ADD:**	.4	.4	.4	.4	.4	.4	.4	.4	.5	.5
Replace spark plug wires,										
4-cylinder	.4	.4	.4	.4	.4	.4	.4	.4	.4	.4
6-cylinder	.5	.5	.5	.5	.5	.5	.5	.5	.5	.5
V-8, small block, Corvette	1.5	1.5	1.5	1.5	1.5	1.5	1.5	1.5	1.5	1.5
V-8, Mark IV, Corvette	1.2	1.2	1.2	1.2	1.2	1.2	1.2	1.2	1.2	1.2
V-8, all others	.7	.7	.7	.7	.7	.7	.7	.7	.7	.7
All models with air conditioning, **ADD:**	.3	.3	.3	.3	.3	.3	.3	.3	.3	.3
Replace ignition coil	.4	.4	.4	.4	.4	.4	.4	.4	.4	.4
Service Fuel System										
Adjust carburetor idle mixture & speed,										
Single barrel	.4	.4	.4	.4	.4	.4	.4	.4	.4	.4
Two or four-barrel	.5	.5	.5	.5	.5	.5	.5	.5	.5	.5
Six-barrel (3x2) or 8-barrel (2x4)	.8	.8	.8	.8	—	—	—	—	—	—
Replace fuel filter	.3	.3	.3	.3	.3	.3	.3	.3	.3	.3
Test & replace fuel pump,										
4-cylinder OHC engine	—	—	—	—	—	.9	.9	.9	.9	.9
L-4 or L-6 engine	.5	.5	.5	.5	.5	.5	.5	.5	.5	.5
V-8, Mark IV, Corvette	.8	.8	.8	.8	.8	.8	.8	.8	.8	.8
V-8, all others	.9	.9	.9	.9	.9	.9	.9	.9	.9	.9
Replace flexible fuel line	.3	.3	.3	.3	.3	.3	.3	.3	.3	.3
Service Driveshaft										
R&R driveshaft & overhaul both U-joints,										
Cross & roller type	1.2	1.2	1.2	1.0	1.0	1.0	1.0	1.0	1.0	1.0
Constant-velocity type	—	—	—	—	—	—	—	—	2.0	2.0
Service Hydraulic Brake System										
Bleed hydraulic system, 4 wheels	.6	.6	.6	.6	.6	.6	.6	.6	.6	.6
Adjust drum brakes, 4 wheels	.5	.5	.5	.5	.5	.5	.5	.5	.5	—
Replace drum brake shoes, 4 wheels	3.5	3.5	3.5	3.5	3.5	3.5	3.5	3.5	3.5	—
Replace disc brake pads, front wheels	1.5	1.5	1.5	1.5	1.5	1.5	1.0	1.0	1.0	1.0
Replace disc brake pads, rear wheels, Corvette	2.0	2.0	2.0	2.0	2.0	2.0	1.5	1.5	1.5	1.5
Overhaul master cylinder	1.3	1.3	1.5	1.5	1.5	1.5	1.8	1.8	1.8	1.8
O/H wheel cylinders, drum brakes (4)	4.1	4.1	4.1	4.1	4.1	4.2	4.2	4.2	4.2	—
O/H front calipers, incl. turn rotors	4.0	4.0	4.0	4.0	4.0	4.0	4.0	4.0	4.0	4.0
O/H rear calipers, incl. turn rotors, Corvette	4.8	4.8	4.8	4.8	4.8	4.8	4.8	4.8	4.8	4.8
With 4-piston unit, ea., **ADD:**	1.0	1.0	1.0	1.0	1.0	1.0	1.0	1.0	1.0	1.0
Service Parking Brakes										
Adjust parking brakes	.4	.4	.4	.4	.4	.4	.4	.4	.4	.4
Replace forward cable,										
Corvette	1.0	1.0	1.0	1.0	1.0	1.0	1.0	1.0	1.0	1.0
All others	.8	.8	.8	.8	.8	.8	.8	.8	.8	.8
Replace rear cable, one side,										
Camaro	1.0	1.0	1.0	1.0	1.0	1.0	1.0	1.0	1.0	1.0
Vega	—	—	—	—	—	.7	.7	.7	.7	.7
All others	.8	.8	.8	.8	.8	.8	.8	.8	.8	.8
Replace rear cable, both sides,										
Camaro	1.6	1.6	1.6	1.6	1.6	1.6	1.6	1.6	1.6	1.6
Vega	—	—	—	—	—	1.1	1.1	1.1	1.1	1.1
All others	1.5	1.5	1.5	1.5	1.5	1.5	1.5	1.5	1.5	1.5

(THIS SCHEDULE CONTINUED ON NEXT PAGE.)

CHEVROLET/CORVETTE 85

SERVICE STATION MAINTENANCE Continued

MODEL	1966	1967	1968	1969	1970	1971	1972	1973	1974	1975
Service Parking Brakes Continued										
Replace intermediate cable	.4	.4	.4	.4	.4	.4	.4	.4	.4	.4
Replace parking brake shoes, both sides, Corvette	*7.0	*7.0	*7.0	*7.0	*7.0	2.6	2.6	2.6	2.6	2.6
*Includes R&R rear spindle.										
Service Suspension System										
Replace front shock absorber, both sides	.9	.9	.9	.9	.9	.9	.9	.9	.9	.9
Replace rear shock absorber, both sides	.8	.8	.8	.8	.8	.8	.8	.8	.8	.8
Replace rear coil spring, both sides,										
Vega	—	—	—	—	—	1.0	1.0	1.0	1.0	1.0
All others	1.5	1.5	1.5	1.5	1.5	1.5	1.5	1.5	1.5	1.5
Replace shackle and bushings; eye bolt and bushings,										
Camaro	1.1	1.1	1.1	1.1	1.1	1.1	1.1	1.1	1.1	1.1
Nova	.9	.9	.9	.9	.9	.9	.9	.9	.9	.9
All others	.7	.7	.7	.7	.7	.7	.7	.7	.7	.7
Adjust rear wheel toe-out, Corvette	.6	.6	.6	.6	.6	.6	.6	.6	.6	.6
Replace rear leaf spring, one side, & shim to align pinion angle,										
Camaro, Nova	1.7	1.7	1.7	1.7	1.7	1.7	1.7	1.7	1.7	1.7
Station wagon	1.4	1.4	1.4	1.4	1.4	1.4	1.4	1.4	1.4	1.4
Corvette, transverse spring, adjust camber & toe-out	1.8	1.8	1.8	1.8	1.8	1.8	1.8	1.8	1.8	1.8
Replace center bolt & liners, **ADD:**	.2	.2	.2	.2	.2	.2	.2	.2	.2	.2
Service Front End & Steering System										
Adjust toe-in only	.4	.4	.4	.4	.4	.4	.4	.4	.4	.4
Repack wheel brgs. only, including new seals,										
Drum brakes, both sides	.9	.9	.9	.9	.9	.9	.9	.9	.9	—
Disc brakes	1.3	1.3	1.3	1.3	1.3	1.3	1.3	1.3	1.3	1.3
Replace wheel brgs. only, each side,										
Drum brakes, inner or outer bearing	.5	.5	.5	.5	.5	.5	.5	.5	.5	.5
Disc brakes, inner or outer bearing	.8	.8	.8	.8	.8	.9	.9	.9	.9	.9
Replace tie-rods or tie-rod ends, (4),										
Corvette	1.7	1.7	1.7	1.7	1.7	1.7	1.7	1.7	1.7	1.7
All others	1.4	1.4	1.4	1.4	1.4	1.4	1.4	1.4	1.4	1.4
Replace Pitman arm, includes toe-in,										
Vega	—	—	—	—	—	1.0	1.0	1.0	1.0	1.0
All others	.8	.8	.8	.8	.8	.8	.8	.8	.8	.8
Replace steering idler arm or bushing, includes adjust toe-in,										
Corvette	.9	.9	.9	.9	.9	.9	.9	.9	.9	.9
All others	.7	.7	.7	.7	.7	.7	.7	.7	.7	.7
Vega with air conditioning, **ADD:**	—	—	—	—	—	.5	.5	.5	.5	.5
Replace power steering pump drive belt	.3	.3	.3	.3	.3	.3	.3	.3	.3	.3
With air conditioning, **ADD:**	.2	.2	.2	.2	.2	.2	.2	.2	.2	.2
Check & replenish reservoir fluid	.2	.2	.2	.2	.2	.2	.2	.2	.2	.2
Replace pressure hoses, either set, includes adjust drive belt,										
4 or 6-cylinder	.3	.3	.3	.3	.3	.3	.3	.3	.3	.3
V-8 engine	.6	.6	.6	.6	.6	.6	.6	.6	.6	.6
With air conditioning, **ADD:**	.1	.1	.1	.1	.1	.1	.1	.1	.1	.1
Balance four wheels on car,										
With drum brakes	1.2	1.2	1.2	1.2	1.2	1.2	1.2	1.2	1.2	—
With disc brakes	1.5	1.5	1.5	1.5	1.5	1.5	1.5	1.5	1.5	1.5
Rotate five wheels	.6	.6	.6	.6	.6	.6	.6	.6	.6	.6
Service Charging System										
Test system and/or adjust regulator	.6	.6	.6	.6	.6	.6	.6	.6	.6	.6
R&R alternator including pulley	.6	.6	.6	.6	.7	.7	.7	.7	.7	.7
With air conditioning, **ADD:**	.1	.1	.1	.1	.1	.1	.1	.1	.1	.1
With AIR, **ADD:**	.2	.2	.2	.2	.2	.2	.2	.2	.2	.2

(THIS SCHEDULE CONTINUED ON NEXT PAGE.)

CHEVROLET/CORVETTE

SERVICE STATION MAINTENANCE Continued

MODEL	1966	1967	1968	1969	1970	1971	1972	1973	1974	1975
Service Charging System Continued										
Overhaul alternator after removal	2.3	2.3	1.5	1.5	1.5	1.5	1.5	1.5	1.5	1.5
Replace regulator	.5	.5	.5	.5	.5	.5	.5	—	—	—
Service Cranking System										
R&R starter,										
4 or 6-cylinder	.7	.7	.7	.7	.7	.8	.8	.8	.8	.8
V-8, small block (265-400 CID)	1.8	1.8	1.8	1.3	1.3	1.3	1.3	1.3	1.3	1.3
V-8, Mark IV (396-454 CID except 400)	.9	.9	.9	.9	.9	.9	1.1	1.1	1.1	1.1
Overhaul starter after removal	1.7	1.7	1.7	1.7	1.7	1.7	1.7	1.7	1.7	1.7
Replace starter battery cable	.3	.3	.3	.3	.3	.3	.3	.3	.3	.3
Replace starter solenoid, includes system test,										
4 or 6-cylinder	1.7	1.7	1.7	1.7	1.7	1.7	1.7	1.7	1.7	1.7
V-8, small block (265-400 CID)	2.7	2.6	2.6	2.0	1.9	1.9	1.9	1.9	1.8	1.8
V-8, Mark IV (396-454 CID except 400)	1.9	1.9	1.9	1.9	2.4	2.4	2.3	2.0	2.0	2.0
Service Lighting System										
Adjust two headlights	.4	.4	.4	.4	.4	.4	.4	.4	.4	.4
Adjust four headlights	.6	.6	.6	.6	.6	.6	.6	.6	.6	.6
Replace sealed beam unit, ea.	.3	.3	.3	.3	.3	.3	.3	.3	.3	.3
Replace foot dimmer switch	.3	.3	.3	.3	.3	.3	.3	.3	.3	.3
Replace headlamp vacuum actuator	.8	.8	.8	.8	.8	.8	.8	.8	.8	.8
Replace signal/hazard flasher	.3	.3	.3	.3	.3	.3	.3	.3	.3	.3
Replace signal/hazard switch,										
With standard column	.8	.8	.8	.8	.8	.8	.8	.8	.8	.8
With tilt or telescopic column	1.0	1.0	1.0	1.0	1.0	1.0	1.0	1.0	1.0	1.0
Replace back-up light switch,										
Corvette	1.4	1.4	1.4	1.4	1.4	1.4	1.0	1.0	1.0	1.0
All others	.4	.4	.4	.4	.4	.4	.4	.4	.4	.4
Replace stoplight switch,										
Corvette	.5	.5	.4	.4	.4	.4	.4	.4	.4	.4
All others	.3	.3	.3	.3	.3	.3	.3	.3	.3	.3
Perform minor tune-up,										
4-cylinder	1.3	1.3	1.3	1.3	1.5	1.5	1.5	1.8	1.8	2.0
6-cylinder	1.5	1.5	1.5	1.5	1.9	1.9	1.9	2.2	2.2	2.4
V-8, small block (265-400 CID)	1.8	1.8	1.8	2.0	2.0	2.0	2.0	2.4	2.4	2.7
V-8, Mark IV (396-454 CID except 400)	2.5	2.5	2.5	2.5	2.7	2.7	2.7	2.9	2.9	3.0
Corvette, small block	2.0	2.0	2.0	2.2	2.2	2.2	2.2	2.6	2.6	3.0
Corvette, Mark IV	2.7	2.7	2.7	2.7	3.0	3.0	3.0	3.2	3.2	3.5

Note: See minor tune-up section for work included and additions.

Perform major tune-up,										
4-cylinder	4.6	4.6	4.6	4.6	4.6	4.8	4.8	4.8	4.8	5.0
L-6 engine	5.3	5.3	5.3	5.3	5.3	5.8	5.8	5.8	5.8	6.0
V-8, small block (265-400 CID)	6.0	6.0	6.0	6.0	6.0	6.2	6.2	6.5	6.5	6.7
V-8, Mark IV (396-454 CID except 400)	6.6	6.6	6.6	6.8	6.8	6.8	6.8	7.0	7.0	7.3
Corvette, small block	6.3	6.3	6.3	6.3	6.3	6.5	6.5	6.8	6.8	7.0
Corvette, Mark IV	7.0	7.0	7.0	7.0	7.0	7.1	7.1	7.3	7.3	7.5

Note: See major tune-up section for work included and additions.

CHEVROLET/CORVETTE 87

TUNE-UP, MINOR

Includes:

Basic Job: Perform the following work.
1. Service air cleaner element.
2. Replace PCV valve.
3. Replace crankcase ventilation filter in air cleaner.
4. Clean battery terminals.
5. Check condition and tension of all drive belts.
6. Check all hoses and hose connections.
7. Check operation of heated-air system (air cleaner), manifold heat valve (EFE valve since 1975) and automatic choke. Service where necessary.
8. Replace fuel filter.
9. Perform compression test.
10. Replace spark plugs.
11. Replace ignition points and condenser.
12. Check dwell or reluctor air gap and adjust ignition timing.
13. Adjust carburetor idle mixture and speed.
14. Make necessary ignition and carburetor adjustments to obtain satisfactory exhaust system analyzer readings.

Additions to Basic Job: Allowances for special equipment and carburetor combinations.

MODEL	1966	1967	1968	1969	1970	1971	1972	1973	1974	1975
Basic Job:										
Perform minor tune-up,										
4-cylinder	1.3	1.3	1.3	1.3	1.5	1.5	1.5	1.8	1.8	2.0
6-cylinder	1.5	1.5	1.5	1.5	1.9	1.9	1.9	2.2	2.2	2.4
V-8, small block (265-400 CID)	1.8	1.8	1.8	2.0	2.0	2.0	2.0	2.4	2.4	2.7
V-8, Mark IV (396-454 CID except 400)	2.5	2.5	2.5	2.5	2.7	2.7	2.7	2.9	2.9	3.0
Corvette, small block	2.0	2.0	2.0	2.2	2.2	2.2	2.2	2.6	2.6	3.0
Corvette, Mark IV	2.7	2.7	2.7	2.7	3.0	3.0	3.0	3.2	3.2	3.5
Note: 1975 Monza 2+2, V-8 engine must be raised to remove #3 spark plug, ADD:	—	—	—	—	—	—	—	—	—	1.1
Additions to Basic Job:										
With 4-bbl. carb. (V-8 small block only) ADD:	.2	.2	.2	.2	.2	.2	.3	.3	.3	.3
With 6-bbl. or 8-bbl. carbs., ADD:	.4	.4	.4	.4	—	—	—	—	—	—
With AIR pump, ADD:	.3	.3	.3	.3	.3	.3	.3	.3	.3	.3
With air conditioning, ADD:	.6	.6	.6	.6	.6	.6	.6	.6	.6	.6

Approximate parts cost:

Spark plugs, each	$1.50	Air cleaner element	$5.50
Points & condenser	5.00	Fuel filter	3.50
PCV valve	3.00		

TUNE-UP, MAJOR

Includes:

Basic Job: Perform the following work.
1. Service air cleaner element.
2. Replace crankcase ventilation filter in air cleaner.
3. Replace PCV valve.
4. Check drive belts and adjust for proper tension.
5. Check all hoses and hose connections.
6. Clean battery terminals.
7. Check operation of manifold heat valve (EFE valve since 1975) and automatic choke. Service where necessary.
8. Check operation of heated-air system.
9. Check exhaust and evaporative emission control systems.
10. Replace fuel filter.
11. Perform compression check.
12. Replace spark plugs.
13. Replace ignition points and condenser.
14. Check dwell or reluctor air gap and adjust ignition timing.
15. Check distributor cap and rotor.
16. Tighten cylinder head bolts.
17. Adjust valve lash (where applicable).
18. Overhaul carburetor(s).
19. Adjust carburetor(s) idle mixture and speed.
20. Make necessary ignition and carburetor adjustments to obtain satisfactory exhaust system analyzer readings.

Additions to Basic Job: Allowances for special equipment and/or carburetor combinations.

(THIS SCHEDULE CONTINUED ON NEXT PAGE.)

CHEVROLET/CORVETTE

MAJOR TUNE-UP Continued

MODEL	1966	1967	1968	1969	1970	1971	1972	1973	1974	1975
Basic Job:										
Perform major tune-up,										
4-cylinder	4.6	4.6	4.6	4.6	4.6	4.8	4.8	4.8	4.8	5.0
L-6 engine	5.3	5.3	5.3	5.3	5.3	5.8	5.8	5.8	5.8	6.0
V-8, small block (265-400 CID)	6.0	6.0	6.0	6.0	6.0	6.2	6.2	6.5	6.5	6.7
V-8, Mark IV (396-400 CID except 400)	6.6	6.6	6.6	6.8	6.8	6.8	6.8	7.0	7.0	7.3
Corvette, small block	6.3	6.3	6.3	6.3	6.3	6.5	6.5	6.8	6.8	7.0
Corvette, Mark IV	7.0	7.0	7.0	7.0	7.0	7.1	7.1	7.3	7.3	7.5
Note: 1975 Monza 2+2, V-8 engine must be raised to remove #3 spark plug, **ADD:**	—	—	—	—	—	—	—	—	—	1.1
Additions to Basic Job:										
With AIR pump, **ADD:**	.7	.7	.7	.7	.7	.7	.7	.7	.7	.7
Replace hydraulic valve lifter, one, **ADD:**	2.0	2.0	2.0	2.0	2.0	2.0	2.0	2.0	2.0	2.0
With 4-bbl. carb. (V-8 small block only) **ADD:**	1.0	1.0	1.0	1.0	1.0	1.0	1.1	1.1	1.1	1.1
With 6-bbl. carbs. (3x2), **ADD:**	4.0	4.0	4.0	4.0	—	—	—	—	—	—
With 8-bbl. carbs. (2x4), **ADD:**	2.5	2.5	2.5	2.5	—	—	—	—	—	—
With air conditioning, **ADD:**	.6	.6	.6	.6	.6	.6	.6	.6	.6	.6

Approximate parts cost:

Spark plugs, each	$1.50
Points & condenser	5.00
PCV valve	3.00
Air cleaner element	5.50
Fuel filter	$ 3.50
Carburetor repair kit, ea.	10.00
Ignition coil	14.00
HEI coil	25.00

EMISSION CONTROL SYSTEMS, TESTS FOR SMOG STATION CERTIFICATION

Includes:

Basic Job: Test crankcase, exhaust and evaporative emission control systems. Check heated-air system. Check HC/CO level with exhaust analyzer. Sign certification certificate. (No adjustments or repairs included in basic job.)

Related Jobs: Service any defective emission control system. Perform minor or major tune-up as required.

Additions to Related Jobs: Service or replace defective part(s) in the system. Allowances for special equipment installed and carburetor combinations.

MODEL	1966	1967	1968	1969	1970	1971	1972	1973	1974	1975
Basic Job:										
Test all systems & sign certificate,										
4 or 6-cylinder	.5	.5	.5	.5	.5	.8	.8	.8	.8	.9
V-8 engine	1.0	1.0	1.0	1.0	1.0	1.3	1.3	1.3	1.3	1.4
Related Jobs:										
Service crankcase emission control system	.3	.3	.3	.3	.3	.3	.3	.3	.3	.3
Service evaporative emission control system	—	—	—	—	.4	.4	.4	.4	.4	.4
Exhaust emission control systems,										
Service heated-air system	—	—	—	—	.3	.3	.3	.3	.3	.3
Service transmission controlled spark (TCS)	—	—	—	—	.5	.5	.5	.5	.5	—
Service EGR system	—	—	—	—	—	—	.4	.4	.4	.4
Service air injection (AIR) system	.5	.5	.5	.5	.5	.5	.5	.5	.5	.5
Replace catalytic converter pellets	—	—	—	—	—	—	—	—	—	1.0

Note: See separate section for replacement of components in each system.

(THIS SCHEDULE CONTINUED ON NEXT PAGE.)

CHEVROLET/CORVETTE 89

EMISSION CONTROL SYSTEMS, TESTS FOR SMOG STATION CERTIFICATION Continued

MODEL	1966	1967	1968	1969	1970	1971	1972	1973	1974	1975
Related Jobs Continued										
Perform minor tune-up,										
4-cylinder	1.3	1.3	1.3	1.3	1.5	1.5	1.5	1.8	1.8	2.0
6-cylinder	1.5	1.5	1.5	1.5	1.9	1.9	1.9	2.2	2.2	2.4
V-8, small block (265-400 CID)	1.8	1.8	1.8	2.0	2.0	2.0	2.0	2.4	2.4	2.7
V-8, Mark IV (396-454 CID except 400)	2.5	2.5	2.5	2.5	2.7	2.7	2.7	2.9	2.9	3.0
Corvette, small block	2.0	2.0	2.0	2.2	2.2	2.2	2.2	2.6	2.6	3.0
Corvette, Mark IV	2.7	2.7	2.7	2.7	3.0	3.0	3.0	3.2	3.2	3.5
Note: 1975 Monza 2+2, V-8 engine must be raised to remove #3 spark plug, **ADD:**	—	—	—	—	—	—	—	—	—	1.1
Perform major tune-up,										
4-cylinder	4.6	4.6	4.6	4.6	4.6	4.8	4.8	4.8	4.8	5.0
L-6 engine	5.3	5.3	5.3	5.3	5.3	5.8	5.8	5.8	5.8	6.0
V-8, small block (265-400 CID)	6.0	6.0	6.0	6.0	6.0	6.2	6.2	6.5	6.5	6.7
V-8, Mark IV (396-400 CID except 400)	6.6	6.6	6.6	6.8	6.8	6.8	6.8	7.0	7.0	7.3
Corvette, small block	6.3	6.3	6.3	6.3	6.3	6.5	6.5	6.8	6.8	7.0
Corvette, Mark IV	7.0	7.0	7.0	7.0	7.0	7.1	7.1	7.3	7.3	7.5
Note: 1975 Monza 2+2, V-8 engine must be raised to remove #3 spark plug, **ADD:**	—	—	—	—	—	—	—	—	—	1.1
Additions to Related Jobs:										
Minor Tune-up										
With 4-bbl. carb. (V-8 small block) **ADD:**	.3	.3	.3	.3	.3	.3	.3	.3	.3	.3
With 6-bbl. or 8-bbl. carbs., **ADD:**	.4	.4	.4	.4	—	—	—	—	—	—
Major Tune-up										
With 4-bbl. carb. (V-8 small block) **ADD:**	1.0	1.0	1.0	1.0	1.0	1.0	1.1	1.1	1.1	1.1
With 6-bbl. carbs. (3x2), **ADD:**	4.0	4.0	4.0	4.0	—	—	—	—	—	—
With 8-bbl. carbs. (2x4), **ADD:**	2.5	2.5	2.5	2.5	—	—	—	—	—	—
With CCS or AIR pump, **ADD:**	.3	.3	.3	.3	.3	.3	.3	.3	.3	.3
With air conditioning, **ADD:**	.6	.6	.6	.6	.6	.6	.6	.6	.6	.6

Approximate parts cost:
See minor or major tune-up section for cost of tune-up parts.
Catalytic converter pellets & kit $70.00

EMISSION CONTROL SYSTEMS, COMPLETE TEST OR SERVICE

Includes:

Basic Job: Make all necessary tests and repairs. Sign certification certificate.

1. Replace PCV valve, check all vacuum passageways and hoses.
2. Replace crankcase ventilation filter in air cleaner.
3. Test purge-control valve, gas ank filler cap, vent lines, and hoses for leakage.
4. Replace evaporation canister filter.
5. Clean EGR valve and test the control system.
6. Check transmission control spark (TCS) or CEC system.
7. Check operation of manifold heat valve (or EFE valve since 1975) and automatic choke. Free-up where necessary.
8. Check and adjust tension of drive belts.
9. Check operation of heated-air system.
10. Check AIR air pump flow.
11. Check routing and condition of hoses.
12. Check operation of diverter or bypass valve.
13. Check AIR manifold and hoses.
14. Replace catalytic converter or pellets, if necessary.
15. Determine if engine tune-up is required.

Related Jobs: Minor or major tune-up as required.

MODEL	1966	1967	1968	1969	1970	1971	1972	1973	1974	1975
Basic Job:										
Perform emission control sys. tune-up,										
4 or 6-cylinder	2.8	2.8	2.8	2.8	2.8	3.3	3.3	3.3	3.3	3.5
V-8 engine	3.1	3.1	3.1	3.1	3.1	3.5	3.5	3.5	3.5	3.7

(THIS SCHEDULE CONTINUED ON NEXT PAGE.)

CHEVROLET/CORVETTE

EMISSION CONTROL SYSTEMS, COMPLETE TEST OR SERVICE Continued

MODEL	1966	1967	1968	1969	1970	1971	1972	1973	1974	1975
Additions to Basic Job:										
With AIR, all models, **ADD**:	.5	.5	.5	.5	.5	.5	.5	.5	.5	.5
Replace catalytic converter pellets, **ADD**:	—	—	—	—	—	—	—	—	—	1.0
Related Jobs:										
Perform minor tune-up,										
4-cylinder	1.3	1.3	1.3	1.3	1.5	1.5	1.5	1.8	1.8	2.0
6-cylinder	1.5	1.5	1.5	1.5	1.9	1.9	1.9	2.2	2.2	2.4
V-8, small block (265-400 CID)	1.8	1.8	1.8	2.0	2.0	2.0	2.0	2.4	2.4	2.7
V-8, Mark IV (396-454 CID except 400)	2.5	2.5	2.5	2.5	2.7	2.7	2.7	2.9	2.9	3.0
Corvette, small block	2.0	2.0	2.0	2.2	2.2	2.2	2.2	2.6	2.6	3.0
Corvette, Mark IV	2.7	2.7	2.7	2.7	3.0	3.0	3.0	3.2	3.2	3.5
Note: 1975 Monza 2+2, V-8 engine must be raised to remove #3 spark plug, **ADD**:	—	—	—	—	—	—	—	—	—	1.1
Perform major tune-up,										
4-cylinder	4.6	4.6	4.6	4.6	4.6	4.8	4.8	4.8	4.8	5.0
L-6 engine	5.3	5.3	5.3	5.3	5.3	5.8	5.8	5.8	5.8	6.0
V-8, small block (265-400 CID)	6.0	6.0	6.0	6.0	6.0	6.2	6.2	6.5	6.5	6.7
V-8, Mark IV (396-454 CID except 400)	6.6	6.6	6.6	6.8	6.8	6.8	6.8	7.0	7.0	7.3
Corvette, small block	6.3	6.3	6.3	6.3	6.3	6.5	6.5	6.8	6.8	7.0
Corvette, Mark IV	7.0	7.0	7.0	7.0	7.0	7.1	7.1	7.3	7.3	7.5
Note: 1975 Monza 2+2, V-8 engine must be raised to remove #3 spark plug, **ADD**:	—	—	—	—	—	—	—	—	—	1.1
Additions to Related Jobs:										
Minor Tune-up										
With 4-bbl. carb. (V-8 small block), **ADD**:	.3	.3	.3	.3	.3	.3	.3	.3	.3	.3
With 6-bbl. or 8-bbl. carbs., **ADD**:	.4	.4	.4	.4	—	—	—	—	—	—
Major Tune-up										
With 4-bbl. carb. (V-8 small block), **ADD**:	1.0	1.0	1.0	1.0	1.0	1.0	1.1	1.1	1.1	1.1
With 6-bbl. carbs. (3x2), **ADD**:	4.0	4.0	4.0	4.0	—	—	—	—	—	—
With 8-bbl. carbs. (2x4), **ADD**:	2.5	2.5	2.5	2.5	—	—	—	—	—	—
With CCS or AIR pump, **ADD**:	.3	.3	.3	.3	.3	.3	.3	.3	.3	.3
With air conditioning, **ADD**:	.6	.6	.6	.6	.6	.6	.6	.6	.6	.6

Approximate parts cost:

Catalytic converter pellets	$70.00
PCV valve	3.00
Hose, per ft.	0.75
Canister filter	1.00
Purge control valve	4.00
Drive belt	$ 3.00
Diverter valve	12.00
Air pump	50.00
Catalytic converter	175.00

See minor or major tune-up section for cost of tune-up parts.

HEATED-AIR SYSTEM, TEST AND SERVICE

Includes:
  Basic Job: Check heated-air door, temperature sensor, and vacuum motor.
  Additions to Basic Job: Replace defective parts.

MODEL	1966	1967	1968	1969	1970	1971	1972	1973	1974	1975
Basic Job:										
Test heated-air system	—	—	—	.3	.3	.3	.3	.3	.3	.3
Additions to Basic Job:										
Replace vacuum motor, **ADD**:	—	—	—	.4	.4	.4	.4	.4	.4	.4
Replace temperature sensor, **ADD**:	—	—	—	.5	.5	.5	.5	.5	.5	.5

Approximate parts cost:

Vacuum motor assembly	$5.00
Temperature sensor	$4.50

CHEVROLET/CORVETTE 91

EVAPORATIVE EMISSION CONTROL SYSTEM, TEST AND SERVICE

Includes:
Basic Job: Test purge control valve, gas tank filler cap, vent lines, and hoses.
Additions to Basic Job: Replace defective part.

MODEL	1966	1967	1968	1969	1970	1971	1972	1973	1974	1975
Basic Job:										
Test evap. emission control system	—	—	—	—	.4	.4	.4	.4	.4	.4
Additions to Basic Job:										
Replace purge control valve, **ADD:**	—	—	—	—	.5	.5	.5	—	—	—
Replace charcoal canister filter, **ADD:**	—	—	—	—	.3	.3	.3	.3	.3	.3
Replace charcoal canister, **ADD:**	—	—	—	—	.5	.5	.5	.5	.5	.5
Replace hose, each, **ADD:**	—	—	—	—	.2	.2	.2	.2	.2	.2

Approximate parts cost:
Purge control valve .... $ 4.00
Canister filter 1.50
Hose, per ft. .... $ 0.75
Charcoal canister 32.00

POSITIVE CRANKCASE VENTILATION (PCV) SYSTEM, TEST AND SERVICE

Includes:
Basic Job: Test PCV valve, check all vacuum passageways, and inspect hoses. Clean or replace air filter.
Additions to Basic Job: Replace defective parts. (Do not attempt to clean PCV valve, replace if valve is not free.)

MODEL	1966	1967	1968	1969	1970	1971	1972	1973	1974	1975
Basic Job:										
Test PCV system, all models	.3	.3	.3	.3	.3	.3	.3	.3	.3	.3
Additions to Basic Job:										
Replace PCV valve, **ADD:**	.3	.3	.3	.3	.3	.3	.3	.3	.3	.3
Replace all hoses, **ADD:**	.6	.6	.6	.6	.6	.6	.6	.6	.6	.6

Approximate parts cost:
PCV valve $3.00
Hose, per ft. $0.75

EXHAUST-GAS RECIRCULATION (EGR), TEST AND SERVICE

Includes:
Basic Job: Test EGR valve, control system, and engine idling condition.
Additions to Basic Job: Replace defective parts. Test & repair thermostatic control system.

MODEL	1966	1967	1968	1969	1970	1971	1972	2973	1974	1975
Basic Job:										
Test EGR system, all models	—	—	—	—	—	—	.4	.4	.4	.4
Additions to Basic Job:										
Service EGR valve, **ADD:**	—	—	—	—	—	—	.7	.7	.7	.7
Replace EGR valve, **ADD:**	—	—	—	—	—	—	.4	.4	.4	.4
Test & repair thermo. control system, **ADD:**	—	—	—	—	—	—	.6	.6	.6	.6

Approximate parts cost:
EGR valve $10.00
Thermal vacuum switch $12.00

CHEVROLET/CORVETTE

TRANSMISSION CONTROLLED SPARK (TCS) SYSTEM, TEST AND SERVICE

Includes:
  Basic Job: Check engine speed in gear using tachometer and timing light, test TCS solenoid or CEC valve, and transmission switch.
  Additions to Basic Job: Replace defective parts.

MODEL	1966	1967	1968	1969	1970	1971	1972	1973	1974	1975
Basic Job:										
Test TCS system, all models	—	—	—	—	.6	.5	.5	.5	.5	—
Additions to Basic Job:										
Replace TCS or CEC solenoid, **ADD:**	—	—	—	—	.3	.3	.3	.3	.3	—
Adjust CEC valve, **ADD:**	—	—	—	—	—	—	—	.2	.2	—
Replace TCS switch,										
With standard transmission, **ADD:**	—	—	—	—	.4	.4	.4	.4	.4	—
With THM 400 transmission, **ADD:**	—	—	—	—	.8	.8	.8	.8	.8	—
All other automatic transmissions, **ADD:**	—	—	—	—	.5	.5	.5	.5	.5	—
Replace TCS relay, **ADD:**	—	—	—	—	.2	.2	.2	.2	.2	—
Replace thermostatic vacuum switch or TCS temperature switch, **ADD:**	—	—	—	—	.3	.3	.3	.3	.3	.3
Replace idle stop solenoid, **ADD:**	—	—	—	—	.3	.3	.3	.3	.3	.3

Approximate parts cost:
  TCS switch $5.00
  Thermostatic vacuum switch 6.50
  TCS relay 2.50
  TCS solenoid $11.50
  Idle stop solenoid 11.00
  CEC solenoid 12.00

AIR INJECTION REACTOR (AIR) SYSTEM, TEST AND SERVICE

Includes:
  Basic Job: Test air pump flow, check routing and condition of hoses, determine operation of diverter valve, verify check valve operation, inspect air manifold and hoses. Check and adjust drive belt tension.
  Additions to Basic Job: Replace defective part. Replace the drive belt, includes adjust tension. Replacement of hose(s), includes soapy water test.

MODEL	1966	1967	1968	1969	1970	1971	1972	1973	1974	1975
Basic Job:										
Test AIR system, all models	.5	.5	.5	.5	.5	.5	.5	.5	.5	.5
Additions to Basic Job:										
Replace and adjust drive belt,										
4 or 6-cylinder, **ADD:**	.4	.4	.4	.4	.4	.4	.4	.4	.4	.4
V-8 engine, **ADD:**	.5	.5	.5	.5	.5	.5	.5	.5	.5	.5
Replace AIR pump,										
4 or 6-cylinder, **ADD:**	.5	.5	.5	.5	.5	.5	.5	.5	.5	.5
V-8 engine, **ADD:**	.7	.7	.7	.7	.7	.7	.7	.7	.7	.7
Replace diverter valve, **ADD:**	.4	.4	.4	.4	.4	.4	.4	.4	.4	.4
Replace check valve assembly, **ADD:**	.3	.3	.3	.3	.3	.3	.3	.3	.3	.3
Repl. hose, includes soapy water test, **ADD:**	.4	.4	.4	.4	.4	.4	.4	.4	.4	.4

Approximate parts cost:
  Drive belt $3.00
  Air pump 50.00
  Check valve 7.00
  Diverter valve $12.00
  Hose, per ft. 0.75

CHEVROLET/CORVETTE 93

IGNITION SYSTEM, SERVICE

Includes:
Basic Jobs: 1. Adjust and install new spark plugs.
2. Replace points and condenser, adjust dwell and ignition timing.
3. R&R distributor, overhaul and test centrifugal and vacuum advances, set dwell or check reluctor air gap and ignition timing.
Related Jobs: Replace additional defective part(s) as required.
Additions: Allowances for special equipment installed or replacement of associated defective part(s).

MODEL	1966	1967	1968	1969	1970	1971	1972	1973	1974	1975
Basic Job #1										
Adjust & install new spark plugs,										
4-cylinder	.4	.4	.4	.4	.4	.4	.4	.4	.4	.4
6-cylinder	.6	.6	.6	.6	.6	.6	.6	.6	.6	.6
V-8 engine	.8	.8	.8	.8	.8	.8	.8	.8	.8	.8
Corvette, small block	1.4	1.4	1.4	1.4	1.4	1.4	1.4	1.4	1.4	1.4
Corvette, Mark IV	1.2	1.2	1.2	1.2	1.2	1.2	1.2	1.2	1.2	1.2
With air conditioning, **ADD:**	.3	.3	.3	.3	.3	.3	.3	.3	.3	.3
With AIR, **ADD:**	.3	.3	.3	.3	.3	.3	.3	.3	.3	.3
Note: 1975 Monza 2+2, V-8 engine must be raised to remove #3 spark plug, **ADD:**	—	—	—	—	—	—	—	—	—	1.1
Basic Job #2										
Replace points and condenser and adjust ignition timing,										
4 or 6-cylinder	.5	.5	.5	.5	.5	.5	.5	.5	.5	—
V-8 engine	.7	.7	.7	.7	.7	.7	.7	.7	.7	—
Replace distributor cap,										
4 or 6-cylinder, **ADD:**	.3	.3	.3	.3	.3	.3	.3	.3	.3	.4
V-8, Corvette	.5	.5	.5	.5	.5	.5	.5	.5	.6	.6
V-8, all others	.4	.4	.4	.4	.4	.4	.4	.4	.5	.5
Basic Job #3										
R&R and overhaul distributor and adjust ignition timing,										
4 or 6-cylinder	1.5	1.5	1.5	1.5	1.5	1.5	1.5	1.5	1.5	—
Corvette	1.8	1.8	1.8	1.8	1.8	1.8	1.8	1.8	1.8	—
Models with High Energy Ignition (HEI)	—	—	—	—	—	—	—	—	.8	.8
All others	1.6	1.6	1.6	1.6	1.6	1.6	1.6	1.6	1.6	—
Replace vacuum advance unit, **ADD:**	.2	.2	.2	.2	.2	.2	.2	.2	.2	.2
Related Jobs:										
Replace ignition coil	.4	.4	.4	.4	.4	.4	.4	.4	.4	.4
Replace spark plug wires,										
4-cylinder	.4	.4	.4	.4	.4	.4	.4	.4	.4	.4
6-cylinder	.5	.5	.5	.5	.5	.5	.5	.5	.5	.5
V-8 engine	.7	.7	.7	.7	.7	.7	.7	.7	.7	.7
Corvette, small block	1.5	1.5	1.5	1.5	1.5	1.5	1.5	1.5	1.5	1.5
Corvette, Mark IV	1.2	1.2	1.2	1.2	1.2	1.2	1.2	1.2	1.2	1.2
All models with air conditioning, **ADD:**	.3	.3	.3	.3	.3	.3	.3	.3	.3	.3
Replace ignition switch	.6	.6	.6	—	—	—	—	—	—	—
With air conditioning, **ADD:**	.5	.5	.5	—	—	—	—	—	—	—
Replace steering and ignition lock,										
Corvette	—	—	1.6	1.6	1.6	1.6	1.6	1.6	1.6	1.6
All others	—	—	—	1.4	1.4	1.4	1.4	1.4	1.4	1.4
Replace ignition buzzer switch	—	—	—	.6	.6	.6	.6	.6	.6	.6

(THIS SCHEDULE CONTINUED ON NEXT PAGE.)

CHEVROLET/CORVETTE

IGNITION SYSTEM Continued

Approximate parts cost:

Spark plugs, each	$1.50
Point set	3.00
Condenser	1.50
Distributor cap	4.50
Distributor parts	10.00
Ignition switch	6.00
HEI ignition coil	25.00
Vacuum control unit	$4.00
Ignition coil	12.50
Spark plug wires, 4-cylinder	5.00
6-cylinder	7.00
V-8 engine	12.00-20.00
Corvette	13.00-27.50
Ignition buzzer switch	2.50

CRANKING SYSTEM, TEST AND SERVICE

Includes:
Basic Job: Test battery and cranking system. Clean battery cable terminals.
Related Jobs: Replace defective part, including test when necessary.

MODEL	1966	1967	1968	1969	1970	1971	1972	1973	1974	1975
Basic Job:										
Test cranking system	.5	.5	.5	.5	.5	.5	.5	.5	.5	.5
Related Jobs:										
R&R starter,										
4 or 6-cylinder	.7	.7	.7	.7	.7	.8	.8	.8	.8	.8
V-8, small block (265-400 CID)	1.8	1.8	1.8	1.3	1.3	1.3	1.3	1.3	1.3	1.3
V-8, Mark IV (396-454 CID except 400)	.9	.9	.9	.9	.9	.9	1.1	1.1	1.1	1.1
Overhaul starter after removal	1.7	1.7	1.7	1.7	1.7	1.7	1.7	1.7	1.7	1.7
Replace starter-battery cable	.3	.3	.3	.3	.3	.3	.3	.3	.3	.3
Replace starter solenoid, includes system test,										
4 or 6-cylinder	1.7	1.7	1.7	1.7	1.7	1.7	1.7	1.7	1.7	1.7
V-8, small block (265-400 CID)	2.7	2.6	2.6	2.0	1.9	1.9	1.9	1.9	1.8	1.8
V-8, Mark IV (396-454 CID except 400)	1.9	1.9	1.9	1.9	2.4	2.4	2.3	2.0	2.0	2.0
Repl. starter/neutral switch & adjust.,										
With column shift	.4	.4	.4	.4	.4	.4	.4	.4	.4	.4
With floor shift	.6	.6	.6	.6	.6	.6	.6	.6	.6	.6

Approximate parts cost:

Starter, new	$80.00
Starter, rebuilt w/o solenoid	30.00
Starter-battery cable	4.50-8.50
Solenoid switch	$14.00
Starter/neutral switch	4.00

CHARGING SYSTEM, TEST AND SERVICE

Includes:
Basic Job: Test battery voltage and gravity, clean battery cable terminals, test alternator output, test and/or adjust regulator.
Related Jobs: Replace or overhaul defective component.

MODEL	1966	1967	1968	1969	1970	1971	1972	1973	1974	1975
Basic Job:										
Test system and adjust regulator	.6	.6	.6	.6	.6	.6	.6	.4	.4	.4
Related Jobs:										
R&R alternator incl. pulley	.6	.6	.6	.6	.7	.7	.7	.7	.7	.7
With air conditioning, **ADD:**	.1	.1	.1	.1	.1	.1	.1	.1	.1	.1
With AIR, **ADD:**	.2	.2	.2	.2	.2	.2	.2	.2	.2	.2
Overhaul alternator after removal	2.3	2.3	1.5	1.5	1.5	1.5	1.5	1.5	1.5	1.5
Test & replace regulator	.5	.5	.5	.5	.5	.5	.5	—	—	—

(THIS SCHEDULE CONTINUED ON NEXT PAGE.)

CHEVROLET/CORVETTE 95

CHARGING SYSTEM, TEST AND SERVICE Continued

Approximate parts cost:
Alternator, new $75.00-80.00
Alternator, rebuilt 35.00
Regulator $13.00-27.00

FUEL SYSTEM, ADJUST AND SERVICE

Includes:
Basic Job: Adjust idle mixture and speed for performance and to obtain satisfactory exhaust system analyzer readings.
Related Jobs: R&R carburetor, overhaul carburetor(s), R&R associated fuel components.

MODEL	1966	1967	1968	1969	1970	1971	1972	1973	1974	1975
Basic Job:										
Adjust carburetor idle mixture & speed,										
Single barrel	.4	.4	.4	.4	.4	.4	.4	.4	.4	.4
Two or four-barrel	.5	.5	.5	.5	.5	.5	.5	.5	.5	.5
Six-barrel (3x2) or 8-barrel (2x4)	.8	.8	.8	.8	—	—	—	—	—	—
Related Jobs:										
Replace carb. incl. compl. adjustments,										
Single barrel	.6	.6	.5	.5	.7	.7	.7	.7	.7	.7
Two or four-barrel	1.0	1.0	1.0	1.0	1.0	1.0	1.0	1.0	1.0	1.0
Multiple carbs., ea., **ADD:**	.8	.8	.8	.8	—	—	—	—	—	—
O/H carb., incl. R&R and compl. adjust.,										
Single or two-barrel, ea.	2.6	2.6	2.6	2.5	2.7	2.2	2.4	2.4	2.4	2.4
Four-barrel	4.0	4.0	4.0	4.0	3.2	3.2	3.2	3.2	3.4	3.4
Test & replace fuel pump,										
4-cylinder OHC engine	—	—	—	—	—	.9	.9	.9	.9	.9
L-4 or L-6 engine	.5	.5	.5	.5	.5	.5	.5	.5	.5	.5
V-8, Mark IV, Corvette	.8	.8	.8	.8	.8	.8	.8	.8	.8	.8
V-8, all others	.9	.9	.9	.9	.9	.9	.9	.9	.9	.9
Replace fuel filter	.3	.3	.3	.3	.3	.3	.3	.3	.3	.3
Replace fuel tank sending unit,										
Corvette	1.5	1.5	1.5	1.5	1.5	1.5	1.5	1.5	1.5	1.5
Station wagon	1.2	1.2	1.2	1.2	1.2	1.2	1.4	1.4	1.4	1.4
All others	1.2	1.2	1.2	1.2	1.2	1.2	1.2	1.2	1.2	1.2
Replace dashboard fuel gauge,										
Corvette	2.0	2.0	1.3	1.3	1.3	1.3	1.3	1.3	1.3	1.3
All others	.4	.4	.8	.5	.5	.5	.5	.5	.5	.5
With air conditioning, **ADD:**	.2	.2	.2	.2	.2	.2	.2	.2	.2	.2
Replace fuel tank, includes transfer fuel tank sending unit,										
Corvette	3.3	3.3	3.3	2.8	2.8	2.8	2.8	2.8	2.8	2.8
Station wagon	1.9	1.9	1.9	1.9	1.9	1.9	1.9	1.9	1.9	1.9
All others	1.6	1.6	1.6	1.6	1.6	1.6	1.6	1.6	1.6	1.6
Replace flexible fuel line	.3	.3	.3	.3	.3	.3	.3	.3	.3	.3

Approximate parts cost:
Carburetor repair kit, ea. $10.00-20.00
Carburetor, new, ea., single bbl. 40.00
   Two bbl. 70.00
   Four bbl. 100.00
Carburetor, rebuilt, single bbl. 15.00
   Two bbl. 22.00
   Four bbl. 40.00

Fuel pump $15.00
Fuel tank sending unit 13.00-24.00
Fuel gauge, dash 9.00-14.00
Flexible fuel line 0.50
Fuel tank 50.00-65.00

CHEVROLET/CORVETTE

ENGINE OVERHAUL, IN-CAR

Includes:

Basic Job: Remove ring ridge, deglaze cylinder walls, fit piston pins, align connecting rods, install new piston rings and rod bearings, install new main bearing inserts and oil seals, overhaul oil pump, clean carbon, grind valves, and perform major tune-up.

Note: Overhaul in-car not possible for 1966-68 Chevelle with V-8 small block.

Additions to Basic Job: Associated work that is required during basic job and allowances for special equipment.

MODEL	1966	1967	1968	1969	1970	1971	1972	1973	1974	1975
Basic Job:										
Overhaul engine,										
L-4 engine	16.0	16.0	16.0	16.0	16.0	—	—	—	—	—
4-cylinder, OHC engine	—	—	—	—	—	17.6	17.6	17.6	17.6	17.8
L-6 engine	21.0	21.0	21.0	21.2	21.2	21.2	20.4	20.6	20.6	20.8
V-8, small block (265-400 CID) Corvette	26.9	26.9	26.9	27.1	27.1	27.3	27.3	27.3	27.3	27.5
V-8, small block, all others	26.1	26.1	26.3	26.3	26.5	26.5	26.5	26.5	26.5	26.8
V-8, Mark IV (396-454 CID except 400), Corvette	28.3	28.3	28.3	28.7	28.7	28.7	29.1	29.1	29.1	29.3
V-8, Mark IV, all others	26.7	26.7	26.7	27.1	27.1	27.1	27.5	27.5	27.5	27.7
Additions to Basic Job:										
Rebore cylinders,										
4-cylinder, **ADD:**	3.0	3.0	3.0	3.0	3.0	3.0	3.0	3.0	3.0	3.0
6-cylinder, **ADD:**	4.0	4.0	4.0	4.0	4.0	4.0	4.0	4.0	4.0	4.0
V-8 engine, **ADD:**	5.0	5.0	5.0	5.0	5.0	5.0	5.0	5.0	5.0	5.0
Expand pistons,										
4-cylinder, **ADD:**	1.2	1.2	1.2	1.2	1.2	1.2	1.2	1.2	1.2	1.2
6-cylinder, **ADD:**	1.8	1.8	1.8	1.8	1.8	1.8	1.8	1.8	1.8	1.8
V-8 engine, **ADD:**	2.4	2.4	2.4	2.4	2.4	2.4	2.4	2.4	2.4	2.4
Regroove top piston ring groove,										
4-cylinder, **ADD:**	1.2	1.2	1.2	1.2	1.2	1.2	1.2	1.2	1.2	1.2
6-cylinder, **ADD:**	1.8	1.8	1.8	1.8	1.8	1.8	1.8	1.8	1.8	1.8
V-8 engine, **ADD:**	2.4	2.4	2.4	2.4	2.4	2.4	2.4	2.4	2.4	2.4
Replace hydraulic valve lifters, **ADD:**	1.0	1.0	1.0	1.0	1.0	1.0	1.0	1.0	1.0	1.0
Replace rocker arm stud, each, **ADD:**	.3	.3	.3	.3	.3	.3	.3	.3	.3	.3
Ream valve guides oversize,										
4-cylinder, **ADD:**	.5	.5	.5	.5	.5	.5	.5	.5	.5	.5
6-cylinder, **ADD:**	.7	.7	.7	.7	.7	.7	.7	.7	.7	.7
V-8 engine, **ADD:**	.9	.9	.9	.9	.9	.9	.9	.9	.9	.9
With AIR pump, **ADD:**	.7	.7	.7	.7	.7	.7	.7	.7	.7	.7
With air conditioning, **ADD:**	.7	.7	.7	.7	.7	.7	.7	.7	.7	.7
With 4-bbl. carb. (V-8 small block), **ADD:**	1.0	1.0	1.0	1.0	1.0	1.0	1.0	1.0	1.0	1.0
With 6-bbl carbs, (3x2), **ADD:**	4.0	4.0	4.0	4.0	—	—	—	—	—	—
With 8-bbl. carbs (2x4), **ADD:**	2.5	2.5	2.5	2.5	—	—	—	—	—	—

Approximate parts cost:

Hydraulic valve lifters, ea.	$ 4.00
Major tune-up parts	20.00-35.00
Carburetor repair kit, ea.	10.00-20.00
Complete gasket set, 4-cylinder	24.00
6-cylinder	26.00
8-cylinder	30.00
Rod bearing inserts, 4-cylinder	16.00
6-cylinder	24.00
8-cylinder	32.00
Rear main bearing oil seal	3.00
Main bearing inserts, 4-cylinder	$20.00
6-cylinder	27.00
8-cylinder	22.00
Piston rings, complete set, 4-cylinder	18.00
6-cylinder	27.00
8-cylinder	36.00
Piston pins, set, 4-cylinder	8.00
6-cylinder	12.00
8-cylinder	16.00
Piston assemblies, set, 4-cylinder	75.00
6-cylinder	85.00
8-cylinder	128.00

CHEVROLET/CORVETTE

ENGINE OVERHAUL, OUT-OF-CAR

Includes:

Basic Job: R&R engine, remove ring ridge, rebore or hone cylinder walls, regrind crankshaft and camshaft, replace camshaft bushings and line ream, replace timing chain and gears and oil seal, install main bearing inserts and seals, install piston pins, align connecting rods, install new piston rings and rod bearings, overhaul oil pump, clean carbon, grind valves, overhaul rocker arm mechanism, and perform major tune-up.

Additions to Basic Job: Associated work that is required during basic job and allowances for special equipment installed.

MODEL	1966	1967	1968	1969	1970	1971	1972	1973	1974	1975
Basic Job:										
Overhaul engine,										
L-4 engine	25.5	25.5	25.5	25.5	25.5	—	—	—	—	—
4-cylinder, OHC engine	—	—	—	—	—	28.7	28.7	28.7	28.7	28.9
L-6 engine	35.2	35.2	35.2	35.2	34.4	34.4	34.4	35.0	35.0	35.2
V-8, small block (265-400 CID) Corvette	43.2	43.2	43.2	43.4	42.6	42.6	41.3	41.6	41.6	41.8
V-8, small block, all others	41.8	41.8	41.8	42.0	41.3	41.3	41.3	41.3	41.3	41.5
V-8, Mark IV (396-454 CID except 400) Corvette	44.8	44.8	44.8	45.0	43.6	43.6	42.3	42.5	42.5	42.8
V-8, Mark IV, all others	42.3	42.3	42.3	42.5	42.3	42.3	42.1	42.3	42.3	42.6
Additions to Basic Job:										
Regroove top piston ring groove,										
4-cylinder, **ADD:**	1.2	1.2	1.2	1.2	1.2	1.2	1.2	1.2	1.2	1.2
6-cylinder, **ADD:**	1.8	1.8	1.8	1.8	1.8	1.8	1.8	1.8	1.8	1.8
V-8 engine, **ADD:**	2.4	2.4	2.4	2.4	2.4	2.4	2.4	2.4	2.4	2.4
Replace rocker arm stud, ea., **ADD:**	.3	.3	.3	.3	.3	.3	.3	.3	.3	.3
Ream valve guides oversize,										
4-cylinder, **ADD:**	.5	.5	.5	.5	.5	.5	.5	.5	.5	.5
6-cylinder, **ADD:**	.7	.7	.7	.7	.7	.7	.7	.7	.7	.7
V-8 engine, **ADD:**	.9	.9	.9	.9	.9	.9	.9	.9	.9	.9
Replace all engine mounts, **ADD:**	.6	.6	.6	.6	.6	.6	.6	.6	.6	.6
Replace worn clutch parts, **ADD:**	.5	.5	.5	.5	.5	.5	.5	.5	.5	.5
With AIR pump, **ADD:**	.7	.7	.7	.7	.7	.7	.7	.7	.7	.7
With air conditioning, incl. chg. sys., **ADD:**	1.8	1.8	1.8	1.8	1.8	1.8	1.8	1.8	1.8	1.8
With 4-bbl. carb. (V-8 small block), **ADD:**	1.0	1.0	1.0	1.0	1.0	1.0	1.0	1.0	1.0	1.0
With 6-bbl. carbs. (3x2), **ADD:**	4.0	4.0	4.0	4.0	—	—	—	—	—	—

Approximate parts cost:

Complete gasket set, 4-cylinder	$24.00
6-cylinder	26.00
8-cylinder	30.00
Piston rings, complete set, 4-cylinder	18.00
6-cylinder	27.00
8-cylinder	36.00
Piston pins, set, 4-cylinder	8.00
6-cylinder	12.00
8-cylinder	16.00
Piston assemblies, set, 4-cylinder	75.00
6-cylinder	85.00
8-cylinder	128.00
Major tune-up parts	22.00-35.00
Rod bearing inserts, set, 4-cylinder	$16.00
6-cylinder	24.00
8-cylinder	32.00
Main bearing inserts, set 4-cylinder	20.00
6-cylinder	27.00
8-cylinder	22.00
Rear main bearing oil seal set	3.00
Hydraulic valve lifters, ea.	4.00
Engine mounts	7.00
Pressure plate	30.00-60.00
Clutch disc	21.00-48.00
Thrust bearing	5.00-15.00
Flywheel pilot bearing	1.50
Carburetor repair kit, ea.	10.00

98 CHEVROLET/CORVETTE

SHORT BLOCK, REPLACE

Includes:

Basic Job: R&R engine, clean and reface valves, scrape carbon, grind valve seats, replace valve seals, overhaul rocker arm mechanism, transfer all parts, and perform major tune-up.

Additions to Basic Job: Associated work that is required during basic job and allowances for special equipment installed and/or carburetor combinations.

MODEL	1966	1967	1968	1969	1970	1971	1972	1973	1974	1975
Basic Job:										
Replace short block,										
L-4 engine	14.5	14.5	14.5	14.5	14.5	—	—	—	—	—
4-cylinder, OHC engine	—	—	—	—	—	13.3	13.3	13.3	13.3	13.5
L-6 engine	15.5	15.5	15.5	15.8	14.7	14.7	14.7	15.3	15.3	15.5
V-8, small block (265-400 CID) Corvette	22.2	22.2	22.2	22.4	22.6	22.6	22.6	21.6	21.6	21.8
V-8, small block, all others	19.6	19.6	19.6	19.8	19.1	19.1	19.1	19.1	19.1	19.3
V-8, Mark IV (396-454 CID except 400) Corvette	23.6	23.6	23.6	23.8	22.4	22.4	22.1	22.3	22.3	22.5
V-8, Mark IV, all others	20.1	20.1	20.1	20.3	20.1	20.1	19.9	20.1	20.1	20.4
Additions to Basic Job:										
Ream valve guides oversize,										
4-cylinder, **ADD:**	.5	.5	.5	.5	.5	.5	.5	.5	.5	.5
6-cylinder, **ADD:**	.7	.7	.7	.7	.7	.7	.7	.7	.7	.7
V-8 engine, **ADD:**	.9	.9	.9	.9	.9	.9	.9	.9	.9	.9
Replace rocker arm stud, ea., **ADD:**	.3	.3	.3	.3	.3	.3	.3	.3	.3	.3
Service/replace hyd. valve lifters, **ADD:**	2.0	2.0	2.0	2.0	2.0	2.0	2.0	2.0	2.0	2.0
Replace all engine mounts, **ADD:**	.6	.6	.6	.6	.6	.6	.6	.6	.6	.6
Replace worn clutch parts, **ADD:**	.5	.5	.5	.5	.5	.5	.5	.5	.5	.5
With AIR pump, **ADD:**	.7	.7	.7	.7	.7	.7	.7	.7	.7	.7
With air conditioning, incl. chg. sys., **ADD:**	1.8	1.8	1.8	1.8	1.8	1.8	1.8	1.8	1.8	1.8
With 4-bbl. carb. (V-8 small block), **ADD:**	1.0	1.0	1.0	1.0	1.0	1.0	1.0	1.0	1.0	1.0
With 6-bbl. carbs. (3x2), **ADD:**	4.0	4.0	4.0	4.0	4.0	—	—	—	—	—
With 8-bbl. carbs. (2x4), **ADD:**	2.5	2.5	2.5	2.5	2.5	—	—	—	—	—

Approximate parts cost:

Complete gasket set, 4-cylinder	$24.00	Oil and air filters	$ 9.00
L-6 engine	26.00	Pressure plate	30.00-60.00
V-8 engine	30.00	Clutch disc	21.00-48.00
Engine mounts	7.00	Thrust bearing	5.00-15.00
Short block: Call supplier for price quote.		Flywheel pilot bearing	1.50
		Carburetor repair kit, ea.	10.00-20.00

TIMING CHAIN MECHANISM, SERVICE

Includes:

Basic Job #1 OHC engines: Replace camshaft drive belt, adjust tension, and perform minor tune-up.
      #2 L-4 and L-6 engines: Replace timing gear, cover gasket, oil seal, and perform minor tune-up.
      #3 V-8 engines: Replace timing cover oil seal, timing chain, and minor tune-up.

Additions to Basic Job: Associated work required during basic job and allowances for special equipment installed.

MODEL	1966	1967	1968	1969	1970	1971	1972	1973	1974	1975
Basic Job #1										
Replace camshaft drive belt, adjust tension, and minor tune-up,										
4-cylinder OHC engine	—	—	—	—	—	2.6	2.6	2.9	2.9	3.1

(THIS SCHEDULE CONTINUED ON NEXT PAGE.)

CHEVROLET/CORVETTE 99

TIMING CHAIN MECHANISM, SERVICE Continued

MODEL	1966	1967	1968	1969	1970	1971	1972	1973	1974	1975
Additions to Basic Job #1										
Replace camshaft sprocket, **ADD**:	—	—	—	—	—	.2	.2	.2	.2	.2
Replace camshaft oil seal, **ADD**:	—	—	—	—	—	.2	.2	.2	.2	.2
Replace crankshaft sprocket, **ADD**:	—	—	—	—	—	.3	.3	.3	.3	.3
With air conditioning, **ADD**:	—	—	—	—	—	.5	.5	.5	.5	.5
With AIR, **ADD**:	—	—	—	—	—	.2	.2	.2	.2	.2
Basic Job #2										
Replace camshaft gear, cover oil seal and perform minor tune-up,										
L-4 engine	4.7	4.7	4.7	4.7	4.9	—	—	—	—	—
L-6 engine	7.5	7.5	7.5	7.5	7.9	6.7	6.7	7.0	7.0	7.2
Additions to Basic Job #2										
Replace crankshaft gear, **ADD**:	.2	.2	.2	.2	.2	.2	.2	.2	.2	.2
With air conditioning, **ADD**:	.2	.2	.2	.2	.2	.2	.2	.2	.2	.2
With power steering, **ADD**:	.2	.2	.2	.2	.2	.2	.2	.2	.2	.2
With AIR, **ADD**:	.3	.3	.3	.3	.3	.3	.3	.3	.3	.3
Basic Job #3										
Replace timing cover oil seal, timing chain, and minor tune-up.										
V-8, small block (265-400 CID) Corvette	4.3	4.3	4.3	4.5	4.5	4.5	4.6	5.0	5.0	5.3
V-8, small block, Chevelle	5.9	5.9	5.9	6.1	6.1	6.1	4.9	5.3	5.3	5.6
V-8, small block, all others	5.5	5.5	5.0	5.2	5.2	5.2	5.2	5.6	5.6	5.9
V-8, Mark IV (396-454 CID except 400) Corvette	5.3	5.3	5.3	5.3	5.6	5.6	6.5	6.4	6.4	6.7
V-8, Mark IV, Chevelle	7.4	7.4	7.4	7.4	7.7	7.7	7.6	6.5	6.5	6.8
V-8, Mark IV, all others	6.5	6.5	6.5	6.5	6.8	6.8	6.3	6.5	6.5	6.8
Additions to Basic Job #3										
Replace crankshaft sprocket, **ADD**:	.2	.2	.2	.2	.2	.2	.2	.2	.2	.2
With air conditioning, **ADD**:	.5	.5	.5	.5	.5	.5	.5	.5	.5	.5
With AIR, **ADD**:	.2	.2	.2	.2	.2	.2	.2	.2	.2	.2
With power steering, **ADD**:	.2	.2	.2	.2	.2	.2	.2	.2	.2	.2

Approximate parts cost:

Timing cover gasket	$1.00
Timing cover oil seal	2.00
Timing chain	9.00
Camshaft sprocket	6.00
Crankshaft sprocket	4.50
Minor tune-up parts	$25.00-30.00
Crankshaft sprocket (OHC engine)	9.00
Camshaft drive belt (OHC engine)	9.00
Camshaft gear	14.00
Crankshaft gear	6.00

OIL PUMP SERVICE

Includes:

Basic Job: R&R oil pan, service oil pump, and replace oil filter element.

MODEL	1966	1967	1968	1969	1970	1971	1972	1973	1974	1975
Basic Job:										
R&R oil pan, service oil pump, and replace oil filter element,										
4-cylinder OHC engine	—	—	—	—	—	3.8	3.8	3.8	3.8	3.8
L-4 or L-6 engine	2.5	2.5	2.5	2.5	2.0	2.0	2.0	2.0	2.0	2.0
V-8, small block (265-400 CID) Corvette	1.4	1.4	1.4	1.4	1.4	1.4	1.7	1.7	1.7	1.7
V-8, small block, Chevelle	6.1	6.1	6.1	2.2	2.2	2.2	2.2	2.2	2.2	2.2
Chevelle with manual trans., **ADD**:	.9	.9	.9	.9	.9	.9	.2	.2	.2	.2
V-8, small block, all others	2.4	2.4	2.4	2.4	2.4	2.4	2.3	2.3	2.3	2.3
V-8, Mark IV (396-454 CID except 400), Corvette	1.6	1.6	1.6	1.6	1.6	1.6	1.9	1.9	1.9	1.9
V-8, Mark IV, Chevelle	3.8	3.8	3.8	3.8	3.8	3.8	2.0	2.0	2.0	2.0
V-8, Mark IV, all others	3.0	3.0	3.0	3.0	3.0	3.0	2.3	2.3	2.3	2.3

(THIS SCHEDULE CONTINUED ON NEXT PAGE.)

100 CHEVROLET/CORVETTE

OIL PUMP SERVICE Continued

MODEL	1966	1967	1968	1969	1970	1971	1972	1973	1974	1975
Additions to Basic Job:										
Overhaul oil pump, **ADD:**	.8	.8	.8	.8	.8	.8	.8	.8	.8	.8
Replace rear main bearing insert & seals,										
4-cylinder OHC, **ADD:**	—	—	—	—	—	.4	.4	.4	.4	.4
L-4 or L-6 engine, **ADD:**	.3	.3	.3	.3	.3	.3	.3	.3	.3	.3
V-8 engine, **ADD:**	.4	.4	.4	.4	.4	.4	.4	.4	.4	.4
Replace other main bearing inserts, ea. set, **ADD:**	.6	.6	.6	.6	.6	.6	.6	.6	.6	.6

Approximate parts cost:
Oil pan	$24.00	Oil pump 4-cylinder, OHC engine	$25.00
Oil pan gasket	4.00	L-4 or L-6 engine	18.00
Oil pump shaft & rotor kit	8.00	V-8 engine	24.00
Oil pump screen	2.50	Oil filter element	5.00

BEARINGS, MAIN AND/OR RODS, REPLACE

Includes:
Basic Job: R&R oil pan, measure connecting rod bearing oil clearance with Plastigage, install new connecting rod bearing inserts, replace rear main bearing oil seals, overhaul oil pump, and replace oil filter element.

Additions to Basic Job: Measure main bearing oil clearance with Pastigage, replace all main bearing inserts.

MODEL	1966	1967	1968	1969	1970	1971	1972	1973	1974	1975
Basic Job:										
Install rod bearing inserts, oil seals,										
4-cylinder OHC engine	—	—	—	—	—	3.7	3.7	3.7	3.7	3.7
L-4 engine	3.2	3.2	3.2	3.2	3.2	—	—	—	—	—
L-6 engine	4.9	4.9	4.9	4.9	4.9	4.4	4.4	4.4	4.4	4.4
V-8, small block (265-400 CID) Corvette	5.4	5.4	5.4	5.3	5.3	5.3	5.3	5.3	5.3	5.3
V-8, small block, Chevelle w/A.T.	4.7	4.7	4.7	4.7	4.7	4.7	5.4	5.4	5.4	5.4
V-8, small block, Chevelle w/M.T.	6.3	6.3	6.3	6.3	6.3	6.3	5.4	5.4	5.4	5.4
V-8, small block, Camaro, Nova, Chevy II	4.7	4.7	4.7	4.7	4.7	4.7	5.7	5.7	5.7	5.7
V-8, small block, all others	5.6	5.6	5.6	5.6	5.6	5.6	5.4	5.4	5.4	5.4
V-8, Mark IV (396-454 CID except 400) Corvette	3.8	3.8	3.8	3.8	3.8	3.8	5.2	5.2	5.2	5.2
V-8, Mark IV, Chevelle	6.3	6.3	6.3	6.3	6.3	6.3	6.9	5.3	5.3	5.3
V-8, Mark IV, all others	5.4	5.4	5.4	5.4	5.4	5.4	5.6	5.3	5.3	5.3
Additions to Basic Job:										
Use Plastigage — all main bearings,										
4-cylinder, **ADD:**	.5	.5	.5	.5	.5	.5	.5	.5	.5	.5
6-cylinder, **ADD:**	.7	.7	.7	.7	.7	.7	.7	.7	.7	.7
V-8 engine, **ADD:**	.5	.5	.5	.5	.5	.5	.5	.5	.5	.5
Replace main inserts,										
4-cylinder, **ADD:**	2.5	2.5	2.5	2.5	2.5	2.5	2.5	2.5	2.5	2.5
6-cylinder, **ADD:**	3.5	3.5	3.5	3.5	3.5	3.5	3.5	3.5	3.5	3.5
V-8 engine, **ADD:**	2.5	2.5	2.5	2.5	2.5	2.5	2.5	2.5	2.5	2.5

Approximate parts cost:
Rod bearing inserts, 4-cylinder	$16.00	Oil pan gasket	$ 4.00
6-cylinder	24.00	Oil filter element	5.00
8-cylinder	32.00	Oil pump, 4-cylinder OHC engine	25.00
Rear main bearing oil seal	3.00	L-6 engine	18.00
Main bearing inserts, 4-cylinder	20.00	V8- engine	24.00
6-cylinder	27.00	Oil pump shaft & rotor kit	8.00
8-cylinder	22.00	Oil pump screen	2.50

CHEVROLET/CORVETTE 101

CYLINDER HEAD AND/OR GASKET, REPLACE

Includes:
Basic Jobs: 1. R&R intake manifold and cylinder head to install new gasket. Clean head and block surfaces and perform minor tune-up.
2. Install new cylinder head, including recondition valves and perform minor tune-up.
Additions to Basic Job: Allowances for special equipment and/or carburetor combinations.

MODEL	1966	1967	1968	1969	1970	1971	1972	1973	1974	1975
Basic Job #1										
Replace head gasket,										
4-cylinder OHC engine	—	—	—	—	—	4.1	4.1	4.4	4.4	4.6
L-4 engine	4.3	4.3	4.3	4.5	4.5	—	—	—	—	—
L-6 engine	5.1	5.1	5.1	5.3	5.3	5.3	4.9	4.9	4.9	5.1
V-8, small block, Corvette, one head	7.1	7.1	7.1	7.1	7.1	7.1	7.3	7.3	7.5	7.7
V-8, small block, Corvette, both heads	10.4	10.4	10.4	10.6	10.6	10.6	10.6	9.8	9.8	10.0
V-8, small block, all others, one head	6.8	6.8	6.8	7.0	7.0	7.0	7.0	7.2	7.2	7.5
V-8, small block, all others, both heads	9.9	9.9	9.9	9.9	9.9	9.9	8.7	8.7	8.7	8.9
V-8, Mark IV, Corvette, one head	8.9	8.9	8.9	8.9	8.9	8.9	8.7	8.7	9.0	9.2
V-8, Mark IV, Corvette, both heads	11.0	11.0	11.0	11.0	11.0	11.0	10.1	10.1	10.4	10.6
V-8, Mark IV, all others, one head	8.3	8.3	8.3	8.5	8.5	8.5	8.5	8.7	8.7	9.0
V-8, Mark IV, all others, both heads	12.9	12.9	12.9	12.9	12.9	12.9	10.4	10.4	10.7	10.9
Basic Job #2										
Install new cylinder head,										
4-cylinder OHC engine	—	—	—	—	—	7.0	7.0	7.3	7.3	7.5
L-4 engine	5.1	5.1	5.1	5.3	5.3	—	—	—	—	—
L-6 engine	6.3	6.3	6.3	6.5	6.5	6.5	6.1	6.1	6.1	6.3
V-8, small block, one head, Corvette	7.9	7.9	7.9	7.9	7.9	7.9	8.1	8.1	8.3	8.5
V-8, small block, one head, all others	7.6	7.6	7.6	7.8	7.8	7.8	7.8	8.0	8.0	8.3
V-8, small block, both heads, Corvette	12.0	12.0	12.0	12.2	12.2	12.2	12.2	11.4	11.4	11.6
V-8, small block, both heads, all others	11.5	11.5	11.5	11.5	11.5	11.5	10.3	10.3	10.3	10.5
V-8, Mark IV, one head, Corvette	10.5	10.5	10.5	10.5	10.5	10.5	9.2	9.2	9.5	9.7
V-8, Mark IV, one head, all others	9.1	9.1	9.1	9.3	9.3	9.3	9.3	9.5	9.5	9.8
V-8, Mark IV, both heads, Corvette	14.5	14.5	14.5	14.5	14.5	14.5	13.7	13.7	14.0	14.2
V-8, Mark IV, both heads, all others	14.0	14.0	14.0	14.0	14.0	14.0	13.1	13.1	13.3	13.5
Additions to Basic Job:										
With air conditioning, **ADD:**	.5	.5	.5	.5	.5	.5	.5	.5	.5	.5
With AIR pump, **ADD:**	.3	.3	.3	.3	.3	.3	.3	.3	.3	.3
With 4-bbl. carb. (V-8 small block only), **ADD:**	.2	.2	.2	.2	.2	.2	.2	.2	.2	.2
With 6-bbl. or 8-bbl. carbs., **ADD:**	.4	.4	.4	.4	—	—	—	—	—	—

Approximate parts cost:

Head gasket, ea.	$ 4.00	Valve grind gasket set, 4-cylinder, OHC	$14.00
Cylinder head, 4-cylinder OHC engine	90.00	L-4 engine	7.00
L-4 engine	60.00	L-6 engine	9.00
L-6 engine	80.00	V-8 engine	18.00
V-8 engine, cast iron, ea.	90.00	Minor tune-up parts	25.00-30.00
V-8 aluminum, ea.	225.00		

102 CHEVROLET/CORVETTE

VALVE MECHANISM, SERVICE

Includes:
Adjustment and Tune-up: Adjust valve lash and perform minor tune-up.
Basic Job: Clean and reface valves, scrape carbon, grind valve seats, replace valve seals, adjust valves, and perform major tune-up.
Additions to Basic Job: Associated work required during basic job and allowances for special equipment installed.

MODEL	1966	1967	1968	1969	1970	1971	1972	1973	1974	1975
Adjustment & tune-up,										
4-cylinder OHC engine	—	—	—	—	—	2.0	2.0	2.3	2.3	2.5
L-4 engine	1.7	1.7	1.7	1.7	1.9	—	—	—	—	—
L-6 engine	2.5	2.5	2.5	2.5	2.9	2.9	2.9	3.1	3.1	3.3
V-8 engine with mechanical lifters	3.2	3.2	3.2	3.2	—	—	—	—	—	—
Basic Job:										
Service valve mechanism,										
4-cylinder OHC engine	—	—	—	—	—	13.8	13.8	13.8	13.8	14.0
L-4 engine	8.3	8.3	8.3	8.3	8.3	—	—	—	—	—
L-6 engine	10.6	10.6	10.6	10.6	10.6	11.1	11.1	11.1	11.1	11.3
V-8, small block (265-400 CID) Corvette	15.4	15.4	15.4	15.4	15.4	15.6	15.6	15.9	15.9	16.1
V-8, small block, all others	14.8	14.8	14.8	14.8	14.8	15.0	15.0	15.3	15.3	15.6
V-8, Mark IV (396-454 CID except 400), Corvette	17.8	17.8	17.8	18.0	16.9	17.0	17.0	17.2	17.2	17.4
V-8, all others	17.2	17.2	17.2	17.4	16.3	16.4	16.4	16.6	16.6	16.8
Additions to Basic Job:										
Ream valve guides oversize,										
L-4 engine, **ADD:**	.6	.6	.6	.6	.6	—	—	—	—	—
L-6 engine, **ADD:**	.7	.7	.7	.7	.7	.7	.7	.7	.7	.7
V-8 engine, **ADD:**	.9	.9	.9	.9	.9	.9	.9	.9	.9	.9
Replace rocker arm stud, ea., **ADD:**	.3	.3	.3	.3	.3	.3	.3	.3	.3	.3
Replace hydraulic valve lifters, **ADD:**	1.0	1.0	1.0	1.0	1.0	1.0	1.0	1.0	1.0	1.0
With 4-bbl. carb. (V-8 small block only), **ADD:**	1.0	1.0	1.0	1.0	1.0	1.0	1.0	1.0	1.0	1.0
With 6-bbl. carbs. (3x2), **ADD:**	4.0	4.0	4.0	4.0	—	—	—	—	—	—
With 8-bbl. carbs. (2x4), **ADD:**	2.5	2.5	2.5	2.5	—	—	—	—	—	—
With air conditioning, **ADD:**	.6	.6	.6	.6	.6	.6	.6	.6	.6	.6
With AIR pump, **ADD:**	.7	.7	.7	.7	.7	.7	.7	.7	.7	.7

Approximate parts cost:
Valve grind gasket set, 4-cyl. OHC	$14.00
L-4 engine	9.00
L-6 engine	10.00
V-8 engine	20.00
Major tune-up parts	$22.00-35.00
Hydraulic valve lifters, ea.	4.00
Valve spring, ea.	2.00

EXHAUST SYSTEM, TEST AND SERVICE

Includes:
Basic Job: Test exhaust system for leaks and/or exhaust odors. Use HC/CO exhaust analyzer to trace carbon monoxide leaks.
Related Jobs: Replace defective parts. Each job includes basic job tests and installation of new hangers as required.

MODEL	1966	1967	1968	1969	1970	1971	1972	1973	1974	1975
Basic Job:										
Complete test of exhaust system	.4	.4	.4	.4	.4	.4	.4	.4	.4	.4
Related Jobs:										
Replace muffler,										
Front, single or dual, one	1.3	1.3	1.3	1.3	1.3	1.3	1.3	1.3	1.3	1.3
Rear, single or dual, one	1.2	1.2	1.2	1.2	1.2	1.2	1.2	1.2	1.2	1.2
One side, single or dual, two	1.8	1.8	1.8	1.8	1.8	1.8	1.8	1.8	1.8	1.8
One each side, dual, two	1.9	1.9	1.9	1.9	1.9	1.9	1.9	1.9	1.9	1.9

(THIS SCHEDULE CONTINUED ON NEXT PAGE.)

CHEVROLET/CORVETTE 103

EXHAUST SYSTEM, TEST AND SERVICE Continued

MODEL	1966	1967	1968	1969	1970	1971	1972	1973	1974	1975
Related Jobs Continued										
Replace tail pipe,										
Single or dual, one	1.1	1.1	1.1	1.1	1.1	1.1	1.1	1.1	1.1	1.1
Dual, two	1.4	1.4	1.4	1.4	1.4	1.4	1.4	1.4	1.4	1.4
Replace exhaust pipe flange gasket, ea.	1.0	1.0	1.0	1.0	1.0	1.0	1.0	1.0	1.0	1.0
Replace exhaust manifold gasket,										
4 or 6-cylinder	2.0	2.0	2.0	2.0	2.0	2.9	2.9	2.9	2.9	2.9
Free-up or O/H heat control or EFE valve,										
4/6-cylinder	1.5	1.5	1.5	1.5	1.5	1.5	1.5	1.5	1.5	1.5
V-8 engine	1.8	1.8	1.8	1.8	1.8	1.8	1.8	1.8	1.8	1.8
Replace exhaust pipe,										
4/6-cylinder	1.3	1.3	1.3	1.3	1.3	1.3	1.3	1.3	1.3	1.3
V-8 single exhaust	1.4	1.4	1.4	1.4	1.4	1.4	1.4	1.4	1.4	1.4
V-8 dual exhaust, one pipe	1.2	1.2	1.2	1.2	1.2	1.2	1.2	1.2	1.2	1.2
V-8 dual exhaust, both pipes	2.0	2.0	2.0	2.0	2.0	2.0	2.0	2.0	2.0	2.0
Replace catalytic converter pellets	—	—	—	—	—	—	—	—	—	1.0
Replace catalytic converter	—	—	—	—	—	—	—	—	—	1.8

Approximate parts cost:
Muffler	$28.00	Exhaust pipe, each	$ 15.00
Tail pipe, each	12.00	Exhaust manifold gasket, each	3.00
Catalytic converter pellets	70.00	Catalytic converter	175.00

COOLING SYSTEM, TEST AND SERVICE

Includes:
  Basic Job: Drain and back-flush system, check for leaks and tighten all hose connections, pressure-test radiator cap and system.
  Related Jobs: Replace defective part. Work performed independently of basic job.
  Additions to Related Jobs: Allowances for special equipment installed.

MODEL	1966	1967	1968	1969	1970	1971	1972	1973	1974	1975
Basic Job:										
Drain, flush, fill, and pressure-test system	.9	.9	.9	.9	.9	.9	.9	.9	.9	.9
Related Jobs:										
Replace upper hose	.4	.4	.4	.4	.4	.4	.4	.4	.4	.4
Replace lower hose	.5	.5	.5	.5	.5	.5	.5	.5	.5	.5
Replace both hoses	.7	.7	.7	.7	.7	.7	.7	.7	.7	.7
Replace thermostat & pressure-test system	.6	.6	.6	.6	.6	.6	.6	.6	.6	.6
Replace water pump drive belt & adjust tension,										
OHC engine	—	—	—	—	—	1.0	1.0	1.0	1.0	1.0
All others	.3	.3	.3	.3	.3	.3	.3	.4	.4	.4
Replace water pump, pressure-test system,										
OHC engines	—	—	—	—	—	1.3	1.3	1.3	1.3	1.3
Corvette	1.4	1.4	1.4	1.4	1.4	1.4	1.4	1.4	1.4	1.4
All others	1.2	1.2	1.2	1.2	1.2	1.2	1.2	1.2	1.2	1.2
With air conditioning, **ADD:**	.2	.2	.2	.2	.2	.2	.2	.2	.2	.2
With power steering, **ADD:**	.2	.2	.2	.2	.2	.2	.2	.2	.2	.2
With AIR pump, **ADD:**	.2	.2	.2	.2	.2	.2	.2	.2	.2	.2
Replace radiator, pressure-test system,										
OHC engine	—	—	—	—	—	.7	.7	.7	.7	.7
L-4 or L-6 engine	.8	.8	.8	.8	.8	.8	.8	.8	.8	.8
V-8, Corvette	1.5	1.5	1.5	1.5	1.5	1.5	1.8	1.8	2.3	2.3
V-8, all others	1.0	1.0	1.0	1.0	1.0	1.0	1.0	1.2	1.2	1.2

(THIS SCHEDULE CONTINUED ON NEXT PAGE.)

CHEVROLET/CORVETTE

COOLING SYSTEM, TEST AND SERVICE Continued

MODEL	1966	1967	1968	1969	1970	1971	1972	1973	1974	1975
Related Jobs Continued										
Replace water temperature gauge, engine,	.4	.4	.4	.4	.4	.4	.4	.4	.4	.4
With air conditioning, **ADD**:	.1	.1	.1	.1	.1	.1	.1	.1	.1	.1
Replace water temperature gauge, dash,										
Corvette	2.5	2.5	1.6	1.6	1.6	1.6	1.6	1.6	1.6	1.6
Chevelle	1.7	1.7	1.7	1.7	1.7	1.7	.6	.6	.6	.6
With air conditioning, **ADD**:	.4	.4	.4	.4	.4	.4	1.5	1.5	1.5	1.5
Camaro	.5	.5	.5	.5	.5	1.0	1.0	1.0	1.0	1.0
Monza 2+2, Vega	.5	.5	.5	.5	.5	.5	.5	.5	.5	.5
All others	1.0	1.0	1.0	1.0	1.0	1.0	1.0	1.0	1.0	1.0
Replace water jacket expansion plug,										
L-6 engine, head, ea.	.5	.5	.5	.5	.5	.5	.5	.5	.5	.5
Block, rear	3.0	3.0	3.0	3.0	3.0	3.0	3.0	3.0	3.0	3.0
Block, side, front or rear	.7	.7	.7	.7	.7	.7	.7	.7	.7	.7
Block side, center	1.1	1.1	1.1	1.1	1.1	1.1	1.1	1.1	1.1	1.1
V-8 engine, head, front	.5	.5	.5	.5	.5	.5	.5	.5	.5	.5
Side of block, ea.	1.2	1.2	1.2	1.2	1.2	1.2	1.2	1.2	1.2	1.2
Rear of block, automatic transmission	2.5	2.5	2.5	2.5	2.5	2.5	2.5	2.5	2.5	2.5
Rear of block, standard transmission	3.2	3.2	3.2	3.2	3.2	3.2	3.2	3.2	3.2	3.2

Approximate parts cost:

Radiator, new	$100.00-160.00
Upper or lower hose, ea.	5.00
Thermostat	4.00
Water pump, OHC engine	25.00
L-6 engine	20.00
V-8 engine	30.00
Camshaft drive belt (OHC engine)	$ 9.00
Drive belt, ea.	3.00
Temperature gauge, engine	4.00
Temperature gauge, dash	10.00
Expansion plug, ea.	1.50

SHIFT LINKAGE, SERVICE

Includes:
  Adjust: Adjust shift linkage.
  Basic Job: Replace one control rod and/or grommet and adjust linkage.
  Additions to Basic Job: Associated work that is required during basic job.

MODEL	1966	1967	1968	1969	1970	1971	1972	1973	1974	1975
Adjust shift linkage:										
3-speed transmission	.5	.5	.5	.5	.5	.5	.5	.5	.5	.5
4-speed transmission	.6	.6	.6	.6	.6	.6	.6	.6	.6	.6
Basic Job:										
Repl. one rod and/or grommet & adjust										
3-speed transmission	.8	.8	.8	.8	.8	.8	.8	.8	.8	.8
4-speed transmission	.9	.9	.9	.9	.9	.9	.9	.9	.9	.9
Additions to Basic Job:										
Replace additional rod, **ADD**:	.3	.3	.3	.3	.3	.3	.3	.3	.3	.3
Repl. shift lever oil seals, both, **ADD**:	.5	.5	.5	.5	.5	.5	.5	.5	.5	.5

Approximate parts cost:

Shift rod, each	$2.00
Rear oil seal	2.50
Shift lever oil seals	$1.50

CHEVROLET/CORVETTE 105

CLUTCH MECHANISM, SERVICE

Includes:
Adjust: Adjust clutch pedal play.
Basic Job: Replace thrust bearing, pressure plate and disc. Adjust clutch pedal play.
Additions to Basic Job: Associated work that is required during basic job and allowances for special engines.

MODEL	1966	1967	1968	1969	1970	1971	1972	1973	1974	1975
Adjustment:										
Adjust clutch pedal play	.3	.3	.3	.3	.3	.3	.3	.3	.3	.3
Basic Job:										
Replace thrust bearing, pressure plate and disc,										
3-speed, Corvette	3.5	3.5	3.4	3.4	3.4	—	—	—	—	—
3-speed, Camaro	2.4	2.4	2.4	2.4	2.4	2.4	2.4	2.4	2.4	2.4
3-speed, all others	1.7	1.7	1.7	1.7	1.7	1.7	1.7	1.7	1.7	1.7
4-speed, Corvette	3.8	3.8	3.8	3.8	3.8	3.8	3.8	3.8	3.8	3.8
4-speed, Camaro	2.5	2.5	2.5	2.5	2.5	2.5	2.5	2.5	2.5	2.5
4-speed, all others	2.0	2.0	2.0	2.0	2.0	2.0	2.0	2.0	2.0	2.0
Additions to Basic Job:										
Remove, reface, and instl. flywheel, **ADD:**	1.8	1.8	1.8	1.8	1.8	1.8	1.8	1.8	1.8	1.8
Replace flywheel ring gear, **ADD:**	1.0	1.0	1.0	1.0	1.0	1.0	1.0	1.0	1.0	1.0
Resurface clutch pressure plate, **ADD:**	.8	.8	.8	.8	.8	.8	.8	.8	.8	.8
Replace flywheel bearing, **ADD:**	.2	.2	.2	.2	.2	.2	.2	.2	.2	.2
Replace clutch release (throwout) bearing, **ADD:**	.2	.2	.2	.2	.2	.2	.2	.2	.2	.2

Approximate parts cost:
Pressure plate	$25.00-60.00
Clutch disc	20.00-35.00
Clutch release bearing	5.00-17.00
Flywheel pilot bearing	$ 1.50
Flywheel w/ring gear	36.00-56.00

STANDARD TRANSMISSION, OVERHAUL

Includes:
Basic Job: R&R transmission, disassemble, replace worn parts, and adjust linkage.
Additions to Basic Job: Associated work that is required during basic job.

MODEL	1966	1967	1968	1969	1970	1971	1972	1973	1974	1975
Basic Job:										
R&R, overhaul transmission, and adjust linkage										
3-speed transmission	5.4	5.4	5.4	5.4	5.4	5.4	5.4	5.4	5.4	5.4
4-speed transmission, Corvette	8.1	8.1	8.1	8.1	8.1	8.1	8.1	8.1	8.1	8.1
4-speed transmission, all others	6.9	6.9	6.9	6.9	6.9	6.9	6.9	6.9	6.9	6.9
With Muncie transmission, **ADD:**	.7	.7	.7	.7	.7	.7	.7	.7	.7	.7
Additions to Basic Job:										
Recondition transmission cover,										
3-speed transmission, **ADD:**	.3	.3	.3	.3	.3	.3	.3	.3	.3	.3
4-speed transmission, **ADD:**	.4	.4	.4	.4	.4	.4	.4	.4	.4	.4
Resurface clutch pressure plate, **ADD:**	.8	.8	.8	.8	.8	.8	.8	.8	.8	.8
R&R and resurface flywheel, **ADD:**	1.8	1.8	1.8	1.8	1.8	1.8	1.8	1.8	1.8	1.8
Replace flywheel ring gear, **ADD:**	1.0	1.0	1.0	1.0	1.0	1.0	1.0	1.0	1.0	1.0
Replace flywheel pilot bushing or bearing, **ADD:**	.2	.2	.2	.2	.2	.2	.2	.2	.2	.2
Replace clutch release (throwout) bearing, **ADD:**	.2	.2	.2	.2	.2	.2	.2	.2	.2	.2

Approximate parts cost:
Phone supplier for price quote on transmission parts required.

Speedometer gear	$ 2.00
Gasket set	8.00
Flywheel pilot bearing	$ 1.50
Clutch release bearing	5.00-17.00
Clutch pressure plate	25.00-60.00

CHEVROLET/CORVETTE

AUTOMATIC TRANSMISSION, SHIFT AND LINKAGE CONTROLS, REPLACE AND ADJUST

Includes:
Replace and Adjust: Replace defective part and make necessary adjustments.

MODEL	1966	1967	1968	1969	1970	1971	1972	1973	1974	1975
Replace part and adjust:										
Repl. control rod, carb. or trans. & adjust:	.9	.9	.9	.9	.9	.9	.9	.9	.9	.9
Replace each additional rod, **ADD:**	.4	.4	.4	.4	.4	.4	.4	.4	.4	.4
Replace carb./throttle link, **ADD:**	.3	.3	.3	.3	.3	.3	.3	.3	.3	.3
Replace throttle control cable, **ADD:**	.5	.5	.5	.5	.5	.5	.5	.5	.5	.5
Front control rod, column shift, **ADD:**	.3	.3	.3	.3	.3	.3	.3	.3	.3	.3
Rear control rod or swivel, **ADD:**	.4	.4	.4	.4	.4	.4	.4	.4	.4	.4
Control torque shaft or bushings, **ADD:**	.6	.6	.6	.6	.6	.6	.6	.6	.6	.6
Replace shift contr. key lock assy.	.7	.7	.7	.7	.7	.7	.7	.7	.7	.7
Replace vac. modulator hose & adjust linkage	.6	.6	.6	.6	.6	.6	.6	.6	.6	.6
Replace and adjust floor shift contr. assy.	.8	.8	.8	.8	.8	.8	.8	.8	.8	.8
With console equipped, **ADD:**	.5	.5	.5	.5	.5	.5	.5	.5	.5	.5

Approximate parts cost:
Linkage rod, ea. ... $1.50	Modulator hose, per ft. ... $0.25
Control cable ... 8.00	Floor shift contr. assy. ... 40.00

AUTOMATIC TRANSMISSION, PERFORMANCE CHECK

Includes:
Basic Job: Conduct transmission performance check. Clean transmission case and operate unit to check case, oil cooler and oil cooler lines for external leaks. Remove oil pan, clean pan, screen or filter. Torque valve body mounting bolts. Adjust band/s where applicable. Adjust throttle and shift linkage. Perform pressure checks of mainline, throttle, and accumulator. Road test.
Related Jobs: Work which does not include R&R transmission and may be done as separate job.

MODEL	1966	1967	1968	1969	1970	1971	1972	1973	1974	1975
Basic Job:										
Complete trans. performance check	2.1	2.1	2.1	2.1	2.1	2.1	2.1	2.1	2.1	2.1
Related Jobs:										
Drain & fill transmission, clean filter	.8	.8	.8	.8	.8	.8	.8	.8	.8	.8
Check for oil leaks	.7	.7	.7	.7	.7	.7	.7	.7	.7	.7
Replace oil pan gasket, incl. clean filter	.9	.9	.9	.9	.9	.9	.9	.9	.9	.9
Replace rear oil seal & O-ring	1.0	1.0	.7	.5	.5	.5	.5	.5	.5	.5
Replace neutral safety switch	.5	.5	.5	.5	.5	.5	.5	.5	.5	.5
Overhaul governor, includes complete transmission performance check,										
2-speed Powerglide	4.0	3.5	3.5	3.5	3.5	3.5	3.5	3.5	—	—
250/350 THM	3.1	3.1	3.1	3.1	3.1	3.1	3.1	3.1	2.9	2.9
375/400 THM	2.9	2.9	2.9	2.9	2.9	2.9	2.9	2.9	2.8	2.8
Overhaul valve body assembly	2.0	2.0	2.0	2.0	2.0	2.0	2.0	2.0	2.0	2.0
Adjust throttle and shift linkage	1.0	1.0	1.0	1.0	1.0	1.0	1.0	1.0	1.0	1.0
Adjust band/s where applicable	1.3	1.3	1.3	1.3	1.3	1.3	1.3	1.3	1.3	1.3

Approximate parts cost:
Transmission fluid, per qt. ... $1.20	Neutral safety switch ... $3.50
Oil pan gasket ... 1.00	Governor body repair kit ... 18.00
Rear oil seal ... 4.50	Valve body assy., new ... 80.00

CHEVROLET/CORVETTE 107

AUTOMATIC TRANSMISSION, MAJOR SERVICE

Includes:

Basic Jobs:
1. Overhaul transmission. Disassemble, clean, inspect and replace all worn parts as needed. Replace all oil seals. Adjust throttle and shift linkage as required. Flush converter and cooler lines. Perform pressure checks of mainline, throttle, and accumulator. Road test.
2. Replace torque converter. R&R transmission. Flush oil cooler and lines. Replace transmission oil and oil filter. Perform pressure checks of mainline, throttle, and accumulator. Adjust throttle and shift linkage as required.
3. Reseal transmission. R&R transmission. Replace all seals and gaskets. Replace transmission oil and oil filter. Check oil cooler for leaks. Perform pressure checks of mainline, throttle, and accumulator. Adjust throttle and shift linkage as required. Road test.

Additions to Basic Jobs: Associated work that is performed while the transmission is out during one of basic jobs.

MODEL	1966	1967	1968	1969	1970	1971	1972	1973	1974	1975
Basic Job #1										
Overhaul transmission,										
2-speed Powerglide	6.9	6.9	6.9	6.9	6.9	6.9	6.9	6.9	—	—
250/350 THM	8.0	8.0	8.0	8.0	8.0	8.0	8.0	8.7	8.7	8.7
375/400 THM	7.2	7.2	7.2	7.2	7.2	7.2	7.2	7.9	8.6	8.6
Basic Job #2										
Replace torque converter,										
2-speed Powerglide	4.2	4.2	4.2	4.2	4.2	4.2	4.2	4.2	—	—
250/350 THM	4.8	4.8	4.8	4.8	4.8	4.8	4.8	4.8	4.6	4.6
375/400 THM	4.4	4.4	4.4	4.4	4.4	4.4	4.4	4.6	4.6	4.6
Basic Job #3										
Reseal transmission,										
2-speed Powerglide	6.6	6.6	6.6	6.6	6.6	6.6	6.6	6.6	—	—
250/350 THM	6.3	6.3	6.3	6.3	6.3	6.3	6.3	6.8	6.8	6.8
375/400 THM	5.8	5.8	5.8	5.8	5.8	5.8	5.8	6.3	6.3	6.3
Additions to Basic Jobs:										
Replace oil cooler pipes, both, **ADD:**	.9	.9	.9	.9	.9	.9	.9	.9	.9	.9
Replace oil filler pipe and/or seal, **ADD:**	.5	.5	.5	.5	.5	.5	.5	.5	.5	.5
Replace torque converter ring gear, **ADD:**	.5	.5	.5	.5	.5	.5	.5	.5	.5	.5

Approximate parts cost:

Transmission seal and gasket kit	$20.00	Oil filler pipe	$ 4.00
Transmission partial overhaul kit	60.00	Oil filler pipe seal	0.25
Oil cooler pipe, each	9.00	Oil pan	8.00
Torque converter assembly	200.00	Oil pan gasket	1.00
Torque converter ring gear	8.00	Governor kit	19.00

DRIVESHAFT, SERVICE

Includes:

Basic Job: R&R driveshaft and overhaul or replace front and rear U-joints.

MODEL	1966	1967	1968	1969	1970	1971	1972	1973	1974	1975
Basic Job:										
R&R driveshaft with joints	.8	.8	.8	.8	.8	.8	.8	.8	.8	.8
R&R driveshaft & overhaul both U-joints,										
Cross & roller type	1.2	1.2	1.2	1.2	1.2	1.2	1.2	1.2	1.2	1.2
Constant-velocity type	—	—	—	—	—	—	—	—	2.0	2.0

Approximate parts cost:

U-joint package, cross & roller type	$11.00	Driveshaft with joints	$120.00
Constant-velocity joint	60.00	Constant-velocity joint kit	12.00

CHEVROLET/CORVETTE

REAR AXLE, SERVICE, EXCEPT CORVETTE

Includes:

Basic Jobs: 1. R&R driveshaft, R&R axle shafts, overhaul differential assembly, check pinion nose angle. Measure and adjust U-joint and driveshaft angles. Balance driveshaft.
2. R&R driveshaft and replace pinion bearing oil seal. Check pinion bearing preload. Measure and adjust driveshaft angles. Balance driveshaft.

Related Jobs: R&R axle shaft (one side) and/or bearing and seals. Replace axle shaft wheel mounting stud.

MODEL	1966	1967	1968	1969	1970	1971	1972	1973	1974	1975
Basic Job #1										
Overhaul differential assembly,										
Removable-type	5.5	5.5	5.5	5.5	5.5	5.5	5.5	5.5	5.5	5.5
Integral-type	5.0	5.0	5.0	5.0	5.0	5.0	5.0	5.0	5.0	5.0
Either type with Posi-traction, **ADD:**	.6	.6	.6	.6	.6	.6	.6	.6	.6	.6
Basic Job #2										
Replace drive pinion bearing oil seal	1.2	1.2	1.2	1.7	1.7	1.7	1.7	1.7	1.7	1.7
Related Jobs:										
R&R axle shaft (one side) and/or bearing and seals	1.3	1.3	1.3	1.3	1.3	1.3	1.3	1.3	1.3	1.3
Replace axle shaft wheel mounting stud	.8	.8	.8	.8	.8	.8	.8	.8	.8	.8

Approximate parts cost:

Axle shaft	$30.00	Pinion bearing oil seal	$ 3.00
Inner or outer seal	2.00	Cover gasket	1.00
Posi-traction repair kit	25.00	Ring & pinion gear set	70.00-120.00

REAR AXLE, SERVICE, CORVETTE ONLY

Includes:

Adjust Wheels: Adjust rear wheel camber and toe-out, both sides.

Basic Jobs: 1. R&R driveshaft, R&R axle shafts, overhaul differential assembly, overhaul axle shaft U-joints (4), adjust rear wheel camber and toe-out.
2. R&R driveshaft, and replace pinion bearing oil seal, adjust pinion bearing preload, overhaul axle shaft U-joints, and adjust rear wheel camber and toe-out.
3. Replace spindle bearings, both sides and adjust camber and toe-out.

Related Jobs: R&R driveshaft & overhaul front and rear U-joints.

MODEL	1966	1967	1968	1969	1970	1971	1972	1973	1974	1975
Adjust Wheels:										
Adjust camber and toe-out	.6	.6	.6	.6	.6	.6	.6	.6	.6	.6
Basic Job #1										
Overhaul differential	10.6	10.6	10.6	10.6	10.6	10.6	10.6	10.6	10.6	10.6
Basic Job #2										
Replace pinion bearing oil seal	4.2	4.2	4.2	4.2	4.2	4.2	4.2	4.2	4.2	4.2
Basic Job #3										
Replace spindle bearings, both sides	5.1	5.1	5.1	5.1	5.1	5.1	5.1	5.1	5.4	5.4
Related Jobs:										
Overhaul front & rear driveshaft U-joints	1.5	1.5	1.5	1.5	1.5	1.5	1.5	1.5	1.5	1.5

Approximate parts cost:

Axle U-joint repair kit	$12.00	Pinion bearing oil seal	$ 2.50
Ring & pinion gear set	85.00	Cover gasket	1.00
Axle shaft oil seal, inner or outer	1.50	Posi-traction repair kit	25.00
Axle shaft	26.00	Spindle bearings, set, outer & inner	15.00

CHEVROLET/CORVETTE 109

REAR SUSPENSION, SERVICE

Includes:
Service for the rear suspension system listed as individual jobs. Add times if more than one job is performed.

MODEL	1966	1967	1968	1969	1970	1971	1972	1973	1974	1975
Adjust camber & toe-out, Corvette	.6	.6	.6	.6	.6	.6	.6	.6	.6	.6
Replace leaf spring, one side, & shim to align pinion angle,										
Camaro, Nova	1.7	1.7	1.7	1.7	1.7	1.7	1.7	1.7	1.7	1.7
Station Wagon	1.4	1.4	1.4	1.4	1.4	1.4	1.4	1.4	1.4	1.4
Corvette, transverse spring, adjust camber & toe-out	1.8	1.8	1.8	1.8	1.8	1.8	1.8	1.8	1.8	1.8
Replace center bolt & liners, **ADD:**	.2	.2	.2	.2	.2	.2	.2	.2	.2	.2
Replace coil spring, both sides,										
Vega	—	—	—	—	—	1.0	1.0	1.0	1.0	1.0
All others	1.5	1.5	1.5	1.5	1.5	1.5	1.5	1.5	1.5	1.5
Replace control arm, includes pinion angle adjustment,										
Upper arm, one	1.1	1.1	1.1	1.1	1.1	1.1	1.1	1.1	1.1	1.1
Lower arm, one	1.5	1.5	1.5	1.5	1.5	1.5	1.5	1.5	1.5	1.5
Replace shackle and bushings; eye bolt and bushings,										
Camaro	1.1	1.1	1.1	1.1	1.1	1.1	1.1	1.1	1.1	1.1
Nova	.9	.9	.9	.9	.9	.9	.9	.9	.9	.9
All others	.7	.7	.7	.7	.7	.7	.7	.7	.7	.7
Replace shock absorber, both sides	.8	.8	.8	.8	.8	.8	.8	.8	.8	.8
Replace strut rod, both sides, Corvette	1.2	1.2	1.2	1.2	1.2	1.2	1.2	1.2	1.2	1.2
Replace strut rod bushings, both sides, Corvette	1.5	1.5	1.5	1.5	1.5	1.5	1.5	1.5	1.5	1.5
Replace tie rod & stabilizer shaft, one	.9	.9	.9	.9	.9	.9	.9	.9	.9	.9

Approximate parts cost:

Shock absorber	$14.00	Tie rod & stabilizer shaft	$ 9.00
Coil spring	26.00	Strut rod bushing, ea.	3.00
Leaf spring	53.00	Strut rod assembly	8.50
Shackle package	9.00	Upper arm assembly	13.00
Shackle bushing package	1.00	Lower arm assembly	14.00
Upper or lower control arm bushing, ea.	3.00		

STANDARD STEERING GEAR, ADJUST AND SERVICE

Includes:
Basic Job: Adjust steering gear, worm and sector mesh, adjust wheel bearings and toe-in.
Related Job: R&R steering gear assembly and complete adjustments.
Addition to Related Job: Overhaul steering gear.

MODEL	1966	1967	1968	1969	1970	1971	1972	1973	1974	1975
Basic Job:										
Complete steering gear, wheel bearings, & toe-in adjustments,										
With drum brakes	1.4	1.4	1.4	1.4	1.4	1.4	1.4	1.4	1.4	—
With disc brakes	1.8	1.8	1.8	1.8	1.8	1.8	1.8	1.8	1.8	1.8
Related Job:										
R&R steering gear assembly & complete adjustment	1.9	1.9	1.9	1.9	1.9	1.9	1.9	1.9	1.9	1.9
Additions to Related Job:										
Overhaul steering gear assembly, **ADD:**	1.0	1.0	1.0	1.0	1.0	1.0	1.0	1.0	1.0	1.0

Approximate parts cost:

Standard steering gear overhaul kit	$14.00	Worm thrust bearing	$1.00
Shaft dust seal	1.00	Pitman shaft seal	1.50
Pitman shaft bushing	2.00		

CHEVROLET/CORVETTE

FRONT END, TEST, SERVICE, AND ADJUST

Includes:
Basic Job: Check and adjust car height, caster, camber, steering axis inclination, turning radius, toe-in. Pack and adjust front wheel bearings, replace seals.
Related Jobs: Perform individual adjustments. Replace or overhaul defective components and make necessary adjustments.

MODEL	1966	1967	1968	1969	1970	1971	1972	1973	1974	1975
Basic Job:										
Complete test and adjustments,										
With drum brakes	2.5	2.5	2.5	2.5	2.5	2.5	2.5	2.5	2.5	—
With disc brakes	3.0	3.0	3.0	3.0	3.0	3.0	3.0	3.0	3.0	3.0
Related Jobs:										
Adjust toe-in only	.4	.4	.4	.4	.4	.4	.4	.4	.4	.4
Repack wheel brgs. only, incl. new seals,										
Drum brakes, both sides	.9	.9	.9	.9	.9	.9	.9	.9	.9	—
Disc brakes, both sides	1.3	1.3	1.3	1.3	1.3	1.3	1.3	1.3	1.3	1.3
Replace wheel brgs. only, each side,										
Drum brakes, inner or outer brg.	.5	.5	.5	.5	.5	.5	.5	.5	.5	—
Disc brakes, inner or outer brg.	.8	.8	.8	.8	.8	.9	.9	.9	.9	.9
Balance four wheels on car,										
With drum brakes	1.2	1.2	1.2	1.2	1.2	1.2	1.2	1.2	1.2	—
With disc brakes	1.5	1.5	1.5	1.5	1.5	1.5	1.5	1.5	1.5	1.5
Overhaul front suspension, incl. disassemble, replace nec. parts, lube., & complete front end adjustments,										
With drum brakes	7.9	7.9	7.9	7.9	7.9	7.9	7.9	7.9	7.9	—
With disc brakes, Corvette	8.8	8.8	8.8	8.8	8.8	8.8	8.8	8.8	8.8	8.8
With disc brakes, all others	—	8.5	8.5	8.5	8.5	8.5	8.5	8.5	8.5	8.5
Replace coil spring, incl. complete front end adjustments,										
With drum brakes	3.9	3.9	3.9	3.9	3.9	3.6	3.6	3.6	3.6	—
With disc brakes	4.4	4.4	4.4	4.4	4.4	4.1	4.1	4.1	4.1	4.1
Replace upper and lower ball joints, both sides, incl. complete front end adjustment,										
With drum brakes	3.9	3.9	3.9	3.9	3.9	3.9	3.7	3.7	3.7	—
With disc brakes	4.4	4.4	4.4	4.4	4.4	4.4	4.1	4.1	4.1	4.1
Replace steering knuckle, one side, incl. complete front end adjustment,										
With drum brakes	3.1	3.1	3.1	3.1	3.1	3.1	3.1	3.1	3.1	—
With disc brakes	3.8	3.8	3.8	3.8	3.8	3.8	3.8	3.8	3.8	3.8
Replace shock absorber, both sides	.9	.9	.9	.9	.9	.9	.9	.9	.9	.9
Replace control arm rubber bumpers, ea. side	.3	.3	.3	.3	.3	.3	.3	.3	.3	.3
Replace strut rod or bushings, ea. side	.4	.4	.4	.4	.4	.4	.4	.4	.4	.4
Replace stabilizer shaft and bushings,										
Corvette	1.1	1.1	1.1	1.1	1.1	1.1	1.1	1.1	1.1	1.1
All others	.8	.8	.8	.8	.8	.8	.8	.8	.8	.8
Replace front stabilizer links or grommets	.7	.7	.7	.7	.7	.7	.7	.7	.7	.7

Approximate parts cost:

Coil spring, ea. $16.00	Control arm rubber bumpers, ea. .... $ 1.50
Upper ball joint 12.00	Strut rod & bushing 6.00
Lower ball joint 14.00	Stabilizer shaft & bushings 15.00
Steering knuckle 40.00	Stabilizer links or grommets 2.00
Shock absorber, ea. 15.00	Wheel bearing seals 2.00
Wheel bearing, outer 5.00	Wheel bearing, inner 6.00

CHEVROLET/CORVETTE 111

POWER STEERING UNIT, TEST AND SERVICE

Includes:
  Basic Job: Adjust drive belt tension; hook-up gauges to check pressure on left and right turns. Adjust steering gear box over-center torque and control valve to balance left and right steering effort.
  Additions to Basic Job: Service power steering unit.
  Related Jobs: R&R power steering unit, pump, or other associated parts.
  Additions to Related Jobs: Overhaul steering unit or pump including replacement of all seals and worn parts.

MODEL	1966	1967	1968	1969	1970	1971	1972	1973	1974	1975
Basic Job:										
Complete test and adjustment of power steering unit	1.0	1.0	1.0	1.0	1.0	1.0	1.0	1.0	1.0	1.0
Adjust control valve, Corvette, **ADD:**	.5	.5	—	—	—	—	—	—	—	—
Additions to Basic Job:										
Replace power steering pump drive belt, **ADD:**	.3	.3	.3	.3	.3	.3	.3	.3	.3	.3
With air conditioning, **ADD:**	.2	.2	.2	.2	.2	.2	.2	.2	.2	.2
Check & replenish reservoir fluid, **ADD:**	.2	.2	.2	.2	.2	.2	.2	.2	.2	.2
Related Jobs:										
Replace pressure hoses, either set, includes adjust drive belt,										
4 or 6-cylinder	.3	.3	.3	.3	.3	.3	.3	.3	.3	.3
V-8 engine	.6	.6	.6	.6	.6	.6	.6	.6	.6	.6
With air conditioning, **ADD:**	.1	.1	.1	.1	.1	.1	.1	.1	.1	.1
Replace pump reservoir or O-ring seals,										
4 or 6-cylinder	1.0	1.0	1.0	1.0	1.0	1.0	1.0	1.0	1.1	1.1
Corvette	1.4	1.4	1.4	1.4	1.4	1.4	1.5	1.5	1.5	1.5
All other V-8	1.1	1.1	1.1	1.1	1.1	1.1	1.2	1.2	1.2	1.2
V-8 with air conditioning, **ADD:**	.1	.1	.1	.1	.1	.1	.1	.1	.2	.2
Replace pump, includes pressure-test original pump and transfer pulley,										
4 or 6-cylinder	.7	.7	.7	.7	.7	.7	.7	.7	.7	.7
Corvette	1.1	1.1	1.1	1.1	1.1	1.1	1.1	1.1	1.1	1.1
All other V-8	.8	.8	.8	.8	.8	.8	.8	.8	.8	.8
Replace control valve	1.1	1.1	1.1	1.1	1.1	1.1	1.1	1.1	1.1	1.1
Overhaul control valve, **ADD:**	.6	.6	.6	.6	.6	.6	.6	.6	.6	.6
R&R power steering unit, includes test original unit and complete adjustment,										
4 or 6-cylinder	2.5	2.5	2.5	2.5	2.5	2.5	2.5	2.5	2.5	2.5
V-8 engine	2.3	2.3	2.3	2.3	2.3	2.3	2.3	2.3	2.3	2.3
Additions to Related Jobs:										
Overhaul power steering unit, **ADD:**	2.2	2.2	2.2	2.2	2.4	2.4	2.4	2.4	3.0	3.0
O/H pump, incl. new kit & seals, **ADD:**	.8	.8	.8	.8	.8	.8	.8	.6	.6	.6

Approximate parts cost:

Drive belt	$ 4.00	Power cylinder	$33.00
Pressure hose	12.00	Power cylinder piston rod seal kit	2.50
Return hose	4.00	Hydraulic pump	62.00
Control valve	42.00	Hydraulic reservoir	15.00
Control valve seal kit	2.00	Hydraulic pump seals	4.00
Power steering unit, valve assembly	85.00	Hydraulic pump repair kit	14.00

CHEVROLET/CORVETTE

STEERING LINKAGE, SERVICE AND ADJUST

Includes:
　Basic Job: Adjust toe-in.
　Related Jobs: Replace defective parts and adjust toe-in.

MODEL	1966	1967	1968	1969	1970	1971	1972	1973	1974	1975
Basic Job:										
Adjust toe-in	.4	.4	.4	.4	.4	.4	.4	.4	.4	.4
Related Jobs:										
Replace tie-rods or tie-rod ends, (4),										
Corvette	1.7	1.7	1.7	1.7	1.7	1.7	1.7	1.7	1.7	1.7
All others	1.4	1.4	1.4	1.4	1.4	1.4	1.4	1.4	1.4	1.4
Repl. Pitman arm, includes adjust toe-in,										
Vega	—	—	—	—	—	1.0	1.0	1.0	1.0	1.0
All others	.8	.8	.8	.8	.8	.8	.8	.8	.8	.8
Replace steering idler arm or bushing, includes adjust toe-in,										
Corvette	.9	.9	.9	.9	.9	.9	.9	.9	.9	.9
All others	.7	.7	.7	.7	.7	.7	.7	.7	.7	.7
Vega with air conditioning, **ADD:**	—	—	—	—	—	.5	.5	.5	.5	.5

Approximate parts cost:
Tie-rod end pkg. .... $10.00-15.00　　Idler arm $17.00
Pitman arm .... 9.00　　Tie rod 15.00

HYDRAULIC BRAKE SYSTEM, OVERHAUL

Includes:
　Basic Job: Overhaul, including hone or replace master cylinder, all wheel cylinders or calipers; bleed hydraulic system; and adjust brakes.
　Related Jobs: Performed at time other than during basic job. Overhaul or replace master cylinder only; overhaul wheel cylinders or calipers.
　Addition to Related Jobs: Allowance for power brakes.

MODEL	1966	1967	1968	1969	1970	1971	1972	1973	1974	1975
Basic Job:										
Complete job, including master & wheel cylinders,										
Drum brakes, 4 wheels	4.7	4.7	4.7	4.7	4.7	4.7	4.7	4.6	4.6	—
Disc front, drum rear	—	3.9	3.9	3.9	3.9	3.9	3.9	3.9	3.9	3.9
Disc front and rear, Corvette	3.3	3.3	3.3	3.3	3.3	3.3	3.3	3.3	3.3	3.3
With 4-piston unit, ea., **ADD:**	1.0	1.0	1.0	1.0	1.0	1.0	1.0	1.0	1.0	1.0
Related Jobs: (Not during basic job)										
Overhaul master cylinder, including hone,										
Drum or disc brakes	1.3	1.3	1.5	1.5	1.5	1.5	1.8	1.8	1.8	1.8
Replace master cylinder	.5	.5	.8	.8	.8	.8	1.1	1.1	1.1	1.1
O/H wheel cylinder, drum brakes (4)	4.1	4.1	4.1	4.1	4.1	4.1	4.2	4.2	4.2	—
O/H front calipers, incl. turn rotors	4.0	4.0	4.0	4.0	4.0	4.0	4.0	4.0	4.0	4.0
O/H rear calipers, incl. turn rotors	4.8	4.8	4.8	4.8	4.8	4.8	4.8	4.8	4.8	4.8
With 4-piston unit, ea., **ADD:**	1.0	1.0	1.0	1.0	1.0	1.0	1.0	1.0	1.0	1.0
Bleed hydraulic system, 4 wheels	.6	.6	.6	.6	.6	.6	.6	.6	.6	.6
Addition to Related Jobs:										
With power brakes, **ADD:**	.2	.2	.2	.2	.2	.2	.2	.2	.2	.2

Approximate parts cost:
Master cylinder repair kit .... $18.00　　Master cylinder $27.00-40.00
Wheel cylinder repair kit, ea. .... 2.00　　Wheel cylinder seal, boot & bushing pkg. 6.00
Caliper repair kit, single piston 4.00
　　four piston 10.00

CHEVROLET/CORVETTE 113

BRAKES, SERVICE

Includes:
Basic Job: Install new linings or pads, turn brake drums or rotors, lubricate and adjust front wheel bearings, replace rear oil seals, bleed hydraulic system, and adjust brakes.
Additions to Basic Job: Overhaul four wheel cylinders, overhaul or replace front calipers, overhaul or replace rear calipers.
Related Jobs: Performed at time other than during basic job. Overhaul or replace front calipers, overhaul or replace rear calipers.

MODEL	1966	1967	1968	1969	1970	1971	1972	1973	1974	1975
Basic Job:										
Complete job incl. turn drums or rotors,										
Drum (4), all models	6.0	6.0	6.3	6.3	6.3	6.3	6.6	6.6	6.6	—
Disc front, drum rear, all models	—	6.5	6.8	6.8	6.8	6.8	7.1	7.1	7.1	7.1
Disc front & rear, Corvette	5.5	5.5	5.8	5.8	5.8	5.8	5.8	5.8	5.8	5.8
Additions to Basic Job:										
O/H 4 wheel cylinders, incl. hone, **ADD:**	1.6	2.3	2.3	2.3	2.3	2.4	2.4	2.4	2.4	—
Overhaul front calipers (both), **ADD:**	3.5	3.5	3.5	2.9	2.9	2.9	2.9	2.9	2.9	2.9
Replace front calipers (both), **ADD:**	.4	.4	.4	.4	.4	.4	.4	.4	.4	.4
Overhaul rear calipers Corvette (both), **ADD:**	3.1	3.1	3.1	3.1	3.1	3.1	3.1	3.1	3.1	3.1
Replace rear calipers Corvette (both), **ADD:**	.6	.6	.6	.6	.6	.6	.6	.6	.6	.6
Overhaul master cylinder, **ADD:**	.8	.8	.8	.8	.8	.8	.8	.8	.8	.8
Related Jobs: (Not during basic job)										
Bleed hydraulic system, 4 wheels	.6	.6	.6	.6	.6	.6	.6	.6	.6	.6
Adjust drum brakes, 4 wheels	.5	.5	.5	.5	.5	.5	.5	.5	.5	—
Replace drum brake shoes, 4 wheels	3.5	3.5	3.5	3.5	3.5	3.5	3.5	3.5	3.5	—
Replace disc brake pads, front wheels	1.5	1.5	1.5	1.5	1.5	1.5	1.0	1.0	1.0	1.0
Replace disc brake pads, rear wheels, Corvette	2.0	2.0	2.0	2.0	2.0	2.0	1.5	1.5	1.5	1.5
O/H front calipers, incl. turn rotors	4.0	4.0	4.0	4.0	4.0	4.0	4.0	4.0	4.0	4.0
Replace front caliper, incl. turn rotor, ea.	2.4	2.4	2.4	2.4	2.4	2.4	2.4	2.4	2.4	2.4
O/H rear calipers, incl. turn rotors, Corvette	4.8	4.8	4.8	4.8	4.8	4.8	4.8	4.8	4.8	4.8
Replace rear caliper, incl. turn rotor, ea., Corvette	2.3	2.3	2.3	2.3	2.3	2.3	2.3	2.3	2.3	2.3
With 4-piston unit, ea., **ADD:**	1.0	1.0	1.0	1.0	1.0	1.0	1.0	1.0	1.0	1.0
Overhaul master cylinder	1.3	1.3	1.5	1.5	1.5	1.5	1.8	1.8	1.8	1.8

Approximate parts cost:
Wheel cylinder seal, boot & bushing pkg. . . . . $ 6.00	Wheel cylinder repair kit, ea. . . . . $ 2.00
Brake shoes and lining sets, front or rear 25.00	Caliper brake housing 50.00
Disc brake pads, set of 2 . . . . 24.00	Oil seal, ea. 2.00
Master cylinder repair kit 18.00	Caliper repair kit, single piston 4.00
	4-piston 10.00

POWER BRAKE UNIT, SERVICE

Includes:
Basic Job: R&R with new unit, test, and adjust brakes.
Additions to Basic Job: Replace vacuum hose or vacuum check valve. Allowance for air conditioning.

MODEL	1966	1967	1968	1969	1970	1971	1972	1973	1974	1975
Basic Job:										
R&R power unit, test, & adj. brakes	1.6	1.6	1.6	1.6	1.5	1.5	1.5	1.5	1.5	1.5
Additions to Basic Job:										
With air conditioning, **ADD:**	.3	.3	.3	.3	.3	.3	.3	.3	.3	.3
Install new hose, **ADD:**	.2	.2	.2	.2	.2	.2	.2	.2	.2	.2
Install new vacuum check valve, **ADD:**	.2	.2	.2	.2	.2	.2	.2	.2	.2	.2

Approximate parts cost:
Power brake unit $30.00-70.00	Vacuum check valve $1.75
Vacuum hose, per ft. 0.90	

CHEVROLET/CORVETTE

PARKING BRAKES, SERVICE AND ADJUST

Includes:
Basic Jobs: Replace defective cable or brake shoes and adjust parking brakes.

MODEL	1966	1967	1968	1969	1970	1971	1972	1973	1974	1975
Basic Jobs:										
Adjust parking brakes	.4	.4	.4	.4	.4	.4	.4	.4	.4	.4
Replace forward cable,										
Corvette	1.0	1.0	1.0	1.0	1.0	1.0	1.0	1.0	1.0	1.0
All others	.8	.8	.8	.8	.8	.8	.8	.8	.8	.8
Replace rear cable, one side,										
Camaro	1.0	1.0	1.0	1.0	1.0	1.0	1.0	1.0	1.0	1.0
Vega	—	—	—	—	—	.7	.7	.7	.7	.7
All others	.8	.8	.8	.8	.8	.8	.8	.8	.8	.8
Replace rear cable both sides,										
Camaro	1.6	1.6	1.6	1.6	1.6	1.6	1.6	1.6	1.6	1.6
Vega	—	—	—	—	—	1.1	1.1	1.1	1.1	1.1
All others	1.5	1.5	1.5	1.5	1.5	1.5	1.5	1.5	1.5	1.5
Replace intermediate cable	.4	.4	.4	.4	.4	.4	.4	.4	.4	.4
Replace parking brake shoes, both sides, Corvette	*7.0	*7.0	*7.0	*7.0	*7.0	2.6	2.6	2.6	2.6	2.6

*Includes R&R rear spindle.

Approximate parts cost:
Front cable	$5.00	Parking brake shoes	$35.00
Intermediate cable	3.50	Rear cable	8.00

LIGHTING SYSTEM, ADJUST AND SERVICE

Includes:
Basic Job: 1. Adjust headlights to inspection requirements.
2. Replace defective parts in rear lighting system.
Additions to Basic Job: Replace associated parts affecting headlight adjustment.
Related Jobs: Replace associated parts not affecting headlight adjustment.

MODEL	1966	1967	1968	1969	1970	1971	1972	1973	1974	1975
Basic Job #1										
Adjust two lights	.4	.4	.4	.4	.4	.4	.4	.4	.4	.4
Adjust four lights	.6	.6	.6	.6	.6	.6	.6	.6	.6	.6
Basic Job #2										
Replace stoplight switch,										
Corvette	.5	.5	.4	.4	.4	.4	.4	.4	.4	.4
All others	.3	.3	.3	.3	.3	.3	.3	.3	.3	.3
Replace back-up light switch,										
Corvette	1.4	1.4	1.4	1.4	1.4	1.4	1.0	1.0	1.0	1.0
All others	.4	.4	.4	.4	.4	.4	.4	.4	.4	.4
Additions to Basic Job:										
Replace sealed beam unit, ea., **ADD:**	.3	.3	.3	.3	.3	.3	.3	.3	.3	.3
Related Jobs:										
Replace headlamp vacuum actuator, one side	.8	.8	.8	.8	.8	.8	.8	.8	.8	.8
Replace headlamp switch,										
Corvette	.4	.4	1.0	1.0	1.0	.8	.8	.8	.8	.8
All others	.6	.6	.4	.4	.4	.4	.4	.4	.4	.4
Replace foot dimmer switch	.3	.3	.3	.3	.3	.3	.3	.3	.3	.3

(THIS SCHEDULE CONTINUED ON NEXT PAGE.)

CHEVROLET/CORVETTE 115

LIGHTING SYSTEM, ADJUST AND SERVICE Continued

MODEL	1966	1967	1968	1969	1970	1971	1972	1973	1974	1975
Related Jobs Continued										
Replace signal/hazard flasher	.3	.3	.3	.3	.3	.3	.3	.3	.3	.3
Replace signal/hazard switch,										
With standard column	.8	.8	.8	.8	.8	.8	.8	.8	.8	.8
With tilt or telescopic column	1.0	1.0	1.0	1.0	1.0	1.0	1.0	1.0	1.0	1.0

Approximate parts cost:
Sealed beam unit ..... $ 4.00	Vacuum actuator $20.00
Signal/hazard flasher 2.00	Headlamp switch 7.00
Signal/hazard switch 15.00	Back-up light switch 3.00-11.00

HEATING SYSTEM, TEST AND SERVICE

Includes:
Basic Job: Drain back-flush, and fill radiator, check radiator and heater hoses and connections, pressure-test radiator cap and system.
Related Jobs: Replace defective parts. Work performed individually and independently of basic job.

MODEL	1966	1967	1968	1969	1970	1971	1972	1973	1974	1975
Basic Job:										
Drain, flush, fill, check, & pressure-test	.9	.9	.9	.9	.9	.9	.9	.9	.9	.9
Related Jobs:										
Replace heater hose, one, inlet or outlet	.5	.5	.5	.5	.5	.5	.5	.5	.5	.5
Replace each additional hose, **ADD:**	.2	.2	.2	.2	.2	.2	.2	.2	.2	.2
With air conditioning, **ADD:**	.3	.3	.3	.3	.3	.3	.3	.3	.3	.3
Replace blower motor and/or impeller,										
Camaro	2.1	2.1	2.1	2.1	2.1	2.1	1.0	1.0	1.0	1.0
Chevy II, Chevy, Nova	1.0	1.0	1.0	1.0	1.0	1.0	.8	.8	.8	.8
Corvette	.3	.3	.3	.3	.3	.3	.6	.6	.6	.6
All others	.8	.8	.8	.8	.8	.8	.8	.8	.8	.8
With air conditioning, see Air Conditioning Blower Motor Section										
Replace heater core, **with** air conditioning,										
Chevelle, Monte Carlo, Four Season	4.1	4.1	2.4	2.4	2.4	2.4	2.7	2.7	2.7	2.7
Chevrolet, Comfortron	3.9	3.9	3.9	3.9	3.9	3.9	2.7	2.7	2.7	2.7
Chevy II, Camaro, Four Season	2.7	2.7	2.7	2.7	2.7	2.7	2.9	2.9	2.7	2.7
Corvette, Four Season	—	—	2.2	2.2	2.2	2.2	3.0	3.0	3.0	3.0
All others, Four Season	2.9	2.9	2.9	2.9	2.9	2.9	2.8	2.8	2.8	2.8
Replace heater core, **without** air conditioning,										
Camaro	2.2	2.2	2.2	2.2	2.2	2.2	1.4	1.4	1.4	1.4
Corvette	1.7	1.7	1.8	1.8	1.8	1.8	2.6	2.6	2.6	2.6
Vega	—	—	—	—	—	1.1	1.1	1.1	1.1	1.1
All others	1.6	1.6	1.6	1.6	1.6	1.6	1.6	1.6	1.6	1.6
Replace blower motor switch,										
Chevelle, Monte Carlo	.7	.7	.7	.7	.7	.7	.7	.7	.7	.7
Corvette, Nova	.5	.5	.5	.5	.5	.5	.6	.6	.6	.6
All others	.5	.5	.5	.5	.5	.5	.5	.5	.5	.5

Approximate parts cost:
Heater hose, per ft. ..... $ 0.75	Heater core $45.00
Blower motor 30.00	Blower motor switch 2.00-10.00

CHEVROLET/CORVETTE

AIR CONDITIONING SYSTEM, SPRING TUNE-UP

Includes:

Basic Job: Clean condenser fins; adjust drive belt tension; test anti-freeze; tighten compressor, condenser, and evaporator mounts. Pressure-test and leak-check system. Check system for performance.

Additions to Basic Job: Replace defective parts.

MODEL	1966	1967	1968	1969	1970	1971	1972	1973	1974	1975
Basic Job:										
Perform complete spring tune-up	2.0	2.0	2.0	2.0	2.0	2.0	2.0	2.0	2.0	2.0
Additions to Basic Job:										
Replace compressor belt & adjust, **ADD:**	.4	.4	.4	.4	.4	.4	.4	.4	.4	.4
Replace compr. clutch pulley w/hub assy., **ADD:**	.5	.5	.5	.5	.5	.5	.5	.5	.5	.5
Replace compr. clutch coil, **ADD:**	.8	.8	.8	.8	.8	.8	.8	.8	.8	.8
Replace compr. clutch bearing, **ADD:**	.8	.8	.8	.8	.8	.8	.8	.8	.8	.8

Approximate parts cost:

Compressor drive belt	$ 3.00	Compressor clutch coil	$28.00
Compressor clutch pulley w/hub	75.00	Compressor clutch bearing	23.00
Freon, per 14 oz. can	2.50	Anti-freeze, per gal.	9.50

AIR CONDITIONING SYSTEM, MAJOR SERVICE

Includes:

Basic Job: Drain system in order to replace defective component; evacuate, dehydrate, and recharge system; pressure-test and leak-check; clean condenser fins; adjust drive belt tension; tighten compressor, condenser, and evaporator mounts; and conduct performance test.

Additions to Basic Job: Replace or overhaul compressor. Replace other defective parts.

MODEL	1966	1967	1968	1969	1970	1971	1972	1973	1974	1975
Basic Job:										
Drain, evacuate, dehydrate, charge & test	3.0	3.0	3.0	3.0	3.0	3.0	3.0	3.0	3.0	3.0
Additions to Basic Job:										
Replace compressor, **ADD:**	1.2	1.2	1.2	1.2	1.2	1.2	1.2	1.2	1.2	1.2
Overhaul compressor, incl. R&R, **ADD:**	2.9	2.9	2.9	2.9	2.9	2.9	2.9	2.9	2.9	2.9
Replace relief valve, **ADD:**	1.5	1.5	1.5	1.5	.8	.8	.8	.8	.8	.8
Replace compr. front head or reed valve, **ADD:**	1.4	1.4	1.4	1.4	1.4	1.4	.5	.5	.5	.5
Replace compr. rear head or reed valve, **ADD:**	1.1	1.1	1.1	1.1	1.1	1.1	.6	.6	.6	.6
Replace suction throttling valve, **ADD:**	.6	.6	.6	.6	.6	.6	.6	.6	.6	.6
Replace condenser, **ADD:**	1.3	1.3	1.3	1.3	1.3	1.3	1.3	1.3	1.3	1.3
Replace evaporator core,										
Corvette, Four Season, **ADD:**	3.2	3.2	1.6	1.6	1.6	1.6	1.2	1.2	1.2	1.2
Chevelle, Camaro, Four Season, **ADD:**	4.1	4.1	2.2	2.2	2.2	2.2	1.9	1.9	1.9	1.9
Chevy II, Nova, Four Season, **ADD:**	3.9	3.9	2.8	2.8	2.8	2.8	2.3	2.3	1.8	1.8
All others, Comfortron, GMC/AC, **ADD:**	3.1	3.1	3.1	3.1	3.1	3.1	2.6	2.6	2.6	2.6
With AIR, **ADD:**	.2	.2	.2	.2	.2	.2	.2	.2	.2	.2
Replace sight-glass, **ADD:**	1.4	1.4	1.4	1.4	1.4	1.4	.9	.9	.9	.9
Replace dehydrator-receiver tank, **ADD:**	1.0	1.0	1.0	.8	.8	.8	.5	.5	.5	.5
Replace expansion valve, **ADD:**	1.5	1.5	1.5	.8	.8	.8	.8	.8	.8	.8
Replace POA valve,										
Corvette, **ADD:**	1.8	1.8	1.1	1.1	1.1	1.1	.9	.9	.9	.9
All others, **ADD:**	.7	.7	.7	.7	.7	.7	.5	.5	.5	.5
Replace compressor shaft seal, **ADD:**	1.4	1.4	1.4	1.4	1.4	1.4	.9	.9	.9	.9
Replace valves-in-receiver (VIR) assy.,										
Corvette, **ADD:**	—	—	—	—	—	—	—	1.4	1.4	1.4
All others, **ADD:**	—	—	—	—	—	—	—	.5	.5	.5

(THIS SCHEDULE CONTINUED ON NEXT PAGE.)

CHEVROLET/CORVETTE 117

AIR CONDITIONING SYSTEM, MAJOR SERVICE Continued

MODEL	1966	1967	1968	1969	1970	1971	1972	1973	1974	1975
Additions to Basic Job Continued										
O/H VIR assy. incl. repl. nec. parts, **ADD:**	—	—	—	—	—	—	—	1.0	1.0	1.0
Replace one hose, **ADD:**	.4	.4	.4	.4	.4	.4	.4	.4	.4	.4

Approximate parts cost:

Compressor	$ 85.00	Expansion valve	$36.00
Compressor front head & valve assy.	20.00	Pressure-operated absolute (POA) valve	30.00
Compressor rear head & valve assy.	65.00	Hose, per ft.	2.75
Compressor pressure relief valve	7.00	Hose fitting, ea.	1.00
Condenser	75.00-125.00	Freon, per 14 oz. can	2.50
Evaporator core assy.	90.00-160.00	Anti-freeze, per gal.	9.50
Compressor shaft seal assy.	8.00	Valves-in-receiver (VIR) assembly	80.00

AIR CONDITIONING SYSTEM BLOWER MOTOR OR CONTROLS, SERVICE

Includes:

Basic Jobs: Conduct performance test of system to determine defective part; R&R component; clean condenser fins; adjust drive belt tension; tighten all mounts; and test system.

MODEL	1966	1967	1968	1969	1970	1971	1972	1973	1974	1975
Basic Jobs:										
R&R blower motor. Includes R&R components to gain access,										
Chevy II, Nova, w/Four Season	1.2	1.2	1.2	1.2	1.2	1.2	1.2	1.2	.8	.8
Camaro, w/Four Season	2.4	2.4	2.4	2.4	2.4	2.4	.9	.9	.9	.9
Corvette, w/Four Season	.7	.7	.7	.7	.7	.7	.7	.7	.7	.4
All others with GM Chevrolet A/C	2.7	2.7	2.7	2.7	2.7	2.7	1.1	1.1	1.1	1.1
R&R blower motor switch, test system,										
Chevelle, Monte Carlo	.7	.7	.7	.7	.7	.7	.7	.7	.7	.7
Corvette, Nova	.5	.5	.5	.5	.5	.5	.6	.6	.6	.6
All others	.5	.5	.5	.5	.5	.5	.5	.5	.5	.5
R&R compressor clutch switch, test system,										
Corvette, Chevy II, Nova w/Four Season	1.2	1.2	1.2	1.2	1.2	—	—	—	—	—
All others	1.5	1.5	1.5	1.5	1.5	—	—	—	—	—
R&R evaporator thermostatic switch	1.1	1.1	1.1	1.1	1.1	1.1	1.1	1.1	1.1	1.1
R&R control assembly. Includes R&R components to gain access.										
Corvette	1.2	1.2	1.2	1.2	1.2	1.2	1.2	1.2	1.2	1.2
All others	1.6	1.6	1.6	1.6	1.6	1.6	1.6	1.6	1.6	1.6
Replace control cable, temperature door,										
Camaro, Chevelle, Corvette, w/Four Season	.7	.7	1.0	1.0	1.0	1.0	1.2	1.2	1.2	1.2
All others	.7	.7	.7	.7	.7	.7	1.0	1.0	1.0	1.0
Replace Comfortron programmer, including test	—	—	—	—	—	1.0	1.0	1.0	1.0	1.0

Approximate parts cost:

Blower motor	$23.00	Control cable, per ft.	$ 0.80
Blower motor switch	3.00	Control cable fittings, ea.	0.75
Evaporator thermostatic switch	4.00	Control assembly	24.00
Compressor clutch switch	2.50		

118 CHRYSLER/PLYMOUTH/DODGE

SERVICE STATION MAINTENANCE

Includes:
Basic Job: Lubricate chassis, drain oil, change filters, repack front wheel bearings, repack U-joints, and lubricate front end. Check fluid levels of battery, radiator, air conditioner, brake master cylinder, power steering reservoir, transmission, and differential. Check condition of hoses and drive belts. Lubricate miscellaneous moving parts, latches, hinges, etc.
Related Jobs: Service individual systems or components. See detailed description of work included for each job in separate major section.
Additions to Basic or Related Jobs: Allowances for special equipment installed.

MODEL	1966	1967	1968	1969	1970	1971	1972	1973	1974	1975
Basic Job:										
General lubrication & systems check,										
6-cylinder	1.0	1.0	1.0	1.0	1.0	1.0	1.0	1.0	1.0	1.0
Imperial	1.5	1.5	1.5	1.5	1.5	1.5	1.5	1.5	1.5	1.5
All other V-8 engines	1.1	1.1	1.1	1.1	1.1	1.1	1.1	1.1	1.1	1.1
With air conditioning, **ADD:**	.3	.3	.3	.3	.3	.3	.3	.3	.3	.3
With CAS or AIR pump, **ADD:**	.2	.2	.2	.2	.2	.2	.2	.2	.2	.2
With disc brakes, **ADD:**	.9	.9	.9	.9	.9	.9	.9	.9	.9	.9
Related Jobs:										
Service Battery Clean, test, & fill	.3	.3	.3	.3	.3	.3	.3	.3	.3	.3
Clean terminals	.2	.2	.2	.2	.2	.2	.2	.2	.2	.2
Replace ground cable	.2	.2	.2	.2	.2	.2	.2	.2	.2	.2
Replace starter cable	.3	.3	.3	.3	.3	.3	.3	.3	.3	.3
Replace battery	.3	.3	.3	.3	.3	.3	.3	.3	.3	.3
Service Cooling System										
Back-flush, fill, & pressure test system	.9	.9	.9	.9	.9	.9	.9	.9	.9	.9
Replace upper hose	.3	.3	.3	.3	.3	.3	.3	.3	.3	.3
Replace lower hose	.4	.5	.4	.4	.4	.4	.4	.4	.4	.4
Replace water pump bypass hose,										
6-cylinder	.9	.9	.9	.9	.9	.9	.9	—	—	—
V-8 engine	.3	.3	.3	.3	.3	.3	.3	—	—	—
Replace thermostat	.5	.5	.5	.5	.5	.5	.5	.5	.5	.5
Repl. water pump drive belt & adjust	.6	.6	.6	.6	.6	.6	.6	.6	.6	.6
Replace water pump,										
6-cylinder	.9	.9	.9	.9	.9	.9	.9	.9	.9	.9
V-8 small block	1.2	1.2	1.2	1.2	1.2	1.2	1.2	1.2	1.2	1.2
V-8 large block	1.2	1.2	1.2	.8	.8	.8	.8	.8	.8	.8
V-8 Hemi engine	1.4	1.4	1.4	1.4	1.4	1.4	—	—	—	—
Service Hydraulic Brake System										
Adjust drum brakes	.5	.5	.5	.5	.5	.5	.5	.5	.5	.5
Replace brake shoes	3.5	3.5	3.5	3.5	3.5	3.5	3.5	3.5	3.5	3.5
Bleed hydraulic system	.6	.6	.6	.6	.6	.6	.6	.6	.6	.6
Replace front disc brake pads	.6	.6	.6	.6	.6	.6	.6	.6	.6	.6
Replace rear disc brake pads	—	—	—	—	—	—	—	—	.8	.8
Overhaul master cylinder	1.6	2.3	2.3	2.3	2.3	2.4	2.4	2.4	2.4	2.4
O/h wheel cylinders, drum brakes, (4)	3.4	3.4	4.4	4.4	4.4	4.4	4.0	4.0	4.0	4.0
O/h fr. calipers, incl. turn rotors	5.3	5.3	5.3	5.3	4.6	4.6	4.6	4.6	4.6	4.6
O/h rear calipers, incl. turn rotors	—	—	—	—	—	—	—	—	4.8	4.8
With power brakes, **ADD:**	.2	.2	.2	.2	.2	.2	.2	.2	.2	.2
Service Parking Brakes										
Replace forward cable,										
Imperial	1.0	1.0	1.0	1.0	1.0	1.0	1.0	1.3	1.3	1.3
All others	1.0	1.0	1.0	1.0	1.0	1.0	1.0	1.0	1.0	1.0
Replace rear cable, one side	1.0	1.0	1.0	1.0	1.0	1.0	1.0	1.0	1.0	1.0
Replace parking brake shoes, both sides	—	—	—	—	—	—	—	—	1.9	1.9

(THIS SCHEDULE CONTINUED ON NEXT PAGE.)

CHRYSLER/PLYMOUTH/DODGE

SERVICE STATION MAINTENANCE Continued

MODEL	1966	1967	1968	1969	1970	1971	1972	1973	1974	1975
Service Suspension System										
Replace front shock absorber, both sides										
Imperial	1.8	1.8	1.8	1.8	1.8	1.8	1.8	1.3	1.3	1.3
All others	.9	.9	.9	.9	.9	.9	.9	.6	.6	.6
Replace rear shock absorber, both sides	.8	.8	.8	.8	.8	.8	.8	.8	.8	.8
Replace spring shackle and bushings; eye bolt and bushings	.7	.7	.7	.7	.7	.7	.7	.7	.7	.7
Replace rear leaf spring & shim to align pinion angle,										
Imperial	—	2.2	2.2	1.8	1.8	1.8	1.8	2.0	2.0	2.0
All others	1.6	1.6	1.6	1.6	1.8	1.8	1.8	1.7	1.7	1.7
Service Front End & Steering System										
Adjust toe-in only	.4	.4	.4	.4	.4	.4	.4	.4	.4	.4
Replace tie-rods or tie-rod ends, (4)	1.6	1.6	1.5	1.5	1.5	1.5	1.5	1.5	1.5	1.5
Repl. Pitman arm, incl. adjust toe-in	.8	.8	.8	.8	.8	.8	.8	.8	.8	.8
Repl. steering idler arm or bushing, including adjust toe-in	.8	.8	.8	.8	.8	.8	.8	.8	.8	.8
Repl. pwr. steer. pump drive belt	.3	.3	.3	.3	.3	.3	.3	.3	.3	.3
With air conditioning, **ADD**:	.2	.2	.2	.2	.2	.2	.2	.2	.2	.2
Check & replenish reservoir fluid	.2	.2	.2	.2	.2	.2	.2	.2	.2	.2
Repl. press. hose, incl. adjust dr. belt	.5	.5	.6	.6	.6	.6	.6	.6	.6	.6
Repl. return hose, incl. adjust dr. belt	.4	.4	.4	.4	.4	.4	.4	.4	.4	.4
Balance four wheels on car,										
With drum brakes	1.2	1.2	1.2	1.2	1.2	1.2	1.2	1.2	1.2	1.2
With disc/drum brakes	1.5	1.5	1.5	1.5	1.5	1.5	1.5	1.5	1.5	1.5
Service Ignition System										
Adjust & install new spark plugs,										
6-cylinder	.6	.6	.6	.6	.6	.6	.6	.6	.6	.6
V-8 400 & 440 engine	.9	.9	.9	.9	.9	.9	.9	.9	.9	.9
All others	.8	.8	.8	.8	.8	.8	.8	.8	.8	.8
With air conditioning, **ADD**:	.3	.3	.3	.3	.3	.3	.3	.3	.3	.3
With CAS or AIR, **ADD**:	.3	.3	.3	.3	.3	.3	.3	.3	.3	.3
Replace points & condenser & adjust ign. timing	1.1	1.1	1.0	1.0	1.3	1.3	1.1	—	—	—
Replace distributor cap, **ADD**:	.4	.4	.4	.3	.3	.3	.3	.3	.3	.3
Check reluctor air gap and ign. timing	—	—	—	—	—	—	.4	.4	.4	.4
Replace spark plug wires,										
6-cylinder	.5	.5	.6	.6	.8	.8	.6	.6	.6	.6
V-8 engine	.7	.7	.8	.9	.9	.8	.8	.8	.8	.8
With air conditioning, **ADD**:	.5	.5	.5	.5	.5	.5	.5	.5	.5	.5
V-8 Hemi engine, **ADD**:	.4	.4	.4	.4	.4	.4	—	—	—	—
Replace ignition coil	.4	.4	.4	.4	.4	.4	.4	.4	.4	.4
Perform Minor Tune-up										
6-cylinder										
V-8 small & large block										
V-8 Hemi engine										
Note: See minor tune-up section for work included and additions.										
Perform Major Tune-up										
6-cylinder	5.8	5.8	5.8	5.8	6.1	6.1	6.1	6.3	6.3	6.5
V-8 small block	6.3	6.3	6.3	6.5	6.5	6.5	6.5	6.8	6.8	7.0
V-8 large block	6.6	6.6	6.6	6.8	6.8	6.8	6.8	7.1	7.1	7.3
V-8 Hemi engine	10.0	10.0	10.0	10.2	10.2	10.2	—	—	—	—
Note: See major tune-up section for work included and additions.										

120 CHRYSLER/PLYMOUTH/DODGE

SERVICE STATION MAINTENANCE Continued

MODEL	1966	1967	1968	1969	1970	1971	1972	1973	1974	1975
Service Fuel System										
Complete carburetor adjustments,										
Single barrel	.4	.4	.4	.4	.4	.4	.4	.4	.4	.4
Two or four-barrel	.6	.6	.6	.6	.6	.6	.6	.6	.6	.6
Six-barrel (3x2) or 8-barrel (2x4)	.8	.8	.8	.8	.8	.8	.8	.8	.8	.8
Replace fuel filter	.3	.3	.3	.3	.3	.3	.3	.3	.3	.3
Test & replace fuel pump,										
6-cylinder	.5	.5	.5	.5	.5	.5	.5	.5	.5	.5
V-8 engine	.7	.7	.7	.7	.7	.7	.8	.8	.8	.8
Electric pump	—	—	—	—	—	—	.6	.6	.6	.6
Replace flexible fuel line	.3	.3	.3	.3	.3	.3	.3	.3	.3	.3
Service Driveshaft										
R&R driveshaft & overhaul both U-joints,										
Cross & roller type	1.2	1.2	1.2	1.0	1.0	1.0	1.0	1.0	1.0	1.0
Constant velocity type	2.0	2.0	2.0	2.0	2.0	2.0	2.0	2.0	2.0	2.0
Service Charging System										
Test system and adjust regulator	.6	.6	.6	.6	.6	.6	.6	.6	.6	.6
R&R alternator incl. pulley	.6	.6	.6	.6	.7	.7	.7	.7	.7	.7
With air conditioning, **ADD:**	.1	.1	.1	.1	.1	.1	.1	.1	.1	.1
With AIR, **ADD:**	.2	.2	.2	.2	.2	.2	.2	.2	.2	.2
Overhaul alternator after removal	2.3	2.3	1.5	1.5	1.5	1.5	1.5	1.5	1.5	1.5
Replace regulator	.3	.3	.3	.3	.4	.4	.4	.3	.3	.3
Service Cranking System										
R&R starter,										
6-cylinder	.7	.7	.7	.7	.7	.8	.8	.8	.8	.8
V-8 small block	1.8	1.8	1.8	1.3	1.3	1.3	1.3	1.3	1.3	1.3
V-8 large block	.9	.9	.9	.9	.9	.9	1.1	1.1	1.1	1.1
Overhaul starter after removal	1.7	1.7	1.7	1.7	1.7	1.7	1.7	1.7	1.7	1.7
Replace starter battery cable	.3	.3	.3	.3	.3	.3	.3	.3	.3	.3
Replace starter solenoid, incl. sys. test										
6-cylinder	1.7	1.7	1.7	1.7	1.7	1.7	1.7	1.7	1.7	1.7
V-8 small block	2.7	2.6	2.6	2.0	1.9	1.9	1.9	1.9	1.8	1.8
V-8 large block	1.9	1.9	1.9	1.9	2.4	2.4	2.3	2.0	2.0	2.0
Service Lighting System										
Adjust two headlights	.4	.4	.4	.4	.4	.4	.4	.4	.4	.4
Adjust four headlights	.6	.6	.6	.6	.6	.6	.6	.6	.6	.6
Replace sealed beam unit, ea.	.3	.3	.3	.3	.3	.3	.3	.3	.3	.3
Replace foot dimmer switch	.3	.3	.3	.3	.3	.3	.3	.3	.3	.3
Replace rotating motor	.7	.7	.4	.4	.4	.4	.4	.4	.4	.4
Replace rotating motor relay	.4	.4	.6	.6	.6	.6	.6	.6	.6	.6
Replace signal/hazard flasher	.2	.2	.2	.2	.2	.2	.2	.2	.2	.2
Replace turn signal/hazard switch,										
With standard column	.8	.8	.8	.8	.8	.8	.8	.8	.8	.8
With tilt or telescopic column	1.0	1.0	1.0	1.0	1.0	1.0	1.0	1.0	1.0	1.0
Replace back-up light switch	.4	.4	.4	.4	.4	.4	.4	.4	.4	.4
Replace stoplight switch	.4	.4	.4	.4	.4	.4	.4	.4	.4	.4

CHRYSLER/PLYMOUTH/DODGE

TUNE-UP, MINOR

Includes:

Basic Job: Perform the following work:
1. Service air cleaner element.
2. Replace PCV valve.
3. Replace crankcase ventilation filter in air cleaner.
4. Clean battery terminals.
5. Check condition and tension of all drive belts.
6. Check all hoses and hose connections.
7. Check operation of heated air system (air cleaner), manifold heat valve, and automatic choke. Service where necessary.
8. Replace fuel filter.
9. Perform compression test.
10. Replace spark plugs.
11. Replace ignition points and condenser.
12. Adjust dwell or reluctor air gap and ignition timing.
13. Adjust carburetor idle mixture and speed.
14. Make necessary ignition and carburetor adjustments to obtain satisfactory exhaust system analyzer readings.

Additions to Basic Job: Allowances for special equipment and carburetor combinations.

MODEL	1966	1967	1968	1969	1970	1971	1972	1973	1974	1975
Basic Job:										
Perform minor tune-up,										
6-cylinder	2.2	2.2	2.2	2.2	2.4	2.4	2.4	2.4	2.4	2.4
V-8 small & large block	2.7	2.7	2.7	2.7	2.9	2.9	2.9	2.9	2.9	2.9
V-8 Hemi engine	3.5	3.5	3.5	3.5	3.5	3.5	—	—	—	—
Additions to Basic Job:										
With 4-bbl. carb. (V-8 sm. bl. only) ADD:	.2	.2	.2	.2	.2	.2	.3	.3	.3	.3
With 6-bbl. or 8-bbl. carbs., ADD:	.4	.4	.4	.4	.4	—	—	—	—	—
With CAS or AIR pump, ADD:	.3	.3	.3	.3	.3	.3	.3	.3	.3	.3
With air conditioning, ADD:	.6	.6	.6	.6	.6	.6	.6	.6	.6	.6

Approximate parts cost:

Spark plugs, each .... $ 1.50
Points & condenser 5.00
PCV valve 3.00
Air cleaner element .... $ 5.50
Fuel filter 3.50

TUNE-UP, MAJOR

Includes:

Basic Job: Perform the following work:
1. Service air cleaner element.
2. Replace crankcase ventilation filter in air cleaner.
3. Replace PCV valve.
4. Check drive belts and adjust for proper tension.
5. Check all hoses and hose connections.
6. Clean battery terminals.
7. Check operation of manifold heat valve and automatic choke. Service where necessary.
8. Check operation of heated-air system.
9. Check exhaust and evaporative emission control systems for proper operation.
10. Replace fuel filter.
11. Perform compression check.
12. Replace spark plugs.
13. Replace ignition points and condenser.
14. Adjust dwell or reluctor air gap and ignition timing.
15. Check distributor cap and rotor.
16. Tighten cylinder head bolts.
17. Adjust valve lash (where applicable).
18. Overhaul carburetor(s).
19. Adjust carburetor(s) idle mixture and speed.
20. Make necessary ignition and carburetor adjustments to obtain satisfactory exhaust system analyzer readings.

Additions to Basic Job: Allowances for special equipment and carburetor combinations.

MODEL	1966	1967	1968	1969	1970	1971	1972	1973	1974	1975
Basic Job:										
Perform major tune-up										
6-cylinder	5.8	5.8	5.8	5.8	6.1	6.1	6.1	6.3	6.3	6.5
V-8 small block	6.3	6.3	6.3	6.5	6.5	6.5	6.5	6.8	6.8	7.0
V-8 large block	6.6	6.6	6.6	6.8	6.8	6.8	6.8	7.1	7.1	7.3
V-8 Hemi engine	10.0	10.0	10.0	10.2	10.2	10.2	—	—	—	—

122 CHRYSLER/PLYMOUTH/DODGE

MAJOR TUNE-UP Continued

MODEL	1966	1967	1968	1969	1970	1971	1972	1973	1974	1975
Additions to Basic Job:										
With CAS or AIR pump, **ADD**:	.7	.7	.7	.7	.7	.7	.7	.7	.7	.7
Replace hydraulic valve lifter, one, **ADD**:	2.0	2.0	2.0	2.0	2.0	2.0	2.0	2.0	2.0	2.0
Hemi engine with pwr. brakes, **ADD**:	.4	.4	.4	.4	.4	.4	—	—	—	—
With 4-bbl. carb. (V-8 sm. bl. only) **ADD**:	1.0	1.0	1.0	1.0	1.0	1.0	1.1	1.1	1.1	1.1
With 6-bbl. carbs. (3x2), **ADD**:	4.0	4.0	4.0	4.0	4.0	—	—	—	—	—
With 8-bbl. carbs. (2x4), **ADD**:	2.5	2.5	2.5	2.5	2.5	—	—	—	—	—
With air conditioning, **ADD**:	.6	.6	.6	.6	.6	.6	.6	.6	.6	.6

Approximate parts cost:

Spark plugs, each	$1.50	Fuel filter	$ 3.50
Points & condenser	5.00	Carburetor repair kit, Carter	10.00
PCV valve	3.00	Stromberg	6.00
Air cleaner element	5.50	Holley	11.00

EMISSION CONTROL SYSTEMS, TESTS FOR SMOG STATION CERTIFICATION

Includes:
Basic Job: Test crankcase, exhaust and evaporative emission control systems. Check heated-air system. Check HC/CO level with exhaust analyzer. Sign certification certificate. (No adjustments or repairs included in basic job.)
Related Jobs: Service any defective emission control system. Perform minor or major tune-up as required.
Additions to Related Jobs: Service or replace defective part(s) in the system. Allowances for special equipment installed and carburetor combinations.

MODEL	1966	1967	1968	1969	1970	1971	1972	1973	1974	1975
Basic Job:										
Test all systems & sign certificate,										
Dart and Valiant	.8	.8	.8	.8	.8	.8	.8	.8	.8	.8
Imperial	1.2	1.2	1.2	1.2	1.2	1.2	1.2	1.2	1.2	1.2
All others	1.0	1.0	1.0	1.0	1.0	1.0	1.0	1.0	1.0	1.0
Related Jobs:										
Service crankcase emission control system	.3	.3	.3	.3	.3	.3	.3	.3	.3	.3
Service evaporative emission contr. system	—	—	—	—	.4	.4	.4	.4	.4	.4
Exhaust emission control systems,										
Service clean air package (CAP)	.4	.4	.4	.4	—	—	—	—	—	—
Service heated-air system	.3	.3	.3	.3	.3	.3	.3	.3	.3	.3
Service distributor retard system	.3	.3	.3	.3	.3	.3	.3	.3	.3	.3
Service NOx control system	—	—	—	—	—	.5	.5	.5	.5	.5
Service EGR system	—	—	—	—	—	—	.4	.4	.4	.4
Service OSAC system	—	—	—	—	—	—	—	.4	.4	—
Service exhaust port air inj. (AIR) sys.	—	—	—	—	—	—	.5	.5	.5	.5
Replace catalytic converter	—	—	—	—	—	—	—	—	—	1.8
Note: See separate section for replacement of components in each system.										
Perform minor tune-up,										
6-cylinder	2.2	2.2	2.2	2.2	2.4	2.4	2.4	2.4	2.4	2.4
V-8 small & large block	2.7	2.7	2.7	2.7	2.9	2.9	2.9	2.9	2.9	2.9
V-8 Hemi engine	3.5	3.5	3.5	3.5	3.5	3.5	—	—	—	—
Perform major tune-up,										
6-cylinder	5.8	5.8	5.8	5.8	6.1	6.1	6.1	6.3	6.3	6.5
V-8 small block	6.3	6.3	6.3	6.5	6.5	6.5	6.5	6.8	6.8	7.0
V-8 large block	6.6	6.6	6.6	6.8	6.8	6.8	6.8	7.1	7.1	7.3
V-8 Hemi engine	10.0	10.0	10.0	10.2	10.2	10.2	—	—	—	—

(THIS SCHEDULE CONTINUED ON NEXT PAGE.)

CHRYSLER/PLYMOUTH/DODGE

EMISSION CONTROL SYSTEMS, TESTS FOR SMOG STATION CERTIFICATION Continued

MODEL	1966	1967	1968	1969	1970	1971	1972	1973	1974	1975
Additions to Related Jobs:										
Major Tune-up										
With 4-bbl. carb. (V-8 sm. bl.) **ADD:**	1.0	1.0	1.0	1.0	1.0	1.0	1.1	1.1	1.1	1.1
With 6-bbl. carbs. (3x2), **ADD:**	4.0	4.0	4.0	4.0	4.0	—	—	—	—	—
With 8-bbl. carbs. (2x4), **ADD:**	2.5	2.5	2.5	2.5	2.5	—	—	—	—	—
Minor Tune-up										
With 4-bbl. carb. (V-8 sm. bl.) **ADD:**	.2	.2	.2	.2	.2	.2	.3	.3	.3	.3
With 6-bbl. or 8-bbl. carbs., **ADD:**	.4	.4	.4	.4	.4	—	—	—	—	—
With CAS or AIR pump, **ADD:**	.3	.3	.3	.3	.3	.3	.3	.3	.3	.3
With air conditioning, **ADD:**	.6	.6	.6	.6	.6	.6	.6	.6	.6	.6

Approximate parts cost:
Catalytic converter $175.00
Minor tune-up parts 25.00-30.00
Major tune-up parts $35.00

EMISSION CONTROL SYSTEMS, COMPLETE TEST OR SERVICE

Includes:
Basic Job: Make all necessary tests and repairs. Sign certification certificate.

1. Replace PCV valve, check all vacuum passageways and hoses.
2. Replace crankcase ventilation filter in air cleaner.
3. Test purge-control valve, gas tank filler cap, vent lines, and hoses for leakage.
4. Replace evaporation system charcoal canister filter.
5. Clean EGR valve and test control system.
6. Check distributor retard system.
7. Check NOx system.
8. Check Orfice Spark Advance Control (OSAC) system.
9. Check operation of manifold heat control valve and automatic choke. Free-up where necessary.
10. Check and adjust tension of drive belts.
11. Check operation of heated air system.
12. Check AIR pump air flow.
13. Check routing and condition of hoses.
14. Check operation of diverter or bypass valve.
15. Inspect air manifold and hoses.
16. Replace catalytic converter, if necessary.
17. Determine if engine tune-up is required.

Related Jobs: Minor or major tune-up as required.

MODEL	1966	1967	1968	1969	1970	1971	1972	1973	1974	1975
Basic Job:										
Perform emission control system tune-up,										
6-cylinder	2.8	2.8	2.8	2.8	3.3	3.3	3.3	3.3	3.3	3.5
V-8 small or large block	3.3	3.3	3.3	3.3	38	3.8	3.8	3.8	3.8	4.0
Additions to Basic Job:										
With AIR installed, all models, **ADD:**	.5	.5	.5	.5	.5	.5	.5	.5	.5	.5
Replace catalytic converter, **ADD:**	—	—	—	—	—	—	—	—	—	1.8
Related Jobs:										
Perform minor tune-up,										
6-cylinder	2.2	2.2	2.2	2.2	2.4	2.4	2.4	2.4	2.4	2.4
V-8 small or large block	2.7	2.7	2.7	2.7	2.9	2.9	2.9	2.9	2.9	2.9
V-8 Hemi engine	3.5	3.5	3.5	3.5	3.5	3.5	—	—	—	—
Perform major tune-up,										
6-cylinder	5.8	5.8	5.8	5.8	6.1	6.1	6.1	6.3	6.3	6.5
V-8 small block	6.3	6.3	6.3	6.5	6.5	6.5	6.5	6.8	6.8	7.0
V-8 large block	6.6	6.6	6.6	6.8	6.8	6.8	6.8	7.1	7.1	7.3
V-8 Hemi engine	10.0	10.0	10.0	10.2	10.2	10.2	—	—	—	—

CHRYSLER/PLYMOUTH/DODGE

EMISSION CONTROL SYSTEMS, COMPLETE TEST OR SERVICE Continued

MODEL	1966	1967	1968	1969	1970	1971	1972	1973	1974	1975
Additions to Related Jobs:										
With 4 bbl. carb. (V-8 sm. bl. only) ADD:	.2	.2	.2	.2	.2	.2	.3	.3	.3	.3
With 6 bbl. or 8 bbl. carbs., ADD:	.4	.4	.4	.4	.4	—	—	—	—	—
With air conditioning, ADD:	.6	.6	.6	.6	.6	.6	.6	.6	.6	.6

Approximate parts cost:
PCV valve	$ 3.00	Drive belt	$ 3.00
Hose, per ft.	0.75	Catalytic converter	175.00
Canister filter	1.00	Diverter valve	12.00
Purge control valve	4.00	Air pump	50.00
Minor tune-up parts	25.00-35.00	Major tune-up parts	35.00

POSITIVE CRANKCASE VENTILATION (PCV) SYSTEM, TEST AND SERVICE

Includes:
Basic Job: Test PCV valve, check all vacuum passageways, and inspect hoses. Clean or replace air filter.
Additions to Basic Job: Replace defective parts. (Do not attempt to clean PCV valve; replace if valve is not free.)

MODEL	1966	1967	1968	1969	1970	1971	1972	1973	1974	1975
Basic Job:										
Test PCV system, all models	.3	.3	.3	.3	.3	.3	.3	.3	.3	.3
Additions to Basic Job:										
Replace PCV valve, ADD:	.3	.3	.3	.3	.3	.3	.3	.3	.3	.3
Replace all hoses, ADD:	.6	.6	.6	.6	.6	.6	.6	.6	.6	.6

Approximate parts cost:
PCV valve	$3.00	Hose, per ft.	$0.75

NOx CONTROL SYSTEM, TEST AND SERVICE

Includes:
Basic Job: Check engine speed in gear using tachometer and timing light, test NOx solenoid and transmission switch.
Additions to Basic Job: Replace defective parts.

MODEL	1966	1967	1968	1969	1970	1971	1972	1973	1974	1975
Basic Job:										
Test NOx control system, all models	—	—	—	—	—	.5	.5	.5	.5	.5
Additions to Basic Job:										
Replace NOx solenoid vacuum valve, ADD:	—	—	—	—	—	1.1	1.1	1.1	1.1	1.1
Replace NOx trans. position switch,										
Manual transmission, ADD:	—	—	—	—	—	.8	.8	.8	.8	.8
Automatic transmission, ADD:	—	—	—	—	—	1.1	1.1	1.1	1.1	1.1
Replace NOx thermal switch, ADD:	—	—	—	—	—	1.1	1.1	1.1	1.1	1.1
Replace idle stop solenoid, ADD:	—	—	—	—	—	.7	.7	.7	.7	.7

Approximate parts cost:
Solenoid vacuum valve	$12.00	Thermal switch	$ 6.00
Transmission-position switch	6.00	Idle stop solenoid	11.00

CHRYSLER/PLYMOUTH/DODGE

EXHAUST PORT AIR INJECTION (AIR) SYSTEM, TEST AND SERVICE

Includes:
Basic Job: Test air pump flow, check routing and condition of hoses, determine operation of diverter valve, verify check valve operation, inspect air manifold and hoses. Check and adjust drive belt tension.
Additions to Basic Job: Replace defective part. Replace drive belt, includes adjust tension. Replacement of hose(s), includes soapy water test.

MODEL	1966	1967	1968	1969	1970	1971	1972	1973	1974	1975
Basic Job:										
Test AIR system, all models	—	—	—	—	—	—	.5	.5	.5	.5
Additions to Basic Job:										
Replace and adjust drive belt, **ADD:**	—	—	—	—	—	—	.5	.5	.5	.5
Replace AIR pump,										
Imperial, **ADD:**	—	—	—	—	—	—	1.5	1.6	1.6	1.6
All others, **ADD:**	—	—	—	—	—	—	1.1	1.1	1.1	1.1
Replace diverter valve,										
Imperial, **ADD:**	—	—	—	—	—	—	1.4	1.4	1.4	1.4
All others, **ADD:**	—	—	—	—	—	—	.7	.7	.7	.7
Replace check valve assembly,										
Imperial, **ADD:**	—	—	—	—	—	—	1.2	1.2	1.2	1.2
All others, **ADD:**	—	—	—	—	—	—	1.0	1.0	1.0	1.0
Replace hose, incl. soapy wtr. test,										
Imperial, **ADD:**	—	—	—	—	—	—	.5	.5	.5	.5
All others, **ADD:**	—	—	—	—	—	—	.4	.4	.4	.4

Approximate parts cost:
Drive belt	$ 3.00	Diverter valve	$12.00
Air pump	50.00	Hose, per ft.	0.75
Check valve	7.00		

EVAPORATIVE EMISSION CONTROL SYSTEM, TEST AND SERVICE

Includes:
Basic Job: Test purge control valve (or crankcase inlet filter 1970-71), gas tank filler cap, vent lines, and hoses.
Additions to Basic Job: Replace defective part.

MODEL	1966	1967	1968	1969	1970	1971	1972	1973	1974	1975
Basic Job:										
Test evap. emission control system	—	—	—	—	.4	.4	.4	.4	.4	.4
Additions to Basic Job:										
Replace purge control valve, **ADD:**	—	—	—	—	—	—	.5	—	—	—
Replace charcoal canister filter, **ADD:**	—	—	—	—	—	—	.3	.3	.3	.3
Replace charcoal canister, **ADD:**	—	—	—	—	—	—	.5	.5	.5	.5
Replace hose, each, **ADD:**	—	—	—	—	—	—	.2	.2	.2	.2
Replace liquid vapor separator or standpipe,										
Dart, **ADD:**	—	—	—	—	1.0	1.0	1.0	1.0	1.0	1.0
Imperial, **ADD:**	—	—	—	—	.8	.8	.8	.8	.8	.8
All others, **ADD:**	—	—	—	—	.6	.6	.6	.6	.6	.6

Approximate parts cost:
Purge control valve	$ 4.00	Hose, per ft.	$ .75
Canister filter	1.00	Liquid vapor separator	9.00
Charcoal canister	25.00		

126 CHRYSLER/PLYMOUTH/DODGE

HEATED-AIR SYSTEM, TEST AND SERVICE

Includes:
 Basic Job: Check cold/heated-air door, temperature sensor, and vacuum motor.
 Additions to Basic Job: Replace defective parts.

MODEL	1966	1967	1968	1969	1970	1971	1972	1973	1974	1975
Basic Job:										
Test heated-air system	—	—	—	.3	.3	.3	.3	.3	.3	.3
Additions to Basic Job:										
Replace vacuum motor, **ADD:**	—	—	—	.4	.4	.4	.4	.4	.4	.4
Replace temperature sensor, **ADD:**	—	—	—	.5	.5	.5	.5	.5	.5	.5

Approximate parts cost:
Vacuum motor assembly .... $5.00   Temperature sensor $4.50

EXHAUST-GAS RECIRCULATION (EGR), TEST AND SERVICE

Includes:
 Basic Job: Test EGR valve, control system, and engine idling condition.
 Additions to Basic Job: Replace defective parts. Test & repair thermostatic control system.

MODEL	1966	1967	1968	1969	1970	1971	1972	1973	1974	1975
Basic Job:										
Test EGR system, all models	—	—	—	—	—	—	.4	.4	.4	.4
Additions to Basic Job:										
Service EGR valve, **ADD:**	—	—	—	—	—	—	.7	.7	.7	.7
Replace EGR valve, **ADD:**	—	—	—	—	—	—	.4	.4	.4	.4
Test & repair thermo. control sys., **ADD:**	—	—	—	—	—	—	.6	.6	.6	.6

Approximate parts cost:
EGR valve $10.00

ORFICE SPARK ADVANCE CONTROL (OSAC) SYSTEM, TEST AND SERVICE

Includes:
 Basic Job: Check all hoses and hose connections; check operation of OSAC valve using vacuum gauge.
 Related Jobs: Replace defective part(s).

MODEL	1966	1967	1968	1969	1970	1971	1972	1973	1974	1975
Basic Job:										
Check OSAC valve, hoses & connections	—	—	—	—	—	—	—	.4	.4	—
Related Jobs:										
Replace vacuum amplifier	—	—	—	—	—	—	—	.5	.5	—
Replace all hoses	—	—	—	—	—	—	—	.6	.6	—
Replace OSAC valve	—	—	—	—	—	—	—	.3	.3	—

Approximate parts cost:
Hose, per ft. .... $ 1.45   OSAC valve $10.00
Amplifier 12.00

CHRYSLER/PLYMOUTH/DODGE

FUEL SYSTEM, ADJUST AND SERVICE

Includes:
Basic Job: Adjust idle mixture and speed for performance and to obtain satisfactory exhaust system analyzer readings.
Related Jobs: R&R carburetor, overhaul carburetor(s), R&R associated fuel components.

MODEL	1966	1967	1968	1969	1970	1971	1972	1973	1974	1975
Basic Job:										
Complete carburetor(s) adjustments,										
Single barrel	.4	.4	.4	.4	.4	.4	.4	.4	.4	.4
Two-barrel	.6	.6	.6	.6	.6	.6	.6	.6	.6	.6
Four-barrel	.7	.7	.7	.7	.7	.7	.7	.7	.7	.7
Six-barrel (3x2) or 8-barrel (2x4)	.8	.8	.8	.8	.8	—	—	—	—	—
Related Jobs:										
Replace carb. incl. compl. adjustments,										
Single or 2-barrel	.6	.6	.5	.5	.7	.7	.7	.7	.7	.7
Four-barrel	1.0	1.0	1.0	1.0	1.0	1.0	1.0	1.0	1.0	1.0
Multiple carbs., ea., **ADD:**	.8	.8	.8	.8	.8	—	—	—	—	—
O/H carb., incl. R&R and compl. adjust.,										
Single or two-barrel, ea.	2.6	2.6	2.6	2.5	2.7	2.2	2.4	2.4	2.4	2.4
Four-barrel	4.0	4.0	4.0	4.0	3.2	3.2	3.2	3.2	3.4	3.4
Two 4-barrel, both	6.1	6.1	6.1	6.1	6.1	6.1	—	—	—	—
Holley tri-carb., all three	—	—	—	—	7.9	7.9	7.9	—	—	—
Test & replace fuel pump,										
6-cylinder	.5	.5	.5	.5	.5	.5	.5	.5	.5	.5
V-8 engine	.7	.7	.7	.7	.7	.7	.8	.8	.8	.8
Electric pump	—	—	—	—	—	.6	.6	.6	.6	.6
Replace fuel filter	.3	.3	.3	.3	.3	.3	.3	.3	.3	.3
Replace fuel tank sending unit,										
Station wagon	1.0	1.0	1.0	1.0	1.0	1.0	1.0	1.0	1.0	1.0
All others	.9	.8	.8	.8	.8	.8	.8	.8	.8	.8
Replace dashboard fuel gauge,										
Chrysler, Imperial	1.4	1.4	1.4	2.0	2.0	2.0	2.0	2.0	1.3	.6
Plymouth, Dodge	1.0	.9	1.5	1.5	1.5	1.5	1.5	1.5	1.1	1.1
Replace fuel tank,										
Station wagon	1.7	1.2	1.2	1.2	1.2	1.5	1.5	1.5	1.5	1.5
Dodge Charger	—	—	1.4	1.4	1.4	1.4	1.1	1.1	.8	.8
Dart, Valiant	.8	.8	.8	.8	1.6	1.6	1.6	1.6	1.6	1.6
All others	1.1	1.1	1.1	1.1	1.1	1.1	1.1	1.1	.8	.8
Replace flexible fuel line	.3	.3	.3	.3	.3	.3	.3	.3	.3	.3
Repl. intake manifold gasket, incl. adj. carb. & ign. timing,										
6-cylinder	2.7	2.7	2.7	2.7	2.7	2.7	2.7	2.7	2.7	2.7
V-8 small block	2.3	2.3	2.3	1.7	1.7	1.7	1.7	1.7	1.7	1.7
With air conditioning, **ADD:**	.4	.4	.4	.4	.4	.4	.4	.4	.4	.4
With two carburetors, **ADD:**	.3	.3	.3	.3	.3	—	—	—	—	—
With three carburetors, **ADD:**	—	—	—	—	.5	.5	.5	—	—	—

Approximate parts cost:

Carburetor repair kit, ea.	$10.00
Carburetor, new, ea. single bbl.	40.00
Two bbl.	70.00
Four bbl.	80.00-120.00
Carburetor, rebuilt, single bbl.	15.00
Two bbl.	22.00
Four bbl.	40.00
Fuel pump	$15.00
Electric fuel pump	80.00
Fuel tank sending unit	13.00
Fuel gauge, dash	7.00-15.00
Fuel tank	50.00-65.00
Gasket, manifold	4.00

CHRYSLER/PLYMOUTH/DODGE

IGNITION SYSTEM, SERVICE

Includes:
1. Adjust and install new spark plugs.
2. Replace points and condenser, adjust dwell and ignition timing.
3. R&R distirbutor, overhaul and test centrifugal and vacuum advances, set dwell or adjust reluctor air gap and ignition timing.

Related Jobs: Replace additional defective part(s) as required.
Additions: Allowances for special equipment installed or replacement of associated defective part(s).

MODEL	1966	1967	1968	1969	1970	1971	1972	1973	1974	1975
Basic Job #1										
Adjust & install new spark plugs,										
6-cylinder	.6	.6	.6	.6	.6	.6	.6	.6	.6	.6
V-8, 400, 440 engine	.9	.9	.9	.9	.9	.9	.9	.9	.9	.9
All others	.8	.8	.8	.8	.8	.8	.8	.8	.8	.8
With air conditioning, **ADD:**	.3	.3	.3	.3	.3	.3	.3	.3	.3	.3
With CAS or AIR, **ADD:**	.3	.3	.3	.3	.3	.3	.3	.3	.3	.3
Basic Job #2										
Replace points and condenser & adjust	1.1	1.1	1.0	1.0	1.3	1.3	1.1	—	—	—
Replace distributor cap, **ADD:**	.4	.4	.4	.3	.3	.3	.3	.3	.3	.3
Basic Job #3										
R&R and overhaul distributor & adjust	2.2	2.2	2.2	2.2	2.4	2.4	2.4	1.5	1.5	1.5
Replace vacuum advance unit, **ADD:**	.2	.2	.2	.2	.2	.2	.2	.2	.2	.2
Related Jobs:										
Replace ignition coil	.4	.4	.4	.4	.4	.4	.4	.4	.4	.4
Replace spark plug wires,										
6-cylinder	.5	.5	.6	.6	.8	.8	.6	.6	.6	.6
V-8 engine	.7	.7	.8	.8	.9	.9	.8	.8	.8	.8
With air conditioning, **ADD:**	.5	.5	.5	.5	.5	.5	.5	.5	.5	.5
V-8 Hemi engine, **ADD:**	.4	.4	.4	.4	.4	.4	—	—	—	—
Replace ignition switch,										
With standard column	.6	.6	.6	.6	1.4	1.4	1.4	1.4	1.4	1.4
With tilt or telescopic column	.8	.8	.8	.8	.8	.8	.8	.8	.8	.8

Approximate parts cost:

Spark plugs, each	$ 1.50
Point set	3.00
Condenser	1.50
Distributor cap	4.50
Distributor parts	10.00
Vacuum control unit	$ 4.00
Ignition coil	12.50
Spark plug wires, 6-cylinder	8.00
V-8 engine	12.00-27.00
Ignition switch	9.00

CHARGING SYSTEM, TEST AND SERVICE

Includes:
Basic Job: Test battery voltage and gravity, clean battery cable terminals, test alternator output, test and adjust regulator.
Related Jobs: Replace or overhaul defective part(s).

MODEL	1966	1967	1968	1969	1970	1971	1972	1973	1974	1975
Basic Job:										
Test system and adjust regulator	.6	.6	.6	.6	.6	.6	.6	.6	.6	.6
Related Jobs:										
R&R alternator incl. pulley	.6	.6	.6	.6	.7	.7	.7	.7	.7	.7
With air conditioning, **ADD:**	.1	.1	.1	.1	.1	.1	.1	.1	.1	.1
With AIR, **ADD:**	.2	.2	.2	.2	.2	.2	.2	.2	.2	.2
Overhaul alternator after removal	2.3	2.3	1.5	1.5	1.5	1.5	1.5	1.5	1.5	1.5
Replace regulator	.3	.3	.3	.3	.4	.4	.4	.3	.3	.3

(THIS SCHEDULE CONTINUED ON NEXT PAGE.)

CHRYSLER/PLYMOUTH/DODGE

CHARGING SYSTEM, TEST AND SERVICE Continued

MODEL	1966	1967	1968	1969	1970	1971	1972	1973	1974	1975

Approximate parts cost:
Alternator, new $75.00-80.00
Alternator, rebuilt 35.00
Regulator $13.00-27.00

CRANKING SYSTEM, TEST AND SERVICE

Includes:
Basic Job: Test battery and cranking system. Clean battery cable terminals.
Related Jobs: Replace defective part including test when necessary.

MODEL	1966	1967	1968	1969	1970	1971	1972	1973	1974	1975
Basic Job:										
Test cranking system	.5	.5	.5	.5	.5	.5	.5	.5	.5	.5
Related Jobs:										
R&R starter,										
6-cylinder	.7	.7	.7	.7	.7	.8	.8	.8	.8	.8
V-8 small block	1.8	1.8	1.8	1.3	1.3	1.3	1.3	1.3	1.3	1.3
V-8 large block	.9	.9	.9	.9	.9	.9	1.1	1.1	1.1	1.1
Overhaul starter after removal	1.7	1.7	1.7	1.7	1.7	1.7	1.7	1.7	1.7	1.7
Replace starter-battery cable	.3	.3	.3	.3	.3	.3	.3	.3	.3	.3
Repl. starter solenoid, incl. sys. test,										
6-cylinder	1.7	1.7	1.7	1.7	1.7	1.7	1.7	1.7	1.7	1.7
V-8 small block	2.7	2.6	2.6	2.0	1.9	1.9	1.9	1.9	1.8	1.8
V-8 large block	1.9	1.9	1.9	1.9	2.4	2.4	2.3	2.0	2.0	2.0
Repl. starter/neutral switch & adjust.,										
With column shift	.4	.4	.4	.4	.4	.4	.4	.4	.4	.4
With floor shift	.6	.6	.6	.6	.6	.6	.6	.6	.6	.6

Approximate parts cost:
Starter, new $100.00
Starter, rebuilt w/o solenoid 30.00
Starter-battery cable 4.50-8.50
Solenoid switch $4.00-10.00
Starter/neutral switch 4.00

ENGINE OVERHAUL, IN-CAR Continued

MODEL	1966	1967	1968	1969	1970	1971	1972	1973	1974	1975

ENGINE OVERHAUL, IN-CAR

Includes:
Basic Job: Remove ring ridge, deglaze cylinders walls, fit piston pins, align connecting rods, install new piston rings and rod bearings, install new main bearing inserts and oil seals, overhaul oil pump, clean carbon, grind valves, and perform major tune-up.
Additions to Basic Job: Associated work that is required during basic job and allowances for special equipment installed.

MODEL	1966	1967	1968	1969	1970	1971	1972	1973	1974	1975
Basic Job:										
Overhaul engine										
6-cylinder	21.5	21.5	21.5	21.5	21.8	21.8	21.0	21.2	21.2	21.4
V-8, small block	26.4	26.4	26.4	26.6	26.6	26.6	26.3	26.5	26.5	26.9
V-8, large block	28.9	28.9	28.9	29.1	29.1	29.1	28.7	29.0	29.0	29.4
V-8, Hemi engine	33.1	33.1	34.9	34.9	34.9	34.9	—	—	—	—

130 CHRYSLER/PLYMOUTH/DODGE

ENGINE OVERHAUL, IN-CAR Continued

MODEL	1966	1967	1968	1969	1970	1971	1972	1973	1974	1975
Additions to Basic Job:										
Rebore cylinders,										
6-cylinder, **ADD:**	4.0	4.0	4.0	4.0	4.0	4.0	4.0	4.0	4.0	4.0
V-8 engine, **ADD:**	5.0	5.0	5.0	5.0	5.0	5.0	5.0	5.0	5.0	5.0
Expand pistons,										
6-cylinder, **ADD:**	1.8	1.8	1.8	1.8	1.8	1.8	1.8	1.8	1.8	1.8
V-8 engine, **ADD:**	2.4	2.4	2.4	2.4	2.4	2.4	2.4	2.4	2.4	2.4
Regroove top piston ring groove,										
6-cylinder, **ADD:**	1.8	1.8	1.8	1.8	1.8	1.8	1.8	1.8	1.8	1.8
V-8 engine, **ADD:**	2.4	2.4	2.4	2.4	2.4	2.4	2.4	2.4	2.4	2.4
Replace hydraulic valve lifters, **ADD:**	1.0	1.0	1.0	1.0	1.0	1.0	1.0	1.0	1.0	1.0
Replace rocker arm stud, each, **ADD:**	.3	.3	.3	.3	.3	.3	.3	.3	.3	.3
Overhaul rocker arm mechanism,										
6-cylinder, **ADD:**	1.0	1.0	1.0	1.0	1.0	1.0	1.0	1.0	1.0	1.0
V-8 engine, **ADD:**	1.9	1.9	1.9	1.9	1.9	1.9	1.9	1.9	1.9	1.9
Ream valve guides oversize,										
6-cylinder, **ADD:**	.7	.7	.7	.7	.7	.7	.7	.7	.7	.7
V-8 engine, **ADD:**	.9	.9	.9	.9	.9	.9	.9	.9	.9	.9
With CAS or AIR pump, **ADD:**	.7	.7	.7	.7	.7	.7	.7	.7	.7	.7
With 4-bbl. carb. (V-8 sm. bl. only), **ADD:**	1.0	1.0	1.0	1.0	1.0	1.0	1.0	1.0	1.0	1.0
With 6-bbl. carbs, (3x2), **ADD:**	4.0	4.0	4.0	4.0	4.0	—	—	—	—	—
With 8-bbl. carbs, (2x4), **ADD:**	2.5	2.5	2.5	2.5	2.5	—	—	—	—	—
With air conditioning, **ADD:**	.7	.7	.7	.7	.7	.7	.7	.7	.7	.7

Approximate parts cost:

Rod bearing inserts, 6-cylinder	$18.00	Valve spring, each	$ 2.00
V-8 engine	32.00	Major tune-up parts	35.00
Piston pins, set, 6-cylinder	12.00	Complete gasket set, 6-cylinder	26.00
V-8 engine	16.00	V-8 engine	30.00
Piston assembly, set, 6-cylinder	72.00	Piston ring set, 6-cylinder	36.00
V-8 engine	150.00	V-8 engine	53.00
Hydraulic valve lifters, each	4.00	Carburetor repair kit, ea.	6.00-13.00

ENGINE OVERHAUL, OUT-OF-CAR

Includes:

Basic Job: R&R engine, remove ring ridge, rebore or hone cylinder walls, regrind crankshaft and camshaft, replace camshaft bushings and line ream, replace timing chain and gears and oil seal, install main bearing inserts and seals, install piston pins, align connecting rods, install new piston rings and rod bearings, overhaul oil pump, clean carbon, grind valves, overhaul rocker arm mechanism, and perform major tune-up.

Additions to Basic Job: Associated work that is required during basic job and allowances for special equipment installed.

MODEL	1966	1967	1968	1969	1970	1971	1972	1973	1974	1975
Basic Job:										
Overhaul engine,										
6-cylinder	34.5	34.5	34.5	34.5	34.8	34.8	34.8	35.0	35.3	35.5
V-8, small block	42.4	42.4	40.7	40.9	41.7	41.7	41.1	41.7	41.7	42.1
V-8, large block	42.6	43.5	41.9	42.5	42.5	42.1	42.1	42.7	42.7	42.9
V-8, Hemi engine	48.4	48.4	48.4	48.6	48.6	48.6	—	—	—	—
Additions to Basic Job:										
Regroove top piston ring groove,										
6-cylinder, **ADD:**	1.8	1.8	1.8	1.8	1.8	1.8	1.8	1.8	1.8	1.8
V-8 engine, **ADD:**	2.4	2.4	2.4	2.4	2.4	2.4	2.4	2.4	2.4	2.4

(THIS SCHEDULE CONTINUED ON NEXT PAGE.)

CHRYSLER/PLYMOUTH/DODGE 131

ENGINE OVERHAUL, OUT-OF-CAR Continued

MODEL	1966	1967	1968	1969	1970	1971	1972	1973	1974	1975
Additions to Basic Job Continued										
Replace rocker arm stud, each, **ADD**:	.3	.3	.3	.3	.3	.3	.3	.3	.3	.3
Ream valve guides oversize,										
6-cylinder, **ADD**:	.7	.7	.7	.7	.7	.7	.7	.7	.7	.7
V-8 engine, **ADD**:	.9	.9	.9	.9	.9	.9	.9	.9	.9	.9
Replace all engine mounts, **ADD**:	.6	.6	.6	.6	.6	.6	.6	.6	.6	.6
Replace worn clutch parts, **ADD**:	.5	.5	.5	.5	.5	.5	.5	.5	.5	.5
With CAS or AIR pump, **ADD**:	.7	.7	.7	.7	.7	.7	.7	.7	.7	.7
With 4-bbl. carb. (V-8 sm. bl. only) **ADD**:	1.0	1.0	1.0	1.0	1.0	1.0	1.0	1.0	1.0	1.0
With 6-bbl. carbs., (3x2), **ADD**:	4.0	4.0	4.0	4.0	4.0	—	—	—	—	—
With 8-bbl. carbs., (2x4), **ADD**:	2.5	2.5	2.5	2.5	2.5	—	—	—	—	—
With air cond., incl. rechg. system, **ADD**:	1.8	1.8	1.8	1.8	1.8	1.8	1.8	1.8	1.8	1.8

Approximate parts cost:

Complete gasket set, 6-cylinder ... $26.00	Piston pins, set, 6-cylinder ... $12.00
V-8 engine ... 30.00	V-8 engine ... 16.00
Piston ring set, 6-cylinder ... 36.00	Piston assembly, set, 6-cylinder ... 72.00
V-8 engine ... 53.00	V-8 engine ... 150.00
Connecting rod bearing set, 6-cylinder ... 18.00	Engine mounts, 6-cylinder ... 6.00
V-8 engine ... 32.00	V-8 engine ... 7.50
Main bearing oil seals ... 5.00	Pressure plate ... 30.00-60.00
Main bearing insert set, 6-cylinder ... 18.00	Clutch disc ... 21.00-40.00
V-8 engine ... 30.00	Clutch release bearing ... 5.00-15.00
Carburetor repair kit, ea. ... 6.00-13.00	Major tune-up parts ... 35.00

SHORT BLOCK, REPLACE

Includes:

  Basic Job: R&R engine, clean and reface valves, scrape carbon, grind valve seats, replace valve seals, overhaul rocker arm mechanism, transfer all parts, and perform major tune-up.

  Additions to Basic Job: Associated work that is required during basic job and allowances for special equipment installed and/or carburetor combinations.

MODEL	1966	1967	1968	1969	1970	1971	1972	1973	1974	1975
Basic Job:										
Replace short block										
6-cylinder	14.8	14.8	14.8	14.8	15.1	15.1	15.1	15.3	15.3	15.5
V-8, small block	19.6	19.6	18.5	18.7	18.7	18.7	18.7	19.0	19.2	19.4
V-8, large block	20.7	20.7	19.7	19.9	19.9	19.5	19.5	20.1	20.1	20.3
V-8, Hemi engine	25.6	25.6	25.6	25.8	25.8	25.8	—	—	—	—
Additions to Basic Job:										
Ream valve guides oversize, **ADD**:										
6-cylinder	.7	.7	.7	.7	.7	.7	.7	.7	.7	.7
V-8 engine	.9	.9	.9	.9	.9	.9	.9	.9	.9	.9
Replace rocker arm stud, each, **ADD**:										
All models	.3	.3	.3	.3	.3	.3	.3	.3	.3	.3
With air cond., incl. chg. sys., **ADD**:	1.8	1.8	1.8	1.8	1.8	1.8	1.8	1.8	1.8	1.8
With CAS or AIR pump, **ADD**:	.3	.3	.3	.3	.3	.3	.3	.3	.3	.3
With 4-bbl. carb., **ADD**:	.3	.3	.3	.3	.3	.3	.3	.3	.3	.3
With 6-bbl. or 8 bbl. carbs., **ADD**:	.4	.4	.4	.4	.4	.4	.4	.4	.4	.4
Replace all engine mounts, **ADD**:	.6	.6	.6	.6	.6	.6	.6	.6	.6	.6
Replace worn clutch parts, **ADD**:	.5	.5	.5	.5	.5	.5	.5	.5	.5	.5

132 CHRYSLER/PLYMOUTH/DODGE

SHORT BLOCK, REPLACE Continued

MODEL	1966	1967	1968	1969	1970	1971	1972	1973	1974	1975

Approximate parts cost:

Major tune-up parts $35.00	Oil and air filters .... $ 9.00
Complete gasket set, 6-cylinder 26.00	Pressure plate 30.00-60.00
V-8 engine 30.00	Clutch disc 21.00-40.00
Short block: Call supplier for price.	Clutch release bearing 5.00-15.00
Engine mounts, each 2.00-6.00	Carburetor repair kit, ea. 6.00-13.00

TIMING CHAIN MECHANISM, SERVICE

Includes:

  Basic Job: Replace timing cover oil seal and timing chain. Perform minor tune-up.
  Additions to Basic Job: Replace camshaft timing sprocket or crankshaft timing sprocket.

MODEL	1966	1967	1968	1969	1970	1971	1972	1973	1974	1975
Basic Job:										
Replace timing cover oil seal & chain; perform minor tune-up										
6-cylinder	4.2	4.2	4.2	4.2	4.4	4.4	4.3	4.3	4.1	4.1
V-8 small block	3.6	3.6	3.6	3.6	3.8	3.8	4.1	4.1	4.1	4.1
V-8 large block	3.6	3.6	3.6	3.6	3.6	3.6	4.0	4.0	4.0	4.0
V-8 Hemi	5.5	5.5	5.5	5.5	5.5	5.5	—	—	—	—
Additions to Basic Job:										
Replace camshaft timing sprocket, **ADD:**	.2	.2	.2	.2	.2	.2	.2	.2	.2	.2
Replace crankshaft timing sprocket, **ADD:**	.2	.2	.2	.2	.2	.2	.2	.2	.2	.2
With air conditioning, **ADD:**	.5	.5	.5	.5	.5	.5	.5	.5	.5	.5

Approximate parts cost:

Timing cover gasket .... $ 1.00	Camshaft sprocket .... $ 6.00
Timing cover oil seal 2.00	Crankshaft sprocket 6.00
Timing chain 14.00	Minor tune-up parts 25.00-30.00

OIL PUMP, SERVICE

Includes:

  Basic Job: R&R oil pan, service oil pump and replace oil filter element.
  Additions to Basic Job: Allowances for associated work that is required during basic job.

MODEL	1966	1967	1968	1969	1970	1971	1972	1973	1974	1975
Basic Job:										
R&R oil pan, serv. pump & repl. filter element,										
6-cylinder	2.4	2.4	2.4	2.4	2.8	2.8	2.8	2.8	2.2	2.2
V-8 small block	2.7	2.7	2.7	2.7	2.7	2.4	2.4	2.4	2.4	2.4
V-8 large block	2.8	2.8	2.8	2.8	2.1	2.1	2.1	2.1	2.0	2.0
V-8 Hemi	2.0	2.0	2.0	2.1	2.1	2.1	—	—	—	—
Additions to Basic Job:										
Overhaul oil pump, **ADD:**	.8	.8	.8	.8	.8	.8	.8	.8	.8	.8
Repl. rear main brg. insert & seals, **ADD:**										
6-cylinder	.3	.3	.3	.3	.3	.3	.3	.3	.3	.3
V-8 small block	.4	.4	.4	.4	.4	.4	.4	.4	.4	.4
V-8 large block	.3	.3	.3	.3	.3	.3	.3	.3	.3	.3
V-8 Hemi	.2	.2	.2	.2	.2	.2	—	—	—	—
Repl. other main brg. inserts, ea. pair, **ADD:**	.6	.6	.6	.6	.6	.6	.6	.6	.6	.6

(THIS SCHEDULE CONTINUED ON NEXT PAGE.)

CHRYSLER/PLYMOUTH/DODGE

OIL PUMP SERVICE Continued

MODEL	1966	1967	1968	1969	1970	1971	1972	1973	1974	1975

Approximate parts cost:

Oil pan $24.00	Oil pump drive gear, 6-cyl. $2.00
Oil pan gasket 4.00	V-8 .... 8.00
Oil pump shaft & rotor kit 8.00	Oil pump shaft & inner rotor 7.00
Oil pump outer rotor 3.00	Oil filter element 4.50

BEARINGS, MAIN AND/OR RODS, REPLACE

Includes:

Basic Job: R&R oil pan, measure connecting rod bearing oil clearance with Plastigage, install new connecting rod bearing inserts, and oil filter element.

Additions to Basic Job: Measure main bearing oil clearance with Plastigage, replace all main bearing inserts and rear main bearing oil seals, repair or replace oil pump.

MODEL	1966	1967	1968	1969	1970	1971	1972	1973	1974	1975
Basic Job:										
R&R pan, measure, install inserts & filter										
6-cylinder	4.8	4.8	4.8	4.8	5.2	5.2	5.2	5.2	4.3	4.3
V-8 small block	6.6	6.6	6.6	6.6	5.9	6.1	6.1	6.1	5.0	5.0
V-8 large block	6.6	6.6	5.9	5.9	5.5	5.5	5.5	5.5	4.4	4.4
V-8 Hemi	6.6	6.6	6.6	6.6	5.3	5.3	—	—	—	—
Additions to Basic Job:										
Use Plastigage — all main brgs.,										
6-cylinder, **ADD:**	.4	.4	.4	.4	.4	.4	.4	.4	.4	.4
V-8 engine, **ADD:**	.5	.5	.5	.5	.5	.5	.5	.5	.5	.5
Replace main inserts & rear oil seals,										
6-cylinder, **ADD:**	1.2	1.2	1.2	1.2	1.2	1.2	1.2	1.2	1.2	1.2
V-8 engine, **ADD:**	2.0	2.0	2.0	2.0	2.0	2.0	2.0	2.0	2.0	2.0
R&R oil pump,										
6-cylinder, **ADD:**	.5	.5	.5	.5	.5	.5	.5	.5	.5	.5
V-8 small block, **ADD:**	.3	.3	.3	.3	1.0	1.0	.4	.4	.6	.6
V-8 large block, **ADD:**	.4	.4	.4	.8	.8	.8	.8	.8	.8	.8
V-8 Hemi, **ADD:**	.5	.5	.5	.5	.5	.5	—	—	—	—
Overhaul oil pump, **ADD:**	.8	.8	.8	.8	.8	.8	.8	.8	.8	.8

Approximate parts cost:

Oil pan gasket $4.00	Rear main brg. oil seal, set $3.00
Rod bearing inserts, set, each 4.00	Oil filter element 4.50
Main brg. inserts, set, ea. 4.00-7.00	Oil pump shaft & rotor kit 8.00

CYLINDER HEAD AND/OR GASKET, REPLACE

Includes:

Basic Jobs: 1. R&R intake manifold and cylinder head to install new gasket. Clean head and block surfaces and perform minor tune-up.
2. Install new cylinder head, including recondition valves and perform minor tune-up.

Additions to Basic Jobs: Recondition second head on V-type engines. Allowances for special equipment and/or carburetor combinations.

MODEL	1966	1967	1968	1969	1970	1971	1972	1973	1974	1975
Basic Job #1										
Replace head gasket, incl. minor tune-up,										
6-cylinder	4.2	4.6	4.6	4.6	4.8	4.8	4.8	4.8	4.8	4.8
V-8, small block, one side	6.2	6.2	5.7	5.7	5.9	5.9	6.0	6.0	6.0	6.0
V-8, small block, both sides	7.8	7.8	7.3	7.3	7.5	7.5	7.5	7.5	7.5	7.5
V-8, large block, one side	6.2	6.0	6.0	6.0	6.2	6.1	6.1	6.4	6.4	6.4
V-8, large block, both sides	7.8	7.8	8.1	8.1	8.3	8.5	8.5	8.5	8.5	8.5

CHRYSLER/PLYMOUTH/DODGE

CYLINDER HEAD AND/OR GASKET, REPLACE Continued

MODEL	1966	1967	1968	1969	1970	1971	1972	1973	1974	1975
Basic Job #2										
Install new cyl. head, incl. minor tune-up,										
6-cylinder	6.9	7.3	7.3	7.3	7.5	7.5	7.5	7.5	7.5	7.5
V-8, small block, one side	8.6	8.6	8.1	8.1	8.3	8.4	8.4	8.4	8.4	8.4
V-8, large block, one side	8.6	8.4	8.4	8.4	8.6	8.5	8.5	8.8	8.8	8.8
Additions to Basic Jobs:										
Recondition second head, V-type engines,										
V-8, small block, **ADD:**	2.0	2.0	2.0	2.0	2.0	2.3	2.3	2.3	2.3	2.3
V-8, large block, **ADD:**	2.5	2.5	2.5	2.5	2.5	2.8	2.8	2.8	2.8	2.8
With air conditioning, **ADD:**	.5	.5	.5	.5	.5	.5	.5	.5	.5	.5
With CAS or AIR pump, **ADD:**	.3	.3	.3	.3	.3	.3	.3	.3	.3	.3
With 4-bbl. carb. (V-8 sm. bl. only), **ADD:**	.2	.2	.2	.2	.2	.2	.2	.2	.2	.2
With 6-bbl. or 8-bbl. carbs., **ADD:**	.4	.4	.4	.4	.4	—	—	—	—	—

Approximate parts cost:

Head gasket, each .... $ 4.00	Valve grind gasket set, 6-cylinder .... $ 9.00
Cylinder head, each 90.00	V-8 engine 18.00
	V-8, 426 CID 38.00

VALVE MECHANISM, SERVICE

Includes:

Adjustment and Tune-up: Adjust valve lash and perform minor tune-up.
Basic Job: Clean and reface valves, scrape carbon, grind valve seats, replace valve seals, adjust valves, and perform major tune-up.
Additions to Basic Job: Associated work required during basic job and allowances for special equipment installed.

MODEL	1966	1967	1968	1969	1970	1971	1972	1973	1974	1975
Adjustment & Tune-up,										
6-cylinder engine	2.8	2.8	2.8	2.8	3.0	3.0	3.0	3.0	3.0	3.0
Basic Job:										
Service valve mechanism,										
6-cylinder	10.4	10.4	10.4	10.8	10.8	11.1	11.1	10.9	10.9	11.1
V-8, small block	16.9	15.1	•14.1	14.3	14.3	14.7	14.7	15.0	14.2	14.4
V-8, large block	14.4	15.6	15.6	15.8	15.8	16.0	16.0	15.3	15.3	15.5
V-8, Hemi engine	17.8	19.0	19.0	19.2	19.2	19.2	—	—	—	—
Additions to Basic Job:										
Ream valve guides oversize,										
6-cylinder, **ADD:**	.7	.7	.7	.7	.7	.7	.7	.7	.7	.7
V-8 engine, **ADD:**	.9	.9	.9	.9	.9	.9	.9	.9	.9	.9
Replace rocker arm stud, ea., **ADD:**	.3	.3	.3	.3	.3	.3	.3	.3	.3	.3
Overhaul rocker arm mechanism,										
6-cylinder, **ADD:**	1.0	1.0	1.0	1.0	1.0	1.0	1.0	1.0	1.0	1.0
V-8 engine, **ADD:**	1.9	1.9	1.9	1.9	1.9	1.9	1.9	1.9	1.9	1.9
Replace hydraulic valve lifters, **ADD:**	1.0	1.0	1.0	1.0	1.0	1.0	1.0	1.0	1.0	1.0
With 4-bbl. carb. (V-8 sm. bl. only) **ADD:**	1.0	1.0	1.0	1.0	1.0	1.0	1.0	1.0	1.0	1.0
With 6-bbl. carbs. (3x2), **ADD:**	4.0	4.0	4.0	4.0	4.0	—	—	—	—	—
With 8-bbl. carbs. (2x4), **ADD:**	2.5	2.5	2.5	2.5	2.5	—	—	—	—	—
With air conditioning, **ADD:**	.6	.6	.6	.6	.6	.6	.6	.6	.6	.6
With CAS or AIR pump, **ADD:**	.7	.7	.7	.7	.7	.7	.7	.7	.7	.7

Approximate parts cost:

Major tune-up parts $35.00	Valve grind gasket set, 6-cylinder .... $ 9.00
Hydraulic valve lifters, each 4.00	V-8 engine 18.00
Valve spring, each 2.00	426 CID 38.00

CHRYSLER/PLYMOUTH/DODGE 135

COOLING SYSTEM, TEST AND SERVICE

Includes:
Basic Job: Drain and back-flush system, check for leaks and tighten all hose connections, pressure-test radiator cap and system.
Related Jobs: Replace defective part. Work performed independently of basic job.

MODEL	1966	1967	1968	1969	1970	1971	1972	1973	1974	1975
Basic Job:										
Drain, flush, fill, & pressure-test system	.9	.9	.9	.9	.9	.9	.9	.9	.9	.9
Related Jobs:										
Replace upper hose	.3	.3	.3	.3	.3	.3	.3	.3	.3	.3
Replace lower hose	.4	.5	.4	.4	.4	.4	.4	.4	.4	.4
Replace water pump bypass hose,										
6-cylinder	.9	.9	.9	.9	.9	.9	.9	—	—	—
V-8 engine	.3	.3	.3	.3	.3	.3	.3	—	—	—
Replace thermostat	.5	.5	.5	.5	.5	.5	.5	.5	.5	.5
Replace water pump drive belt & adjust	.6	.6	.6	.6	.6	.6	.6	.6	.6	.6
Replace water pump,										
6-cylinder	.9	.9	.9	.9	.9	.9	.9	.9	.9	9
V-8 small block	1.2	1.2	1.2	1.2	1.2	1.2	1.2	1.2	1.2	1.2
V-8 large block	1.2	1.2	1.2	.8	.8	.8	.8	.8	.8	.8
V-8 Hemi engine	1.4	1.4	1.4	1.4	1.4	1.4	—	—	—	—
Replace radiator, incl. R&R fan shroud,										
6-cylinder	.6	.6	.6	.6	.6	.6	.6	.6	.6	.6
V-8 engine	.9	.9	.9	.9	.9	.9	.9	.9	.9	.9
With air conditioning, **ADD:**	.3	.3	.2	.2	.2	.2	.2	.2	.2	.2
Replace water temp. gauge, engine	.5	.5	.5	.5	.5	.5	.5	.5	.5	.5
Replace water temp. gauge, dash,										
Chrysler, Imperial	1.4	1.4	1.4	2.0	3.5	3.5	3.5	3.5	.6	.6
Dodge	.9	.9	1.5	1.5	2.3	2.3	2.3	2.3	.6	.6
Plymouth	.7	1.0	1.5	1.5	2.3	2.3	2.3	2.3	.6	.6
Replace water jacket expansion plug,										
6-cylinder engine										
Left front	.5	.5	.5	.5	.5	.5	.5	.5	.5	.5
Left center	1.2	1.2	1.2	1.2	1.2	1.2	1.2	1.2	1.2	1.2
Left rear	.7	.7	.7	.7	.7	.7	.7	.7	.7	.7
Right front	.6	.6	.6	.6	.6	.6	.6	.6	.6	.6
V-8, 273 CID engine,										
Right front	1.3	1.3	1.3	1.3	—	—	—	—	—	—
Right center	.6	.6	.6	.6	—	—	—	—	—	—
Right rear	.7	.7	.7	.7	—	—	—	—	—	—
Left front or left center	3.2	3.2	3.2	3.2	—	—	—	—	—	—
Left rear	2.1	2.1	2.1	2.1	—	—	—	—	—	—
V-8, 383, 400, 426, 440 CID engine,										
Right or left front	1.3	1.3	1.3	1.3	1.3	1.3	1.3	1.3	1.3	1.3
Right or left center	.6	.6	.6	.6	.6	.6	.6	.6	.6	.6
Right or left rear	.7	.7	.7	.7	.7	.7	.7	.7	.7	.7
V-8, 318, 340 & 360 CID engine,										
Right front	—	—	1.3	1.3	1.3	1.3	1.3	1.3	1.3	1.3
Right center	—	—	.6	.6	.6	.6	.6	.6	.6	.6
Left front or left center	—	—	3.2	3.2	3.2	3.2	3.2	3.2	3.2	3.2
Left rear	—	—	2.1	2.1	2.1	2.1	2.1	2.1	2.1	2.1

Approximate parts cost:

Radiator, new	$75.00-125.00
Upper or lower hose, ea.	4.00-7.00
Thermostat	4.00
Water pump	24.00
Drive belt, ea.	$ 4.00
Temperature gauge, engine	4.00
Temperature gauge, dash	12.00
Expansion plug, ea.	1.50

CHRYSLER/PLYMOUTH/DODGE

EXHAUST SYSTEM, TEST AND SERVICE

Includes:
Basic Job: Test exhaust system for leaks and/or exhaust odors. Use HC/CO exhaust analyzer to trace carbon monoxide leaks.
Related Jobs: Replace defective parts. Each job includes basic job tests and install new hangers as required.

MODEL	1966	1967	1968	1969	1970	1971	1972	1973	1974	1975
Basic Job:										
Complete test of exhaust system	.4	.4	.4	.4	.4	.4	.4	.4	.4	.4
Related Jobs:										
Replace muffler,										
Front, single or dual, one	1.3	1.3	1.3	1.3	1.3	1.3	1.3	1.3	1.3	1.3
Rear, single or dual, one	1.2	1.2	1.2	1.2	1.2	1.2	1.2	1.2	1.2	1.2
One side, single or dual, two	1.8	1.8	1.8	1.8	1.8	1.8	1.8	1.8	1.8	1.8
One each side, dual, two	1.9	1.9	1.9	1.9	1.9	1.9	1.9	1.9	1.9	1.9
Replace tail pipe,										
Single or dual, one	1.1	1.1	1.1	1.1	1.1	1.1	1.1	1.1	1.1	1.1
Dual, two	1.4	1.4	1.4	1.4	1.4	1.4	1.4	1.4	1.4	1.4
Replace exhaust pipe flange gasket, ea.	1.0	1.0	1.0	1.0	1.0	1.0	1.0	1.0	1.0	1.0
Replace exhaust manifold gasket,										
6-cylinder	2.0	2.0	2.0	2.0	2.0	2.9	2.9	2.9	2.9	2.9
V-8, small block, left side	1.4	1.4	1.4	1.4	1.4	1.8	1.8	1.8	1.8	1.8
V-8, small block, right side	1.4	1.4	1.4	1.4	1.4	1.6	1.6	1.6	1.6	1.6
V-8, large block, left side	1.4	1.4	1.6	2.4	2.4	2.4	2.4	2.4	2.4	2.4
V-8, large block, right side	1.4	1.4	1.4	1.9	1.9	1.9	1.9	1.9	1.9	1.9
V-8, Hemi engine, left side	1.9	1.9	1.9	2.2	2.2	2.2	—	—	—	—
V-8, Hemi engine, right side	2.1	2.1	2.1	2.4	2.4	2.4	—	—	—	—
Free-up or O/H heat control valve,										
6-cylinder	1.5	1.5	1.5	1.5	1.5	1.5	1.5	1.5	1.5	1.5
V-8 engine	1.8	1.8	1.8	1.8	1.8	1.8	1.8	1.8	1.8	1.8
Replace exhaust pipe,										
6-cylinder	1.3	1.3	1.3	1.3	1.3	1.3	1.3	1.3	1.3	1.3
V-8 single exhaust	1.4	1.4	1.4	1.4	1.4	1.4	1.4	1.4	1.4	1.4
V-8 dual exhaust, one pipe	1.2	1.2	1.2	1.2	1.2	1.2	1.2	1.2	1.2	1.2
V-8 dual exhaust, both pipes	2.0	2.0	2.0	2.0	2.0	2.0	2.0	2.0	2.0	2.0
Replace catalytic converter	—	—	—	—	—	—	—	—	—	1.8

Approximate parts cost:
Muffler $28.00
Tail pipe, each 12.00
Catalytic converter 175.00
Exhaust pipe, each $15.00
Exhaust manifold gasket, each 3.00

CLUTCH MECHANISM, SERVICE

Includes:
Adjust: Adjust clutch pedal play.
Basic Job: Replace thrust bearing, pressure plate and disc. Adjust clutch pedal play.
Additions to Basic Job: Associated work that is required during basic job and allowances for special engines.

MODEL	1966	1967	1968	1969	1970	1971	1972	1973	1974	1975
Adjust clutch pedal play	.3	.3	.3	.3	.3	.3	.3	.3	.3	.3
Basic Job:										
Replace thrust brg., pressure plate & disc.										
3-speed transmission	2.1	2.1	2.1	2.1	2.1	2.1	2.2	2.2	2.2	2.2
4-speed transmission	2.6	2.6	2.6	2.6	3.0	3.0	3.0	2.8	2.8	2.8

(THIS SCHEDULE CONTINUED ON NEXT PAGE.)

CHRYSLER/PLYMOUTH/DODGE

CLUTCH MECHANISM, SERVICE Continued

MODEL	1966	1967	1968	1969	1970	1971	1972	1973	1974	1975
Additions to Basic Job:										
Remove, reface, and instl. flywheel, **ADD:**	1.8	1.8	1.8	1.8	1.8	1.8	1.8	1.8	1.8	1.8
Replace flywheel ring gear, **ADD:**	1.0	1.0	1.0	1.0	1.0	1.0	1.0	1.0	1.0	1.0
Resurface clutch pressure plate, **ADD:**	.8	.8	.8	.8	.8	.8	.8	.8	.8	.8
Replace pilot bearing, **ADD:**	.2	.2	.2	.2	.2	.2	.2	.2	.2	.2
With 440 hi-performance engine, **ADD:**	.9	.9	.9	.9	.9	.9	.9	.9	.9	.9
With Hemi engine, **ADD:**	2.1	2.1	2.1	2.1	2.1	2.1	—	—	—	—

Approximate parts cost:
Pressure plate $25.00-60.00
Clutch disc 20.00-35.00
Clutch release bearing 5.00-17.00
Pilot bearing .... $ 1.00
Flywheel w/ring gear 36.00-56.00

SHIFT LINKAGE, SERVICE

Includes:
Adjust: Adjust shift linkage.
Basic Job: Replace one control rod and/or grommet and adjust linkage.
Additions to Basic Job: Associated work that is required during basic job.

MODEL	1966	1967	1968	1969	1970	1971	1972	1973	1974	1975
Adjust shift linkage:										
3-speed transmission	.5	.5	.5	.5	.5	.5	.5	.5	.5	.5
4-speed transmission	.6	.6	.6	.6	.6	.6	.6	.6	.6	.6
Basic Job:										
Replace one rod and/or grommet & adjust,										
3-speed transmission	.8	.8	.8	.8	.8	.8	.8	.8	.8	.8
4-speed transmission	.9	.9	.9	.9	.9	.9	.9	.9	.9	.9
Additions to Basic Job:										
Replace additional rod, **ADD:**	.3	.3	.3	.3	.3	.3	.3	.3	.3	.3
Replace shift lever oil seals, both, **ADD:**	.5	.5	.5	.5	.5	.5	.5	.5	.5	.5

Approximate parts cost:
Shift rod, each $2.00
Rear oil seal 2.50
Shift lever oil seals $1.50

STANDARD TRANSMISSION, OVERHAUL

Includes:
Basic Job: R&R transmission, disassemble, replace worn parts, and adjust linkage.
Additions to Basic Job: Associated work that is required during basic job.

MODEL	1966	1967	1968	1969	1970	1971	1972	1973	1974	1975
Basic Job:										
R&R, overhaul, and adjust linkage										
3-speed transmission	5.4	5.4	5.4	5.4	5.4	5.4	5.4	5.4	5.4	5.4
4-speed transmission	6.9	6.9	6.9	6.9	6.9	6.9	6.9	6.9	6.9	6.9

138   CHRYSLER/PLYMOUTH/DODGE

STANDARD TRANSMISSION, OVERHAUL Continued

MODEL	1966	1967	1968	1969	1970	1971	1972	1973	1974	1975
Additions to Basic Job:										
Recondition transmission cover,										
3-speed transmission, **ADD**:	.3	.3	.3	.3	.3	.3	.3	.3	.3	.3
4-speed transmission, **ADD**:	.4	.4	.4	.4	.4	.4	.4	.4	.4	.4
Resurface clutch pressure plate, **ADD**:	.8	.8	.8	.8	.8	.8	.8	.8	.8	.8
R&R and resurface flywheel, **ADD**:	1.8	1.8	1.8	1.8	1.8	1.8	1.8	1.8	1.8	1.8
Replace flywheel ring gear, **ADD**:	1.0	1.0	1.0	1.0	1.0	1.0	1.0	1.0	1.0	1.0
Replace pilot bearing, **ADD**:	.2	.2	.2	.2	.2	.2	.2	.2	.2	.2
Replace crankshaft trans. drive pinion bushing, **ADD**:	.7	.7	.7	.7	.7	.7	.7	.7	.7	.7

Approximate parts cost:
Phone supplier for price quote on transmission parts required.
Speedometer gear .... $ 2.00
Gasket set 8.00
Clutch pressure plate 25.00-60.00
Flywheel w/ring gear 36.00-56.00
Crankshaft trans. drive pinion bushing $1.50
Pilot bearing 1.00
Clutch release bearing 5.00-17.00

AUTOMATIC TRANSMISSION, SHIFT AND LINKAGE CONTROLS, REPLACE AND ADJUST

Includes:
Replace defective part and make necessary adjustment(s).

MODEL	1966	1967	1968	1969	1970	1971	1972	1973	1974	1975
Replace control rod, carb. or trans. & adjust	.9	.9	.9	.9	.9	.9	.9	.9	.9	.9
Replace each additional rod, **ADD**:	.4	.4	.4	.4	.4	.4	.4	.4	.4	.4
Replace carb./throttle link, **ADD**:	.3	.3	.3	.3	.3	.3	.3	.3	.3	.3
Replace throttle control cable, **ADD**:	.5	.5	.5	.5	.5	.5	.5	.5	.5	.5
Replace contr. rod, column shift, **ADD**:	.3	.3	.3	.3	.3	.3	.3	.3	.3	.3
Replace rear contr. rod or swivel, **ADD**:	.4	.4	.4	.4	.4	.4	.4	.4	.4	.4
Replace contr. torque shaft or bushings, **ADD**:	.6	.6	.6	.6	.6	.6	.6	.6	.6	.6
Replace shift contr. key lock assy.	.7	.7	.7	.7	.7	.7	.7	.7	.7	.7
Replace and adjust floor shift contr. assy.	.8	.8	.8	.8	.8	.8	.8	.8	.8	.8
With console equipped, **ADD**:	.5	.5	.5	.5	.5	.5	.5	.5	.5	.5

Approximate parts cost:
Linkage rod, ea. $1.50
Control cable 8.00
Floor shift contr. assy. $40.00

TORQUEFLITE AUTOMATIC TRANSMISSION, PERFORMANCE CHECK

Includes:
Basic Job: Conduct transmission performance check. Clean transmission case and operate unit to check case, oil cooler and oil cooler lines for external leaks. Remove oil pan, clean pan, screen or filter. Torque valve body mounting bolts. Adjust kickdown and reverse bands. Adjust throttle and shift linkage. Perform pressure checks of mainline, throttle, and accumulator. Road test.
Related Jobs: Work which does not include R&R transmission and may be done as separate job.

MODEL	1966	1967	1968	1969	1970	1971	1972	1973	1974	1975
Basic Job:										
Complete trans. performance check	2.1	2.1	2.1	2.1	2.1	2.1	2.1	2.1	2.1	2.1

(THIS SCHEDULE CONTINUED ON NEXT PAGE.)

CHRYSLER/PLYMOUTH/DODGE

TORQUEFLITE AUTOMATIC TRANSMISSION, PERFORMANCE CHECK Continued

MODEL	1966	1967	1968	1969	1970	1971	1972	1973	1974	1975
Related Jobs:										
Drain & fill trans., clean filter	.8	.8	.8	.8	.8	.8	.8	.8	.8	.8
Check for oil leaks	.7	.7	.7	.7	.7	.7	.7	.7	.7	.7
Replace oil pan gasket, incl. clean filter	.9	.9	.9	.9	.9	.9	.9	.9	.9	.9
Replace rear oil seal & O-ring	1.0	1.0	.7	.5	.5	.5	.5	.5	.5	.5
Replace neutral safety switch	.5	.5	.5	.5	.5	.5	.5	.5	.5	.5
Overhaul governor,										
Imperial	3.0	3.0	3.0	3.0	3.0	3.0	3.0	2.4	2.4	2.4
Hemi or Hi-perf. engine	3.9	3.9	3.9	3.9	3.9	3.9	3.9	3.3	3.3	3.3
All others	2.5	2.5	2.5	2.5	2.5	2.5	2.5	1.9	1.9	1.9
Overhaul valve body assembly	2.0	2.0	2.0	2.0	2.0	2.0	2.0	2.0	2.0	2.0
Adjust throttle and shift linkage	1.0	1.0	1.0	1.0	1.0	1.0	1.0	1.0	1.0	1.0
Adjust kickdown and reverse bands	1.3	1.3	1.3	1.3	1.3	1.3	1.3	1.3	1.3	1.3

Approximate parts cost:
Transmission fluid, per qt.	$1.20
Oil pan gasket	1.00
Rear oil seal	4.50
Neutral safety switch	$ 3.50
Governor body repair kit	18.00
Valve body assy., new	80.00

TORQUEFLITE AUTOMATIC TRANSMISSION, MAJOR SERVICE

Includes:
Basic Jobs:
1. **Overhaul transmission.** R&R transmission disassemble, clean, inspect and replace all worn parts as needed. Replace all oil seals. Adjust throttle and shift linkage as required. Flush converter and cooler lines. Perform pressure checks of mainline, throttle, and accumulator. Road test.
2. **Replace torque converter.** R&R transmission. Flush oil cooler and lines. Replace transmission oil and oil filter. Perform pressure checks of mainline, throttle, and accumulator. Adjust throttle and shift linkage as required. Road test.
3. **Reseal transmission.** R&R transmission. Replace all seals and gaskets. Replace transmission oil and oil filter. Check oil cooler for leaks. Perform pressure checks of mainline, throttle, and accumulator. Adjust throttle and shift linkage as required. Road test.

Additions to Basic Jobs: Associated work that is performed while the transmission is out during one of basic jobs.

MODEL	1966	1967	1968	1969	1970	1971	1972	1973	1974	1975
Basic Job #1										
Overhaul transmission,										
Imperial	10.3	10.3	10.3	9.5	9.5	9.5	9.5	9.5	9.2	9.2
Hemi or 440 hi-perf. engine	11.2	11.2	11.2	10.4	10.4	10.4	10.4	10.4	10.1	10.1
All others	9.2	9.2	9.2	8.4	8.4	8.4	8.4	8.4	8.1	8.1
Basic Job #2										
Replace torque converter,										
Imperial	6.8	6.8	6.8	5.4	5.4	5.4	5.4	4.9	4.9	4.9
Hemi or 440 hi-perf. engine	7.7	7.7	7.7	6.3	6.3	6.3	6.3	5.8	5.8	5.8
All others	5.9	5.9	5.9	5.4	5.4	5.4	5.3	4.6	4.6	4.6
Basic Job #3										
Reseal transmission,										
Imperial	7.9	7.9	6.3	6.3	6.3	6.3	6.3	6.0	6.0	6.0
Hemi or 440 engine	8.8	8.8	7.2	7.2	7.2	7.2	7.2	6.9	6.9	6.9
All others	7.0	7.0	7.0	6.0	6.0	6.0	6.0	6.0	6.0	6.0
Additions to Basic Jobs:										
Replace oil cooler pipes, both, **ADD:**	.9	.9	.9	.9	.9	.9	.9	.9	.9	.9
Replace oil filler pipe and/or seal, **ADD:**	.5	.5	.5	.5	.5	.5	.5	.5	.5	.5
Replace torque converter ring gear, **ADD:**	.5	.5	.5	.5	.5	.5	.5	.5	.5	.5

CHRYSLER/PLYMOUTH/DODGE

TORQUEFLITE AUTOMATIC TRANSMISSION, MAJOR SERVICE Continued

Approximate parts cost:
Transmission seal and gasket kit	$20.00-40.00
Transmission partial overhaul kit	44.00
Oil cooler pipe, each	9.00
Torque converter assembly	200.00
Torque converter ring gear	8.00
Oil filler pipe	$ 4.00
Oil filler pipe seal	0.25
Oil pan	8.00
Oil pan gasket	1.00
Governor kit	19.00

DRIVESHAFT, SERVICE

Includes:
Basic Job: R&R driveshaft and overhaul or replace front and rear U-joints.

MODEL	1966	1967	1968	1969	1970	1971	1972	1973	1974	1975
Basic Job:										
R&R driveshaft & overhaul both U-joints,										
Cross & roller type	1.7	1.7	1.7	1.5	1.5	1.5	1.5	1.5	1.5	1.5
Constant velocity type	2.5	2.5	2.5	2.5	2.5	2.5	2.5	2.5	2.5	2.5
R&R driveshaft with joints	.8	.8	.8	.8	.8	.8	.8	.8	.8	.8

Approximate parts cost:
U-joint package, cross & roller type	$11.00
Constant velocity joint kit	12.00
Driveshaft with joints	$120.00

REAR AXLE, SERVICE

Includes:
Basic Jobs: 1. R&R driveshaft, R&R axle shafts, overhaul differential assembly, and check and adjust pinion nose angle.
    2. R&R driveshaft and replace pinion bearing oil seal.
Related Jobs: R&R axle shaft (one side) and/ or bearing and seals and adjust end-play. Replace axle shaft wheel mounting stud.

MODEL	1966	1967	1968	1969	1970	1971	1972	1973	1974	1975
Basic Job #1										
Overhaul differential assembly										
Removable-type, standard	7.0	7.0	6.6	6.6	6.6	6.6	6.6	6.6	5.8	5.8
Removable-type, Sure Grip	7.4	7.4	7.0	7.0	7.0	7.0	7.0	7.0	5.5	5.5
Integral-type, standard	7.8	7.8	6.1	6.1	6.1	6.1	6.1	6.1	5.6	5.6
Integral-type, Sure Grip	8.4	8.4	8.4	8.4	8.4	8.4	8.4	8.4	5.5	5.5
Basic Job #2										
Replace drive pinion bearing oil seal	.8	.8	.8	1.3	1.3	1.3	1.3	.8	.8	.8
Related Jobs:										
R&R axle shaft (one side), and/or brg. and seals and adjust end-play	1.7	1.7	1.5	1.5	1.5	1.5	1.5	1.5	1.5	1.5
Replace axle shaft wheel mounting stud	.8	.8	.8	.8	.8	.8	.8	.8	.8	.8

Approximate parts cost:
Axle shaft	$30.00
Inner or outer seal	2.00
Sure Grip repair kit	30.00
Pinion bearing oil seal	$ 3.00
Cover gasket	1.00
Ring & pinion gear set	70.00-120.00

CHRYSLER/PLYMOUTH/DODGE

REAR SUSPENSION, SERVICE

Includes:
Service for the rear suspension system listed as individual jobs. Add times if more than one job is performed.

MODEL	1966	1967	1968	1969	1970	1971	1972	1973	1974	1975
Repl. rear leaf spring & shim to align pinion angle,										
Imperial	2.2	2.2	2.2	1.8	1.8	1.8	1.8	2.0	2.0	2.0
All others	1.6	1.6	1.6	1.6	1.8	1.8	1.8	1.7	1.7	1.7
Repl. shackle and bushings; eye bolt & bushings	.7	.7	.7	.7	.7	.7	.7	.7	.7	.7
Replace shock absorber, both sides	.8	.8	.8	.8	.8	.8	.8	.8	.8	.8
Repl. sway bar and bushings	.9	.9	.9	.9	.9	.9	.9	.9	.9	.9

Approximate parts cost:
Shock absorber $14.00
Rear spring 40.00
Sway bar and bushings 37.00
Shackle package $4.00-7.00
Shackle bushing package 1.00

STEERING LINKAGE, SERVICE AND ADJUST

Includes:
Basic Job: Adjust toe-in.
Related Jobs: Replace defective parts and adjust toe-in.

MODEL	1966	1967	1968	1969	1970	1971	1972	1973	1974	1975
Basic Job:										
Adjust toe-in	.4	.4	.4	.4	.4	.4	.4	.4	.4	.4
Related Jobs:										
Replace tie-rods or tie-rod ends, (4)	1.6	1.6	1.5	1.5	1.5	1.5	1.5	1.5	1.5	1.5
Replace Pitman arm, includes adjust toe-in	.8	.8	.8	.8	.8	.8	.8	.8	.8	.8
Replace steering idler arm or bushing, including adjust toe-in	.8	.8	.8	.8	.8	.8	.8	.8	.8	.8

Approximate parts cost:
Tie-rod end pkg. .... $ 7.00
Pitman arm 11.00
Tie rod 3.00
Idler arm, Imperial $23.00
Idler arm, all others 13.00

STANDARD STEERING GEAR, ADJUST AND SERVICE

Includes:
Basic Job: Adjust steering gear end play, worm and sector mesh; adjust wheel bearings and toe-in.
Related Job: Replace steering gear assembly.
Addition to Related Job: Overhaul steering gear.

MODEL	1966	1967	1968	1969	1970	1971	1972	1973	1974	1975
Basic Job:										
Complete gear, wheel brgs. & toe-in adj.	1.4	1.4	1.4	1.4	1.4	1.4	1.4	1.4	1.4	1.4
Related Job:										
Replace steering gear assy.	2.4	2.6	2.6	2.6	2.4	2.4	2.4	2.4	2.0	2.0
Addition to Related Job:										
Overhaul steering gear, ADD:	1.2	1.2	1.2	1.2	1.2	1.2	1.2	1.2	.9	.9

Approximate parts cost:
Standard steering gear overhaul kit $12.00
Standard steering gear, new $90.00

CHRYSLER/PLYMOUTH/DODGE

FRONT END, TEST, SERVICE, AND ADJUST

Includes:
Basic Job: Check and adjust car height, caster, camber, steering axis inclination, turning radius, and toe-in; pack and adjust front wheel bearings; replace seals.
Related Jobs: Perform individual adjustments. Replace or overhaul defective part(s) and make necessary adjustments.

MODEL	1966	1967	1968	1969	1970	1971	1972	1973	1974	1975
Basic Job:										
Complete test and adjustments,										
With drum brakes	2.5	2.5	2.5	2.5	2.5	2.5	2.5	2.5	2.5	2.5
With disc brakes	3.0	3.0	3.0	3.0	3.0	3.0	3.0	3.0	3.0	3.0
Related Jobs:										
Adjust toe-in only	.4	.4	.4	.4	.4	.4	.4	.4	.4	.4
Repack wheel brgs. only, incl. new seals,										
Drum brakes, both sides	.9	.9	.9	.9	.9	.9	.9	.9	.9	.9
Disc brakes, both sides	1.5	1.5	1.5	1.2	1.9	1.9	1.9	1.5	1.5	1.5
Replace wheel brgs. only, each side,										
Drum brakes, inner or outer brg.	.5	.5	.5	.5	.5	.5	.5	.5	.5	.5
Disc brakes, inner or outer brg.	.8	.8	.8	.7	1.1	1.1	1.1	.9	.9	.9
Balance four wheels, on car,										
With drum brakes	1.2	1.2	1.2	1.2	1.2	1.2	1.2	1.2	1.2	1.2
With disc/drum brakes	1.5	1.5	1.5	1.5	1.5	1.5	1.5	1.5	1.5	1.5
Overhaul front suspension, incl. disassemble, replace nec. parts, lube., & complete adjustment,										
With drum brakes	7.9	7.9	7.9	7.9	7.9	7.9	7.9	7.9	7.9	7.9
With disc brakes	8.8	8.8	8.8	8.8	8.8	8.8	8.8	8.8	8.8	8.8
Replace torsion bar spring, one side, incl. complete front end adjustments,										
Imperial	2.8	2.8	2.8	2.8	2.8	2.8	2.8	2.8	2.8	2.8
All others	2.6	2.6	2.6	2.6	2.6	2.6	2.6	2.6	2.6	2.6
Replace upper ball joints, both sides, incl. complete front end adjustments	3.7	3.7	3.7	3.7	3.7	3.7	3.7	3.7	3.7	3.7
Replace steering knuckle, one side, incl. complete front end adjustment,										
With drum brakes	2.9	2.9	2.9	2.9	2.9	2.9	2.9	2.9	2.9	2.9
With disc brakes	3.2	3.2	3.2	3.2	3.2	3.2	3.2	3.2	3.2	3.2
Replace shock absorber, both sides,										
Imperial	1.8	1.8	1.8	1.8	1.8	1.8	1.8	1.3	1.3	1.3
All others	.9	.9	.9	.9	.9	.9	.9	.6	.6	.6
Replace lwr. control arm struts, or bushing,										
Imperial, drum or disc brakes	1.3	1.3	1.3	1.3	1.3	1.3	1.3	1.3	1.1	1.1
All others, drum brakes	3.3	3.3	2.3	2.3	2.3	2.3	2.4	2.4	2.4	2.4
All others, disc brakes	3.6	3.6	3.6	3.6	3.6	3.8	3.4	1.3	1.1	1.1
Replace control arm rubber bumper, one	.4	.4	.4	.4	.4	.4	.4	.4	.4	.4
Replace stabilizer bar and bushings	.7	.7	.7	.7	.7	.7	.7	.7	.7	.7

Approximate parts cost:

Front wheel brg., outer ... $2.00	Steering knuckle ... $50.00
Wheel bearing inner ... 3.00	Rubber bumper, each ... 1.50
Seals ... 1.50	Shock absorber, each ... 13.00
Stabilizer bar & bushing, ea. side ... 5.00	Control arm strut ... 10.00
Torsion bar ... 17.00	Ball joint ... 13.00

CHRYSLER/PLYMOUTH/DODGE

POWER STEERING UNIT, TEST AND SERVICE

Includes:
Basic Job: Adjust drive belt tension; hook-up gauges to check pressure on left and right turns. Adjust steering gear box over-center torque and control valve to balance left and right steering effort.
Additions to Basic Job: Service power steering unit.
Related Jobs: R&R power steering unit, pump, or other associated parts.
Additions to Related Jobs: Overhaul steering unit or pump including replacement of all seals and worn parts.

MODEL	1966	1967	1968	1969	1970	1971	1972	1973	1974	1975
Basic Job:										
Compl. test and adj. pwr. steer. unit	1.0	1.0	1.0	1.0	1.0	1.0	1.0	1.0	1.0	1.0
Additions to Basic Job:										
Repl. pwr. steer. pump drive belt, **ADD**:	.3	.3	.3	.3	.3	.3	.3	.3	.3	.3
With air conditioning, **ADD**:	.2	.2	.2	.2	.2	.2	.2	.2	.2	.2
Check & replenish reservoir fluid, **ADD**:	.2	.2	.2	.2	.2	.2	.2	.2	.2	.2
Related Jobs:										
Repl. press. hose, incl. adjust dr. belt	.5	.5	.6	.6	.6	.6	.6	.6	.6	.6
Repl. return hose, incl. adjust dr. belt	.4	.4	.4	.4	.4	.4	.4	.4	.4	.4
Repl. pump reservoir or O-ring seals	1.0	1.3	1.0	1.0	1.0	1.0	1.0	1.0	1.0	1.0
Repl. pump, incl. pressure-test orig. pump and transf. pulley	1.8	1.8	1.8	1.8	1.8	1.8	1.8	1.8	1.8	1.8
Repl. pwr. steering unit, incl. test orig. unit and compl. adjust,										
Imperial	3.6	3.6	3.6	2.8	2.8	2.8	2.8	2.8	2.2	2.2
Coronet, Charger, Satellite	2.1	2.1	2.1	2.1	2.6	2.6	2.6	2.6	2.6	2.6
All others	3.0	2.8	2.8	2.1	2.2	2.2	2.2	2.2	2.2	2.2
Addtions to Related Jobs:										
O/H power steering unit, **ADD**:	2.2	2.2	2.2	2.4	2.4	2.4	2.4	2.4	3.0	3.0
O/H pump, incl. new kit & seals, **ADD**:	.8	.8	.8	.8	.8	.8	.8	.6	.6	.6

Approximate parts cost:
Drive belt	$ 4.00	Rotor kit	$28.00
Pressure hose	12.00	Reservoir	5.00-11.00
Return hose	4.00	Pump assembly	85.00
Valve assembly	19.00	Worm with piston	35.00
Seal kit	14.00	Pwr. steering gear unit	250.00

POWER BRAKE UNIT, SERVICE

Includes:
Basic Job: R&R with new unit, test, and adjust brakes.
Additions to Basic Job: Replace vacuum hose or vacuum check valve.

MODEL	1966	1967	1968	1969	1970	1971	1972	1973	1974	1975
Basic Job:										
R&R pwr. unit, test, & adj. brakes	1.6	1.6	1.8	1.5	1.5	1.5	1.5	1.5	1.5	1.5
Additions to Basic Job:										
Install new hose, **ADD**:	.2	.2	.2	.2	.2	.2	.2	.2	.2	.2
Install new vacuum check valve, **ADD**:	.2	.2	.2	.2	.2	.2	.2	.2	.2	.2

Approximate parts cost:
Power brake unit	$48.00-62.00	Vacuum check valve	$1.75
Vacuum hose, per ft.	0.90		

CHRYSLER/PLYMOUTH/DODGE

BRAKES, SERVICE

Includes:

Basic Job: Install new linings or pads, turn brake drums or rotors, lubricate and adjust front wheel bearings, replace rear oil seals, bleed hydraulic system, and adjust drakes.

Additions to Basic Job: Overhaul four wheel cylinders, overhaul or replace front calipers, overhaul or replace rear calipers.

Related Jobs: Performed at time other than during basic job. Overhaul or replace front calipers, overhaul or replace rear calipers.

MODEL	1966	1967	1968	1969	1970	1971	1972	1973	1974	1975
Basic Job:										
Complete job incl. turn drums or rotors,										
Drum (4), all models	7.4	7.4	7.4	7.4	7.4	7.4	7.4	7.4	7.4	7.4
Disc front, drum rear, all models	7.6	7.6	7.6	7.6	7.8	7.8	7.8	7.8	7.8	7.8
Disc (4), Imperial	—	—	—	—	—	—	—	—	7.2	7.2
With floating caliper type, ADD:	—	—	—	—	1.0	1.0	1.1	1.1	1.1	1.1
With 4-piston calipers, ADD:	—	—	—	.5	.5	.5	.5	.5	.5	.5
Additions to Basic Job:										
Overhaul 4 wheel cyl. incl. hone, ADD:	1.6	2.3	2.3	2.3	2.3	2.4	2.4	2.4	2.4	2.4
Overhaul front calipers (both), ADD:	3.5	3.5	3.5	2.9	2.9	2.9	2.9	2.9	2.9	2.9
Replace front calipers (both), ADD:	.4	.4	.4	.4	.4	.4	.4	.4	.4	.4
Overhaul rear calipers, ADD:	—	—	—	—	—	—	—	—	3.1	3.1
Replace rear calipers, ADD:	—	—	—	—	—	—	—	—	.6	.6
Related Jobs: (Not during basic job)										
Bleed hyd. sys., 4 wheels	.6	.6	.6	.6	.6	.6	.6	.6	.6	.6
O/h fr. calipers, incl. turn rotors	5.3	5.3	5.3	5.3	4.6	4.6	4.6	4.6	4.6	4.6
Rpl. fr. caliper, incl. turn rotor, ea.	2.4	2.4	2.4	2.4	2.4	2.4	2.4	2.4	2.4	2.4
O/h rear calipers, incl. turn rotors	—	—	—	—	—	—	—	—	4.8	4.8
Repl. rear caliper, incl. turn rotor, ea.	—	—	—	—	—	—	—	—	2.3	2.3
O/h with 4-piston-type caliper, both	—	—	—	—	5.9	5.9	5.9	5.9	5.9	5.9

Approximate parts cost:

Wheel cyl. seal, boot & bush pkg.	$ 6.00	Caliper brake housing	$50.00
Brake shoes and lining sets, front or rear	25.00	Oil seal, ea.	2.00
Disc brake pads, set of 2	24.00	Master cylinder repair kit	20.00
Wheel cylinder repair kit, ea.	2.00		

PARKING BRAKES, SERVICE AND ADJUST

Includes:

Basic Jobs: Replace defective cable or brake shoes and adjust parking brakes.

MODEL	1966	1967	1968	1969	1970	1971	1972	1973	1974	1975
Basic Job:										
Replace forward cable,										
Imperial	1.0	1.0	1.0	1.0	1.0	1.0	1.0	1.3	1.3	1.3
All others	1.0	1.0	1.0	1.0	1.0	1.0	1.0	1.0	1.0	1.0
Replace rear cable, one side	1.0	1.0	1.0	1.0	1.0	1.0	1.0	1.0	1.0	1.0
Replace rear cable, both sides,										
Imperial	1.5	1.5	1.5	1.5	1.5	1.5	1.5	1.3	1.3	1.3
All others	1.5	1.5	1.5	1.5	1.5	1.5	1.5	1.5	1.5	1.5
Replace parking brake shoes, both sides	—	—	—	—	—	—	—	—	1.9	1.9

Approximate parts cost:

Rear cable, each	$5.00-8.00	Parking brake shoes	$24.00
Front cable	8.00		

CHRYSLER/PLYMOUTH/DODGE   145

HYDRAULIC BRAKE SYSTEM, OVERHAUL

Includes:
Basic Job: Overhaul or replace master cylinder, all wheel cylinders or calipers, bleed hydraulic system, and adjust brakes.
Related Jobs: Performed at time other than during basic job. Overhaul or replace master cylinder only, overhaul wheel cylinders or calipers.

MODEL	1966	1967	1968	1969	1970	1971	1972	1973	1974	1975
Basic Job:										
Compl. job, incl. mstr. & wh. cylinders,										
Drum brakes, all models	5.0	5.0	6.0	6.0	6.0	6.0	5.2	5.2	5.2	5.2
Disc front, drum rear, all models	4.6	4.6	5.6	5.6	5.6	5.6	4.8	4.8	4.8	4.8
Related Jobs: (Not during basic job)										
Overhaul mstr. cylinder only	1.6	2.3	2.3	2.3	2.3	2.4	2.4	2.4	2.4	2.4
Replace mstr. cylinder	1.0	1.1	.9	.9	.9	.9	1.0	1.0	1.0	1.0
With power brakes, **ADD:**	.2	.2	.2	.2	.2	.2	.2	.2	.2	.2
O/h wheel cylinders, drum brakes, (4)	3.4	3.4	4.4	4.4	4.4	4.4	4.0	4.0	4.0	4.0
O/h fr. calipers, incl. turn rotors	5.3	5.3	5.3	5.3	4.6	4.6	4.6	4.6	4.6	4.6
O/h rear calipers, incl. turn rotors	—	—	—	—	—	—	—	—	4.8	4.8
Bleed hydraulic system	.6	.6	.6	.6	.6	.6	.6	.6	.6	.6

Approximate parts cost:
Master cylinder repair kit $18.00	Master cylinder $32.00
Wheel cylinder repair kit, ea. 2.00	Wheel cyl. seal, boot & bushing pkg. 6.00

LIGHTING SYSTEM, ADJUST AND SERVICE

Includes:
Basic Jobs: 1. Adjust headlights to inspection requirements.
              2. Replace defective parts in rear lighting system.
Additions to Basic Jobs: Replace associated parts affecting headlight adjustment.
Related Jobs: Replace associated parts not affecting headlight adjustment.

MODEL	1966	1967	1968	1969	1970	1971	1972	1973	1974	1975
Basic Job #1										
Adjust two lights	.4	.4	.4	.4	.4	.4	.4	.4	.4	.4
Adjust four lights	.6	.6	.6	.6	.6	.6	.6	.6	.6	.6
Basic Job #2										
Replace stoplight switch	.4	.4	.4	.4	.4	.4	.4	.4	.4	.4
Replace back-up light switch	.4	.4	.4	.4	.4	.4	.4	.4	.4	.4
Additions to Basic Job:										
Replace sealed beam unit, each, **ADD:**	.3	.3	.3	.3	.3	.3	.3	.3	.3	.3
Replace rotating motor, **ADD:**	.7	.7	.4	.4	.4	.4	.4	.4	.4	.4
Replace rotating motor relay, **ADD:**	.4	.4	.6	.6	.6	.6	.6	.6	.6	.6
Related Jobs:										
Replace headlight switch,										
Dodge Polara, Monaco, 880	.4	.4	.4	1.1	1.1	1.1	1.1	1.1	1.1	1.1
All others	.5	1.0	1.0	1.5	1.5	1.5	1.5	1.5	1.5	1.5
Replace foot dimmer switch	.3	.3	.3	.3	.3	.3	.3	.3	.3	.3
Replace signal/hazard flasher	.2	.2	.2	.2	.2	.2	.2	.2	.2	.2
Replace turn signal/hazard switch,										
With standard column	.8	.8	.8	.8	.8	.8	.8	.8	.8	.8
With tilt or telescopic column	1.0	1.0	1.0	1.0	1.0	1.0	1.0	1.0	1.0	1.0

Approximate parts cost:
Sealed beam unit .... $ 3.00	Rotating motor $50.00-60.00
Signal/hazard flasher 2.00	Rotating motor relay 6.00
Signal/hazard switch 6.00-16.00	Headlight switch 8.50
Stoplight switch 4.00	Back-up light switch 7.00

CHRYSLER/PLYMOUTH/DODGE

HEATING SYSTEM, TEST AND SERVICE

Includes:
   Basic Job: Drain, back-flush, and fill radiator, check radiator and heater hoses and connections, pressure-test radiator cap and system.
   Related Jobs: Replace defective parts. Work performed individually and independently of basic job.

MODEL	1966	1967	1968	1969	1970	1971	1972	1973	1974	1975
Basic Job:										
Drain, flush, fill, check, & pressure-test	.9	.9	.9	.9	.9	.9	.9	.9	.9	.9
Related Jobs:										
Replace heater hose, front, one	.4	.4	.4	.4	.4	.4	.4	.4	.4	.4
Replace heater hose, rear, one	.8	.8	.8	.8	.8	.8	.8	.8	.8	.8
Replace heater blower motor, front	1.9	1.9	1.9	1.3	1.3	1.3	1.3	1.3	1.3	1.3
Replace heater blower motor, rear	.3	.3	.3	.3	.3	.3	.3	.3	.3	.3
Replace heater core, front, w/o A/C	1.9	1.9	1.9	1.0	1.0	1.0	1.0	1.0	1.0	1.0
Replace heater core, rear	1.6	1.6	1.6	1.6	1.6	1.6	1.6	1.6	1.6	1.6
Replace heater core with air conditioning,										
Plymouth	1.8	1.8	1.8	1.8	1.8	1.8	1.8	1.8	1.8	1.8
All others	3.1	3.1	3.1	3.1	3.1	3.1	3.1	3.1	3.1	3.1
Replace heater switch, front	.9	.9	.7	.7	.8	.8	.8	.8	.8	.8
Replace heater switch, rear	1.5	1.5	1.5	1.5	1.5	1.5	.5	.5	.5	.5

Approximate parts cost:
Heater hose, per ft. $0.75
Blower motor 21.00
Heater core $18.00-45.00
Heater switch 5.00

AIR CONDITIONING SYSTEM, SPRING TUNE-UP

Includes:
   Basic Job: Clean condenser fins; adjust drive belt tension; test anti-freeze; tighten compressor, condenser, and evaporator mounts. Pressure-test and leak-check system. Check system for performance.
   Additions to Basic Job: Replacement of defective parts.

MODEL	1966	1967	1968	1969	1970	1971	1972	1973	1974	1975
Basic Job:										
Perform complete spring tune-up	2.0	2.0	2.0	2.0	2.0	2.0	2.0	2.0	2.0	2.0
Additions to Basic Job:										
Replace compressor belt, **ADD:**	.4	.4	.4	.4	.4	.4	.4	.4	.4	.4
Replace compr. clutch pulley w/hub assy., **ADD:**	.5	.5	.5	.5	.5	.5	.5	.5	.5	.5
Replace compr. clutch coil, **ADD:**	.8	.8	.8	.8	.8	.8	.8	.8	.8	.8
Replace compr. clutch bearing, **ADD:**	.8	.8	.8	.8	.8	.8	.8	.8	.8	.8

Approximate parts cost:
Compressor drive belt ....$ 3.00
Compressor clutch pulley w/hub 76.00
Freon, per 14 oz. can 2.50
Compressor clutch coil $28.00
Compressor clutch bearing 23.00
Anti-freeze, per gal. 9.50

CHRYSLER/PLYMOUTH/DODGE 147

AIR CONDITIONING SYSTEM, MAJOR SERVICE

Includes:
Basic Job: Drain system in order to replace defective part(s), evacuate, dehydrate, and recharge system, pressure test, and leak check, clean condenser fins, adjust drive belt tension, tighten compressor, condenser, and evaporator mounts, and conduct performance test.
Additions to Basic Job: Replace or overhaul compressor. Replace other defective parts.

MODEL	1966	1967	1968	1969	1970	1971	1972	1973	1974	1975
Basic Job:										
Drain, evacuate, dehydrate, charge & test	3.0	3.0	3.0	3.0	3.0	3.0	3.0	3.0	3.0	3.0
Additions to Basic Job:										
Replace compressor, ADD:	1.2	1.2	1.2	1.2	1.2	1.2	1.2	1.2	1.2	1.2
Overhaul compressor, incl. R&R, ADD:	2.9	2.9	2.9	2.9	2.9	2.9	2.9	2.9	2.9	2.9
Replace relief valve (EPR), ADD:	1.5	1.5	1.5	1.5	.8	.8	.8	.8	.8	.8
Replace compr. front head or reed valve, ADD:	1.4	1.4	1.4	1.4	1.4	1.4	.4	.4	.4	.4
Replace compr. oil pump seal, ADD:	.9	.9	.9	.9	1.1	1.1	.9	.9	.9	.9
Replace compr. rear head or valve assy., ADD:	1.1	1.1	1.1	1.1	1.1	1.1	.6	.6	.6	.6
Replace condenser, ADD:	2.1	2.1	2.1	1.3	1.3	1.3	1.3	1.3	1.3	1.3
Replace evaporator coil,										
Chrys., Polara, Monanco, 880, Fury, ADD:	4.8	4.8	4.8	4.2	4.2	4.2	4.2	4.2	4.2	4.2
All others, ADD:	3.6	3.6	3.6	3.6	3.6	3.6	3.6	3.6	3.6	3.6
Imperial rear unit, ADD:	1.7	1.7	1.7	1.7	1.7	1.8	1.8	1.8	1.8	1.8
Replace sight-glass, ADD:	1.4	1.4	1.4	1.4	1.4	1.4	.9	.9	.9	.9
Replace receiver-dehydrator, ADD:	1.0	1.0	1.0	.8	.8	.8	.4	.4	.4	.4
Replace expansion valve, ADD:	1.7	1.7	1.1	.8	.8	.8	.8	.8	.8	.8
Replace one hose, ADD:	.4	.4	.4	.4	.4	.4	.4	.4	.4	.4

Approximate parts cost:
Compressor	$120.00
Compressor seal pkg.	8.00
Relief valve	27.00
Condenser	100.00
Compressor front head & gasket	7.00
Compressor rear head & gasket	7.00
Expansion valve	35.00
Hose, per ft.	$2.75
Hose fittings, each	1.00
Evaporator coil	130.00
With blower	190.00
Freon, per 14 oz. can	2.50
Anti-freeze, per gal.	9.50

AIR CONDITIONING SYSTEM BLOWER MOTOR OR CONTROLS, SERVICE

Includes:
Basic Jobs: Conduct performance test of system to determine defective part(s), R&R part, and test system following installation.

MODEL	1966	1967	1968	1969	1970	1971	1972	1973	1974	1975
Basic Jobs:										
R&R blower motor, test system after install,										
Imperial, front unit	2.2	1.4	1.4	2.1	2.1	2.1	2.1	2.1	2.1	2.1
Imperial, rear unit, one	1.4	1.4	1.4	1.4	2.4	2.4	2.4	2.4	2.4	2.4
Mopar unit	3.0	3.0	3.0	3.0	3.0	3.0	3.0	3.0	3.0	3.0
All others	2.7	1.8	1.8	1.8	2.4	2.4	2.4	2.4	2.4	2.4
R&R blower motor switch, test system	1.8	1.8	1.8	1.8	1.8	1.8	1.8	1.8	1.8	1.8
R&R compr. clutch switch, test system	1.4	1.4	1.4	1.4	1.4	1.4	1.3	1.3	1.3	1.3
R&R evap. temp. contr. switch, test system	1.4	1.4	1.4	1.4	1.4	1.4	1.4	1.4	1.4	1.4
R&R contr. unit, test system after install	1.4	1.4	1.4	1.4	1.4	1.4	1.4	1.4	1.4	1.4

Approximate parts cost:
Blower motor	$30.00
Blower motor switch	3.50
1969-70 Imperial	14.00
Compressor clutch switch	$10.00
Evap. temperature control switch	6.00
Control unit	67.00

FORD/LINCOLN/MERCURY

SERVICE STATION MAINTENANCE

Includes:
Basic Job: Lubricate chassis, drain oil, change filters, repack front wheel bearings, repack U-joints, and lubricate front end. Check fluid levels of battery, radiator, air conditioner, brake master cylinder, power steering reservoir, transmission, and differential. Check condition of hoses and drive belts. Lubricate miscellaneous moving parts and joints, hinges, etc.

Related Jobs: Service individual systems or components. See detailed description of work included for each job in separate major section.

Additions to Basic or Related Jobs: Allowances for special equipment installed.

MODEL	1966	1967	1968	1969	1970	1971	1972	1973	1974	1975
Basic Job:										
General lubrication & systems check,										
4-cylinder	—	—	—	—	—	1.2	1.2	1.2	1.2	1.2
6-cylinder, in-line	1.0	1.0	1.0	1.0	1.0	1.0	1.0	1.0	1.0	1.0
V-6 engine	—	—	—	—	—	—	—	—	1.3	1.3
V-8, Continental	1.5	1.5	1.5	1.5	1.5	1.5	1.5	1.5	1.5	1.5
V-8, all others	1.1	1.1	1.1	1.1	1.1	1.1	1.1	1.1	1.1	1.1
With air conditioning, **ADD:**	.3	.3	.3	.3	.3	.3	.3	.3	.3	.3
With Thermactor, **ADD:**	.2	.2	.2	.2	.2	.2	.2	.2	.2	.2
With disc brakes, **ADD:**	.9	.9	.9	.9	.9	.9	.9	.9	.9	.9
Related Jobs:										
Service Battery.										
Clean, test, & fill	.3	.3	.3	.3	.3	.3	.3	.3	.3	.3
Clean terminals	.2	.2	.2	.2	.2	.2	.2	.2	.2	.2
Replace ground cable	.2	.2	.2	.2	.2	.2	.2	.2	.2	.2
Replace starter cable	.3	.3	.3	.3	.3	.3	.3	.3	.3	.3
Replace battery	.4	.4	.4	.4	.4	.4	.4	.4	.4	.4
Service Cooling System.										
Back-flush, fill, & pressure-test cap & system,										
Replace upper hose	.4	.4	.4	.4	.4	.4	.4	.4	.4	.4
Replace lower hose,										
V-8, large block (383-462 CID)	.7	.7	.7	.7	.7	.7	.7	.7	.7	.7
All other engines	.5	.5	.5	.5	.5	.5	.5	.5	.5	.5
Replace water pump bypass hose,										
V-8, 429 & 460 engines	1.5	1.5	1.5	1.5	1.5	1.5	1.8	1.8	1.8	1.8
V-8, 302 & 351 CID engines	.3	.3	.3	.3	.3	.3	.3	.3	.3	.3
V-8, all others	1.0	1.0	1.0	1.0	1.0	1.0	—	—	—	—
With air conditioning, **ADD:**	.2	.2	.2	.2	.2	.2	.2	.2	.2	.2
Replace thermostat, includes test,										
4-cylinder	—	—	—	—	—	.8	1.0	1.0	1.0	1.0
V-6 engine	—	—	—	—	—	—	—	—	.8	.8
6-cylinder, in line	.8	.8	.8	.8	.8	.8	.8	.8	.8	.8
V-8, 302 CID engine	.9	.9	.9	.9	.9	.9	.9	.9	.9	.9
V-8, 462 CID engine (inblock)	1.4	1.4	1.4	—	—	—	—	—	—	—
V-8, all others	.7	.7	.7	.7	.7	.7	.7	.7	.7	.7
6-cylinder with power steering, **ADD:**	.1	.1	.1	.1	.1	.1	.1	.1	.1	.1
With Thermactor, **ADD:**	—	—	—	—	—	—	—	—	.1	.1
With air conditioning, **ADD:**	.2	.2	.2	.2	.2	.2	.2	.2	.2	.2
Replace water pump drive belt & adjust	.6	.6	.6	.6	.6	.6	.6	.6	.6	.6
4-cylinder OHC	—	—	—	—	—	1.0	1.0	1.0	1.0	1.0
All other engines	.4	.4	.4	.4	.4	.4	.4	.4	.4	.4
With Thermactor, **ADD:**	.1	.1	.1	.1	.1	.1	.1	.1	.1	.1
With power steering, **ADD:**	.1	.1	.1	.1	.1	.1	.1	.1	.1	.1
With air conditioning, **ADD:**	.2	.2	.2	.2	.2	.2	.2	.2	.2	.2

(THIS SCHEDULE CONTINUED ON NEXT PAGE.)

FORD/LINCOLN/MERCURY

SERVICE STATION MAINTENANCE Continued

MODEL	1966	1967	1968	1969	1970	1971	1972	1973	1974	1975
Service Cooling System Continued										
Replace water pump,										
4-cylinder OHC	—	—	—	—	—	1.0	1.0	1.0	1.0	1.0
6-cylinder, in-line	1.3	1.3	1.3	1.3	1.3	1.3	1.3	1.3	1.3	1.3
With air cond. & pwr. steering, ADD:	.6	.6	.6	.6	.6	.6	.4	.4	.4	.4
V-6 engine	—	—	—	—	—	—	—	—	1.6	1.6
With air conditioning, ADD:	—	—	—	—	—	—	—	—	.2	.2
V-8, 429 & 460 CID engines	1.9	1.9	1.9	1.9	1.9	1.9	2.1	2.1	2.1	2.1
With air cond. & pwr. steering, ADD:	.2	.2	.2	.2	.2	.2	.4	.4	.4	.4
V-8, all others	1.3	1.3	1.3	1.3	1.3	1.3	1.3	1.3	1.4	1.4
With air cond. & pwr. steering, ADD:	.6	.6	.6	.6	.6	.6	.4	.4	.4	.4
All models with Thermactor, ADD:	.2	.2	.2	.2	.2	.2	.1	.1	.1	.1
Service Ignition System.										
Adjust & install new spark plugs,										
4-cylinder	—	—	—	—	—	.4	.4	.4	.4	.4
6-cylinder	.6	.6	.6	.6	.6	.6	.6	.6	.6	.6
V-8 engine	.9	.9	.9	.9	.9	.9	.9	.9	.9	.9
With air conditioning, ADD:	.3	.3	.3	.3	.3	.3	.3	.3	.3	.3
With Thermactor, ADD:	.3	.3	.3	.3	.3	.3	.3	.3	.3	.3
V-8, 390, 428 CID with Thermactor, ADD:	1.0	1.0	1.0	1.0	1.0	—	—	—	—	—
Replace points & condenser & adjust ignition timing,										
4-cylinder	—	—	—	—	—	.6	.6	.6	.6	—
6-cylinder, in-line	.7	.7	.7	.7	.7	.7	.7	.7	—	—
V-6 engine	—	—	—	—	—	—	—	—	.7	—
V-8 engine	.7	.7	.7	.7	.7	.7	.7	.7	—	—
Replace distributor cap,										
4 or 6-cylinder, ADD:	.3	.3	.3	.3	.3	.3	.3	.3	.3	.4
V-8 engine, ADD:	.4	.4	.4	.4	.4	.4	.4	.4	.4	.5
Check reluctor air gap and ignition timing	—	—	—	—	—	—	—	—	.5	.5
Replace spark plug wires,										
4-cylinder	—	—	—	—	—	.4	.4	.4	.4	.4
6-cylinder, in-line	.5	.5	.6	.6	.6	.6	.6	.6	.6	.6
V-6 engine	—	—	—	—	—	—	—	—	.7	.7
V-8 engine	.7	.7	.8	.8	.8	.8	.8	.8	.8	.8
With air conditioning, ADD:	.3	.3	.3	.3	.3	.3	.3	.3	.3	.3
Replace ignition coil	.4	.4	.4	.4	.4	.4	.4	.4	.4	.4
Perform Minor Tune-up.										
4-cylinder	—	—	—	—	—	1.6	1.6	1.8	1.8	2.0
6-cylinder, in-line	1.6	1.6	1.6	1.6	1.8	1.8	1.8	2.0	2.0	2.2
V-6 engine	—	—	—	—	—	—	—	—	2.2	2.4
V-8, small block (221-351 CID)	1.8	1.8	1.8	2.0	2.0	2.0	2.0	2.2	2.4	2.6
V-8, large block (383-462 CID)	2.5	2.5	2.5	2.5	2.5	2.5	2.5	2.7	2.9	3.0
Note: See minor tune-up section for work included and additions.										
Perform Major Tune-up.										
4-cylinder	—	—	—	—	—	4.8	4.8	4.8	5.0	5.0
6-cylinder, in-line	5.0	5.0	5.0	5.0	5.3	5.3	5.3	5.3	5.5	5.5
V-6 engine	—	—	—	—	—	—	—	—	6.2	6.2
V-8, small block (221-351 CID)	6.0	6.0	6.0	6.0	6.3	6.5	6.5	6.8	6.8	7.0
V-8, large block (383-462 CID)	6.6	6.6	6.6	6.8	6.8	7.0	7.0	7.4	7.4	7.5
Note: See major tune-up section for work included and additions.										

(THIS SCHEDULE CONTINUED ON NEXT PAGE.)

150 FORD/LINCOLN/MERCURY

SERVICE STATION MAINTENANCE Continued

MODEL	1966	1967	1968	1969	1970	1971	1972	1973	1974	1975
Service Fuel System.										
Complete carburetor adjustments,										
Single barrel	.4	.4	.4	.4	.4	.4	.4	.4	.4	.4
Two or four barrel	.6	.6	.6	.6	.6	.6	.6	.6	.6	.6
Replace fuel filter	.3	.3	.3	.3	.3	.3	.3	.3	.3	.3
Test & replace fuel pump,										
4-cylinder OHC	—	—	—	—	—	.9	.9	.9	.9	.9
4-cyl. OHV or 6-cyl. in-line	.5	.5	.5	.5	.5	.5	.5	.5	.5	.5
V-6 engine	—	—	—	—	—	—	—	—	.7	.7
V-8 engine	.7	.7	.7	.7	.7	.7	.8	.8	.8	.8
With air conditioning, **ADD:**	.2	.2	.2	.2	.2	.2	.2	.2	.2	.2
Replace flexible fuel line	.3	.3	.3	.3	.3	.3	.3	.3	.3	.3
Service Driveshaft.										
R&R driveshaft & overhaul both U-joints and check driveshaft alignment,										
Continental	2.1	2.1	2.1	2.1	2.2	2.2	2.2	2.2	2.2	2.2
All others	1.6	1.6	1.6	1.6	1.6	1.6	1.6	1.6	1.6	1.6
Service Hydraulic Brake System.										
Adjust drum brakes	.5	.5	.5	.5	.5	.5	.5	.5	.5	.5
Replace drum brake shoes, 4 wheels	3.5	3.5	3.5	3.5	3.5	3.5	3.5	3.5	3.5	3.5
Bleed hydraulic system, 4 wheels	.6	.6	.6	.6	.6	.6	.6	.6	.6	.6
Replace front disc brake pads	.6	.6	.6	.6	.6	.6	.6	.6	.6	.6
Replace rear disc brake pads	—	—	—	—	—	—	—	—	—	.8
Overhaul master cylinder	1.0	1.2	1.2	1.2	1.2	1.2	1.2	1.2	1.2	1.2
With power brakes, **ADD:**	.2	.2	.2	.2	.2	.2	.2	.2	.2	.2
O/h wheels cylinders, drum brakes, (4)	3.4	3.4	4.4	4.4	4.4	4.4	4.0	4.0	4.0	4.0
O/h fr. calipers, incl. turn rotors	5.3	5.3	5.3	5.3	4.6	4.6	4.6	4.6	4.6	4.6
O/h rear calipers, incl. turn rotors	—	—	—	—	—	—	—	—	—	4.8
Service Parking Brakes.										
Replace forward cable,										
Continental	1.0	1.0	1.0	1.0	1.0	1.0	1.0	1.3	1.3	1.3
All others	1.0	1.0	1.0	1.0	1.0	1.0	1.0	1.0	1.0	1.0
Replace rear cable, one side	1.0	1.0	1.0	1.0	1.0	1.0	1.0	1.0	1.0	1.0
Service Suspension System										
Replace front shock absorber, both sides	.9	.9	.9	.9	.9	.9	.9	.9	.9	.9
Replace rear shock absorber, both sides	.8	.8	.8	.8	.8	.8	.8	.8	.8	.8
Replace shackle and bushings; eye bolt and bushings	.7	.7	.7	.7	.7	.7	.7	.7	.7	.7
Replace rear leaf spring & shim to align pinion angle,										
Continental	1.9	1.9	1.9	1.9	—	—	—	—	—	—
All others	1.7	1.7	1.7	1.7	1.7	1.7	1.7	1.7	1.7	1.7
Replace rear coil spring and make pinion angle adjustment	.8	.8	.8	.8	.8	.8	.8	.8	.8	.8
Service Front End & Steering System										
Adjust toe-in only	.4	.4	.4	.4	.4	.4	.4	.4	.4	.4
Replace tie-rods or tie-rod ends, (4),										
Pinto, Bobcat, Mustang II	—	—	—	—	—	1.7	1.7	1.7	1.7	1.7
All others	1.6	1.6	1.5	1.5	1.5	1.5	1.5	1.5	1.5	1.5
Repl. Pitman arm, incl. adjust toe-in	.8	.8	.8	.8	.8	.8	.8	.8	.8	.8
Repl. steering idler arm or bushing, including adjust toe-in	.8	.8	.8	.8	.8	.8	.8	.8	.8	.8
Repl. pwr. steer. pump drive belt	.3	.3	.3	.3	.3	.3	.3	.3	.3	.3
With air conditioning, **ADD:**	.2	.2	.2	.2	.2	.2	.2	.2	.2	.2
Check & replenish reservoir fluid	.2	.2	.2	.2	.2	.2	.2	.2	.2	.2

(THIS SCHEDULE CONTINUED ON NEXT PAGE.)

FORD/LINCOLN/MERCURY

SERVICE STATION MAINTENANCE Continued

MODEL	1966	1967	1968	1969	1970	1971	1972	1973	1974	1975
Service Front End & Steering System Continued										
Repl. pressure hose, incl. adjust dr. belt	.5	.5	.6	.6	.6	.6	.6	.6	.6	.6
Repl. return hose, incl. adjust dr. belt	.4	.4	.4	.4	.4	.4	.4	.4	.4	.4
Balance four wheels on car,										
Drum brakes	1.2	1.2	1.2	1.2	1.2	1.2	1.2	1.2	1.2	1.2
Disc brakes	1.5	1.5	1.5	1.5	1.5	1.5	1.5	1.5	1.5	1.5
Rotate five wheels	.6	.6	.6	.6	.6	.6	.6	.6	.6	.6
Service Charging System										
Test system and adjust regulator	.6	.6	.6	.6	.6	.6	.6	.6	.6	.6
R&R alternator incl. pulley,										
Continental, Mark IV	.9	.9	.9	.9	.9	.9	.9	.9	.9	.9
Pinto, Bobcat, Mustang II	—	—	—	—	—	.7	.7	.7	.7	.7
All others	.6	.6	.6	.6	.7	.7	.7	.7	.7	.7
Overhaul alternator after removal	2.3	2.3	1.5	1.5	1.5	1.5	1.5	1.5	1.5	1.5
Replace regulator	.3	.3	.3	.3	.4	.4	.4	.3	.3	.3
With air conditioning, **ADD:**	.1	.1	.1	.1	.1	.1	.1	.1	.1	.1
With Thermactor, **ADD:**	.2	.2	.2	.2	.2	.2	.2	.2	.2	.2
Service Cranking System.										
R&R starter,										
4-cylinder	—	—	—	—	—	.5	.5	.5	.5	.5
6-cylinder, in-line	.7	.7	.7	.7	.7	.8	.8	.8	.8	.8
V-6 engine	—	—	—	—	—	—	—	—	.9	.9
V-8, Continental, Mark IV, T-Bird	.8	.8	.8	.8	.9	.9	1.0	1.0	1.0	1.0
V-8, all others	.6	.6	.6	.6	.6	.6	.7	.7	.7	.7
Overhaul starter after removal, **ADD:**	1.7	1.7	1.7	1.7	1.7	1.7	1.7	1.7	1.7	1.7
Replace starter battery cable	.3	.3	.3	.3	.3	.3	.3	.3	.3	.3
Replace starter solenoid switch	.8	.8	.8	.8	.9	.9	1.1	1.1	1.1	1.1
Service Lighting System.										
Adjust two head lights	.4	.4	.4	.4	.4	.4	.4	.4	.4	.4
Adjust four head lights	.6	.6	.6	.6	.6	.6	.6	.6	.6	.6
Replace sealed beam unit, ea.	.3	.3	.3	.3	.3	.3	.3	.3	.3	.3
Replace foot dimmer switch	.3	.3	.3	.3	.3	.3	.3	.3	.3	.3
Replace headlamp cover vacuum actuator	—	—	.7	.7	.7	.5	.5	.6	.6	.6
Replace signal/hazard flasher	.3	.3	.3	.3	.3	.3	.3	.3	.3	.3
Replace turn signal/hazard switch,										
With standard column	.8	.8	.8	.8	.8	.8	.8	.8	.8	.8
With tilt wheel, Continental	1.6	1.6	1.6	1.6	1.6	1.0	1.0	1.0	1.0	1.0
With tilt wheel, all others	1.0	1.0	1.0	1.0	1.0	1.0	1.0	1.0	1.0	1.0
Replace back-up light switch	.4	.4	.4	.4	.4	.4	.4	.4	.4	.4
Replace stoplight switch	.4	.4	.4	.4	.4	.4	.4	.4	.4	.4

FORD/LINCOLN/MERCURY

TUNE-UP, MINOR

Includes:

Basic Job: Perform the following work.
1. Service air cleaner element.
2. Replace PCV valve.
3. Replace crankcase ventilation filter in air cleaner.
4. Clean battery terminals.
5. Check condition and tension of all drive belts.
6. Check all hoses and hose connections.
7. Check operation of heated air system (air cleaner), manifold heat valve, and thermostatic and electric automatic choke. Service where necessary.
8. Replace fuel filter.
9. Perform compression test.
10. Replace spark plugs.
11. Replace ignition points and condenser.
12. Check dwell or reluctor air gap and adjust ignition timing.
13. Adjust carburetor idle mixture and speed.
14. Make necessary ignition and carburetor adjustments to obtain satisfactory scope or HC/CO exhaust system analyzer readings.

Additions to Basic Job: Allowances for special equipment and carburetor.

MODEL	1966	1967	1968	1969	1970	1971	1972	1973	1974	1975
Basic Job:										
Perform minor tune-up,										
4-cylinder	—	—	—	—	—	1.6	1.6	1.8	1.8	2.0
6-cylinder, in-line	1.6	1.6	1.6	1.6	1.8	1.8	1.8	2.0	2.0	2.2
V-6 engine	—	—	—	—	—	—	—	—	2.2	2.4
V-8, small block (221-351 CID)	1.8	1.8	1.8	2.0	2.0	2.0	2.0	2.2	2.4	2.6
V-8, large block (383-462 CID)	2.5	2.5	2.5	2.5	2.5	2.5	2.5	2.7	2.9	3.0
Additions to Basic Job:										
V-8 small block with 4-bbl. carb., **ADD:**	.2	.2	.2	.2	.2	.2	.2	.2	.2	.2
V-8 with 8-bbl. carbs. (2x4), **ADD:**	.4	.4	—	—	—	—	—	—	—	—
With Thermactor, **ADD:**	.3	.3	.3	.3	.3	.3	.3	.3	.3	.3
With air conditioning, **ADD:**	.6	.6	.6	.6	.6	.6	.6	.6	.6	.6

Approximate parts cost:

Spark plugs, each	$1.50	Air cleaner element	$5.50
Points & condenser	5.00	Fuel filter	3.50
PCV valve	3.00		

TUNE-UP, MAJOR

Includes:

Basic Job: Perform the following work.
1. Service air cleaner element.
2. Replace crankcase ventilation filter in air cleaner.
3. Replace PCV valve.
4. Check drive belts and adjust for proper tension.
5. Check all hoses and hose connections.
6. Clean battery terminals.
7. Check operation of manifold heat valve and thermostatic automatic choke. Service where necessary.
8. Check operation of heated-air system.
9. Check exhaust and evaporative emission control systems for proper operation.
10. Replace fuel filter.
11. Perform compression check.
12. Replace spark plugs.
13. Replace ignition points and condenser.
14. Adjust dwell or reluctor air gap and ignition timing.
15. Check distributor cap and rotor.
16. Tighten cylinder head bolts.
17. Adjust valve lash (where applicable).
18. Overhaul carburetor.
19. Adjust carburetor idle mixture and speed.
20. Make necessary ignition and carburetor adjustments to obtain satisfactory scope or HC/CO exhaust system analyzer readings.

Additions to Basic Job: Allowances for special equipment and carburetor.

MODEL	1966	1967	1968	1969	1970	1971	1972	1973	1974	1975
Basic Job:										
Perform major tune-up,										
4-cylinder	—	—	—	—	—	4.8	4.8	4.8	5.0	5.0
6-cylinder, in-line	5.0	5.0	5.0	5.0	5.3	5.3	5.3	5.3	5.5	5.5
V-6 engine	—	—	—	—	—	—	—	—	6.2	6.2
V-8, small block (221-351 CID)	6.0	6.0	6.0	6.0	6.3	6.5	6.5	6.8	6.8	7.0
V-8, large block (383-462 CID)	6.6	6.6	6.6	6.8	6.8	7.0	7.0	7.4	7.4	7.5

(THIS SCHEDULE CONTINUED ON NEXT PAGE.)

FORD/LINCOLN/MERCURY

TUNE-UP, MAJOR Continued

MODEL	1966	1967	1968	1969	1970	1971	1972	1973	1974	1975
Additions to Basic Job:										
Replace hydraulic valve lifter, ea., ADD:	2.0	2.0	2.0	2.0	2.0	2.0	2.0	2.0	2.0	2.0
V-8 small block with 4-bbl. carb., ADD:	1.0	1.0	1.0	1.0	1.0	1.0	1.0	1.0	1.0	1.0
V-8 with 8-bbl. carbs. (2x4), ADD:	2.5	2.5	—	—	—	—	—	—	—	—
With Thermactor, ADD:	.3	.3	.3	.3	.3	.3	.3	.3	.3	.3
With air conditioning, ADD:	.6	.6	.6	.6	.6	.6	.6	.6	.6	.6

Approximate parts cost:

Spark plugs, each $1.50	Fuel filter $3.50
Points & condenser 5.00	Carburetor repair kit, ea. 6.00-10.00
PCV valve 3.00	Carburetor gasket kit 2.50
Air cleaner element 5.50	Hydraulic valve lifter, each 4.00
Valve rocker cover gasket(s) 3.00-6.00	

EMISSION CONTROL SYSTEMS, TESTS FOR SMOG STATION CERTIFICATION

Includes:

Basic Job: Test crankcase, exhaust and evaporative emission control systems. Check heated-air system. Check HC/CO level with exhaust analyzer. Sign certification certificate. (No adjustments or repairs included in basic job.)

Related Jobs: Service any defective emission control system. Perform minor or major tune-up as required.

Additions to Related Jobs: Service or replace defective part(s) in the system and allowances for special equipment and carburetor.

MODEL	1966	1967	1968	1969	1970	1971	1972	1973	1974	1975
Basic Job:										
Test all systems & sign certificate,										
4 or 6-cylinder	.8	.8	.8	.8	.8	.8	.8	.8	.8	1.3
V-8, small block (221-351 CID)	1.0	1.0	1.0	1.0	1.0	1.0	1.0	1.0	1.0	1.5
V-8, large block (383-462 CID)	1.2	1.2	1.2	1.2	1.2	1.2	1.2	1.2	1.2	1.7
Related Jobs:										
Service crankcase emission control sys.	.3	.3	.3	.3	.3	.3	.3	.3	.3	.3
Service crankcase emission control system	—	—	—	—	.4	.4	.4	.4	.4	.4
Service evaporative emission control system										
Service heated-air system	.3	.3	.3	.3	.3	.3	.3	.3	.3	.3
Service ECS or TRS system	—	—	—	—	—	.5	.5	.5	.5	.5
Service EGR system	—	—	—	—	—	—	.4	.4	.4	.4
Service spark delay system (SDS)	—	—	—	—	—	—	—	.4	.4	.4
Service Thermactor (AIR) system	—	—	—	—	—	—	.5	.5	.5	.5
Replace catalytic converter	—	—	—	—	—	—	—	—	—	1.0
Note: See separate section for replacement of components in each system.										
Perform minor tune-up,										
4-cylinder	—	—	—	—	—	1.6	1.6	1.8	1.8	2.0
6-cylinder, in-line	1.6	1.6	1.6	1.6	1.8	1.8	1.8	2.0	2.0	2.2
V-6 engine	—	—	—	—	—	—	—	—	2.2	2.4
V-8, small block (221-351 CID)	1.8	1.8	1.8	2.0	2.0	2.0	2.0	2.2	2.4	2.6
V-8, large block (383-462 CID)	2.5	2.5	2.5	2.5	2.5	2.5	2.5	2.7	2.9	3.0
Perform major tune-up,										
4-cylinder	—	—	—	—	—	4.8	4.8	4.8	5.0	5.0
6-cylinder, in-line	5.0	5.0	5.0	5.0	5.3	5.3	5.3	5.3	5.5	5.5
V-6 engine	—	—	—	—	—	—	—	—	6.2	6.2
V-8, small block (221-351 CID)	6.0	6.0	6.0	6.0	6.3	6.5	6.5	6.8	6.8	7.0
V-8, large block (383-462 CID)	6.6	6.6	6.6	6.8	6.8	7.0	7.0	7.4	7.4	7.5

(THIS SCHEDULE CONTINUED ON NEXT PAGE.)

154 FORD/LINCOLN/MERCURY

EMISSION CONTROL SYSTEMS, TESTS FOR SMOG STATION CERTIFICATION Continued

MODEL	1966	1967	1968	1969	1970	1971	1972	1973	1974	1975
Additions to Related Jobs:										
Minor Tune-up										
V-8, small block with 4-bbl. carb., **ADD:**	.2	.2	.2	.2	.2	.2	.2	.2	.2	.2
V-8, with 8 bbl. carbs., **ADD:**	.4	.4	—	—	—	—	—	—	—	—
Major Tune-up										
V-8, small block with 4-bbl. carb., **ADD:**	1.0	1.0	1.0	1.0	1.0	1.0	1.0	1.0	1.0	1.0
V-8, with 8-bbl. carbs., **ADD:**	2.5	2.5	—	—	—	—	—	—	—	—
With Thermactor, **ADD:**	.3	.3	.3	.3	.3	.3	.3	.3	.3	.3
With air conditioning, **ADD:**	.6	.6	.6	.6	.6	.6	.6	.6	.6	.6

Approximate parts cost:
See major or minor tune-up section for cost of tune-up parts.   Catalytic converter $125.00-185.00

EMISSION CONTROL SYSTEMS, COMPLETE TEST OR SERVICE

Includes:
Basic Job: Make all necessary tests and repairs. Sign certification certificate.
1. Replace PCV valve, check all vacuum passageways and hoses.
2. Replace crankcase ventilation filter in air cleaner.
3. Test evaporative emission system, gas tank filler cap, vent lines, and hoses for leakage.
4. Replace evaporation canister filter.
5. Clean EGR valve and test the control system.
6. Check ECS or TRS system.
7. Check spark delay system (SDS).
8. Check operation of manifold heat control valve; thermostatic and electric automatic choke. Free up where necessary.
9. Check and adjust tension of drive belts.
10. Check operation of heated-air system.
11. Check Thermactor air pump flow.
12. Check routing and condition of hoses.
13. Check operation of diverter or bypass valve.
14. Inspect air manifold and hoses.
15. Replace catalytic converter, when necessary.
16. Measure exhaust HC/CO levels with analyzer to determine if an engine tune-up is required.

Related Jobs: Minor or major tune-up as required.

MODEL	1966	1967	1968	1969	1970	1971	1972	1973	1974	1975
Basic Job:										
Perform emission control system tune-up,										
4 or 6-cylinder	2.8	2.8	2.8	2.8	3.3	3.3	3.3	3.3	3.3	4.1
V-8 engine, small or large block	3.3	3.3	3.3	3.3	3.8	3.8	3.8	3.8	3.8	4.6
Additions to Basic Job:										
With Thermactor, all models, **ADD:**	.5	.5	.5	.5	.5	.5	.5	.5	.5	.5
Related Jobs:										
Perform minor tune-up,										
4-cylinder	—	—	—	—	—	1.6	1.6	1.8	1.8	2.0
6-cylinder, in-line	1.6	1.6	1.6	1.6	1.8	1.8	1.8	2.0	2.0	2.2
V-6 engine	—	—	—	—	—	—	—	—	2.2	2.4
V-8, small block (221-351 CID)	1.8	1.8	1.8	2.0	2.0	2.0	2.0	2.2	2.4	2.6
V-8, large block (383-462 CID)	2.5	2.5	2.5	2.5	2.5	2.5	2.5	2.7	2.9	3.0
Perform major tune-up,										
4-cylinder	—	—	—	—	—	4.8	4.8	4.8	5.0	5.0
6-cylinder, in-line	5.0	5.0	5.0	5.0	5.3	5.3	5.3	5.3	5.5	5.5
V-6 engine	—	—	—	—	—	—	—	—	6.2	6.2
V-8, small block (221-351 CID)	6.0	6.0	6.0	6.0	6.3	6.5	6.5	6.8	6.8	7.0
V-8, large block (383-462 CID)	6.6	6.6	6.6	6.8	6.8	7.0	7.0	7.4	7.4	7.5

(THIS SCHEDULE CONTINUED ON NEXT PAGE.)

FORD/LINCOLN/MERCURY 155

EMISSION CONTROL SYSTEMS, COMPLETE TEST OR SERVICE Continued

MODEL	1966	1967	1968	1969	1970	1971	1972	1973	1974	1975
Additions to Related Jobs:										
V-8 small block with 4-bbl. carb., **ADD:**	1.0	1.0	1.0	1.0	1.0	1.0	1.0	1.0	1.0	1.0
With air conditioning, **ADD:**	.6	.6	.6	.6	.6	.6	.6	.6	.6	.6
V-8 with 8-bbl. carbs. (2x4) minor, **ADD:**	.4	.4	—	—	—	—	—	—	—	—
V-8 with 8-bbl. carbs. (2x4) major, **ADD:**	2.5	2.5	—	—	—	—	—	—	—	—

Approximate parts cost:

PCV valve	$3.00	Drive belt	$ 3.00
Hose, per ft.	0.75	Catalytic converter	125.00-185.00
Canister filter	1.00	Diverter valve	12.00
See major or minor tune-up section for cost of tune-up parts.		Thermactor (AIR) pump	80.00

POSITIVE CRANKCASE VENTILATION (PCV) SYSTEM, TEST AND SERVICE

Includes:
  Basic Job: Test PCV valve, check all vacuum passageways, and inspect hoses. Clean or replace air filter.
  Additions to Basic Job: Replace defective parts. (Do not attempt to clean PCV valve, replace if valve is not free.)

MODEL	1966	1967	1968	1969	1970	1971	1972	1973	1974	1975
Basic Job:										
Test PCV system, all models	.3	.3	.3	.3	.3	.3	.3	.3	.3	.3
Additions to Basic Job:										
Replace PCV valve, **ADD:**	.3	.3	.3	.3	.3	.3	.3	.3	.3	.3
Replace all hoses, **ADD:**	.6	.6	.6	.6	.6	.6	.6	.6	.6	.6

Approximate parts cost:

PCV valve	$3.00	Hose, per ft.	$0.75

TRANSMISSION REGULATED SPARK (TRS), OR ELECTRONIC SPARK CONTROL (ESC) SYSTEM, TEST AND SERVICE

Includes:
  Basic Job: Check spark advance in gear using tachometer and timing light, test TRS or ESC solenoid and transmission or speed-control switch. Check electronic amplifier.
  Additions to Basic Job: Replace defective parts.

MODEL	1966	1967	1968	1969	1970	1971	1972	1973	1974	1975
Basic Job:										
Test TRS or ESC system	—	—	—	—	—	—	.5	.5	.5	—
Additions to Basic Job:										
Replace TRS or ESC solenoid vacuum valve, **ADD:**	—	—	—	—	—	—	.3	.3	.3	—
Replace TRS trans. position switch,										
Manual transmission, **ADD:**	—	—	—	—	—	—	.4	.4	.4	—
Automatic transmission, **ADD:**	—	—	—	—	—	—	.3	.3	.3	—
Replace TRS or ESC temperature switch, **ADD:**	—	—	—	—	—	—	.3	.3	.3	—
Replace idle stop solenoid, **ADD:**	—	—	—	—	—	—	.2	.2	.2	—
Replace ESC amplifier, **ADD:**	—	—	—	—	—	—	.6	.6	.6	—
Replace ESC speed-control switch, **ADD:**	—	—	—	—	—	—	.3	.3	.3	—

Approximate parts cost:

Solenoid vacuum valve	$12.00	TRS temperature switch	$ 6.00
Transmission position switch	6.00	Idle stop solenoid	11.00
ESC amplifier	80.00	ESC speed-control switch	17.00

FORD/LINCOLN/MERCURY

HEATED-AIR SYSTEM, TEST AND SERVICE

Includes:
  Basic Job: Check cold/heated-air door, temperature sensor, and vacuum motor or capsule-type thermostatic valve.
  Additions to Basic Job: Replace defective parts.

MODEL	1966	1967	1968	1969	1970	1971	1972	1973	1974	1975
Basic Job:										
Test heated-air system	—	—	—	.3	.3	.3	.3	.3	.3	.3
Additions to Basic Job:										
Replace vacuum motor, ADD:	—	—	—	—	—	.4	.4	.4	.4	.4
Replace temperature sensor, ADD:	—	—	—	—	—	.5	.5	.5	.5	.5
Replace thermostatic valve, ADD:	—	—	—	.6	.6	.6	.6	.6	.6	.6

Approximate parts cost:
Vacuum motor assembly .... $5.00   Temperature sensor $4.50
Thermostatic valve 3.00

EVAPORATIVE EMISSION CONTROL SYSTEM, TEST AND SERVICE

Includes:
  Basic Job: Test gas tank filler cap, vent lines, and hoses.
  Additions to Basic Job: Replace defective part.

MODEL	1966	1967	1968	1969	1970	1971	1972	1973	1974	1975
Basic Job:										
Test evap. emission control system	—	—	—	—	.4	.4	.4	.4	.4	.4
Additions to Basic Job:										
Replace float-type vapor separator, ADD:	—	—	—	—	—	.6	.6	.6	.6	.6
Replace fuel vapor canister, ADD:	—	—	—	—	.5	.5	.5	.5	.5	.5
Replace hose, each, ADD:	—	—	—	—	.2	.2	.2	.2	.2	.2

Approximate parts cost:
Fuel vapor canister .... $25.00   Vapor separator $1.75
Hose, per ft. 0.75

EXHAUST-GAS RECIRCULATION (EGR), TEST AND SERVICE

Includes:
  Basic Job: Test EGR valve, control system, and engine idling condition.
  Additions to Basic Job: Service or replace defective parts. Test & repair thermostatic control system.

MODEL	1966	1967	1968	1969	1970	1971	1972	1973	1974	1975
Basic Job:										
Test EGR system, all models	—	—	—	—	—	—	—	.4	.4	.4
Additions to Basic Job:										
Service EGR valve, ADD:	—	—	—	—	—	—	—	.7	.7	.7
Replace EGR valve, ADD:	—	—	—	—	—	—	—	.4	.4	.4
Test & repair thermo. control sys., ADD:	—	—	—	—	—	—	—	.6	.6	.6

Approximate parts cost:
EGR valve .... $10.00   Thermostatic (PVS) valve $6.00

FORD/LINCOLN/MERCURY

SPARK DELAY SYSTEM (SDS), TEST AND SERVICE

Includes:
  Basic Job: Check all hoses and hose connections; check operation of delay control valve using vacuum gauge.
  Related Jobs: Replace defective part(s).

MODEL	1966	1967	1968	1969	1970	1971	1972	1973	1974	1975
Basic Job:										
Check SDS valve, hoses & connections	—	—	—	—	—	—	—	.4	.4	.4
Related Jobs:										
Replace vacuum amplifier	—	—	—	—	—	—	—	.5	.5	.5
Replace all hoses	—	—	—	—	—	—	—	.6	.6	.6
Replace SDS valve	—	—	—	—	—	—	—	.3	.3	.3

Approximate parts cost:
Hose, per ft. .... $ 1.45   SDS valve $4.50
Amplifier 12.00

THERMACTOR (AIR) SYSTEM, TEST AND SERVICE

Includes:
  Basic Job: Test air pump flow; check routing and condition of hoses; determine operation of bypass valve, solenoid-controlled bypass valve (1975); verify check valve operation; inspect air manifold and hoses; check and adjust drive belt tension.
  Additions to Basic Job: Replace defective part. Replace drive belt includes adjust tension. Replacement of hose(s) includes soapy water test.

MODEL	1966	1967	1968	1969	1970	1971	1972	1973	1974	1975
Basic Job:										
Test AIR system, all models	.5	.5	.5	.5	.5	.5	.5	.5	.5	.8
Additions to Basic Job:										
Replace and adjust drive belt, ADD:	.5	.5	.5	.5	.5	.5	.5	.5	.5	.5
Replace AIR pump	.4	.4	.4	.4	.4	.4	.4	.4	.4	.4
Replace bypass valve, ADD:	.4	.4	.4	.4	.4	.4	.4	.4	.4	.4
Replace hose, incl. soapy water test,										
Continental, ADD:	.5	.5	.5	.5	.5	.5	.5	.5	.5	.5
All others, ADD:	.4	.4	.4	.4	.4	.4	.4	.4	.4	.4

Approximate parts cost:
Drive belt .... $ 3.00   Bypass valve $13.50
Thermactor (AIR) pump .... 80.00   Hose, per ft. 0.75

CRANKING SYSTEM, TEST AND SERVICE

Includes:
  Basic Job: Test battery and cranking system. Clean battery cable terminals.
  Related Jobs: Replace defective part including test when necessary.

MODEL	1966	1967	1968	1969	1970	1971	1972	1973	1974	1975
Basic Job:										
Test cranking system	.5	.5	.5	.5	.5	.5	.5	.5	.5	.5

(THIS SCHEDULE CONTINUED ON NEXT PAGE.)

FORD/LINCOLN/MERCURY

CRANKING SYSTEM, TEST AND SERVICE Continued

MODEL	1966	1967	1968	1969	1970	1971	1972	1973	1974	1975
Related Jobs:										
R&R starter,										
4-cylinder	—	—	—	—	—	.5	.5	.5	.5	.5
6-cylinder, in-line	.7	.7	.7	.7	.7	.8	.8	.8	.8	.8
V-6 engine	—	—	—	—	—	—	—	—	.9	.9
V-8, Continental, Mark IV, T-Bird	.8	.8	.8	.8	.9	.9	1.0	1.0	1.0	1.0
V-8, all others	.6	.6	.6	.6	.6	.6	.7	.7	.7	.7
R&R starter relay switch, **ADD:**	.3	.3	.3	.3	.3	.3	.3	.3	.3	.3
Replace starter solenoid switch, **ADD:**	.2	.2	.2	.2	.2	.2	.2	.2	.2	.2
Overhaul starter after removal, **ADD:**	1.7	1.7	1.7	1.7	1.7	1.7	1.7	1.7	1.7	1.7
Replace starter-battery cable	.3	.3	.3	.3	.3	.3	.3	.3	.3	.3
Replace starter/neutral switch & adjust,										
With column shift	.4	.4	.4	.4	.4	.4	.4	.4	.4	.4
With floor shift	.7	.7	.7	.7	.7	.7	.7	.7	.7	.7
Mustang, Cougar with FMX	1.0	1.0	1.0	1.0	1.0	1.0	1.0	1.0	—	—

Approximate parts cost:

Starter, new	$70.00
Starter, rebuilt	30.00
Starter-battery cable	3.00-12.00
Starter solenoid switch	$4.00-12.00
Starter neutral switch	7.00

CHARGING SYSTEM, TEST AND SERVICE

Includes:
    Basic Job: Test battery voltage and gravity, clean battery cable terminals, test alternator output, test and adjust regulator.
    Related Jobs: Replace or overhaul defective part(s).

MODEL	1966	1967	1968	1969	1970	1971	1972	1973	1974	1975
Basic Job:										
Test system and adjust regulator	.6	.6	.6	.6	.6	.6	.6	.6	.6	.6
Related Jobs:										
R&R alternator incl. pulley,										
Continental, Mark IV	.9	.9	.9	.9	.9	.9	.9	.9	.9	.9
Pinto, Mustang II, Bobcat	—	—	—	—	—	.7	.7	.7	.7	.7
All others	.6	.6	.6	.6	.7	.7	.7	.7	.7	.7
Overhaul alternator after removal	1.5	1.5	1.5	1.5	1.5	1.5	1.5	1.5	1.5	1.5
Replace regulator	.3	.3	.3	.3	.4	.4	.4	.4	.4	.4
With air conditioning, **ADD:**	.1	.1	.1	.1	.1	.1	.1	.1	.1	.1
With Thermactor, **ADD:**	.2	.2	.2	.2	.2	.2	.2	.2	.2	.2

Approximate parts cost:

Alternator, new	$75.00-95.00
Alternator, rebuilt	35.00
Regulator	$18.00

FORD/LINCOLN/MERCURY

IGNITION SYSTEM, SERVICE

Includes:
Basic Jobs: 1. Adjust and install new spark plugs.
2. Replace points and condenser, adjust dwell or check reluctor air gap, and ignition timing.
3. R&R distributor, overhaul and test centrifugal and vacuum advances, set dwell or adjust reluctor air gap and ignition timing.

Related Jobs: Replace additional defective part(s) as required.
Additions: Allowances for special equipment installed or replacement of associated defective part(s).

MODEL	1966	1967	1968	1969	1970	1971	1972	1973	1974	1975
Basic Job #1										
Adjust & install new spark plugs,										
4-cylinder	—	—	—	—	—	.4	.4	.4	.4	.4
6-cylinder	.6	.6	.6	.6	.6	.6	.6	.6	.6	.6
V-8 engine	.8	.8	.8	.8	.8	.8	.8	.8	.8	.8
With air conditioning, **ADD:**	.3	.3	.3	.3	.3	.3	.3	.3	.3	.3
With Thermactor, **ADD:**	.3	.3	.3	.3	.3	.3	.3	.3	.3	.3
V-8, 390, 428 CID with Thermactor, **ADD:**	1.0	1.0	1.0	1.0	1.0	—	—	—	—	—
Basic Job #2										
Replace points and condenser & adjust ignition timing,										
4-cylinder	—	—	—	—	—	.6	.6	.6	.6	—
6-cylinder, in-line	.7	.7	.7	.7	.7	.7	.7	.7	—	—
V-6 engine	—	—	—	—	—	—	—	—	.7	—
V-8 engine	.7	.7	.7	.7	.7	.7	.7	.7	—	—
Replace distributor cap,										
4 or 6-cylinder, **ADD:**	.3	.3	.3	.3	.3	.3	.3	.3	.3	.4
V-8 engine, **ADD:**	.4	.4	.4	.4	.4	.4	.4	.4	.4	.5
Basic Job #3										
R&R and overhaul distributor & adjust ignition timing,										
4-cylinder	—	—	—	—	—	1.8	1.8	1.8	1.8	1.4
6-cylinder, in-line	1.9	1.9	1.9	1.9	1.9	1.9	1.9	1.9	1.9	1.4
V-6 engine	—	—	—	—	—	—	—	—	2.1	1.6
V-8 engine	2.3	2.3	2.3	2.3	2.3	2.3	2.3	2.3	2.3	1.8
Replace vacuum advance unit, **ADD:**	.2	.2	.2	.2	.2	.2	.2	.2	.2	.2
Related Jobs:										
Replace ignition coil	.4	.4	.4	.4	.4	.4	.4	.4	.4	.4
Replace spark plug wires,										
4-cylinder	—	—	—	—	—	.4	.4	.4	.4	.4
6-cylinder, in-line	.5	.5	.6	.6	.6	.6	.6	.6	.6	.6
V-6 engine	—	—	—	—	—	—	—	—	.7	.7
V-8 engine	.7	.7	.8	.8	.8	.8	.8	.8	.8	.8
With air conditioning, **ADD:**	.3	.3	.3	.3	.3	.3	.3	.3	.3	.3
Replace ignition switch,										
With standard column	.6	.6	.6	.6	1.1	1.1	1.1	1.1	1.1	1.1
With tilt or telescopic column	.8	.8	.8	.8	.8	.8	.8	.8	.8	.8

Approximate parts cost:

Spark plugs, each ..... $ 1.50	Ignition coil $15.00
Point set 4.00	Spark plug wires, 4-cylinder 5.00
Condenser 1.50	6-cylinder 8.00
Distributor cap 4.50	V-8 engine 12.00-27.00
Distributor parts 10.00	Ignition switch 9.00
Vacuum control unit 10.00	Ignition modulator assembly 86.00

160 FORD/LINCOLN/MERCURY

FUEL SYSTEM, ADJUST AND SERVICE

Includes:
Basic Job: Adjust idle speed, fast-idle speed and idle mixture for performance and to obtain satisfactory exhaust system analyzer readings.
Related Jobs: R&R carburetor, overhaul carburetor. R&R associated fuel components. Adjust carburetor as in basic job.

MODEL	1966	1967	1968	1969	1970	1971	1972	1973	1974	1975
Basic Job:										
Adjust carburetor idle mixture & speed,										
Single barrel	.4	.4	.4	.4	.4	.4	.4	.4	.4	.4
Two- or four-barrel	.6	.6	.6	.6	.6	.6	.6	.6	.6	.6
Related Jobs:										
Replace carb, incl. compl. adjustments,										
Single or 2-barrel	.6	.6	.5	.5	.7	.7	.7	.7	.7	.7
Four-barrel	1.0	1.0	1.0	1.0	1.0	1.0	1.0	1.0	1.0	1.0
O/H carb., incl. R&R and compl. adjust.,										
Single or two-barrel, ea.	2.6	2.6	2.6	2.5	2.7	2.2	2.4	2.4	2.4	2.4
Four-barrel	4.0	4.0	4.0	4.0	3.2	3.2	3.2	3.2	3.4	3.4
Test & replace fuel pump,										
4-cylinder OHC	—	—	—	—	—	.9	.9	.9	.9	.9
4-cyl. or 6-cyl. in-line	.5	.5	.5	.5	.5	.5	.5	.5	.5	.5
V-6 engine	—	—	—	—	—	—	—	—	.7	.7
V-8 engine	.7	.7	.7	.7	.7	.7	.8	.8	.8	.8
With air conditioning, **ADD:**	.2	.2	.2	.2	.2	.2	.2	.2	.2	.2
Replace fuel filter	.3	.3	.3	.3	.3	.3	.3	.3	.3	.3
Replace fuel tank sending unit,										
Pinto, Bobcat, Mustang II	.5	.5	.5	.5	.5	.5	.5	.5	.5	.5
All others	.8	.8	.8	.8	.8	.8	.8	.8	.8	.8
Replace fuel gauge, instrument panel,										
Merc., Montego, Mustang, Cougar, Falcon	1.5	1.5	1.5	1.5	1.5	1.1	1.1	.8	.8	.8
Pinto, Bobcat, Mustang II	—	—	—	—	—	.5	.5	.5	.5	.5
All others	1.0	1.0	1.0	1.0	1.0	1.0	1.0	1.0	1.0	1.0
Replace fuel tank	.9	.9	.9	.9	1.1	1.1	1.1	1.1	1.1	1.1
Clean fuel tank, **ADD:**	.6	.6	.6	.6	.6	.6	.6	.6	.6	.6
Replace flexible fuel line	.3	.3	.3	.3	.3	.3	.3	.3	.3	.3
Repl. intake manifold gasket, includes adjust carb. & ignition timing,										
4-cylinder	—	—	—	—	—	1.2	1.2	1.2	1.2	1.2
6-cylinder, in-line	1.5	1.5	1.5	1.5	1.5	1.5	1.5	—	—	—
V-6 engine	—	—	—	—	—	—	—	—	2.7	2.7
V-8 small block (221-351 CID)	2.0	2.0	2.0	2.0	2.0	2.0	2.0	2.0	2.0	2.0
V-8 large block (383-462 CID)	3.1	3.1	3.1	3.1	2.9	2.9	2.9	2.9	2.9	2.9
With Thermactor, **ADD:**	.3	.3	.3	.3	.3	.3	.3	.3	.3	.3
V-8 small block with 4-bbl. carb., **ADD:**	.2	.2	.2	.2	.2	.2	.2	.2	.2	.2
With air conditioning, **ADD:**	.6	.6	.6	.6	.6	.6	.6	.6	.6	.6

Approximate parts cost:
Carburetor, new, single bbl.	$40.00
Two bbl.	60.00
Four bbl.	80.00-120.00
Carburetor, rebuilt, single bbl.	15.00
Two bbl.	22.00
Four bbl.	40.00
Carburetor repair kit	$10.00-20.00
Fuel pump	15.00-20.00
Fuel tank sending unit	13.00-27.00
Fuel gauge, dashboard	7.00-15.00
Fuel tank	50.00-65.00
Gasket, manifold	4.00

FORD/LINCOLN/MERCURY

ENGINE OVERHAUL, IN-CAR

Includes:

Basic Job: R&R piston-and-rod assembly, remove ring ridge, deglaze cylinders walls, fit piston pins, align connecting rods, install new piston rings and rod bearings, install new main bearing inserts and oil seals, overhaul oil pump, clean carbon, grind valves, and perform major tune-up.

Additions to Basic Job: Associated work that is required during basic job and allowances for special equipment installed.

MODEL	1966	1967	1968	1969	1970	1971	1972	1973	1974	1975
Basic Job:										
Overhaul engine,										
4-cylinder OHC (2300 CID)*	—	—	—	—	—	17.0	17.0	17.0	17.2	17.2
4-cylinder OHV	—	—	—	—	—	15.5	15.5	15.5	—	—
6-cylinder, in-line*	21.5	21.5	21.5	21.5	21.8	21.8	21.0	21.2	21.2	21.4
V-6 engine*	—	—	—	—	—	—	—	—	23.6	23.6
V-8, small block (221-351 CID)	26.4	26.4	26.4	26.6	26.6	26.6	26.3	26.5	26.5	26.9
V-8, large block (383-462 CID)	28.9	28.9	28.9	29.1	29.1	29.1	28.7	29.0	29.0	29.4

*4-cyl. OHC 200 CID, 6-cyl. 2400 CID, and V-6 engines, complete overhaul not possible in car due to inability to R&R main bearings.

	1966	1967	1968	1969	1970	1971	1972	1973	1974	1975
Additions to Basic Job:										
Rebore cylinders,										
4-cylinder, **ADD:**	—	—	—	—	—	3.0	3.0	3.0	3.0	3.0
6-cylinder, **ADD:**	4.0	4.0	4.0	4.0	4.0	4.0	4.0	4.0	4.0	4.0
V-8 engine, **ADD:**	5.0	5.0	5.0	5.0	5.0	5.0	5.0	5.0	5.0	5.0
Expand pistons,										
4-cylinder, **ADD:**	—	—	—	—	—	1.2	1.2	1.2	1.2	1.2
6-cylinder, **ADD:**	1.8	1.8	1.8	1.8	1.8	1.8	1.8	1.8	1.8	1.8
V-8 engine, **ADD:**	2.4	2.4	2.4	2.4	2.4	2.4	2.4	2.4	2.4	2.4
Regroove top piston ring groove,										
4-cylinder, **ADD:**	—	—	—	—	—	1.2	1.2	1.2	1.2	1.2
6-cylinder, **ADD:**	1.8	1.8	1.8	1.8	1.8	1.8	1.8	1.8	1.8	1.8
V-8 engine, **ADD:**	2.4	2.4	2.4	2.4	2.4	2.4	2.4	2.4	2.4	2.4
Replace hydraulic valve lifters, **ADD:**	1.0	1.0	1.0	1.0	1.0	1.0	1.0	1.0	1.0	1.0
Replace rocker arm stud, each, **ADD:**	.3	.3	.3	.3	.3	.3	.3	.3	.3	.3
Overhaul rocker arm mechanism,										
4-cylinder OHV, **ADD:**	—	—	—	—	—	.6	.6	.6	—	—
6-cylinder, **ADD:**	1.0	1.0	1.0	1.0	1.0	1.0	1.0	1.0	1.0	1.0
V-8 engine, **ADD:**	1.9	1.9	1.9	1.9	1.9	1.9	—	—	—	—
Ream valve guides oversize,										
4-cylinder, **ADD:**	—	—	—	—	—	.5	.5	.5	.5	.5
6-cylinder, **ADD:**	.7	.7	.7	.7	.7	.7	.7	.7	.7	.7
V-8 engine, **ADD:**	.9	.9	.9	.9	.9	.9	.9	.9	.9	.9
With Thermactor, **ADD:**	.7	.7	.7	.7	.7	.7	.7	.7	.7	.7
V-8 small block with 4-bbl. carb., **ADD:**	.2	.2	.2	.2	.2	.2	.2	.2	.2	.2
With air conditioning, **ADD:**	.6	.6	.6	.6	.6	.6	.6	.6	.6	.6

Approximate parts cost:

Hydraulic valve lifters, each	$ 4.00
Valve spring, each	2.00
Complete gasket set, 4-cylinder	24.00
6-cylinder	26.00
8-cylinder	30.00
Rod bearing inserts, 4-cylinder	8.00
6-cylinder	12.00
8-cylinder	16.00
Main bearing inserts, 4-cylinder	16.00
6-cylinder, in-line	40.00
V-6 engine	17.00
V-8 engine	17.00
Carburetor repair kit	$10.00-20.00
Major tune-up parts	30.00-45.00
Piston rings, complete set, 4-cylinder	10.00-20.00
6-cylinder	45.00
8-cylinder	60.00
Piston pins, set, 4-cylinder	8.00
6-cylinder	12.00
8-cylinder	16.00
Piston assemblies, set, 4-cylinder	52.00
6-cylinder	60.00
8-cylinder	130.00

FORD/LINCOLN/MERCURY

ENGINE OVERHAUL, OUT-OF-CAR

Includes:
   Basic Job: R&R engine, remove ring ridge, rebore or hone cylinder walls, regrind crankshaft and camshaft, replace camshaft bushings and line ream, replace timing chain, gears and oil seal, install main bearing inserts and seals, install piston pins, align connecting rods, install new piston rings and rod bearings, overhaul oil pump, clean carbon, grind valves, overhaul rocker arm mechanism, and perform major tune-up.
   Additions to Basic Job: Associated work that is required during basic job and allowances for special equipment installed.

MODEL	1966	1967	1968	1969	1970	1971	1972	1973	1974	1975
Basic Job:										
Overhaul engine,										
4-cylinder, OHC	—	—	—	—	—	27.6	27.6	27.8	—	—
4-cylinder, OHV	—	—	—	—	—	26.5	26.5	26.7	26.7	26.9
6-cylinder, in-line	34.5	34.5	34.5	34.5	34.8	34.8	34.8	35.0	35.3	35.5
V-6 engine	—	—	—	—	—	—	—	—	31.8	31.8
V-8, small block (221-353 CID)	37.6	37.6	37.6	37.6	37.9	37.9	37.9	38.2	38.2	38.4
V-8, large block (383-462 CID)	42.6	43.5	41.9	42.5	42.5	42.1	42.1	42.7	42.7	42.9
Additions to Basic Job:										
Regroove top piston ring groove,										
4-cylinder	—	—	—	—	—	1.2	1.2	1.2	1.2	1.2
6-cylinder, ADD:	1.8	1.8	1.8	1.8	1.8	1.8	1.8	1.8	1.8	1.8
V-8 engine, ADD:	2.4	2.4	2.4	2.4	2.4	2.4	2.4	2.4	2.4	2.4
Replace rocker arm stud, each, ADD:	.3	.3	.3	.3	.3	.3	.3	.3	.3	.3
Ream valve guides oversize,										
4-cylinder	—	—	—	—	—	.5	.5	.5	.5	.5
6-cylinder, ADD:	.7	.7	.7	.7	.7	.7	.7	.7	.7	.7
V-8 engine, ADD:	.9	.9	.9	.9	.9	.9	.9	.9	.9	.9
Replace all engine mounts, ADD:	.6	.6	.6	.6	.6	.6	.6	.6	.6	.6
Replace worn clutch parts, ADD:	.5	.5	.5	.5	.5	.5	.5	.5	.5	.5
With auto. transmission, ADD:	.6	.6	.6	.6	.6	.6	.6	.6	.6	.6
With Thermactor, ADD:	.7	.7	.7	.7	.7	.7	.7	.7	.7	.7
With air conditioning, ADD:	.6	.6	.6	.6	.6	.6	.6	.6	.6	.6

Approximate parts cost:

Main bearing oil seals	$ 5.00
Engine mounts, 4 or 6-cylinder, pr.	6.00
V-8 engine, pr.	7.50
Pressure plate	30.00-60.00
Clutch disc	21.00-40.00
Thrust bearing	5.00-15.00
Complete gasket set, 4-cylinder	24.00
6-cylinder	26.00
8-cylinder	30.00
Rod bearing inserts, 4-cylinder	8.00
6-cylinder	12.00
8-cylinder	16.00
Main bearing inserts, 4-cylinder	16.00
6-cylinder, in-line	40.00
V-6 engine	17.00
V-8 engine	17.00
Major tune-up parts	$30.00-45.00
Carburetor repair kit	10.00-20.00
Piston rings, complete set, 4-cylinder	10.00-20.00
6-cylinder	45.00
8-cylinder	60.00
Piston pins, set, 4-cylinder	8.00
6-cylinder	12.00
8-cylinder	16.00
Piston assemblies, set, 4-cylinder	52.00
6-cylinder	60.00
8-cylinder	130.00
Valve grind gasket set, 4-cylinder OHC	14.00
4-cylinder OHV	8.00
6-cylinder, in-line	9.00
V-6 engine	20.00
V-8 engine	20.00-30.00

FORD/LINCOLN/MERCURY 163

SHORT BLOCK, REPLACE

Includes:
Basic Job: R&R engine, clean and reface valves, scrape carbon, grind valve seats, replace valve seals, overhaul rocker arm mechanism, transfer all parts, and perform major tune-up.

Additions to Basic Job: Associated work that is required during basic job and allowances for special equipment and/or carburetor.

MODEL	1966	1967	1968	1969	1970	1971	1972	1973	1974	1975
Basic Job:										
Replace short block										
4-cylinder OHV	—	—	—	—	—	11.9	11.9	11.9	—	—
4-cylinder OHC	—	—	—	—	—	13.2	13.2	13.2	13.4	13.4
6-cylinder, in-line, 240 CID	16.9	16.9	16.9	16.9	17.2	17.2	—	—	—	—
6-cylinder, in-line, all others	15.5	15.5	15.5	15.5	15.8	15.8	15.8	15.8	16.0	16.0
V-6 engine	—	—	—	—	—	—	—	—	18.1	18.1
V-8, small block (221-353 CID)	16.7	16.7	16.7	16.7	17.0	17.2	17.2	17.2	17.2	17.4
V-8, large block (383-462 CID)	19.2	19.2	19.2	19.2	19.2	19.4	19.4	19.4	19.4	19.6
Additions to Basic Job:										
Ream valve guides oversize, **ADD:**										
4-cylinder	—	—	—	—	.5	.5	.5	.5	.5	.5
6-cylinder	.7	.7	.7	.7	.7	.7	.7	.7	.7	.7
V-8 engine	.9	.9	.9	.9	.9	.9	.9	.9	.9	.9
Replace rocker arm stud, each, **ADD:**	.3	.3	.3	.3	.3	.3	.3	.3	.3	.3
With auto. transmission, **ADD:**	.6	.6	.6	.6	.6	.6	.6	.6	.6	.6
With air cond., incl. partial chg. sys., **ADD:**	1.5	1.5	1.5	1.5	1.5	1.5	1.5	1.5	1.5	1.5
Replace all engine mounts, **ADD:**	.6	.6	.6	.6	.6	.6	.6	.6	.6	.6
Replace worn clutch parts, **ADD:**	.5	.5	.5	.5	.5	.5	.5	.5	.5	.5
With Thermactor, **ADD:**	.7	.7	.7	.7	.7	.7	.7	.7	.7	.7
V-8 small block with 4-bbl. carb., **ADD:**	.2	.2	.2	.2	.2	.2	.2	.2	.2	.2

Approximate parts cost:

Major tune-up parts	$30.00-45.00
Oil and air filters	9.00
Pressure plate	30.00-60.00
Clutch disc	21.00-40.00
Thrust bearing	5.00-15.00
Complete gasket set, 4-cylinder	24.00
6-cylinder	26.00
8-cylinder	30.00
Carburetor repair kit	$10.00-20.00
Short block, 4-cylinder	700.00-800.00
6-cylinder, in-line	550.00
V-6 engine	900.00
V-8, small block	600.00
V-8, large block	650.00-750.00
Engine mounts, 4 or 6-cylinder, pr.	6.00
V-8 engine, pr.	7.50

CYLINDER HEAD AND/OR GASKET, REPLACE

Includes:
Basic Jobs: 1. R&R intake manifold and cylinder head to install new gasket. Clean head and block surfaces and perform minor tune-up.
2. Install new cylinder head, including recondition valves and perform minor tune-up.

Additions to Basic Jobs: Recondition second head on V-type engines. Allowances for special equipment and/or carburetor.

MODEL	1966	1967	1968	1969	1970	1971	1972	1973	1974	1975
Basic Job #1										
Replace head gasket, (one head),										
4-cylinder OHC	—	—	—	—	—	4.2	4.2	4.4	4.4	4.6
4-cylinder OHV	—	—	—	—	—	3.5	3.5	3.7	—	—
6-cylinder, in-line	3.9	3.9	3.9	3.9	4.1	4.1	4.1	4.3	4.3	4.5
V-6, one side	—	—	—	—	—	—	—	—	5.6	5.8
V-8, small block (221-351 CID), one side	4.9	4.9	4.9	5.1	5.1	5.1	5.1	5.3	5.5	5.7
V-8, large block (383-462 CID), one side	7.0	7.0	7.0	7.0	7.0	7.0	7.0	7.2	7.4	7.5

(THIS SCHEDULE CONTINUED ON NEXT PAGE.)

FORD/LINCOLN/MERCURY

CYLINDER HEAD AND/OR GASKET, REPLACE Continued

MODEL	1966	1967	1968	1969	1970	1971	1972	1973	1974	1975
Basic Job #2										
Replace one cylinder head,										
4-cylinder OHC	—	—	—	—	—	7.9	7.9	8.1	8.1	8.3
4-cylinder OHV	—	—	—	—	—	6.0	6.0	6.2	—	—
6-cylinder, in-line	7.7	7.7	7.7	7.7	7.9	7.9	7.9	8.1	8.1	8.3
V-6, one side	—	—	—	—	—	—	—	—	7.2	7.4
V-8, small block (221-351 CID), one side	7.1	7.1	7.1	7.3	7.3	7.3	7.3	7.5	7.7	7.9
V-8, large block (383-462 CID), one side	9.4	9.4	9.4	9.4	9.4	9.4	9.4	9.6	9.8	9.9
Additions to Basic Jobs:										
Recondition second head, V-type engines,										
V-6, **ADD**:	—	—	—	—	—	—	—	—	1.8	1.8
V-8, small block, **ADD**:	2.0	2.0	2.0	2.0	2.0	2.2	2.2	2.2	2.2	2.2
V-8, large block, **ADD**:	2.5	2.5	2.5	2.5	2.5	2.7	2.7	2.7	2.7	2.7
V-8 small block with 4-bbl. carb., **ADD**:	.2	.2	.2	.2	.2	.2	.2	.2	.2	.2
With Thermactor, **ADD**:	.3	.3	.3	.3	.3	.3	.3	.3	.3	.3
With air conditioning, **ADD**:	.6	.6	.6	.6	.6	.6	.6	.6	.6	.6

Approximate parts cost:

Head gasket, each	$ 4.00	Valve grind gasket set, 4-cylinder OHC	$14.00
Cylinder head, 4-cylinder OHC	100.00	4-cylinder OHV	8.00
4-cylinder OHV	80.00	6-cylinder, in-line	9.00
6-cylinder, in-line	90.00	V-6 engine	20.00
V-6, ea.	135.00	V-8 engine	20.00-30.00
V-8, small clock, ea.	90.00	Minor tune-up parts	23.00-30.00
V-8, large block, ea.	90.00-160.00		

VALVE MECHANISM, SERVICE

Includes:

Adjustment and Tune-up: Adjust mechanical valve lash and perform minor tune-up.

Basic Job: Clean and reface valves, scrape carbon, grind valve seats, replace valve seals, adjust valves, or check collapsed hydraulic lifter clearance, and perform minor tune-up.

Additions to Basic Job: Major tune-up, associated work required during basic job, and allowances for special equipment and carburetor.

MODEL	1966	1967	1968	1969	1970	1971	1972	1973	1974	1975
Adjustment & Tune-up:										
4-cylinder OHV	—	—	—	—	—	2.2	2.2	2.4	—	—
4-cylinder OHC	—	—	—	—	—	2.7	2.7	2.9	2.9	2.9
V-6 engine	—	—	—	—	—	—	—	—	3.5	3.7
V-8, 302 CID	2.7	2.7	2.7	2.9	2.9	3.0	—	—	—	—
V-8, 427, 429 CID	3.6	3.6	3.6	3.6	3.6	3.6	3.6	—	—	—
Basic Job:										
Service valve mechanism,										
4-cylinder OHV	—	—	—	—	—	5.5	5.5	5.7	—	—
Major tune-up, **ADD**:	—	—	—	—	—	3.2	3.2	3.0	—	—
4-cylinder OHC	—	—	—	—	—	7.0	7.0	7.2	7.2	7.4
Major tune-up, **ADD**:	—	—	—	—	—	3.2	3.2	3.0	3.2	3.0
6-cylinder, in-line	6.8	6.8	6.8	6.8	7.0	7.0	7.0	6.9	6.9	7.1
Major tune-up, **ADD**:	3.4	3.4	3.4	3.4	3.5	3.5	3.5	3.3	3.5	3.3
V-6 engine	—	—	—	—	—	—	—	—	9.1	9.3
Major tune-up, **ADD**:	—	—	—	—	—	—	—	—	3.3	3.1
V-8, 351C Boss, 302 Boss	—	—	—	10.4	10.4	10.4	10.4	10.6	—	—
Major tune-up, **ADD**:	—	—	—	4.0	4.3	4.5	4.5	4.6	—	—

(THIS SCHEDULE CONTINUED ON NEXT PAGE.)

FORD/LINCOLN/MERCURY

VALVE MECHANISM, SERVICE Continued

MODEL	1966	1967	1968	1969	1970	1971	1972	1973	1974	1975
Basic Job Continued										
V-8, small block (221-351 CID)	9.8	9.8	9.8	10.0	10.0	10.0	10.0	10.2	10.4	10.6
Major tune-up, **ADD:**	4.2	4.2	4.2	4.0	4.3	4.5	4.5	4.6	4.4	4.4
V-8, 429, 460 CID T-Bird	12.6	12.6	12.6	12.4	12.2	12.2	12.1	12.3	12.5	12.6
Major tune-up, **ADD:**	4.1	4.1	4.1	4.3	4.3	4.5	4.5	4.7	4.5	4.5
V-8, (383-462 CID), Continental, Mark IV	13.0	13.0	13.1	12.7	12.5	12.8	12.4	12.6	12.8	12.9
Major tune-up, **ADD:**	4.1	4.1	4.1	4.3	4.3	4.5	4.5	4.7	4.5	4.5
V-8, large block (383-462 CID), all others	11.9	11.9	11.9	11.9	11.9	11.9	11.6	11.8	12.0	12.1
Major tune-up, **ADD:**	4.1	4.1	4.1	4.3	4.3	4.5	4.5	4.7	4.5	4.5
With Thermactor, all models, **ADD:**	.3	.3	.3	.3	.3	.3	.3	.3	.3	.3
With air conditioning, all models, **ADD:**	.5	.5	.5	.5	.5	.5	.5	.5	.5	.5
Additions to Basic Job:										
Ream valve guides oversize,										
4-cylinder, **ADD:**	—	—	—	—	—	.6	.6	.6	.6	.6
6-cylinder, **ADD:**	.7	.7	.7	.7	.7	.7	.7	.7	.7	.7
V-8 engine, **ADD:**	.9	.9	.9	.9	.9	.9	.9	.9	.9	.9
Replace rocker arm stud, ea., **ADD:**	.3	.3	.3	.3	.3	.3	.3	.3	.3	.3
Overhaul rocker arm mechanism,										
4-cylinder OHV, 1600CC, **ADD:**	—	—	—	—	—	.4	.4	.4	—	—
6-cylinder, in-line, **ADD:**	.5	.5	.5	.5	.5	.5	.5	.5	.5	.5
V-6 engine, **ADD:**	—	—	—	—	—	—	—	—	.8	.8
V-8, 390, 427, 428, 462 CID, **ADD:**	.9	.9	.9	.9	.9	.9	—	—	—	—
Replace hydraulic valve lifters, **ADD:**	1.0	1.0	1.0	1.0	1.0	1.0	1.0	1.0	1.0	1.0

Approximate parts cost:

Valve grind gasket set, 4-cylinder OHC	$14.00
4-cylinder OHV	8.00
6-cylinder, in-line	9.00
V-6 engine	20.00
V-8 engine	20.00-30.00
Minor tune-up parts	$24.00-30.00
Major tune-up parts	$30.00-45.00
Hydraulic valve lifters, each	4.00
Valve spring, each	2.00

OIL PUMP, SERVICE

Includes:
  Basic Job: 1. R&R oil pump (externally mounted), service pump, and install new oil filter element.
                  2. R&R oil pan, oil pump, clean oil pump pickup tube and screen, install new oil filter element.
  Additions to Basic Job: Allowances for associated work that is required during basic job.

MODEL	1966	1967	1968	1969	1970	1971	1972	1973	1974	1975
Basic Job #1										
R&R pump & service,										
4-cylinder OHV, 1600cc	—	—	—	—	—	1.1	1.1	1.1	—	—
Basic Job #2										
R&R oil pan, gasket, pump, & filter,										
4-cylinder OHC	—	—	—	—	—	2.6	2.6	2.6	2.6	2.6
6-cylinder, in-line, 170 CID	3.2	3.2	3.2	2.8	2.8	2.8	2.8	—	—	—
6-cylinder, in-line, 200, 250 CID	2.3	2.3	2.3	2.3	2.6	2.6	2.5	2.5	2.5	2.5
V-6 engine	—	—	—	—	—	—	—	—	2.9	2.9
V-8, Continental, Mark IV	3.2	3.2	3.2	3.3	2.9	2.9	2.9	2.9	2.9	2.9
V-8, all others	2.2	2.2	2.2	2.2	2.3	2.3	2.3	2.3	2.3	2.3
Additions to Basic Job:										
Overhaul oil pump, **ADD:**	.5	.5	.5	.5	.5	.5	.5	.5	.5	.5

(THIS SCHEDULE CONTINUED ON NEXT PAGE.)

FORD/LINCOLN/MERCURY

OIL PUMP SERVICE Continued

Approximate parts cost:
Oil pan gasket .... $ 4.00
Oil pan 25.00
Oil pump assembly, new 30.00
Oil filter element $4.50
Oil pump shaft and rotor kit 4.00

TIMING CHAIN MECHANISM, SERVICE

Includes:
Basic Job:
1. OHC engine: Replace camshaft drive belt, adjust tension, and perform minor tune-up.
2. V-6 engine: Replace timing gears, cover oil seal, and perform minor tune-up.
3. 4-cylinder OHV, 6-cylinder in-line, V-8 engines: Replace timing chain, cover oil seal, and perform minor tune-up.

Additions to Basic Job: Associated work required during basic job and allowances for special equipment installed.

MODEL	1966	1967	1968	1969	1970	1971	1972	1973	1974	1975
Basic Job #1										
Replace camshaft drive belt, adjust tension, and minor tune-up,										
4-cylinder OHC engine	—	—	—	—	—	2.6	2.6	2.8	2.8	3.0
Additions to Basic Job #1										
Replace camshaft sprocket, **ADD:**	—	—	—	—	—	.2	.2	.2	.2	.2
Replace camshaft oil seal, **ADD:**	—	—	—	—	—	.2	.2	.2	.2	.2
Replace crankshaft sprocket, **ADD:**	—	—	—	—	—	.3	.3	.3	.3	.3
With air conditioning, **ADD:**	—	—	—	—	—	.5	.5	.5	.5	.5
With Thermactor, **ADD:**	—	—	—	—	—	.2	.2	.2	.2	.2
Basic Job #2										
Replace camshaft timing gear, oil seal, and perform minor tune-up,										
V-6 engine	—	—	—	—	—	—	—	—	*9.7	*10.1
*Includes R&R engine and camshaft.										
Additions to Basic Job #2										
Replace crankshaft gear, **ADD:**	—	—	—	—	—	—	—	—	.2	.2
With air conditioning, **ADD:**	—	—	—	—	—	—	—	—	.2	.2
With power steering, **ADD:**	—	—	—	—	—	—	—	—	.2	.2
With Thermactor, **ADD:**	—	—	—	—	—	—	—	—	.3	.3
Basic Job #3										
Replace timing chain, oil seal, and minor tune-up,										
4-cylinder OHV	—	—	—	—	—	2.8	2.8	3.0	—	—
6-cylinder, in-line, 240, 250 CID	5.1	5.1	5.1	4.7	4.9	4.9	4.9	5.0	5.0	5.2
6-cylinder, in-line, all others	3.5	3.5	3.5	3.5	3.7	3.7	3.7	3.9	3.9	4.1
V-8, small block (221-351 CID)	4.1	4.1	4.1	4.3	4.3	4.3	4.5	4.7	4.9	5.1
V-8, large block (383-462 CID)	5.1	5.1	5.1	5.1	5.1	5.1	5.1	5.3	5.5	5.6
Additions to Basic Job #3										
Replace camshaft sprocket, **ADD:**	.2	.2	.2	.2	.2	.2	.2	.2	.2	.2
Replace crankshaft sprocket, **ADD:**	.2	.2	.2	.2	.2	.2	.2	.2	.2	.2
With air conditioning, **ADD:**	.5	.5	.5	.5	.5	.5	.5	.5	.5	.5
With power steering, **ADD:**	.3	.3	.3	.3	.3	.3	.3	.3	.3	.3
With Thermactor, **ADD:**	.2	.2	.2	.2	.2	.2	.2	.2	.2	.2

Approximate parts cost:
Timing cover gasket .... $ 1.00
Timing cover oil seal 2.00
Timing chain 14.00
Camshaft drive belt (OHC engine) 9.00
Minor tune-up parts 23.00-30.00
Camshaft gear $6.00-12.00
Crankshaft gear 6.00
Crankshaft sprocket (OHC engine) 9.00
Tension pulley assy. (OHC engine) 7.00

FORD/LINCOLN/MERCURY

BEARINGS, MAIN AND/OR RODS, REPLACE

Includes:

Basic Job 1. R&R oil pan, measure connecting rod bearing oil clearance with Plastigage, install new connecting rod bearing inserts, and oil filter element.

Additions to Basic Job #1. Measure main bearing oil clearance with Plastigage, replace all main bearing inserts and rear main bearing oil seals, repair or replace oil pump.

Basic Job: 2. Replace rear main bearing oil seal, includes R&R pan, R&R engine, or move transmission, as required.

MODEL	1966	1967	1968	1969	1970	1971	1972	1973	1974	1975
Basic Job #1										
R&R pan, measure rod clearance, install inserts & oil filter,										
4-cylinder OHC	—	—	—	—	—	3.6	3.6	3.6	3.6	3.6
4-cylinder OHV	—	—	—	—	—	3.3	3.3	3.3	—	—
6-cylinder, in-line	4.0	4.0	4.0	4.0	4.0	4.0	4.0	4.0	4.0	4.0
V-6 engine	—	—	—	—	—	—	—	—	4.5	4.5
V-8, small block (221-351 CID)	4.4	4.4	4.4	4.4	4.4	4.5	4.5	4.5	4.5	4.5
V-8, large block (383-462 CID)	5.4	5.4	5.4	5.4	5.1	5.1	5.1	5.1	5.1	5.1
Additions to Basic Job #1										
Use Plastigage — all main brgs.,										
4-cylinder, ADD:	—	—	—	—	—	.5	.5	.5	.5	.5
V-6 engine, ADD:	—	—	—	—	—	—	—	—	.4	.4
6-cylinder, in-line, ADD:	.7	.7	.7	.7	.7	.7	.7	.7	.7	.7
V-8 engine, ADD:	.5	.5	.5	.5	.5	.5	.5	.5	.5	.5
Replace main inserts & rear oil seals,										
4-cylinder OHC, std. trans., ADD:	—	—	—	—	—	*5.5	*5.5	*5.5	*5.5	*5.5
4-cylinder OHC, auto. trans., ADD:	—	—	—	—	—	*6.4	*6.4	*6.4	*6.4	*6.4
4-cylinder OHV, 1600CC (rear oil seal not included), ADD:	—	—	—	—	—	1.8	1.8	1.8	—	—
6-cylinder, in-line 240 CID, ADD:	*6.6	*6.6	*6.6	*6.6	*6.6	*6.6	*6.6	—	—	—
6-cylinder, in-line 200, 250 CID, ADD:	3.5	3.5	3.5	3.5	3.5	3.5	3.5	3.5	3.5	3.5
6-cylinder, in-line, 170 CID, ADD:	2.3	2.3	2.3	2.3	—	—	—	—	—	—
V-6 engine, ADD:	—	—	—	—	—	—	—	—	*6.3	*6.3
V-8 engine, ADD:	3.1	3.1	3.1	3.1	3.1	3.1	3.1	3.1	3.1	3.1
*Includes R&R engine.										
R&R oil pump, overhaul,										
4-cylinder OHC, ADD	—	—	—	—	—	.7	.7	.7	.7	.7
4-cylinder OHV, ADD:	—	—	—	—	—	1.3	1.3	1.3	—	—
All other engines, ADD:	.5	.5	.5	.5	.5	.5	.5	.5	.5	.5
Basic Job #2										
Replace rear main bearing oil seal,										
4-cyl. OHV, 1600CC (R&R engine)	—	—	—	—	—	4.5	4.5	4.5	—	—
4-cyl. OHC, 2000CC (move trans.), w/std. trans.	—	—	—	—	—	2.3	2.5	2.5	2.5	2.5
w/auto. trans.	—	—	—	—	—	3.3	3.5	3.5	3.5	3.5
4-cyl. OHC 2300CC (R&R pan)	—	—	—	—	—	—	—	—	3.5	3.5
6-cyl. in-line, 240 CID (move trans.)	2.3	2.3	2.3	2.3	2.3	2.3	2.3	—	—	—
6-cyl. in-line, all others (R&R pan)	2.9	2.9	2.9	2.9	2.9	2.9	2.9	2.9	2.9	2.9
V-6 engine (move trans.) w/std. trans.	—	—	—	—	—	—	—	—	2.5	2.5
w/auto. trans.	—	—	—	—	—	—	—	—	3.8	3.8
V-8, 221-351 CID, (R&R pan)	2.8	2.8	2.8	2.8	2.8	2.8	2.8	2.8	2.8	2.8
V-8, 427, 462 CID (R&R engine)	8.4	8.4	8.4	—	—	—	—	—	—	—
V-8, 383-460 exc. 427 & 462, (R&R pan)	3.8	3.8	3.8	3.8	3.8	3.8	3.8	3.8	3.8	3.8

(THIS SCHEDULE CONTINUED ON NEXT PAGE.)

168 FORD/LINCOLN/MERCURY

BEARINGS, MAIN- AND/OR RODS, REPLACE Continued

Approximate parts cost:

Oil pan gasket	$ 4.00
Rod bearing inserts, 4-cylinder	8.00
6-cylinder	12.00
8-cylinder	16.00
Main bearing inserts 4-cylinder	16.00
6-cylinder, in-line	40.00
V-6 engine	17.00
V-8 engine	17.00
Rear main brg. oil seal, set	$ 3.00
Oil filter element	4.50
Oil pump shaft & rotor kit	8.00
Oil pump, 4-cylinder	24.00
6-cylinder	30.00
V-6 engine	28.00
V-8 engine	32.00
Oil pump screen	2.50

COOLING SYSTEM, TEST AND SERVICE

Includes:

Basic Job: Drain and back-flush system, check for leaks and tighten all hose connections, pressure-test radiator cap and system.
Related Jobs: Replace defective part. Work performed independently of basic job.
Additions to Related Jobs: Allowances for special equipment installed.

MODEL	1966	1967	1968	1969	1970	1971	1972	1973	1974	1975
Basic Job:										
Drain, flush, fill, & pressure-test system	.9	.9	.9	.9	.9	.9	.9	.9	.9	.9
Related Jobs:										
Replace upper hose	.4	.4	.4	.4	.4	.4	.4	.4	.4	.4
Replace lower hose,										
V-8, large block (383-462 CID)	.7	.7	.7	.7	.7	.7	.7	.7	.7	.7
All other engines	.5	.5	.5	.5	.5	.5	.5	.5	.5	.5
Replace radiator bypass hose,										
V-8, 429 & 460 CID engines	1.5	1.5	1.5	1.5	1.5	1.5	1.8	1.8	1.8	1.8
V-8, 302 & 351 CID engines	.3	.3	.3	.3	.3	.3	.3	.3	.3	.3
V-8, all others	1.0	1.0	1.0	1.0	1.0	1.0	—	—	—	—
With air conditioning, **ADD:**	.2	.2	.2	.2	.2	.2	.2	.2	.2	.2
Replace thermostat, includes test,										
4-cylinder	—	—	—	—	—	.8	1.0	1.0	1.0	1.0
V-6 & 6-cylinder in-line	.8	.8	.8	.8	.8	.8	.8	.8	.8	.8
V-8, 302 CID engine	.9	.9	.9	.9	.9	.9	.9	.9	.9	.9
V-8, 460 CID engine	1.4	1.4	1.4	1.4	1.4	—	—	—	—	—
All others	.7	.7	.7	.7	.7	.7	.7	.7	.7	.7
With Thermactor, **ADD:**	.2	.2	.2	.2	.2	.2	.2	.2	.2	.2
6-cylinder in-line with power steering, **ADD:**	.1	.1	.1	.1	.1	.1	.1	.1	.1	.1
With air conditioning, **ADD:**	.2	.2	.2	.2	.2	.2	.2	.2	.2	.2
Replace water pump drive belt & adjust,										
4-cylinder OHC	—	—	—	—	—	1.0	1.0	1.0	1.0	1.0
All other engines	.4	.4	.4	.4	.4	.4	.4	.4	.4	.4
With Thermactor, **ADD:**	.1	.1	.1	.1	.1	.1	.1	.1	.1	.1
With power steering, **ADD:**	.1	.1	.1	.1	.1	.1	.1	.1	.1	.1
With air conditioning, **ADD:**	.2	.2	.2	.2	.2	.2	.2	.2	.2	.2
Replace water pump,										
4-cylinder OHC	—	—	—	—	—	1.0	1.0	1.0	1.0	1.0
6-cylinder, in-line	1.3	1.3	1.3	1.3	1.3	1.3	1.3	1.3	1.3	1.3
V-6 engine	—	—	—	—	—	—	—	—	1.6	1.6
With air conditioning, **ADD:**	—	—	—	—	—	—	—	—	.2	.2
With air cond. & pwr. steering, **ADD:**	.6	.6	.6	.6	.6	.6	.4	.4	.4	.4
V-8, 429 & 460 CID engines	1.9	1.9	1.9	1.9	1.9	1.9	2.1	2.1	2.1	2.1
With air cond. & pwr. steering, **ADD:**	.2	.2	.2	.2	.2	.2	.4	.4	.4	.4

(THIS SCHEDULE CONTINUED ON NEXT PAGE.)

FORD/LINCOLN/MERCURY

COOLING SYSTEM, TEST AND SERVICE Continued

MODEL	1966	1967	1968	1969	1970	1971	1972	1973	1974	1975
Related Jobs: Continued										
Replace water pump continued										
V-8, all others	1.3	1.3	1.3	1.3	1.3	1.3	1.3	1.3	1.4	1.4
With air cond. & pwr. steering, **ADD:**	.6	.6	.6	.6	.6	.6	.4	.4	.4	.4
All models with Thermactor, **ADD:**	.2	.2	.2	.2	.2	.2	—	—	.1	.1
Replace radiator,										
4-cylinder OHC	—	—	—	—	—	.7	.7	.7	.7	.7
6-cylinder, in-line	.8	.8	.8	.8	.8	.8	.8	.8	.8	.8
V-6 engine	—	—	—	—	—	—	—	—	.9	.9
V-8 engine	.9	.9	.9	.9	.9	.9	1.1	1.1	1.1	1.1
With air conditioning, **ADD:**	.3	.3	.2	.2	.2	.2	.2	.2	.2	.2
Replace water temp. sending unit, engine	.5	.5	.5	.5	.5	.5	.5	.5	.5	.5
Replace water temp. gauge, dash,										
Mustang, Cougar, Continental	1.3	1.3	1.3	1.3	1.3	1.3	1.3	1.3	.8	.8
All others	1.1	1.1	1.1	1.1	1.1	1.1	1.1	1.1	.8	.8
With performance cluster, **ADD:**	—	—	—	—	.2	.2	.2	.2	.2	.2
Replace water jacket expansion plug	.3	.3	.3	.3	.3	.3	.3	.3	.3	.3

Note: Add time to gain access to plug.

Approximate parts cost:

Radiator, new	$100.00-160.00	Drive belt, each	$ 4.00
Upper or lower hose, each	6.00	Temperature sending unit	4.00
Thermostat	4.00	Temperature gauge, dash	12.00
Water pump	21.00-40.00	Expansion plug, each	1.50

EXHAUST SYSTEM, TEST AND SERVICE

Includes:

Basic Job: Test exhaust system for leaks and/or exhaust odors. Use HC/CO exhaust analyzer to trace carbon monoxide leaks.

Related Jobs: Replace defective parts. Each job includes basic job tests and installation of new hangers as required.

MODEL	1966	1967	1968	1969	1970	1971	1972	1973	1974	1975
Basic Job:										
Complete test of exhaust system	.4	.4	.4	.4	.4	.4	.4	.4	.4	.4
Related Jobs:										
Replace muffler,										
Single or dual, one	1.0	1.0	1.0	1.0	1.0	1.0	1.0	1.0	1.0	1.0
Dual, both	1.4	1.4	1.4	1.4	1.4	1.4	1.4	1.4	1.4	1.4
Replace resonator,										
One	.9	.9	.9	.9	.9	.9	.9	.9	.9	.9
Dual, both, Continental	1.5	1.5	1.5	1.5	—	—	—	—	—	—
Dual, both, all others	1.1	1.1	1.1	1.1	1.1	1.1	1.1	1.1	1.1	1.1
Replace tail pipe,										
Single or dual, one	1.1	1.1	1.1	1.1	1.1	1.1	1.1	1.1	1.1	1.1
Dual, both	1.4	1.4	1.4	1.4	1.4	1.4	1.4	1.4	1.4	1.4
Replace exhaust pipe flange gasket, each	1.0	1.0	1.0	1.0	1.0	1.0	1.0	1.0	1.0	1.0
Free-up or o/h heat control valve,										
4 or 6-cylinder in-line engine	1.5	1.5	1.5	1.5	1.5	1.5	1.5	1.5	1.5	1.5
V-6 engine	—	—	—	—	—	—	—	—	1.7	1.7
V-8 engine	1.8	1.8	1.8	1.8	1.8	1.8	1.8	1.8	1.8	1.8
Replace exhaust pipe,										
4 or 6-cylinder in-line engine	1.3	1.3	1.3	1.3	1.3	1.3	1.3	1.3	1.3	1.3
V-6 or V-8 engine, single exhaust	1.4	1.4	1.4	1.4	1.4	1.4	1.4	1.4	1.4	1.4
V-8 engine, dual exhaust, one pipe	1.2	1.2	1.2	1.2	1.2	1.2	1.2	1.2	1.2	1.2
V-8 engine, dual exhaust, both pipes	2.0	2.0	2.0	2.0	2.0	2.0	2.0	2.0	2.0	2.0
Replace catalytic converter, ea.	—	—	—	—	—	—	—	—	—	1.0

(THIS SCHEDULE CONTINUED ON NEXT PAGE.)

170 FORD/LINCOLN/MERCURY

EXHAUST SYSTEM, TEST AND SERVICE Continued

Approximate parts cost:

Muffler	$25.00-60.00
Exhaust pipe	15.00
Catalytic converter	125.00-185.00
Heat control valve (through 1974)	$12.00
Resonator	40.00
Vacuum operated heat control valve (since 1975)	3.00

SHIFT LINKAGE, SERVICE

Includes:
  Adjust: Adjust shift linkage.
  Basic Job: Replace one control rod and/or grommet and adjust linkage.
  Additions to Basic Job: Associated work that is required during basic job.

MODEL	1966	1967	1968	1969	1970	1971	1972	1973	1974	1975
Adjust shift linkage:										
3-speed transmission	.5	.5	.5	.5	.5	.5	.5	.5	.5	.5
4-speed transmission	.6	.6	.6	.6	.6	.6	.6	.6	.6	.6
Basic Job:										
Replace one rod and/or grommet & adjust,										
3-speed transmission	.8	.8	.8	.8	.8	.8	.8	.8	.8	.8
4-speed transmission	.9	.9	.9	.9	.9	.9	.9	.9	.9	.9
Additions to Basic Job:										
Replace additional rod, ADD:	.3	.3	.3	.3	.3	.3	.3	.3	.3	.3
Replace shift lever oil seals, both, ADD:	.5	.5	.5	.5	.5	.5	.5	.5	.5	.5

Approximate parts cost:

Shift rod, each	$2.00
Shift lever oil seals	$1.50

CLUTCH MECHANISM, SERVICE

Includes:
  Adjust: Adjust clutch pedal play.
  Basic Job: Replace thrust bearing, pressure plate and disc. Adjust clutch pedal play.
  Additions to Basic Job: Associated work that is required during basic job.

MODEL	1966	1967	1968	1969	1970	1971	1972	1973	1974	1975
Adjust										
Clutch pedal play	.3	.3	.3	.3	.3	.3	.3	.3	.3	.3
Basic Job:										
Replace thrust bearing, pressure plate & disc.										
3-speed transmission	2.1	2.1	2.1	2.1	2.1	2.1	2.2	2.2	2.2	2.2
4-speed transmission	2.6	2.6	2.6	2.6	3.0	3.0	3.0	2.8	2.8	2.8
Additions to Basic Job:										
Remove, reface, and instl. flywheel, ADD:	1.8	1.8	1.8	1.8	1.8	1.8	1.8	1.8	1.8	1.8
Replace flywheel ring gear, ADD:	1.0	1.0	1.0	1.0	1.0	1.0	1.0	1.0	1.0	1.0
Resurface clutch pressure plate, ADD:	.8	.8	.8	.8	.8	.8	.8	.8	.8	.8
Replace clutch pilot bearing, ADD:	.2	.2	.2	.2	.2	.2	.2	.2	.2	.2

Approximate parts cost:

Pressure plate	$25.00-60.00
Clutch disc	20.00-35.00
Clutch release bearing	5.00-17.00
Pilot bearing	$ 2.00
Flywheel w/ring gear	36.00-56.00

FORD/LINCOLN/MERCURY 171

STANDARD TRANSMISSION, OVERHAUL

Includes:
Basic Job: R&R transmission, disassemble, replace worn parts, and adjust linkage.
Additions to Basic Job: Associated work that is required during basic job.

MODEL	1966	1967	1968	1969	1970	1971	1972	1973	1974	1975
Basic Job:										
R&R, overhaul, and adjust linkage										
3-speed transmission	5.4	5.4	5.4	5.4	5.4	5.4	5.4	5.4	5.4	5.4
4-speed transmission	6.9	6.9	6.9	6.9	6.9	6.9	6.9	6.9	6.9	6.9
Additions to Basic Job:										
Recondition transmission cover,										
3-speed trans., ADD:	.3	.3	.3	.3	.3	.3	.3	.3	.3	.3
4-speed trans., ADD:	.4	.4	.4	.4	.4	.4	.4	.4	.4	.4
Resurface clutch pressure plate, ADD:	.8	.8	.8	.8	.8	.8	.8	.8	.8	.8
R&R and resurface flywheel, ADD:	1.8	1.8	1.8	1.8	1.8	1.8	1.8	1.8	1.8	1.8
Replace flywheel ring gear, ADD:	1.0	1.0	1.0	1.0	1.0	1.0	1.0	1.0	1.0	1.0
Replace clutch pilot bearing, ADD:	.2	.2	.2	.2	.2	.2	.2	.2	.2	.2
Replace crankshaft trans. drive pinion bushing, ADD:	.7	.7	.7	.7	.7	.7	.7	.7	.7	.7

Approximate parts cost:
Phone supplier for price quote on transmission parts required.
Speedometer gear .... $ 2.00
Gasket and seals 8.00
Clutch pressure plate 25.00-60.00
Flywheel and ring gear $20.00-75.00
Clutch release bearing 5.00-17.00
Pilot bearing 2.00

AUTOMATIC TRANSMISSION, PERFORMANCE CHECK

Includes:
Basic Job: Conduct transmission performance check. Clean transmission case and operate unit to check case, oil cooler and oil cooler lines for external leaks. Remove oil pan, clean pan, screen or filter. Torque valve body mounting bolts. Adjust forward and reverse bands. Adjust throttle and shift linkage. Perform pressure checks of mainline, throttle and accumulator. Road test.
Related Jobs: Work which does not include R&R transmission and may be done as separate job.

MODEL	1966	1967	1968	1969	1970	1971	1972	1973	1974	1975
Basic Job:										
Complete trans. performance check	2.1	2.1	2.1	2.1	2.1	2.1	2.1	2.1	2.1	2.1
Related Jobs:										
Drain & fill trans., clean filter	.8	.8	.8	.8	.8	.8	.8	.8	.8	.8
Check for oil leaks	.7	.7	.7	.7	.7	.7	.7	.7	.7	.7
Repl. oil pan gasket, incl. clean filter	.9	.9	.9	.9	.9	.9	.9	.9	.9	.9
Repl. rear oil seal & O-ring	1.0	1.0	.7	.5	.5	.5	.5	.5	.5	.5
Repl. neutral safety switch	.5	.5	.5	.5	.5	.5	.5	.5	.5	.5
R&R and overhaul governor, pressure & road tests,										
C-3 transmission	—	—	—	—	—	—	—	—	2.4	2.4
C-4 transmission	2.3	2.3	2.3	2.3	2.3	2.3	2.3	2.3	2.3	2.3
C-6 transmission	2.5	2.5	2.5	2.5	2.5	2.5	2.5	2.5	2.5	2.5
FMX transmission	2.7	2.7	2.7	2.7	2.7	2.7	2.7	2.7	2.7	2.7
R&R and o/h control valve assy. and test	2.9	2.9	2.9	2.9	2.9	2.9	2.9	2.9	2.9	2.9
Adjust throttle and shift linkage	1.0	1.0	1.0	1.0	1.0	1.0	1.0	1.0	1.0	1.0
Adjust forward and reverse bands	1.3	1.3	1.3	1.3	1.3	1.3	1.3	1.3	1.3	1.3

Approximate parts cost:
Transmission fluid, per qt. $1.20
Oil pan gasket 1.00
Rear oil seal 4.50
Neutral safety switch $5.00-12.00
Governor body repair kit 16.00
Valve body assy., new 80.00

FORD/LINCOLN/MERCURY

AUTOMATIC TRANSMISSION, SHIFT AND LINKAGE CONTROLS, REPLACE AND ADJUST

Includes:
Replace defective part and make necessary adjustment(s).

MODEL	1966	1967	1968	1969	1970	1971	1972	1973	1974	1975
Replace control rod, carb. or trans., & adjust	.9	.9	.9	.9	.9	.9	.9	.9	.9	.9
Replace each additional rod, **ADD:**	.4	.4	.4	.4	.4	.4	.4	.4	.4	.4
Replace carb./throttle link, **ADD:**	.3	.3	.3	.3	.3	.3	.3	.3	.3	.3
Replace throttle control cable, **ADD:**	.5	.5	.5	.5	.5	.5	.5	.5	.5	.5
Replace front control rod, column shift, **ADD:**	.3	.3	.3	.3	.3	.3	.3	.3	.3	.3
Replace rear control rod or swivel, **ADD:**	.4	.4	.4	.4	.4	.4	.4	.4	.4	.4
Replace control torque shaft or bushings, **ADD:**	.6	.6	.6	.6	.6	.6	.6	.6	.6	.6
Replace shift control key lock assy.	.7	.7	.7	.7	.7	.7	.7	.7	.7	.7
Replace vac. modulator hose & adj. linkage	.6	.6	.6	.6	.6	.6	.6	.6	.6	.6
Replace and adjust floor shift control assy.	.8	.8	.8	.8	.8	.8	.8	.8	.8	.8

Approximate parts cost:
Linkage rod, ea. ... $1.50	Modulator hose, per ft. ... $0.25
Control cable ... 8.00	Floor shift contr. assy. ... 40.00

AUTOMATIC TRANSMISSION, MAJOR SERVICE

Includes:
Basic Jobs:
1. **Overhaul transmission.** Disassemble, clean, inspect and replace all worn parts as needed. Adjust throttle and shift linkage as required. Flush converter and cooler lines. Perform pressure checks of mainline, throttle, and accumulator. Road test.
2. **Replace torque converter.** R&R transmission. Flush oil cooler and lines. Replace transmission oil and oil filter. Perform pressure checks of mainline, throttle, and accumulator. Adjust throttle and shift linkage as required. Road test.
3. **Reseal transmission.** R&R transmission. Replace all seals and gaskets. Replace transmission oil and oil filter. Check oil cooler for leaks. Perform pressure checks of mainline, throttle, and accumulator. Adjust throttle and shift linkage as required. Road test.

Additions to Basic Jobs: Associated work that is performed while the transmission is out during one of basic jobs.

MODEL	1966	1967	1968	1969	1970	1971	1972	1973	1974	1975
Basic Job #1										
Overhaul transmission,										
C-3 transmission	—	—	—	—	—	—	—	—	9.0	9.0
C-4 transmission	9.2	9.2	9.2	9.2	9.2	9.2	9.2	9.2	9.2	9.2
C-6 transmission	10.0	10.0	10.0	10.0	10.0	10.0	10.0	10.0	10.0	10.0
FMX transmission	11.9	11.9	11.9	11.9	11.9	11.9	11.9	11.9	11.9	11.9
Basic Job #2										
Replace torque converter,										
C-3 transmission	—	—	—	—	—	—	—	—	5.0	5.0
C-4 transmission	5.1	5.1	5.1	5.1	5.1	5.1	5.1	5.1	5.1	5.1
C-6 transmission	5.7	5.7	5.7	5.7	5.7	5.7	5.7	5.7	5.7	5.7
FMX transmission	5.7	5.7	5.7	5.7	5.7	5.2	5.2	5.2	5.2	5.2
Flush & clean, **ADD:**	.5	.5	.5	.5	.5	.5	.5	.5	.5	.5
Basic Job #3										
Reseal transmission,										
C3, C-4 transmission	6.8	6.8	6.8	6.8	6.8	6.8	6.8	6.8	6.8	6.8
C-6 transmission	7.6	7.6	7.6	7.6	7.6	7.6	7.6	7.6	7.6	7.6
FMX transmission	9.5	9.5	9.5	9.5	9.5	9.5	9.5	9.5	9.5	9.5
Additions to Basic Jobs:										
Replace oil cooler pipes, both, **ADD:**	.9	.9	.9	.9	.9	.9	.9	.9	.9	.9
Replace oil filler pipe and/or seal, **ADD:**	.5	.5	.5	.5	.5	.5	.5	.5	.5	.5
Replace torque converter ring gear, **ADD:**	.5	.5	.5	.5	.5	.5	.5	.5	.5	.5

(THIS SCHEDULE CONTINUED ON NEXT PAGE.)

FORD/LINCOLN/MERCURY

AUTOMATIC TRANSMISSION, MAJOR SERVICE Continued

Approximate parts cost:

Transmission seal and gasket kit ... $20.00	Oil filler pipe ... $ 3.00
Transmission partial overhaul kit ... 50.00	Oil filler pipe seal ... 0.25
Oil cooler pipe, each ... 9.00	Oil pan ... 5.00
Torque converter assembly ... 200.00	Oil pan gasket ... 1.00
Torque converter ring gear ... 8.00	Governor kit ... 16.00
Transmission fluid, per qt. ... 1.20	

DRIVESHAFT, SERVICE

Includes:
  Basic Job: R&R driveshaft and overhaul or replace front and rear U-joints, adjust pinion nose angle.
  Addition to Basic Job: Replace axle pinion oil seal.

MODEL	1966	1967	1968	1969	1970	1971	1972	1973	1974	1975
Basic Job:										
R&R driveshaft & overhaul both U-joints, and check driveshaft alignment,										
Continental	2.1	2.1	2.1	2.1	2.2	2.2	2.2	2.2	2.2	2.2
All others	1.6	1.6	1.6	1.6	1.6	1.6	1.6	1.6	1.6	1.6
Addition to Basic Job:										
Replace axle drive pinion oil seal, **ADD**:	.5	.5	.5	.5	.5	.5	.5	.5	.5	.5

Approximate parts cost:

Universal joint kit ... $12.00	Pinion shaft oil seal ... $3.50

REAR AXLE, SERVICE

Includes:
  Basic Jobs: 1. R&R driveshaft, R&R axle shafts, overhaul differential assembly, and check and adjust pinion nose angle.
              2. R&R driveshaft and replace pinion bearing oil seal.
  Related Jobs: Associated work that is performed independently of basic jobs.

MODEL	1966	1967	1968	1969	1970	1971	1972	1973	1974	1975
Basic Job #1										
Overhaul differential assembly, removeable carrier-type,										
Standard	5.3	5.3	5.3	5.3	5.3	5.3	5.3	5.3	5.3	5.3
Solid spacer	5.8	5.8	5.8	5.8	5.8	5.8	5.8	5.8	5.8	5.8
Locking differential	5.5	5.5	5.5	5.5	5.5	5.5	5.5	5.5	5.5	5.5
Overhaul differential assembly, integral carrier-type,										
Standard	4.3	4.3	4.3	4.3	4.3	4.3	4.3	4.3	4.3	4.3
Locking differential	4.8	4.8	4.8	4.8	4.8	4.8	4.8	4.8	4.8	4.8
Basic Job #2										
Replace drive pinion bearing oil seal.	1.0	1.0	1.0	1.0	1.0	1.0	1.0	1.0	1.0	1.0
Related Jobs:										
R&R axle shaft (one side), and/or bearing and seals	1.5	1.5	1.5	1.5	1.5	1.5	1.5	1.5	1.5	1.5
Replace axle shaft wheel mounting stud	.8	.8	.8	.8	.8	.8	.8	.8	.8	.8

Approximate parts cost:

Axle shaft & bearing assy. ... $40.00	Cover gasket ... $ 1.00
Axle shaft oil seal ... 2.00	Ring & pinion gear set ... 80.00
Pinion shaft oil seal ... 3.50	Pinion gear kit ... 9.00
Side gear kit ... 18.00	Wheel bearing oil seal ... 3.00
Universal joint flange assembly ... 12.00	Rear wheel bearing ... 16.00

174 FORD/LINCOLN/MERCURY

REAR SUSPENSION, SERVICE

Includes:
Service for the rear suspension system is listed as individual jobs. Add times if more than one job is performed.

MODEL	1966	1967	1968	1969	1970	1971	1972	1973	1974	1975
Repl. rear coil spring and make pinion angle adjustment	.8	.8	.8	.8	.8	.8	.8	.8	.8	.8
Repl. rear leaf spring & shim to align pinion angle,										
Continental	1.9	1.9	1.9	1.9	—	—	—	—	—	—
All others	1.7	1.7	1.7	1.7	1.7	1.7	1.7	1.7	1.7	1.7
Repl. shackle and bushings; eye bolt & bushings	.7	.7	.7	.7	.7	.7	.7	.7	.7	.7
Repl. rear suspension arm, including pinion angle adjustment,										
Upper arm, one	1.5	1.5	1.5	1.5	1.5	1.5	1.1	1.1	1.1	1.1
Lower arm, one	1.1	1.1	1.1	1.1	1.1	1.1	1.1	1.1	1.1	1.1
Repl. shock absorber, both sides,										
Torino, Montego	1.0	1.0	1.0	1.0	1.0	1.0	.8	.8	.8	.8
All others	.9	.9	.9	.9	.8	.8	.8	.8	.8	.8
Install stabilizer bar end kit	.9	.9	.9	.9	.9	.9	.9	.9	.9	.9
Repl. stabilizer bar	.7	.7	.7	.7	.7	.7	.7	.7	.7	.7

Approximate parts cost:
Rear leaf spring	$40.00	Shackle bushing package	$1.00
Coil spring, each	25.00	Stabilizer bar end kit	10.00
Shackle package	7.50	Stabilizer bar	35.00
Suspension arm, upper	12.00	Suspension arm, lower	13.00

STANDARD STEERING GEAR, ADJUST AND SERVICE

Includes:
Basic Job:
1. Worm & ball gear: Adjust steering gear, worm and sector mesh; adjust wheel bearings and toe-in.
2. Worm & ball gear: R&R steering gear assembly.
3. Rack & pinion gear: R&R steering gear assembly; make pinion preload and yoke support adjustments; adjust toe-in.

Addition to Basic Jobs: Overhaul steering gear assembly.

MODEL	1966	1967	1968	1969	1970	1971	1972	1973	1974	1975
Basic Job #1										
Complete worm & ball gear, wheel brgs, & toe-in adjustments	1.4	1.4	1.4	1.4	1.4	1.4	1.4	1.4	1.4	1.4
Basic Job #2										
R&R worm & ball gear assembly	1.0	1.0	1.0	1.0	1.0	1.0	1.0	1.0	1.0	1.0
Additions:										
Overhaul worm & ball gear assembly, **ADD:**	1.0	1.0	1.0	1.0	1.0	1.0	1.0	1.0	1.0	1.0
Basic Job #3										
R&R rack & pinion assembly & adjust, Pinto, Bobcat, Mustang II	—	—	—	—	—	1.3	1.3	1.3	2.3	2.3
Additions:										
Overhaul rack & pinion assembly, **ADD:**	—	—	—	—	—	.8	.8	.8	.8	1.6

Approximate parts cost:
Housing & bushing assembly, worm & ball gear	$40.00	Worm & ball kit	$7.00
Rack & pinion shaft	23.00	Sector shaft seal	1.00
Rack & pinion gasket, seal & dust cover kit	5.00	Rack & pinion yoke	2.50

FORD/LINCOLN/MERCURY

POWER STEERING UNIT, TEST AND SERVICE

Includes:
Basic Job: 1. Worm & ball gear: Adjust drive belt tension; hook-up gauges to check pressure on left and right turns. Adjust steering gear box over-center torque and control valve to balance left and right steering effort.
2. Rack & pinion gear: R&R gear assembly; make pinion preload and yoke support adjustment; adjust drive belt tension; adjust toe-in; check pump output pressure.
Additions to Basic Job: Service power steering unit.
Related Jobs: R&R power steering unit, (worm & ball unit), pump, or other associated parts.
Additions to Related Jobs: Overhaul steering unit or pump including replacement of all seals and worn parts.

MODEL	1966	1967	1968	1969	1970	1971	1972	1973	1974	1975
Basic Job #1										
Worm & ball gear, test and adjust	1.0	1.0	1.0	1.0	1.0	1.0	1.0	1.0	1.0	1.0
Basic Job #2										
Rack & pinion, R&R and adjust,										
Pinto, Bobcat	—	—	—	—	—	—	—	—	1.8	1.6
Mustang II	—	—	—	—	—	—	—	—	2.2	2.2
Additions to Basic Jobs:										
Replace pwr. steering pump drive belt, **ADD:**	.3	.3	.3	.3	.3	.3	.3	.3	.3	.3
With air conditioning, **ADD:**	.2	.2	.2	.2	.2	.2	.2	.2	.2	.2
Check & replenish reservoir fluid, **ADD:**	.2	.2	.2	.2	.2	.2	.2	.2	.2	.2
Related Jobs:										
Replace pressure hose, incl. adjust drive belt	.5	.5	.6	.6	.6	.6	.6	.6	.6	.6
Replace return hose, incl. adjust drive belt	.4	.4	.4	.4	.4	.4	.4	.4	.4	.4
Replace pump reservoir or O-ring seals	1.0	1.3	1.0	1.0	1.0	1.0	1.0	1.0	1.0	1.0
Replace pump, includes pressure-test original pump and transfer pulley,										
Continental, 462 CID	1.6	1.6	1.6	—	—	—	—	—	—	—
All others	1.2	1.2	1.2	1.2	1.2	1.2	1.2	1.2	1.2	1.2
With air conditioning, **ADD:**	.2	.2	.2	.2	.2	.2	.2	.2	.2	.2
Replace worm & ball power gear unit, includes test original unit and complete adjustment,										
Continental	2.5	2.5	2.5	2.5	2.0	2.0	2.0	2.0	2.0	2.0
Mustang, Cougar, 428 CID	2.6	2.6	2.6	2.6	2.6	—	—	—	—	—
Maverick, Comet, V-8, 302 CID, Std. Trans.	—	—	—	—	—	2.7	2.7	2.7	2.7	2.7
All others	2.0	2.0	2.0	2.0	2.0	2.0	2.0	2.0	2.0	2.0
Additions to Related Jobs:										
Overhaul worm & ball power gear unit, **ADD:**	2.2	2.2	2.2	2.4	2.4	2.4	2.4	2.4	2.4	2.4
Overhaul rack & pinion power gear unit, **ADD:**	—	—	—	—	—	—	—	—	2.3	2.3
Overhaul pump, incl. new kit & seals, **ADD:**	.6	.6	.6	.6	.6	.6	.6	.6	.6	.6

Approximate parts cost:

Drive belt	$ 4.00
Pressure hose	12.00
Return hose	4.00
Rack & pinion unit parts	
Valve assembly	100.00
Sector shaft	35.00
Worm bearing set	4.00
Dust seals, right & left	7.00
Sector shaft bushing	2.00
Pump assembly, Lincoln, Mark, IV, 1966-69	$135.00
Pump assembly, all others	65.00
Worm & ball unit parts	
Bearing kit	5.00
Valve kit	13.00
Piston seal	2.50
Sector shaft and worm gear	35.00
Seal kit	14.00

FORD/LINCOLN/MERCURY

FRONT END; TEST, SERVICE, AND ADJUST

Includes:

Basic Job: Check and adjust car height, caster, camber, steering axis inclination, turning radius, toe-in; pack and adjust front wheel bearings, replace seals.

Related Jobs: Perform individual adjustments. Replace or overhaul defective parts and make necessary adjustment.

MODEL	1966	1967	1968	1969	1970	1971	1972	1973	1974	1975
Basic Job:										
Complete test and adjustments,										
With drum brakes	2.5	2.5	2.5	2.5	2.5	2.5	2.5	2.5	2.5	2.5
With disc brakes	3.0	3.0	3.0	3.0	3.0	3.0	3.0	3.0	3.0	3.0
Related Jobs:										
Adjust toe-in only	.4	.4	.4	.4	.4	.4	.4	.4	.4	.4
Repack wheel brgs. only, incl. new seals,										
Drum brakes, both sides	.9	.9	.9	.9	.9	.9	.9	.9	.9	.9
Disc brakes, both sides	1.5	1.5	1.5	1.2	1.9	1.9	1.9	1.5	1.5	1.5
Replace wheel brgs. only, each side,										
Drum brakes, inner or outer brg.	.5	.5	.5	.5	.5	.5	.5	.5	.5	.5
Disc brakes, inner or outer brg.	.8	.8	.8	.7	1.1	1.1	1.1	.9	.9	.9
Balance four wheels on car,										
Drum brakes	1.2	1.2	1.2	1.2	1.2	1.2	1.2	1.2	1.2	—
Disc brakes	1.5	1.5	1.5	1.5	1.5	1.5	1.5	1.5	1.5	1.5
Overhaul front suspension, incl. disassemble, replace nec. parts, lube., & complete adjust,										
With drum brakes	7.9	7.9	7.9	7.9	7.9	7.9	7.9	7.9	7.9	7.9
With disc brakes	8.8	8.8	8.8	8.8	8.8	8.8	8.8	8.8	8.8	8.8
Replace coil spring, one side, incl. complete front end adjustments,										
Continental, Mark IV	2.8	2.8	2.8	2.8	2.8	2.8	2.8	2.8	2.8	2.8
All others	2.6	2.6	2.6	2.6	2.6	2.6	2.6	2.6	2.6	2.6
Replace upper ball joints, both sides, incl. complete front end adjustments	3.7	3.7	3.7	3.7	3.7	3.7	3.7	3.7	3.7	3.7
Replace steering knuckle, one side, incl. complete front end adjustment,										
With drum brakes	2.9	2.9	2.9	2.9	2.9	2.9	2.9	2.9	2.9	2.9
With disc brakes	3.2	3.2	3.2	3.2	3.2	3.2	3.2	3.2	3.2	3.2
Replace shock absorber, both sides	.9	.9	.9	.9	.9	.9	.9	.9	.9	.9
Replace lwr. control arm struts or bushing,										
With drum brakes	3.3	3.3	2.3	2.3	2.3	2.3	2.4	2.4	2.4	2.4
With disc brakes	3.6	3.6	3.6	3.6	3.6	3.8	3.4	1.3	1.1	1.1
Replace control arm rubber bumper, one	.4	.4	.4	.4	.4	.4	.4	.4	.4	.4
Replace stabilizer bar and bushings	.7	.7	.7	.7	.7	.7	.7	.7	.7	.7

Approximate parts cost:

Front wheel brg., outer	$ 2.00
Wheel bearing inner	3.00
Wheel bearing, package	4.50
Seals	1.50
Stabilizer bar & bushing	16.00
Coil spring	20.00
Steering knuckle	$50.00
Rubber bumper, ea.	1.50
Shock absorber, ea.	13.00
Control arm strut	10.00
Ball joint	13.00

FORD/LINCOLN/MERCURY

STEERING LINKAGE, SERVICE AND ADJUST

Includes:
  Basic Job: Adjust toe-in.
  Related Jobs: Replace defective parts and adjust toe-in.

MODEL	1966	1967	1968	1969	1970	1971	1972	1973	1974	1975
Basic Job:										
Adjust toe-in	.4	.4	.4	.4	.4	.4	.4	.4	.4	.4
Related Jobs:										
Replace tie-rods or tie-rod ends, (4),										
Pinto, Bobcat, Mustang II	—	—	—	—	—	1.7	1.7	1.7	1.7	1.7
All others	1.6	1.6	1.5	1.5	1.5	1.5	1.5	1.5	1.5	1.5
Repl. Pitman arm, includes adjust toe-in	.8	.8	.8	.8	.8	.8	.8	.8	.8	.8
Repl. steering idler arm or bushing, including adjust toe-in	1.4	1.4	1.4	1.4	1.4	1.4	1.4	1.4	1.4	1.4

Approximate parts cost:
Tie-rod end pkg. .... $ 7.00
Pitman arm 11.00
Tie rod 9.00
Idler arm, kit $9.00-20.00
Tie rod end kit 10.00

BRAKES, SERVICE

Includes:
  Basic Job: Install new linings or pads, turn brake drums or rotors, lubricate and adjust front wheel bearings, replace rear oil seals, bleed hydraulic system, and adjust brakes.
  Additions to Basic Job: Overhaul four wheel cylinders, overhaul or replace front calipers, overhaul or replace rear calipers, overhaul master cylinder.
  Related Jobs: Performed at time other than during basic job. Overhaul or replace front calipers, overhaul or replace rear calipers, overhaul master cylinder.

MODEL	1966	1967	1968	1969	1970	1971	1972	1973	1974	1975
Basic Job:										
Complete job incl. turn drums or rotors,										
Drum (4), all models	6.4	6.4	6.4	6.4	6.6	6.6	6.6	6.1	6.1	6.0
Disc front, drum rear, all models	7.3	7.3	7.3	7.3	7.3	7.3	6.7	6.7	6.7	6.7
With floating caliper type, ADD:	—	—	1.0	1.0	1.0	1.0	1.1	1.1	1.1	1.1
Additions to Basic Job:										
Overhaul 4 wheel cyl. incl. hone, ADD:	1.6	2.3	2.3	2.3	2.3	2.4	2.4	2.4	2.4	2.4
Overhaul front calipers (both), ADD:	3.5	3.5	3.5	2.9	2.9	2.9	2.9	2.9	2.9	2.9
Replace front calipers (both), ADD:	.4	.4	.4	.4	.4	.4	.4	.4	.4	.4
Overhaul rear calipers, ADD:	—	—	—	—	—	—	—	—	—	3.1
Replace rear calipers, ADD:	—	—	—	—	—	—	—	—	—	.6
Overhaul master cylinder, ADD:	.6	.8	.8	.8	.8	.8	.8	.8	.8	.8
Related Jobs: (Not during basic job)										
Bleed hyd. system, 4 wheels	.6	.6	.6	.6	.6	.6	.6	.6	.6	.6
Adjust drum brakes, 4 wheels	.5	.5	.5	.5	.5	.5	.5	.5	.5	.5
Replace drum brake shoes, 4-wheels	3.5	3.5	3.5	3.5	3.5	3.5	3.5	3.5	3.5	3.5
Replace disc brake pads, front wheels	1.6	1.6	1.6	1.6	1.6	1.6	1.0	1.0	1.0	1.0
Replace disc brake pads, rear wheels,										
Continental	—	—	—	—	—	—	—	—	—	1.5
All others	—	—	—	—	—	—	—	—	—	1.3
O/h front calipers, incl. turn rotors	5.3	5.3	5.3	5.3	4.6	4.6	4.6	4.6	4.6	4.6
Replace front caliper, incl. turn rotor, ea.	2.4	2.4	2.4	2.4	2.4	2.4	2.4	2.4	2.4	2.4
O/h rear calipers, incl. turn rotors	—	—	—	—	—	—	—	—	—	4.8
Replace rear caliper, incl. turn rotor, ea.	—	—	—	—	—	—	—	—	—	2.3
Overhaul master cylinder	1.0	1.2	1.2	1.2	1.2	1.2	1.2	1.2	1.2	1.2

(THIS SCHEDULE CONTINUED ON NEXT PAGE.)

FORD/LINCOLN/MERCURY

BRAKES SERVICE Continued

Approximate parts cost:
Wheel cyl. seal, boot & bushing pkg. ... $ 6.00	Wheel cylinder repair kit, ea. ... $ 2.00
Brake shoes and lining sets, front or rear ... 25.00	Caliper brake housing ... 50.00
Disc brake pads, set of 2 ... 24.00	Oil seal, set ... 2.00
Master cylinder repair kit (dual) ... 18.00	

HYDRAULIC BRAKE SYSTEM, OVERHAUL

Includes:
Basic Job: Overhaul or replace master cylinder, overhaul all wheel cylinders, including hone if necessary, overhaul calipers, replace rear wheel oil seals, bleed hydraulic system, and adjust brakes.

Related Jobs: Work performed at time other than during basic job. Front wheel work includes pack & adjust wheel bearings. Rear wheel work includes R&R rear oil seals.

MODEL	1966	1967	1968	1969	1970	1971	1972	1973	1974	1975
Basic Job:										
Complete job, incl. master & wheel cylinders,										
Drum brakes, all models	4.7	4.7	4.7	4.7	4.7	4.7	4.7	4.6	4.6	4.6
Disc front, drum rear, all models	3.9	3.9	3.9	3.9	3.9	3.9	3.9	3.9	3.9	3.9
Disc front and rear	—	—	—	—	—	—	—	—	—	3.3
Related Jobs: (Not during basic job)										
Bleed hyd. system, 4 wheels	.6	.6	.6	.6	.6	.6	.6	.6	.6	.6
Overhaul master cylinder, incl. hone, and bleed system,										
Drum brakes	.9	1.4	1.2	1.2	1.2	1.2	1.2	1.2	1.2	1.2
Disc brakes	1.1	1.6	1.2	1.2	1.2	1.2	1.2	1.2	1.2	1.2
Replace master cylinder and bleed system	1.2	1.2	1.2	1.0	1.0	1.0	1.0	1.0	1.1	1.1
With power brakes, **ADD:**	.2	.2	.2	.2	.2	.2	.2	.2	.2	.2
O/h wheel cylinders, drum brakes (4)	4.4	4.4	4.4	4.4	4.4	4.4	4.1	4.1	4.1	4.1
O/h front calipers, incl. turn rotors	4.0	4.0	4.0	4.0	4.0	4.0	4.0	4.0	4.0	4.0
O/h rear calipers, incl. turn rotors	—	—	—	—	—	—	—	—	—	4.8

Approximate parts cost:
Master cylinder repair kit (dual) ... $18.00	Master cylinder ... $35.00
Wheel cylinder repair kit, ea. ... 2.00	Wheel cyl. seal, boot & bush. pkg. ... 6.00

PARKING BRAKES, SERVICE AND ADJUST

Includes:
Basic Jobs: Replace defective cable and adjust parking brakes.

MODEL	1966	1967	1968	1969	1970	1971	1972	1973	1974	1975
Basic Job:										
Adjust parking brakes	.4	.4	.4	.4	.4	.4	.4	.4	.4	.4
Replace forward cable,										
Continental	1.0	1.0	1.0	1.0	1.0	1.0	1.0	1.1	1.1	1.1
All others	.8	.8	.8	.8	.8	.8	.8	.8	.8	.8
Replace rear cable, one side	.8	.8	.8	.8	.8	.8	.8	.8	.8	.8
Replace rear cables, both sides	1.1	1.1	1.1	1.1	1.1	1.1	1.1	1.1	1.1	1.1

Approximate parts cost:
Front cable ... $9.00-15.00	Rear cable, each ... $6.00-12.00

FORD/LINCOLN/MERCURY 179

BRAKE BOOSTER OR SKID CONTROL ASSEMBLY, REPLACE OR SERVICE

Includes:
Basic Job: R&R with new booster assy., test and adjust brakes.
Related Jobs: Test and replace associated defective parts.

MODEL	1966	1967	1968	1969	1970	1971	1972	1973	1974	1975
Basic Job:										
R&R booster assy., test, & adj. brakes,										
Mustang, Cougar	1.7	1.7	1.7	1.7	2.0	2.0	1.8	1.8	1.3	1.3
All others	1.4	1.4	1.4	1.4	1.4	1.4	1.6	1.6	1.6	1.6
Related Jobs:										
Replace brake booster check valve	.4	.4	.4	.4	.4	.4	.4	.4	.4	.4
Replace differential pressure valve, incl. bleed system,										
Drum brakes, all models	1.1	1.1	1.1	1.1	1.1	1.1	1.1	1.1	1.1	1.1
Disc brakes, Continental, Mark IV, Mercury, Meteor	1.6	1.6	1.6	1.6	1.2	1.2	1.2	1.2	1.2	1.2
Replace skid control sensor,										
On axle shaft	—	—	—	—	.9	.9	—	—	—	—
On axle pinion	—	—	—	—	.7	.7	.7	.7	.7	.7
Replace skid control module	—	—	—	.6	.6	.6	.6	.6	.6	.6
Replace skid control actuator,										
Thunderbird, Mark IV	—	—	—	2.0	2.0	2.0	1.5	1.5	1.5	1.5
Continental	—	—	—	—	1.5	1.5	1.5	1.5	1.5	1.1
Mercury	—	—	—	—	—	—	—	—	—	1.1

Approximate parts cost:
Brake booster assembly	$90.00
Booster check valve	5.00
Differential pressure valve	15.00
Skid control sensor	$ 50.00
Skid control module	160.00
Skid control actuator	165.00

LIGHTING SYSTEM, ADJUST AND SERVICE

Includes:
Basic Jobs: 1. Adjust headlights to inspection requirements.
              2. Replace defective parts in rear lighting system.
Additions to Basic Job: Replace associated parts affecting headlight adjustment.
Related Jobs: Replace associated parts not affecting headlight adjustment.

MODEL	1966	1967	1968	1969	1970	1971	1972	1973	1974	1975
Basic Job #1										
Adjust two lights	.4	.4	.4	.4	.4	.4	.4	.4	.4	.4
Adjust four lights	.6	.6	.6	.6	.6	.6	.6	.6	.6	.6
Basic Job #2										
Replace stoplight switch	.4	.4	.4	.4	.4	.4	.4	.4	.4	.4
Replace back-up light switch	.4	.4	.4	.4	.4	.4	.4	.4	.4	.4
Additions to Basic Job:										
Replace sealed beam unit, each, **ADD:**	.3	.3	.3	.3	.3	.3	.3	.3	.3	.3
Related Jobs:										
Replace headlamp vacuum motor	.7	.7	.7	.7	.7	.5	.5	.6	.6	.6
Replace headlamp switch,										
T-Bird, Mark IV	.6	.6	.6	.6	.6	.8	.8	.8	.8	.8
All others	.7	.7	.7	.7	.7	.8	.8	.8	.8	.8

(THIS SCHEDULE CONTINUED ON NEXT PAGE.)

FORD/LINCOLN/MERCURY

LIGHTING SYSTEM, ADJUST AND SERVICE Continued

MODEL	1966	1967	1968	1969	1970	1971	1972	1973	1974	1975
Related Jobs Continued										
Replace foot dimmer switch	.3	.3	.3	.3	.3	.3	.3	.3	.3	.3
Replace signal/hazard flasher	.3	.3	.3	.3	.3	.3	.3	.3	.3	.3
Replace signal/hazard switch,										
With standard column	.8	.8	.8	.8	.8	.8	.8	.8	.8	.8
With tilt wheel, Continental	1.6	1.6	1.6	1.6	1.6	1.0	1.0	1.0	1.0	1.0
With tilt wheel, all others	1.0	1.0	1.0	1.0	1.0	1.0	1.0	1.0	1.0	1.0

Approximate parts cost:
Sealed beam unit	$4.00
Signal/hazard flasher	2.00
Signal/hazard switch	4.00
Vacuum actuator	$25.00
Headlamp switch	8.00-18.00
Back-up light switch	7.00

HEATING SYSTEM, TEST AND SERVICE

Includes:
Basic Job: Drain, back-flush, and fill radiator, check radiator and heater hoses and connections, pressure-test radiator cap and system.
Related Jobs: Replace defective parts. Work performed individually and independently of basic job.

MODEL	1966	1967	1968	1969	1970	1971	1972	1973	1974	1975
Basic Job:										
Drain, flush, fill, check, & pressure-test	.9	.9	.9	.9	.9	.9	.9	.9	.9	.9
Related Jobs:										
Replace heater hose, one, inlet or outlet,										
Mustang	.7	.7	.7	.7	.7	.4	.4	.4	1.3	1.3
Cougar	.7	.7	.7	.7	.7	.4	.4	.4	.4	.4
Pinto, Bobcat	—	—	—	—	—	1.1	1.1	1.1	1.1	1.1
All others	.4	.4	.4	.4	.4	.4	.4	.4	.4	.4
R&R heater core w/air conditioning, includes partial charge system,										
Torino, Falcon, Montego, T-bird, Mark IV	2.6	2.6	2.6	2.6	2.6	2.6	1.5	1.5	1.6	1.6
Mustang, Maverick, Comet	3.2	3.2	3.2	3.2	3.2	3.4	3.4	3.4	3.4	3.4
Cougar	3.2	3.2	3.2	3.2	3.2	2.4	2.4	2.4	1.5	1.5
Pinto, Bobcat	—	—	—	—	—	1.4	1.4	1.8	1.8	1.8
All others	1.3	1.3	1.3	1.3	1.3	1.3	1.3	1.3	1.3	1.3
Boil out and repair core, **ADD:**	1.2	1.2	1.2	1.2	1.2	1.2	1.2	1.2	1.2	1.2
R&R heater core without air conditioning,										
Mustang	1.8	1.8	1.8	1.8	1.8	1.8	1.8	1.8	1.8	1.8
Thunderbird	2.0	2.0	2.0	2.0	1.9	1.9	.8	.8	.8	.8
Cougar	1.8	1.8	1.8	1.8	1.8	1.7	1.7	1.7	.9	.9
Pinto, Bobcat	—	—	—	—	—	1.1	1.1	1.1	1.1	1.1
All others	.9	.9	.9	.9	.9	.9	.9	.9	.9	.9
Boil out and repair core, **ADD:**	1.2	1.2	1.2	1.2	1.2	1.2	1.2	1.2	1.2	1.2
Replace heater blower motor, test system, after installation,										
Ford, Merc., Meteor, T-bird, Mark IV	2.1	2.1	2.1	2.1	2.1	1.7	1.7	1.7	1.7	1.7
Pinto, Bobcat	—	—	—	—	—	1.8	1.8	1.8	1.8	1.8
Mustang II	—	—	—	—	—	—	—	—	2.0	2.0
All others	1.6	1.6	1.6	1.6	1.6	1.6	1.6	1.6	1.4	1.4
Replace heater switch	.7	.7	.7	.7	.7	.7	.7	.7	.7	.7

Approximate parts cost:
Heater hose, per ft.	$0.75
Heater switch	3.00-12.00
Heater core	$15.00-40.00
Blower motor	25.00-50.00

FORD/LINCOLN/MERCURY

AIR CONDITIONING SYSTEM, SPRING TUNE-UP

Includes:
 Basic Job: Clean condenser fins; adjust drive belt tension; test anti-freeze; tighten compressor, condenser, and evaporator mounts. Pressure-test and leak-check system. Check system for performance.
 Additions to Basic Job: Replacement of defective parts.

MODEL	1966	1967	1968	1969	1970	1971	1972	1973	1974	1975
Basic Job:										
Perform complete spring tune-up	2.0	2.0	2.0	2.0	2.0	2.0	2.0	2.0	2.0	2.0
Additions to Basic Job:										
Replace compressor belt, **ADD:**	.4	.4	.4	.4	.4	.4	.4	.4	.4	.4
Replace compr. clutch pulley/hub assy., **ADD:**	.5	.5	.5	.5	.5	.5	.5	.5	.5	.7
Replace compr. clutch brush assy., **ADD:**	.8	.8	.8	.8	.8	.8	.8	.8	.8	.8
Replace compr. clutch bearing, **ADD:**	.8	.8	.8	.8	.8	.8	1.0	1.0	1.0	1.2

Approximate parts cost:
Compressor drive belt	$ 3.00
Compressor clutch pulley w/hub	67.00
Freon, per 14 oz. can	2.50
Compressor clutch brush assy.	$ 7.00
Compressor clutch bearing	12.00
Anti-freeze, per gal.	9.50

AIR CONDITIONING SYSTEM, MAJOR SERVICE

Includes:
 Basic Job: Drain system in order to replace defective component, evacuate, dehydrate, and recharge system, pressure test, and leak check, clean condenser fins, adjust drive belt tension, tighten compressor, condenser, and evaporator mounts, and conduct performance test.
 Additions to Basic Job: Replace or overhaul compressor. Replace other defective parts.

MODEL	1966	1967	1968	1969	1970	1971	1972	1973	1974	1975
Basic Job:										
Drain, evacuate, dehydrate, charge & test	3.0	3.0	3.0	3.0	3.0	3.0	3.0	3.0	3.0	3.0
Additions to Basic Job:										
Replace compressor,										
Pinto, Bobcat, **ADD:**	—	—	—	—	—	.8	.8	.8	.8	.8
Continental, **ADD:**	1.5	1.5	1.5	.9	.9	1.6	1.2	1.2	1.2	1.2
Mark IV, T-Bird, **ADD:**	.9	.9	.9	.9	.9	1.2	1.2	1.2	1.2	1.2
All others, **ADD:**	.9	.9	.9	.9	.9	.9	.9	.9	.9	.9
Overhaul compressor, incl. R&R, **ADD:**	2.9	2.9	2.9	2.9	2.9	2.9	2.9	2.9	2.9	2.9
Replace compr. oil pump seal, **ADD:**	.9	.9	.9	.9	1.1	1.1	.9	.9	.9	.9
Replace suction throttling valve, **ADD:**	.6	.6	.6	.6	.6	.6	.6	.6	.6	.6
Replace condenser, **ADD:**	1.3	1.3	1.3	1.3	1.3	1.3	1.3	1.3	1.3	1.3
Replace evaporator core,										
Continental, **ADD:**	3.0	3.0	3.0	3.0	1.5	1.5	1.5	1.5	1.5	1.5
Mustang, Mustang II, **ADD:**	2.0	2.0	2.0	3.0	3.0	1.7	1.7	1.7	3.5	3.5
Pinto, Bobcat, **ADD:**	—	—	—	—	—	1.3	1.6	1.6	2.0	2.0
T-Bird, Mark IV, Torino, Falcon, Montego, **ADD:**	2.4	2.4	2.4	2.4	2.5	2.5	1.0	1.0	1.0	1.0
Cougar, **ADD:**	2.0	2.0	2.0	3.0	3.0	1.7	1.7	1.7	1.0	1.0
All others, **ADD:**	1.5	1.5	1.5	.9	.9	.7	.7	.8	.8	.8
Replace sight-glass, **ADD:**	1.4	1.4	1.4	1.4	1.4	1.4	.9	.9	.9	.9
Replace dehydrator-receiver tank,										
Maverick, Comet, **ADD:**	—	—	—	—	.4	.4	.4	.4	.4	.4
Pinto, Bobcat, **ADD:**	—	—	—	—	—	.3	.3	.3	.3	.3
Continental, **ADD:**	.7	.7	.7	.7	.5	.5	.5	.5	.4	.4
All others, **ADD:**	1.0	1.0	1.0	.8	.8	.8	.8	.8	.8	.8
Replace expansion valve, **ADD:**	1.1	1.1	1.1	.8	.8	.8	.8	.8	.8	.8
Replace one hose, **ADD:**	.4	.4	.4	.4	.4	.4	.4	.4	.4	.4

(THIS SCHEDULE CONTINUED ON NEXT PAGE.)

182 FORD/LINCOLN/MERCURY

AIR CONDITIONING SYSTEM, MAJOR SERVICE Continued

Approximate parts cost:
Compressor $85.00	Expansion valve $35.00
Compressor repair kit 15.00	Hose, per ft. 2.75
Compressor oil pump seal 9.00	Hose fittings, each. 1.00
Condenser 120.00	Evaporator coil 110.00
Evaporator core 100.00	Freon, per 14 oz. can 2.50
Suction throttling valve 40.00	Anti-freeze, per gal. 9.50

AIR CONDITIONING SYSTEM BLOWER MOTOR OR CONTROLS, SERVICE

Includes:
Basic Jobs: Performance-test system to determine defective part, R&R component, and test system following installation.

MODEL	1966	1967	1968	1969	1970	1971	1972	1973	1974	1975
Basic Jobs:										
R&R blower mtr., test system after installation.										
Ford, Merc. Meteor, T-Bird, Mark IV	2.1	2.1	2.1	2.1	2.1	2.1	1.7	1.7	1.7	1.7
Pinto, Bobcat	—	—	—	—	—	1.8	1.8	1.8	1.8	1.8
Mustang II	—	—	—	—	—	—	—	—	2.0	2.0
All others	1.6	1.6	1.6	1.6	1.6	1.6	1.6	1.6	1.4	1.4
R&R blower motor switch, test system	1.8	1.8	1.8	1.8	1.8	1.8	1.8	1.8	1.8	1.8
R&R compr. clutch switch, test system	1.4	1.4	1.4	1.4	1.4	1.4	1.3	1.3	1.3	1.3
R&R evap. thermostatic switch, test system	1.4	1.4	1.4	1.4	1.4	1.4	1.4	1.4	1.4	1.4
R&R control unit, test system after installation	1.4	1.4	1.4	1.4	1.4	1.4	1.4	1.4	1.4	1.4

Approximate parts cost:
Blower motor $30.00	Compressor clutch switch $10.00
Blower motor switch 3.50	Evaporator thermostatic switch 15.00

OLDSMOBILE 183

SERVICE STATION MAINTENANCE

Includes:

Basic Job: Lubricate chassis, drain oil, change filters, repack front wheel bearings, repack U-joints, and lubricate front end. Check fluid levels of battery, radiator, air conditioner, brake master cylinder, power steering reservoir, transmission, and differential. Check condition of hoses and drive belts. Lubricate miscellaneous moving parts, latches, hinges, etc.

Related Jobs: Service individual systems or components. See detailed description of work included for each job in separate major section.

Additions to Basic or Related Jobs: Allowances for special equipment installed.

MODEL	1966	1967	1968	1969	1970	1971	1972	1973	1974	1975
Basic Job:										
General lubrication & system check,										
L-6 engine	1.0	1.0	1.0	1.0	1.0	1.0	—	1.0	1.1	1.1
V-6 engine	—	—	—	—	—	—	—	—	—	1.3
V-8 engine	1.4	1.4	1.4	1.4	1.4	1.4	1.4	1.4	1.5	1.5
With air conditioning, **ADD:**	.3	.3	.3	.3	.3	.3	.3	.3	.3	.3
With AIR pump, **ADD:**	.2	.2	.2	.2	.2	.2	.2	.2	.2	.2
With disc brakes, **ADD:**	—	.9	.9	.9	.9	.9	.9	.9	.9	.9
Related Jobs:										
Service Battery										
Clean, test, & fill	.3	.3	.3	.3	.3	.3	.3	.3	.3	.3
Replace ground cable	.2	.2	.2	.2	.2	.2	.2	.2	.2	.2
Replace starter cable	.3	.3	.3	.3	.3	.3	.3	.3	.3	.3
Replace battery	.4	.4	.4	.4	.4	.4	.4	.4	.4	.4
Service Cooling System										
Back-flush, fill, & pressure-test system	.9	.9	.9	.9	.9	.9	.9	.9	.9	.9
Replace upper hose	.4	.4	.4	.4	.4	.4	.4	.4	.4	.4
Replace lower hose	.5	.5	.5	.5	.5	.5	.5	.5	.5	.5
Replace both hoses	.7	.7	.7	.7	.7	.7	.7	.7	.7	.7
Replace thermostat & pressure-test system	.6	.6	.6	.6	.6	.6	.6	.6	.6	.6
Replace water pump drive belt & adjust tension	.4	.4	.4	.4	.4	.4	.4	.4	.4	.4
Replace water pump, pressure-test system,										
L-6 engine	1.0	1.0	1.0	1.0	1.0	1.0	—	1.0	1.0	1.0
V-6 or V-8 engine	1.3	1.3	1.3	1.3	1.3	1.3	1.3	1.3	1.3	1.3
With air conditioning, **ADD:**	.2	.2	.2	.2	.2	.2	.2	.2	.2	.2
With power steering, **ADD:**	.2	.2	.2	.2	.2	.2	.2	.2	.2	.2
With AIR, **ADD:**	.2	.2	.2	.2	.2	.2	.2	.2	.2	.2
Service Ignition System										
Adjust & install spark plugs,										
6-cylinder	.6	.6	.6	.6	.6	.6	—	.6	.6	.6
V-8 engine	.8	.8	.8	.8	.8	.8	.8	.8	.8	.8
With air conditioning, **ADD:**	.3	.3	.3	.3	.3	.3	.3	.3	.3	.3
With AIR, **ADD:**	.3	.3	.3	.3	.3	.3	.3	.3	.3	.3
Replace points and condenser & adjust ignition timing,										
6-cylinder	.5	.5	.5	.5	.5	.5	—	—	—	—
V-8 engine	.7	.7	.7	.7	.7	.7	.7	—	—	—
Replace distributor cap,										
6-cylinder, **ADD:**	.3	.3	.3	.3	.3	.3	—	.3	.3	.3
V-8 engine, **ADD:**	.4	.4	.4	.4	.4	.4	.4	.4	.4	.4
Check reluctor air gap, & adjust ignition timing	—	—	—	—	—	—	—	.5	.5	.5
Replace ignition coil	.4	.4	.4	.4	.4	.4	.4	.4	.4	.4
Replace spark plug wires,										
L-6 or V-6 engine	.6	.6	.6	.6	.6	.6	—	.6	.6	.6
V-8 engine	.8	.8	.8	.8	.8	.8	.8	.8	.8	.8
With air conditioning, **ADD:**	.3	.3	.3	.3	.3	.3	.3	.3	.3	.3

184 OLDSMOBILE

SERVICE STATION MAINTENANCE Continued

MODEL	1966	1967	1968	1969	1970	1971	1972	1973	1974	1975
Perform Minor Tune-up										
L-6 engine	1.5	1.5	1.5	1.5	1.9	1.9	—	2.2	2.2	2.4
V-6 engine	—	—	—	—	—	—	—	—	—	2.7
V-8 engine	2.7	2.7	2.7	2.7	2.9	2.9	2.9	2.9	2.9	3.0
V-8, small block, w/4-bbl. carb., **ADD:**	.2	.2	.2	.2	.2	.3	.3	.3	.3	.3
With AIR pump, **ADD:**	.3	.3	.3	.3	.3	.3	.3	.3	.3	.3
With air conditioning, **ADD:**	.6	.6	.6	.6	.6	.6	.6	.6	.6	.6
Note: See minor tune-up section for work included and additions.										
Perform Major Tune-up										
L-6 engine	5.3	5.3	5.3	5.3	5.3	5.4	—	5.4	5.4	5.5
V-6 engine	—	—	—	—	—	—	—	—	—	6.3
V-8, small block	6.0	6.0	6.0	6.0	6.0	6.2	6.2	6.5	6.5	6.7
V-8, large block	6.6	6.6	6.6	6.8	6.8	6.8	6.8	7.0	7.0	7.2
With AIR pump, **ADD:**	.7	.7	.7	.7	.7	.7	.7	.7	.7	.7
V-8, small block, w/4-bbl. carb., **ADD:**	1.0	1.0	1.0	1.0	1.0	1.0	1.1	1.1	1.1	1.1
With air conditioning, **ADD:**	.6	.6	.6	.6	.6	.6	.6	.6	.6	.6
Note: See major tune-up section for work included and additions.										
Service Fuel System										
Adjust carburetor idle mixture & speed,										
Single barrel	.4	.4	.4	.4	.4	.4	.4	.4	.4	.4
Two or four-barrel	.6	.6	.6	.6	.6	.6	.6	.6	.6	.6
Replace fuel filter	.3	.3	.3	.3	.3	.3	.3	.3	.3	.3
Replace fuel pump,										
L-6 engine	.5	.5	.5	.5	.5	.5	—	.5	.5	.5
V-6 engine	—	—	—	—	—	—	—	—	—	.9
V-8 engine	.7	.7	.7	.7	.7	.7	.8	.8	.8	.8
With air conditioning, **ADD:**	.2	.2	.2	.2	.2	.2	.2	.2	.2	.2
Replace flexible fuel line	.3	.3	.3	.3	.3	.3	.3	.3	.3	.3
Service Driveshaft										
R&R driveshaft & overhaul both U-joints,										
Cross & roller joints	1.5	1.5	1.5	1.5	1.5	1.5	1.5	1.5	1.5	1.5
Constant velocity joints	1.8	1.8	1.8	1.8	1.8	1.8	1.8	1.8	1.8	1.8
Service Hydraulic Brake System										
Adjust drum brakes, (4 wheels)	.5	.5	.5	.5	.5	.5	.5	.5	.5	—
Replace drum brake shoes, 4 wheels, incl. bleed system	3.5	3.5	3.5	3.5	3.5	3.5	3.5	3.5	3.5	—
Bleed hydraulic system, 4 wheels	.6	.6	.6	.6	.6	.6	.6	.6	.6	—
Replace front disc brake pads & rear brake linings, incl. bleed system	3.3	3.3	3.3	3.3	3.3	3.3	3.3	3.3	3.3	3.3
Overhaul master cylinder	1.3	1.3	1.5	1.5	1.5	1.5	1.8	1.8	1.8	1.8
Overhaul wheel cylinders, drum brakes (4)	4.1	4.1	4.1	4.1	4.1	4.1	4.2	4.2	4.2	—
Overhaul front calipers, incl. turn rotors	5.3	5.3	5.3	5.3	4.6	4.6	4.6	4.6	4.6	4.6
Service Parking Brakes										
Adjust parking brakes	.4	.4	.4	.4	.4	.4	.4	.4	.4	.4
Replace forward cable	.7	.7	.7	.7	.7	.7	.7	.7	.7	.7
Replace center cable	.4	.4	.4	.4	.4	.4	.4	.4	.4	.4
Replace rear cable, one side	.6	.6	.6	.6	.6	.6	.6	.6	.6	.6
Replace rear cable, both sides	1.0	1.0	1.0	1.0	1.0	1.0	1.0	1.0	1.0	1.0
Service Suspension System										
Replace front shock absorber, both sides	.9	.9	.9	.9	.9	.9	.9	.9	.9	.9
Replace rear shock absorber, both sides	.8	.8	.8	.8	.8	.8	.8	.8	.8	.8
Replace rear leaf spring & shim to align pinion angle	1.6	1.6	1.6	1.6	1.8	1.8	1.8	1.7	1.7	1.7
Replace shackle and bushings; eye bolt and bushings	.7	.7	.7	.7	.7	.7	.7	.7	.7	.7

(THIS SCHEDULE CONTINUED ON NEXT PAGE.)

OLDSMOBILE

SERVICE STATION MAINTENANCE Continued

MODEL	1966	1967	1968	1969	1970	1971	1972	1973	1974	1975
Service Front End & Steering System										
Adjust toe-in only	.4	.4	.4	.4	.4	.4	.4	.4	.4	.4
Replace tie-rods or tie-rod ends, (4)	1.4	1.4	1.4	1.4	1.4	1.4	1.4	1.4	1.4	1.4
Replace Pitman arm, incl. adjust toe-in	.8	.8	.8	.8	.8	.8	.8	.8	.8	.8
Replace steering idler arm or bushing, incl. adjust toe-in	.7	.7	.7	.7	.7	.7	.7	.7	.7	.7
Replace power steering pump drive belt	.3	.3	.3	.3	.3	.3	.3	.3	.3	.3
With air conditioning, **ADD:**	.2	.2	.2	.2	.2	.2	.2	.2	.2	.2
Check & replenish reservoir fluid	.2	.2	.2	.2	.2	.2	.2	.2	.2	.2
Replace pressure hoses, either set, incl. adjust drive belt,										
L-6 engine	.3	.3	.3	.3	.3	.3	—	.3	.3	.3
V-6 or V-8 engine	.6	.6	.6	.6	.6	.6	.6	.6	.6	.6
Balance four wheels on car,										
Drum brakes	1.2	1.2	1.2	1.2	1.2	1.2	1.2	1.2	1.2	1.2
Disc/drum brakes	1.5	1.5	1.5	1.5	1.5	1.5	1.5	1.5	1.5	1.5
Rotate five wheels	.6	.6	.6	.6	.6	.6	.6	.6	.6	.6
Service Charging System										
Test system and/or adjust regulator	.6	.6	.6	.6	.6	.6	.6	.4	.4	.4
R&R alternator, incl. pulley	.6	.6	.6	.6	.7	.7	.7	.7	.7	.7
With air conditioning, **ADD:**	.1	.1	.1	.1	.1	.1	.1	.1	.1	.1
With AIR, **ADD:**	.2	.2	.2	.2	.2	.2	.2	.2	.2	.2
Overhaul alternator after removal	2.3	2.3	1.5	1.5	1.5	1.5	1.5	1.5	1.5	1.5
Test & replace regulator	.3	.3	.3	.3	.4	.4	.4	—	—	—
Service Cranking System										
R&R starter,										
L-6 engine	.7	.7	.7	.7	.7	.8	—	.8	.8	.8
V-6 engine	—	—	—	—	—	—	—	—	—	1.3
V-8 engine	.9	.9	.9	.9	.9	.9	1.1	1.1	1.1	1.1
Overhaul starter after removal	1.7	1.7	1.7	1.7	1.7	1.7	1.7	1.7	1.7	1.7
Replace starter-battery cable	.3	.3	.3	.3	.3	.3	.3	.3	.3	.3
Replace starter solenoid, incl. system test,										
L-6 engine	1.7	1.7	1.7	1.7	1.7	1.7	—	1.7	1.7	1.7
V-6 engine	—	—	—	—	—	—	—	—	—	1.8
V-8 engine	1.9	1.9	1.9	1.9	2.4	2.4	2.3	2.0	2.0	2.0
Replace starter/neutral switch & adjust,										
With column shift	.4	.4	.4	.4	.4	.4	.4	.4	.4	.4
With floor shift	.6	.6	.6	.6	.6	.6	.6	.6	.6	.6
Service Lighting System										
Adjust two headlights	.4	.4	.4	.4	.4	.4	.4	.4	.4	.4
Adjust four headlights	.6	.6	.6	.6	.6	.6	.6	.6	.6	.6
Replace sealed beam unit, ea.	.3	.3	.3	.3	.3	.3	.3	.3	.3	.3
Replace foot dimmer switch	.3	.3	.3	.3	.3	.3	.3	.3	.3	.3
Replace headlamp vacuum motor, one side	.8	.8	.8	—	—	—	—	—	—	—
Replace signal/hazard flasher	.2	.2	.2	.2	.2	.2	.2	.2	.2	.2
Replace turn signal/hazard switch,										
With standard column	1.2	1.2	1.2	1.0	1.0	1.0	1.0	1.0	1.0	1.0
With tilt or telescopic column	1.5	1.5	1.5	1.3	1.3	1.3	1.3	1.3	1.3	1.3
Replace back-up light switch	.4	.4	.4	.4	.4	.4	.4	.4	.4	.4
Replace stoplight switch	.3	.3	.3	.3	.3	.3	.3	.3	.3	.3

186 OLDSMOBILE

TUNE-UP, MINOR

Includes:

Basic Job: Perform the following work:
1. Service air cleaner element.
2. Replace PVC valve.
3. Replace crankcase ventilation filter in air cleaner.
4. Clean battery terminals.
5. Check condition and tension of all drive belts.
6. Check all hoses and hose connections.
7. Check operation of heated air system (air cleaner), manifold heat valve (EFE valve since 1975), and automatic choke. Service where necessary.
8. Replace fuel filter.
9. Perform compression test.
10. Replace spark plugs.
11. Replace ignition points and condenser.
12. Check dwell or reluctor air gap and adjust ignition timing.
13. Adjust carburetor idle mixture and speed.
14. Make necessary ignition and carburetor adjustments to obtain satisfactory exhaust system analyzer readings.

Additions to Basic Job: Allowances for special equipment and carburetor

MODEL	1966	1967	1968	1969	1970	1971	1972	1973	1974	1975
Basic Job:										
Perform minor tune-up,										
L-6 engine	1.5	1.5	1.5	1.5	1.9	1.9	—	2.2	2.2	2.4
V-6 engine	—	—	—	—	—	—	—	—	—	2.7
V-8 engine	2.7	2.7	2.7	2.7	2.9	2.9	2.9	2.9	2.9	3.0
Additions to Basic Job:										
With 4-bbl. carb. (V-8 small block only), ADD:	.2	.2	.2	.2	.2	.2	.3	.3	.3	.3
With AIR pump, ADD:	.3	.3	.3	.3	.3	.3	.3	.3	.3	.3
With air conditioning, ADD:	.6	.6	.6	.6	.6	.6	.6	.6	.6	.6

Approximate parts cost:

Spark plugs, each	$1.50
Points & condenser	5.00
PCV valve	3.00
Air cleaner element	$5.50
Fuel filter	3.50

TUNE-UP, MAJOR

Includes:

Basic Job: Perform the following work:
1. Service air cleaner element.
2. Replace crankcase ventilation filter in air cleaner.
3. Replace PCV valve.
4. Check drive belts and adjust for proper tension.
5. Check all hoses and hose connections.
6. Clean battery terminals.
7. Check operation of manifold heat valve (EFE valve since 1975) and automatic choke. Service where necessary.
8. Check operation of heated-air system.
9. Check exhaust and evaporative emission control systems for proper operation.
10. Replace fuel filter.
11. Perform compression check.
12. Replace spark plugs.
13. Replace ignition points and condenser.
14. Check dwell or reluctor air gap and adjust ignition timing.
15. Check distributor cap and rotor.
16. Tighten cylinder head bolts.
17. Adjust valve lash (where applicable).
18. Overhaul carburetor(s).
19. Adjust carburetor(s) idle mixture and speed.
20. Make necessary ignition and carburetor adjustments to obtain satisfactory exhaust system analyzer readings.

Additions to Basic Job: Allowances for special equipment and carburetor.

MODEL	1966	1967	1968	1969	1970	1971	1972	1973	1974	1975
Basic Job:										
Perform major tune-up,										
L-6 engine	5.3	5.3	5.3	5.3	5.3	5.4	—	5.4	5.4	5.5
V-6 engine	—	—	—	—	—	—	—	—	—	6.3
V-8, small block	6.0	6.0	6.0	6.0	6.0	6.2	6.2	6.5	6.5	6.7
V-8, large block	6.6	6.6	6.6	6.8	6.8	6.8	6.8	7.0	7.0	7.2

(THIS SCHEDULE CONTINUED ON NEXT PAGE.)

OLDSMOBILE 187

TUNE-UP, MAJOR Continued

MODEL	1966	1967	1968	1969	1970	1971	1972	1973	1974	1975
Additions to Basic Job:										
With AIR pump, ADD:	.7	.7	.7	.7	.7	.7	.7	.7	.7	.7
Replace hydraulic valve lifter, one, ADD:	2.0	2.0	2.0	2.0	2.0	2.0	2.0	2.0	2.0	2.0
With 4-bbl. carb. (V-8 small block only), ADD:	1.0	1.0	1.0	1.0	1.0	1.0	1.1	1.1	1.1	1.1
With air conditioning, ADD:	.6	.6	.6	.6	.6	.6	.6	.6	.6	.6

Approximate parts cost:

Spark plugs, each	$1.50	Fuel filter	$ 3.50
Points & condenser	5.00	Carburetor repair kit, ea.	10.00-20.00
PCV valve	3.00	Ignition coil	14.00
Air cleaner element	5.50	HEI coil	25.00

EMISSION CONTROL SYSTEMS, TESTS FOR SMOG STATION CERTIFICATION

Includes:

Basic Job: Test crankcase, exhaust and evaporative emission control systems. Check heated-air system. Check HC/CO level with exhaust analyzer. Sign certification certificate. (No adjustments or repairs included in basic job.)

Related Jobs: Service any defective emission control system. Perform minor or major tune-up as required.

Additions to Related Jobs: Service or replace defective part(s) in the system. Allowances for special equipment installed and carburetor.

MODEL	1966	1967	1968	1969	1970	1971	1972	1973	1974	1975
Basic Job:										
Test all systems & sign certificate,										
6-cylinder	.5	.5	.5	.5	.5	.8	—	.8	.9	.9
V-8 engine	1.0	1.0	1.0	1.0	1.0	1.0	1.3	1.3	1.3	1.4
Related Jobs:										
Service crankcase emission control system	.3	.3	.3	.3	.3	.3	.3	.3	.3	.3
Service evaporative emission control system	—	—	—	—	.4	.4	.4	.4	.4	.4
Exhaust emission control systems,										
Service heated-air system	—	—	—	.3	.3	.3	.3	.3	.3	.3
Service transmission controlled spark (TCS/SCS)	—	—	—	—	.5	.5	.5	.5	.5	.5
Service EGR system	—	—	—	—	—	—	.4	.4	.4	.4
Service air injection (AIR) system	.5	.5	.5	.5	.5	.5	.5	.5	.5	.5
Replace catalytic converter pellets	—	—	—	—	—	—	—	—	—	1.0

Note: See separate section for replacement of components in each system.

	1966	1967	1968	1969	1970	1971	1972	1973	1974	1975
Perform minor tune-up,										
L-6 engine	1.5	1.5	1.5	1.5	1.9	1.9	—	2.2	2.2	2.4
V-6 engine	—	—	—	—	—	—	—	—	—	2.7
V-8 engine	2.7	2.7	2.7	2.7	2.9	2.9	2.9	2.9	2.9	3.0
Perform major tune-up,										
L-6 engine	5.3	5.3	5.3	5.3	5.3	5.4	—	5.4	5.4	5.5
V-6 engine	—	—	—	—	—	—	—	—	—	6.3
V-8, small block	6.0	6.0	6.0	6.0	6.0	6.2	6.2	6.5	6.5	6.7
V-8, large block	6.6	6.6	6.6	6.8	6.8	6.8	6.8	7.0	7.0	7.2
Additions to Related Jobs:										
Minor Tune-up										
With 4-bbl. carb. (V-8 small block only), ADD:	.2	.2	.2	.2	.2	.3	.3	.3	.3	.3
Major Tune-up										
With 4-bbl. carb. (V-8 small block only), ADD:	1.0	1.0	1.0	1.0	1.0	1.0	1.1	1.1	1.1	1.1
With AIR pump, ADD:	.3	.3	.3	.3	.3	.3	.3	.3	.3	.3
With air conditioning, ADD:	.6	.6	.6	.6	.6	.6	.6	.6	.6	.6

Approximate parts cost:

Catalytic converter pellets .... $70.00   See minor or major tune-up section for cost of tune-up parts.

188 OLDSMOBILE

EMISSION CONTROL SYSTEMS, COMPLETE TEST OR SERVICE

Includes:

Basic Job: Make all necessary tests and repairs. Sign certification certificate.

1. Replace PCV valve, check all vacuum passageways and hoses.
2. Replace crankcase ventilation filter in air cleaner.
3. Test purge-control valve, gas tank filler cap, vent lines, and hoses for leakage.
4. Replace evaporation canister filter.
5. Clean EGR valve and test the control system.
6. Check transmission control spark (TCS or CEC) system.
7. Check operation of manifold heat valve (or EFE valve since 1975) and automatic choke. Free-up where necessary.
8. Check and adjust tension of drive belts.
9. Check operation of heated-air system.
10. Check AIR air pump flow.
11. Check routing and condition of hoses.
12. Check operation of diverter or bypass valve.
13. Check AIR manifold and hoses.
14. Replace catalytic converter or pellets, if necessary.
15. Determine if engine tune-up is required.

Related Jobs: Minor or major tune-up as required.

MODEL	1966	1967	1968	1969	1970	1971	1972	1973	1974	1975
Basic Job:										
Perform emission control system tune-up,										
6-cylinder	.8	.8	.8	.8	2.8	3.3	—	3.3	3.5	3.5
V-8 engine	.8	.8	.8	.8	3.8	3.8	3.8	3.8	3.8	4.0
Additions to Basic Job:										
With AIR, all models, **ADD**:	.5	.5	.5	.5	.5	.5	.5	.5	.5	.5
Replace catalytic converter pellets, **ADD**:	—	—	—	—	—	—	—	—	—	1.0
Related Jobs:										
Perform minor tune-up,										
L-6 engine	1.5	1.5	1.5	1.5	1.9	1.9	—	2.2	2.2	2.4
V-6 engine	—	—	—	—	—	—	—	—	—	2.7
V-8 engine	2.7	2.7	2.7	2.7	2.9	2.9	2.9	2.9	2.9	3.0
Perform major tune-up,										
L-6 engine	5.3	5.3	5.3	5.3	5.3	5.4	—	5.4	5.4	5.5
V-6 engine	—	—	—	—	—	—	—	—	—	6.3
V-8, small block	6.0	6.0	6.0	6.0	6.0	6.2	6.2	6.5	6.5	6.7
V-8, large block	6.6	6.6	6.6	6.8	6.8	6.8	6.8	7.0	7.0	7.2
Additions to Related Jobs:										
Minor Tune-up										
With 4-bbl. carb. (V-8 small block only), **ADD**:	.3	.3	.3	.3	.3	.3	.3	.3	.3	.3
Major Tune-up										
With 4-bbl. carb. (V-8 small block only), **ADD**:	1.0	1.0	1.0	1.0	1.0	1.0	1.1	1.1	1.1	1.1

Approximate parts cost:

Catalytic converter pellets	$70.00
PCV valve	3.00
Hose, per ft.	0.75
Canister filter	1.00
Purge control valve	4.00
Drive belt	$ 3.00
Diverter valve	12.00
Air pump	50.00
Catalytic converter	175.00

See minor or major tune-up section for cost of tune-up parts.

OLDSMOBILE

AIR INJECTION REACTOR (AIR) SYSTEM, TEST AND SERVICE

Includes:
Basic Job: Test AIR air pump flow, check routing and condition of hoses, determine operation of diverter valve, verify check valve operation, inspect air manifold and hoses. Check and adjust drive belt tension.
Additions to Basic Job: Replace defective parts. Replace drive belt, includes adjust tension. Replacement of hose(s), includes soapy water test.

MODEL	1966	1967	1968	1969	1970	1971	1972	1973	1974	1975
Basic Job:										
Test AIR system, all models	.5	.5	.5	.5	.5	.5	.5	.5	.5	.5
Additions to Basic Job:										
Replace and adjust drive belt,										
6-cylinder, **ADD:**	.4	.4	.4	.4	.4	.4	.4	.4	.4	.4
V-6 or V-8 engine, **ADD:**	.5	.5	.5	.5	.5	.5	.5	.5	.5	.5
Replace AIR pump,										
6-cylinder, **ADD:**	.5	.5	.5	.5	.5	.5	.5	.5	.5	.5
V-8 engine, **ADD:**	.7	.7	.7	.7	.7	.7	.7	.7	.7	.7
Replace diverter valve, all models, **ADD:**	.4	.4	.4	.4	.4	.4	.4	.4	.4	.4
Replace check valve assembly, **ADD:**	.3	.3	.3	.3	.3	.3	.3	.3	.3	.3
Replace hose, incl. soapy water test, **ADD:**	.4	.4	.4	.4	.4	.4	.4	.4	.4	.4

Approximate parts cost:
Drive belt ..... $ 3.00
Air pump 50.00
Check valve 7.00
Diverter valve $12.00
Hose, per ft. 0.75

TRANSMISSION CONTROLLED SPARK (TCS) SYSTEM, TEST AND SERVICE

Includes:
Basic Job: Check engine speed in gear using tachometer and timing light, test TCS solenoid or CEC valve, and transmission switch.
Additions to Basic Job: Replace defective parts.

MODEL	1966	1967	1968	1969	1970	1971	1972	1973	1974	1975
Basic Job:										
Test TCS system, all models	—	—	—	—	.6	.5	.5	.5	.5	—
Additions to Basic Job:										
Replace TCS or CEC solenoid, **ADD:**	—	—	—	—	.3	.3	.3	.3	.3	—
Adjust CEC valve, **ADD:**	—	—	—	—	—	.2	.2	.2	.2	—
Replace TCS switch,										
With standard transmission, **ADD:**	—	—	—	—	.4	.4	.4	.4	.4	—
With THM 400 transmission, **ADD:**	—	—	—	—	.8	.8	.8	.8	.8	—
All other automatic transmissions, **ADD:**	—	—	—	—	.5	.5	.5	.5	.5	—
Replace TCS relay, **ADD:**	—	—	—	—	.2	.2	.2	.2	.2	—
Replace thermostatic vacuum switch or TCS temperature switch, **ADD:**	—	—	—	—	.3	.3	.3	.3	.3	.3
Replace idle stop solenoid, **ADD:**	—	—	—	—	.3	.3	.3	.3	.3	.3

Approximate parts cost:
TCS switch $5.00
Thermostatic vacuum switch 6.50
TCS relay 2.50
TCS solenoid $11.50
Idle stop solenoid 11.00
CEC solenoid 12.00

190 OLDSMOBILE

POSITIVE CRANKCASE VENTILATION (PCV) SYSTEM, TEST AND SERVICE

Includes:
Basic Job: Test PCV valve, check all vacuum passageways, and inspect hoses. Clean or replace air filter.
Additions to Basic Job: Replace defective parts. (Do not attempt to clean PCV valve, replace if valve is not free.)

MODEL	1966	1967	1968	1969	1970	1971	1972	1973	1974	1975
Basic Job:										
Test PCV system, all models	.3	.3	.3	.3	.3	.3	.3	.3	.3	.3
Additions to Basic Job:										
Replace PCV valve, **ADD:**	.3	.3	.3	.3	.3	.3	.3	.3	.3	.3
Replace all hoses, **ADD:**	.6	.6	.6	.6	.6	.6	.6	.6	.6	.6

Approximate parts cost:
PCV valve .... $3.00   Hose, per ft. $0.75

EVAPORATIVE EMISSION CONTROL SYSTEM, TEST AND SERVICE

Includes:
Basic Job: Test purge control valve, gas tank filler cap, vent lines, and hoses.
Additions to Basic Job: Replace defective part.

MODEL	1966	1967	1968	1969	1970	1971	1972	1973	1974	1975
Basic Job:										
Test evap. emission control system	—	—	—	—	.4	.4	.4	.4	.4	.4
Additions to Basic Job:										
Replace purge control valve, **ADD:**	—	—	—	—	.5	.5	.5	—	—	—
Replace charcoal canister filter, **ADD:**	—	—	—	—	.3	.3	.3	.3	.3	.3
Replace charcoal canister, **ADD:**	—	—	—	—	.5	.5	.5	.5	.5	.5
Replace hose, each, **ADD:**	—	—	—	—	.2	.2	.2	.2	.2	.2

Approximate parts cost:
Purge control valve .... $4.00   Hose, per ft. $0.75
Canister filter .... 1.50   Charcoal canister 32.00

EXHAUST-GAS RECIRCULATION (EGR), TEST AND SERVICE

Includes:
Basic Job: Test EGR valve, control system, and engine idling condition.
Additions to Basic Job: Replace defective parts. Test & repair thermostatic control system.

MODEL	1966	1967	1968	1969	1970	1971	1972	1973	1974	1975
Basic Job:										
Test EGR system, all models	—	—	—	—	—	—	.4	.4	.4	.4
Additions to Basic Job:										
Service EGR valve, **ADD:**	—	—	—	—	—	—	.7	.7	.7	.7
Replace EGR valve, **ADD:**	—	—	—	—	—	—	.4	.4	.4	.4
Test & repair thermo. control sys., **ADD:**	—	—	—	—	—	—	.6	.6	.6	.6

Approximate parts cost:
EGR valve .... $10.00   Thermal vacuum switch $12.00

OLDSMOBILE

HEATED-AIR SYSTEM, TEST AND SERVICE

Includes:
  Basic Job: Check heated-air door, temperature sensor, and vacuum motor.
  Additions to Basic Job: Replace defective parts.

MODEL	1966	1967	1968	1969	1970	1971	1972	1973	1974	1975
Basic Job:										
Test heated-air system	—	—	—	.3	.3	.3	.3	.3	.3	.3
Additions to Basic Job:										
Replace vacuum motor, **ADD:**	—	—	—	.4	.4	.4	.4	.4	.4	.4
Replace temperature sensor, **ADD:**	—	—	—	.5	.5	.5	.5	.5	.5	.5

Approximate parts cost:
Vacuum motor assembly .... $5.00   Temperature sensor $4.50

IGNITION SYSTEM, SERVICE

Includes:
  Basic Jobs: 1. Adjust and install new spark plugs.
  2. Replace points and condenser, adjust dwell and ignition timing.
  3. R&R distributor, overhaul and test centrifugal and vacuum advances, set dwell or check reluctor air gap and ignition timing.
  Related Jobs: Replace additional defective part(s) as required.
  Additions: Allowances for special equipment installed or replacement of associated defective part(s).

MODEL	1966	1967	1968	1969	1970	1971	1972	1973	1974	1975
Basic Job #1										
Adjust & install new spark plugs,										
6-cylinder	.6	.6	.6	.6	.6	.6	—	.6	.6	.6
V-8 engine	.8	.8	.8	.8	.8	.8	.8	.8	.8	.8
With air conditioning, **ADD:**	.3	.3	.3	.3	.3	.3	.3	.3	.3	.3
With AIR, **ADD:**	.3	.3	.3	.3	.3	.3	.3	.3	.3	.3
Basic Job #2										
Replace points and condenser & adjust ignition timing,										
6-cylinder	.5	.5	.5	.5	.5	.5	—	—	—	—
V-8 engine	.7	.7	.7	.7	.7	.7	.7	—	—	—
Replace distributor cap,										
6-cylinder, **ADD:**	.3	.3	.3	.3	.3	.3	—	.3	.3	.3
V-8 engine, **ADD:**	.4	.4	.4	.4	.4	.4	.4	.4	.4	.4
Check reluctor air gap & adjust ignition timing	—	—	—	—	—	—	.5	.5	.5	.5
Basic Job #3										
R&R and overhaul distributor & adjust ignition timing,										
All models	1.4	1.4	1.4	1.4	1.4	1.4	1.4	1.4	1.4	1.4
Replace vacuum advance unit, **ADD:**	.2	.2	.2	.2	.2	.2	.2	.2	.2	.2
Related Jobs:										
Replace ignition coil	.4	.4	.4	.4	.4	.4	.4	.4	.4	.4
Replace spark plug wires,										
L-6 or V-6 engine	.6	.6	.6	.6	.6	.6	—	.6	.6	.6
V-8 engine	.8	.8	.8	.8	.8	.8	.8	.8	.8	.8
With air conditioning, **ADD:**	.3	.3	.3	.3	.3	.3	.3	.3	.3	.3
Replace ignition switch, all models	.6	.6	.6	.6	.6	.6	.6	.6	.6	.6
Replace ign. sw. lock cyl. or buzzer sw.	—	—	—	.4	.4	.7	.7	.7	.7	.7
Change code tumblers, **ADD:**	.2	.2	.2	.2	.2	.2	.2	.2	.2	.2

(THIS SCHEDULE CONTINUED ON NEXT PAGE.)

OLDSMOBILE

IGNITION SYSTEM, SERVICE Continued

Approximate parts cost:

Spark plugs, each	$ 1.50
Point set	3.00
Condenser	1.50
Distributor cap	4.50
Distributor parts	10.00
Ignition switch	7.00
Vacuum control unit	$ 4.00
Ignition coil	12.50
HEI ignition coil	25.00
Spark plug wires, 4-cylinder	6.00
6-cylinder	7.00
V-8 engine	10.00-17.00

CRANKING SYSTEM, TEST AND SERVICE

Includes:
Basic Job: Test battery and cranking system. Clean battery cable terminals.
Related Jobs: Replace defective part(s), including test when necessary.

MODEL	1966	1967	1968	1969	1970	1971	1972	1973	1974	1975
Basic Job:										
Test cranking system	.5	.5	.5	.5	.5	.5	.5	.5	.5	.5
Related Jobs:										
R&R starter,										
L-6 engine	.7	.7	.7	.7	.7	.8	—	.8	.8	.8
V-6 engine	—	—	—	—	—	—	—	—	—	1.3
V-8 engine	.9	.9	.9	.9	.9	.9	1.1	1.1	1.1	1.1
Overhaul starter after removal	1.7	1.7	1.7	1.7	1.7	1.7	1.7	1.7	1.7	1.7
Replace starter-battery cable	.3	.3	.3	.3	.3	.3	.3	.3	.3	.3
Replace starter solenoid, incl. system test,										
L-6 engine	1.7	1.7	1.7	1.7	1.7	1.7	—	1.7	1.7	1.7
V-6 engine	—	—	—	—	—	—	—	—	—	1.8
V-8 engine	1.9	1.9	1.9	1.9	2.4	2.4	2.3	2.0	2.0	2.0
Replace starter/neutral switch & adjust,										
With column shift	.4	.4	.4	.4	.4	.4	.4	.4	.4	.4
With floor shift	.6	.6	.6	.6	.6	.6	.6	.6	.6	.6

Approximate parts cost:

Starter, new	$80.00
Starter, rebuilt w/o solenoid	30.00
Starter-battery cable	4.50-8.50
Solenoid switch	$4.00-10.00
Starter/neutral switch	4.00

CHARGING SYSTEM, TEST AND SERVICE

Includes:
Basic Job: Test battery voltage and gravity, clean battery cable terminals, test alternator output, test and/or adjust regulator.
Related Jobs: Replace or overhaul defective component.

MODEL	1966	1967	1968	1969	1970	1971	1972	1973	1974	1975
Basic Job:										
Test system and/or adjust regulator	.6	.6	.6	.6	.6	.6	.6	.4	.4	.4
Related Jobs:										
R&R alternator incl. pulley	.6	.6	.6	.6	.7	.7	.7	.7	.7	.7
With air conditioning, **ADD:**	.1	.1	.1	.1	.1	.1	.1	.1	.1	.1
With AIR, **ADD:**	.2	.2	.2	.2	.2	.2	.2	.2	.2	.2
Overhaul alternator after removal	2.3	2.3	1.5	1.5	1.5	1.5	1.5	1.5	1.5	1.5
Test & replace regulator	.3	.3	.3	.3	.4	.4	.4	—	—	—

Approximate parts cost:

Alternator, new	$75.00-80.00
Alternator, rebuilt	35.00
Regulator	$13.00-27.00

OLDSMOBILE

FUEL SYSTEM, ADJUST AND SERVICE

Includes:
Basic Job: Adjust idle mixture and speed for performance and to obtain satisfactory exhaust system analyzer readings.
Related Jobs: R&R carburetor, overhaul carburetor, R&R associated fuel components.

MODEL	1966	1967	1968	1969	1970	1971	1972	1973	1974	1975
Basic Job:										
Adjust carburetor idle mixture & speed,										
Single barrel	.4	.4	.4	.4	.4	.4	.4	.4	.4	.4
Two or four barrel	.6	.6	.6	.6	.6	.6	.6	.6	.6	.6
Related Jobs:										
Replace carb. incl. complete adjustments,										
Single or two-barrel	.6	.6	.5	.5	.7	.7	.7	.7	.7	.7
Four-barrel	1.0	1.0	1.0	1.0	1.0	1.0	1.0	1.0	1.0	1.0
O/H carb., incl. R&R and complete adjustments,										
Single or two-barrel	2.6	2.6	2.6	2.5	2.7	2.2	2.4	2.4	2.4	2.4
Four-barrel	4.0	4.0	4.0	4.0	3.2	3.2	3.2	3.2	3.4	3.4
Test & replace fuel pump,										
L-6 engine	.5	.5	.5	.5	.5	.5	—	.5	.5	.5
V-6 engine	—	—	—	—	—	—	—	—	—	.9
V-8 engine	.7	.7	.7	.7	.7	.7	.8	.8	.8	.8
Replace fuel filter	.3	.3	.3	.3	.3	.3	.3	.3	.3	.3
Replace fuel tank sending unit, incl. R&R tank,										
Station wagon	1.4	1.4	1.4	1.4	1.4	1.4	1.4	1.4	1.4	1.4
All others	.9	.8	.8	.8	.8	.9	.9	.9	1.0	1.0
Replace dashboard fuel gauge,										
Omega	—	—	—	—	—	—	—	1.4	1.4	1.4
All others	.6	.6	.6	.6	.6	.6	.6	1.0	1.0	1.0
Replace fuel tank,										
Station wagon	1.5	1.5	1.5	1.5	1.5	1.5	1.5	1.5	1.5	1.5
Omega	—	—	—	—	—	—	—	1.0	1.0	1.0
All others	1.6	1.6	1.6	1.6	1.6	1.6	1.6	1.4	1.4	1.4
Replace flexible fuel line	.3	.3	.3	.3	.3	.3	.3	.3	.3	.3

Approximate parts cost:
Carburetor repair kit, ea. $10.00-20.00
Carburetor, new, ea., single-bbl. 40.00
  Two-bbl. 75.00
    Four-bbl. 110.00
Carburetor, rebuilt, single-bbl. 15.00
  Two-bbl. 22.00
    Four-bbl. 40.00

Fuel pump $15.00
Fuel tank sending unit 13.00-24.00
Fuel gauge, dash 9.00-14.00
Flexible fuel line, per ft. 0.50
Fuel tank 50.00-65.00

ENGINE OVERHAUL, IN-CAR

Includes:
Basic Job: Remove ring ridge, deglaze cylinder walls, fit piston pins, align connecting rods, install new piston rings and rod bearings, install new main bearing inserts and oil seals, overhaul oil pump, clean carbon, grind valves, and perform major tune-up.
Additions to Basic Job: Associated work that is required during basic job and allowances for special equipment.

MODEL	1966	1967	1968	1969	1970	1971	1972	1973	1974	1975
Basic Job:										
Overhaul engine,										
L-6 engine	—	—	—	—	22.0	22.0	—	22.5	22.5	22.5
V-6 engine	—	—	—	—	—	—	—	—	—	25.0
V-8, small block	27.3	27.3	27.3	27.3	27.3	27.5	27.5	27.8	27.8	27.9
V-8, large block	29.0	29.0	29.0	29.2	29.2	29.2	29.2	29.4	29.4	29.6

Note: L-6, 1966-69 & V-8 Toronado, overhaul not performed in-car.

(THIS SCHEDULE CONTINUED ON NEXT PAGE.)

OLDSMOBILE

ENGINE OVERHAUL, IN-CAR Continued

MODEL	1966	1967	1968	1969	1970	1971	1972	1973	1974	1975
Additions to Basic Job:										
Rebore cylinders,										
6-cylinder, **ADD**:	—	—	—	—	4.0	4.0	—	4.0	4.0	4.0
V-8 engine, **ADD**:	5.0	5.0	5.0	5.0	5.0	5.0	5.0	5.0	5.0	5.0
Expand pistons,										
6-cylinder, **ADD**:	—	—	—	—	1.8	1.8	—	1.8	1.8	1.8
V-8 engine, **ADD**:	2.4	2.4	2.4	2.4	2.4	2.4	2.4	2.4	2.4	2.4
Regroove top piston ring groove,										
6-cylinder, **ADD**:	—	—	—	—	1.8	1.8	—	1.8	1.8	1.8
V-8 engine, **ADD**:	2.4	2.4	2.4	2.4	2.4	2.4	2.4	2.4	2.4	2.4
Replace hydraulic valve lifters, **ADD**:	1.0	1.0	1.0	1.0	1.0	1.0	1.0	1.0	1.0	1.0
Replace rocker arm stud, each, **ADD**:	.3	.3	.3	.3	.3	.3	.3	.3	.3	.3
Overhaul rocker arm mechanism, **ADD**:	1.5	1.5	1.5	1.5	1.5	1.5	1.5	1.5	1.5	1.5
Ream valve guides oversize,										
6-cylinder, **ADD**:	—	—	—	—	.7	.7	—	.7	.7	.7
V-8 engine, **ADD**:	.9	.9	.9	.9	.9	.9	.9	.9	.9	.9
With AIR pump, **ADD**:	.7	.7	.7	.7	.7	.7	.7	.7	.7	.7
With air conditioning, **ADD**:	.7	.7	.7	.7	.7	.7	.7	.7	.7	.7
With 4-bbl. carb. (V-8 small block only), **ADD**:	1.0	1.0	1.0	1.0	1.0	1.0	1.0	1.0	1.0	1.0

Approximate parts cost:

Hydraulic valve lifters, ea.	$ 4.00
Major tune-up parts	20.00-35.00
Carburetor repair kit	10.00-20.00
Rod bearing inserts, 6-cylinder	24.00
8-cylinder	32.00
Rear main brg. oil seal set	3.00
Complete gasket set, L-6 engine	24.00
V-6 engine	28.00
V-8 engine	30.00
Main bearing inserts, L-6 engine	$ 27.00
V-6 engine	20.00
V-8 engine	22.00
Piston rings, complete set, 6-cylinder	27.00
8-cylinder	36.00
Piston pins, set, 6-cylinder	12.00
8-cylinder	16.00
Piston assemblies, set, 6-cylinder	85.00
8-cylinder	128.00

ENGINE OVERHAUL, OUT-OF-CAR

Includes:

Basic Job: R&R engine, remove ring ridge, rebore or hone cylinder walls, regrind crankshaft and camshaft, replace camshaft bushings and line ream, replace timing chain and gears and oil seal, install main bearing inserts and seals, install piston pins, align connecting rods, install new piston rings and rod bearings, overhaul oil pump, clean carbon, grind valves, overhaul rocker arm mechanism, and perform major tune-up.

Additions to Basic Job: Associated work that is required during basic job and allowances for special equipment installed.

MODEL	1966	1967	1968	1969	1970	1971	1972	1973	1974	1975
Basic Job:										
Overhaul engine,										
L-6 engine	35.2	35.2	35.2	35.2	35.2	35.3	—	35.3	35.3	35.4
V-6 engine	—	—	—	—	—	—	—	—	—	38.5
V-8, small block	41.8	41.8	41.8	41.8	41.8	42.0	42.0	42.3	42.3	42.5
V-8, large block	42.3	42.3	42.3	42.5	42.5	42.5	42.5	42.7	42.7	42.9
V-8, Toronado	42.8	42.8	42.8	42.8	43.0	43.0	43.0	43.3	43.3	43.5
Additions to Basic Job:										
Regroove top piston ring groove,										
6-cylinder, **ADD**:	1.8	1.8	1.8	1.8	1.8	1.8	—	1.8	1.8	1.8
V-8 engine, **ADD**:	2.4	2.4	2.4	2.4	2.4	2.4	2.4	2.4	2.4	2.4
Replace rocker arm stud, ea., **ADD**:	.3	.3	.3	.3	.3	.3	.3	.3	.3	.3
Ream valve guides oversize,										
6-cylinder, **ADD**:	.7	.7	.7	.7	.7	.7	—	.7	.7	.7
V-8 engine, **ADD**:	.9	.9	.9	.9	.9	.9	.9	.9	.9	.9

(THIS SCHEDULE CONTINUED ON NEXT PAGE.)

OLDSMOBILE 195

ENGINE OVERHAUL, OUT-OF-CAR Continued

MODEL	1966	1967	1968	1969	1970	1971	1972	1973	1974	1975
Additions to Basic Job Continued										
Replace all engine mounts, **ADD**:	.6	.6	.6	.6	.6	.6	.6	.6	.6	.6
Replace worn clutch parts, **ADD**:	.5	.5	.5	.5	.5	.5	.5	.5	.5	.5
With AIR pump, **ADD**:	.7	.7	.7	.7	.7	.7	.7	.7	.7	.7
With air conditioning, incl. charge system, **ADD**:	1.8	1.8	1.8	1.8	1.8	1.8	1.8	1.8	1.8	1.8

Approximate parts cost:

Complete gasket set, L-6 engine	$ 24.00
V-6 engine	28.00
V-8 engine	30.00
Hydraulic valve lifters, ea.	4.00
Piston rings, complete set, 6-cylinder	27.00
8-cylinder	36.00
Piston pins, 6-cylinder	12.00
8-cylinder	16.00
Piston assemblies, 6-cylinder	85.00
8-cylinder	128.00
Carburetor repair kit	10.00-20.00
Major tune-up parts	20.00-35.00
Rod bearing inserts, 6-cylinder	$24.00
8-cylinder	32.00
Rear main bearing oil seal set	3.00
Main bearing inserts, V-6 engine	20.00
L-6 engine	27.00
V-8 engine	22.00
Engine mounts	7.00
Pressure plate	30.00-60.00
Clutch disc	21.00-48.00
Clutch release bearing	5.00-15.00
Pilot bearing	1.50

SHORT BLOCK, REPLACE

Includes:

Basic Job: R&R engine, clean and reface valves, scrape carbon, grind valve seats, replace valve seals, overhaul rocker arm mechanism, transfer all parts, and perform major tune-up.

Additions to Basic Job: Associated work that is required during basic job and allowances for special equipment installed and/or carburetor.

MODEL	1966	1967	1968	1969	1970	1971	1972	1973	1974	1975
Basic Job:										
Replace short block,										
L-6 engine	15.5	15.5	15.5	15.5	15.5	15.6	—	15.6	15.6	15.7
V-6 engine	—	—	—	—	—	—	—	—	—	17.5
V-8, small block	20.2	20.2	20.2	20.2	20.2	19.5	19.5	19.5	19.5	19.7
V-8, large block	20.7	20.7	20.7	20.7	20.7	18.5	18.5	18.5	18.5	18.7
V-8, Toronado	25.0	25.0	25.0	25.0	25.0	22.0	22.0	22.2	22.2	22.4
Additions to Basic Job:										
Ream valve guides oversize,										
6-cylinder, **ADD**:	.7	.7	.7	.7	.7	.7	—	.7	.7	.7
V-8 engine, **ADD**:	.9	.9	.9	.9	.9	.9	.9	.9	.9	.9
Replace rocker arm stud, ea., **ADD**:	.3	.3	.3	.3	.3	.3	.3	.3	.3	.3
Replace all engine mounts, **ADD**:	.6	.6	.6	.6	.6	.6	.6	.6	.6	.6
Replace worn clutch parts, **ADD**:	.5	.5	.5	.5	.5	.5	.5	.5	.5	.5
With AIR pump, **ADD**:	.7	.7	.7	.7	.7	.7	.7	.7	.7	.7
With air conditioning, incl. charge system, **ADD**:	1.8	1.8	1.8	1.8	1.8	1.8	1.8	1.8	1.8	1.8
With 4-bbl. carb. (V-8 small block only), **ADD**:	1.0	1.0	1.0	1.0	1.0	1.0	1.0	1.0	1.0	1.0

Approximate parts cost:

Complete gasket set, L-6 engine	$24.00
V-6 engine	28.00
V-8 engine	30.00
Engine mounts, front or rear	7.00
Oil and air filters	9.00
Short block: Call supplier for price quote.	
Pressure plate	$30.00-60.00
Clutch disc	21.00-40.00
Clutch release bearing	5.00-15.00
Carburetor repair kit	10.00-20.00
Pilot bearing	1.50

OLDSMOBILE

TIMING CHAIN MECHANISM, SERVICE

Includes:
Basic Job #1 L-6 engines: Replace camshaft gear, cover gasket, oil seal, and minor tune-up.
    #2 V-6 and V-8 engines: Replace timing cover oil seal, timing chain, and minor tune-up.
Additions to Basic Job: Associated work required during basic job and allowances for special equipment installed.

MODEL	1966	1967	1968	1969	1970	1971	1972	1973	1974	1975
Basic Job #1										
Replace camshaft gear, cover gasket, oil seal & minor tune-up,										
L-6 engine	7.5	7.5	7.5	7.5	7.9	6.7	—	7.0	7.0	7.2
Additions to Basic Job #1										
Replace crankshaft gear, ADD:	.2	.2	.2	.2	.2	.2	—	.2	.2	.2
With air conditioning, ADD:	.2	.2	.2	.2	.2	.2	—	.2	.2	.2
With power steering, ADD:	.2	.2	.2	.2	.2	.2	—	.2	.2	.2
With AIR, ADD:	.3	.3	.3	.3	.3	.3	—	.3	.3	.3
With manual transmission, ADD:	.6	.6	.6	.6	.6	.6	—	.6	.6	.6
Basic Job #2										
Replace timing cover oil seal, timing chain, and minor tune-up,										
V-6 engine	—	—	—	—	—	—	—	—	—	5.0
V-8, Toronado	8.0	8.0	8.0	8.0	8.2	8.2	8.2	8.2	8.2	8.3
V-8, all others	5.3	5.3	5.3	5.3	5.5	5.5	5.5	5.5	5.5	5.6
Additions to Basic Job #2										
Replace crankshaft sprocket, ADD:	.2	.2	.2	.2	.2	.2	.2	.2	.2	.2
With air conditioning, ADD:	.5	.5	.5	.5	.5	.5	.5	.5	.5	.5
With AIR, ADD:	.2	.2	.2	.2	.2	.2	.2	.2	.2	.2
With power steering, ADD:	.2	.2	.2	.2	.2	.2	.2	.2	.2	.2

Approximate parts cost:

Timing cover gasket	$ 1.00	Crankshaft gear	$ 6.00
Timing cover oil seal	2.00	Camshaft sprocket	6.00
Timing chain	9.00	Crankshaft sprocket	4.50
Camshaft gear	14.00	Minor tune-up parts	25.00-30.00

OIL PUMP, SERVICE

Includes:
Basic Job: R&R oil pan, service oil pump, and replace oil filter element.
Additions to Basic Job: Allowances for associated work that is required during basic job.

MODEL	1966	1967	1968	1969	1970	1971	1972	1973	1974	1975
Basic Job:										
Service oil pump, and replace oil filter element,										
L-6 engine	*4.1	*4.1	*4.1	*4.1	2.2	2.2	—	2.2	2.2	2.2
With manual transmission, ADD:	.6	.6	.6	.6	—	—	—	—	—	—
With air conditioning, ADD:	.3	.3	.3	.3	—	—	—	—	—	—
With power steering, ADD:	.2	.2	.2	.2	—	—	—	—	—	—
V-6 engine	—	—	—	—	—	—	—	—	—	1.0
V-8, small block	2.0	2.0	2.0	2.0	2.0	2.2	2.2	2.2	2.2	2.2
V-8, large block	2.4	2.4	2.4	2.4	2.4	2.6	2.6	2.6	2.6	2.6
V-8, Toronado	*5.0	*5.0	*5.0	*5.0	*5.0	*5.0	*5.0	*5.0	*5.0	*5.0
With air conditioning, ADD:	.4	.4	.4	.4	.4	.4	.4	.4	.4	.4
With Cruise Control, ADD:	.2	.2	.2	.2	.2	.2	.2	.2	.2	.2

*Includes R&R engine.

(THIS SCHEDULE CONTINUED ON NEXT PAGE.)

OLDSMOBILE

OIL PUMP, SERVICE Continued

MODEL	1966	1967	1968	1969	1970	1971	1972	1973	1974	1975
Additions to Basic Job:										
Overhaul oil pump, **ADD:**	.8	.8	.8	.8	.8	.8	.8	.8	.8	.8
Replace rear main bearing inserts & seals,										
L-6 engine, **ADD:**	.3	.3	.3	.3	.5	.5	.5	.5	.5	.5
V-6 engine, **ADD:**	—	—	—	—	—	—	—	—	—	.4
V-8 engine, **ADD:**	.6	.6	.6	.6	.6	.6	.6	.6	.6	.6
Use Plastigage, repl. addl.										
main bearing inserts, ea. pair, **ADD:**	.6	.6	.6	.6	.6	.6	.6	.6	.6	.6

Approximate parts cost:

Oil pan $25.00	Oil pump screen .... $ 2.50
Oil pan gasket 4.00	Oil filter element 5.00
Oil pump shaft & rotor kit 8.00	Oil pump 18.00-24.00

BEARINGS, MAIN AND/OR RODS, REPLACE

Includes:

   Basic Job: R&R oil pan, measure connecting rod bearing oil clearance with Plastigage, install new connecting rod bearing inserts, and oil filter element.

   Additions to Basic Job: Measure main bearing oil clearance with Plastigage, replace all main bearing inserts and rear main bearing oil seals, repair or replace oil pump.

MODEL	1966	1967	1968	1969	1970	1971	1972	1973	1974	1975
Basic Job:										
R&R pan, use Plastigage, install rod inserts & filter element,										
L-6 engine	*6.1	*6.1	*6.1	*6.1	4.2	4.2	—	4.2	4.2	4.2
With manual transmission, **ADD:**	.6	.6	.6	.6	—	—	—	—	—	—
With air conditioning, **ADD:**	.3	.3	.3	.3	—	—	—	—	—	—
With power steering, **ADD:**	.2	.2	.2	.2	—	—	—	—	—	—
V-6 engine	—	—	—	—	—	—	—	—	—	3.6
V-8, small block	4.9	4.9	4.9	4.9	4.9	5.1	5.1	5.1	5.1	5.1
V-8, large block	5.3	5.3	5.3	5.3	5.3	5.5	5.5	5.5	5.5	5.5
V-8, Toronado	*7.9	*7.9	*7.9	*7.9	*7.9	*7.9	*7.9	*7.9	*7.9	*7.9
With air conditioning, **ADD:**	.4	.4	.4	.4	.4	.4	.4	.4	.4	.4
With Cruise Control, **ADD:**	.2	.2	.2	.2	.2	.2	.2	.2	.2	.2
*Includes R&R engine.										
Additions to Basic Job:										
Use Plastigage — all main bearings,										
L-6 engine, **ADD:**	.7	.7	.7	.7	.7	.7	—	.7	.7	.7
V-6 engine, **ADD:**	—	—	—	—	—	—	—	—	—	.4
V-8 engine, **ADD:**	.5	.5	.5	.5	.5	.5	.5	.5	.5	.5
Replace main bearing inserts & rear oil seals,										
L-6 engine, **ADD:**	3.5	3.5	3.5	3.5	3.5	3.5	—	3.5	3.5	3.5
V-6 engine, **ADD:**	—	—	—	—	—	—	—	—	—	2.0
V-8 engine, **ADD:**	2.5	2.5	2.5	2.5	2.5	2.5	2.5	2.5	2.5	2.5

Approximate parts cost:

Rod bearing inserts, 6-cylinder $24.00	Oil pan gasket .... $ 4.00
8-cylinder 32.00	Oil filter element 5.00
Rear main bearing oil seal set 3.00	Oil pump 18.00-24.00
Main bearing inserts, L-6 engine 27.00	Oil pump shaft & rotor kit 8.00
V-6 engine 20.00	
V-8 engine 22.00	

198 OLDSMOBILE

VALVE MECHANISM, SERVICE

Includes:
Adjustment and Tune-up: Adjust valve lash and perform minor tune-up.
Basic Job: Clean and reface valves, scrape carbon, grind valve seats, replace valve seals, adjust valves, and perform major tune-up.
Additions to Basic Job: Associated work required during basic job and allowances for special equipment installed.

MODEL	1966	1967	1968	1969	1970	1971	1972	1973	1974	1975
Adjustment & tune-up:										
L-6 engine	2.5	2.5	2.5	2.5	2.9	2.9	—	3.1	3.1	3.3
Basic Job:										
Service valve mechanism,										
L-6 engine	10.6	10.6	10.6	10.6	11.0	11.0	—	11.3	11.3	11.4
V-6 engine	—	—	—	—	—	—	—	—	—	14.0
V-8, small block	14.8	14.8	14.8	14.8	15.0	15.0	15.0	15.0	15.0	15.1
V-8, large block	17.2	17.2	17.2	17.2	16.0	16.0	16.0	16.0	16.2	16.3
Additions to Basic Job:										
Ream valve guides oversize,										
6-cylinder, **ADD:**	.7	.7	.7	.7	.7	.7	—	.7	.7	.7
V-8 engine, **ADD:**	.9	.9	.9	.9	.9	.9	.9	.9	.9	.9
Replace rocker arm stud, ea., **ADD:**	.3	.3	.3	.3	.3	.3	.3	.3	.3	.3
Overhaul rocker arm mechanism, **ADD:**	1.5	1.5	1.5	1.5	1.5	1.5	1.5	1.5	1.5	1.5
Replace hydraulic valve lifters, **ADD:**	1.0	1.0	1.0	1.0	1.0	1.0	1.0	1.0	1.0	1.0
With 4-bbl. carb. (V-8 small block only), **ADD:**	1.0	1.0	1.0	1.0	1.0	1.0	1.0	1.0	1.0	1.0
With air conditioning, **ADD:**	.6	.6	.6	.6	.6	.6	.6	.6	.6	.6
With AIR pump, **ADD:**	.7	.7	.7	.7	.7	.7	.7	.7	.7	.7

Approximate parts cost:
Valve grind gasket set, L-6 engine	$10.00
V-6 engine	18.00
V-8 engine	20.00
Minor tune-up parts	25.00-30.00
Hydraulic valve lifters, ea.	$4.00
Valve spring, ea.	2.00
Major tune-up parts	30.00-35.00

CYLINDER HEAD AND/OR GASKET, REPLACE

Includes:
Basic Jobs: 1. R&R intake manifold and cylinder head to install new gasket. Clean head and block surfaces and perform minor tune-up.
2. Install new cylinder head, including recondition valves and perform minor tune-up.
Additions to Basic Job: Allowances for special equipment and/or carburetor.

MODEL	1966	1967	1968	1969	1970	1971	1972	1973	1974	1975
Basic Job #1										
Replace head gasket, (one head), minor tune-up,										
L-6 engine	4.3	4.3	4.3	4.3	4.7	4.7	—	4.7	4.7	4.9
V-6 engine	—	—	—	—	—	—	—	—	—	5.2
V-8, small block	6.1	6.1	6.1	6.1	6.3	6.3	6.3	6.3	6.3	6.4
V-8, large block	7.6	7.6	7.6	7.6	7.8	7.8	7.8	7.8	7.8	7.9
Basic Job #2										
Replace one cylinder head,										
L-6 engine	6.5	6.5	6.5	6.5	6.5	6.5	—	6.7	6.7	6.8
V-6 engine	—	—	—	—	—	—	—	—	—	6.5
V-8, small block	7.5	7.5	7.5	7.5	7.7	7.7	7.7	7.7	7.7	7.8
V-8, large block	9.0	9.0	9.0	9.0	9.2	9.2	9.2	9.2	9.2	9.3

(THIS SCHEDULE CONTINUED ON NEXT PAGE.)

OLDSMOBILE

CYLINDER HEAD AND/OR GASKET, REPLACE Continued

MODEL	1966	1967	1968	1969	1970	1971	1972	1973	1974	1975
Additions to Basic Jobs:										
Recondition second head, V-type engines,										
V-6, **ADD**:	—	—	—	—	—	—	—	—	—	1.8
V-8, small block, **ADD**:	2.0	2.0	2.0	2.0	2.0	2.0	2.2	2.2	2.2	2.2
V-8, large block, **ADD**:	2.5	2.5	2.5	2.5	2.5	2.5	2.7	2.7	2.7	2.7
V-8 small block with 4-bbl. carb., **ADD**:	.2	.2	.2	.2	.2	.2	.2	.2	.2	.2
With AIR, **ADD**:	.3	.3	.3	.3	.3	.3	.3	.3	.3	.3
With air conditioning, **ADD**:	.5	.5	.5	.5	.5	.5	.5	.5	.5	.5
With power steering, left side, **ADD**:	.3	.3	.3	.3	.3	.3	.3	.3	.3	.3

Approximate parts cost:

Head gasket, ea. .... $ 4.00	Valve grind gasket set, L-6 engine $10.00
Cylinder head, L-6 engine 95.00	V-6 engine 18.00
V-6 engine, ea. 90.00	V-8 engine 20.00
V-8 engine, ea. 75.00-95.00	Minor tune-up parts 25.00-30.00

EXHAUST SYSTEM, TEST AND SERVICE

Includes:

  Basic Job: Test exhaust system for leaks and/or exhaust odors. Use HC/CO exhaust analyzer to trace carbon monoxide leaks.
  Related Jobs: Replace defective parts. Each job includes basic job tests and installation of new hangers as required.

MODEL	1966	1967	1968	1969	1970	1971	1972	1973	1974	1975
Basic Job:										
Complete test of exhaust system	.4	.4	.4	.4	.4	.4	.4	.4	.4	.4
Related Jobs:										
Replace muffler,										
Front, single or dual, one	1.3	1.3	1.3	1.3	1.3	1.3	1.3	1.3	1.3	1.3
Rear, single or dual, one	1.2	1.2	1.2	1.2	1.2	1.2	1.2	1.2	1.2	1.2
One side, single or dual, two	1.8	1.8	1.8	1.8	1.8	1.8	1.8	1.8	1.8	1.8
One each side, dual, two	1.9	1.9	1.9	1.9	1.9	1.9	1.9	1.9	1.9	1.9
Replace tail pipe,										
Single or dual, one	1.1	1.1	1.1	1.1	1.1	1.1	1.1	1.1	1.1	1.1
Dual, two	1.4	1.4	1.4	1.4	1.4	1.4	1.4	1.4	1.4	1.4
Replace exhaust pipe flange gasket, ea.	1.0	1.0	1.0	1.0	1.0	1.0	1.0	1.0	1.0	1.0
Replace exhaust manifold gasket,										
L-6 engine	2.0	2.0	2.0	2.0	2.0	2.9	—	2.9	2.9	2.9
Free-up or O/H heat control or EFE valve,										
L-6 engine	1.5	1.5	1.5	1.5	1.5	1.5	—	1.5	1.5	1.6
V-6 engine	—	—	—	—	—	—	—	—	—	1.7
V-8 engine	1.8	1.8	1.8	1.8	1.8	1.8	1.8	1.8	1.8	1.9
Test & replace Early Fuel Evaporation (EFE) valve	—	—	—	—	—	—	—	—	—	.6
Replace exhaust pipe,										
L-6 engine	1.3	1.3	1.3	1.3	1.3	1.3	—	1.3	1.3	1.3
V-6 or V-8 single exhaust	1.4	1.4	1.4	1.4	1.4	1.4	1.4	1.4	1.4	1.4
V-8 dual exhaust, one pipe	1.2	1.2	1.2	1.2	1.2	1.2	1.2	1.2	1.2	1.2
V-8 dual exhaust, both pipes	2.0	2.0	2.0	2.0	2.0	2.0	2.0	2.0	2.0	2.0
Replace catalytic converter pellets	—	—	—	—	—	—	—	—	—	1.0
Replace catalytic converter	—	—	—	—	—	—	—	—	—	1.8

Approximate parts cost:

Muffler $28.00	Catalytic converter pellets $70.00
Tail pipe, ea. 12.00	Catalytic converter 175.00
Exhaust pipe, ea. 15.00	Heat control valve (through 1974) 12.00
Exhaust manifold gasket, L-6 .... 3.00	Early Fuel Evaporation (EFE) valve 30.00

200 OLDSMOBILE

COOLING SYSTEM, TEST AND SERVICE

Includes:
  Basic Job: Drain and back-flush system, check for leaks and tighten all hose connections, pressure-test radiator cap and system.
  Related Jobs: Replace defective part. Work performed independently of basic job.
  Additions to Related Jobs: Allowances for special equipment installed.

MODEL	1966	1967	1968	1969	1970	1971	1972	1973	1974	1975
Basic Job:										
Drain, flush, fill, and pressure-test system	.9	.9	.9	.9	.9	.9	.9	.9	.9	.9
Related Jobs:										
Replace upper hose	.4	.4	.4	.4	.4	.4	.4	.4	.4	.4
Replace lower hose	.5	.5	.5	.5	.5	.5	.5	.5	.5	.5
Replace both hoses	.7	.7	.7	.7	.7	.7	.7	.7	.7	.7
Replace thermostat & pressure-test system	.6	.6	.6	.6	.6	.6	.6	.6	.6	.6
Replace water pump drive belt & adjust tension	.4	.4	.4	.4	.4	.4	.4	.4	.4	.4
Replace water pump, pressure-test system,										
L-6 engine	1.0	1.0	1.0	1.0	1.0	1.0	—	1.0	1.0	1.0
V-6 or V-8 engine	1.3	1.3	1.3	1.3	1.3	1.3	1.3	1.3	1.3	1.3
With air conditioning, **ADD:**	.2	.2	.2	.2	.2	.2	.2	.2	.2	.2
With power steering, **ADD:**	.2	.2	.2	.2	.2	.2	.2	.2	.2	.2
With AIR, **ADD:**	.2	.2	.2	.2	.2	.2	.2	.2	.2	.2
Replace radiator, incl. pressure-test system,										
L-6 engine	.6	.6	.6	.6	.6	.6	—	.8	.8	.8
V-6 engine	—	—	—	—	—	—	—	—	—	1.1
V-8 engine	.8	.8	.8	.8	.8	.8	1.0	1.0	1.0	1.0
With automatic transmission, **ADD:**	.2	.2	.2	.2	.2	2	.2	.2	.2	.2
Replace water temp. gauge, engine	.4	.4	.4	.4	.4	4	.4	.4	.4	.4
With air conditioning, **ADD:**	.1	.1	.1	.1	.1	.1	.1	.1	.1	.1
Replace water temp. gauge, dash, Rally Pack units	.8	.8	.5	.5	.5	.5	.5	.5	.5	.5
Replace water jacket expansion plug,										
L-6 engine, head, ea.	.5	.5	.5	.5	.5	.5	—	.5	.5	.5
Block, rear	3.0	3.0	3.0	3.0	3.0	3.0	—	3.0	3.0	3.0
Block, side, front or rear	.7	.7	.7	.7	.7	.7	—	.7	.7	.7
Block side, center	1.1	1.1	1.1	1.1	1.1	1.1	—	1.1	1.1	1.1
V-8 engine, head, front	.5	.5	.5	.5	.5	.5	.5	.5	.5	.5
Side of block, ea.	1.2	1.2	1.2	1.2	1.2	1.2	1.2	1.2	1.2	1.2
Rear of block, auto. trans.	2.5	2.5	2.5	2.5	2.5	2.5	2.5	2.5	2.5	2.2
Rear of block, std. trans.	3.2	3.2	3.2	3.2	3.2	3.2	3.2	3.2	3.2	3.2

Approximate parts cost:

Radiator, new	$100.00-160.00
Upper or lower hose, ea.	5.00
Thermostat	4.00
Water pump, L-6 engine	20.00
V-6 or V-8 engine	40.00
Drive belt, ea.	$ 3.00
Temperature gauge, engine	4.00
Temperature gauge, dash	10.00
Expansion plug, ea.	1.50

CLUTCH MECHANISM, SERVICE

Includes:
  Adjust: Adjust clutch pedal play.
  Basic Job: Replace thrust bearing, pressure plate, and disc. Adjust clutch pedal play.
  Additions to Basic Job: Associated work that is required during basic job.

MODEL	1966	1967	1968	1969	1970	1971	1972	1973	1974	1975
Adjustment:										
Adjust clutch pedal play	.3	.3	.3	.3	.3	.3	.3	.3	.3	.3

(THIS SCHEDULE CONTINUED ON NEXT PAGE.)

OLDSMOBILE 201

CLUTCH MECHANISM, SERVICE Continued

MODEL	1966	1967	1968	1969	1970	1971	1972	1973	1974	1975
Basic Job:										
Replace thrust brg., pressure plate & disc,										
3-speed transmission	2.1	2.1	2.1	2.1	2.1	2.1	2.2	2.2	2.2	2.2
4-speed transmission	2.6	2.6	2.6	2.6	3.0	3.0	3.0	2.8	2.8	2.8
Additions to Basic Job:										
Remove, reface, and instl. flywheel, **ADD:**	1.8	1.8	1.8	1.8	1.8	1.8	1.8	1.8	1.8	1.8
Replace flywheel ring gear, **ADD:**	1.0	1.0	1.0	1.0	1.0	1.0	1.0	1.0	1.0	1.0
Resurface clutch pressure plate, **ADD:**	.8	.8	.8	.8	.8	.8	.8	.8	.8	.8
Replace flywheel bearing, **ADD:**	.2	.2	.2	.2	.2	.2	.2	.2	.2	.2
Replace clutch release (throwout) bearing, **ADD:**	.2	.2	.2	.2	.2	.2	.2	.2	.2	.2

Approximate parts cost:
Pressure plate $25.00-60.00
Clutch disc 20.00-35.00
Clutch release bearing 5.00-15.00
Pilot bearing .... $ 1.00
Flywheel w/ring gear 36.00-56.00

SHIFT LINKAGE, SERVICE

Includes:
  Adjust: Adjust manual transmission shift linkage.
  Basic Job: Replace one control rod and/or grommet and adjust linkage.
  Additions to Basic Job: Associated work that is required during basic job.

MODEL	1966	1967	1968	1969	1970	1971	1972	1973	1974	1975
Adjust shift linkage:										
3-speed transmission	.5	.5	.5	.5	.5	.5	.5	.5	.5	.5
4-speed transmission	.6	.6	.6	.6	.6	.6	.6	.6	.6	.6
Basic Job:										
Replace one rod and/or grommet & adjust,										
3-speed transmission	.8	.8	.8	.8	.8	.8	.8	.8	.8	.8
4-speed transmission	.9	.9	.9	.9	.9	.9	.9	.9	.9	.9
Additions to Basic Job:										
Replace additional rod, **ADD:**	.3	.3	.3	.3	.3	.3	.3	.3	.3	.3
Replace shift lever oil seals, both, **ADD:**	.5	.5	.5	.5	.5	.5	.5	.5	.5	.5

Approximate parts cost:
Shift rod, each $2.00
Rear oil seal 2.50
Shift lever oil seals $1.50

STANDARD TRANSMISSION, OVERHAUL

Includes:
  Basic Job: R&R transmission, disassemble, replace worn parts, and adjust linkage.
  Additions to Basic Job: Associated work that is required during basic job.

MODEL	1966	1967	1968	1969	1970	1971	1972	1973	1974	1975
Basic Job:										
R&R, overhaul transmission, and adjust linkage,										
3-speed transmission	5.4	5.4	5.4	5.4	5.4	5.4	5.4	5.4	5.4	5.4
4-speed transmission	6.9	6.9	6.9	6.9	6.9	6.9	6.9	6.9	6.9	6.9

(THIS SCHEDULE CONTINUED ON NEXT PAGE.)

202 OLDSMOBILE

STANDARD TRANSMISSION, OVERHAUL Continued

MODEL	1966	1967	1968	1969	1970	1971	1972	1973	1974	1975
Additions to Basic Job:										
Recondition transmission cover,										
3-speed trans., **ADD:**	.3	.3	.3	.3	.3	.3	.3	.3	.3	.3
4-speed trans., **ADD:**	.4	.4	.4	.4	.4	.4	.4	.4	.4	.4
Resurface clutch pressure plate, **ADD:**	.8	.8	.8	.8	.8	.8	.8	.8	.8	.8
R&R and resurface flywheel, **ADD:**	1.8	1.8	1.8	1.8	1.8	1.8	1.8	1.8	1.8	1.8
Replace flywheel ring gear, **ADD:**	1.0	1.0	1.0	1.0	1.0	1.0	1.0	1.0	1.0	1.0
Replace flywheel pilot bearing, **ADD:**	.2	.2	.2	.2	.2	.2	.2	.2	.2	.2
Replace clutch release (throwout) bearing, **ADD:**	.7	.7	.7	.7	.7	.7	.7	.7	.7	.7

Approximate parts cost:
Phone supplier for price quote on transmission parts required.
Gasket set .... $ 8.00
Clutch pressure plate 25.00-60.00
Speedometer gear .... $ 2.00
Pilot bearing 1.50
Clutch release bearing 5.00-15.00

AUTOMATIC TRANSMISSION, MAJOR SERVICE

Includes:
Basic Jobs:
1. R&R transmission. Overhaul transmission. Disassemble, clean, inspect and replace all worn parts as needed. Replace all oil seals. Adjust throttle and shift linkage as required. Flush converter and cooler lines. Perform pressure checks of mainline, throttle, and accumulator. Road test.
2. Replace torque converter. R&R transmission. Flush oil cooler and lines. Replace transmission oil and oil filter. Perform pressure checks of mainline, throttle, and accumulator. Adjust throttle and shift linkage as required.
3. Reseal transmission. R&R transmission. Replace all seals and gaskets. Replace transmission oil and oil filter. Check oil cooler for leaks. Perform pressure checks of mainline, throttle, and accumulator. Adjust throttle and shift linkage as required. Road test.

Additions to Basic Jobs: Associated work that is performed while the transmission is out during one of basic jobs.

MODEL	1966	1967	1968	1969	1970	1971	1972	1973	1974	1975
Basic Job #1										
Overhaul transmission,										
250/350 THM	8.0	8.0	8.0	8.0	8.0	8.0	8.0	8.7	8.7	8.7
375/400 THM	7.2	7.2	7.2	7.2	7.2	7.2	7.2	7.9	8.6	8.6
425 THM, Toronado	12.3	12.3	12.3	12.3	12.3	12.3	12.3	12.5	12.5	12.5
Basic Job #2										
Replace torque converter,										
250/350 THM	4.8	4.8	4.8	4.8	4.8	4.8	4.8	4.8	4.6	4.6
375/400 THM	4.4	4.4	4.4	4.4	4.4	4.4	4.4	4.6	4.6	4.6
425 THM, Toronado	6.1	6.1	6.1	6.1	6.3	6.3	6.3	6.3	6.3	6.3
Basic Job #3										
Reseal transmission,										
250/350 THM	6.3	6.3	6.3	6.3	6.3	6.3	6.3	6.8	6.8	6.8
375/400 THM	5.8	5.8	5.8	5.8	5.8	5.8	5.8	6.3	6.3	6.3
425 THM, Toronado	7.7	7.7	7.7	7.7	7.7	7.9	7.9	9.5	9.5	9.5
Additions to Basic Jobs:										
Replace oil cooler pipes, both, **ADD:**	.9	.9	.9	.9	.9	.9	.9	.9	.9	.9
Replace oil filler pipe and/or seal, **ADD:**	.5	.5	.5	.5	.5	.5	.5	.5	.5	.5
Replace torque converter ring gear, **ADD:**	.5	.5	.5	.5	.5	.5	.5	.5	.5	.5

Approximate parts cost:
Transmission seal and gasket kit $20.00
Transmission partial overhaul kit 60.00
Oil cooler pipe, each 9.00
Torque converter assembly 70.00-140.00
Torque converter ring gear 8.00
Oil filler pipe .... $ 4.00
Oil filler pipe seal 0.25
Oil pan 8.00
Oil pan gasket 1.00
Governor kit 19.00

OLDSMOBILE

AUTOMATIC TRANSMISSION, PERFORMANCE CHECK

Includes:
Basic Job: Conduct transmission performance check. Clean transmission case and operate unit to check case, oil cooler and oil cooler lines for external leaks. Remove oil pan, clean pan, screen or filter. Torque valve body mounting bolts. Adjust band/s where applicable. Adjust throttle and shift linkage. Perform pressure checks of mainline, throttle, and accumulator. Road test.

Related Jobs: Work which does not include R&R transmission and may be done as separate job.

MODEL	1966	1967	1968	1969	1970	1971	1972	1973	1974	1975
Basic Job:										
Complete transmission performance check	2.1	2.1	2.1	2.1	2.1	2.1	2.1	2.1	2.1	2.1
Related Jobs:										
Drain & fill trans., clean filter	.8	.8	.8	.8	.8	.8	.8	.8	.8	.8
Check for oil leaks	.7	.7	.7	.7	.7	.7	.7	.7	.7	.7
Replace oil pan gasket, incl. clean filter	.9	.9	.9	.9	.9	.9	.9	.9	.9	.9
Replace rear oil seal & O-ring	1.0	1.0	.7	.5	.5	.5	.5	.5	.5	.5
Replace neutral safety switch	.5	.5	.5	.5	.5	.5	.5	.5	.5	.5
Overhaul governor, includes complete trans. performance check,										
250/350 THM	3.1	3.1	3.1	3.1	3.1	3.1	3.1	3.1	2.9	2.9
375/400 THM	2.9	2.9	2.9	2.9	2.9	2.9	2.9	2.9	2.8	2.8
425 THM, Toronado	3.0	3.0	3.0	3.0	3.0	3.0	3.0	3.0	3.0	3.0
Overhaul valve body assembly	2.0	2.0	2.0	2.0	2.0	2.0	2.0	2.0	2.0	2.0
Adjust throttle and shift linkage	1.0	1.0	1.0	1.0	1.0	1.0	1.0	1.0	1.0	1.0
Adjust band/s where applicable	1.3	1.3	1.3	1.3	1.3	1.3	1.3	1.3	1.3	1.3

Approximate parts cost:
Transmission fluid, per qt.	$1.20
Oil pan gasket	1.00
Rear oil seal	4.50
Neutral safety switch	$ 3.50
Governor body repair kit	18.00
Valve body assy., new	80.00

AUTOMATIC TRANSMISSION, SHIFT AND LINKAGE CONTROLS, REPLACE AND ADJUST

Includes:
Replace and Adjust: Replace defective part and make necessary adjustments.

MODEL	1966	1967	1968	1969	1970	1971	1972	1973	1974	1975
Replace Part and Adjust:										
Replace control rod, carb. or trans. & adjust	.9	.9	.9	.9	.9	.9	.9	.9	.9	.9
Replace each additional rod, **ADD:**	.4	.4	.4	.4	.4	.4	.4	.4	.4	.4
Replace carb./throttle link, **ADD:**	.3	.3	.3	.3	.3	.3	.3	.3	.3	.3
Replace throttle control cable, **ADD:**	.5	.5	.5	.5	.5	.5	.5	.5	.5	.5
Replace front control rod, column shift, **ADD:**	.3	.3	.3	.3	.3	.3	.3	.3	.3	.3
Replace rear control rod or swivel, **ADD:**	.4	.4	.4	.4	.4	.4	.4	.4	.4	.4
Replace control torque shaft or bushings, **ADD:**	.6	.6	.6	.6	.6	.6	.6	.6	.6	.6
Replace shift control key lock assy.	.7	.7	.7	.7	.7	.7	.7	.7	.7	.7
Replace vacuum modulator hose & adjust linkage	.6	.6	.6	.6	.6	.6	.6	.6	.6	.6
Replace and adjust floor shift control assy.	.8	.8	.8	.8	.8	.8	.8	.8	.8	.8
With console equipped, **ADD:**	.5	.5	.5	.5	.5	.5	.5	.5	.5	.5

Approximate parts cost:
Linkage rod, ea.	$ 1.50
Control cable	8.00
Vacuum modulator	18.00
Modulator hose, per ft.	$ 0.25
Floor shift control assy.	40.00

OLDSMOBILE

REAR AXLE/FINAL DRIVE, SERVICE

Includes:
- **Basic Jobs:** 1. (Except Toronado) R&R driveshaft, R&R axle shafts, overhaul differential assembly. Measure and adjust U-joint and driveshaft angles. Balance driveshaft.
- 2. (Except Toronado) R&R driveshaft and replace pinion bearing oil seal. Check pinion bearing preload. Measure and adjust driveshaft angles. Balance driveshaft.
- **Related Jobs:** R&R axle shaft (one side) and/or bearing and seals. Replace axle shaft wheel mounting stud.
- **Basic Job:** 3. (Toronado) Replace final drive unit and related parts. **Note:** Final drive unit cannot be serviced but must be replaced as an assembly, with the exception of external seals. Jobs listed below in the schedule can be individually performed as indicated.
- **Related Work to Basic Job 3 (Toronado):** Service axle shafts, constant-velocity joints, and output shaft.

MODEL	1966	1967	1968	1969	1970	1971	1972	1973	1974	1975
Basic Job #1										
Overhaul differential assembly	5.5	5.5	5.5	5.5	5.5	5.5	5.5	5.5	5.5	5.5
With Posi-traction, **ADD:**	.6	.6	.6	.6	.6	.6	.6	.6	.6	.6
Basic Job #2										
Replace drive pinion bearing oil seal	1.2	1.2	1.2	1.7	1.7	1.7	1.7	1.7	1.7	1.7
Related Jobs:										
R&R axle shaft (one side), and/or bearing & seals	1.3	1.3	1.3	1.3	1.3	1.3	1.3	1.3	1.3	1.3
Replace axle shaft wheel mounting stud	.8	.8	.8	.8	.8	.8	.8	.8	.8	.8
Basic Job #3 (Toronado)										
R&R final drive unit. No service	3.0	3.0	3.0	3.0	3.0	3.0	3.0	3.0	3.0	3.0
Replace pinion brg. cover and/or O-ring seal, **ADD:**	.3	.3	.3	.3	.3	.3	.3	.3	.3	.3
Replace pinion bearing seal and/or vent pin seal, **ADD:**	.4	.4	.4	.4	.4	.4	.4	.4	.4	.4
Replace output shaft seal, **ADD:**	.2	.2	.2	.2	.2	.2	.2	.2	.2	.2
Replace final drive cover gasket, **ADD:**	.4	.4	.4	.4	.4	.4	.4	.4	.4	.4
Replace final drive chain, **ADD:**	.6	.6	.6	.6	.6	.6	.6	.6	.6	.6
Related Work to Basic Job #3 (Toronado)										
Replace axle shaft assemblies,										
Right axle	.7	.7	.7	.7	.7	.7	.7	.7	.7	.7
Left axle	1.1	1.1	1.1	1.1	1.1	1.1	1.1	1.1	1.1	1.1
Both axles	1.7	1.7	1.7	1.7	1.7	1.7	1.7	1.7	1.7	1.7
Repack or replace right or left outer C.V. joint, **ADD:**	.5	.5	.5	.5	.5	.5	.5	.5	.5	.5
Repack or replace right or left inner C.V. joint, **ADD:**	.8	.8	.8	.8	.8	.8	.8	.8	.8	.8
Repack or repl. both right or both left C.V. joints, **ADD:**	1.2	1.2	1.2	1.2	1.2	1.2	1.2	1.2	1.2	1.2
Replace output shaft,										
Right side	.5	.5	.5	.5	.5	.5	.5	.5	.5	.5
Left side	1.1	1.1	1.1	1.1	1.1	1.1	1.1	1.1	1.1	1.1
Both sides	1.5	1.5	1.5	1.5	1.5	1.5	1.5	1.5	1.5	1.5
Replace bearing or retainer on right shaft, **ADD:**	.3	.3	.3	.3	.3	.3	.3	.3	.3	.3
Replace output shaft seal,										
Right side	.6	.6	.6	.6	.6	.6	.6	.6	.6	.6
Left side	1.2	1.2	1.2	1.2	1.2	1.2	1.2	1.2	1.2	1.2

Approximate parts cost: (Except Toronado)
Axle shaft	$45.00
Inner or outer seal	2.00
Posi-traction repair kit	25.00
Pinion bearing oil seal	$ 3.00
Cover gasket	1.00
Ring & pinion gear set	100.00-125.00

Approximate parts cost: (Toronado)
Final drive housing	$130.00
Axle assy., w/shaft & joints	300.00
Pinion bearing O-ring	1.50
Output shaft seal	3.50
Output shaft bearing	17.00
Link belt & gear pkg.	220.00
Final drive cover gasket	$ 1.00
Right or left outer C.V. joint	160.00
Right or left inner C.V. joint	70.00
Right output shaft	74.00
Left output shaft	32.00

OLDSMOBILE

DRIVESHAFT, SERVICE

Includes:
Basic Job: R&R driveshaft and overhaul or replace front and rear U-joints.

MODEL	1966	1967	1968	1969	1970	1971	1972	1973	1974	1975
Basic Job:										
R&R driveshaft & overhaul both U-joints,										
Cross & roller joints	1.5	1.5	1.5	1.5	1.5	1.5	1.5	1.5	1.5	1.5
Constant velocity joint	1.8	1.8	1.8	1.8	1.8	1.8	1.8	1.8	1.8	1.8
R&R driveshaft with joints	1.1	1.1	1.1	1.1	1.1	1.1	1.1	1.1	1.1	1.1

Approximate parts cost:
U-joint package, cross & roller $11.00
Constant velocity joint kit 12.00
Driveshaft with joints (2) $120.00
Constant velocity joint 60.00

REAR SUSPENSION, SERVICE

Includes:
Service for the rear suspension system listed as individual jobs. Add times if more than one job is performed.

MODEL	1966	1967	1968	1969	1970	1971	1972	1973	1974	1975
Replace rear leaf spring & shim to align pinion angle	1.6	1.6	1.6	1.6	1.8	1.8	1.8	1.7	1.7	1.7
Replace coil spring	1.5	1.5	1.5	1.5	1.5	1.5	1.5	1.5	1.5	1.5
Replace control arm, incl. pinion angle adjustment,										
Upper arm, one	1.1	1.1	1.1	1.1	1.1	1.1	1.1	1.1	1.1	1.1
Lower arm, one	1.5	1.5	1.5	1.5	1.5	1.5	1.1	1.1	1.1	1.1
Replace shackle and bushings; eye bolt and bushings	.7	.7	.7	.7	.7	.7	.7	.7	.7	.7
Replace shock absorber, both sides	.8	.8	.8	.8	.8	.8	.8	.8	.8	.8
Replace tie rod & stabilizer shaft (one)	.9	.9	.9	.9	.9	.9	.9	.9	.9	.9

Approximate parts cost:
Shock absorber $14.00
Coil spring 26.00
Leaf spring 53.00
Shackle package .... $ 9.00
Shackle bushing package 1.00
Tie rod & stabilizer shaft 23.00

STEERING LINKAGE, SERVICE AND ADJUST

Includes:
Basic Job: Adjust toe-in.
Related Jobs: Replace defective parts and adjust toe-in.

MODEL	1966	1967	1968	1969	1970	1971	1972	1973	1974	1975
Basic Job:										
Adjust toe-in	.4	.4	.4	.4	.4	.4	.4	.4	.4	.4
Related Jobs:										
Replace tie-rods or tie-rod ends, (4)	1.4	1.4	1.4	1.4	1.4	1.4	1.4	1.4	1.4	1.4
Replace Pitman arm, includes adjust toe-in	.8	.8	.8	.8	.8	.8	.8	.8	.8	.8
Replace steering idler arm or bushing	.7	.7	.7	.7	.7	.7	.7	.7	.7	.7

Approximate parts cost:
Tie-rod end pkg. $10.00-15.00
Pitman arm 9.00
Idler arm $17.00
Tie rod 15.00

206 OLDSMOBILE

STANDARD STEERING GEAR, ADJUST AND SERVICE

Includes:
   Basic Job: Adjust steering gear, worm and sector mesh, adjust wheel bearings and toe-in.
   Related Job: R&R steering gear assembly and complete adjustments.
   Additions to Related Job: Overhaul steering gear.

MODEL	1966	1967	1968	1969	1970	1971	1972	1973	1974	1975
Basic Job:										
Complete steering gear, wheel bearings, & toe-in adjustments,										
With drum brakes	1.4	1.4	1.4	1.4	1.4	1.4	1.4	1.4	1.4	—
With disc brakes	1.8	1.8	1.8	1.8	1.8	1.8	1.8	1.8	1.8	1.8
Related Job:										
R&R steering gear assembly & complete adjustments	1.9	1.9	1.9	1.9	1.9	1.9	1.9	1.9	1.9	1.9
Additions to Related Job:										
Overhaul steering gear assembly, **ADD:**	1.0	1.0	1.0	1.0	1.0	1.0	1.0	1.0	1.0	1.0

Approximate parts cost:
   Pitman shaft bushing .... $2.00   Worm thrust bearing $1.00
   Shaft dust seal .... 1.00   Pitman shaft seal 1.50

POWER STEERING UNIT, TEST AND SERVICE

Includes:
   Basic Job: Adjust drive belt tension; hook-up gauges to check pressure on left and right turns. Adjust steering gear box overcenter torque and control valve to balance left and right steering effort.
   Additions to Basic Job: Service power steering unit.
   Related Jobs: R&R power steering unit, pump, or other associated parts.
   Additions to Related Jobs: Overhaul steering unit or pump including replacement of all seals and worn parts.

MODEL	1966	1967	1968	1969	1970	1971	1972	1973	1974	1975
Basic Job:										
Complete test and adjustment of power steering unit	1.0	1.0	1.0	1.0	1.0	1.0	1.0	1.0	1.0	1.0
Additions to Basic Job:										
Replace power steering pump drive belt, **ADD:**	.3	.3	.3	.3	.3	.3	.3	.3	.3	.3
With air conditioning, **ADD:**	.2	.2	.2	.2	.2	.2	.2	.2	.2	.2
Check & replenish reservoir fluid, **ADD:**	.2	.2	.2	.2	.2	.2	.2	.2	.2	.2
Related Jobs:										
Replace pressure hoses, either set, includes adjust drive belt,										
L-6 engine	.3	.3	.3	.3	.3	.3	—	.3	.3	.3
V-6 or V-8 engine	.6	.6	.6	.6	.6	.6	.6	.6	.6	.6
With air conditioning, **ADD:**	.1	.1	.1	.1	.1	.1	.1	.1	.1	.1
Replace pump reservoir or O-ring seals,										
L-6 engine	1.0	1.0	1.0	1.0	1.0	1.0	—	1.0	1.1	1.1
V-6 engine	—	—	—	—	—	—	—	—	—	1.5
V-8 engine	1.1	1.1	1.1	1.1	1.1	1.1	1.2	1.2	1.2	1.2
With air conditioning, **ADD:**	.1	.1	.1	.1	.1	.1	.1	.1	.2	.2
Replace pump, includes pressure-test original pump and transfer pulley,										
L-6 engine	.7	.7	.7	.7	.7	.7	—	.7	.7	.7
V-6 engine	—	—	—	—	—	—	—	—	—	1.1
V-8 engine	.8	.8	.8	.8	.8	.8	.8	.8	.8	.8
With air conditioning, **ADD:**	.1	.1	.1	.1	.1	.1	.1	.2	.2	.2
Replace control valve, includes adjust	1.1	1.1	1.1	1.1	1.1	1.1	1.1	1.1	1.1	1.1
Overhaul control valve, **ADD:**	.6	.6	.6	.6	.6	.6	.6	.6	.6	.6

(THIS SCHEDULE CONTINUED ON NEXT PAGE.)

OLDSMOBILE 207

POWER STEERING UNIT, TEST AND SERVICE Continued

MODEL	1966	1967	1968	1969	1970	1971	1972	1973	1974	1975
R&R power steering unit, includes test original unit and complete adjustment,										
L-6 engine	1.9	1.9	1.9	1.9	1.9	1.9	—	1.9	1.9	1.9
V-6 engine	—	—	—	—	—	—	—	—	—	2.6
V-8 engine	2.3	2.3	2.3	2.3	2.3	2.3	2.3	2.3	2.3	2.3
Additions to Related Jobs:										
Overhaul power steering unit, **ADD:**	2.2	2.2	2.2	2.2	2.4	2.4	2.4	2.4	3.0	3.0
O/H pump, incl. new kit & seals, **ADD:**	.8	.8	.8	.8	.8	.8	.8	.6	.6	.6

Approximate parts cost:

Drive belt .... $ 4.00	Power cylinder $33.00
Pressure hose 12.00	Power cylinder piston rod seal kit 2.50
Return hose 4.00	Hydraulic pump 62.00
Control valve 42.00	Hydraulic reservoir 15.00
Control valve seal kit 2.00	Hydraulic pump seals 4.00
Power steering unit, valve assembly 85.00	Hydraulic pump repair kit 14.00

FRONT END, TEST, SERVICE, AND ADJUST

Includes:

Basic Job: (All models) Check and adjust car height, caster, camber, steering axis inclination, turning radius, toe-in; pack and adjust front wheel bearings; replace seals.

Related Jobs: 1. (Except Eldorado) Perform individual adjustments. Replace or overhaul defective components and make necessary adjustments.
2. (Eldorado) Perform individual adjustments. Replace or overhaul defective components and make necessary adjustments.

MODEL	1966	1967	1968	1969	1970	1971	1972	1973	1974	1975
Basic Job:										
Complete front end test and adjustment,										
Toronado	—	3.0	3.0	3.0	3.0	3.0	3.0	3.0	3.0	3.0
All others	2.7	2.7	2.7	2.7	2.7	2.7	2.7	2.7	2.7	2.7
Related Jobs: #1 (Except Toronado)										
Adjust toe-in only	.4	.4	.4	.4	.4	.4	.4	.4	.4	.4
Repack wheel bearings only, incl. new seals	1.3	1.3	1.3	1.3	1.3	1.3	1.3	1.3	1.3	1.3
Replace wheel bearings only, each side	.8	.8	.8	.8	.8	.9	.9	.9	.9	.9
Balance four wheels on car,										
With drum brakes	1.2	1.2	1.2	1.2	1.2	1.2	1.2	1.2	1.2	1.2
With disc brakes	1.5	1.5	1.5	1.5	1.5	1.5	1.5	1.5	1.5	1.5
Overhaul front suspension, incl. disassemble, replace necessary parts, lube., & complete front end adjustment	7.9	7.9	7.9	7.9	7.9	7.9	7.9	7.9	7.9	7.9
Replace coil spring, one side, incl. complete front end adjustment	4.4	4.4	4.4	4.4	4.4	4.1	4.1	4.1	4.1	4.1
Replace lower spherical joint, one side, includes R&R lower control arm and complete front end adjustment	4.6	4.6	4.6	4.6	4.6	4.6	4.6	4.6	4.6	4.6
Replace upper spherical joint, one side, (replaced as an assembly with upper control arm), incl. compl. front end adjust.	5.5	5.5	5.5	5.5	5.5	5.5	5.5	5.5	5.5	5.5
Replace steering knuckle, one side, incl. complete front end adjustment	3.6	3.6	3.6	3.6	3.6	3.6	3.6	3.6	3.6	3.6
Replace shock absorber, both sides	.9	.9	.9	.9	.9	.9	.9	.9	.9	.9
Replace control arm rubber bumpers, ea. side	.3	.3	.3	.3	.3	.3	.3	.3	.3	.3
Replace tie strut, one side, incl. disconnect and connect stabilizer link	.6	.6	.6	.6	.6	.6	.6	.6	.6	.6
Replace stabilizer bar and bushings	1.1	1.1	1.1	1.1	1.1	1.1	1.1	1.1	1.1	1.1
Replace both stabilizer links or grommets	.7	.7	.7	.7	.7	.7	.7	.7	.7	.7

(THIS SCHEDULE CONTINUED ON NEXT PAGE.)

OLDSMOBILE

FRONT END, TEST, SERVICE, AND ADJUST Continued

MODEL	1966	1967	1968	1969	1970	1971	1972	1973	1974	1975
Related Jobs #2 (Toronado)										
Adjust toe-in only	.4	.4	.4	.4	.4	.4	.4	.4	.4	.4
Adjust torsion bar (car height)	.3	.3	.3	.3	.3	.3	.3	.3	.3	.3
Balance four wheels on car,										
With drum brakes	1.2	1.2	1.2	1.2	1.2	1.2	1.2	1.2	1.2	—
With disc brakes	1.5	1.5	1.5	1.5	1.5	1.5	1.5	1.5	1.5	1.5
Overhaul front suspension, incl. disassemble, replace necessary parts, lube, & complete front end adjustment	10.8	10.8	10.8	10.8	10.8	10.8	10.8	10.8	10.8	10.8
Replace torsion bar, one side, incl. compl. front end adjust	3.3	3.3	3.3	3.3	3.3	3.3	3.3	2.8	2.8	2.8
Replace steering knuckle inner seal, one side, incl. complete front end adjustment	4.8	4.8	4.8	4.8	4.8	4.7	4.7	4.7	4.7	4.7
Replace hub, bearings, cups & seals, **ADD:**	.7	.7	.7	.7	.7	.7	.7	.7	.7	.7
Replace axle shaft assemblies,										
Right axle	.7	.7	.7	.7	.7	.7	.7	.7	.7	.7
Left axle	1.1	1.1	1.1	1.1	1.1	1.1	1.1	1.1	1.1	1.1
Both axles	1.7	1.7	1.7	1.7	1.7	1.7	1.7	1.7	1.7	1.7
Repack or replace right or left outer C.V. joint, **ADD:**	.5	.5	.5	.5	.5	.5	.5	.5	.5	.5
Repack or replace right or left inner C.V. joint, **ADD:**	.8	.8	.8	.8	.8	.8	.8	.8	.8	.8
Repack or repl. both right or both left C.V. joints, **ADD:**	1.2	1.2	1.2	1.2	1.2	1.2	1.2	1.2	1.2	1.2
Replace output shaft,										
Right side	.5	.5	.5	.5	.5	.5	.5	.5	.5	.5
Left side	1.1	1.1	1.1	1.1	1.1	1.1	1.1	1.1	1.1	1.1
Both sides	1.5	1.5	1.5	1.5	1.5	1.5	1.5	1.5	1.5	1.5
Replace bearing or retainer on right shaft, **ADD:**	.3	.3	.3	.3	.3	.3	.3	.3	.3	.3
Replace output shaft seal,										
Right side	.6	.6	.6	.6	.6	.6	.6	.6	.6	.6
Left side	1.2	1.2	1.2	1.2	1.2	1.2	1.2	1.2	1.2	1.2
Replace lower spherical joint, one side, includes R&R lower control arm and complete front end adjustment	5.2	5.2	5.2	5.2	5.2	5.2	5.2	5.2	5.2	5.2
Replace upper spherical joint, one side, (replaced as an assy. with upper control arm), incl. compl. front end adjust	6.8	6.8	6.8	6.8	6.8	6.8	6.1	6.1	6.1	6.1
Replace stabilizer bar & bushings	1.1	1.1	1.1	1.1	1.1	1.1	1.1	1.1	1.1	1.1
Replace both stabilizer links or grommets	.7	.7	.7	.7	.7	.7	.7	.7	.7	.7
Replace tie strut, one side, incl. disconnect and connect stabilizer link	.6	.6	.6	.6	.6	.6	.6	.6	.6	.6
Replace shock absorber, both sides	.9	.9	.9	.9	.9	.9	.9	.9	.9	.9

Approximate parts cost: (except Toronado)

Coil spring, ea.	$25.00
Lower spherical joint kit	16.00
Upper spherical joint and control arm assembly	35.00
Steering knuckle	50.00
Shock absorber, ea.	15.00
Stabilizer link kit, ea.	$ 2.50
Stabilizer bar and bushings	17.00
Tie strut	15.00
Wheel bearing, outer	5.00
Wheel bearing, inner	6.00
Wheel bearing seals	2.00

Approximate parts cost: (Toronado)

Torsion bar	$30.00
Lower spherical joint kit	16.00
Upper spherical joint and control arm assembly	35.00
Steering knuckle	50.00
Shock absorber, ea.	15.00
Tie strut	15.00
Stabilizer link kit, ea.	2.50
Right or left outer C.V. joint	$160.00
Right or left inner C.V. joint	70.00
Output shaft bearing	17.00
Right output shaft	74.00
Left output shaft	32.00
Output shaft seal	3.50
Stabilizer bar and bushing	17.00

OLDSMOBILE

HYDRAULIC BRAKE SYSTEM, OVERHAUL

Includes:
Basic Job: Overhaul including hone or replace master cylinder, all wheel cylinders or calipers; bleed hydraulic system; and adjust brakes.
Related Jobs: Performed at time other than during basic job. Overhaul or replace master cylinder only; overhaul wheel cylinders or calipers.
Addition to Related Jobs: Allowance for power brakes.

MODEL	1966	1967	1968	1969	1970	1971	1972	1973	1974	1975
Basic Job:										
Complete job, including master & wheel cylinders,										
Drum brakes		4.7	4.7	4.7	4.7	4.7	4.7	4.6	4.6	—
Disc front, drum rear	3.9	3.9	3.9	3.9	3.9	3.9	3.9	3.9	3.9	3.9
Related Jobs: (Not during basic job)										
Overhaul master cylinder, including hone,										
Drum or disc brakes	1.3	1.3	1.5	1.5	1.5	1.5	1.8	1.8	1.8	1.8
Replace master cylinder	.5	.5	.8	.8	.8	.8	1.1	1.1	1.1	1.1
O/H wheel cylinder, drum brakes (4)	4.1	4.1	4.1	4.1	4.1	4.1	4.2	4.2	4.2	—
O/H front calipers, incl. turn rotors	4.0	4.0	4.0	4.0	4.0	4.0	4.0	4.0	4.0	4.0
Bleed hydraulic system, 4 wheels	.6	.6	.6	.6	.6	.6	.6	.6	.6	.6
Addition to Related Jobs:										
With power brakes, **ADD:**	.2	.2	.2	.2	.2	.2	.2	.2	.2	.2
Service True Track System										
Replace one sensor	—	—	—	—	.5	.9	.9	.5	.5	.5
Replace both sensors	—	—	—	—	.8	1.3	1.3	.8	.8	.8
Replace controller	—	—	—	—	.5	.5	.5	.5	.5	.5
Replace solenoid valve assembly	—	—	—	—	.5	.5	.5	.5	.5	.5
Replace modulator assembly, **ADD:**	—	—	—	—	.9	.9	.9	.7	.7	.7
Replace hydraulic line, includes bleed system,										
Modulator to rear connector	—	—	—	—	.9	.9	.9	.7	.7	.7
Balance valve to modulator	—	—	—	—	.9	.9	.9	.7	.7	.7
Balance valve to distributor or combination valve	—	—	—	—	.7	.7	.7	.7	.7	.7

Approximate parts cost:

Master cylinder repair kit	$18.00
Wheel cylinder repair kit, ea.	2.00
Caliper repair kit	4.00
Master cylinder	27.00-40.00
Wheel cylinder seal, boot & bushing pkg.	6.00
True Track sensor	$55.00-70.00
True Track controller	130.00
True Track solenoid	56.00
True Track modulator	250.00
True Track hose pkg.	5.00

PARKING BRAKES, SERVICE AND ADJUST

Includes:
Basic Jobs: Replace defective cable and/or adjust parking brakes.

MODEL	1966	1967	1968	1969	1970	1971	1972	1973	1974	1975
Basic Job:										
Adjust parking brakes	.4	.4	.4	.4	.4	.4	.4	.4	.4	.4
Replace forward cable	.7	.7	.7	.7	.7	.7	.7	.7	.7	.7
Replace center cable	.4	.4	.4	.4	.4	.4	.4	.4	.4	.4
Replace rear cable, one side	.6	.6	.6	.6	.6	.6	.6	.6	.6	.6
Replace rear cable, both sides	1.0	1.0	1.0	1.0	1.0	1.0	1.0	1.0	1.0	1.0

Approximate parts cost:

Front cable	$5.00
Center cable	3.50
Rear cable, ea.	$8.00

210 OLDSMOBILE

BRAKES, SERVICE

Includes:

Basic Job: Install new linings or pads, turn brake drums or rotors, lubricate and adjust front wheel bearings, replace rear oil seals, bleed hydraulic system, and adjust brakes.

Additions to Basic Job: Overhaul four wheel cylinders, overhaul or replace front calipers.

Related Jobs: Work performed at time other than during basic job.

MODEL	1966	1967	1978	1969	1970	1971	1972	1973	1974	1975
Basic Job:										
Complete job incl. turn drums or rotors,										
Drum (4), all models	6.5	6.5	6.5	6.5	6.5	6.5	6.5	6.5	6.5	—
Disc front, drum rear, all models	6.9	6.9	6.9	6.9	6.9	6.9	6.9	6.9	6.9	6.9
Additions to Basic Job:										
O/H 4 wheel cylinders, incl. hone, ADD:	2.3	2.3	2.3	2.3	2.3	2.4	2.4	2.4	2.4	—
Overhaul front calipers (both), ADD:	3.5	3.5	3.5	2.9	2.9	2.9	2.9	2.9	2.9	2.9
Replace front calipers (both), ADD:	.4	.4	.4	.4	.4	.4	.4	.4	.4	.4
Overhaul master cylinder, ADD:	.8	.8	.8	.8	.8	.8	.8	.8	.8	.8
Related Jobs: (Not during basic job)										
Bleed hydraulic system, 4 wheels	.6	.6	.6	.6	.6	.6	.6	.6	.6	.6
Adjust drum brakes, 4 wheels	.5	.5	.5	.5	.5	.5	.5	.5	.5	—
Replace front disc brake pads & rear brake linings, incl. bleed system	3.3	3.3	3.3	3.3	3.3	3.3	3.3	3.3	3.3	3.3
Replace drum brake shoes, 4 wheels, incl. bleed system	3.5	3.5	3.5	3.5	3.5	3.5	3.5	3.5	3.5	—
O/H front calipers, incl. turn rotors	4.6	4.6	4.6	4.0	4.0	4.0	4.0	4.0	4.0	4.0
Replace front caliper, incl. turn rotor, ea.	3.0	3.0	3.0	2.4	2.4	2.4	2.4	2.4	2.4	2.4
Overhaul master cylinder	1.3	1.3	1.5	1.5	1.5	1.5	1.8	1.8	1.8	1.8

Approximate parts cost:

Wheel cylinder seal, boot & bushing pkg.	$ 6.00
Brake shoes and lining sets, front or rear	25.00
Disc brake pads, set of 2	24.00
Master cylinder repair kit	18.00
Wheel cylinder repair kit, ea.	$ 2.00
Caliper brake housing	50.00
Oil seal, ea.	2.00

POWER BRAKE UNIT, SERVICE

Includes:

Basic Job: R&R with new unit, test, and adjust brakes.

Additions to Basic Job: Replace vacuum hose or vacuum check valve. Allowance for air conditioning.

MODEL	1966	1967	1968	1969	1970	1971	1972	1973	1974	1975
Basic Job:										
R&R power unit, test, & adj. brakes	1.6	1.6	1.6	1.6	1.5	1.5	1.5	1.5	1.5	1.5
Additions to Basic Job:										
With air conditioning, ADD:	.3	.3	.3	.3	.3	.3	.3	.3	.3	.3
Install new hose, ADD:	.2	.2	.2	.2	.2	.2	.2	.2	.2	.2
Install new vacuum check valve, ADD:	.2	.2	.2	.2	.2	.2	.2	.2	.2	.2

Approximate parts cost:

Power brake unit	$50.00-70.00
Vacuum hose, per ft.	0.90
Vacuum check valve	$1.75

OLDSMOBILE 211

LIGHTING SYSTEM, ADJUST AND SERVICE

Includes:
Basic Job: 1. Adjust headlights to inspection requirements.
2. Replace defective parts in rear lighting system.
Additions to Basic Job: Replace associated parts affecting headlight adjustment.
Related Jobs: Replace associated parts not affecting headlight adjustment.

MODEL	1966	1967	1968	1969	1970	1971	1972	1973	1974	1975
Basic Job #1										
Adjust two lights	.4	.4	.4	.4	.4	.4	.4	.4	.4	.4
Adjust four lights	.6	.6	.6	.6	.6	.6	.6	.6	.6	.6
Basic Job #2										
Replace stoplight switch	.3	.3	.3	.3	.3	.3	.3	.3	.3	.3
Replace back-up light switch	.4	.4	.4	.4	.4	.4	.4	.4	.4	.4
Additions to Basic Job:										
Replace sealed beam unit, ea., **ADD:**	.3	.3	.3	.3	.3	.3	.3	.3	.3	.3
Related Jobs:										
Replace headlamp vacuum actuator, one side	.8	.8	.8	—	—	—	—	—	—	—
Replace headlamp switch,										
88, 98, & Toronado	.4	.4	.4	.4	.4	.4	.4	.4	.6	.6
All others	.5	.5	.5	.5	.5	.5	.5	.5	.5	.5
Replace foot dimmer switch	.3	.3	.3	.3	.3	.3	.3	.3	.3	.3
Replace signal/hazard flasher	.2	.2	.2	.2	.2	.2	.2	.2	.2	.2
Replace signal/hazard switch,										
With standard column	1.2	1.2	1.2	1.0	1.0	1.0	1.0	1.0	1.0	1.0
With tilt or telescopic column	1.5	1.5	1.5	1.3	1.3	1.3	1.3	1.3	1.3	1.3

Approximate parts cost:
Sealed beam unit	$ 4.00	Vacuum motor	$20.00
Signal/hazard flasher	2.00	Headlamp switch	7.00
Signal/hazard switch	15.00	Back-up light switch	8.00

HEATING SYSTEM, TEST AND SERVICE

Includes:
Basic Job: Drain back-flush, and fill radiator, check radiator and heater hoses and connections, pressure-test radiator cap and system.
Related Jobs: Replace defective parts. Work performed individually and independently of basic job.

MODEL	1966	1967	1968	1969	1970	1971	1972	1973	1974	1975
Basic Job:										
Drain, flush, fill, check, & pressure-test	.9	.9	.9	.9	.9	.9	.9	.9	.9	.9
Related Jobs:										
Replace heater hose, one, inlet or outlet	.5	.5	.5	.5	.5	.5	.5	.5	.5	.5
Replace each additional hose, **ADD:**	.2	.2	.2	.2	.2	.2	.2	.2	.2	.2
With air conditioning, **ADD:**	.3	.3	.3	.3	.3	.3	.3	.3	.3	.3
Replace blower motor, includes R&R front fender filler panel,										
Toronado	1.0	1.0	1.0	.7	1.2	1.2	2.0	2.0	2.0	2.0
Omega	—	—	—	—	—	—	—	.9	.9	.9
All others	1.2	1.2	1.2	1.0	1.0	1.0	1.0	1.0	1.0	1.0
Replace heater core w/o air conditioning,										
Toronado	1.2	1.2	1.2	1.2	.8	.8	.8	.8	.8	.8
Omega	—	—	—	—	—	—	—	1.0	1.0	1.0
F-85	1.0	1.0	1.0	1.0	1.1	1.1	1.1	1.2	1.2	1.2
All others	.9	.9	.9	.9	.9	.9	.9	.9	.9	.9

(THIS SCHEDULE CONTINUED ON NEXT PAGE.)

OLDSMOBILE

HEATING SYSTEM, TEST AND SERVICE Continued

MODEL	1966	1967	1968	1969	1970	1971	1972	1973	1974	1975
Related Jobs Continued										
Replace heater core with air conditioning,										
Omega	—	—	—	—	—	—	—	2.3	2.3	2.3
All others	1.8	1.8	1.8	1.8	1.8	1.8	1.8	1.8	1.8	1.8
Replace heater switch,										
Omega	—	—	—	—	—	—	—	.8	.8	.8
Toronado	1.3	1.3	1.3	1.3	1.3	.8	.8	.8	.8	.8
All others	.4	.4	.4	.4	1.0	.8	.8	.8	.8	.8

Approximate parts cost:
Heater hose, per ft. .... $ 0.75
Blower motor 32.00
Heater core $45.00
Blower motor switch 9.00

AIR CONDITIONING SYSTEM, SPRING TUNE-UP

Includes:
Basic Job: Clean condenser fins; adjust drive belt tension; test anti-freeze; tighten compressor, condenser, and evaporator mounts. Pressure-test and leak-check system. Check system for performance.
Additions to Basic Job: Replace defective parts.

MODEL	1966	1967	1968	1969	1970	1971	1972	1973	1974	1975
Basic Job:										
Perform complete spring tune-up	2.0	2.0	2.0	2.0	2.0	2.0	2.0	2.0	2.0	2.0
Additions to Basic Job:										
Replace compressor belt & adjust, ADD:	.4	.4	.4	.4	.4	.4	.4	.4	.4	.4
Replace compr. clutch pulley w/hub assy., ADD:	.5	.5	.5	.5	.5	.5	.5	.5	.5	.5
Replace compr. clutch coil, ADD:	.8	.8	.8	.8	.8	.8	.8	.8	.8	.8
Replace compr. clutch bearing, ADD:	.8	.8	.8	.8	.8	.8	.8	.8	.8	.8

Approximate parts cost:
Compressor drive belt .... $ 3.00
Compressor clutch pulley w/hub 75.00
Freon, per 14 oz. can 2.50
Compressor clutch coil $28.00
Compressor clutch bearing 23.00
Cnti-freeze, per gal. 9.50

AIR CONDITIONING SYSTEM, MAJOR SERVICE

Includes:
Basic Job: Drain system in order to replace defective component; evacuate, dehydrate, and recharge system; pressure-test and leak-check; clean condenser fins; adjust drive belt tension; tighten compressor, condenser, and evaporator mounts; and conduct performance test.
Additions to Basic Job: Replace or overhaul compressor. Replace other defective part(s) and performance test following installation of new part.

MODEL	1966	1967	1968	1969	1970	1971	1972	1973	1974	1975
Basic Job:										
Drain, evacuate, dehydrate, charge & test	3.0	3.0	3.0	3.0	3.0	3.0	3.0	3.0	3.0	3.0
Additions to Basic Job:										
Replace compressor, includes transfer parts and test, ADD:	1.1	1.1	1.1	1.1	1.1	1.1	1.1	1.1	1.1	1.1
R&R and overhaul complete compressor assy., ADD:	3.0	3.0	3.0	3.0	3.0	3.0	3.0	3.0	3.0	3.0
Replace compressor front seal, incl. R&R driven plate, disconnect & connect compressor, ADD:	1.1	1.1	1.1	1.1	1.1	1.1	1.1	1.1	1.1	1.1
Replace O-rings, compressor, intake and discharge, ADD:	.5	.5	.5	.5	.5	.5	.5	.5	.5	.5

(THIS SCHEDULE CONTINUED ON NEXT PAGE.)

OLDSMOBILE 213

AIR CONDITIONING SYSTEM, MAJOR SERVICE Continued

MODEL	1966	1967	1968	1969	1970	1971	1972	1973	1974	1975
Additions to Basic Job Continued										
Replace O-rings, receiver or VIR inlet or outlet, **ADD:**	—	—	—	—	.7	.7	.7	.7	.5	.5
Replace pressure relief valve and/or O-ring, **ADD:**	—	—	—	—	.5	.5	.5	.5	.5	.5
Replace compressor front head, **ADD:**	1.4	1.4	1.4	1.4	1.4	.8	.8	.8	.8	.8
Replace compressor rear head and/or oil pump gears, **ADD:**	1.3	1.3	1.3	1.3	1.3	1.3	1.3	1.3	1.3	1.3
Replace refrigerant line, one, add oil, bleed system, **ADD:**	1.0	1.0	1.0	1.0	1.0	1.0	1.0	1.0	1.0	1.0
Replace condenser,										
Omega, **ADD:**	—	—	—	—	—	—	—	.9	.9	.9
Toronado, **ADD:**	1.1	1.1	.8	.8	.8	.8	.8	.8	.8	.8
All others, **ADD:**	.6	.6	.6	.6	.6	.6	.6	1.2	1.2	1.2
Add oil to compressor, **ADD:**	.3	.3	.3	.3	.3	.3	.3	.3	.3	.3
Replace sight glass,										
Toronado, **ADD:**	.6	.6	.2	.2	.2	.2	.2	.2	.2	.2
All others, **ADD:**	.2	.2	.2	.2	.2	.2	.2	.2	.2	.2
Replace evaporator core,										
Omega, **ADD:**	—	—	—	—	—	—	—	1.8	1.8	1.8
F-85, **ADD:**	2.5	2.5	2.1	2.1	1.8	1.8	1.8	1.8	1.8	1.8
All others, **ADD:**	1.4	1.4	1.4	1.4	1.8	1.8	1.8	1.8	1.8	1.8
Replace evaporator expansion valve,										
Toronado, **ADD:**	1.8	1.8	1.8	1.8	1.7	1.7	1.7	1.7	1.7	1.7
F-85, **ADD:**	2.4	2.4	2.4	2.4	1.7	1.7	1.7	1.7	1.7	1.7
All others, **ADD:**	1.0	1.0	1.0	1.0	1.2	1.2	1.2	1.2	1.2	1.2
Replace POA valve, **ADD:**	.6	.6	.6	.6	.6	.5	.5	.2	.2	.2
R&R valves-in receiver (VIR) assy., **ADD:**	—	—	—	—	—	—	—	.5	.5	.5
Overhaul VIR assy., **ADD:**	—	—	—	—	—	—	—	1.0	1.0	1.0
Replace suction throttling valve, **ADD:**	.6	.6	.6	.6	.6	.6	.6	.6	.6	.6

Approximate parts cost:

Compressor	$ 85.00
Compressor front head & valve assy.	20.00
Compressor rear head & valve assy.	65.00
Compressor pressure relief valve	7.00
Condenser	75.00-125.00
Evaporator core assy.	90.00-160.00
Compressor shaft seal assy.	8.00
Expansion valve	$36.00
Pressure-operated absolute (POA) valve	30.00
Hose, per ft.	2.75
Hose fitting, ea.	1.00
Freon, per 14 oz. can	2.50
Anti-freeze, per gal.	9.50
Suction throttling valve	35.00

AIR CONDITIONING SYSTEM BLOWER MOTOR OR CONTROLS, SERVICE

Includes:

Basic Jobs: Conduct performance test of system to determine defective part; R&R component; clean condenser fins; adjust drive belt tension; tighten all mounts; and test system

MODEL	1966	1967	1968	1969	1970	1971	1972	1973	1974	1975
Basic Jobs:										
R&R blower motor, test system after installation,										
Toronado	1.4	1.4	1.4	1.4	1.4	1.6	1.6	1.6	1.6	1.6
Omega	—	—	—	—	—	—	—	1.3	1.3	1.3
All others	1.3	1.3	1.3	1.3	1.3	1.4	1.4	1.4	1.4	1.4
R&R control assy., includes blower switch,										
Toronado	1.6	1.6	1.6	1.6	1.6	1.2	1.2	1.2	1.3	1.3
Omega	—	—	—	—	—	—	—	1.4	1.4	1.4
All others	1.3	1.3	1.3	1.5	1.5	1.3	1.3	1.3	1.3	1.3

(THIS SCHEDULE CONTINUED ON NEXT PAGE.)

OLDSMOBILE

AIR CONDITIONING SYSTEM BLOWER MOTOR OR CONTROLS, SERVICE Continued

MODEL	1966	1967	1968	1969	1970	1971	1972	1973	1974	1975
Basic Jobs Continued										
Replace compressor clutch switch,										
Toronado	1.0	1.0	1.0	1.0	1.0	—	—	—	—	—
All others	1.4	1.4	1.4	1.4	1.4	—	—	—	—	—
R&R evaporator thermostatic switch	1.1	1.1	1.1	1.1	1.1	1.1	1.1	1.1	1.1	1.1
Replace control cable, temperature door	.7	.7	.7	.7	.7	.7	1.0	1.0	1.0	1.0
R&R programmer	—	—	—	—	—	1.3	1.3	1.3	1.3	1.3
Test programmer, **ADD:**	—	—	—	—	—	.7	.7	.7	.7	.7
Replace defective parts, ea., **ADD:**	—	—	—	—	—	.2	.2	.2	.2	.2

Approximate parts cost:

Blower motor	$23.00	Control cable, per ft.	$ 0.80
Blower motor switch	3.00	Control cable fittings, ea.	0.75
Evaporator thermostatic switch	4.00	Control assembly, manual	35.00
Compressor clutch switch	2.50	automatic	90.00
Programmer	80.00		

PONTIAC 215

SERVICE STATION MAINTENANCE

Includes:
Basic Job: Lubricate chassis, drain oil, change filters, repack front wheel bearings, repack U-joints, and lubricate front end. Check fluid levels of battery, radiator, air conditioner, brake master cylinder, power steering reservoir, transmission, and differential. Check condition of hoses and drive belts. Lubricate miscellaneous moving parts, latches, hinges, etc.

Related Jobs: Service individual systems or components. See detailed description of work included for each job in separate major section.

Additions to Basic or Related Jobs: Allowances for special equipment installed.

MODEL	1966	1967	1968	1969	1970	1971	1972	1973	1974	1975
Basic Job:										
General lubrication & system check,										
4/6 cylinder OHC engine	1.2	1.2	1.2	1.2	—	—	—	—	—	1.3
L-6 engine	—	—	—	—	1.0	1.0	1.0	1.0	1.1	1.1
V-8 engine	1.4	1.4	1.4	1.4	1.4	1.4	1.4	1.4	1.5	1.5
With air conditioning, **ADD:**	.3	.3	.3	.3	.3	.3	.3	.3	.3	.3
With AIR pump, **ADD:**	.2	.2	.2	.2	.2	.2	.2	.2	.2	.2
With disc brakes, **ADD:**	—	.9	.9	.9	.9	.9	.9	.9	.9	.9
Related Jobs:										
Service Battery										
Clean, test, & fill	.3	.3	.3	.3	.3	.3	.3	.3	.3	.3
Replace ground cable	.2	.2	.2	.2	.2	.2	.2	.2	.2	.2
Replace starter cable	.3	.3	.3	.3	.3	.3	.3	.3	.3	.3
Replace battery	.4	.4	.4	.4	.4	.4	.4	.4	.4	.4
Service Cooling System										
Back-flush, fill, & pressure-test system	.9	.9	.9	.9	.9	.9	.9	.9	.9	.9
Replace upper hose	.4	.4	.4	.4	.4	.4	.4	.4	.4	.4
Replace lower hose	.5	.5	.5	.5	.5	.5	.5	.5	.5	.5
Replace both hoses	.7	.7	.7	.7	.7	.7	.7	.7	.7	.7
Replace thermostat & pressure-test system	.6	.6	.6	.6	.6	.6	.6	.6	.6	.6
Replace water pump drive belt & adjust tension,										
OHC engines	1.0	1.0	1.0	1.0	—	—	—	—	—	1.0
All others	.4	.4	.4	.4	.4	.4	.4	.4	.4	.4
Replace water pump, pressure-test system,										
OHC engines	1.3	1.3	1.3	1.3	—	—	—	—	—	1.3
All others	1.0	1.0	1.0	1.0	1.0	1.0	1.0	1.0	1.0	1.0
With air conditioning, **ADD:**	.2	.2	.2	.2	.2	.2	.2	.2	.2	.2
With power steering, **ADD:**	.2	.2	.2	.2	.2	.2	.2	.2	.2	.2
With AIR, **ADD:**	.2	.2	.2	.2	.2	.2	.2	.2	.2	.2
Service Ignition System										
Adjust & install spark plugs										
4-cylinder	—	—	—	—	—	—	—	—	—	.4
6-cylinder	.6	.6	.6	.6	.6	.6	.6	.6	.6	.6
V-8 engine	.8	.8	.8	.8	.8	.8	.8	.8	.8	.8
With air conditioning, **ADD:**	.3	.3	.3	.3	.3	.3	.3	.3	.3	.3
With AIR, **ADD:**	.3	.3	.3	.3	.3	.3	.3	.3	.3	.3
Replace points and condenser & adjust ignition timing,										
4 or 6-cylinder	.5	.5	.5	.5	.5	.5	.5	.5	.5	—
V-8 engine	.7	.7	.7	.7	.7	.7	.7	.7	.7	—
replace distributor cap,										
4 or 6-cylinder, **ADD:**	.3	.3	.3	.3	.3	.3	.3	.3	.3	.3
V-8 engine, **ADD:**	.4	.4	.4	.4	.4	.4	.4	.4	.4	.4
Check reluctor air gap, and adjust ignition timing	—	—	—	—	—	—	—	—	—	.4

(THIS SCHEDULE CONTINUED ON NEXT PAGE.)

216 PONTIAC

SERVICE STATION MAINTENANCE Continued

MODEL	1966	1967	1968	1969	1970	1971	1972	1973	1974	1975
Service Ignition System Continued										
Replace spark plug wires,										
4-cylinder	—	—	—	—	—	—	—	—	—	.4
6-cylinder	.6	.6	.6	.6	.6	.6	.6	.6	.6	.6
V-8 engine	.8	.8	.8	.8	.8	.8	.8	.8	.8	.8
With air conditioning, **ADD:**	.5	.5	.5	.5	.5	.5	.5	.5	.5	.5
Replace ignition coil	.4	.4	.4	.4	.4	.4	.4	.4	.4	.6
Perform Minor Tune-up										
4-cylinder	—	—	—	—	—	—	—	—	—	2.1
6-cylinder	2.2	2.2	2.2	2.2	2.4	2.4	2.4	2.4	2.5	2.5
V-8 engine	2.7	2.7	2.7	2.7	2.9	2.9	2.9	2.9	2.9	3.0
Note: See minor tune-up section for work included and additions.										
Perform Major Tune-up										
4-cylinder	—	—	—	—	—	—	—	—	—	5.5
6-cylinder	5.0	5.0	5.0	5.0	5.5	5.5	5.5	5.5	5.7	5.7
V-8 engine	6.5	6.5	6.5	6.5	6.7	6.7	6.7	6.7	7.0	7.0
Note: See major tune-up section for work included and additions.										
Service Fuel System										
Complete carburetor adjustments,										
Single barrel	.4	.4	.4	.4	.4	.4	.4	.4	.4	.4
Two or four-barrel	.6	.6	.6	.6	.6	.6	.6	.6	.6	.6
Six-barrel (3x2)	.8	.8	.8	.8	—	—	—	—	—	—
Replace fuel filter	.3	.3	.3	.3	.3	.3	.3	.3	.3	.3
Test & replace fuel pump,										
4 or 6-cylinder OHC engine	.9	.9	.9	.9	—	—	—	—	—	.9
L-6 engine	.5	.5	.5	.5	.5	.5	.5	.5	.5	.5
V-8 engine	.7	.7	.7	.7	.7	.7	.8	.8	.8	.8
Replace flexible fuel line	.3	.3	.3	.3	.3	.3	.3	.3	.3	.3
Service Driveshaft										
R&R driveshaft & overhaul U-joints and adjust pinion nose angle,										
Cross & roller joints	1.5	1.5	1.5	1.5	1.5	1.5	1.5	1.5	1.5	1.5
Service Hydraulic Brake System										
Adjust drum brakes	.5	.5	.5	.5	.5	.5	.5	.5	.5	—
Replace drum brake shoes, 4 wheels	2.5	2.5	2.5	2.5	2.5	2.5	2.5	2.5	2.5	—
Bleed hydraulic system, 4 wheels	.6	.6	.6	.6	.6	.6	.6	.6	.6	.6
Replace front disc brake pads	—	1.5	1.5	1.5	1.5	1.5	1.0	1.0	1.0	1.0
Overhaul master cylinder	1.3	1.3	1.5	1.5	1.5	1.5	1.8	1.8	1.8	1.8
O/H wheel cylinders, drum brakes (4)	4.1	4.1	4.1	4.1	4.1	4.1	4.2	4.2	4.2	—
O/H fr. calipers incl. turn rotors	—	4.6	4.6	4.0	4.0	4.0	4.0	4.0	4.0	4.0
With power brakes, **ADD:**	.2	.2	.2	.2	.2	.2	.2	.2	.2	.2
Service Parking Brakes										
Replace forward cable,										
Pontiac, Tempest	1.4	1.4	1.4	1.4	1.4	1.4	1.4	1.4	1.4	1.4
All others	.8	.8	.8	.8	.8	.8	.8	.8	.8	.8
Replace rear cable, one side, all models	1.0	1.0	1.0	1.0	1.0	1.0	1.0	1.0	1.0	1.0
Replace rear cable, both sides, all models	1.5	1.5	1.5	1.5	1.5	1.5	1.5	1.5	1.5	1.5
Replace intermediate cable, all models	.4	.4	.4	.4	.4	.4	.4	.4	.4	.4

(THIS SCHEDULE CONTINUED ON NEXT PAGE.)

PONTIAC

SERVICE STATION MAINTENANCE (CONTINUED)

MODEL	1966	1967	1968	1969	1970	1971	1972	1973	1974	1975
Service Suspension System										
Replace front shock absorber, both sides	.9	.9	.9	.9	.9	.9	.9	.9	.9	.9
Replace rear shock absorber, both sides	.8	.8	.8	.8	.8	.8	.8	.8	.8	.8
Replace spring shackle and bushings; eye bolt and bushings	.7	.7	.7	.7	.7	.7	.7	.7	.7	.7
Replace rear leaf spring & shim to align pinion angle, Station Wagon, Firebird, Ventura, GTO	1.6	1.6	1.6	1.6	1.8	1.8	1.8	1.7	1.7	1.7
Service Front End & Steering System										
Adjust toe-in only	.4	.4	.4	.4	.4	.4	.4	.4	.4	.4
Replace tie-rods or tie-rod ends, (4)	1.4	1.4	1.4	1.4	1.4	1.4	1.4	1.4	1.4	1.4
Repl. Pitman arm, incl. adjust toe-in	.8	.8	.8	.8	.8	.8	.8	.8	.8	.8
Repl. steering idler arm or bushing, including adjust toe-in	.7	.7	.7	.7	.7	.7	.7	.7	.7	.7
Repl. pwr. steering pump drive belt	.3	.3	.3	.3	.3	.3	.3	.3	.3	.3
With air conditioning, **ADD:**	.2	.2	.2	.2	.2	.2	.2	.2	.2	.2
Check & replenish reservoir fluid	.2	.2	.2	.2	.2	.2	.2	.2	.2	.2
Replace pressure hoses, either set, includes adjust drive belt tension,										
4/6 cylinder	.3	.3	.3	.3	.3	.3	.3	.3	.3	.3
V-8 engine	.6	.6	.6	.6	.6	.6	.6	.6	.6	.6
With air conditioning, **ADD:**	.1	.1	.1	.1	.1	.1	.1	.1	.1	.1
Balance four wheels on car,										
With drum brakes	1.2	1.2	1.2	1.2	1.2	1.2	1.2	1.2	1.2	—
With disc/drum brakes	—	1.5	1.5	1.5	1.5	1.5	1.5	1.5	1.5	1.5
Rotate five wheels	.6	.6	.6	.6	.6	.6	.6	.6	.6	.6
Service Charging System										
Test system and/or adjust regulator	.6	.6	.6	.6	.6	.6	.6	.6	.6	.6
R&R alternator including pulley	.6	.6	.6	.6	.7	.7	.7	.7	.7	.7
With air conditioning, **ADD:**	.1	.1	.1	.1	.1	.1	.1	.1	.1	.1
With AIR, **ADD:**	.2	.2	.2	.2	.2	.2	.2	.2	.2	.2
Overhaul alternator after removal	2.3	2.3	1.5	1.5	1.5	1.5	1.5	1.5	1.5	1.5
Replace regulator	.3	.3	.3	.3	.3	.4	.4	.3	.3	.3
Service Cranking System										
R&R starter,										
4 or 6-cylinder	.7	.7	.7	.7	.7	.8	.8	.8	.8	.8
350/400 CID engines	2.7	2.6	2.6	2.0	1.9	1.9	1.9	1.9	1.8	1.8
All other V-8 engines	1.9	1.9	1.9	1.9	2.4	2.4	2.3	2.0	2.0	2.0
Overhaul starter after removal	1.7	1.7	1.7	1.7	1.7	1.7	1.7	1.7	1.7	1.7
Replace starter battery cable	.3	.3	.3	.3	.3	.3	.3	.3	.3	.3
Replace starter solenoid, incl. test sys.,										
4 or 6 cylinder	1.7	1.7	1.7	1.7	1.7	1.7	1.7	1.7	1.7	1.7
350/400 CID engines	2.7	2.6	2.6	2.0	1.9	1.9	1.9	1.9	1.8	1.8
All other V-8 engines	1.9	1.9	1.9	1.9	2.4	2.4	2.3	2.0	2.0	2.0
Service Lighting System										
Adjust two headlights	.4	.4	.4	.4	.4	.4	.4	.4	.4	.4
Adjust four headlights	.6	.6	.6	.6	.6	.6	.6	.6	.6	.6
Replace sealed beam unit, ea.	.3	.3	.3	.3	.3	.3	.3	.3	.3	.3
Replace foot dimmer switch	.3	.3	.3	.3	.3	.3	.3	.3	.3	.3
Replace headlamp vacuum motor, one side	.8	.8	.8	.8	.8	.8	.8	.8	.8	.8
Replace signal/hazard flasher	.2	.2	.2	.2	.2	.2	.2	.2	.2	.2
Replace turn signal/hazard switch,										
With standard column	1.2	1.2	1.2	1.0	1.0	1.0	1.0	1.0	1.0	1.0
With tilt or telescopic column	1.5	1.5	1.5	1.3	1.3	1.3	1.3	1.3	1.3	1.3
Replace back-up light switch	.4	.4	.4	.4	.4	.4	.4	.4	.4	.4
Replace stoplight switch	.3	.3	.3	.3	.3	.3	.3	.3	.3	.3

218 PONTIAC

TUNE-UP, MINOR

Includes:

Basic Job: Perform the following work:
1. Service air cleaner element.
2. Replace PCV valve.
3. Replace crankcase ventilation filter in air cleaner.
4. Clean battery terminals.
5. Check condition and tension of all drive belts.
6. Check all hoses and hose connections
7. Check operation of heated air system (air cleaner), manifold heat valve (EFE valve since 1975) and automatic choke. Service where necessary.
8. Replace fuel filter.
9. Perform compression test.
10. Replace spark plugs.
11. Replace ignition points and condenser.
12. Check dwell or reluctor air gap and adjust ignition timing.
13. Adjust carburetor idle mixture and speed.
14. Make necessary ignition and carburetor adjustments to obtain satisfactory exhaust system analyzer readings.

Additions to Basic Job: Allowances for special equipment and carburetor combinations.

MODEL	1966	1967	1968	1969	1970	1971	1972	1973	1974	1975
Basic Job:										
Perform minor tune-up,										
4-cylinder	—	—	—	—	—	—	—	—	—	2.1
6-cylinder	2.2	2.2	2.2	2.2	2.4	2.4	2.4	2.4	2.5	2.5
V-8 engine	2.7	2.7	2.7	2.7	2.9	2.9	2.9	2.9	2.9	3.0
Additions to Basic Job:										
350/400 CID engines w/4 bbl. carb., **ADD:**	.2	.2	.2	.2	.2	.2	.3	.3	.3	.3
V-8 with 6-bbl. (3x2) carbs., **ADD:**	.4	.4	.4	.4	—	—	—	—	—	—
With AIR pump, **ADD:**	.3	.3	.3	.3	.3	.3	.3	.3	.3	.3
With air conditioning, **ADD:**	.6	.6	.6	.6	.6	.6	.6	.6	.6	.6

Approximate parts cost:

Spark plugs, each	$1.50	Air cleaner element	$5.50
Points & condenser	5.00	Fuel filter	3.50
PCV valve	3.00		

TUNE-UP, MAJOR

Includes:

Basic Job: Perform the following work:
1. Service air cleaner element.
2. Replace crankcase ventilation filter in air cleaner.
3. Replace PCV valve.
4. Check drive belts and adjust for proper tension.
5. Check all hoses and hose connections.
6. Clean battery terminals.
7. Check operation of manifold heat valve (EFE valve since 1975) and automatic choke. Service where necessary.
8. Check operation of heated-air system.
9. Check exhaust and evaporative emission control systems for proper operation.
10. Replace fuel filter.
11. Perform compression check.
12. OHC 4-cylinder engine only: Make valve lash adjustment.
13. Replace spark plugs.
14. Replace ignition points and condenser.
15. Check dwell or reluctor air gap and adjust ignition timing.
16. Check distributor cap and rotor.
17. Tighten cylinder head bolts.
18. Adjust valve lash (where applicable).
19. Overhaul carburetor(s).
20. Adjust carburetor(s) idle mixture and speed.
21. Make necessary ignition and carburetor adjustments to obtain satisfactory exhaust system analyzer readings.

Additions to Basic Job: Allowances for special equipment and carburetor combinations.

MODEL	1966	1967	1968	1969	1970	1971	1972	1973	1974	1975
Basic Job:										
Perform major tune-up,										
4-cylinder	—	—	—	—	—	—	—	—	—	5.5
6-cylinder	5.0	5.0	5.0	5.0	5.5	5.5	5.5	5.5	5.7	5.7
V-8 engine	6.5	6.5	6.5	6.5	6.7	6.7	6.7	6.7	7.0	7.0

(THIS SCHEDULE CONTINUED ON NEXT PAGE.)

PONTIAC 219

TUNE-UP MAJOR Continued

MODEL	1966	1967	1968	1969	1970	1971	1972	1973	1974	1975
Additions to Basic Job:										
With AIR pump, ADD:	.7	.7	.7	.7	.7	.7	.7	.7	.7	.7
Replace hydraulic valve lifter, one, ADD:	2.0	2.0	2.0	2.0	2.0	2.0	2.0	2.0	2.0	2.0
350/400 CID engines, w/4-bbl. carb., ADD:	1.0	1.0	1.0	1.0	1.0	1.0	1.1	1.1	1.1	1.1
V-8 with 6-bbl. (3x2) carbs., ADD:	4.0	4.0	4.0	4.0	—	—	—	—	—	—
With air conditioning, ADD:	.6	.6	.6	.6	.6	.6	.6	.6	.6	.6

Approximate parts cost:

Spark plugs, each	$1.50
Points & condenser	5.00
PCV valve	3.00
Air cleaner element	5.50
Fuel filter	$ 3.50
Carburetor repair kit, ea.	10.00
Ignition coil	14.00
HEI coil	25.00

EMISSION CONTROL SYSTEMS, COMPLETE TEST OR SERVICE

Includes:

Basic Job: Make all necessary tests and repairs. Sign certification certificate.

1. Replace PCV valve, check all vacuum passageways and hoses.
2. Replace crankcase ventilation filter in air cleaner.
3. Test purge-control valve, gas tank filler cap and vent lines, and hoses for leakage.
4. Replace evaporation canister filter.
5. Clean EGR valve and test the control system.
6. Check transmission control spark (TCS) system.
7. Check operation of manifold heat valve and automatic choke. Free-up where necessary.
8. Check and adjust tension of drive belts.
9. Check operation of heated-air system.
10. Check AIR air pump flow.
11. Check routing and condition of hoses.
12. Check operation of diverter of bypass valve.
13. Check AIR manifold and hoses.
14. Replace catalytic converter or pellets, if necessary.
15. Determine if engine tune-up is required.

Related Jobs: Minor or major tune-up as required.

MODEL	1966	1967	1968	1969	1970	1971	1972	1973	1974	1975
Basic Job:										
Perform emission control sys. tune-up,										
4-cylinder	—	—	—	—	—	—	—	—	—	3.1
6-cylinder	.8	.8	.8	.8	2.8	3.3	3.3	3.3	3.5	3.5
V-8 engine	.8	.8	.8	.8	3.8	3.8	3.8	3.8	3.8	4.0
Additions to Basic Job:										
With AIR, all models, ADD:	.5	.5	.5	.5	.5	.5	.5	.5	.5	.5
Related Jobs:										
Perform minor tune-up,										
4-cylinder	—	—	—	—	—	—	—	—	—	2.1
6-cylinder	2.2	2.2	2.2	2.2	2.4	2.4	2.4	2.4	2.5	2.5
V-8 engine	2.7	2.7	2.7	2.7	2.9	2.9	2.9	2.9	2.9	3.0
Perform major tune-up,										
4-cylinder	—	—	—	—	—	—	—	—	—	5.5
6-cylinder	5.0	5.0	5.0	5.0	5.5	5.5	5.5	5.5	5.7	5.7
V-8 engine	6.5	6.5	6.5	6.5	6.7	6.7	6.7	6.7	7.0	7.0
Additions to Related Jobs:										
Minor Tune-up										
350/400 CID engines w/4-bbl. carb., ADD:	.3	.3	.3	.3	.3	.3	.3	.3	.3	.3
V-8 with 6-bbl. (3x2) carbs., ADD:	.4	.4	.4	.4	—	—	—	—	—	—
Major Tune-up										
350/400 CID engines w/4 bbl. carb., ADD:	1.0	1.0	1.0	1.0	1.0	1.0	1.1	1.1	1.1	1.1
V-8 with 6-bbl. (3x2) carbs., ADD:	4.0	4.0	4.0	4.0	—	—	—	—	—	—

(THIS SCHEDULE CONTINUED ON NEXT PAGE.)

220 PONTIAC

EMISSION CONTROL SYSTEMS, COMPLETE TEST OR SERVICE Continued

Approximate parts cost:
Catalytic converter pellets & kit	$70.00
PCV valve	3.00
Hose, per ft.	0.75
Canister filter	1.00
Purge control valve	4.00
Drive belt	$ 3.00
Diverter valve	12.00
Air pump	50.00
Catalytic converter	175.00

See minor or major tune-up section for cost of tune-up parts.

EMISSION CONTROL SYSTEMS, TESTS FOR SMOG STATION CERTIFICATION

Includes:
Basic Job: Test crankcase, exhaust and evaporative emission control systems. Check heated-air system. Check HC/CO level with exhaust analyzer. Sign certification certificate. (No adjustments or repairs included in basic job.)
Related Jobs: Service any defective emission control system. Perform minor or major tune-up as required.
Additions to Related Jobs: Service or replace defective part(s) in the system. Allowances for special equipment installed and carburetor combinations.

MODEL	1966	1967	1968	1969	1970	1971	1972	1973	1974	1975
Basic Job:										
Test all systems & sign certificate,										
4-cylinder	—	—	—	—	—	—	—	—	—	.9
6-cylinder	.5	.5	.5	.5	.5	.8	.8	.8	.9	.9
V-8 engine	1.0	1.0	1.0	1.0	1.0	1.0	1.3	1.3	1.3	1.3
Related Jobs:										
Service crankcase emission control system	.3	.3	.3	.3	.3	.3	.3	.3	.3	.3
Service evaporative emission control system	—	—	—	—	.4	.4	.4	.4	.4	.4
Exhaust emission control systems,										
Service heated-air system	—	—	—	.3	.3	.3	.3	.3	.3	.3
Service transmission controlled spark (TCS/SCS)	—	—	—	—	.5	.5	.5	.5	.5	.5
Service EGR system	—	—	—	—	—	—	.4	.4	.4	.4
Service air injection (AIR) system	.5	.5	.5	.5	.5	.5	.5	.5	.5	.5
Replace catalytic converter pellets	—	—	—	—	—	—	—	—	—	1.0

Note: See separate section for replacement of components in each system.

	1966	1967	1968	1969	1970	1971	1972	1973	1974	1975
Perform minor tune-up,										
4-cylinder	—	—	—	—	—	—	—	—	—	2.1
6-cylinder	2.2	2.2	2.2	2.2	2.4	2.4	2.4	2.4	2.5	2.5
V-8 engine	2.7	2.7	2.7	2.7	2.9	2.9	2.9	2.9	2.9	3.0
Perform major tune-up,										
4-cylinder	—	—	—	—	—	—	—	—	—	5.5
6-cylinder	5.0	5.0	5.0	5.0	5.5	5.5	5.5	5.5	5.7	5.7
V-8 engine	6.5	6.5	6.5	6.5	6.7	6.7	6.7	6.7	7.0	7.0
Additions to Related Jobs:										
Minor Tune-up										
350/400 CID engines w/4-bbl. carb., ADD:	.3	.3	.3	.3	.3	.3	.3	.3	.3	.3
V-8 with 6-bbl. (3x2) carbs., ADD:	.4	.4	.4	.4	—	—	—	—	—	—
Major Tune-up										
350/400 CID engines w/4-bbl. carb., ADD:	1.0	1.0	1.0	1.0	1.0	1.0	1.1	1.1	1.1	1.1
V-8 with 6 bbl. (3x2) carbs., ADD:	4.0	4.0	4.0	4.0	—	—	—	—	—	—
With CCS or AIR pump, ADD:	.3	.3	.3	.3	.3	.3	.3	.3	.3	.3
With air conditioning, ADD:	.6	.6	.6	.6	.6	.6	.6	.6	.6	.6

Approximate parts cost:
Catalytic converter pellets .... $70.00   See minor or major tune-up section for cost of tune-up parts.

PONTIAC 221

POSITIVE CRANKCASE VENTILATION (PCV) SYSTEM, TEST AND SERVICE

Includes:
Basic Job: Test PCV valve, check all vacuum passageways, and inspect hoses. Clean or replace air filter.
Additions to Basic Job: Replace defective parts. (Do not attempt to clean PCV valve, replace if valve is not free.)

MODEL	1966	1967	1968	1969	1970	1971	1972	1973	1974	1975
Basic Job:										
Test PCV system, all models	.3	.3	.3	.3	.3	.3	.3	.3	.3	.3
Additions to Basic Job:										
Replace PCV valve, ADD:	.3	.3	.3	.3	.3	.3	.3	.3	.3	.3
Replace all hoses, ADD:	.6	.6	.6	.6	.6	.6	.6	.6	.6	.6

Approximate parts cost:
PCV valve .... $3.00   Hose, per ft. $0.75

EVAPORATIVE EMISSION CONTROL SYSTEM, TEST AND SERVICE

Includes:
Basic Job: Test purge control valve, gas tank filler cap, vent lines, and hoses.
Additions to Basic Job: Replace defective part.

MODEL	1966	1967	1968	1969	1970	1971	1972	1973	1974	1975
Basic Job:										
Test evap. emission control system	—	—	—	—	.4	.4	.4	.4	.4	.4
Additions to Basic Job:										
Replace purge control valve, ADD:	—	—	—	—	.5	.5	.5	—	—	—
Replace charcoal canister filter, ADD:	—	—	—	—	.3	.3	.3	.3	.3	.3
Replace charcoal canister, ADD:	—	—	—	—	.5	.5	.5	.5	.5	.5
Replace hose, each, ADD:	—	—	—	—	.2	.2	.2	.2	.2	.2

Approximate parts cost:
Purge control valve .... $4.00   Hose, per ft. $0.75
Canister filter .... 1.50   Charcoal canister 32.00

HEATED-AIR SYSTEM, TEST AND SERVICE

Includes:
Basic Job: Check cold/heated-air door, temperature sensor, and vacuum motor.
Additions to Basic Job: Replace defective parts.

MODEL	1966	1967	1968	1969	1970	1971	1972	1973	1974	1975
Basic Job:										
Test heated-air system	—	—	—	.3	.3	.3	.3	.3	.3	.3
Additions to Basic Job:										
Replace vacuum motor, ADD:	—	—	—	.4	.4	.4	.4	.4	.4	.4
Replace temperature sensor, ADD:	—	—	—	.5	.5	.5	.5	.5	.5	.5

Approximate parts cost:
Vacuum motor assembly .... $5.00   Temperature sensor $4.50

222 PONTIAC

AIR INJECTION REACTOR (AIR) SYSTEM, TEST AND SERVICE

Includes:
 Basic Job: Test AIR air pump flow, check routing and condition of hoses, determine operation of diverter valve, verify check valve operation, inspect air manifold and hoses. Check and adjust drive belt tension.
 Additions to Basic Job: Replace defective parts. Replace drive belt, includes adjust tension. Replacement of hose(s), includes soapy water test.

MODEL	1966	1967	1968	1969	1970	1971	1972	1973	1974	1975
Basic Job:										
Test AIR system, all models	.5	.5	.5	.5	.5	.5	.5	.5	.5	.5
Additions to Basic Job:										
Replace and adjust drive belt,										
4 or 6 cylinder, **ADD:**	.4	.4	.4	.4	.4	.4	.4	.4	.4	.4
V-8 engine, **ADD:**	.5	.5	.5	.5	.5	.5	.5	.5	.5	.5
Replace AIR pump,										
4 or 6 cylinder, **ADD:**	.5	.5	.5	.5	.5	.5	.5	.5	.5	.5
V-8 engine, **ADD:**	.7	.7	.7	.7	.7	.7	.7	.7	.7	.7
Replace diverter valve, all models, **ADD:**	.4	.4	.4	.4	.4	.4	.4	.4	.4	.4
Replace check valve assembly, **ADD:**	.3	.3	.3	.3	.3	.3	.3	.3	.3	.3
Repl. hose, incl. soapy water test, **ADD:**	.4	.4	.4	.4	.4	.4	.4	.4	.4	.4

Approximate parts cost:
Drive belt .... $ 3.00
Air pump 50.00
Check valve 7.00
Diverter valve $12.00
Hose, per ft. 0.75

TRANSMISSION CONTROLLED SPARK (TCS) SYSTEM, TEST AND SERVICE

Includes:
 Basic Job: Check engine speed in gear using tachometer and timing light, test TCS solenoid or CEC valve, and transmission switch.
 Additions to Basic Job: Replace defective parts.

MODEL	1966	1967	1968	1969	1970	1971	1972	1973	1974	1975
Basic Job:										
Test TCS system, all models	—	—	—	—	.6	.5	.5	.5	.5	.5
Additions to Basic Job:										
Replace TCS or CEC solenoid, **ADD:**	—	—	—	—	.3	.3	.3	.3	.3	.3
Adjust CEC valve, **ADD:**	—	—	—	—	—	—	—	—	.2	.2
Replace TCS switch,										
With standard transmission, **ADD:**	—	—	—	—	.4	.4	.4	.4	.4	.4
With THM 400 transmission, **ADD:**	—	—	—	—	.8	.8	.8	.8	.8	.8
All other automatic transmissions, **ADD:**	—	—	—	—	.5	.5	.5	.5	.5	.5
Replace TCS relay, **ADD:**	—	—	—	—	.2	.2	.2	.2	.2	.2
Replace thermostatic vacuum switch or TCS temperature switch, **ADD:**	—	—	—	—	.3	.3	.3	.3	.3	.3
Replace idle stop solenoid, **ADD:**	—	—	—	—	.3	.3	.3	.3	.3	.3

Approximate parts cost:
TCS switch $5.00
Thermostatic vacuum switch 6.50
TCS relay 2.50
TCS solenoid $11.50
Idle stop solenoid 11.00
CEC solenoid 12.00

PONTIAC 223

EXHAUST-GAS RECIRCULATION (EGR), TEST AND SERVICE

Includes:
Basic Job: Test EGR valve, control system, and engine idling condition.
Additions to Basic Job: Replace defective parts. Test & repair thermostatic control system.

MODEL	1966	1967	1968	1969	1970	1971	1972	1973	1974	1975
Basic Job:										
Test EGR system, all models	—	—	—	—	—	—	.4	.4	.4	.4
Additions to Basic Job:										
Service EGR valve, **ADD:**	—	—	—	—	—	—	.7	.7	.7	.7
Replace EGR valve, **ADD:**	—	—	—	—	—	—	.4	.4	.4	.4
Test & repair thermo. control sys., **ADD:**	—	—	—	—	—	—	.6	.6	.6	.6

Approximate parts cost:
EGR valve .... $10.00   Thermal vacuum switch $12.00

IGNITION SYSTEM, SERVICE

Includes:
Basic Jobs: 1. Adjust and install new spark plugs.
2. Replace points and condenser, adjust dwell and ignition timing.
3. R&R distributor, overhaul and test centrifugal and vacuum advances, set dwell or check reluctor air gap and ignition timing.
Related Jobs: Replace additional defective part(s) as required.
Additions: Allowances for special equipment installed or replacement of associated defective part(s).

MODEL	1966	1967	1968	1969	1970	1971	1972	1973	1974	1975
Basic Job #1										
Adjust & install new spark plugs,										
4-cylinder	—	—	—	—	—	—	—	—	—	.4
6-cylinder	.6	.6	.6	.6	.6	.6	.6	.6	.6	.6
V-8 engine	.8	.8	.8	.8	.8	.8	.8	.8	.8	.8
With air conditioning, **ADD:**	.3	.3	.3	.3	.3	.3	.3	.3	.3	.3
With AIR, **ADD:**	.3	.3	.3	.3	.3	.3	.3	.3	.3	.3
Basic Job #2										
Replace points and condenser & adjust ignition timing,										
4 or 6-cylinder	.5	.5	.5	.5	.5	.5	.5	.5	.5	—
V-8 engine	.7	.7	.7	.7	.7	.7	.7	.7	.7	—
Replace distributor cap,										
4 or 6-cylinder, **ADD:**	.3	.3	.3	.3	.3	.3	.3	.3	.3	.3
V-8 engine, **ADD:**	.4	.4	.4	.4	.4	.4	.4	.4	.4	.4
Basic Job #3										
R&R and overhaul distirbutor & adjust ignition timing,										
All models	1.4	1.4	1.4	1.4	1.4	1.4	1.4	1.4	1.4	.8
Replace vacuum advance unit, **ADD:**	.2	.2	.2	.2	.2	.2	.2	.2	.2	.2
Related Jobs:										
Replace ignition coil	.4	.4	.4	.4	.4	.4	.4	.4	.4	.6
Replace spark plug wires,										
4-cylinder	—	—	—	—	—	—	—	—	—	.4
6-cylinder	.6	.6	.6	.6	.6	.6	.6	.6	.6	.6
V-8 engine	.8	.8	.8	.8	.8	.8	.8	.8	.8	.8
With air conditioning, **ADD:**	.5	.5	.5	.5	.5	.5	.5	.5	.5	.5
Replace ignition switch, all models	.6	.6	.6	.6	.6	.6	.6	.6	.6	.6
Replace ign. sw. lock cyl. or buzzer sw.	.4	.4	.4	.4	.4	.4	.7	.7	.7	.7

(THIS SCHEDULE CONTINUED ON NEXT PAGE.)

224 PONTIAC

IGNITION SYSTEM, SERVICE Continued

Approximate parts cost:

Spark plugs, each .... $ 1.50	Vacuum control unit .... $ 4.00
Point set 3.00	Ignition coil 12.50
Condenser 1.50	Spark plug wires, 4-cylinder 6.00
Distributor cap 4.50	6-cylinder 7.00
Distributor parts 10.00	V-8 engine 10.00-17.00
Ignition switch 7.00	HEI ignition coil 25.00

CRANKING SYSTEM, TEST AND SERVICE

Includes:
Basic Job: Test battery and cranking system. Clean battery cable terminals.
Related Jobs: Replace defective part(s), including test when necessary.

MODEL	1966	1967	1968	1969	1970	1971	1972	1973	1974	1975
Basic Job:										
Test cranking system	.5	.5	.5	.5	.5	.5	.5	.5	.5	.5
Related Jobs:										
R&R starter,										
4 or 6-cylinder	.7	.7	.7	.7	.7	.8	.8	.8	.8	.8
350/400 CID engines	1.8	1.8	1.8	1.3	1.3	1.3	1.3	1.3	1.3	1.3
All other V-8 engines	.9	.9	.9	.9	.9	.9	1.1	1.1	1.1	1.1
Overhaul starter after removal	1.7	1.7	1.7	1.7	1.7	1.7	1.7	1.7	1.7	1.7
Replace starter-battery cable	.3	.3	.3	.3	.3	.3	.3	.3	.3	.3
Repl. starter solenoid, incl. sys. test,										
4 or 6-cylinder	1.7	1.7	1.7	1.7	1.7	1.7	1.7	1.7	1.7	1.7
350/400 CID engines	2.7	2.6	2.6	2.0	1.9	1.9	1.9	1.9	1.8	1.8
All other V-8 engines	1.9	1.9	1.9	1.9	2.4	2.4	2.3	2.0	2.0	2.0
Repl. starter/neutral switch & adjust,										
With column shift	.4	.4	.4	.4	.4	.4	.4	.4	.4	.4
With floor shift	.6	.6	.6	.6	.6	.6	.6	.6	.6	.6

Approximate parts cost:

Starter, new $80.00	Solenoid switch $4.00-10.00
Starter, rebuilt w/o solenoid 30.00	Starter/neutral switch 4.00
Starter-battery cable 4.50-8.50	

CHARGING SYSTEM, TEST AND SERVICE

Includes:
Basic Job: Test battery voltage and gravity, clean battery cable terminals, test alternator output, test and/or adjust regulator.
Related Jobs: Replace or overhaul defective part(s)

MODEL	1966	1967	1968	1969	1970	1971	1972	1973	1974	1975
Basic Job:										
Test system and/or adjust regulator	.6	.6	.6	.6	.6	.6	.6	.6	.6	.6
Related Jobs:										
R&R alternator incl. pulley	.6	.6	.6	.6	.7	.7	.7	.7	.7	.7
With air conditioning, **ADD:**	.1	.1	.1	.1	.1	.1	.1	.1	.1	.1
With AIR, **ADD:**	.2	.2	.2	.2	.2	.2	.2	.2	.2	.2
Overhaul alternator after removal	2.3	2.3	1.5	1.5	1.5	1.5	1.5	1.5	1.5	1.5
Replace regulator	.3	.3	.3	.3	.4	.4	.4	.3	.3	.3

(THIS SCHEDULE CONTINUED ON NEXT PAGE.)

PONTIAC 225

CHARGING SYSTEM, TEST AND SERVICE Continued

Approximate parts cost:
Alternator, new $75.00-80.00
Alternator, rebuilt 35.00
Regulator $13.00-27.00

FUEL SYSTEM, ADJUST AND SERVICE

Includes:
Basic Job: Adjust idle mixture and speed for performance and to obtain satisfactory exhaust system analyzer readings.
Related Jobs: R&R carburetor, overhaul carburetor(s), R&R associated fuel components.

MODEL	1966	1967	1968	1969	1970	1971	1972	1973	1974	1975
Basic Job:										
Complete carburetor(s) adjustments,										
Single barrel	.4	.4	.4	.4	.4	.4	.4	.4	.4	.4
Two or four-barrel	.6	.6	.6	.6	.6	.6	.6	.6	.6	.6
Six-barrel (3x2)	.8	.8	.8	.8	—	—	—	—	—	—
Related Jobs:										
Replace carb. incl. compl. adjustments,										
Single barrel	.6	.6	.5	.5	.7	.7	.7	.7	.7	.7
Two or four-barrel	1.0	1.0	1.0	1.0	1.0	1.0	1.0	1.0	1.0	1.0
Multiple carbs., ea., **ADD:**	.8	.8	.8	.8	—	—	—	—	—	—
O/H carb., incl. R&R and compl. adjust.,										
Single or two-barrel, ea.	2.6	2.6	2.6	2.5	2.7	2.2	2.4	2.4	2.4	2.4
Four-barrel	4.0	4.0	4.0	4.0	3.2	3.2	3.2	3.2	3.4	3.4
Six-barrel (3x2), all three	7.5	7.5	7.5	7.5	—	—	—	—	—	—
Test & replace fuel pump,										
4 or 6 cylinder OHC engine	.9	.9	.9	.9	—	—	—	—	—	.9
L-6 engine	.5	.5	.5	.5	.5	.5	.5	.5	.5	.5
V-8 engine	.7	.7	.7	.7	.7	.7	.8	.8	.8	.8
Replace fuel filter	.3	.3	.3	.3	.3	.3	.3	.3	.3	.3
Replace fuel tank sending unit,										
Station wagon	1.0	1.0	1.0	1.0	1.0	1.0	1.0	1.0	1.0	1.0
All others	.9	.8	.8	.8	.8	.8	.8	.8	.8	.8
Replace dashboard fuel gauge,										
Gran Prix	1.4	1.4	2.0	2.0	2.0	2.0	2.0	1.4	1.4	1.4
All others	.6	.6	.6	.6	.6	.6	.6	1.0	1.0	1.0
Replace fuel tank,										
Station wagon	1.5	1.5	1.5	1.5	1.5	1.5	1.5	1.5	1.5	1.5
Astre	—	—	—	—	—	—	—	—	—	1.0
All others	1.6	1.6	1.6	1.6	1.6	1.6	1.6	1.4	1.4	1.4
Replace flexible fuel line	.3	.3	.3	.3	.3	.3	.3	.3	.3	.3

Approximate parts cost:
Carburetor repair kit, ea. $10.00
Carburetor, new, ea., single bbl. 40.00
  Two bbl. 70.00
  Four bbl. 110.00
Carburetor, rebuilt, single bbl. 15.00
  Two bbl. 22.00
  Four bbl. 40.00

Fuel pump $15.00
Fuel tank sending unit 13.00-24.00
Fuel gauge, dash 9.00-14.00
Flexible fuel line, per ft. 0.50
Fuel tank 50.00-65.00

226 PONTIAC

ENGINE OVERHAUL, IN-CAR

Includes:
Basic Job: Remove ring ridge, deglaze cylinder walls, fit piston pins, align connecting rods, install new piston rings and rod bearings, install new main bearing inserts and oil seals, overhaul oil pump, clean carbon, grind valves, and perform major tune-up.
Additions to Basic Job: Associated work that is required during basic job and allowances for special equipment.

MODEL	1966	1967	1968	1969	1970	1971	1972	1973	1974	1975
Basic Job:										
Overhaul engine,										
4-cylinder	—	—	—	—	—	—	—	—	—	17.5
6-cylinder OHC engine	23.0	23.0	23.0	23.0	—	—	—	—	—	—
L-6 engine	—	—	—	—	24.5	24.5	24.5	25.0	25.0	25.0
V-8 engine	29.0	29.0	29.0	29.4	29.4	29.4	29.0	29.0	29.0	29.5
Additions to Basic Job:										
Rebore cylinders,										
4-cylinder, **ADD:**	—	—	—	—	—	—	—	—	—	3.0
6-cylinder, **ADD:**	4.0	4.0	4.0	4.0	4.0	4.0	4.0	4.0	4.0	4.0
V-8 engine, **ADD:**	5.0	5.0	5.0	5.0	5.0	5.0	5.0	5.0	5.0	5.0
Expand pistons,										
4-cylinder, **ADD:**	—	—	—	—	—	—	—	—	—	1.2
6-cylinder, **ADD:**	1.8	1.8	1.8	1.8	1.8	1.8	1.8	1.8	1.8	1.8
V-8 engine, **ADD:**	2.4	2.4	2.4	2.4	2.4	2.4	2.4	2.4	2.4	2.4
Regroove top piston ring groove,										
4-cylinder, **ADD:**	—	—	—	—	—	—	—	—	—	1.2
6-cylinder, **ADD:**	1.8	1.8	1.8	1.8	1.8	1.8	1.8	1.8	1.8	1.8
V-8 engine, **ADD:**	2.4	2.4	2.4	2.4	2.4	2.4	2.4	2.4	2.4	2.4
Replace hydraulic valve lifters, **ADD:**	1.0	1.0	1.0	1.0	1.0	1.0	1.0	1.0	1.0	1.0
Replace rocker arm stud, each, **ADD:**	.3	.3	.3	.3	.3	.3	.3	.3	.3	.3
Ream valve guides oversize,										
4-cylinder, **ADD:**	—	—	—	—	—	—	—	—	—	.5
6-cylinder, **ADD:**	.7	.7	.7	.7	.7	.7	.7	.7	.7	.7
V-8 engine, **ADD:**	.9	.9	.9	.9	.9	.9	.9	.9	.9	.9
With AIR pump, **ADD:**	.7	.7	.7	.7	.7	.7	.7	.7	.7	.7
With air conditioning, **ADD:**	.7	.7	.7	.7	.7	.7	.7	.7	.7	.7
350/400 CID engines w/4-bbl. carb., **ADD:**	1.0	1.0	1.0	1.0	1.0	1.0	1.0	1.0	1.0	1.0
V-8 with 6-bbl. carbs. (3x2), **ADD:**	4.0	4.0	4.0	4.0	—	—	—	—	—	—

Approximate parts cost:

Hydraulic valve lifters, ea.	$ 4.00
Major tune-up parts	20.00-35.00
Carburetor repair kit	10.00-20.00
Rod bearing inserts, 4-cylinder	16.00
6-cylinder	24.00
8-cylinder	32.00
Rear main brg. oil seal set	3.00
Complete gasket set, 4-cylinder	24.00
6-cylinder	26.00
8-cylinder	30.00
Main bearing inserts, 4-cylinder	$20.00
6-cylinder	27.00
V-8 engine	22.00
Piston rings, complete set, 4-cylinder	18.00
6-cylinder	27.00
8-cylinder	36.00
Piston pins, 4-cylinder	8.00
6-cylinder	12.00
8-cylinder	16.00
Piston assemblies, 4-cylinder	75.00
6-cylinder	85.00
8-cylinder	128.00

PONTIAC 227

ENGINE OVERHAUL, OUT-OF-CAR

Includes:
Basic Job: R&R engine, remove ring ridge, rebore or hone cylinder walls, regrind crankshaft and camshaft, replace camshaft bushings and line ream, replace timing chain and gears and oil seal, install main bearing inserts and seals, install piston pins, align connecting rods, install new piston rings and rod bearings, overhaul oil pump, clean carbon, grind valves, overhaul rocker arm mechanism, and perform major tune-up.
Additions to Basic Job: Associated work that is required during basic job and allowances for special equipment installed.

MODEL	1966	1967	1968	1969	1970	1971	1972	1973	1974	1975
Basic Job:										
Overhaul engine,										
4-cylinder	—	—	—	—	—	—	—	—	—	28.9
6-cylinder OHC engine	32.0	32.0	32.0	32.0	—	—	—	—	—	—
L-6 engine	—	—	—	—	34.5	34.5	34.5	35.0	35.0	35.4
V-8 engine	42.5	42.5	42.5	42.5	42.5	42.0	42.0	42.0	42.0	42.0
Additions to Basic Job:										
Regroove top piston ring groove,										
4-cylinder, **ADD:**	—	—	—	—	—	—	—	—	—	1.2
6-cylinder, **ADD:**	1.8	1.8	1.8	1.8	1.8	1.8	1.8	1.8	1.8	1.8
V-8 engine, **ADD:**	2.4	2.4	2.4	2.4	2.4	2.4	2.4	2.4	2.4	2.4
Replace rocker arm stud, ea., **ADD:**	.3	.3	.3	.3	.3	.3	.3	.3	.3	.3
Ream valve guides oversize,										
4-cylinder, **ADD:**	—	—	—	—	—	—	—	—	—	.5
6-cylinder, **ADD:**	.7	.7	.7	.7	.7	.7	.7	.7	.7	.7
V-8 engine, **ADD:**	.9	.9	.9	.9	.9	.9	.9	.9	.9	.9
Replace all engine mounts, **ADD:**	.6	.6	.6	.6	.6	.6	.6	.6	.6	.6
Replace worn clutch parts, **ADD:**	.5	.5	.5	.5	.5	.5	.5	.5	.5	.5
With AIR pump, **ADD:**	.7	.7	.7	.7	.7	.7	.7	.7	.7	.7
With air conditioning, incl. chg. sys., **ADD:**	1.8	1.8	1.8	1.8	1.8	1.8	1.8	1.8	1.8	1.8
350/400 CID engines w/4 bbl. carb., **ADD:**	1.0	1.0	1.0	1.0	1.0	1.0	1.0	1.0	1.0	1.0
V-8 with 6-bbl. (3x2) carbs., **ADD:**	4.0	4.0	4.0	4.0	—	—	—	—	—	—

Approximate parts cost:

Complete gasket set, 4-cylinder	$24.00
6-cylinder	26.00
V-8 engine	30.00
Hydraulic valve lifters, ea.	4.00
Piston rings, complete set, 4-cylinder	18.00
6-cylinder	27.00
8-cylinder	36.00
Piston pins, 4-cylinder	8.00
6-cylinder	12.00
8-cylinder	16.00
Piston assemblies, 4-cylinder	75.00
6-cylinder	85.00
8-cylinder	128.00
Rod bearing inserts, 4-cylinder	$16.00
6-cylinder	24.00
8-cylinder	32.00
Rear main bearing oil seal set	3.00
Main bearing inserts, 4-cylinder	20.00
6-cylinder	27.00
V-8 engine	22.00
Engine mounts	7.00
Pressure plate	30.00-60.00
Clutch disc	21.00-48.00
Clutch release bearing	5.00-15.00
Major tune-up parts	22.00-35.00
Carburetor repair kits, ea.	10.00

228 PONTIAC

SHORT BLOCK, REPLACE

Includes:
    Basic Job: R&R engine, clean and reface valves, scrape carbon, grind valve seats, replace valve seals, overhaul rocker arm mechanism, transfer all parts, and perform major tune-up.
    Additions to Basic Job: Associated work that is required during basic job and allowances for special equipment installed and/or carburetor combinations.

MODEL	1966	1967	1968	1969	1970	1971	1972	1973	1974	1975
Basic Job:										
Replace short block,										
4-cylinder	—	—	—	—	—	—	—	—	—	13.2
6-cylinder OHC engine	15.5	15.5	15.5	15.5	—	—	—	—	—	—
L-6 engine	—	—	—	—	17.7	17.7	17.7	17.7	17.3	17.3
V-8 engine	22.5	22.5	22.5	22.0	22.0	20.1	20.1	20.1	20.1	20.1
Additions to Basic Job:										
Ream valve guides oversize,										
4-cylinder, **ADD:**	.5	.5	.5	.5	.5	.5	.5	.5	.5	.5
6-cylinder, **ADD:**	.7	.7	.7	.7	.7	.7	.7	.7	.7	.7
V-8 engine, **ADD:**	.9	.9	.9	.9	.9	.9	.9	.9	.9	.9
Replace rocker arm stud, ea., **ADD:**	.3	.3	.3	.3	.3	.3	.3	.3	.3	.3
Replace all engine mounts, **ADD:**	.6	.6	.6	.6	.6	.6	.6	.6	.6	.6
Replace worn clutch parts, **ADD:**	.5	.5	.5	.5	.5	.5	.5	.5	.5	.5
With AIR pump, **ADD:**	.7	.7	.7	.7	.7	.7	.7	.7	.7	.7
With air conditioning incl. chg. sys., **ADD:**	1.8	1.8	1.8	1.8	1.8	1.8	1.8	1.8	1.8	1.8
350/400 CID engines w/4-bbl. carb., **ADD:**	1.0	1.0	1.0	1.0	1.0	1.0	1.0	1.0	1.0	1.0
V-8 with 6-bbl. (3x2) carbs., **ADD:**	4.0	4.0	4.0	4.0	—	—	—	—	—	—

Approximate parts cost:

Complete gasket set, 4-cylinder	$24.00	Oil and air filters	$ 9.00
6-cylinder	26.00	Pressure plate	30.00-60.00
V-8 engine	30.00	Clutch disc	21.00-40.00
Engine mounts	7.00	Clutch release bearing	5.00-15.00
Short block: Call supplier for price quote.		Carburetor repair kit, ea.	10.00

TIMING CHAIN MECHANISM, SERVICE

Includes:
    Basic Job: 1. OHC engines: Replace camshaft drive belt, adjust tension, and perform minor tune-up.
                   2. L-6 engines: Replace timing gear, cover gasket, oil seal, and perform minor tune-up.
                   3. V-8 engines: Replace timing cover oil seal and timing chain and perform minor tune-up.
    Additions to Basic Job: Associated work required during basic job and allowances for special equipment installed.

MODEL	1966	1967	1968	1969	1970	1971	1972	1973	1974	1975
Basic Job #1										
Replace camshaft drive belt, adjust tension, and minor tune-up,										
4-cylinder OHC engine	—	—	—	—	—	—	—	—	—	3.1
6-cylinder OHC engine	3.2	3.2	3.2	3.2	—	—	—	—	—	—
Additions to Basic Job #1										
Replace camshaft sprocket, **ADD:**	.2	.2	.2	.2	—	—	—	—	—	.2
Replace camshaft oil seal, **ADD:**	.2	.2	.2	.2	—	—	—	—	—	.2
Replace crankshaft sprocket, **ADD:**	.3	.3	.3	.3	—	—	—	—	—	.3
With air conditioning, **ADD:**	.5	.5	.5	.5	—	—	—	—	—	.5
With AIR, **ADD:**	.2	.2	.2	.2	—	—	—	—	—	.2
Basic Job #2										
Replace camshaft gear, cover oil seal and perform minor tune-up,										
L-6 engine	7.5	7.5	7.5	7.5	7.9	6.7	6.7	7.0	7.0	7.2

(THIS SCHEDULE CONTINUED ON NEXT PAGE.)

TIMING CHAIN MECHANISM, SERVICE Continued

MODEL	1966	1967	1968	1969	1970	1971	1972	1973	1974	1975
Additions to Basic Job #2										
Replace crankshaft gear, **ADD**:	.2	.2	.2	.2	.2	.2	.2	.2	.2	.2
With air conditioning, **ADD**:	.2	.2	.2	.2	.2	.2	.2	.2	.2	.2
With power steering, **ADD**:	.2	.2	.2	.2	.2	.2	.2	.2	.2	.2
With AIR, **ADD**:	.3	.3	.3	.3	.3	.3	.3	.3	.3	.3
Basic Job #3										
Replace timing cover oil seal and timing chain. Perform minor tune-up.										
V-8 engine	4.8	4.8	4.8	4.8	4.8	4.5	4.5	4.5	5.0	5.0
Additions to Basic Job #3										
Replace crankshaft sprocket, **ADD**:	.2	.2	.2	.2	.2	.2	.2	.2	.2	.2
With air conditioning, **ADD**:	.5	.5	.5	.5	.5	.5	.5	.5	.5	.5
With AIR, **ADD**:	.2	.2	.2	.2	.2	.2	.2	.2	.2	.2
With power steering, **ADD**:	.3	.3	.3	.3	.3	.3	.3	.3	.3	.3

Approximate parts cost:
Timing cover gasket	$1.00
Timing cover oil seal	2.00
Timing chain	9.00
Camshaft drive belt (OHC engine)	9.00
Crankshaft sprocket (OHC engine)	9.00
Camshaft gear	$14.00
Crankshaft gear	6.00
Camshaft sprocket	6.00-12.00
Crankshaft sprocket	4.50
Minor tune-up parts	25.00-30.00

OIL PUMP SERVICE

Includes:
Basic Job: Service oil pump, and replace oil filter element.

MODEL	1966	1967	1968	1969	1970	1971	1972	1973	1974	1975
Basic Job:										
Service oil pump, and replace oil filter element.										
4-cylinder OHC engine	—	—	—	—	—	—	—	—	—	*3.8
6-cylinder OHC engine	1.0	1.0	1.0	1.0	—	—	—	—	—	—
L-6 engine	—	—	—	—	2.0	2.0	2.0	2.0	2.0	2.0
V-8 engine	2.8	2.8	2.8	2.8	2.8	2.4	2.4	2.4	2.4	2.4
All models with air conditioning, **ADD**:	.4	.4	.4	.4	.4	.4	.4	.4	.4	.4

*Includes: R&R front crossmember, radiator, water pump, oil pump, & clean oil pan.

Additions to Basic Job:										
Overhaul oil pump, **ADD**:	.8	.8	.8	.8	.8	.8	.8	.8	.8	.8
Replace rear main bearing insert & seals,										
4-cylinder, **ADD**:	—	—	—	—	—	—	—	—	—	.4
6-cylinder, **ADD**:	.3	.3	.3	.3	.3	.3	.3	.3	.3	.3
V-8 engine, **ADD**:	.4	.4	.4	.4	.4	.4	.4	.4	.4	.4
Replace other main brg. inserts, ea., **ADD**:	.6	.6	.6	.6	.6	.6	.6	.6	.6	.6

Approximate parts cost:
Oil pan	$24.00
Oil pan gasket	4.00
Oil pump shaft & rotor kit	8.00
Oil pump screen	2.50
Oil filter element	5.00
Oil pump, 4-cylinder OHC engine	$25.00
6-cylinder OHC engine	55.00
L-6 engine	18.00
V-8 engine	24.00

230 PONTIAC

BEARINGS, MAIN AND/OR RODS, REPLACE

Includes:
  Basic Job: R&R oil pan, measure connecting rod bearing oil clearance with Plastigage, install new connecting rod bearing inserts, and oil filter element.
  Additions to Basic Job: Measure main bearing oil clearance with Pastigage, replace all main bearing inserts and rear main bearing oil seals, repair or replace oil pump.

MODEL	1966	1967	1968	1969	1970	1971	1972	1973	1974	1975
Basic Job:										
R&R pan, measure, install inserts & filter,										
4-cylinder OHC engine	—	—	—	—	—	—	—	—	—	*5.4
6-cylinder OHC engine	4.6	4.6	4.6	4.6	—	—	—	—	—	—
L-6 engine	—	—	—	—	4.4	4.4	4.4	4.4	4.4	4.4
V-8 engine	6.0	6.0	6.0	6.0	6.0	5.6	5.6	5.6	5.6	5.6
*Includes: R&R front crossmember, radiator, water pump, oil pan, & service oil pump.										
All models with air conditioning, **ADD:**	.4	.4	.4	.4	.4	.4	.4	.4	.4	.4
Additions to Basic Job:										
Use Plastigage — all main bearings,										
4-cylinder, **ADD:**	—	—	—	—	—	—	—	—	—	.5
6-cylinder, **ADD**	.7	.7	.7	.7	.7	.7	.7	.7	.7	.7
V-8 engine, **ADD:**	.5	.5	.5	.5	.5	.5	.5	.5	.5	.5
Replace main inserts & rear oil seals,										
4-cylinder, **ADD:**	—	—	—	—	—	—	—	—	—	2.5
6-cylinder, **ADD:**	3.5	3.5	3.5	3.5	3.5	3.5	3.5	3.5	3.5	3.5
V-8 engine, **ADD:**	2.5	2.5	2.5	2.5	2.5	2.5	2.5	2.5	2.5	2.5
Overhaul oil pump, **ADD:**	.8	.8	.8	.8	.8	.8	.8	.8	.8	.8

Approximate parts cost:

Oil pan gasket	$ 4.00
Rod bearing inserts, 4-cylinder	16.00
6-cylinder	24.00
8-cylinder	32.00
Rear main bearing oil seal set	3.00
Main bearing inserts, 4-cylinder	20.00
6-cylinder	27.00
V-8 engine	22.00
Oil filter element	$ 5.00
Oil pump, 4-cylinder OHC engine	25.00
6-cylinder OHC engine	55.00
L-6 engine	18.00
V-8 engine	24.00
Oil filter element	5.00
Oil pump shaft & rotor kit	8.00

VALVE MECHANISM, SERVICE

Includes:
  Adjustment and Tune-up: Adjust valve lash and perform minor tune-up.
  Basic Job: Clean and reface valves, scrape carbon, grind valve seats, replace valve seals, adjust valves, and perform major tune-up.
  Additions to Basic Job: Associated work required during basic job and allowances for special equipment installed.

MODEL	1966	1967	1968	1969	1970	1971	1972	1973	1974	1975
Adjustment & Tune-up:										
4-cylinder OHC engine	—	—	—	—	—	—	—	—	—	2.5
L-6 engine	—	—	—	—	3.0	3.0	3.0	3.0	3.1	3.1
Basic Job:										
Service valve mechanism,										
4-cylinder OHC engine	—	—	—	—	—	—	—	—	—	14.5
6-cylinder OHC engine	16.5	16.5	16.5	16.5	—	—	—	—	—	—
L-6 engine	—	—	—	—	10.8	10.8	10.8	10.8	11.0	11.0
V-8 engine	15.8	15.8	15.8	15.8	15.8	16.0	16.0	16.0	16.0	16.1

(THIS SCHEDULE CONTINUED ON NEXT PAGE.)

PONTIAC 231

VALVE MECHANISM, SERVICE Continued

MODEL	1966	1967	1968	1969	1970	1971	1972	1973	1974	1975
Additions to Basic Job:										
Ream valve guides oversize,										
4-cylinder	—	—	—	—	—	—	—	—	—	.6
6-cylinder	.7	.7	.7	.7	.7	.7	.7	.7	.7	.7
V-8 engine	.9	.9	.9	.9	.9	.9	.9	.9	.9	.9
Replace rocker arm stud, ea., ADD:	.3	.3	.3	.3	.3	.3	.3	.3	.3	.3
Replace hydraulic valve lifters, ADD:	1.0	1.0	1.0	1.0	1.0	1.0	1.0	1.0	1.0	1.0
350/400 CID engines, w/4-bbl. carb., ADD:	1.0	1.0	1.0	1.0	1.0	1.0	1.0	1.0	1.0	1.0
V-8 with 6-bbl. carbs. (3x2), ADD:	4.0	4.0	4.0	4.0	—	—	—	—	—	—
With air conditioning, ADD:	.6	.6	.6	.6	.6	.6	.6	.6	.6	.6
With AIR pump, ADD:	.7	.7	.7	.7	.7	.7	.7	.7	.7	.7

Approximate parts cost:

Valve grind gasket set, 4-cyl. OHC	$14.00
6-cyl. OHC	10.00
L-6 engine	9.00
V-8 engine	20.00
Hydraulic valve lifters, each	$ 4.00
Valve spring, each	2.00
Major tune-up parts	35.00

CYLINDER HEAD AND/OR GASKET, REPLACE

Includes:

Basic Jobs: 1. R&R intake manifold and cylinder head to install new gasket. Clean head and block surfaces and perform minor tune-up.
               2. Install new cylinder head, including recondition valves and perform minor tune-up.
Additions to Basic Job: Allowances for special equipment and/or carburetor combinations.

MODEL	1966	1967	1968	1969	1970	1971	1972	1973	1974	1975
Replace head gasket, including minor tune-up,										
4-cylinder OHC engine	—	—	—	—	—	—	—	—	—	4.6
6-cylinder OHC engine	5.2	5.2	5.2	5.2	—	—	—	—	—	—
L-6 engine	—	—	—	—	4.3	4.3	4.3	4.3	4.4	4.4
V-8 engine, one side	6.7	6.7	6.7	6.7	6.9	6.9	6.9	6.9	6.9	7.0
V-8 engine, both sides	8.5	8.5	8.5	8.5	8.7	8.7	8.7	8.7	8.7	8.8
Basic Job #2										
Install new cylinder head, including minor tune-up,										
4-cylinder OHC engine	—	—	—	—	—	—	—	—	—	7.5
6-cylinder OHC engine	8.4	8.4	8.4	8.4	—	—	—	—	—	—
L-6 engine	—	—	—	—	6.0	6.0	6.0	6.0	6.1	6.1
V-8 engine, one side	7.5	7.5	7.5	7.5	7.9	7.9	7.9	7.9	7.9	8.0
V-8 engine, both sides	10.6	10.6	10.6	10.6	10.8	10.8	10.8	10.8	10.8	11.0
Additions to Basic Jobs:										
With air conditioning, ADD:	.5	.5	.5	.5	.5	.5	.5	.5	.5	.5
With AIR pump, ADD:	.3	.3	.3	.3	.3	.3	.3	.3	.3	.3
With power steering, ADD:	.3	.3	.3	.3	.3	.3	.3	.3	.3	.3
350/400 CID engines, w/4 bbl. carb., ADD:	.2	.2	.2	.2	.2	.2	.2	.2	.2	.2
V-8 with 6-bbl. (3x2) carbs., ADD:	.4	.4	.4	.4	—	—	—	—	—	—

Approximate parts cost:

Head gasket, each	$ 4.00
Cylinder head, 4-cylinder OHC engine	90.00
6-cylinder OHC engine	120.00
L-6 engine	95.00
V-8 engine, ea.	75.00-95.00
Valve grind gasket set, 4-cylinder, OHC	$14.00
6-cylinder, OHC	10.00
L-6 engine	9.00
V-8 engine	20.00
Minor tune-up parts	22.00-30.00

232 PONTIAC

COOLING SYSTEM, TEST AND SERVICE

Includes:

Basic Job: Drain and back-flush system, check for leaks and tighten all hose connections, pressure-test radiator cap and system.
Related Jobs: Replace defective part. Work performed independently of basic job.
Additions to Related Jobs: Allowances for special equipment installed.

MODEL	1966	1967	1968	1969	1970	1971	1972	1973	1974	1975
Basic Job:										
Drain, flush, fill, and pressure-test system	.9	.9	.9	.9	.9	.9	.9	.9	.9	.9
Related Jobs:										
Replace upper hose	.4	.4	.4	.4	.4	.4	.4	.4	.4	.4
Replace lower hose	.5	.5	.5	.5	.5	.5	.5	.5	.5	.5
Both hoses	.7	.7	.7	.7	.7	.7	.7	.7	.7	.7
Replace thermostat & pressure-test system	.6	.6	.6	.6	.6	.6	.6	.6	.6	.6
Replace water pump drive belt & adjust tension,										
OHC engines	1.0	1.0	1.0	1.0	—	—	—	—	—	1.0
All others	.4	.4	.4	.4	.4	.4	.4	.4	.4	.4
Replace water pump,										
OHC engines	1.3	1.3	1.3	1.3	—	—	—	—	—	1.3
All others	1.0	1.0	1.0	1.0	1.0	1.0	1.0	1.0	1.0	1.0
With air conditioning, **ADD:**	.2	.2	.2	.2	.2	.2	.2	.2	.2	.2
With power steering, **ADD:**	.2	.2	.2	.2	.2	.2	.2	.2	.2	.2
With AIR, **ADD:**	.2	.2	.2	.2	.2	.2	.2	.2	.2	.2
Replace radiator, incl. pressure-test system,										
OHC engine	.7	.7	.7	.7	—	—	—	—	—	.7
L-6 engine	—	—	—	—	.6	.6	.6	.6	.6	.6
V-8 engine	.8	.8	.8	.8	.8	.8	.8	.8	.8	.8
With automatic transmission, **ADD:**	.2	.2	.2	.2	.2	.2	.2	.2	.2	.2
Replace water temp. gauge, engine	.4	.4	.4	.4	.4	.4	.4	.4	.4	.4
With air conditioning, **ADD:**	.1	.1	.1	.1	.1	.1	.1	.1	.1	.1
Replace water temp. gauge, dash,										
Grand Prix	2.5	2.5	2.5	2.5	2.5	2.5	2.5	1.0	1.0	1.0
Firebird	—	1.0	1.0	1.0	1.0	1.0	1.0	1.0	1.0	1.0
All others	.6	.6	.6	.6	.6	.6	1.0	1.0	1.0	1.0
Replace water jacket expansion plug,										
L-6 engine, head, ea.	—	—	—	—	.5	.5	.5	.5	.5	.5
Block, rear	—	—	—	—	3.0	3.0	3.0	3.0	3.0	3.0
Block, side, front or rear	—	—	—	—	.7	.7	.7	.7	.7	.7
Block side, center	—	—	—	—	1.1	1.1	1.1	1.1	1.1	1.1
V-8 engine, head, front	.5	.5	.5	.5	.5	.5	.5	.5	.5	.5
Side of block, ea.	1.2	1.2	1.2	1.2	1.2	1.2	1.2	1.2	1.2	1.2
Rear of block, auto. trans.	2.5	2.5	2.5	2.5	2.5	2.5	2.5	2.5	2.5	2.5
Rear of block, std. trans.	3.2	3.2	3.2	3.2	3.2	3.2	3.2	3.2	3.2	3.2

Approximate parts cost:

Radiator, new	$100.00-160.00
Upper or lower hose, ea.	5.00
Thermostat	4.00
Water pump, OHC engine	25.00
L-6 engine	20.00
V-8 engine	30.00
Camshaft drive belt (OHC) engine	$ 9.00
Drive belt, ea.	3.00
Temperature gauge, engine	4.00
Temperature gauge, dash	10.00
Expansion plug, ea.	1.50

PONTIAC

EXHAUST SYSTEM, TEST AND SERVICE

Includes:
Basic Job: Test exhaust system for leaks and/or exhaust odors. Use HC/CO exhaust analyzer to trace carbon monoxide leaks.
Related Jobs: Replace defective parts. Each job includes basic job tests and installation of new hangers as required.

MODEL	1966	1967	1968	1969	1970	1971	1972	1973	1974	1975
Basic Job:										
Complete test of exhaust system	.4	.4	.4	.4	.4	.4	.4	.4	.4	.4
Related Jobs:										
Replace muffler,										
Front, single or dual, one	1.3	1.3	1.3	1.3	1.3	1.3	1.3	1.3	1.3	1.3
Rear, single or dual, one	1.2	1.2	1.2	1.2	1.2	1.2	1.2	1.2	1.2	1.2
One side, single or dual, two	1.8	1.8	1.8	1.8	1.8	1.8	1.8	1.8	1.8	1.8
One each side, dual, two	1.9	1.9	1.9	1.9	1.9	1.9	1.9	1.9	1.9	1.9
Replace tail pipe,										
Single or dual, one	1.1	1.1	1.1	1.1	1.1	1.1	1.1	1.1	1.1	1.1
Dual, two	1.4	1.4	1.4	1.4	1.4	1.4	1.4	1.4	1.4	1.4
Replace exhaust pipe flange gasket, ea.	1.0	1.0	1.0	1.0	1.0	1.0	1.0	1.0	1.0	1.0
Replace exhaust manifold gasket,										
4/6-cylinder	2.0	2.0	2.0	2.0	2.0	2.9	2.9	2.9	2.9	2.9
V-8, left side	1.4	1.4	1.4	1.4	1.4	1.8	1.8	1.8	1.8	1.8
V-8, right side	1.4	1.4	1.4	1.4	1.4	1.6	1.6	1.6	1.6	1.6
With air conditioning, **ADD:**	.3	.3	.3	.3	.3	.3	.3	.3	.3	.3
With power steering, **ADD:**	.3	.3	.3	.3	.3	.3	.3	.3	.3	.3
With AIR, **ADD:**	.4	.4	.4	.4	.4	.4	.4	.4	.4	.4
Free-up or O/H heat control or EFE valve,										
4/6-cylinder	1.5	1.5	1.5	1.5	1.5	1.5	1.5	1.5	1.5	1.5
V-8 engine	1.8	1.8	1.8	1.8	1.8	1.8	1.8	1.8	1.8	1.8
Replace exhaust pipe,										
4/6-cylinder	1.3	1.3	1.3	1.3	1.3	1.3	1.3	1.3	1.3	1.3
V-8 single exhaust	1.4	1.4	1.4	1.4	1.4	1.4	1.4	1.4	1.4	1.4
V-8 dual exhaust, one pipe	1.2	1.2	1.2	1.2	1.2	1.2	1.2	1.2	1.2	1.2
V-8 dual exhaust, both pipes	2.0	2.0	2.0	2.0	2.0	2.0	2.0	2.0	2.0	2.0
Replace catalytic converter, ea.	—	—	—	—	—	—	—	—	1.0	1.0
Replace catalytic converter catalyst	—	—	—	—	—	—	—	—	1.5	1.5
Replace bottom cover, **ADD:**	—	—	—	—	—	—	—	—	.5	.5

Approximate parts cost:
Muffler	$28.00	Exhaust pipe, each	$15.00
Tail pipe, each	12.00	Exhaust manifold gasket, each	3.00
Catalytic converter	175.00	Catalytic converter pellets	70.00
Heat control valve (through 1974)	12.00	Early Fuel Evaporation (EFE) valve	30.00

SHIFT LINKAGE, SERVICE

Includes:
Adjust: Adjust manual transmission shift linkage.
Basic Job: Replace one control rod and/or grommet and adjust linkage.
Additions to Basic Job: Associated work that is required during basic job.

MODEL	1966	1967	1968	1969	1970	1971	1972	1973	1974	1975
Adjust shift linkage:										
3-speed transmission	.5	.5	.5	.5	.5	.5	.5	.5	.5	.5
4-speed transmission	.6	.6	.6	.6	.6	.6	.6	.6	.6	.6

(THIS SCHEDULE CONTINUED ON NEXT PAGE.)

PONTIAC

SHIFT LINKAGE, SERVICE Continued

MODEL	1966	1967	1968	1969	1970	1971	1972	1973	1974	1975
Basic Job:										
Replace one rod and/or grommet & adjust,										
3-speed transmission	.8	.8	.8	.8	.8	.8	.8	.8	.8	.8
4-speed transmission	.9	.9	.9	.9	.9	.9	.9	.9	.9	.9
Additions to Basic Job:										
Replace additional rod, **ADD:**	.3	.3	.3	.3	.3	.3	.3	.3	.3	.3
Replace shift lever oil seals, both, **ADD:**	.5	.5	.5	.5	.5	.5	.5	.5	.5	.5

Approximate parts cost:
Shift rod, each $2.00
Rear oil seal 2.50
Shift lever oil seals $1.50

CLUTCH MECHANISM, SERVICE

Includes:
Adjust: Adjust clutch pedal play.
Basic Job: Replace thrust bearing, pressure plate, and disc. Adjust clutch pedal play.
Additions to Basic Job: Associated work that is required during basic job.

MODEL	1966	1967	1968	1969	1970	1971	1972	1973	1974	1975
Adjustment:										
Adjust clutch pedal play	.3	.3	.3	.3	.3	.3	.3	.3	.3	.3
Basic Job:										
Repl. thrust brg., pressure plate & disc,										
3-speed transmission	2.1	2.1	2.1	2.1	2.1	2.1	2.2	2.2	2.2	2.2
4-speed transmission	2.6	2.6	2.6	2.6	3.0	3.0	3.0	2.8	2.8	2.8
Additions to Basic Job:										
Remove, reface, and instl. flywheel, **ADD:**	1.8	1.8	1.8	1.8	1.8	1.8	1.8	1.8	1.8	1.8
Replace flywheel ring gear, **ADD:**	1.0	1.0	1.0	1.0	1.0	1.0	1.0	1.0	1.0	1.0
Resurface clutch pressure plate, **ADD:**	.8	.8	.8	.8	.8	.8	.8	.8	.8	.8
Replace flywheel pilot bearing, **ADD:**	.2	.2	.2	.2	.2	.2	.2	.2	.2	.2
Replace clutch release (throwout) bearing, **ADD:**	.2	.2	.2	.2	.2	.2	.2	.2	.2	.2

Approximate parts cost:
Pressure plate $25.00-60.00
Clutch disc 20.00-35.00
Thrust bearing 5.00-15.00
Flywheel pilot bearing .... $ 1.00
Flywheel w/ring gear 36.00-56.00

STANDARD TRANSMISSION, OVERHAUL

Includes:
Basic Job: R&R transmission, disassemble, replace worn parts, and adjust linkage.
Additions to Basic Job: Associated work that is required during basic job.

MODEL	1966	1967	1968	1969	1970	1971	1972	1973	1974	1975
Basic Job:										
R&R, overhaul transmission, and adjust linkage,										
3-speed transmission	5.4	5.4	5.4	5.4	5.4	5.4	5.4	5.4	5.4	5.4
4-speed transmission	6.9	6.9	6.9	6.9	6.9	6.9	6.9	6.9	6.9	6.9

(THIS SCHEDULE CONTINUED ON NEXT PAGE.)

PONTIAC 235

STANDARD TRANSMISSION, OVERHAUL Continued

MODEL	1966	1967	1968	1969	1970	1971	1972	1973	1974	1975
Additions to Basic Job:										
Reconditition transmission cover,										
3-speed trans., **ADD:**	.3	.3	.3	.3	.3	.3	.3	.3	.3	.3
4-speed trans., **ADD:**	.4	.4	.4	.4	.4	.4	.4	.4	.4	.4
Resurface clutch pressure plate, **ADD:**	.8	.8	.8	.8	.8	.8	.8	.8	.8	.8
R&R and resurface flywheel, **ADD:**	1.8	1.8	1.8	1.8	1.8	1.8	1.8	1.8	1.8	1.8
Replace flywheel ring gear, **ADD:**	1.0	1.0	1.0	1.0	1.0	1.0	1.0	1.0	1.0	1.0
Replace flywheel pilot bearing, **ADD:**	.2	.2	.2	.2	.2	.2	.2	.2	.2	.2
Replace clutch release (throwout) bearing, **ADD:**	.7	.7	.7	.7	.7	.7	.7	.7	.7	.7

Approximate parts cost:

Speedometer gear	$ 2.00	Flywheel pilot bearing	$ 1.50
Gasket set	8.00	Clutch release bearing	5.00-15.00
Clutch pressure plate	25.00-60.00	Phone supplier for price quote on transmission parts required.	

AUTOMATIC TRANSMISSION, MAJOR SERVICE

Includes:

Basic Jobs:
1. Overhaul transmission. Disassemble, clean, inspect and replace all worn parts as needed. Replace all oil seals. Adjust throttle and shift linkage as required. Flush converter and cooler lines. Perform pressure checks of mainline, throttle, and accumulator. Road test.
2. Replace torque converter. R&R transmission. Flush oil cooler and lines. Replace transmission oil and oil filter. Perform pressure checks of mainline, throttle, and accumulator. Adjust throttle and shift linkage as required.
3. Reseal transmission. R&R transmission. Replace all seals and gaskets. Replace transmission oil and oil filter. Check oil cooler for leaks. Perform pressure checks of mainline, throttle, and accumulator. Adjust throttle and shift linkage as required. Road test.

Additions to Basic Jobs: Associated work that is performed while the transmission is out during one of basic jobs.

MODEL	1966	1967	1968	1969	1970	1971	1972	1973	1974	1975
Basic Job #1										
Overhaul transmission,										
2-speed T-300 or M-35	6.9	6.9	6.9	6.9	6.9	6.9	6.9	6.9	—	—
250/350 THM	8.0	8.0	8.0	8.0	8.0	8.0	8.0	8.7	8.7	8.7
375/400 THM	7.2	7.2	7.2	7.2	7.2	7.2	7.2	7.9	8.6	8.6
Basic Job #2										
Replace torque converter,										
2-speed T-300 or M-35	4.2	4.2	4.2	4.2	4.2	4.2	4.2	4.2	—	—
250/350 THM	4.8	4.8	4.8	4.8	4.8	4.8	4.8	4.8	4.6	4.6
375/400 THM	4.4	4.4	4.4	4.4	4.4	4.4	4.4	4.6	4.6	4.6
Basic Job #3										
Reseal transmission,										
2-speed T-300 or M-35	6.6	6.6	6.6	6.6	6.6	6.6	6.6	6.6	—	—
250/350 THM	6.3	6.3	6.3	6.3	6.3	6.3	6.3	6.8	6.8	6.8
375/400 THM	5.8	5.8	5.8	5.8	5.8	5.8	5.8	6.3	6.3	6.3
Additions to Basic Jobs:										
Replace oil cooler pipes, both, **ADD:**	.9	.9	.9	.9	.9	.9	.9	.9	.9	.9
Replace oil filler pipe and/or seal, **ADD:**	.5	.5	.5	.5	.5	.5	.5	.5	.5	.5
Replace torque converter ring gear, **ADD:**	.5	.5	.5	.5	.5	.5	.5	.5	.5	.5

Approximate parts cost:

Transmission seal and gasket kit	$20.00	Oil filler pipe	$ 4.00
Transmission partial overhaul kit	60.00	Oil filler pipe seal	0.25
Oil coller pipe, each	9.00	Oil pan	8.00
Torque converter assembly	70.00-140.00	Oil pan gasket	1.00
Torque converter ring gear	8.00	Governor kit	19.00

PONTIAC

AUTOMATIC TRANSMISSION, PERFORMANCE CHECK

Includes:
Basic Job: Conduct transmission performance check. Clean transmission case and operate unit to check case, oil cooler and oil cooler lines for external leaks. Remove oil pan, clean pan, screen or filter. Torque valve body mounting bolts. Adjust band(s) where applicable. Adjust throttle and shift linkage. Perform pressure checks of mainline, throttle, and accumulator. Road test.
Related Jobs: Work which does not include R&R transmission and may be done as separate job.

MODEL	1966	1967	1968	1969	1970	1971	1972	1973	1974	1975
Basic Job:										
Complete trans. performance check	2.1	2.1	2.1	2.1	2.1	2.1	2.1	2.1	2.1	2.1
Related Jobs:										
Drain & fill trans., clean filter	.8	.8	.8	.8	.8	.8	.8	.8	.8	.8
Check for oil leaks	.7	.7	.7	.7	.7	.7	.7	.7	.7	.7
Repl. oil pan gasket, incl. clean filter	.9	.9	.9	.9	.9	.9	.9	.9	.9	.9
Repl. rear oil seal & O-ring	1.0	1.0	.7	.5	.5	.5	.5	.5	.5	.5
Repl. neutral safety switch	.5	.5	.5	.5	.5	.5	.5	.5	.5	.5
Overhaul governor, includes complete trans. performance check,										
2-speed T-300 or M-35	4.0	3.5	3.5	3.5	3.5	3.5	3.5	3.5	—	—
250/350 THM	3.1	3.1	3.1	3.1	3.1	3.1	3.1	3.1	—	—
375/400 THM	2.9	2.9	2.9	2.9	2.9	2.9	2.9	2.9	2.8	2.8
Overhaul valve body assembly	2.0	2.0	2.0	2.0	2.0	2.0	2.0	2.0	2.0	2.0
Adjust throttle and shift linkage	1.0	1.0	1.0	1.0	1.0	1.0	1.0	1.0	1.0	1.0
Adjust band/s where applicable	1.3	1.3	1.3	1.3	1.3	1.3	1.3	1.3	1.3	1.3

Approximate parts cost:

Transmission fluid, per qt.	$1.20	Neutral safety switch	$ 3.50
Oil pan gasket	1.00	Governor body repair kit	18.00
Rear oil seal	4.50	Valve body assy., new	80.00

AUTOMATIC TRANSMISSION, SHIFT AND LINKAGE CONTROLS, REPLACE AND ADJUST

Includes:
Replace and Adjust: Replace defective part and make necessary adjustments.

MODEL	1966	1967	1968	1969	1970	1971	1972	1973	1974	1975
Replace part and adjust:										
Replace control rod, carb, or trans. & adj.:	.9	.9	.9	.9	.9	.9	.9	.9	.9	.9
Replace each additional rod, **ADD**:	.4	.4	.4	.4	.4	.4	.4	.4	.4	.4
Replace carb./throttle link, **ADD**:	.3	.3	.3	.3	.3	.3	.3	.3	.3	.3
Replace throttle control cable, **ADD**:	.5	.5	.5	.5	.5	.5	.5	.5	.5	.5
Replace front control rod, column shift, **ADD**:	.3	.3	.3	.3	.3	.3	.3	.3	.3	.3
Replace rear control rod or swivel, **ADD**:	.4	.4	.4	.4	.4	.4	.4	.4	.4	.4
Replace contr. torque shaft or bushings, **ADD**:	.6	.6	.6	.6	.6	.6	.6	.6	.6	.6
Replace shift control key lock assy.	.7	.7	.7	.7	.7	.7	.7	.7	.7	.7
Replace vac. modulator hose & adj. linkage	.6	.6	.6	.6	.6	.6	.6	.6	.6	.6
Replace and adjust floor shift control assy.	.8	.8	.8	.8	.8	.8	.8	.8	.8	.8
With console equipped, **ADD**:	.5	.5	.5	.5	.5	.5	.5	.5	.5	.5

Approximate parts cost:

Linkage rod, ea.	$1.50	Modulator hose, per ft.	$ 0.25
Control cable	8.00	Floor shift contr. assy.	40.00

PONTIAC 237

DRIVESHAFT, SERVICE

Includes:
Basic Job: R&R driveshaft and overhaul or replace front and rear U-joints.

MODEL	1966	1967	1968	1969	1970	1971	1972	1973	1974	1975
Basic Job:										
R&R driveshaft & overhaul both U-joints, Cross & roller joints	1.5	1.5	1.5	1.5	1.5	1.5	1.5	1.5	1.5	1.5
R&R driveshaft with joints	1.1	1.1	1.1	1.1	1.1	1.1	1.1	1.1	1.1	1.1

Approximate parts cost:
U-joint package, cross & roller .... $11.00   Driveshaft with joints $120.00

REAR AXLE, SERVICE

Includes:
Basic Jobs: 1. R&R driveshaft, R&R axle shafts, overhaul differential assembly and check and adjust pinion nose angle.
2. R&R driveshaft and replace pinion bearing oil seal.
Related Jobs: R&R axle shaft (one side) and/or bearing and seals and adjust end-play. Replace axle shaft wheel mounting stud.

MODEL	1966	1967	1968	1969	1970	1971	1972	1973	1974	1975
Basic Job #1										
Overhaul differential assembly,										
Removable-type	5.5	5.5	5.5	5.5	5.5	5.5	5.5	5.5	5.5	5.5
Integral-type	5.0	5.0	5.0	5.0	5.0	5.0	5.0	5.0	5.0	5.0
With Posi-traction, **ADD:**	.6	.6	.6	.6	.6	.6	.6	.6	.6	.6
Basic Job #2										
Replace drive pinion bearing oil seal	1.2	1.2	1.2	1.7	1.7	1.7	1.7	1.7	1.7	1.7
Related Jobs:										
R&R axle shaft (one side), and/or bearing and seals and adjust end-play	1.3	1.3	1.3	1.3	1.3	1.3	1.3	1.3	1.3	1.3
Replace axle shaft wheel mounting stud	.8	.8	.8	.8	.8	.8	.8	.8	.8	.8

Approximate parts cost:
Axle shaft .... $30.00   Pinion bearing oil seal .... $ 3.00
Inner or outer seal .... 2.00   Cover gasket 1.00
Posi-traction repair kit .... 25.00   Ring & pinion gear set 70.00-120.00

REAR SUSPENSION, SERVICE

Includes:
Service for the rear suspension system listed as individual jobs. Add times if more than one job is performed.

MODEL	1966	1967	1968	1969	1970	1971	1972	1973	1974	1975
Repl. rear leaf spring & shim to align pinion angle.										
Station Wagon, Firebird, Ventura, GTO	1.6	1.6	1.6	1.6	1.8	1.8	1.8	1.7	1.7	1.7
Replace coil spring	1.5	1.5	1.5	1.5	1.5	1.5	1.5	1.5	1.5	1.5
Replace control arm, incl. pinion angle adjustment,										
Upper arm, one	1.1	1.1	1.1	1.1	1.1	1.1	1.1	1.1	1.1	1.1
Lower arm, one	1.5	1.5	1.5	1.5	1.5	1.5	1.1	1.1	1.1	1.1
Replace shackle and bushings; eye bolt and bushings	.7	.7	.7	.7	.7	.7	.7	.7	.7	.7
Replace shock absorber, both sides	.8	.8	.8	.8	.8	.8	.8	.8	.8	.8
Replace tie rod & stabilizer shaft (one)	.9	.9	.9	.9	.9	.9	.9	.9	.9	.9

Approximate parts cost:
Shock absorber .... $14.00   Shackle package .... $ 9.00
Coil spring .... 26.00   Shackle bushing package 1.00
Leaf spring .... 53.00   Tie rod & stabilizer shaft 23.00

PONTIAC

FRONT END, TEST, SERVICE, AND ADJUST

Includes:
Basic Job: Check and adjust car height, caster, camber, steering axis inclination, turning radius, toe-in; pack and adjust front wheel bearings, replace seals.
Related Jobs: Perform individual adjustments. Replace or overhaul defective components and make necessary adjustments.

MODEL	1966	1967	1968	1969	1970	1971	1972	1973	1974	1975
Basic Job:										
Complete test and adjustments,										
With drum brakes	2.5	2.5	2.5	2.5	2.5	2.5	2.5	2.5	2.5	—
With disc brakes	—	3.0	3.0	3.0	3.0	3.0	3.0	3.0	3.0	3.0
Related Jobs:										
Adjust toe-in only	.4	.4	.4	.4	.4	.4	.4	.4	.4	.4
Repack wheel brgs. only, incl. new seals,										
Drum brakes, both sides	.9	.9	.9	.9	.9	.9	.9	.9	.9	—
Disc brakes, both sides	—	1.3	1.3	1.3	1.3	1.3	1.3	1.3	1.3	1.3
Replace wheel brgs. only each side,										
Drum brakes, inner or outer brg.	.5	.5	.5	.5	.5	.5	.5	.5	.5	—
Disc brakes, inner or outer brg.	—	.8	.8	.8	.8	.9	.9	.9	.9	.9
Balance four wheels on car,										
With drum brakes	1.2	1.2	1.2	1.2	1.2	1.2	1.2	1.2	1.2	—
With disc/drum brakes	—	1.5	1.5	1.5	1.5	1.5	1.5	1.5	1.5	1.5
Overhaul front suspension, incl. disassemble, replace nec. parts, lube., & complete front end adjustments,										
With drum brakes	7.9	7.9	7.9	7.9	7.9	7.9	7.9	7.9	7.9	—
With disc brakes, Grand Prix	—	8.8	8.8	8.8	8.8	8.8	8.8	8.8	8.8	8.8
With disc brakes, all others	—	8.5	8.5	8.5	8.5	8.5	8.5	8.5	8.5	8.5
Replace coil spring, incl. complete front end adjustments,										
With drum brakes	3.9	3.9	3.9	3.9	3.9	3.6	3.6	3.6	3.6	—
With disc brakes	—	4.4	4.4	4.4	4.4	4.1	4.1	4.1	4.1	4.1
Replace upper and lower ball joints, both sides, incl. complete front end adjustment,										
With drum brakes	3.9	3.9	3.9	3.9	3.9	3.9	3.7	3.7	3.7	—
With disc brakes	—	4.4	4.4	4.4	4.4	4.4	4.2	4.2	4.2	4.2
Replace steering knuckle, one side, incl. complete front end adjustment,										
With drum brakes	3.1	3.1	3.1	3.1	3.1	3.1	3.1	3.1	3.1	—
With disc brakes	—	3.6	3.6	3.6	3.6	3.6	3.6	3.6	3.6	3.6
Replace shock absorber, both sides	.9	.9	.9	.9	.9	.9	.9	.9	.9	.9
Replace control arm rubber bumpers, ea. side	.3	.3	.3	.3	.3	.3	.3	.3	.3	.3
Replace strut rod or bushings, ea. side	.4	.4	.4	.4	.4	.4	.4	.4	.4	.4
Replace stabilizer shaft and bushings	1.1	1.1	1.1	1.1	1.1	1.1	1.1	1.1	1.1	1.1
Replace front stabilizer links or grommets	.7	.7	.7	.7	.7	.7	.7	.7	.7	.7

Approximate parts cost:

Coil spring, ea. $16.00	Control arm rubber bumpers, ea. .... $ 1.50
Upper ball joint 12.00	Strut rod & bushing 6.00
Lower ball joint 14.00	Stabilizer shaft & bushings 15.00
Steering knuckle 40.00	Stabilizer links or grommets 2.00
Shock absorber, ea. 15.00	Wheel bearing seals 2.00
Wheel bearing, outer 5.00	Wheel bearing, inner 6.00

PONTIAC 239

STEERING LINKAGE, SERVICE AND ADJUST

Includes:
Basic Job: Adjust toe-in.
Related Jobs: Replace defective parts and adjust toe-in.

MODEL	1966	1967	1968	1969	1970	1971	1972	1973	1974	1975
Basic Job:										
Adjust toe-in	.4	.4	.4	.4	.4	.4	.4	.4	.4	.4
Related Jobs:										
Replace tie-rods or tie-rod ends, (4)	1.4	1.4	1.4	1.4	1.4	1.4	1.4	1.4	1.4	1.4
Replace Pitman arm, includes adjust toe-in	.8	.8	.8	.8	.8	.8	.8	.8	.8	.8
Replace steering idler arm or bushing	.7	.7	.7	.7	.7	.7	.7	.7	.7	.7

Approximate parts cost:
Tie-rod end pkg. $10.00-15.00
Pitman arm...9.00
Idler arm $17.00
Tie rod 15.00

STANDARD STEERING GEAR, ADJUST AND SERVICE

Includes:
Basic Job: Adjust steering gear, worm and sector mesh, adjust wheel bearings and toe-in.
Related Job: R&R steering gear assembly and complete adjustments.
Additions to Related Job: Overhaul steering gear.

MODEL	1966	1967	1968	1969	1970	1971	1972	1973	1974	1975
Basic Job:										
Complete steering gear, wheel bearings, & toe-in adjustments,										
With drum brakes	1.4	1.4	1.4	1.4	1.4	1.4	1.4	1.4	1.4	1.4
With disc brakes	—	1.8	1.8	1.8	1.8	1.8	1.8	1.8	1.8	1.8
Related Job:										
R&R steering gear assembly & complete adjustments	1.9	1.9	1.9	1.9	1.9	1.9	1.9	1.9	1.9	1.9
Additions to Related Job:										
Overhaul steering gear assembly, **ADD:**	1.0	1.0	1.0	1.0	1.0	1.0	1.0	1.0	1.0	1.0

Approximate parts cost:
Pitman shaft bushing $2.00
Shaft dust seal 1.00
Worm thrust bearing $1.00
Pitman shaft seal 1.50

POWER STEERING UNIT, TEST AND SERVICE

Includes:
Basic Job: Adjust drive belt tension; hook-up gauges to check pressure on left and right turns. Adjust steering gear box over center torque and control valve to balance left and right steering effort.
Additions to Basic Job: Service power steering unit.
Related Jobs: R&R power steering unit, pump, or other associated parts.
Additions to Related Jobs: Overhaul steering unit or pump including replacement of all seals and worn parts.

MODEL	1966	1967	1968	1969	1970	1971	1972	1973	1974	1975
Basic Job:										
Complete test and adjustment of power steering unit	1.0	1.0	1.0	1.0	1.0	1.0	1.0	1.0	1.0	1.0
Additions to Basic Job:										
Replace power steering pump drive belt, **ADD:**	.3	.3	.3	.3	.3	.3	.3	.3	.3	.3
With air conditioning, **ADD:**	.2	.2	.2	.2	.2	.2	.2	.2	.2	.2
Check & replenish reservoir fluid, **ADD:**	.2	.2	.2	.2	.2	.2	.2	.2	.2	.2

(THIS SCHEDULE CONTINUED ON NEXT PAGE.)

240 PONTIAC
POWER STEERING UNIT, TEST AND SERVICE Continued

MODEL	1966	1967	1968	1969	1970	1971	1972	1973	1974	1975
Related Jobs:										
Replace pressure hoses, either set, includes adjust drive belt tension,										
4/6-cylinder	.3	.3	.3	.3	.3	.3	.3	.3	.3	.3
V-8 engine	.6	.6	.6	.6	.6	.6	.6	.6	.6	.6
With air conditioning, **ADD:**	.1	.1	.1	.1	.1	.1	.1	.1	.1	.1
Replace pump reservoir or O-ring seals,										
4/6-cylinder	1.0	1.0	1.0	1.0	1.0	1.0	1.0	1.0	1.1	1.1
V-8 engine	1.1	1.1	1.1	1.1	1.1	1.1	1.2	1.2	1.2	1.2
With air conditioning, **ADD:**	.1	.1	.1	.1	.1	.1	.1	.1	.2	.2
Replace pump, includes pressure-test original pump and transfer pulley,										
4/6-cylinder	.7	.7	.7	.7	.7	.7	.7	.7	.7	.7
V-8 engine	.8	.8	.8	.8	.8	.8	.8	.8	.8	.8
With air conditioning, **ADD:**	.1	.1	.1	.1	.1	.1	.1	.2	.2	.2
Replace control valve, includes adjust	1.1	1.1	1.1	1.1	1.1	1.1	1.1	1.1	1.1	1.1
Overhaul control valve, **ADD:**	.6	.6	.6	.6	.6	.6	.6	.6	.6	.6
R&R power steering unit, includes test original unit and complete adjustment,										
4/6-cylinder	2.5	2.5	2.5	2.5	2.5	2.5	2.5	2.5	2.5	2.5
V-8 engine	2.3	2.3	2.3	2.3	2.3	2.3	2.3	2.3	2.3	2.3
Additions to Related Jobs:										
Overhaul power steering unit, **ADD:**	2.2	2.2	2.2	2.2	2.4	2.4	2.4	2.4	3.0	3.0
O/H pump, incl. new kit & seals, **ADD:**	.8	.8	.8	.8	.8	.8	.8	.6	.6	.6

Approximate parts cost:
Drive belt	$ 4.00	Power cylinder	$33.00
Pressure hose	12.00	Power cylinder piston rod seal kit	2.50
Return hose	4.00	Hydraulic pump	62.00
Control valve	42.00	Hydraulic reservoir	15.00
Control valve seal kit	2.00	Hydraulic pump seals	4.00
Power steering unit, valve assembly	85.00	Hydraulic pump repair kit	14.00

PARKING BRAKES, SERVICE AND ADJUST

Includes:
  Basic Jobs: Replace defective cable and/or adjust parking brakes.

MODEL	1966	1967	1968	1969	1970	1971	1972	1973	1974	1975
Basic Jobs:										
Adjust parking brakes	.4	.4	.4	.4	.4	.4	.4	.4	.4	.4
Replace forward cable,										
Pontiac, Tempest	1.4	1.4	1.4	1.4	1.4	1.4	1.4	1.4	1.4	1.4
All others	.8	.8	.8	.8	.8	.8	.8	.8	.8	.8
Replace rear cable, one side	1.0	1.0	1.0	1.0	1.0	1.0	1.0	1.0	1.0	1.0
Replace rear cable both sides	1.5	1.5	1.5	1.5	1.5	1.5	1.5	1.5	1.5	1.5
Replace intermediate cable	.4	.4	.4	.4	.4	.4	.4	.4	.4	.4

Approximate parts cost:
Front cable	$5.00	Rear cable	$8.00
Intermediate cable	3.50		

PONTIAC

BRAKES, SERVICE

Includes:

Basic Job: Install new linings or pads, turn brake drums or rotors, lubricate and adjust front wheel bearings, replace rear oil seals, bleed hydraulic system, and adjust brakes.

Additions to Basic Job: Overhaul four wheel cylinders, overhaul or replace front calipers.

Related Jobs: Performe at time other than during basic job. Overhaul or replace front calipers.

MODEL	1966	1967	1968	1969	1970	1971	1972	1973	1974	1975
Basic Job:										
Complete job incl. turn drums or rotors,										
Drum (4), all models	6.5	6.5	6.5	6.5	6.5	6.5	6.5	6.5	6.5	—
Disc front, drum rear, all models	—	6.9	6.9	6.9	6.9	6.9	6.9	6.9	6.9	6.9
Additions to Basic Job:										
O/H 4 wheel cylinders, incl. hone, **ADD:**	2.3	2.3	2.3	2.3	2.3	2.4	2.4	2.4	2.4	—
Overhaul front calipers (both), **ADD:**	—	3.5	3.5	2.9	2.9	2.9	2.9	2.9	2.9	2.9
Replace front calipers (both), **ADD:**	—	.4	.4	.4	.4	.4	.4	.4	.4	.4
Overhaul master cylinder, **ADD:**	.8	.8	.8	.8	.8	.8	.8	.8	.8	.8
Related Jobs: (Not during basic job)										
Bleed hydraulic system, 4 wheels	.6	.6	.6	.6	.6	.6	.6	.6	.6	.6
Adjust drum brakes, 4 wheels	.5	.5	.5	.5	.5	.5	.5	.5	.5	—
Replace disc brake pads, front wheels	—	1.5	1.5	1.5	1.5	1.5	1.0	1.0	1.0	1.0
Replace drum brake shoes, 4 wheels	3.5	3.5	3.5	3.5	3.5	3.5	3.5	3.5	3.5	—
O/H front calipers, incl. turn rotors	—	4.6	4.6	4.0	4.0	4.0	4.0	4.0	4.0	4.0
Replace front caliper, incl. turn rotor, ea.	—	3.0	3.0	2.4	2.4	2.4	2.4	2.4	2.4	2.4
Overhaul master cylinder	1.3	1.3	1.5	1.5	1.5	1.5	1.8	1.8	1.8	1.8

Approximate parts cost:

Wheel cylinder seal, boot & bushing pkg.	$ 6.00	Wheel cylinder repair kit, ea.	$ 2.00
Brake shoes and lining sets, front or rear	25.00	Caliper brake housing	50.00
Disc brake pads, set of 2	24.00	Oil seal, ea.	2.00
Master cylinder repair kit	18.00		

POWER BRAKE UNIT, SERVICE

Includes:

Basic Job: R&R with new unit, test, and adjust brakes.

Additions to Basic Job: Replace vacuum hose or vacuum check valve. Allowance for air conditioning.

MODEL	1966	1967	1968	1969	1970	1971	1972	1973	1974	1975
Basic Job:										
R&R power unit, test, & adj. brakes	1.6	1.6	1.6	1.6	1.5	1.5	1.5	1.5	1.5	1.5
Additions to Basic Job:										
With air conditioning, **ADD:**	.3	.3	.3	.3	.3	.3	.3	.3	.3	.3
Install new hose, **ADD:**	.2	.2	.2	.2	.2	.2	.2	.2	.2	.2
Install new vacuum check valve, **ADD:**	.2	.2	.2	.2	.2	.2	.2	.2	.2	.2

Approximate parts cost:

Power brake unit	$50.00-70.00	Vacuum check valve	$1.75
Vacuum hose, per ft.	0.90		

242 PONTIAC

HYDRAULIC BRAKE SYSTEM, OVERHAUL

Includes:
Basic Job: Overhaul including hone or replace master cylinder, all wheel cylinders or calipers; bleed hydraulic system; and adjust brakes.
Related Jobs: Performed at time other than during basic job. Overhaul or replace master cylinder only; overhaul wheel cylinders or calipers.
Addition to Related Jobs: Allowance for power brakes.

MODEL	1966	1967	1968	1969	1970	1971	1972	1973	1974	1975
Basic Job:										
Complete job, including master & wheel cylinders,										
Drum brakes	4.7	4.7	4.7	4.7	4.7	4.7	4.7	4.6	4.6	—
Disc front, drum rear	—	3.9	3.9	3.9	3.9	3.9	3.9	3.9	3.9	3.9
Related Jobs: (Not during basic job)										
Overhaul master cylinder, including hone,										
Drum or disc brakes	1.3	1.3	1.5	1.5	1.5	1.5	1.8	1.8	1.8	1.8
Bleed hydraulic system, 4 wheels	.6	.6	.6	.6	.6	.6	.6	.6	.6	.6
Replace master cylinder	.5	.5	.8	.8	.8	.8	1.1	1.1	1.1	1.1
O/H wheel cylinder, drum brakes (4)	4.1	4.1	4.1	4.1	4.1	4.1	4.2	4.2	4.2	—
O/H front calipers, incl. turn rotors	—	4.0	4.0	4.0	4.0	4.0	4.0	4.0	4.0	4.0
Addition to Related Jobs:										
With power brakes, **ADD:**	.2	.2	.2	.2	.2	.2	.2	.2	.2	.2

Approximate parts cost:
Master cylinder repair kit $18.00
Wheel cylinder repair kit, ea. 2.00
Caliper repair kit 4.00
Master cylinder $27.00-40.00
Wheel cylinder seal, boot & bushing pkg. 6.00

LIGHTING SYSTEM, ADJUST AND SERVICE

Includes:
Basic Job: 1. Adjust headlights to inspection requirements.
2. Replace defective parts in rear lighting system.
Additions to Basic Job: Replace associated parts affecting headlight adjustment.
Related Jobs: Replace associated parts not affecting headlight adjustment.

MODEL	1966	1967	1968	1969	1970	1971	1972	1973	1974	1975
Basic Job #1										
Adjust two headlights	.4	.4	.4	.4	.4	.4	.4	.4	.4	.4
Adjust four headlights	.6	.6	.6	.6	.6	.6	.6	.6	.6	.6
Basic Job #2										
Replace stoplight switch	.3	.3	.3	.3	.3	.3	.3	.3	.3	.3
Replace back-up light switch	.4	.4	.4	.4	.4	.4	.4	.4	.4	.4
Additions to Basic Job:										
Replace sealed beam unit, ea., **ADD:**	.3	.3	.3	.3	.3	.3	.3	.3	.3	.3
Related Jobs:										
Replace headlamp vacuum motor, one side	.8	.8	.8	.8	.8	.8	.8	.8	.8	.8
Replace headlamp switch,										
Astre	—	—	—	—	—	—	—	—	—	.3
All others	.5	.5	.5	.5	.5	.5	.5	.5	.5	.5
Replace foot dimmer switch	.3	.3	.3	.3	.3	.3	.3	.3	.3	.3
Replace signal/hazard flasher	.2	.2	.2	.2	.2	.2	.2	.2	.2	.2
Replace signal/hazard switch,										
With standard column	1.2	1.2	1.2	1.0	1.0	1.0	1.0	1.0	1.0	1.0
With tilt or telescopic column	1.5	1.5	1.5	1.3	1.3	1.3	1.3	1.3	1.3	1.3

(THIS SCHEDULE CONTINUED ON NEXT PAGE.)

PONTIAC 243

LIGHTING SYSTEM, ADJUST AND SERVICE Continued

Approximate parts cost:

Sealed beam unit $4.00	Headlamp switch $7.00
Signal/hazard flasher 2.00	Back-up light switch, 1966-68 floor shift 8.00
Signal/hazard switch 15.00	Back-up light switch, all others 4.00
Vacuum motor 20.00	

HEATING SYSTEM, TEST AND SERVICE

Includes:

Basic Job: Drain back-flush, and fill radiator, check radiator and heater hoses and connections, pressure-test radiator cap and system.
Related Jobs: Replace defective parts. Work performed individually and independently of basic job.

MODEL	1966	1967	1968	1969	1970	1971	1972	1973	1974	1975
Basic Job:										
Drain, flush, fill, check, & pressure-test	.9	.9	.9	.9	.9	.9	.9	.9	.9	.9
Related Jobs:										
Replace heater hose, one, inlet or outlet	.5	.5	.5	.5	.5	.5	.5	.5	.5	.5
Replace each additional hose, **ADD:**	.2	.2	.2	.2	.2	.2	.2	.2	.2	.2
With air conditioning, **ADD:**	.3	.3	.3	.3	.3	.3	.3	.3	.3	.3
Replace blower motor and/or impeller,										
Tempest	1.0	1.0	1.0	1.0	.8	.8	.8	.8	.8	.8
Firebird	2.0	2.0	2.0	2.0	.8	.8	.8	.8	.8	.8
Astre	—	—	—	—	—	—	—	—	—	.5
Gran Prix	.5	.5	.5	.5	.5	.5	.5	.5	.5	.5
All others	1.5	1.5	1.5	1.5	1.5	1.5	1.5	1.5	1.5	1.5
With air conditioning, **ADD:**	.7	.7	.7	.7	.7	.7	.7	.7	.7	.7
Replace heater core with air conditioning,										
Astre	—	—	—	—	—	—	—	—	—	2.5
Gran Prix	1.7	1.7	1.7	1.7	1.7	1.9	1.9	1.9	1.9	1.9
Tempest	2.5	2.5	2.5	2.5	2.5	2.5	2.5	2.8	2.8	2.8
All others	1.5	1.5	1.5	1.5	1.5	1.5	1.5	1.5	1.5	1.5
Replace heater core w/o air conditioning,										
Astre	—	—	—	—	—	—	—	—	—	1.0
Tempest	1.5	1.5	1.5	1.5	1.5	1.5	1.5	1.8	1.8	1.8
All others	1.0	1.0	1.0	1.0	1.0	1.0	1.0	1.8	1.8	1.8
Replace blower motor switch,										
Gran Prix	.6	.6	.6	1.0	1.2	1.2	.8	.8	.8	.8
Astre	—	—	—	—	—	—	—	—	—	.5
All others	1.0	1.0	1.0	1.0	1.0	1.0	1.0	1.2	1.2	1.2

Approximate parts cost:

Heater hose, per ft. $0.75	Heater core $45.00
Blower motor 32.00	Blower motor switch 9.00

PONTIAC

AIR CONDITIONING SYSTEM, SPRING TUNE-UP

Includes:
   Basic Job: Clean condenser fins; adjust drive belt tension; test anti-freeze; tighten compressor, condenser, and evaporator mounts. Pressure-test and leak-check system. Check system for performance.
   Additions to Basic Job: Replace defective parts.

MODEL	1966	1967	1968	1969	1970	1971	1972	1973	1974	1975
Basic Job:										
Perform complete spring tune-up	2.0	2.0	2.0	2.0	2.0	2.0	2.0	2.0	2.0	2.0
Additions to Basic Job:										
Replace compressor belt & adjust, ADD:	.4	.4	.4	.4	.4	.4	.4	.4	.4	.4
Replace compr. clutch pulley w/hub assy., ADD:	.5	.5	.5	.5	.5	.5	.5	.5	.5	.5
Replace compr. clutch coil, ADD:	.8	.8	.8	.8	.8	.8	.8	.8	.8	.8
Replace compr. clutch bearing, ADD:	.8	.8	.8	.8	.8	.8	.8	.8	.8	.8

Approximate parts cost:

Compressor drive belt	$ 3.00	Compressor clutch coil	$28.00
Compressor clutch pulley w/hub	75.00	Compressor clutch bearing	23.00
Freon, per 14 oz. can	2.50	Anti-freeze, per gal.	9.50

AIR CONDITIONING SYSTEM, MAJOR SERVICE

Includes:
   Basic Job: Drain system in order to replace defective component; evacuate, dehydrate, and recharge system; pressure-test and leak-check; clean condenser fins; adjust drive belt tension; tighten compressor, condenser, and evaporator mounts; and conduct performance test.
   Additions to Basic Job: Replace or overhaul compressor. Replace other defective parts.

MODEL	1966	1967	1968	1969	1970	1971	1972	1973	1974	1975
Basic Job:										
Drain, evacuate, dehydrate, charge & test	3.0	3.0	3.0	3.0	3.0	3.0	3.0	3.0	3.0	3.0
Additions to Basic Job:										
Replace compressor, ADD:	1.2	1.2	1.2	1.2	1.2	1.2	1.2	1.2	1.2	1.2
Overhaul compressor, incl. R&R, ADD:	2.9	2.9	2.9	2.9	2.9	2.9	2.9	2.9	2.9	2.9
Replace relief valve, ADD:	1.5	1.5	1.5	1.5	.8	.8	.8	.8	.8	.8
Replace compr. front head or reed valve, ADD:	1.4	1.4	1.4	1.4	1.4	1.4	.5	.5	.5	.5
Replace compr. rear head or reed valve, ADD:	1.1	1.1	1.1	1.1	1.1	1.1	.6	.6	.6	.6
Replace suction throttling valve, ADD:	.6	.6	.6	.6	.6	.6	.6	.6	.6	.6
Replace condenser, ADD:	1.3	1.3	1.3	1.3	1.3	1.3	1.3	1.3	1.3	1.3
Replace evaporator core,										
Firebird & Station Wagons, ADD:	1.8	1.8	1.8	1.8	1.8	1.8	1.3	1.3	1.3	1.3
Gran Prix, ADD:	1.1	1.1	1.1	1.1	1.1	1.1	.8	.8	.8	.8
Astre, ADD:	—	—	—	—	—	—	—	—	—	1.5
All others, ADD:	1.0	1.0	1.0	1.0	1.0	1.0	1.0	1.0	1.0	1.0
With AIR, ADD:	.2	.2	.2	.2	.2	.2	.2	.2	.2	.2
Replace sight glass, ADD:	1.4	1.4	1.4	1.4	1.4	1.4	.9	.9	.9	.9
Replace dehydrator-receiver tank, ADD:	1.0	1.0	1.0	.8	.8	.8	.5	.5	.5	.5
Replace expansion valve, ADD:	1.5	1.5	1.5	.8	.8	.8	.8	.8	.8	.8
Replace POA valve, ADD:	.7	.7	.7	.7	.7	.7	.5	.5	.5	.5
Replace compressor shaft seal, ADD:	1.4	1.4	1.4	1.4	1.4	1.4	.9	.9	.9	.9
Replace valves-in-receiver (VIR) assy.	—	—	—	—	—	—	—	.5	.5	.5
O/H VIR assy. incl. repl. nec. parts, ADD:	—	—	—	—	—	—	—	1.0	1.0	1.0
Replace one hose, ADD:	.4	.4	.4	.4	.4	.4	.4	.4	.4	.4

(THIS SCHEDULE CONTINUED ON NEXT PAGE.)

PONTIAC 245

AIR CONDITIONING SYSTEM, MAJOR SERVICE Continued

Approximate parts cost:

Compressor..$85.00	Expansion valve $36.00
Compressor front head & valve assy........................20.00	Pressure-operated absolute (POA) valve 30.00
Compressor rear head & valve assy. 65.00	Hose, per ft..2.75
Compressor pressure relief valve 7.00	Hose fitting, ea. 1.00
Condenser..75.00-125.00	Freon, per 14 oz. can 2.50
Evaporator core assy..................................90.00-160.00	Anti-freeze, per gal.......................................9.50
Compressor shaft seal assy................................8.00	

AIR CONDITIONING SYSTEM BLOWER MOTOR OR CONTROLS, SERVICE

Includes:
Basic Jobs: Conduct performance test of system to determine defective part; R&R component; clean condenser fins; adjust drive belt tension; tighten all mounts; and test system.

MODEL	1966	1967	1968	1969	1970	1971	1972	1973	1974	1975
Basic Jobs:										
R&R blower motor, test system after installation,										
Tempest...	1.7	1.7	1.7	1.7	1.5	1.5	1.5	1.5	1.5	1.5
Firebird..	2.7	2.7	2.7	2.7	1.5	1.5	1.5	1.5	1.5	1.5
Astre	—	—	—	—	—	—	—	—	—	1.2
Gran Prix	1.2	1.2	1.2	1.2	1.2	1.2	1.2	1.2	1.2	1.2
All others	2.2	2.2	2.2	2.2	2.2	2.2	2.2	2.2	2.2	2.2
R&R blower motor switch,										
Gran Prix	.6	.6	.6	1.0	1.2	1.2	.8	.8	.8	.8
Astre	—	—	—	—	—	—	—	—	—	.5
All others	1.0	1.0	1.0	1.0	1.0	1.0	1.0	1.2	1.2	1.2
R&R compressor clutch switch, test system,										
Gran Prix	1.1	1.1	1.1	1.1	1.1	—	—	—	—	—
All others	1.4	1.4	1.4	1.4	1.4	—	—	—	—	—
R&R evaporator thermostatic switch	1.1	1.1	1.1	1.1	1.1	1.1	1.1	1.1	1.1	1.1
R&R control assembly, test system	1.6	1.6	1.6	1.6	1.6	1.6	1.6	1.6	1.6	1.6
Replace control cable, temperature door	.7	.7	.7	.7	.7	.7	1.0	1.0	1.0	1.0
Replace programmer, including test	—	—	—	—	—	1.0	1.0	1.0	1.0	1.0

Approximate parts cost:

Blower motor $23.00	Control cable, per ft. ....$ 0.80
Blower motor switch 3.00	Control cable fittings, ea. 0.75
Evaporator thermostatic switch...........................4.00	Control assembly 24.00
Compressor clutch switch 2.50	